Symmetric and Asymmetric Data in Solution Models

Symmetric and Asymmetric Data in Solution Models

Editors

Edmundas Kazimieras Zavadskas
Jurgita Antuchevičienė
Zenonas Turskis

MDPI • Basel • Beijing • Wuhan • Barcelona • Belgrade • Manchester • Tokyo • Cluj • Tianjin

Editors

Edmundas Kazimieras Zavadskas
Institute of Sustainable Construction
Vilnius Gediminas Technical University
Vilnius
Lithuania

Jurgita Antuchevičienė
Department of Construction Management and Real Estate
Vilnius Gediminas Technical University
Vilnius
Lithuania

Zenonas Turskis
Department of Construction Management and Real Estate,
Institute of Sustainable Construction
Vilnius Gediminas Technical University
Vilnius
Lithuania

Editorial Office
MDPI
St. Alban-Anlage 66
4052 Basel, Switzerland

This is a reprint of articles from the Special Issue published online in the open access journal *Symmetry* (ISSN 2073-8994) (available at: www.mdpi.com/journal/symmetry/special_issues/Symmetric_Asymmetric_Data_Solution_Models).

For citation purposes, cite each article independently as indicated on the article page online and as indicated below:

LastName, A.A.; LastName, B.B.; LastName, C.C. Article Title. *Journal Name* **Year**, *Volume Number*, Page Range.

ISBN 978-3-0365-1612-7 (Hbk)
ISBN 978-3-0365-1611-0 (PDF)

© 2021 by the authors. Articles in this book are Open Access and distributed under the Creative Commons Attribution (CC BY) license, which allows users to download, copy and build upon published articles, as long as the author and publisher are properly credited, which ensures maximum dissemination and a wider impact of our publications.

The book as a whole is distributed by MDPI under the terms and conditions of the Creative Commons license CC BY-NC-ND.

Contents

About the Editors vii

Preface to "Symmetric and Asymmetric Data in Solution Models" ix

Edmundas Kazimieras Zavadskas, Jurgita Antucheviciene and Zenonas Turskis
Symmetric and Asymmetric Data in Solution Models
Reprinted from: *Symmetry* **2021**, *13*, 1045, doi:10.3390/sym13061045 1

Bo Li, Zeshui Xu, Edmundas Kazimieras Zavadskas, Jurgita Antuchevičienė and Zenonas Turskis
A Bibliometric Analysis of Symmetry (2009–2019)
Reprinted from: *Symmetry* **2020**, *12*, 1304, doi:10.3390/sym12081304 11

Sang-Hyang Lee, Jae-Hwan Kim and Jun-Ho Huh
Land Price Forecasting Research by Macro and Micro Factors and Real Estate Market Utilization Plan Research by Landscape Factors: Big Data Analysis Approach
Reprinted from: *Symmetry* **2021**, *13*, 616, doi:10.3390/sym13040616 29

Irina Vinogradova-Zinkevič, Valentinas Podvezko and Edmundas Kazimeras Zavadskas
Comparative Assessment of the Stability of AHP and FAHP Methods
Reprinted from: *Symmetry* **2021**, *13*, 479, doi:10.3390/sym13030479 53

Romualdas Bausys and Giruta Kazakeviciute-Januskeviciene
Qualitative Rating of Lossy Compression for Aerial Imagery by Neutrosophic WASPAS Method
Reprinted from: *Symmetry* **2021**, *13*, 273, doi:10.3390/sym13020273 79

Zdeněk Kala
Global Sensitivity Analysis of Quantiles: New Importance Measure Based on Superquantiles and Subquantiles
Reprinted from: *Symmetry* **2021**, *13*, 263, doi:10.3390/sym13020263 107

Amirhossein Balali, Alireza Valipour, Jurgita Antucheviciene and Jonas Šaparauskas
Improving the Results of the Earned Value Management Technique Using Artificial Neural Networks in Construction Projects
Reprinted from: *Symmetry* **2020**, *12*, 1745, doi:10.3390/sym12101745 129

Edyta Plebankiewicz and Damian Wieczorek
Adaptation of a Cost Overrun Risk Prediction Model to the Type of Construction Facility
Reprinted from: *Symmetry* **2020**, *12*, 1739, doi:10.3390/sym12101739 145

Zdeněk Kala
From Probabilistic to Quantile-Oriented Sensitivity Analysis: New Indices of Design Quantiles
Reprinted from: *Symmetry* **2020**, *12*, 1720, doi:10.3390/sym12101720 161

Mojisola Grace Asogbon, Oluwarotimi Williams Samuel, Yanbing Jiang, Lin Wang, Yanjuan Geng, Arun Kumar Sangaiah, Shixiong Chen, Peng Fang and Guanglin Li
Appropriate Feature Set and Window Parameters Selection for Efficient Motion Intent Characterization towards Intelligently Smart EMG-PR System
Reprinted from: *Symmetry* **2020**, *12*, 1710, doi:10.3390/sym12101710 183

Ingrida Lescauskiene, Romualdas Bausys, Edmundas Kazimieras Zavadskas and Birute Juodagalviene
VASMA Weighting: Survey-Based Criteria Weighting Methodology that Combines ENTROPY and WASPAS-SVNS to Reflect the Psychometric Features of the VAS Scales
Reprinted from: *Symmetry* **2020**, *12*, 1641, doi:10.3390/sym12101641 . . . . **203**

Tetyana Nestorenko, Mangirdas Morkunas, Jana Peliova, Artiom Volkov, Tomas Balezentis and Dalia Streimkiene
A New Model for Determining the EOQ under Changing Price Parameters and Reordering Time
Reprinted from: *Symmetry* **2020**, *12*, 1512, doi:10.3390/sym12091512 . . . . **223**

Flaviu Ionuț Birouaș, Radu Cătălin Țarcă, Simona Dzitac and Ioan Dzitac
Preliminary Results in Testing of a Novel Asymmetric Underactuated Robotic Hand Exoskeleton for Motor Impairment Rehabilitation
Reprinted from: *Symmetry* **2020**, *12*, 1470, doi:10.3390/sym12091470 . . . . **245**

Sun-Weng Huang, James J.H. Liou, William Tang and Gwo-Hshiung Tzeng
Location Selection of a Manufacturing Facility from the Perspective of Supply Chain Sustainability
Reprinted from: *Symmetry* **2020**, *12*, 1418, doi:10.3390/sym12091418 . . . . **261**

Darjan Karabašević, Dragiša Stanujkić, Edmundas Kazimieras Zavadskas, Predrag Stanimirović, Gabrijela Popović, Bratislav Predić and Alptekin Ulutaş
A Novel Extension of the TOPSIS Method Adapted for the Use of Single-Valued Neutrosophic Sets and Hamming Distance for E-Commerce Development Strategies Selection
Reprinted from: *Symmetry* **2020**, *12*, 1263, doi:10.3390/sym12081263 . . . . **285**

Subhadip Roy, Jeong-Gon Lee, Anita Pal and Syamal Kumar Samanta
Similarity Measures of Quadripartitioned Single Valued Bipolar Neutrosophic Sets and Its Application in Multi-Criteria Decision Making Problems
Reprinted from: *Symmetry* **2020**, *12*, 1012, doi:10.3390/sym12061012 . . . . **301**

Kristina Jaukovic Jocic, Goran Jocic, Darjan Karabasevic, Gabrijela Popovic, Dragisa Stanujkic, Edmundas Kazimieras Zavadskas and Phong Thanh Nguyen
A Novel Integrated PIPRECIA–Interval-Valued Triangular Fuzzy ARAS Model: E-Learning Course Selection
Reprinted from: *Symmetry* **2020**, *12*, 928, doi:10.3390/sym12060928 . . . . **317**

Sarfaraz Hashemkhani Zolfani, Morteza Yazdani, Ali Ebadi Torkayesh and Arman Derakhti
Application of a Gray-Based Decision Support Framework for Location Selection of a Temporary Hospital during COVID-19 Pandemic
Reprinted from: *Symmetry* **2020**, *12*, 886, doi:10.3390/sym12060886 . . . . **333**

About the Editors

Edmundas Kazimieras Zavadskas

Edmundas Kazimieras Zavadskas, PhD, DSc, Dr. habil, Dr. H. C. multi, Chief Researcher at the Institute of Sustainable Construction, Vilnius Gediminas Technical University, Lithuania. He received his PhD in Building Structures (1973), Dr Sc. (1987) in Building Technology and Management, Dr. Habil (1993). He is a member of Lithuanian and several foreign Academies of Sciences, Doctore Honoris Causa from Poznan, Saint Petersburg and Kiev Universities, the Honorary International Chair Professor in the National Taipei University of Technology, Honorary Fellowship of International Association of Grey System and Uncertain Analysis (GSUA), honorary membership in Neutrosophic Science - International Association. Chairman of EURO Working Group ORSDCE. Main research interests: multi-criteria decision-making, civil engineering, sustainable development. Over 600 publications in Clarivate Analytic Web of Science, h=72. Highly Cited Researcher in 2014, 2018, 2019, 2020.

Jurgita Antuchevičienė

Jurgita Antucheviciene, PhD, Professor at the Department of Construction Management and Real Estate at Vilnius Gediminas Technical University, Lithuania. She received her PhD in Civil Engineering in 2005. Her research interests include multiple-criteria decision-making theory and applications, sustainable development, construction technology and management. Over 130 publications in Clarivate Analytic Web of Science, h=33. A member of IEEE SMC, Systems Science and Engineering Technical Committee: Grey Systems and of two EURO Working Groups: Multicriteria Decision Aiding (EWG - MCDA) and Operations Research in Sustainable Development and Civil Engineering (EWG - ORSDCE). Deputy Editor in Chief of Journal of Civil Engineering and Management, Editorial Board member of Applied Soft Computing, Sustainability and Buildings. Guest Editor of several special issues in Mathematical Problems in Engineering, Complexity, Symmetry, Sustainability, and Information.

Zenonas Turskis

Zenonas Turskis, PhD, Professor at the Department of Construction Management and Real Estate, Director and Chief Researcher at the Institute of Sustainable Construction, Vilnius Gediminas Technical University, Lithuania. Education and training: 1979 Civil engineer at Vilnius Civil Engineering Institute (now Vilnius Gediminas Technical University); 1990 Applied Mathematics at Kaunas Polytechnic Institute (now Kaunas Technological University), Kaunas (Lithuania); 1993 PhD degree, Technical sciences at Vilnius Technical University (now Vilnius Gediminas Technical University); 2009 Habilitation procedure, Technological Sciences, Civil Engineering at Vilnius Gediminas Technical University. Main research areas: Sustainability in architecture, design and construction; Infrastructure and transport projects; Life cycle analysis; Innovations in construction and management; Decision support models to solve above mentioned problems. Over 170 publications in Clarivate Analytic Web of Science, h=53.

Preface to "Symmetric and Asymmetric Data in Solution Models"

This book is a Printed Edition of the Special Issue which covers research on symmetric and asymmetric data that occur in real-life problems. We invited authors to submit their theoretical or experimental research to present engineering and economic problem solution models that deal with symmetry or asymmetry of different data types. The Special Issue gained interest in the research community and received many submissions. After rigorous scientific evaluation by editors and reviewers, seventeen papers were accepted and published. The authors proposed different solution models, mainly covering uncertain data in multicriteria decision-making (MCDM) problems as complex tools to balance the symmetry between goals, risks, and constraints to cope with the complicated problems in engineering or management. Therefore, we invite researchers interested in the topics to read the papers provided in the Book.

Edmundas Kazimieras Zavadskas, Jurgita Antuchevičienė, Zenonas Turskis

Editors

Editorial

Symmetric and Asymmetric Data in Solution Models

Edmundas Kazimieras Zavadskas [1], Jurgita Antucheviciene [2,*] and Zenonas Turskis [1,2]

[1] Institute of Sustainable Construction, Vilnius Gediminas Technical University, Sauletekio al. 11, LT-10223 Vilnius, Lithuania; edmundas.zavadskas@vilniustech.lt (E.K.Z.); zenonas.turskis@vilniustech.lt (Z.T.)

[2] Department of Construction Management and Real Estate, Vilnius Gediminas Technical University, Sauletekio al. 11, LT-10223 Vilnius, Lithuania

* Correspondence: jurgita.antucheviciene@vilniustech.lt

Abstract: This Special Issue covers symmetric and asymmetric data that occur in real-life problems. We invited authors to submit their theoretical or experimental research to present engineering and economic problem solution models that deal with symmetry or asymmetry of different data types. The Special Issue gained interest in the research community and received many submissions. After rigorous scientific evaluation by editors and reviewers, seventeen papers were accepted and published. The authors proposed different solution models, mainly covering uncertain data in multi-criteria decision-making problems as complex tools to balance the symmetry between goals, risks, and constraints to cope with the complicated problems in engineering or management. Therefore, we invite researchers interested in the topics to read the papers provided in the Special Issue.

Keywords: symmetric data; asymmetric data; solution models; MCDM; fuzzy sets; neutrosophic sets

Citation: Zavadskas, E.K.; Antucheviciene, J.; Turskis, Z. Symmetric and Asymmetric Data in Solution Models. *Symmetry* **2021**, *13*, 1045. https://doi.org/10.3390/sym13061045

Received: 30 April 2021
Accepted: 21 May 2021
Published: 9 June 2021

Publisher's Note: MDPI stays neutral with regard to jurisdictional claims in published maps and institutional affiliations.

Copyright: © 2021 by the authors. Licensee MDPI, Basel, Switzerland. This article is an open access article distributed under the terms and conditions of the Creative Commons Attribution (CC BY) license (https://creativecommons.org/licenses/by/4.0/).

1. Introduction

This Special Issue covers symmetric and asymmetric data that occur in real-life problems. The existence of data asymmetry causes difficulties when achieving an optimal solution. The authors submitted their theoretical and experimental research, presenting engineering and other problem-solving models dealing with symmetry and asymmetry of different data types.

Accurate balance in the real world is an exceptional case. Decision makers need information about a problem's objectives and the importance of many reasonable goals, guidelines and trade-offs [1]. The role of asymmetric information is more important and weightier. Therefore, solution models offer different integrated tools to balance the overall components of work [2], i.e., to find asymmetry axes concerning goals, risks, and constraints to cope with complicated problems. Policymakers need to find a balance between data objectivity and subjectivity.

Symmetrical and asymmetrical information play a decisive role in many problems. Decision makers address these information asymmetry problems in different ways.

Marwala and Hurwitz [3] noted decreased information asymmetry observed between two artificial intelligent agents, compared to two human agents. If these artificial intelligence agents are present in the financial markets, it reduces arbitrage opportunities and makes them more efficient. As the number of artificially intelligent agents in the market increases, the market's commercial volume will decrease because trade is the information asymmetry [4] in the valuation of goods and services. Information asymmetry is applied in various ways in management research, ranging from conceptualisations of information asymmetry to building resolutions to reduce it [5].

Schmidt and Keil's study show that private information's asymmetry affects a business's normal conduct. Firms with a better understanding of such resources can use this information to assess their own and competitors' advantages [6]. Although different team members incorporate diverse, specialised knowledge, values, and perspectives into overall, strategic decision making, there is a lack of equal information sharing [7].

Since the publication of Shepard pioneering articles on multi-dimensional scaling (MDS) [8,9], the MDS methodology has received wide attention and application by researchers in the behavioural and administrative sciences. Over the last decade, researchers in marketing have applied numerous MDS methods of perceptions and preferences. Harshman [10–14] proposed a new family of models called DEDICOM (DEcomposition into DIrectional COMponents), analysing intrinsically asymmetric data matrices to fulfil a gap in the MDS methodology the lack of suitable models for analysing inherently asymmetric data relationships. Such information often has helpful marketing implications.

Arrow, the Nobel Prize winner in Economics in 1972, examined, among other things, uncertainty in the field of medicine. Arrow noted that a patient must defer to the doctor, and trust that they will use their knowledge to the patient's best advantage to provide the best care. According to Arrow, the doctor relies on trust's social obligation to sell their services to the public, even though the patients do not or cannot inspect the doctor's work quality. Last, he notes how this unique relationship demands that doctors attain high education and certification levels to maintain doctors' medical service quality.

High investment, more comprehensive implementation of plans and polished technologies characterise more recent projects [15]. Many decision-making problems stem from the fact that not all know the information necessary to create a reasonable solution. In one market, product developers have to have detailed information on product functions. It is necessary to understand the importance of asymmetric information [16], as the nobility, if this inefficiency were to cause concern, and the degree of asymmetry are essential, economically. Information asymmetry is the most important, usually in areas where information is complex to receive. Asymmetric information is typically for a problem where one party has more information than another. Thus, stakeholders also need to see an incentive for mechanisms that allow for imperfectly beneficial decisions for both parties.

The degree of asymmetry is different and gives the effect of the prevalence of asymmetric learning [17]. People practice various creative solutions [18]. Individuals make scientific and technological measurements of subjective elements [19] by selecting or collecting data to analyse or explain facts. They create an incentive for company employees [20] to gather information and exchange and collaborate with other companies, rather than through covert means [21].

In addition, they receive confirmation; suppose a company pays against a believer to show that it has the financial resources to repay the money. In that case, the believer has an incentive to pay the company a lower interest than was necessary if the company considered the believer to be a risky borrower [22].

Symmetry examines symmetric phenomena concerning mathematics, physics, interdisciplinary fields and others. According to the results, the following topics can be looked at in the future [23]:

1. Processing complex and varied raw data and examining new operators;
2. Examining symmetry phenomena in artificial intelligence;
3. Identifying symmetry in conforming problems aimed at solving social management problems;
4. Predicting trends in possible changes in time and its weight in dynamic issues;
5. Studying intelligent algorithms and encouraging their stability and reliability.

The evolution of humans' creativity highlights the advantages of symmetry principles [24]. Symmetry is an essential element of design that reflects the balance between a product and its factors [25]. It affects such product conditions as structural efficiency, attractive forms, economic production, and functional or aesthetic requirements [26]. Geometric symmetry means symmetry in space. The ideal shape is the most straightforward: round. Simple symmetrical geometry shapes are safer, more efficient, and more predictable than asymmetrical ones [27]. In industry, more material is needed to make asymmetrical items [28]; therefore, designers prefer symmetrical shapes to asymmetrical ones. There are subjective decisions in every objective measurement. Planners first decide which goals and objectives are essential [29].

Information asymmetry is usually most significant in areas where information is complex, challenging to obtain or both. Asymmetric information is typical of a problem where one party has more information than another does. Insufficient info makes market problems more difficult. The degree of asymmetry is different, yielding testable implications for the prevalence of asymmetric learning. Decision makers should acknowledge a critical parameter corresponding to the degree to which the information is asymmetric. Humans necessarily fill scientific and technology measurements with subjective elements by selecting or collecting, analysing, or interpreting data [30].

Many decision-making problems arise from imperfect information. In a market where customers reach balance and product developers need detailed information about product features, it is necessary to understand the importance of asymmetric information so that nobility, should this inefficiency cause concern, and the degree of asymmetry are economically essential. For this reason, decision makers can use interval type-2 fuzzy sets. The project environment is particularly vulnerable during conflict [31].

The perfect symbol of Yin–Yang is a sign of balance, harmony and moderation. There is symmetrical balance when all parts of an object are well balanced. It is about finding unity in the middle of duality. Human balanced product conditions include structural efficiency, attractiveness, and financial, functional, or aesthetic requirements. It includes compliance with standardisation requirements, production of repetitive elements and mass production, which reduce production costs. In many particular situations, using the balance of the Yin–Yang manufacturing theory and product organisation helps decision makers [32].

Modern decision makers (both scientists and experienced users), when stakes are very high, are critical in defining a problem and multiple conflicting criteria properly, and explicitly evaluating multiple criteria instead of making decisions based on only the intuition of one's own experience. Proper systemic analysis of complex problems leads to more informed and better decisions. The beginning of the 21st century led to the development of both new and much more advanced MCDM (Multi-Criteria Decision-Making) tools. The notion of sustainable development, which is increasingly omnipresent in all activity fields, is part of the knowledge that researchers in management have to acquire [33]. The basic premise is rationality. Often, different MCDM methods do not give the same results [34]. The most popular hybrid MCDM methods show benefits over traditional solutions to complex problems, including stakeholder preferences, interrelated or conflicting criteria, and an unsafe environment [35]. The objectivity, balance and symmetry of decision making highlight paradoxes in the envelope on groups and results.

Correct, logical and rational projects are reliable and sound products that meet critical quality and design requirements of safety, price, and influence; they are expected to have a lower, long-term impact on the environment [36].

The lack of information in the multi-criteria analysis stems from two following sources:

6. Imprecise definition of alternatives, assessment criteria and preferences (or preference scenarios);
7. Inaccurate measurement of the impact of other options on the assessment criteria and preferential weights.

Modern decision makers (scientists and expert users) define problems with many conflicting criteria rather than adopting decisions based solely on intuition. As a result, researchers need to research with a wide range of knowledge. Exogenous asymmetric information is the basis of many traditional models of contract theory [37,38]. Thus, some authors have examined theoretical processing models, where asymmetric information appears endogenous if agents decide to collect information. Nowadays, the supply chains' environmental and economic factors have come to the fore due to more critical competition conditions [39].

Environmental restoration, revival and recovery are vital principles for sustainable development and human well-being. There is balance when all the objects' features are symmetrically well balanced [40]. Using interval type-2 fuzzy sets helps decision makers deal more effectively with the uncertainty of experts or decision makers' opinions, judgements and preferences [41].

Civil design and engineering are central to the axes of a multi-disciplinary (multi-dimensional) world, linked to many disciplines, which are, therefore, interrelated. Symmetry and structural regularity are essential concepts in many natural and manufactured objects and play an essential role in the world's design, construction, and development [42]. A project and plan's success depends mainly on balancing needs (symmetry) and its satisfaction on correctly defining many success indicators [43]. Sustainable and efficient development is one of the most significant challenges of modern society if we want to save the world for future generations [44]. In discrete, multi-criteria decision-making processes, the weights of criteria are the essential components on which decision makers make their final decisions. Designers that design products use several different subjective and objective requirements to select materiality and structural solutions, considering impacts on environmental aspects [45]. The Vague Kit is a methodological concept of knowledge that allows people, worldwide, to explore possible examples of medium-sized individual alternatives with a perfect decision-making tool [46].

Market participants avoid investment in new and successful technologies since such decisions are linked to personal training, higher start-up costs, and uncertainties about possible profits [47]. The choice of efficient technological industry systems is a complex task with several criteria. Many decision makers reject innovations that face similar difficulties [48]. Therefore, the most excellent valuation methods try to make, as decision makers, the most economical decisions and, above all, these decisions are only for economic objectives [49].

Over the last 40 years, despite many new and progressive technologies for applied industry projects, the sectors' efficiency has remained relatively low. Older researchers propose that digital technologies allow for fast, flexible forms of project organisation [50]. Technological and social growth shape social preferences to stop non-renewable sources and energy consumption and pollutant emissions into the environment as much as possible. It requires the development of systems and technologies for waste disposal, storage and regulatory enforcement. Old residential buildings consume a considerable amount of European energy [51]. The choice of an excellent site to implement projects is of great importance since the practice collaborates independently in the knowledge-rich and multi-functional working environments. The success of the choice of sites is an abstract concept. It decides, to the greatest extent, whether a project is a success or a failure. Decision theory usually analyses a player's perspective, while game theory emphasises its analysis of many players' interactions [52].

Therefore, it is necessary to retrofit them. There is a mass financial gap between the excellent post armament and its modernisation. The industrial sector uses the most significant parts of natural resources and generates increasing waste. In countries with the most significant growing populations, well-being, and urbanisation, the municipalities' significant challenges are to collect waste to be recycled and disposed of [53].

2. Contributions

After careful evaluation, seventeen papers were accepted and are published in the Special Issue.

The Special Issue raised the interest of researchers from different scientific schools in Europa, Asia and South America. Sixty-seven researchers from sixteen different countries contributed to the published papers (Figure 1). The most significant number of researchers were from Lithuania. Ten authors contributed from Serbia and China. From the other remaining countries, one to four authors participated.

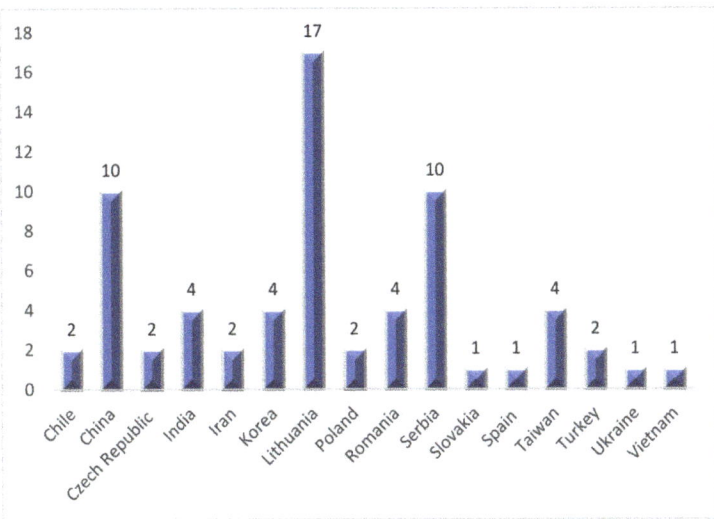

Figure 1. The number of authors from different countries.

Publications were evenly distributed according to whether authors produced them from one country or by international collectives: authors prepared nine papers from one country and the other eight were from international collectives (Table 1). Leading countries by the number of publications are Lithuania (three national collectives and four international collectives) and the Czech Republic (two papers).

Table 1. Publications by countries.

Countries	Number of Papers
Lithuania	3
Czech Republic	2
Poland	1
Romania	1
Taiwan	1
Korea	1
Iran–Lithuania	1
China–Lithuania	1
Ukraine–Slovakia–Lithuania	1
Serbia–Turkey–Lithuania	1
Serbia–Vietnam	1
Korea–India	1
China–India	1
Chile–Spain–Turkey	1

The authors proposed different solution models, mainly covering uncertain data in multi-criteria decision-making problems, as complex tools to deal with complicated problems in engineering or management (Table 2).

Table 2. Publications by solution methods and application areas.

References	Applied/Developed Solution Methods	Type of Data Uncertainty	Application Areas
[54]	AHP, FAHP	Fuzzy sets	Numerical examples, no real case study
[55]	Neutrosophic WASPAS	Single-valued neutrosophic sets	Evaluate the quality of the aerial image
[56]	Global sensitivity analysis of quantiles	Uncertain model inputs as random variables	Resistance of a steel member under compression
[57]	ANN	Crisp data	Construction project management
[58]	Fuzzy inference model	Fuzzy sets	Construction project management
[59]	Quantile-oriented sensitivity analysis	The variance of the input variable	Engineering tasks
[60]	A pattern recognition (PR) algorithm	Neural information	Development of intelligent prosthetic/rehabilitation devices
[61]	ENTROPY, WASPAS-SVNS, VASMA	Single-valued neutrosophic set	The choice of the kindergarten institution
[62]	Wilson's formulation	Varying parameters of the model	Supply chain management
[63]	Pulley-cable transmission and Bowden cable transmission	Geometrical and behavioural parameters of the biological hand	Medical robotics: motor rehabilitation treatment
[64]	DANP, Entropy, VIKOR, DANP-mV	Subjective and objective weights	Supply chain in electronic manufacturing
[23]	Bibliometric analysis	Certain data	Bibliometric analysis of the Journal
[65]	Extended TOPSIS	Single-valued neutrosophic sets	Ranking e-commerce development strategies
[66]	QSVBNS	Quadripartitioned single-valued and bipolar neutrosophic sets (QSVNS and BNS)	Green supplier selection
[67]	PIPRECIA, Interval-valued triangular fuzzy ARAS	Interval-valued triangular fuzzy sets	Evaluation of e-learning courses
[68]	CRITIC, CoCoSo-G	Grey values	Location selection of a temporary hospital during COVID-19 pandemic
[69]	Big data analysis, text mining, correlation analysis	Structured, unstructured and semi-structured data	Real estate market

More than half of the papers proposed different, multiple-criteria decision-making models, mainly dealing with uncertain data. Fuzzy sets [54,57,67] or single-valued neutrosophic sets [55,61,65,66] were the most often applied for modelling uncertain data.

The application fields of the proposed solution models rather often involved different engineering problems. Much attention was given to civil engineering in terms of construction project management [56,58] and the analysis of building structures [59,61]. Three papers analysed the optimisation of supply chains [62,64,66]. Two papers aimed to optimise e-activities, namely, to rank e-commerce development strategies [65] and to evaluate e-learning courses [67]. Two papers solved mechanical medical problems in rehabilitation [60,63]. An up-to-date medical-area problem was solved in [68], namely, location selection of a temporary hospital during the COVID-19 pandemic. It is worth mentioning the excellent article published in the current Special Issue, which is the bibliometric analysis of publications in the *Symmetry* journal from 2009 to 2019 [23], which helps readers to understand past and current research scopes of the journal as well as future trends of its development.

3. Conclusions

The Special Issue raised the interest of researchers from different scientific schools in Europa, Asia and South America. Researchers from sixteen different countries, including eight international collectives, contributed to the papers published in the issue.

As regards solution models, more than half of the papers proposed multiple-criteria decision-making models. These models mostly covered partly uncertain or entirely uncertain data, integrating crisp MCDM methods with interval-valued fuzzy or neutrosophic sets theory. Therefore, we can conclude that the suggested hybrid decision-making techniques are well applicable to symmetric/asymmetric data modelling.

The application fields of the proposed solution models involved both problems of engineering and management sciences. Supply chain management, construction project management or other civil engineering problems, e-activities, and even problems in the medical field can be marked as application areas that received the most attention.

Author Contributions: All authors contributed equally to this work. All authors have read and agreed to the published version of the manuscript.

Funding: This research received no external funding.

Institutional Review Board Statement: Not applicable.

Informed Consent Statement: Not applicable.

Data Availability Statement: Data sharing not applicable.

Acknowledgments: Authors express their gratitude to the journal *Symmetry*.

Conflicts of Interest: The authors declare no conflict of interest.

References

1. Gompf, K.; Traverso, M.; Hetterich, J. Using Analytical Hierarchy Process (AHP) to Introduce Weights to Social Life Cycle Assessment of Mobility Services. *Sustainability* **2021**, *13*, 1258. [CrossRef]
2. Zhang, H.; Sun, Q. An Integrated MCDM Approach to Train Derailment Risk Response Strategy Selection. *Symmetry* **2019**, *12*, 47. [CrossRef]
3. Marwala, T.; Hurwitz, E. *Artificial Intelligence and Economic Theory: Skynet in the Market*; Springer Science and Business Media LLC: London, UK, 2017.
4. Paliwal, V.; Chandra, S.; Sharma, S. Blockchain Technology for Sustainable Supply Chain Management: A Systematic Literature Review and a Classification Framework. *Sustainability* **2020**, *12*, 7638. [CrossRef]
5. Bergh, D.D.; Ketchen, J.D.J.; Orlandi, I.; Heugens, P.P.M.A.R.; Boyd, B.K. Information Asymmetry in Management Research: Past Accomplishments and Future Opportunities. *J. Manag.* **2019**, *45*, 122–158. [CrossRef]
6. Schmidt, J.; Keil, T. What Makes a Resource Valuable? Identifying the Drivers of Firm-Idiosyncratic Resource Value. *Acad. Manag. Rev.* **2013**, *38*, 206–228. [CrossRef]
7. Ozmel, U.; Reuer, J.J.; Gulati, R. Signals across Multiple Networks: How Venture Capital and Alliance Networks Affect Interorganizational Collaboration. *Acad. Manag. J.* **2013**, *56*, 852–866. [CrossRef]
8. Shepard, R.N. The analysis of proximities: Multidimensional scaling with an unknown distance function. I. *Psychometrika* **1962**, *27*, 125–140. [CrossRef]
9. Shepard, R.N. The analysis of proximities: Multidimensional scaling with an unknown distance function. II. *Psychometrika* **1962**, *27*, 219–246. [CrossRef]
10. Harshman, R.A. Models for Analysis of Asymmetrical Relationships among N Objects or Stimuli. In Proceedings of the First Joint Meeting of the Psychometric Society and the Society of Mathematical Psychology, Hamilton, ON, Canada, 25–27 August 1978.
11. Harshman, R.A. *DEDICOM Multidimensional Analysis of Skew-Symmetric Data. Part I: Theory*; Unpublished Technical Memorandum; Bell Laboratories: Murray Hill, NJ, USA, 1981.
12. Harshman, R.A. *Scaling and Rotation DEDICOM solutions*; Unpublished Manuscript; University of Western Ontario: London, ON, Canada, 1982.
13. Harshman, R.A. *DEDICOM: A Family of Models Generalizing Factor Analysis and Multidimensional Scaling for Decomposition of Asymmetric Relationships*; Unpublished Manuscript; University of Western Ontario: London, ON, Canada, 1982.

14. Harshman, R.A.; Green, P.E.; Wind, Y.; Lundy, M.E. A Model for the Analysis of Asymmetric Data in Marketing Research. *Mark. Sci.* **1982**, *1*, 205–242. [CrossRef]
15. Echarri-Iribarren, V.; Sotos-Solano, C.; Espinosa-Fernández, A.; Prado-Govea, R. The Passivhaus Standard in the Spanish Mediterranean: Evaluation of a House's Thermal Behaviour of Enclosures and Airtightness. *Sustainability* **2019**, *11*, 3732. [CrossRef]
16. Łuczak, A.; Just, M. A Complex MCDM Procedure for the Assessment of Economic Development of Units at Different Government Levels. *Mathematics* **2020**, *8*, 1067. [CrossRef]
17. Huang, C.-Y.; Hsieh, H.-L.; Chen, H. Evaluating the Investment Projects of Spinal Medical Device Firms Using the Real Option and DANP-mV Based MCDM Methods. *Int. J. Environ. Res. Public Health* **2020**, *17*, 3335. [CrossRef]
18. Wang, C.-N.; Yang, C.-Y.; Cheng, H.-C. A Fuzzy Multicriteria Decision-Making (MCDM) Model for Sustainable Supplier Evaluation and Selection Based on Triple Bottom Line Approaches in the Garment Industry. *Processes* **2019**, *7*, 400. [CrossRef]
19. Chang, S.-C.; Chang, H.-H.; Lu, M.-T. Evaluating Industry 4.0 Technology Application in SMEs: Using a Hybrid MCDM Approach. *Mathematics* **2021**, *9*, 414. [CrossRef]
20. Turskis, Z.; Goranin, N.; Nurusheva, A.; Boranbayev, S. Information Security Risk Assessment in Critical Infrastructure: A Hybrid MCDM Approach. *Informatica* **2019**, *30*, 187–211. [CrossRef]
21. Zhao, Q.; Tsai, P.-H.; Wang, J.-L. Improving Financial Service Innovation Strategies for Enhancing China's Banking Industry Competitive Advantage during the Fintech Revolution: A Hybrid MCDM Model. *Sustainability* **2019**, *11*, 1419. [CrossRef]
22. Dahooie, J.H.; Hajiagha, S.H.R.; Farazmehr, S.; Zavadskas, E.K.; Antucheviciene, J. A novel dynamic credit risk evaluation method using data envelopment analysis with common weights and combination of multi-attribute decision-making methods. *Comput. Oper. Res.* **2021**, *129*, 105223. [CrossRef]
23. Li, B.; Xu, Z.; Zavadskas, E.K.; Antuchevičienė, J.; Turskis, Z. A Bibliometric Analysis of Symmetry (2009–2019). *Symmetry* **2020**, *12*, 1304. [CrossRef]
24. Liu, G.; Fan, S.; Tu, Y.; Wang, G. Innovative Supplier Selection from Collaboration Perspective with a Hybrid MCDM Model: A Case Study Based on NEVs Manufacturer. *Symmetry* **2021**, *13*, 143. [CrossRef]
25. Zavadskas, E.K.; Turskis, Z.; Antucheviciene, J. Solution Models based on Symmetric and Asymmetric Information. *Symmetry* **2019**, *11*, 500. [CrossRef]
26. Marković, V.; Stajić, L.; Stević, Ž.; Mitrović, G.; Novarlić, B.; Radojičić, Z. A Novel Integrated Subjective-Objective MCDM Model for Alternative Ranking in Order to Achieve Business Excellence and Sustainability. *Symmetry* **2020**, *12*, 164. [CrossRef]
27. Amato, A.; Andreoli, M.; Rovai, M. Adaptive Reuse of a Historic Building by Introducing New Functions: A Scenario Evaluation Based on Participatory MCA Applied to a Former Carthusian Monastery in Tuscany, Italy. *Sustainability* **2021**, *13*, 2335. [CrossRef]
28. Pan, B.; Liu, S.; Xie, Z.; Shao, Y.; Li, X.; Ge, R. Evaluating Operational Features of Three Unconventional Intersections under Heavy Traffic Based on CRITIC Method. *Sustainability* **2021**, *13*, 4098. [CrossRef]
29. Faizi, S.; Sałabun, W.; Rashid, T.; Zafar, S.; Wątróbski, J. Intuitionistic Fuzzy Sets in Multi-Criteria Group Decision Making Problems Using the Characteristic Objects Method. *Symmetry* **2020**, *12*, 1382. [CrossRef]
30. Alyamani, R.; Long, S. The Application of Fuzzy Analytic Hierarchy Process in Sustainable Project Selection. *Sustainability* **2020**, *12*, 8314. [CrossRef]
31. Dobrovolskienė, N.; Pozniak, A.; Tvaronavičienė, M. Assessment of the Sustainability of a Real Estate Project Using Multi-Criteria Decision Making. *Sustainability* **2021**, *13*, 4352. [CrossRef]
32. Zolfani, S.H.; Zavadskas, E.K.; Turskis, Z. Design of Products with Both International and Local Perspectives based on Yin-Yang Balance Theory and Swara Method. *Econ. Res. Ekon. Istraživanja* **2013**, *26*, 153–166. [CrossRef]
33. Studen, L.; Tiberius, V. Social Media, Quo Vadis? Prospective Development and Implications. *Futur. Internet* **2020**, *12*, 146. [CrossRef]
34. Melnik-Leroy, G.A.; Dzemyda, G. How to Influence the Results of MCDM?—Evidence of the Impact of Cognitive Biases. *Mathematics* **2021**, *9*, 121. [CrossRef]
35. Marhavilas, P.K.; Filippidis, M.; Koulinas, G.K.; Koulouriotis, D.E. A HAZOP with MCDM Based Risk-Assessment Approach: Focusing on the Deviations with Economic/Health/Environmental Impacts in a Process Industry. *Sustainability* **2020**, *12*, 993. [CrossRef]
36. Baç, U. An Integrated SWARA-WASPAS Group Decision Making Framework to Evaluate Smart Card Systems for Public Transportation. *Mathematics* **2020**, *8*, 1723. [CrossRef]
37. Baron, D.P.; Myerson, R.B. Regulating a Monopolist with Unknown Costs. *Econometrica* **1982**, *50*, 911. [CrossRef]
38. Maskin, E.; Riley, J. Monopoly with Incomplete Information. *RAND J. Econ.* **1984**, *15*, 171. [CrossRef]
39. Keshavarz Ghorabaee, M.; Amiri, M.; Zavadskas, E.K.; Turskis, Z.; Antucheviciene, J. A new multi-criteria model based on interval type-2 fuzzy sets and EDAS method for supplier evaluation and order allocation with environmental considerations. *Comput. Ind. Eng.* **2017**, *112*, 156–174. [CrossRef]
40. Faizi, S.; Sałabun, W.; Ullah, S.; Rashid, T.; Więckowski, J. A New Method to Support Decision-Making in an Uncertain Environment Based on Normalized Interval-Valued Triangular Fuzzy Numbers and COMET Technique. *Symmetry* **2020**, *12*, 516. [CrossRef]

41. Keshavarz-Ghorabaee, M.; Amiri, M.; Zavadskas, E.K.; Turskis, Z.; Antuchevičienė, J. An Extended Step-Wise Weight Assessment Ratio Analysis with Symmetric Interval Type-2 Fuzzy Sets for Determining the Subjective Weights of Criteria in Multi-Criteria Decision-Making Problems. *Symmetry* **2018**, *10*, 91. [CrossRef]
42. Dahooie, J.H.; Zavadskas, E.K.; Abolhasani, M.; Vanaki, A.; Turskis, Z. A Novel Approach for Evaluation of Projects Using an Interval–Valued Fuzzy Additive Ratio Assessment (ARAS) Method: A Case Study of Oil and Gas Well Drilling Projects. *Symmetry* **2018**, *10*, 45. [CrossRef]
43. Radović, D.; Stević, Ž.; Pamučar, D.; Zavadskas, E.K.; Badi, I.; Antuchevičiene, J.; Turskis, Z. Measuring Performance in Transportation Companies in Developing Countries: A Novel Rough ARAS Model. *Symmetry* **2018**, *10*, 434. [CrossRef]
44. Turskis, Z.; Antuchevičienė, J.; Keršulienė, V.; Gaidukas, G. Hybrid Group MCDM Model to Select the Most Effective Alternative of the Second Runway of the Airport. *Symmetry* **2019**, *11*, 792. [CrossRef]
45. Turskis, Z.; Urbonas, K.; Daniūnas, A. A Hybrid Fuzzy Group Multi-Criteria Assessment of Structural Solutions of the Symmetric Frame Alternatives. *Symmetry* **2019**, *11*, 261. [CrossRef]
46. Turskis, Z.; Dzitac, S.; Stankiuviene, A.; Šukys, R. A Fuzzy Group Decision-making Model for Determining the Most Influential Persons in the Sustainable Prevention of Accidents in the Construction SMEs. *Int. J. Comput. Commun. Control* **2019**, *14*, 90–106. [CrossRef]
47. Zemlickienė, V.; Turskis, Z. Evaluation of the expediency of technology commercialization: A case of information technology and biotechnology. *Technol. Econ. Dev. Econ.* **2020**, *26*, 271–289. [CrossRef]
48. Zavadskas, E.K.; Turskis, Z.; Volvačiovas, R.; Kildiene, S. Multi-criteria Assessment Model of Technologies. *Stud. Inform. Control* **2013**, *22*, 249–258. [CrossRef]
49. Sivilevicius, H.; Zavadskas, E.K.; Turskis, Z. Quality attributes and complex assessment methodology of the asphalt mixing plant. *Balt. J. Road Bridg. Eng.* **2008**, *3*, 161–166. [CrossRef]
50. Erdogan, S.A.; Šaparauskas, J.; Turskis, Z. Decision Making in Construction Management: AHP and Expert Choice Approach. *Procedia Eng.* **2017**, *172*, 270–276. [CrossRef]
51. Ruzgys, A.; Volvačiovas, R.; Ignatavičius, Č.; Turskis, Z. Integrated evaluation of external wall insulation in residential buildings using SWARA-TODIM MCDM method. *J. Civ. Eng. Manag.* **2014**, *20*, 103–110. [CrossRef]
52. Javanmardi, E.; Liu, S. Exploring Grey Systems Theory-Based Methods and Applications in Analyzing Socio-Economic Systems. *Sustainability* **2019**, *11*, 4192. [CrossRef]
53. Turskis, Z.; Lazauskas, M.; Zavadskas, E.K. Fuzzy multiple criteria assessment of construction site alternatives for non-hazardous waste incineration plant in Vilnius city, applying ARAS-F and AHP methods. *J. Environ. Eng. Landsc. Manag.* **2012**, *20*, 110–120. [CrossRef]
54. Vinogradova-Zinkevič, I.; Podvezko, V.; Zavadskas, E. Comparative Assessment of the Stability of AHP and FAHP Methods. *Symmetry* **2021**, *13*, 479. [CrossRef]
55. Bausys, R.; Kazakeviciute-Januskeviciene, G. Qualitative Rating of Lossy Compression for Aerial Imagery by Neutrosophic WASPAS Method. *Symmetry* **2021**, *13*, 273. [CrossRef]
56. Kala, Z. Global Sensitivity Analysis of Quantiles: New Importance Measure Based on Superquantiles and Subquantiles. *Symmetry* **2021**, *13*, 263. [CrossRef]
57. Balali, A.; Valipour, A.; Antucheviciene, J.; Šaparauskas, J.; Balali, A. Improving the Results of the Earned Value Management Technique Using Artificial Neural Networks in Construction Projects. *Symmetry* **2020**, *12*, 1745. [CrossRef]
58. Plebankiewicz, E.; Wieczorek, D. Adaptation of a Cost Overrun Risk Prediction Model to the Type of Construction Facility. *Symmetry* **2020**, *12*, 1739. [CrossRef]
59. Kala, Z. From Probabilistic to Quantile-Oriented Sensitivity Analysis: New Indices of Design Quantiles. *Symmetry* **2020**, *12*, 1720. [CrossRef]
60. Asogbon, M.G.; Samuel, O.W.; Jiang, Y.; Wang, L.; Geng, Y.; Sangaiah, A.K.; Chen, S.; Fang, P.; Li, G. Appropriate Feature Set and Window Parameters Selection for Efficient Motion Intent Characterization towards Intelligently Smart EMG-PR System. *Symmetry* **2020**, *12*, 1710. [CrossRef]
61. Lescauskiene, I.; Bausys, R.; Zavadskas, E.K.; Juodagalviene, B. VASMA Weighting: Survey-Based Criteria Weighting Methodology that Combines ENTROPY and WASPAS-SVNS to Reflect the Psychometric Features of the VAS Scales. *Symmetry* **2020**, *12*, 1641. [CrossRef]
62. Nestorenko, T.; Morkunas, M.; Peliova, J.; Volkov, A.; Balezentis, T.; Streimkiene, D. A New Model for Determining the EOQ under Changing Price Parameters and Reordering Time. *Symmetry* **2020**, *12*, 1512. [CrossRef]
63. Birouaș, F.I.; Țarcă, R.C.; Dzitac, S.; Dzitac, I. Preliminary Results in Testing of a Novel Asymmetric Underactuated Robotic Hand Exoskeleton for Motor Impairment Rehabilitation. *Symmetry* **2020**, *12*, 1470. [CrossRef]
64. Huang, S.-W.; Liou, J.J.; Tang, W.; Tzeng, G.-H. Location Selection of a Manufacturing Facility from the Perspective of Supply Chain Sustainability. *Symmetry* **2020**, *12*, 1418. [CrossRef]
65. Karabašević, D.; Stanujkić, D.; Zavadskas, E.K.; Stanimirović, P.; Popović, G.; Predić, B.; Ulutaş, A. A Novel Extension of the TOPSIS Method Adapted for the Use of Single-Valued Neutrosophic Sets and Hamming Distance for E-Commerce Development Strategies Selection. *Symmetry* **2020**, *12*, 1263. [CrossRef]
66. Roy, S.; Lee, J.-G.; Pal, A.; Samanta, S.K. Similarity Measures of Quadripartitioned Single Valued Bipolar Neutrosophic Sets and Its Application in Multi-Criteria Decision Making Problems. *Symmetry* **2020**, *12*, 1012. [CrossRef]

67. Jocic, K.J.; Jocic, G.; Karabasevic, D.; Popovic, G.; Stanujkic, D.; Zavadskas, E.K.; Nguyen, P.T. A Novel Integrated PIPRECIA–Interval-Valued Triangular Fuzzy ARAS Model: E-Learning Course Selection. *Symmetry* **2020**, *12*, 928. [CrossRef]
68. Zolfani, S.H.; Yazdani, M.; Torkayesh, A.E.; Derakhti, A. Application of a Gray-Based Decision Support Framework for Location Selection of a Temporary Hospital during COVID-19 Pandemic. *Symmetry* **2020**, *12*, 886. [CrossRef]
69. Lee, S.-H.; Kim, J.-H.; Huh, J.-H. Land Price Forecasting Research by Macro and Micro Factors and Real Estate Market Utilization Plan Research by Landscape Factors: Big Data Analysis Approach. *Symmetry* **2021**, *13*, 616. [CrossRef]

Article
A Bibliometric Analysis of Symmetry (2009–2019)

Bo Li [1], Zeshui Xu [2,*], Edmundas Kazimieras Zavadskas [3,*], Jurgita Antuchevičienė [4] and Zenonas Turskis [5]

1. Institute for Disaster Management and Reconstruction, Sichuan University, Chengdu 610207, China; libo_0206@stu.scu.edu.cn
2. Business School, Sichuan University, Chengdu 610064, China
3. Department of Construction Management and Real Estate, Institute of Sustainable Construction, Vilnius Gediminas Technical University, LT–10223 Vilnius, Saulėtekio al. 11, Lithuania
4. Department of Construction Management and Real Estate, Vilnius Gediminas Technical University, LT–10223 Vilnius, Saulėtekio al. 11, Lithuania; jurgita.antucheviciene@vgtu.lt
5. Institute of Sustainable Construction, Vilnius Gediminas Technical University, LT–10223 Vilnius, Saulėtekio al. 11, Lithuania; zenonas.turskis@vgtu.lt
* Correspondence: xuzeshui@263.net (Z.X.); edmundas.zavadskas@vgtu.lt (E.K.Z.)

Received: 20 July 2020; Accepted: 29 July 2020; Published: 5 August 2020

Abstract: *Symmetry* is an international journal in the research fields of physics, chemistry, biology, mathematics, computer science, theory and methods, and other scientific disciplines and engineering. The first paper was published in 2009. Here, we make a bibliometric analysis of publications in *Symmetry* from 2009 to 2019. According to Web of Science (WoS), we obtained 3215 publications in this journal. First, we explore the publications, citation number, and citation structure based on bibliometric indicators. Second, we analyze the most influential objects, including countries/regions, institutions, authors, and papers. Cooperation networks are also presented. Next, the co-citation and burst detection analyses are conducted according to the techniques of visualization tools, i.e., VOSviewer and CiteSpace. Furthermore, the co-occurrence analyses and timeline view analyses of keywords are investigated, aiming to explore the research hotspots. Finally, this paper provides relatively thorough perspectives and reviews and discloses the future development trend of this journal and challenges for scholars, which will promote the development of the journal and in-depth research of scholars.

Keywords: *Symmetry*; bibliometric analysis; Web of Science; co-citation; burst detection analysis

1. Introduction

The bibliometric method has been widely applied in exploring publications' structure and the development of a journal. In recent years, scholars have systematically researched journals, such as *European Journal of Operational Research* [1], *Technological and Economic Development of Economy* [2], *Information Sciences* [3], *IEEE Transactions on Fuzzy Systems* [4], *International Journal of Strategic Property Management* [5], *Journal of Civil Engineering and Management* [6], and *Baltic Journal of Road and Bridge Engineering* [7]. The development trends of various research topics are also conducted, related to fuzzy decision making [8], sustainable energy [9], support vector machines [10], etc. Combining with visualization tools, i.e., VOSviewer [11,12], CiteSpace [13–15], CiteNetExplorer [16], Bicomb [17,18], BibExcel [19,20], etc., the science mapping enriches the contents of bibliometric analyses from co-citation, co-occurrence, co-authorship, and burst detection aspects. It also helps scholars intuitively grasp research trends greatly and main research focuses in different phases [21]. In this paper, VOSviewer and CiteSpace are used to demonstrate the characteristics of the journal. The former conducts the co-citation analysis, co-authorship analysis, and co-occurrence analysis, aiming to present the structure of publications. The latter is chosen to cluster keywords and track development trends in different years of the journal by cluster analysis, burst detection analysis, and timeline analysis.

Symmetry is an international open-access journal indexed by the Science Citation Index Expanded (Web of Science, search for "*Symmetry-Basel*"), Scopus, MathSciNet (American Mathematical Society), and other databases with an impact factor of 2.645 by Journal Citation Reports (2019). It covers research on symmetry phenomena in scientific studies, including physics, chemistry, biology, mathematics, computer science, theory and method, etc. The details are listed as Table 1:

Table 1. The subject areas of *Symmetry*.

Fields	Subject Areas
Physics	conservation laws, Noether's theorem, spatial parity, charge parity, time parity, G-parity, standard model, internal symmetry, Lorentz symmetry, transformations, invariance, conservation, local and global symmetries, laws and symmetry, symmetry breaking, color symmetry, periodic and quasiperiodic crystals, time-reversal symmetry breaking, symmetry and complexity, Curie-Rosen symmetry principles, constants, biophysics, entropy, and indistinguishability
Chemistry	crystal and crystallography; chiral molecules, chiral resolution and asymmetric synthesis, asymmetric induction, chiral auxiliaries and chiral catalysts, stereochemistry, diastereomers, stereogenic, stereoisomers (enantiomers, atropisomers, diastereomers), stability, mixing, and phase separation
Biology	symmetry in biology, radial symmetry (tetramerism, pentamerism, etc.), diversity, preservation, sustainability, morphology, origin of life, and molecular evolution (homochirality)
Mathematics	invariance, transformation, group theory, Lie groups, chirality, achiral or amphichiral, helix and Möbius strip, knot theory, graph theory, isometry, plane of symmetry, skewness, vertex algebra, asymmetry, dissymmetry, nonsymmetry and antisymmetry, supergroups and nonlinear algebraic structures, supersymmetry and supergravity, strings and branes, integrability and geometry, information theory, Felix Klein's Erlangen Program, and continuous symmetry
Computer Science, Theory and Methods	computer-aided design, computational geometry, computer graphics, visualization, image compression, data compression, pattern recognition, diversity, similarity, and conservation and sustainability

To date, *Symmetry* has published over 3000 documents with the development of 12 years. Therefore, it is valuable to explore the development trend based on bibliometric methods and science mapping. Since the first paper published in *Symmetry* in 2009, we analyze the journal from 2009 to 2019 mainly from following aspects (considering the completeness of data, we only searched the publications from 2009 to 2019): (1) the basic characteristics of publications are presented to describe development status, including the type of publications, annual number, citation number, and the productive contributors; (2) the top 15 most cited papers are listed. The influential countries/regions, institutions, and authors in the journal are provided, based on the total number of publications (TP), the total number of citations (TC), the number of citation-year distribution (C), the number of average citation (AC), H-index, the number of publications that satisfy certain citations (i.e., ≥100, ≥50) [22,23], etc. Besides, we also analyze the important cooperation relationship; (3) the co-citation analyses at the level of reference/source/authors, the burst detections of cited authors and cited journals, and the co-occurrence analyses and timeline view analysis of keywords are given, which is conducive to clear the development directions and the changes of research focus; (4) the future challenges of *Symmetry* are also discussed, combining with the above results.

The rest of this paper is organized as follows: Section 2 illustrates the data source and analyzes the basic characteristics, i.e., publications, citation numbers, and citation structure. The influential contributors in terms of papers, countries/regions, institutions, and authors are presented in Section 3. The co-citation and burst detections analyses are given in Section 4. Section 5 focuses on the co-occurrence and timeline view analyses of keywords. Section 6 discusses the characteristics of this journal and presents future suggestions according to the whole analyses. Some conclusions are provided to end this paper in Section 7.

2. Data Source and Basic Characteristics

This paper mainly uses the bibliometric method to study the publications in *Symmetry* from 2009 to 2019. The literature data are from the Web of Science (WoS) Core Collection database on June 24, 2020, using *Symmetry-Basel* (we replace *Symmetry-Basel* with *Symmetry* below). Then, through the search for the journal's name, we found 3125 papers.

Base on the analytic results given by WoS, we obtain Figure 1 and find that the paper types published on *Symmetry* are classified into five kinds. The number of articles is 2941 and far more than other types of publications. This is followed by 161 reviews, 21 editorial material, 2 corrections, and 1 biographic item. This phenomenon shows that *Symmetry* focuses on academic articles. Then, the total number of publications (TP), the total number of citations distribution (TC), and the number of citation-year distribution (C) in the journal from 2009 to 2019 are illustrated in Figure 2. In this paper, we also use AC to denote the average number of citations per publication.

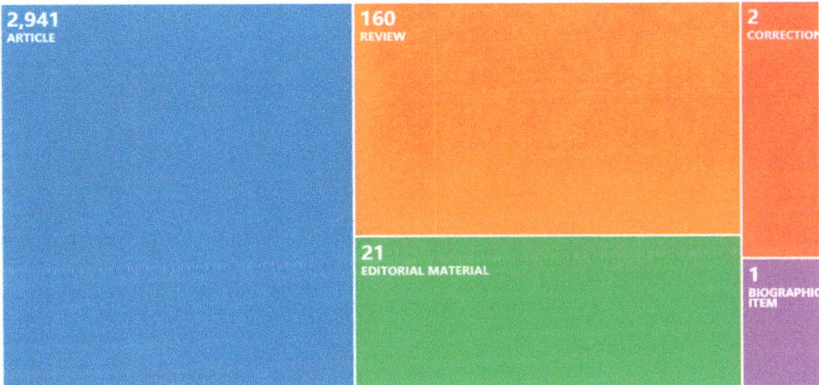

Figure 1. Types of the *Symmetry* publications.

From Figure 2a, the annual number of publications per year shows an increasing trend. To be specific, the annual publications were less than 100 before 2015. Then, it has been increasing rapidly, and the annual publications have been greater than 1000 in 2019, which shows that more and more scholars have paid attention to the journal.

Furthermore, Figure 2a describes the citation numbers of papers published in each year. The publications receive the most citations (3324) in 2018, followed by 2234 citations in 2019, and 1930 citations in 2017. The trend of citations had three peaks, i.e., in 2010 (1388), 2015 (918), and 2018 (3324), respectively. Figure 2b illustrates the citation numbers of each year from 2009 to 2019. We can see that the citation-year distributions increased year by year. In 2009, the number of citations was only 3; since 2011, the annual number of citations was more than 100. By 2018, the number of citations increased to 1840, which denotes that *Symmetry* was paid close attention. The low citation-year, i.e., 2013, does not mean that no excellent studies appeared; the number of citations is dynamic and time is required for publications to be widely recognized and cited [24]. Table 2 is provided to explore more detailed information about *Symmetry*. Among the several indicators, H-index considers both the number of publications and citations; the index without self-citations is an important indicator. A high H-index implies a greater achievement [25]. Furthermore, different intervals reflect the number of citations; for example, ≥50 denotes the number of publications that cited times great than or equal to 50. From Table 2, the paper published in 2018 has the greatest TC (3324) and H-index (24), 2010 has the greatest AC (18). It is obvious that as time goes by, the influence of *Symmetry* has increased. Based on the data collection from WoS, only in 2010 and 2015 were there two papers that satisfy the standard of "≥100", and three papers were high-cited papers.

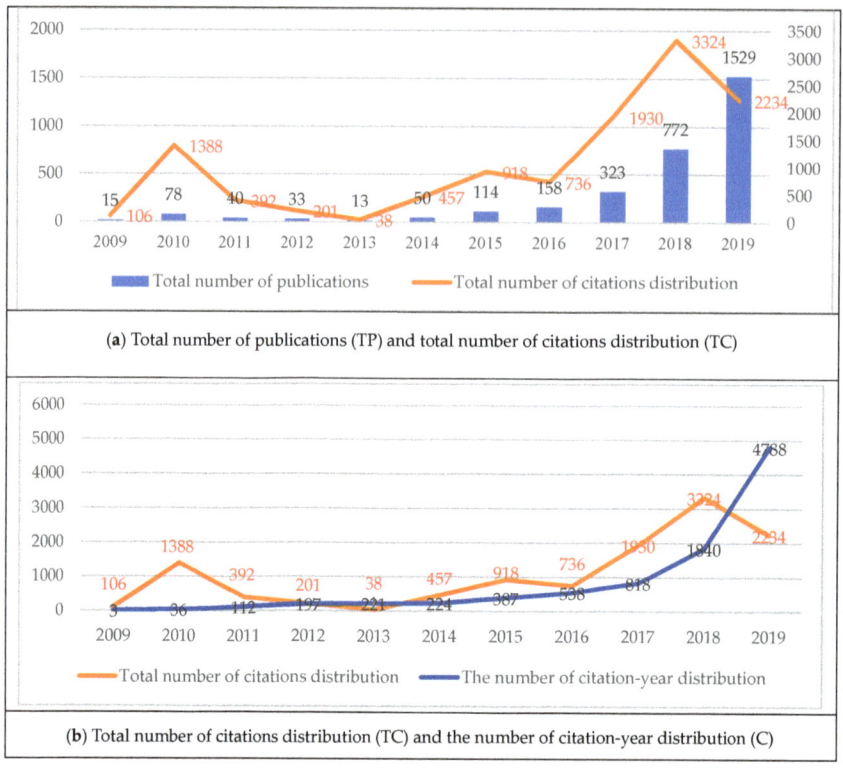

(a) Total number of publications (TP) and total number of citations distribution (TC)

(b) Total number of citations distribution (TC) and the number of citation-year distribution (C)

Figure 2. The number of publications and citations distribution.

Table 2. *Symmetry* publication characteristics from 2009 to 2019.

Year	TP [1]	TC	AC	H-Index	≥100	≥50	≥20	≥10	≥5
2009	15	106	7	6	0	0	2	4	6
2010	78	1388	**18**	18	2	8	16	35	48
2011	40	392	10	12	0	1	4	14	20
2012	33	201	6	7	0	1	0	4	9
2013	13	38	3	4	0	0	0	0	2
2014	50	457	9	9	0	3	5	9	24
2015	114	918	8	13	2	0	8	20	41
2016	158	736	5	14	0	0	7	20	50
2017	323	1930	6	20	0	1	21	57	128
2018	772	**3324**	4	**24**	0	3	31	74	210
2019	**1529**	2234	1	15	0	3	10	37	109
Total	3125	11,724	-	-	4	20	104	274	647

[1] TP: total number of publications; TC: the total number of citations distribution; AC: the average number of citations per publication, the same below.

Next, this paper analyzes the productive objects, including countries/regions, institutions, and authors. The countries/regions with greater than 100 publications are presented in Figure 3 and then the top 10 productive institutions and authors are presented in Table 3. From Figure 3, we can see that the scholars in China have published 1226 papers and rank in the first place. Following, the scholars in the USA and South Korea both published more than 340 papers each, and rank in the second and the third places, respectively. The fourth to eleventh productive countries/regions are Spain (217), Pakistan (207), Saudi Arabia (177), Italy (118), Malaysia (114), Poland (109), Japan (107), and India (106).

In terms of institutions, China Medical University Taiwan published 66 papers and ranks first, followed by the National University of Defense Technology China (59), Beijing Jiaotong University (54), King Abdulaziz University (52), and the University of New Mexico (51), respectively. In the top 10 institutions, 6 of them are from China.

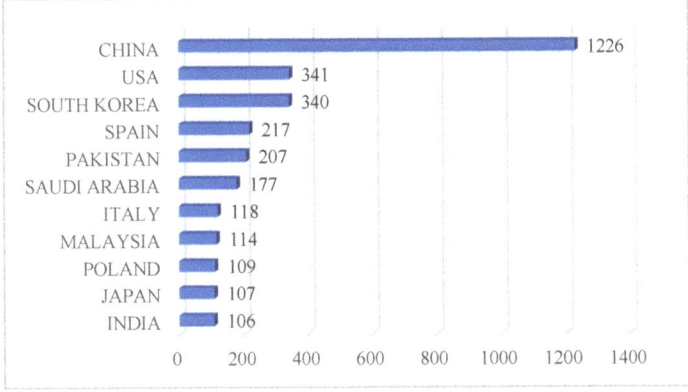

Figure 3. The 11 countries/regions with greater than 100 publications.

On the author's side, Smarandache F., from the USA, and Zhang X. H., from China, rank first and second, with 51 and 31 publications, respectively. Among the top 10 most productive authors, 4 of them are from China, 4 come from South Korea, 1 comes from the USA, and the other is Vietnamese. From the above three aspects, *Symmetry* has aroused special attention for scholars from China, the USA, and Korea.

Table 3. Top 10 productive Institutions/Authors in *Symmetry*.

Institution	TP	Author	TP
China Medical University Taiwan	66	Smarandache F.	51
National University of Defense Technology China	59	Zhang X.H.	31
Beijing Jiaotong University	54	Wang J.	25
King Abdulaziz University	52	Kim J.	24
University of New Mexico	51	Khan I.	22
Harbin Engineering University	47	Chang C.C.	19
Comsats University Islamabad Cui	44	Lee S.	19
Ton Duc Thang University	41	Kim D.S.	18
China Medical University Hospital Taiwan	40	Kim T.	18
Central South University	39	Park J.H.	17

Furthermore, the subject areas of *Symmetry* relate to physics, chemistry, biology, computer science, theory and methods, etc., which is multidisciplinary. Since it published papers, some publications impact the corresponding field. Table 4 lists the details of the top 15 most influential papers, including author, type, year, citation, etc.

Table 4. The top 15 most cited papers in Symmetry from 2009 to 2019.

	Title	Author(s)	Type	Year	Citation	Is it a High-Cited Paper
1	Fluctuating asymmetry: methods, theory, and applications	Graham et al.	Review	2010	183	√
2	Inflationary cosmology in modified gravity theories	Bamba and Odintsov	Review	2015	175	√
3	Analyzing fluctuating asymmetry with geometric morphometrics: concepts, methods, and applications	Klingenberg and Christian	Review	2015	125	√
4	Doubly-special relativity: facts, myths and some key open issues	Giovanni	Article	2010	114	
5	One-sign order parameter in iron based superconductor	Borisenko et al.	Article	2012	90	
6	Behind the looking-glass: a review on human symmetry perception	Trender	Review	2010	90	
7	Organocatalytic enantioselective henry reactions	Yolanda et al.	Review	2011	89	
8	A critical assessment of the performance of magnetic and electronic indices of aromaticity	Sola et al.	Review	2010	87	
9	On the harmonic oscillator model of electron delocalization (homed) index and its application to heteroatomic pi-electron systems	Raczynska et al.	Article	2010	84	√
10	Models for green supplier selection with some 2-tuple linguistic neutrosophic number Bonferroni mean operators	Wang et al.	Article	2018	81	
11	Spontaneous symmetry breaking and nambu-goldstone bosons in quantum many-body systems	Brauner	Review	2010	78	
12	Chiral liquid crystals: structures, phases, effects	Dierking	Review	2014	70	
13	Synthesis and reactions of dibenzo [a,e] pentalenes	Saito	Review	2010	65	
14	Methods for multiple attribute group decision making based on intuitionistic fuzzy dombi hamy mean operators	Li et al.	Article	2018	64	√
15	Chlorophylls, dymmetry, chirality, and photosynthesis	Senge et al.	Review	2014	61	

From Table 4, 5 publications are articles and 10 publications are reviews. The top three cited publications are all reviews [26–28] and high-cited papers. Furthermore, two of them are studying fluctuating asymmetry, which has been widely investigated from basic theories, methods, and applications. Besides, the top 15 most cited papers were mainly published in 2010 (7), 2014 (2), 2015 (2), and 2018 (2). Furthermore, 10 of them have more than one author. Thus, the cooperation of authors also plays a key role in academic research.

3. Influential Contributor Analyses

According to Table 4, the frequency of the most cited paper is 183; it reviewed old and new methods of measuring fluctuation asymmetry and then reviewed the theory, developmental origins, and the applications of fluctuation asymmetry [26].

The paper "Inflationary cosmology in modified gravity theories" was cited 175 times; it reviewed inflationary cosmology in modified gravity [27]. The paper "Analyzing fluctuating asymmetry with geometric morphometrics: concepts, methods, and applications" ranks third place and was cited 125 times. The theme of this paper is the same as the most cited paper, i.e., fluctuating asymmetry. This paper summarized the concepts and morphometric methods for studying fluctuating asymmetry of shape and size.

In the top 15 most cited papers, we can find that there are only 2 papers published in recent years (in 2018); thus, the papers published in recent years still need time to gain attention. These data illustrate that the top 15 most cited papers all promote the development and advance of the journal and the related research fields.

Figure 4 depicts the cooperation network among countries/regions, where the nodes represent the countries/regions, and the sizes denote the citations; that is, the larger the size of the node, the greater the number of citations. The lines between two countries/regions denote that they cooperate. The density of the links of a country indicates the cooperation degree. The denser of the lines, the more collaboration for one country with other countries. From Figure 4, we can see that China, the USA, Pakistan, and the UK have more lines. Therefore, they have more cooperation with other countries.

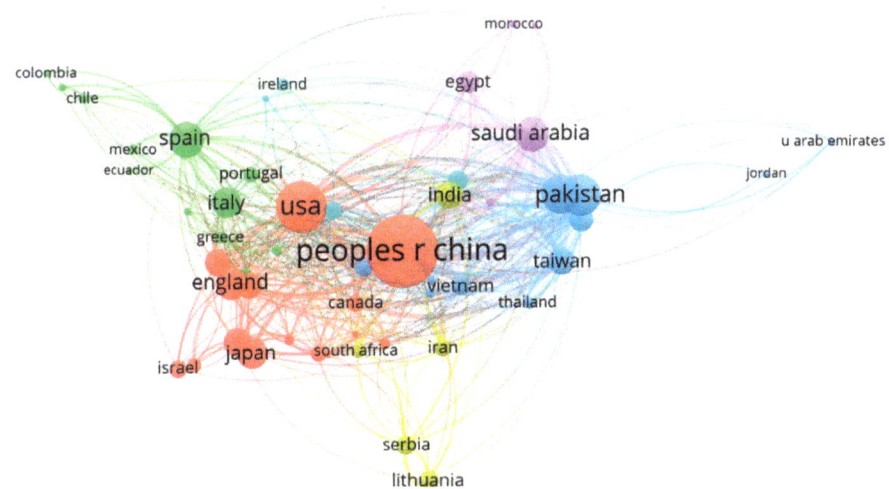

Figure 4. The co-authorship network of countries/regions.

Table 5 gives the top 10 most influential countries/regions and their corresponding data. China has the most citations (4002) and the highest H-index (24), which is consistent with Figure 4. For ≥100, each of the USA, Spain, the UK, Japan, and Italy has one paper. Furthermore, it can be seen that 5 papers from China have more than 50 citations, 36 papers have more than 20 citations, and 86 papers have more than 10 citations. There are 91 papers from the USA with more than 10 citations, which are far more than other countries. Thus, China and the USA are two biggest contributors to this journal. It is noted that, although the UK only has 96 publications on *Symmetry*, it has the highest AC with 7.28, which means that these papers play an important role in the related research fields. China and Saudi Arabia have 10 high-cited papers each. We also find that the top 10 most influential countries/regions are mainly from Asia and Europe.

Table 5. The top 10 most influential countries/regions.

	Countries	Continent	TP	TC	AC	H-Index	≥100	≥50	≥20	≥10	HC [1]	HP
1	China	Asia	1226	4002	3.26	24	0	5	36	86	10	0
2	USA	North American	341	1718	5.04	19	1	3	16	91	3	0
3	Pakistan	Asia	207	1179	5.70	17	0	2	15	74	7	2
4	South Korea	Asia	340	1011	2.97	15	0	0	9	61	1	0
5	Spain	Europe	217	851	3.92	11	1	3	5	18	1	0
6	Saudi Arabia	Asia	177	781	4.41	13	0	2	11	25	10	2
7	UK	Europe	96	699	7.28	12	1	4	7	15	1	0
8	Japan	Asia	107	669	6.25	12	1	3	5	17	1	0
9	Italy	Europe	118	607	5.14	13	1	1	7	16	0	0
10	Poland	Europe	109	505	4.63	11	0	2	6	14	1	0

[1] HC: the number of the high-cited papers; HP: the number of the hot papers, the same below.

Furthermore, the top 10 most cited institutions are presented in Table 6. The University of New Mexico is the most cited institution, with 491 citations and 11 H-index, while its AC is only 9.63. Sichuan Normal University has 362 citations and ranks in second place. The University of Manchester has the greatest AC (43.30), even though it only has 5 papers, which explains the importance of these papers and the related research topics. Its most cited paper, *Analyzing Fluctuating Asymmetry with Geometric Morphometrics: Concepts, Methods, and Applications*, is the third most cited paper of *Symmetry*.

Table 6. The top 10 most influential institutions.

	Institutions	TP	TC	AC	H-Index	≥100	≥50	≥20	≥10	HC	HP
1	Univ New Mexico	51	491	9.63	11	0	1	8	16	1	0
2	Sichuan Normal Univ	9	362	40.22	7	0	3	7	7	4	0
3	Shaoxing Univ	18	261	14.50	8	0	1	5	7	0	0
4	Shaanxi Univ Sci & Technol	30	246	8.20	8	0	0	3	8	2	0
5	Shanghai Maritime Univ	27	241	8.93	8	0	0	4	8	1	0
6	China Med Univ	67	249	3.72	9	0	0	2	7	1	0
7	Univ Manchester	5	217	43.40	4	1	2	2	4	1	0
8	Berry Coll	5	210	42.00	3	1	1	1	2	1	0
9	Vilnius Gediminas Tech Univ	17	207	12.18	8	0	0	1	7	1	0
10	Tomsk State Pedag Univ	10	206	20.60	3	1	1	1	2	1	0

Next, the most cited authors are analyzed and the top 10 most influential authors are presented in Table 7. Smarandache F. has the greatest TC and H-index, ranking in the first place. Besides, even though each of Hel-Or Hagit, Nevo Eviatar, and Raz Shmuel only published two papers in *Symmetry*, their AC is the highest (95.50). Furthermore, they relate to the same paper, i.e., *Fluctuating Asymmetry: Methods, Theory, and Applications*, the most cited paper in Table 4. Graham, John H. ranks in second place of AC and is also the author of the same paper. This phenomenon can be explained by the cooperative relationship among authors. Then, we analyze the cooperation relationship and depict the corresponding science mapping as shown in Figure 5.

Table 7. The top 10 most influential authors.

	Authors	TP	TC	AC	H-Index	≥100	≥50	≥20	≥10	HC	HP
1	Smarandache F.	51	**489**	9.59	11	0	1	8	16	1	0
2	Wei G.W.	8	362	45.25	7	0	3	7	7	4	0
3	Wang J.	11	266	24.18	5	0	2	5	5	3	0
4	Ye J.	17	259	15.24	8	0	1	5	7	0	0
5	Zhang X.H.	30	246	8.20	8	0	0	3	8	2	0
6	Graham J.H.	3	205	68.33	3	1	1	1	2	1	0
7	Zavadskas E.K.	12	194	16.17	8	0	0	3	7	1	0
8	Hel-Or H.	2	191	**95.50**	2	1	1	1	1	1	0
9	Nevo E.	2	191	**95.50**	2	1	1	1	1	1	0
10	Raz S.	2	191	**95.50**	1	1	1	1	1	1	0

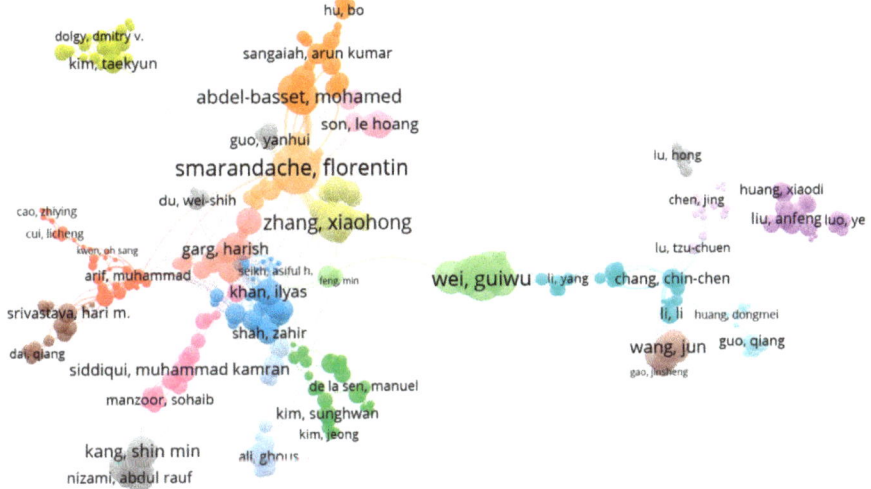

Figure 5. The closest cooperation relationship among authors in *Symmetry*.

The visualization of the cooperation network only presents 296 authors, which is the closest network by setting the minimum number of documents of an author as two. In Figure 5, the size of the node denotes the number of citations, for example, the node for Smarandache F., is the largest, followed by Wei G. W., which is consistent with Table 7. Besides, the links between the two authors mean that they cooperate. The links linked to Smarandache F. are the greatest, therefore having 43 links, 6.1% of the total links (704), and their total link strength is 99, 8% of the whole link strength (1244). Then, Zhang X. H. has 16 links and a total link strength of 56, 4.5% of 1244.

4. The Co-Citation and the Burst Detection Analysis

In this section, we make co-citation and the burst detection analysis by depicting visualizations combining with VOSviewer and CiteSpace. The co-citation analyses are conducted from the following aspects: reference co-citation, source co-citation, and author co-citation. Citation burst detection reflects the explosive data, that is, in a certain period, scholars' attention is attracted [29].

Figure 6 illustrates the closest reference co-citation network, where the threshold that denotes the minimum number of citations of a cited reference is 20, and there are 31 references that satisfy the threshold. The closest network includes 25 references. In Figure 6, a node shows a reference, the size of the node denotes the citations number of the references. A link between two references means a co-citation relationship. The thicker the link is, the more citations the reference has. There are 5 clusters marked with different colors. Furthermore, the paper *Fuzzy sets, Information Control, 1965, 8, 2–3: 30–33* (cited 38,108 times) ranks in first place, with 203 citations in *Symmetry*. Similarly, the author and source co-citation networks are also be displayed. Then, Table 8 presents the top 10 most cited references/sources/authors by publications in *Symmetry*.

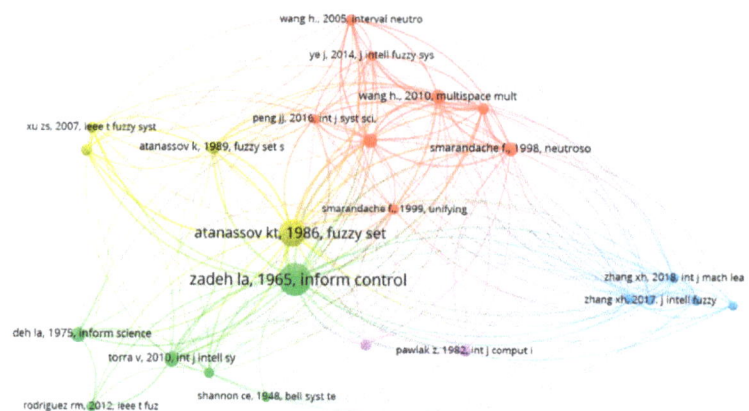

Figure 6. The closest co-citation network of references in *Symmetry*.

Table 8. The top 10 most cited references/sources/authors by publications in the journal.

	Reference	TC	Source	TC	Author	TC
1	Zadeh La, 1965, *Inform. Control*	203	*Phys. Rev. D.*	2226	Ye, J.H.	336
2	Atanassov K, 1986, *Fuzzy Set Syst.*	148	*Symmetry-Basel*	1858	Smarandache, F	331
3	Torra V, 2010, *Int. J. Intell. Syst.*	49	*Phys. Rev. Lett.*	1468	Zadeh, La	307
4	Zadeh La, 1975, *Inform. Sciences*	47	*Inform. Sciences*	951	Liu, P.D.	282
5	Smarandache F., 1998, *Neutrosophy Neutroso*	45	*Lect. Notes Comput. Sc.*	867	Wei, G.W.	267
6	Wang H., 2010, *Multispace Multistru*	43	*Phys. Lett. B*	862	Xu, Z.S.	241
7	Ye J, 2014, *J. Intell. Fuzzy Syst.*	42	*Fuzzy Set. Syst.*	816	Kim, T	229
8	Atanassov K, 1989, *Fuzzy Set. Syst.*	38	*Expert Syst. Appl.*	778	Zhang, X.H.	229
9	Pawlak Z, 1982, *Int. J. Comput. Inf. Sci.*	35	*J. Intell. Fuzzy Syst.*	735	Atanassov, K.T.	184
10	Wang H., 2005, *Interval Neutrosophi*	31	*Phys. Rev. A*	728	Kostelecky, V.A.	176

Table 8 lists the information of the top 10 most cited references/sources/authors by publications in *Symmetry*. Six of references are published before 2010, and the first cited reference is from 1965 by Zadeh [30]. Only two references had a number of citations more than 100. *Phys. Rev. D* ranks the first cited source with 2226 citations. In terms of cited authors, Ye, J. H. received the most citations, with 336, followed by Smarandache, F (331) and Zadeh, La (307).

Through detecting bursts, Table 9 lists the top 10 cited authors of publications in *Symmetry* with the strongest citation bursts. Zadeh La on the top of the list with the maximum burst strength of 17.965. All of them have a citation burst duration with three years and close to the present (from 2018 to 2019), which shows that their work may have formed a hot and leading topic.

Table 9. Top 10 cited authors with the strongest citation bursts.

	Cited Authors	Year	Strength	Begin	End	2009–2019
1	Zadeh La	2009	17.965	2018	2019	
2	Atanassov K.T.	2009	12.435	2018	2019	
3	Smarandache F.	2009	12.1931	2018	2019	
4	Zhang X.H.	2009	11.7661	2018	2019	
5	Ye. J.	2009	11.2671	2018	2019	
6	Xu Z. S.	2009	10.3632	2018	2019	
7	Torra V.	2009	9.7113	2018	2019	
8	Chen S.M.	2009	9.7113	2018	2019	
9	Wang H.	2009	9.5661	2018	2019	
10	Wang J.Q.	2009	9.3017	2018	2019	

Table 10 presents the top 15 cited journals with the strongest citation bursts from 2009 to 2019. The cited journals receive frequent citations by *Symmetry* in a certain period. The citation bursts of the cited journals of *Inform. Control.* had the longest strength (39.1302). Besides, 5 of the top 15 cited journals had the longest duration, with 8 years from 2009 to 2016, which means that the publications in *Symmetry* cited these journals earlier and explosively. Of these 15, 7 are the closest to 2019, such as *Inform. Control.*, *Knowl-Based Syst.*, and *IEEE T. Fuzzy Syst.*, which illustrates that they still have an influence on *Symmetry* and can even influence the future research directions.

Table 10. Top 15 cited journals with the strongest citation bursts.

	Cited journals	Year	Strength	Begin	End	2009–2019
1	*Inform. Control.*	2009	39.1302	2017	2019	
2	*Knowl-Based Syst*	2009	37.1671	2017	2019	
3	*IEEE T. Fuzzy Syst.*	2009	32.2774	2017	2019	
4	*J. Math Phys.*	2009	30.0428	2009	2016	
5	*Soft Comput.*	2009	30.0041	2017	2019	
6	*Int. J. Intell. Syst.*	2009	27.9824	2018	2019	
7	*Int. J. Mach. Learn Cyb.*	2009	26.2151	2018	2019	
8	*J. Phys. A-math Gen.*	2009	24.9067	2009	2016	
9	*IEEE T. Pattern Anal.*	2009	23.3408	2014	2019	
10	*Rev. Mod. Phys.*	2009	20.8109	2009	2016	
11	*Science*	2009	20.0597	2010	2016	
12	*Phys. Lett. B*	2009	19.0243	2010	2016	
13	*Phys. Lett A*	2009	18.7673	2009	2016	
14	*J. Phys. A-math Theor.*	2009	18.3113	2014	2016	
15	*Phys. Rev. B*	2009	17.2365	2009	2016	

5. Co-Occurrence and Timeline Analyses of Keywords

This section analyzes the co-occurrence of author-keywords and presents the timeline view. In the 1980 s, the co-occurrence analysis was first provided and has been widely applied in bibliometrics analyses [31]. When more than or equal to two keywords appear in the same paper, this can be called keywords occurrence [32]. Through the co-occurrence analysis, we can identify the research hotspots of the journal.

There are 11,731 author-keywords of publications in the journal from 2009 to 2019, according to VOSviewer. Figure 7 presents the author-keywords co-occurrence network, where there are 164 author-keywords, by setting the threshold of minimum occurrences to five and giving the closest relationship. They are classified into 16 clusters marked in different colors. The node presents an author-keyword; its size denotes the citations. The bigger the node is, the more citations the keyword has. A link between two nodes means the co-occurrence of the two keywords. In Figure 7, symmetry has the greatest citations; therefore, it has the most links with other clusters. Then, we present the top 20 most frequent author-keywords and their frequencies in Table 11.

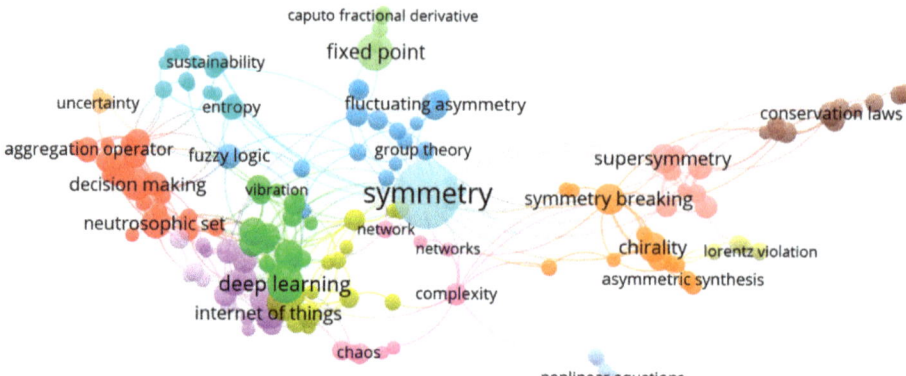

Figure 7. The co-occurrence network of author-keywords.

Table 11. The top 20 most frequent author-keywords in *Symmetry*.

Rank	Author-Keyword	Frequency	Rank	Author-Keyword	Frequency
1	symmetry	92	11	chirality	18
2	decision making	37	12	big data	17
3	deep learning	30	13	convolutional neural network	17
4	fixed point	29	14	fluctuating asymmetry	17
5	machine learning	27	15	cloud computing	16
6	internet of things	22	16	image processing	16
7	symmetry breaking	20	17	clustering	15
8	neural network	19	18	aggregation operator	14
9	neutrosophic set	19	19	classification	14
10	supersymmetry	19	20	data mining	14

The frequency of symmetry is 92 and ranks first. Following, decision making (37), deep learning (30), fixed point (29), and machine learning (27) rank in the second to fifth place, respectively, which explain the research topics of the journal. The frequencies of all the keywords in Table 11 are higher than 10, and seven of them have frequencies greater than 20.

Table 12 explains the top 20 keywords with the strongest citation bursts. Most of them are close to present (2019), such as fuzzy set, decision making, aggregation operator, deep learning, etc., which denote that the research contents in the publications of *Symmetry* closely follow hot topics and leading issues. Comparing Table 11 with Table 12, we can find several of the same keywords, i.e., symmetry, decision making, symmetry breaking, neutrosophic set, and deep learning. This phenomenon explains that these are the research hotspots of the journal from 2009 to 2019; at the same time, the research fever of these may continue. Thus, the scholars interested in the journal can start from these research topics.

Table 12. The top 20 keywords with the strongest citation bursts.

	Keywords	Year	Strength	Begin	End	2009–2019
1	fuzzy set	2009	18.3082	2017	2019	
2	aggregation operator	2009	11.0627	2018	2019	
3	number	2009	10.6203	2018	2019	
4	symmetry	2009	9.8647	2009	2014	
5	similarity measure	2009	9.2729	2018	2019	
6	information	2009	8.9273	2017	2019	
7	decision making	2009	8.7959	2017	2019	
8	operator	2009	8.3778	2018	2019	
9	environment	2009	6.5953	2018	2019	
10	symmetry breaking	2009	6.3503	2010	2010	
11	TOPSIS	2009	5.7079	2018	2019	
12	network	2009	5.6572	2017	2019	
13	neutrosophic set	2009	5.2651	2018	2019	
14	deep learning	2009	5.2651	2018	2019	
15	management	2009	5.2651	2018	2019	
16	evolution	2009	5.0578	2015	2016	
17	intuitionistic-fuzzy	2009	5.0308	2017	2017	
18	group-decision-making	2009	5.0308	2017	2017	
19	attribute-decision-making	2009	5.0308	2017	2017	
20	scheme	2009	4.9364	2018	2019	

Figure 8 shows the keyword clusters visualizations by CiteSpace and summarizes nine clusters for all keywords of publication in *Symmetry*, which are "exact solution", "decision making", "aromaticity", "aesthetic", "deep learning", "cyclic twin", "fixed point", "quantum theory", and "drosophila melanogaster" in order.

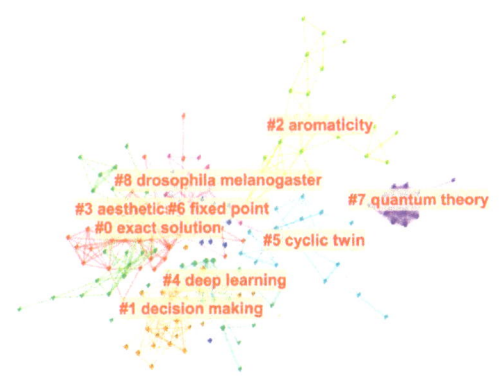

Figure 8. The keywords clusters visualizations.

Then, based on the timeline view of keywords, the development and the research trend of the hotspots from 2009 to 2019 are presented. In Figure 9, there are four stages from the time perspective. Specifically, it focused more on the "symmetry property", "simulation", "aromaticity", "model", and so on, between 2009 and 2010. The keywords of "tilling aperiodicity" and "symmetry group of knot" occurred most from 2010 to 2013. Next, from 2013 to 2016, a large number of research topics emerged, such as "exact solution", "framework", "three-dimensional space", "neural network", "equational simulation", "fluctuating asymmetry", etc. For the next phase, the publication preferred to occur keywords like "operator", "convolutional neural network", and "support vector machine". We can see that keywords continually change over time, and scholars expanded and deepened the research content on the journal.

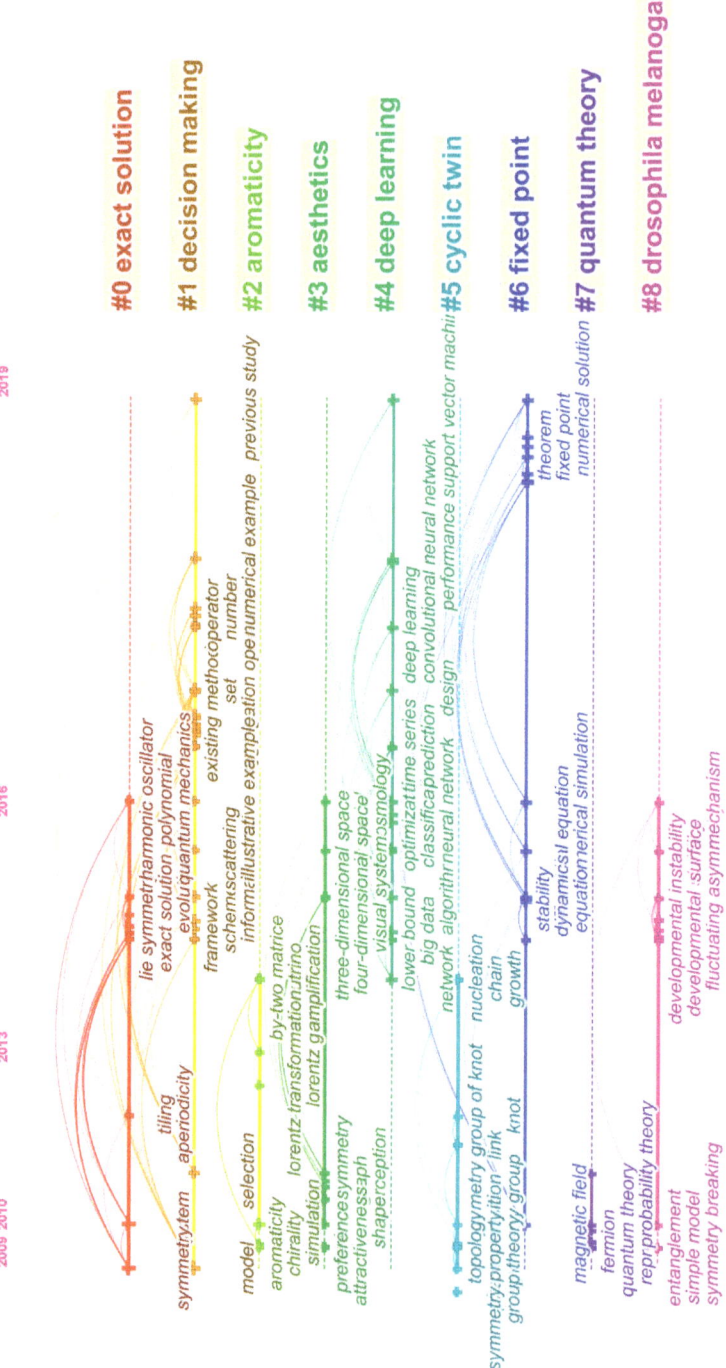

Figure 9. The timeline view of keywords for publications.

Moreover, this paper also retrieves the papers published in 2020 and obtains 691 papers. Figure 10 shows the author-keywords co-occurrence network of these papers by setting the minimum number of occurrences of a keyword to two and displaying the closest network, which is related to 138 keywords. The side of the nodes denotes the frequency of co-occurrence. We can see that machine learning has the greatest frequency (24), followed by symmetry (20), deep learning (9), fixed point (9), asymmetry (8), dark matter (8), classification (7), dark energy (7), fuzzy logic (7), etc. The tenth to twentieth author-keywords are internet of things, particle swarm optimization, sustainability, conservation laws, convergence, hermite-hadamard inequality, stability analysis, ahp, artificial intelligence, bioconvection, and cloud computing.

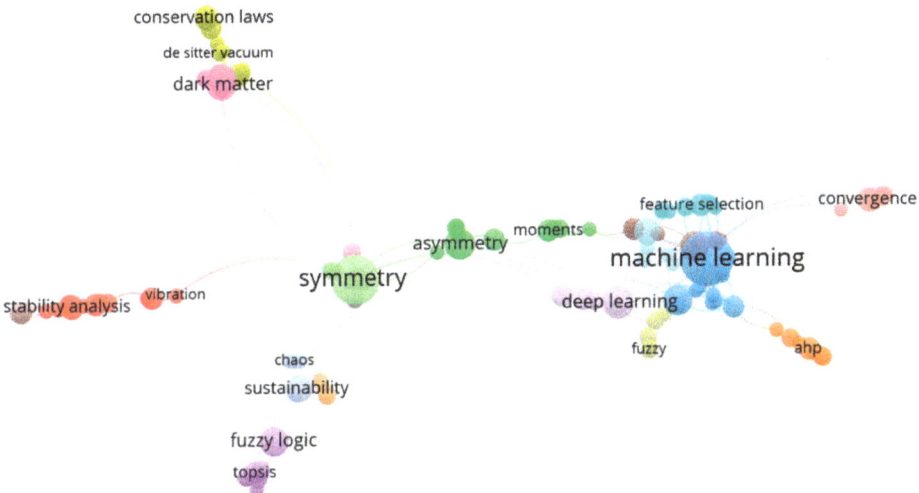

Figure 10. Author-keywords co-occurrence network of publications in 2020.

6. Discussions

This journal explores symmetry phenomena related to mathematical, physics, interdisciplinary fields, etc. After the bibliometric analysis, we further discussed the possible reasons and given future suggestions. According to analyses of *Symmetry*, the basic characteristics, citation structures, and productive objects are summarized as follows:

(1) The most frequent type of publication is the article, occupying 94.11% of the publications. There were more high-quality papers published in 2020, 2017, and 2018, in the view of TC and H-index. The trend of the publication-year distribution increased from 2013 to 2019. As of June, 2020, the publications received the most citations (3324) in 2018. The publications in 2019 were cited 2234 times; this year not only had the greatest number of papers, but also ranks second place in terms of citation frequency, the reason for which may be that an increasing amount of scholars are paying attention to the journal.

(2) Since most of the top 15 cited publications are cooperative, communication plays a key role in improving the level of publications. From the cooperation network, China receives the largest number of cooperation and is at the core place; at the same time, it is the country with the greatest number of publications.

(3) Publications cover 100 countries/regions, and the most influential countries/regions are mainly from Asia and Europe. In terms of TP, TC, and H-index, China led, which shows that publications in *Symmetry* from China have higher influence, followed by the USA. From the top 10 most cited references/sources/authors: (a) the publications cite reference universally; (b) the cited sources are

mostly in the field of physics and fuzzy mathematics; (c) the researchers can pay close attention to the papers of the top cited authors and sources.

(4) Combined with the strong citation burst analyses, we can find that the top 10 lists between Tables 8 and 9 are different. This phenomenon explains that the author citation bursts at various times, and especially the emergence of some new authors, including Torra V. and Wang H. For the same authors, the ranks also exist discrepancy. The reason may be that the research topics of the journal are constantly enriched and there are diverse focuses, i.e., from physics to comprehensive discipline, including decision making, fuzzy mathematic, and deep learning.

(5) Considering the top 20 most frequent author-keywords and the top 20 keywords with the strongest citation bursts, in recent years, the main research contents of *Symmetry* focus on fuzzy set, aggregation operation, etc. The burst detection and the timeline view analyses of keywords show the knowledge structure and research trends in the journal. According to the results, the following topics can be considered in the future: (a) to process the complex and diverse raw data, and investigate new operators; (b) to study the symmetry phenomena in the artificial intelligence; (c) to excavate the symmetry nature in matching problems, aimed at solving more social management problems; (d) to predict the possible time change trends and their weights in dynamic issues; (e) to study the intelligent algorithms and promote their stability and reliability.

Due to the characteristics of publications, the most influential objects, and the co-occurrence analyses of author-keywords, regarding the publications from 2009 to 2019 in *Symmetry*, we find that, although the papers were first published in 2009, the numbers of publications have been increasing until the present. From 2015, the annual number of publications always exceeded 100. This suggests that the journal has constructed its influence on multidisciplinary theory and practice. Especially, authors from Asia and Europe pay more attention to this journal. In the future, it can expand its influence through cooperation. Then, the analyses results suggest that scholars should investigate advanced techniques (such as neural network, data mining, fuzzy decision-making, etc.) to keep pace with the times and solve the practical problems. Besides, with the uncertainty and diversification of the environment, enriching the research contents of the journal, at the same time, promoting the robustness of theory methods, etc. are also challenges for future scholars.

7. Conclusions

This paper presents a bibliometric analysis of *Symmetry* from 2009 to 2019 based on WoS. According to VOSviewer and CiteSpace, the analyses are conducted from the following aspects: basic characteristics, including the publications, citation number and citation structure; the influential objects; co-citation contributors and the burst detection analyses; the author-keywords co-occurrence analyses and timeline view analysis. The number of publications has almost increased every year since 2014. The year 2019 was the year with the largest volume of publications and 2018 was the year with the most citations. China is the most productive and influential country. The top three productive institutions are China Medical University Taiwan (China), National University of Defense Technology China (China), and Beijing Jiaotong University (China), respectively. The prominent author is Smarandache F. According to the results, cooperation among contributors also plays a key role in the publications. In the view of author-keyword analyses, the scopes of *Symmetry* are constantly enriching and no longer limited to the symmetry phenomena in the fields of physics and chemistry. At present, these include decision making, fuzzy mathematics, deep learning, machine learning and classification, etc. We also discuss possible reasons for this and future development.

In summary, this paper is a relatively comprehensive view of *Symmetry* by bibliometric analysis, which helps scholars understand its current status, future trends of development, and research scope. In future, we will continue to collect its productions and pay more attention to its developments, aiming to make the conclusions richer.

Author Contributions: Conceptualization, Z.X.; data curation, J.A.; formal analysis, Z.T.; investigation, B.L.; methodology, Z.X.; project administration, Z.X.; supervision, E.K.Z.; validation, E.K.Z.; writing—original draft,

B.L.; writing—review and editing, J.A. and Z.T. All authors have read and agreed to the published version of the manuscript.

Funding: This work was funded by the National Natural Science Foundation of China under Grant 71771155.

Conflicts of Interest: The authors declare no conflict of interest.

References

1. Laengle, S.; Merigo, J.M.; Miranda, J.; Slowinski, R.; Bomze, I.; Borgonovo, E.; Dyson, R.G.; Oliveira, J.F.; Teunter, R. Forty years of the European Journal of Operational Research: A bibliometric overview. *Eur. J. Oper. Res.* **2017**, *262*, 803–816. [CrossRef]
2. Yu, D.J.; Xu, Z.S.; Saparauskas, J. The evolution of "Technological and Economic Development of Economy": A bibliometric analysis. *Technol. Econ. Dev. Econ.* **2019**, *25*, 369–385. [CrossRef]
3. Yu, D.J.; Xu, Z.S.; Pedrycz, W.; Wang, W.R. Information Sciences 1968–2016: A retrospective analysis with text mining and bibliometric. *Inf. Sci.* **2017**, *418*, 619–634. [CrossRef]
4. Yu, D.J.; Xu, Z.S.; Kao, Y.S.; Lin, C.T. The structure and citation landscape of IEEE Transactions on Fuzzy Systems (1994–2015). *IEEE Trans. Fuzzy Syst.* **2018**, *26*, 430–442. [CrossRef]
5. Zhou, W.; Xu, Z.S.; Zavadskas, E.K. A bibliometric overview of International Journal of Strategic Property Management between 2008 and 2019. *Int. J. Strateg. Prop. Manag.* **2019**, *23*, 366–377. [CrossRef]
6. Yu, D.J.; Xu, Z.S.; Antucheviciene, J. Bibliometric analysis of the Journal of Civil Engineering and Management between 2008 and 2018. *J. Civ. Eng. Manag.* **2019**, *25*, 402–410. [CrossRef]
7. Zhou, W.; Xu, Z.S.; Zavadskas, E.K.; Laurinavičius, A. The knowledge domain of the Baltic Journal of Road and Bridge Engineering between 2006 and 2019. *Balt. J. Road Bridge E.* **2020**, *15*, 1–30. [CrossRef]
8. Liu, W.S.; Liao, H.C. A bibliometric analysis of fuzzy decision research during 1970–2015. *Int. J. Fuzzy Syst.* **2017**, *19*, 1–14. [CrossRef]
9. Hache, E.; Palle, A. Renewable energy source integration into power networks, research trends and policy implications: A bibliometric and research actors survey analysis. *Energy Policy* **2019**, *124*, 23–35. [CrossRef]
10. Yu, D.J.; Xu, Z.S.; Wang, X.X. Bibliometric analysis of support vector machines research trend: A case study in China. *Int. J. Mach. Learn Cybern.* **2019**, *11*, 715–728.
11. Stopar, K.; Bartol, T. Digital competences, computer skills and information literacy in secondary education: Mapping and visualization of trends and concepts. *Scientometrics* **2019**, *118*, 479–498. [CrossRef]
12. Van-Eck, N.J.; Waltman, L.R. VOSviewer: A computer program for bibliometric mapping. *Soc. Sci. Electron Publ.* **2009**, *84*, 523–538.
13. Chen, C.M. CiteSpace II: Detecting and visualizing emerging trends and transient patterns in scientific literature. *J. Am. Soc. Inf. Sci. Technol.* **2006**, *57*, 359–377. [CrossRef]
14. Chen, C.M.; Hu, Z.G.; Liu, S.B.; Tseng, H. Emerging trends in regenerative medicine: A scientometric analysis in CiteSpace. *Expert Opin. Biol. Ther.* **2012**, *12*, 593–608. [CrossRef]
15. Chen, C.M. Science mapping: A systematic review of the literature. *J. Data Inf. Sci.* **2017**, *2*, 1–40. [CrossRef]
16. Eck, N.J.V.; Waltman, L. Citnetexplorer: A new software tool for analyzing and visualizing citation networks. *J. Inf.* **2014**, *8*, 802–823.
17. Lu, Y.; Li, Z.; Arthur, D. Mapping publication status and exploring hotspots in a research field: Chronic disease self-management. *J. Adv. Nurs.* **2014**, *70*, 1837–1844. [CrossRef]
18. Zhao, F.K.; Shi, B.; Liu, R.X.; Zhou, W.K.; Shi, D.; Zhang, J.S. Theme trends and knowledge structure on choroidal neovascularization: A quantitative and co-word analysis. *BMC Ophthalmol.* **2018**, *18*, 86. [CrossRef]
19. Qaiser, F.H.; Ahmed, K.; Sykora, M.; Choudhary, A.; Simpson, M. Decision support systems for sustainable logistics: A review and bibliometric analysis. *Ind. Manag. Data Syst.* **2017**, *117*, 1376–1388. [CrossRef]
20. Tian, X.; Geng, Y.; Zhong, S.Z.; Wilson, J.; Gao, C.X.; Chen, W.; Yu, Z.J.; Hao, H. A bibliometric analysis on trends and characters of carbon emissions from transport sector. *Transp. Res. D Transp. Environ.* **2018**, *59*, 1–10. [CrossRef]
21. Cobo, M.J.; Lopez-Herrera, A.G.; Herrera-Viedma, E.; Herrera, F. Science mapping software tools: Review, analysis, and cooperative sudy among tools. *J. Am. Soc. Inf. Sci. Technol.* **2011**, *62*, 1382–1402. [CrossRef]
22. Wang, X.X.; Xu, Z.S.; Share, M. A bibliometric analysis of Economic Research-Ekonomska Istrazivanja (2007–2019). *Ekono. Istraz.* **2020**, *33*, 865–886. [CrossRef]

23. Xu, Z.S.; Zhou, W.; Baltrenaite, E. Comprehensive bibliometric study of journal of environmental engineering and landscape management from 2007 to 2019. *J. Environ. Eng. Landsc.* **2019**, *27*, 215–227. [CrossRef]
24. Pilkington, A.; Meredith, J. The evolution of the intellectual structure of operations management-1980–2006: A citation/co-citation analysis. *J. Oper. Manag.* **2009**, *27*, 185–202. [CrossRef]
25. Hirsch, J.E. An index to quantify an individual's scientific research output. *Proc. Natl. Acad. Sci. USA* **2005**, *102*, 16569–16572. [CrossRef] [PubMed]
26. Graham, J.H.; Raz, S.; Hel-Or, H.; Nevo, E. Fluctuating asymmetry: Methods, theory, and applications. *Symmetry* **2010**, *2*, 466–540. [CrossRef]
27. Bamba, K.; Odintsov, S.D. Inflationary cosmology in modified gravity theories. *Symmetry* **2015**, *7*, 220–240. [CrossRef]
28. Klingenberg, C.P. Analyzing fluctuating asymmetry with geometric morphometrics: Concepts, methods, and applications. *Symmetry* **2015**, *7*, 843–934. [CrossRef]
29. Kleinberg, J. Bursty and hierarchical structure in streams. *Data Min. Knowl. Discov.* **2003**, *7*, 373–397. [CrossRef]
30. Zadeh, L.A. Fuzzy sets. *Inf. Control* **1965**, *8*, 338. [CrossRef]
31. Ding, Y.; Gobinda, G.C.; Schubert, F. Bibliometric cartography of information retrieval research by using co-word analysis. *Inf. Process Manag.* **2001**, *37*, 817–842. [CrossRef]
32. Su, H.; Lee, P.C. Mapping knowledge structure by keyword cooccurrence: A first look at journal papers in Technology Foresight. *Scientometrics* **2010**, *85*, 65–79. [CrossRef]

© 2020 by the authors. Licensee MDPI, Basel, Switzerland. This article is an open access article distributed under the terms and conditions of the Creative Commons Attribution (CC BY) license (http://creativecommons.org/licenses/by/4.0/).

Article

Land Price Forecasting Research by Macro and Micro Factors and Real Estate Market Utilization Plan Research by Landscape Factors: Big Data Analysis Approach

Sang-Hyang Lee [1], Jae-Hwan Kim [1,2,*] and Jun-Ho Huh [1,2,*]

1. Department of Data Informatics, (National) Korea Maritime and Ocean University, Busan 49112, Korea; euri2017@g.kmou.ac.kr
2. Department of Data Science, (National) Korea Maritime and Ocean University, Busan 49112, Korea
* Correspondence: jhkim@kmou.ac.kr (J.-H.K.); 72networks@kmou.ac.kr (J.-H.H.)

Citation: Lee, S.-H.; Kim, J.-H.; Huh, J.-H. Land Price Forecasting Research by Macro and Micro Factors and Real Estate Market Utilization Plan Research by Landscape Factors: Big Data Analysis Approach. *Symmetry* **2021**, *13*, 616. https://doi.org/10.3390/sym13040616

Academic Editors: Edmundas Kazimieras Zavadskas, Jurgita Antuchevičienė and Zenonas Turskis

Received: 18 March 2021
Accepted: 1 April 2021
Published: 7 April 2021

Publisher's Note: MDPI stays neutral with regard to jurisdictional claims in published maps and institutional affiliations.

Copyright: © 2021 by the authors. Licensee MDPI, Basel, Switzerland. This article is an open access article distributed under the terms and conditions of the Creative Commons Attribution (CC BY) license (https://creativecommons.org/licenses/by/4.0/).

Abstract: In real estate, there are various variables for the forecasting of future land prices, in addition to the macro and micro perspectives used in the current research. Examples of such variables are the economic growth rate, unemployment rate, regional development and important locations, and transportation. Therefore, in this paper, data on real estate and national price fluctuation rates were used to predict the ways in which future land prices will fluctuate, and macro and micro perspective variables were actively utilized in order to conduct land analysis based on Big Data analysis. We sought to understand what kinds of variables directly affect the fluctuation of the land, and to use this for future land price analysis. In addition to the two variables mentioned above, the factor of the landscape was also confirmed to be closely related to the real estate market. Therefore, in order to check the correlation between the landscape and the real estate market, we will examine the factors which change the land price in the landscape district, and then discuss how the landscape and real estate can interact. As a result, re-explaining the previous contents, the future land price is predicted by actively utilizing macro and micro variables in real estate land price prediction. Through this method, we want to increase the accuracy of the real estate market, which is difficult to predict, and we hope that it will be useful in the real estate market in the future.

Keywords: landscape; micro factor; macro factor; real estate market; Big Data analysis; Big Data; land price; R and Python; land Big Data

1. Introduction

Various methods of predicting and analyzing prices in the real estate market have been around since time immemorial. In the case of Joseon, 500 years ago, the biggest factor in determining land price was the crop harvest. Nowadays, however, the factors which determine the price of land can be confirmed to fluctuate due to various side points, such as the use value of the land, the area around the station, and the restricted area. As a result, there are various methods of predicting real estate prices [1,2], and in Korea, they are disclosed to citizens through land indexes.

In this paper, however, we will focus on history and policy. As in the past, the real estate market in the Republic of Korea is still going back and forth between hot and cold water like a roller coaster. In the Republic of Korea, large-scale apartment complexes were created by introducing large-scale residential complex construction in 1962 with the enforcement of the Korea Housing Corporation Act. At that time, Seoul was crowded with people who went to search for jobs across the country, and 80% of Seoul's population was concentrated in Gwanghwamun. Then, as the real estate prices surged, unlicensed buildings entered the scene, and houses became scarce.

Thus, the government promoted the construction of new residential areas or the transfer of administrative functions to the sub-Han River area, providing two alternatives.

The first option was to relocate the capital. Capital relocation involved dispersing the population by distributing administrative demand, which was concentrated in the central part of Seoul City. As it had only been about 10 years since the 6.25 war, Korea could not afford the astronomical costs and abandoned the first option. The second option was to develop the southern part of the Hangang River, particularly Yeongdeungpo, the subcenter of Seoul at the time. It was to be developed by incorporating the southern region into Seoul. At that time, the government formulated an economic development plan for an export-centric system, and sought the construction of national industrial parks in Ansan, Ulsan, Changwon, and Gwangyang. It needed a highway to connect with the national industrial complex and Seoul. The primary alternative was Yeongdeungpo, but it was not selected because of its high price and low site availability.

Thus, the southern part of the Han River was chosen, and Hannam Bridge in 1966 and Gyeongbu Expressway in 1968 were built to facilitate access. Through these two roads, Gangnam was designated as a migration land readjustment project area, and the development was started. In this plan, Yeongdong 1 and 2 earth were to be created; one area was the Gyeongbu Expressway project, and two areas were to have basic infrastructure built, while promoting the housing complex construction project in order to disperse the city center population. In 1972, Nonhyun-dong built public service apartments, apartment complexes, and detached houses. Nonetheless, the district, which used to be empty, was an area that was not of interest to people at the time, so the government shelved the development of Gangbuk and promoted Gangnam's development. As such, Gangbuk implemented large-scale regulatory policies, such as restrictions on the construction of certain facilities and public institutions, the prohibition of entertainment facilities, and the prohibition of the establishment of department stores and universities. In 1973, the Yeongdong district was designated as a development promotion district. With the waiving of property taxes, etc., the number of relocations to the Gangnam district increased; to date, Gangnam's representative apartments—Banpo Jugong Apartment and Apgujeong Hyundai Apartment—have been built and sold. In addition to residential complexes, adult entertainment establishments moved from Gangbuk to Gangnam, which benefitted from large-scale regulatory policies, thus making Gangnam a center of adult entertainment establishments. Moreover, on the transportation side, the construction of subway line 2 in 1975, Banpodaegyo Bridge, and the Namsan No. 3 tunnel in order to facilitate movement within the city center, along with the Gangnam Express Bus Terminal in 1976 were carried out. In terms of education, the prestigious high schools in downtown Gangbuk moved to the Gangnam area; public facilities and public enterprises in Gangnam moved to Jongno, the center of Seoul, but the gap was not as wide as it is now [3].

With low-rise apartments housing more than 5×10^4 households rebuilt in the 21st century, Gangnam's land price skyrocketed. As such, Gangnam, which is still the wealthiest area in the Republic of Korea, has low supply, high demand, and many reconstruction targets. As mentioned above, Gangnam is currently the richest area with the best infrastructure. In the future real estate market, it would be desirable to introduce smart cities which can solve various problems in areas surrounded by landscape areas and areas subject to rebuilding, instead of unreasonable construction. Looking at of the history of the Gangnam real estate market from the 1960s to the present, we can see that the focus was on policy, but there are various factors in the real estate market in addition to policy. The prediction and analysis of land prices are extremely demanding.

Therefore, in this research, we will seek a method for predicting future land prices by combining macro and micro environment variables in the real estate market, in which it is difficult to predict land prices in the future. The target areas of the paper will be set in the six regional living areas in Gangnam-gu, Seoul, based on the apartments of 30 *tsubo* in each area. Furthermore, in the prefecture's research, we would like to use past data to confirm future data, but the current data is the data for 2019, using the data from 2015 to 2018, which has not been released yet. We want to check if it matches. Then, we would like to investigate whether some variables have the greatest effect on land prices using regression analysis [4], and confirm that some variables and land prices are correlated through correlation analysis. In addition, in the real estate market, the factor of the landscape is also relevant, and we would like to investigate the relationship between real estate and landscape, which will be judged as a factor which will affect the future.

In order to confirm the relationship between the landscape and the real estate market, the effect of the landscape district on the real estate was investigated to find ways to interact. In order to explain the previous content again, we predicted land prices in the future by actively utilizing macroscopic and microscopic variables in real estate land price forecasting. We would like to use this method to improve the accuracy in the real estate market, which is difficult to predict, and we hope it will be useful in the future real estate market.

2. Related Research

2.1. The Concept of Real Estate Big Data

For real estate, the data market is of great significance. In the history of Gangnam mentioned above, the real estate market is diversifying and diversifying, moving back and forth between rising and falling curves. Data is a very important factor in the real-time analysis of this diversifying real estate market. However, it will be helpful to use analysis and prediction only when data is generated in each form suitable for real estate market analysis. In the real estate market, real estate data is largely divided into three elements. First, financial data includes information on real estate investment trust companies and REIT-related stocks (Real Estate Investment Trust). The second is transactional data, including real estate sales, mortgage loans that loan long-term housing funds by issuing mortgage securities as collateral for real estate, and financial data such as leases, prices, and taxes. Finally, physical data includes real estate land or structure information, such as real estate structural characteristics or location data. Thus, three types of financial, transactional, and physical data are considered to be real estate data [5,6].

2.2. Real Estate Market Analysis

Real estate market analysis can be a process of providing necessary information on real estate policy and administrative support by analyzing the market, in which prices are determined by the supply and demand of real estate. At the core of the analysis of the real estate market can be the research and analysis of various factors, such as the factors that form supply and demand, and their changing societies, economies, and policies. In addition to the macro and micro environment variables seen in the current paper, the analysis of changes in economic conditions, industrial structure, climate, and global markets that affect demand requires regional character and spatial congestion. The analysis of the location of the area and the regional market is required because the subgroups that have are born. Therefore, the factors that determine real estate prices are diversely distributed, such as psychological, social, policy, economic, individual, and regional factors [7–11].

2.3. Republic of Korea Real Estate Market Land Price Analysis Technology

There is also a method of analyzing the real estate market through data quantification [12], but the analysis method introduced in this related paper aims to explain how to make the real estate market analysis desirable through eight factors. The first is to check the cycle of the real estate market. In the real estate market, government policies, domestic and international economic conditions, and demand and supply aspects have a greater impact on price fluctuations than other factors. Looking at the history of the real estate market in Korea, it has been repeatedly rising and falling. Analyzing the real estate market doing so, it would be desirable to understand when prices rise, and when to adjust and invest. Second, when a new government is in place, the Presidential Commission on Acquisition of Office has the task of setting a new policy stance. It is important to check whether the regulation of real estate policy will be strengthened or relaxed by checking the state roadmap. The third point is similar to the second. If the government continues to use the real estate market stimulus, the land price will naturally rise, such that, if the government induces to buy it, one needs to buy it. Fourth, it is necessary to examine the past trends in the history of real estate, because the regulatory policy was strengthened and then relaxed from 1960 to the present. Fifth, since the real estate market policy regulation and stimulus are repeated in a pattern, it is necessary to invest conservatively during the regulatory period and aggressively during the stimulus period. The sixth point is to view investment as an active economic activity as a defensive measure to prevent the current assets from being thrown away. Considering the ever-increasing inflation rate, investment is necessary because the purchasing power of the product may become zero someday if you deposit assets in a bank without carrying out any investment. The seventh point is that value and price should not be viewed at the same time. If you do not make an investment which exceeds the inflation rate, you will lose money; thus, it is necessary to actively invest. Finally, if you are investing in the real estate market, it is better to stay still unless you know anything [13]. As mentioned earlier, there is a method of analyzing the real estate market by approaching it with data and expressing it by quantifying it, but empirical factors can also be an analysis and collection factor. The following Figure 1 shows the eight factors of the real estate market analysis technique.

Figure 1. Real estate market analysis by eight kinds of techniques.

2.4. Real Estate Big Data: The Domestic Case

2.4.1. Housing Supply Statistics Information System (HIS)

Housing supply statistics (HIS) produce various housing statistics—including national statistics—and builds a housing statistics system, collects statistical data, verifies it, processes and analyzes it, and utilizes it for the establishment of housing policies. Statistical data are used to analyze candidate sites for construction, business feasibility analysis, and sales strategies. In addition, it is very useful for the construction industry and real estate industry as well as general customers to understand the past and present construction industry through monthly housing statistics, such as permits, construction, completion, and sales.

2.4.2. Construction Administration System (Seum-Teo)

The building administration system is a system for computerizing and managing the application and processing of building permits—such as for building, housing, building registers, etc.—without visiting the government office. There is also information which is necessary for housing work, maintenance work, and construction-related business. It shows statistics such as building permits, construction starts, buildings, and house construction.

2.4.3. Real Estate Transaction Management System

This system is designed to enable the quick convenient handling of all real estate transactions, from reporting real estate transaction contracts related to real estate transactions to real estate registration. Thanks to Internet real estate transaction reporting, people need not go to cities, counties, and ward offices. Report documents can be conveniently processed online without the need to reduce the attached documents. The data is used for inquiry when the registration is removed from the Supreme Court's registration system and is utilized by the National Tax Service for assignment duties. In addition, the basic municipality uses it for the task of imposing registration tax, whereas the Ministry of Land, Infrastructure, and Transport uses it for real transaction prices, transaction statistics, and price disclosure [14,15].

2.4.4. Korea Land and Housing Corporation (SEE:REAL)

This is a system built to deliver real estate information through a systematic service based on the Internet. It uses a map as a real estate information portal site which provides 12 kinds of real estate-related information and 50 kinds of real estate information, spatial information, and statistical information data from one place on the Internet. It has the advantage of allowing anyone to use it easily to look up real estate information. This portal provides various kinds of information, such as real estate information, presale information, real estate individual information, and usage area districts when searching on the map, including materials and programs related to real estate, such as 'search for my land' and a real estate transaction information inquiry service portal [16].

2.4.5. Republic of Korea Real Estate Statistics System (R-ONE)

As a Republic of Korea Appraisal Board-based system that provides real estate statistics information to policymakers as well as the general public, this surveys the national land price fluctuation rate, national housing price trend survey, monthly rent price trend survey, apartment housing transaction price index, and commercial rental trends in the investigation of official price trends, etc. Most of the methods used for the sampling involve stratified extraction. In addition, one can check the real estate transaction status and economic and financial statistics, remove errors and outliers from the real transaction data database, create a valid database by creating valid DB (Data Base) and basic statistics, and calculate and verify the actual transaction price index for the disclosure of information [17].

2.4.6. Real Estate *Aptgin*

Real estate acquaintances use convenient data and various analytical methods to provide customers with convenient and easy access to various kinds of information and regulations on real estate in order to disclose freely the information used only in some companies or investment groups to the general public. It provides a differentiated information service by refining and solving various quality data and contents provided by the government. Real estate acquaintances provide customers with regional information that is viewed as Big Data, detailed information on the expected amount of occupancy by region, apartment comparisons, unsold information, transaction volumes by region, and a Big Data map. Figure 2 shows the market price and market strength through the Big Data map provided by the apartment acquaintances [18].

2.4.7. Ziptoss

As a recent example of public data use, Ziptoss has become popular as an on- and offline-owned real estate brokerage service without fees. As one of its advantages, if the customer receives information directly from the landlord and makes the quality of the information transparent, and a customer makes an online inquiry, there is no fee for anyone who connects to a direct store to obtain a room, and only the person who sells the product is charged a fee. Ziptoss operates the building register, road name address information Supreme Court, land use regulation system, and road condition public data to receive information about the building and information related to the rent, building price, and actual trading price.

Figure 2. Analysis of big data area provided by the real estate *aptgin* Gangnam-gu system.

2.5. Real Estate Market Big Data Analysis System and Technique

Real estate big data analysis systems need to analyze using models, integrate predicted results, and perform optimization simulations in order to be utilized as a real estate policy tool. In addition, through the visualization process, the demand of the real estate market displays information such as supply and land price, and an algorithm for the analysis and accuracy of the result is required. In particular, the collection and real-time monitoring of unstructured data such as SNS (Social Network Service) media and newspaper articles should be reflected. This allows you to extract useful information, manage the real estate market in real time through a refining process, and actively manage it on a regular basis in order to stabilize the real estate market and exert policy effects. It is necessary to prepare a compatible system. Then, research using market analysis and prediction models through big data technology which can be applied to various real estates should be continued. Based on these technologies, the technology for analyzing real estate prices of public and private institutions introduced in Section 2.4 was created [7]. In addition, technologies used in real estate-related analysis technologies are being studied through regression analysis [19–22], artificial neural networks [23], data mining [24], predictive modeling [25,26], and machine learning [27]. Research should be conducted based on accuracy and efficiency.

2.6. The Possibility of Using Real Estate Big Data

In the real estate market, Big Data is a suitable technology for approaching current issues and policies. It is believed to be able to support real-estate–related activities through the use of Big Data, and to respond to future problems through future prediction [28]. Therefore, real estate Big Data should be derived to reflect the various factors comprehensively and proceed to the best process. Currently, the Korean market is preparing for difficult or unpredictable situations, such as going back and forth between cold and hot water like riding a roller coaster. It is expected to be effective in solving the problems for the purpose. Therefore, it is necessary to find a way to graft into the real estate market by referring to the use cases of Big Data technology and recent trends [14]. Figure 3 shows the real estate Big Data in the STEEP (Social, Technological, Economic, Ecological, and Political) type.

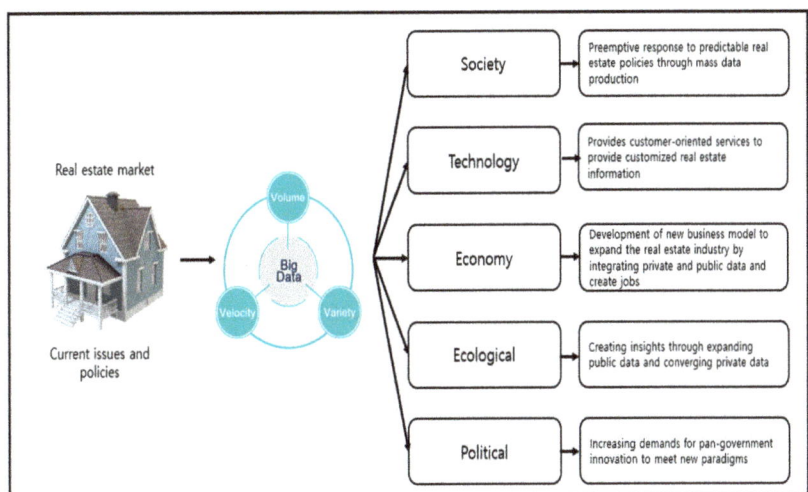

Figure 3. Real estate Big Data utilization plan system.

3. Real Estate Market after Land Price Prediction Study

The real estate market belongs to a typical area in which it is difficult to predict the 'after' situation. As a result, even experts agree that the area of interest is likely to skyrocket. There are various factors for investigating the 'after' of real estate, in addition to macro and micro variables [29]. In this paper, however, we examined the factors for forecasting real estate land prices through macro variables and micro variables. If we look at the entire real estate market over the long term, the macro perspective has a great influence. Likewise, in the short term, the micro perspective has a high impact. Nonetheless, it is necessary to consider both, because their effects may be intertwined. Therefore, the research focused on two factors in the ground prediction.

Currently, the center of real estate investment in the Republic of Korea has changed from 4,50 to 2,30. The reason for the high number of housing transactions for the 20th and 30th generations is that the supply of employment and restrictions on housing construction have been relaxed. If this continues, however, not only will speculation overheating be a concern, but investment risks will increase. That is why real estate transactions are very important to the macro economy. Still, the micro economy is just as important as the macro economy. Just as stock in the 'after' value and credibility of a company, real estate must also look at the location and current situation. Therefore, this paper seeks to confirm that some factors have a high influence on land prices aside from the two factors [30].

Figure 4 is a blueprint of how big data is analyzed in the real estate market, and how to organize it before getting the result. The target area for the analysis is Gangnam-gu, and the data collection is based on information provided by public data portals and public institutions. Subsequently, through multiple regression analysis and correlation analysis, as a result, we seek out the most influential factors for real estate market prices.

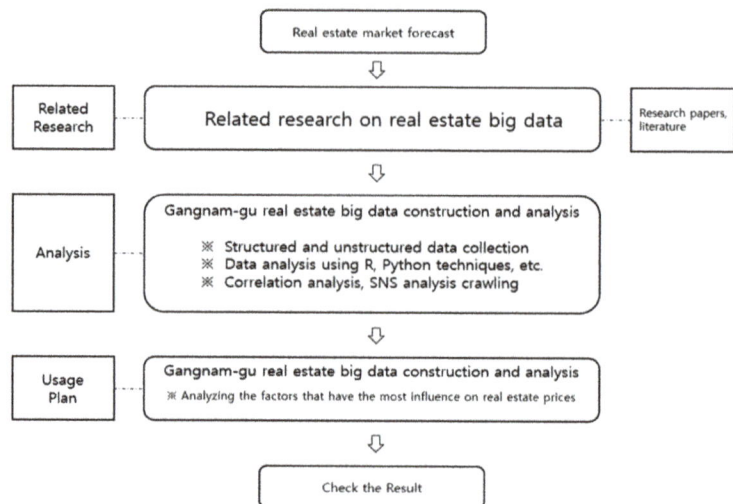

Figure 4. Real estate market future land price forecast research flow chart system.

3.1. Macroscopic View of the Real Estate Market

The macro view is that the social structure dominates an individual's thinking, and assumes that the individual acts in a structured manner under the influence of the social structure [31–33]. Figure 5 explains the factors of the macroscopic data.

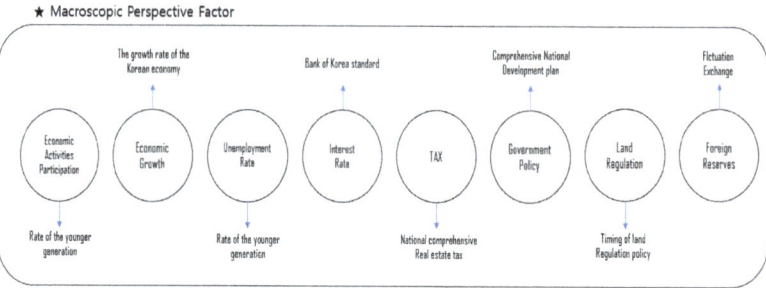

Figure 5. Macroscopic factors in the real estate market system.

3.1.1. Growth Rate of Young People Participating in the Company

Currently, as Korea approaches the age of ultra-aging like its neighbor, Japan, the population of the elderly is increasing, and the proportion of the youth is decreasing. Nevertheless, as of 2018, the value of the real estate market is not falling, but is currently on the rise. As such, what is the biggest reason the land price is not falling when the fertility rate is decreasing and the economic situation is not as good as it was in the past? The value of the real estate market cannot depreciate because they are entering the real estate market due to the increase in the number of young adults owing to the baby boomers from the early 90s to the mid-90s. When the fertility rate reaches a number similar to the present by the 2030s beyond the 2020s, the analysis of statistical institutions confirms that house prices will change significantly from the present. As a result, from a macroscopic point of view, the future situation is not good. The following Figure 6 shows the participation rate of young adults in economic activities, where young people are between 15 and 39 years old.

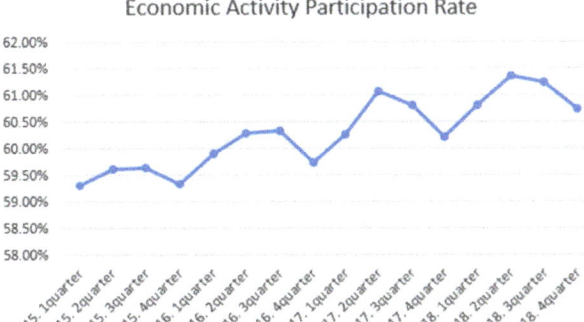

Figure 6. Economic activity participation rate between 15 and 39 years old.

Meanwhile, the macroscopic and microscopic numerical data in Section 3 were created using data provided by public data portals, and data provided by public institutions [34–37].

3.1.2. Economic Growth Rate/Unemplyoment Rate

As the economy grows, the value of stocks, real estate, and existing goods rises as inflation progresses rapidly when people's income and corporate capital investment increase [38]. If the economic growth rate decreases compared to the present, the demand for and value of real estate and stocks will decrease. Moreover, as the income and corporate investment of the people decrease, the growth rate decreases as the number of sales providers increases. Figure 7, below, shows the figure of the economic growth rate, which means the rate of GDP (Gross Domestic Product) growth, and the unemployment rate for 15 to 39 year-olds.

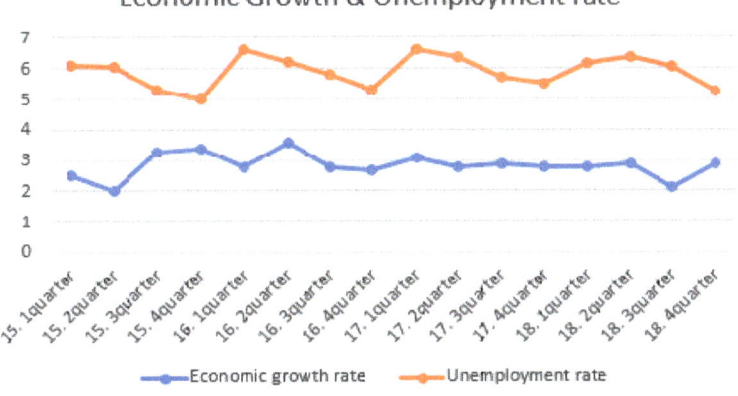

Figure 7. Economic growth rate and unemployment rate.

3.1.3. Interest Rate

The interest rate is a rate expressed as the interest rate per period applied to the principal. The interest rate wields various influences on our lives. If the interest rates rise, the method of depositing in the bank is appropriate, but buying a house by borrowing is burdensome. As a result, the real estate price falls. In this case, the method of depositing in the bank will lower the value; thus, it is effective to buy a house with a loan; of course, this will increase the value of real estate due to the high demand. When a crisis comes, like the current coronavirus situation, if the interest rate falls outside the normal range, the real estate market will overheat or cool down rapidly. Moreover, unlike foreign countries, there is a system called a *jeonse* system. Thus, if the interest rate goes down, the value of the charter decreases for the landholder, resulting in an increase in the value of the *jeonse*. To explain by example, the price of an apartment in Daechi-dong, Gangnam-gu, before the coronavirus incident occurred was 2.215 billion won. The coronavirus pandemic caused the demand for real estate to diminish as the interest rate fluctuated, with trading at 1950 million won. On the other side, the charter price has increased by 100 million won. Currently, apartment prices in Seoul have fallen by 0.02%, but charter prices have risen 0.03%. Figure 8 shows the interest rates from 15 to 18 years.

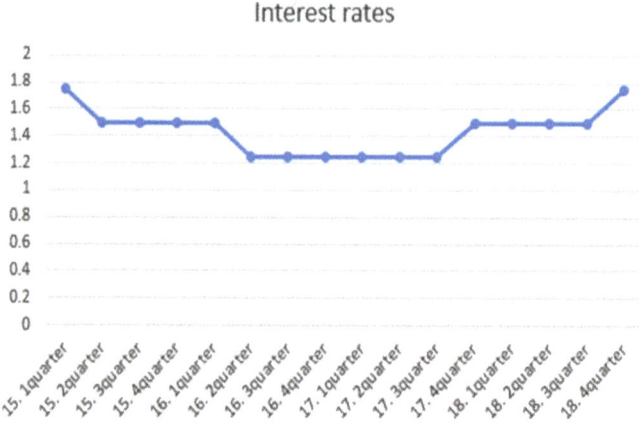

Figure 8. Standard interest rate status.

3.1.4. Comprehensive Real Estate Tax Charge

Comprehensive real estate tax is the tax that is levied on the excess if the total amount of publicly-announced prices exceeds a certain standard amount by dividing the homes and lands of each country by type. The comprehensive real estate tax is imposed on high-value real estate holders, which is based on equity in the tax burden of the people on real estate holdings, and it aims to stabilize real estate prices and contribute to the balanced development of local governments, and the economic development of the Republic of Korea. The base date for taxation is 1 June. Figure 9 shows the history of change in the overall real estate tax.

3.1.5. Government Policy

When planning to deploy government offices on a nationwide basis—such as the Comprehensive Land Development Plan, large-scale residential land developments like the new city development, and the construction of social overhead capital such as roads—the contents from the microscopic perspective should also be viewed from a macroscopic perspective. Increasing the budget to implement policies such as national land development in the country will cause the real estate market to overheat nationwide, but in the opposite case, it will tend to slow down. Figure 10 shows the history of government real estate policy [21].

3.1.6. Land Construction Regulation

Architecture is regulated to suit the environment, economy, culture, and politics, etc., of the land and the type of land used. According to a paper on economic trends, real estate is closely correlated with income, population, and the land regulation level. In fact, it is impossible for the government to change the income and the population artificially, so only the land regulation can be changed. The green belt and other areas of public green space regulation are factors that increase the price of housing, and excessive building regulation is also a policy for the reduction of housing construction, which is why it is causing the price to rise. Looking at overseas cases, San Francisco and Dallas have seen similar income growth since 1980. As a result of checking the land price compared to income, however, San Francisco, where the green space regulation was the most severe, showed an increase rate of over 30%, whereas Dallas had no change. Figure 11 shows the number of building regulations in the current state of the Seoul City Ordinance.

Comprehensive Real Estate Tax Change Process

	Taxation Standard	Tax Base and Tax Rate (b : billion)	Target application rate	Upper limit of tax burden	Taxation box
Introduced in January 2005	Over 900 Million won	0.3b->1%, 0.3b~1.4b ->1.5%, 1.4b~9.4b->2%, more than 9.4b->3%	50% (based on published price)	150%	System of summing By person
Aug. 2005 Reinforcement	Over 600 Million won	0.3b->1%, 0.3b~1.4b ->1.5%, 1.4b~9.4b->2%, more than 9.4b->3%	Increase by 10% point every year (based on official price)	300%	Generational summation method
September 2008 Easing	More than 600 Million won (900 Milion won for single - homeowners)	Less than 0.6b->0.5%, 0.6b~1.2b->0.75%, 1.2b~5b->1%, 5b~9.4b->1.5%, more than 9.4b->2%	80% (based on fair market value)	150%	System of summing By person
June 2018 Reinforcement	More than 600 Million won (900 Milion won for single - homeowners)	Less than 0.6b->0.5%, 0.6b~1.2b->0.8%, 1.2b~5b->1.2%, 5b~9.4b->1.8%, more than 9.4b->2.5%	Increase by 10% point every year (based on fair market value)	150%	System of summing By person

Figure 9. History of the comprehensive real estate tax charge system.

Figure 10. The Republic of Korea's real estate measures system.

Figure 11. Gangnam-gu's urban planning ordinance history system.

3.1.7. Foreign Currency Reserves

Foreign currency reserves are foreign currency funds that a country is stockpiling in preparation for emergencies. Foreign currency reserves are an important means to respond to changes in the external environment and economic crisis. They are a liquid asset that responds to sudden capital inflows when a crisis occurs by reducing the rate of exchange rate fluctuations. As such, macroscopically, the amount of foreign exchange reserves is an external saving in the Korean economy, and external saving is determined at the same time as internal saving. The rapid increase in foreign exchange reserves has led to a decrease in domestic investment in the Korean economy. Thus, if the foreign exchange reserves increase rapidly, an imbalance in the financial sector will result, resulting in over-investment in real estate and stock markets. The following Figure 12 shows the status of foreign exchange reserves in Korea.

Figure 12. Republic of Korea's foreign exchange reserves ($100 million).

3.2. Microscopic View of the Real Estate Market

A micro perspective is a theory which focuses on the interactions between individuals in everyday life or the subjectivity of individuals, and which presupposes the social nominal theory. The micro real estate factors can be seen in Figure 13.

3.2.1. External Capital Inflow

In Korea, the influence of land and building owners is absolute. Thus, even if an outsider contributes to the holder, there is no burden of property tax, capital tax, and taxation. In other words, the so-called 'good news' profits all go to the landholders, not theirs. Industrial complexes, social overhead capital, current local residents and artists, and external investments such as efforts to revive the neighborhood are the so-called 'good news'; the profits all go to the landholders, not them. Therefore, it is important to analyze the impact of good conditions on real estate, and bad conditions need to be analyzed as well.

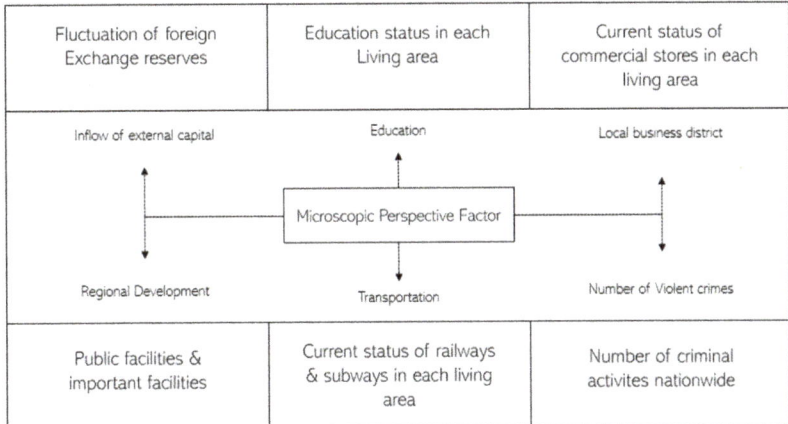

Figure 13. Microscopic perspective factor status system.

3.2.2. Local Development or Public Facilities, and Important Facilities

Not surprisingly, if public facilities or important facilities come in next to residential or commercial areas, the value of the real estate increases as the number of floating populations increases and investment increases. On the other hand, if rumors that public facilities will be transferred to other areas fail to attract important facilities, the value will decrease; in the Republic of Korea, however, it is common to minimize damage by bringing in other major facilities to appease opposing local residents, and to take follow-up measures with lawmakers' politics. In the current paper, the real estate market was focused on Gangnam-gu and divided into six living zones.

3.2.3. Commercial Growth

As the commercial area grows, if the land or building in the area is owned, the profit gained from the rental income or land transaction becomes relatively large. There is a need to be cautious when the existing holders pay for everything and sell all of them at high prices when trading with the right to name the premium commercial zone. Among the commercial districts in Seoul, the most popular commercial districts are Hongdae, Sinchon, Hanyang University, and Keonkuk University, but not all of the commercial districts are growing. Although it plays a part in the flow of traffic, factors which promote the growth of commercial areas are needed. As an example, Hongdae's commercial district has a growing population, unlike other commercial districts. The reason the Hongdae commercial area is gradually growing is that it is expanding into Donggyo-dong, Yeonnam-dong, Sangsu-dong, and Hapjeong-dong, and the charm of the old and new generations overlaps with Korean and exotic ones. As a result, commercial areas grew in the past as residential areas turned into clothing stores and restaurants. The second attraction of the Hongdae area is creative diversity. As shown by the recent SBS (Seoul Broadcasting System) entertainment Jong-won Baek alley restaurant, we can find different charms in the Hongdae area, too, as each block has a new charm. Transportation and important facilities are indicative of the growth of the commercial area, but it can be seen that the attractive part can also promote the growth of a commercial area [39]. Figure 14 shows the variation in the number of stores in each living zone.

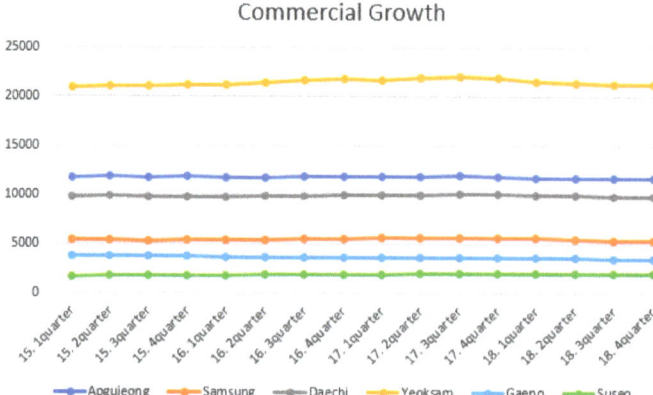

Figure 14. Number of stores in six local living areas.

3.2.4. Traffic

Transportation is considered to have the closest relationship to the real estate market [40]. It also has a great influence on the growth of the commercial area, education, and the location of important facilities and development zones. Therefore, even in real estate, the area is within a 500 m radius centered on the subway, or within 5~10 min on foot. The station area is the most important factor in determining the real estate price. Placing railway- and public transportation-related items as one of the policies is the biggest factor in the real estate market. If the traffic is far from the commercial area or inconvenient, real estate foreclosure will increase due to populations moving to other areas. In this way, traffic may overheat the real estate market; on the contrary, it shows the ability to suppress it. According to a paper in the United States, the way to suppress the rise in real estate prices is the expansion of the railroad network, which extends the radius of people's living to the outskirts. This is to ensure that Korea is distributed to the outlying areas by expanding urban railroads and developing new cities in order to prevent the overheating of the local real estate market. Blast furnace transportation is one of the most important factors in predicting future land prices, as it has a great influence on the land price.

Gangnam-gu opened Line 9 at the beginning of year 15, opening the Samsung Central Station, Bongeunsa Station, Seonjeongneung Station, and Eonju Station. At the end of year 16, an SRT against the Korean high-speed rail KTX was built in the Suseo and Segok regional living zones in Gangnam-gu, with a wide area bus linking other regions introduced in year 17.

3.2.5. Education

In areas where schools have high university admission rates, or where schools and academic costs are concentrated, value increases as real estate demand increases. Representative examples are Daechi-dong, Junggye-dong, Mok-dong, and Noryangjin-dong, which are densely populated by Seoul city standards. In addition, the real estate prices in areas where special high schools and private high schools are located tend to be distributed. As a result, the Ministry of Education has decided to convert foreign high schools, international high schools, and high schools into general high schools in 2025. Therefore, the demand for high school districts may increase. Accordingly, there are concerns that the demand for high school districts in District 8 and Seocho-gu in Gangnam-gu will increase significantly.

There are a total of 88 schools in Gangnam-gu, including elementary, middle, and high schools, special purpose schools, and universities: 13 in the Apgujeong area, 19 in the Daechi area, nine in the Samsung area, ten in the Yeoksam area, 22 in the Gaepo area, and 15 in the Suseo area.

3.2.6. Violent Crime Rate

Strong crime rates are also an important factor in predicting real estate land prices. The more dangerous the area, the poorer the image, and the more difficult it is to fix it in the residential area or commercial area. As a result, the commercial area and the residential area decline, the area becomes less active, and the influx of poor people and the number of criminals increase. From another perspective, it is true that, by taking risks and investing in a region, not only will land prices be cheaper than other regions but if the gamble succeeds, it will mean gaining an advantage in that region. Moreover, with the rise of outside investors, the crime rate will decrease, and real estate land prices can go up again. As was the case in the past, if there are rumors of rental apartments and houses around condominiums, a demonstration opposing it will most likely follow. The correlation between public rental housing and crime occurrence in four years was analyzed, and the rest excluding permanent rental housing were confirmed to have affected the crime rate. Figure 15 shows the results of using the prosecution's crime trend report to set the violent crime rate of 100,100 from 2015 to 2018.

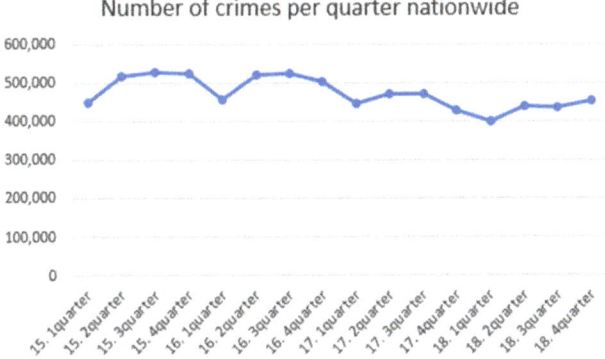

Figure 15. Number of crimes per quarter nationwide.

4. Analysis of Factors from Macroscopic and Microscopic Perspectives for the Prediction of Future Land Prices in the Real Estate Market

Prior to the data analysis, the land prices in the real estate market were analyzed based on apartments where land price transactions occurred smoothly in the living areas of each region. The land price of each regional living area was set as the independent variable, and the dependent variables are the economic activity participation rate of the young people, the economic growth rate, the unemployment rate of the young people, interest rates, the application rate of the comprehensive real estate tax and policy, local building regulations, foreign exchange reserves, the growth in the trading area, and violent crimes. The analysis was carried out with a total of 10 out of the 13 variables mentioned above; when we focused on the quarterly data from 2015 to 2018, the transportation, education, and public facilities sectors fluctuated. These were not used as variables because their effect was not big. As we all know, transportation, education, and public facilities are variables with a huge impact on real estate land prices. Unlike other areas, Gangnam-gu is a region which has been developed since the 1970s, so it has complete transportation, education, and public facilities. Thus, these three variables were not used in this analysis. Figure 16 shows the real estate data analysis through the R and Python programs to determine which factors are related to land prices.

4.1. R Program Data Analysis

As a result of analysis using the macroscopic variable data and microscopic variable data in Section 3, the regression model itself was found to be valid, but the overall independent variables did not significantly affect the dependent variable. Therefore, using the backward elimination method and the stepwise selection method, the analysis was conducted based on the smallest AIC.

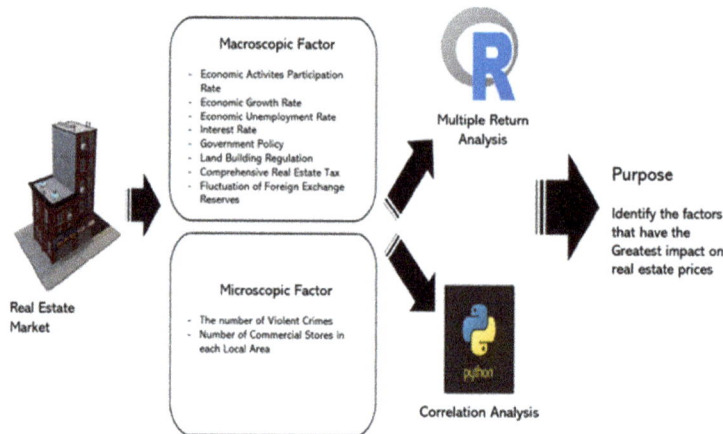

Figure 16. Analysis flow diagram for the estimation of real estate land prices.

From the results above, it was confirmed that the dependent variable explains the large LP (Land Price) fluctuation of 92% and 99.8%. In addition, as a result of testing whether there is a significant relationship between the dependent variable and the set of all of the independent variables, the two were confirmed to be related at a significance level of 95%.

Based on Figure 17, we were able to ascertain the influence of the dependent variables and the independent variables. First, in the case of Apgujeong, we confirmed that dependent variables such as the unemployment rate, interest rate, comprehensive real estate tax, and violent crime rate affect land prices. In the case of the Second Samsung Living Area, dependent variables such as the economic growth rate, policies, land construction regulations, foreign exchange reserves, and violent crime rates were confirmed to have an effect. In the case of the third Daechi Living area, we confirmed that dependent variables such as the unemployment rate, interest rate, foreign exchange reserves, commercial growth, and violent crime rate have an effect. For the Yeoksam living sphere, eight dependent variables—the youth economic activity participation rate, economic growth rate, interest rate and policy, land construction regulation, foreign exchange reserves, commercial growth, and violent crime rate—have an effect. In the case of the fifth Gaepo living area, dependent variables such as the youth economic activity participation rate, interest rate, comprehensive real estate tax, policy, foreign exchange reserves, and commercial growth have an effect. Finally, in the case of the Suseo living areas, the youth economic activity participation rates, comprehensive real estate tax, and policy dependent variables were confirmed to have an effect.

As a result, we were able to confirm whether the ten factors affect land prices. Nonetheless, four factors policy, interest rate, violent crime rate, and foreign exchange reserves were found to have more influence than the other factors. In addition, the F TEST confirmed that the dependent variables of the six regional living spaces were significant together with the independent variables.

4.2. Python Program Data Analysis

In Section 4.1, multi-regression analysis was used to analyze the independent variables affecting the dependent variables using variable data from the macroscopic point of view and variable data from the microscopic point of view; this time, we tried to find the factors that correlate with the real estate price through correlation analysis. Correlation analysis is designed to understand the degree of association between two variables, not to explain causality.

(a)

```
Coefficients:
              Estimate Std. Error t value Pr(>|t|)
(Intercept)  2.313e+01  1.438e+01   1.608  0.13610
UR          -3.138e+00  7.594e-01  -4.132  0.00167 **
IR          -1.084e+01  2.251e+00  -4.815  0.00054 ***
FT           5.862e+01  9.561e+00   6.131  7.4e-05 ***
VCR         -4.519e-05  1.147e-05  -3.939  0.00232 **
---
Signif. codes:  0 '***' 0.001 '**' 0.01 '*' 0.05 '.' 0.1 ' ' 1

Residual standard error: 1.249 on 11 degrees of freedom
Multiple R-squared:  0.908,	Adjusted R-squared:  0.8745
F-statistic: 27.14 on 4 and 11 DF,  p-value: 1.199e-05
```

(b)

```
Coefficients:
              Estimate Std. Error t value Pr(>|t|)
(Intercept)  1.784e+01  2.080e+01   0.858  0.41122
UR          -1.074e+00  2.605e-01  -4.124  0.00206 **
IR          -2.662e+00  1.046e+00  -2.545  0.02913 *
FER          1.276e-02  8.914e-04  14.315 5.47e-08 ***
CG          -3.674e-03  1.658e-03  -2.215  0.05111 .
VCR         -2.086e-05  5.227e-06  -3.991  0.00255 **
---
Signif. codes:  0 '***' 0.001 '**' 0.01 '*' 0.05 '.' 0.1 ' ' 1

Residual standard error: 0.3287 on 10 degrees of freedom
Multiple R-squared:  0.9822,	Adjusted R-squared:  0.9733
F-statistic: 110.3 on 5 and 10 DF,  p-value: 2.057e-08
```

(c)

```
Coefficients:
              Estimate Std. Error t value Pr(>|t|)
(Intercept) -4.340e+01  4.847e+00  -8.954 4.33e-06 ***
EGR          5.968e-01  2.189e-01   2.726  0.02133 *
Policy       4.339e-01  1.441e-01   3.010  0.01311 *
LCR         -2.834e-01  8.798e-02  -3.221  0.00916 **
FER          1.720e-02  9.650e-04  17.829 6.58e-09 ***
VCR         -2.037e-05  3.223e-06  -6.382 8.02e-05 ***
---
Signif. codes:  0 '***' 0.001 '**' 0.01 '*' 0.05 '.' 0.1 ' ' 1

Residual standard error: 0.3259 on 10 degrees of freedom
Multiple R-squared:  0.9917,	Adjusted R-squared:  0.9876
F-statistic: 240.1 on 5 and 10 DF,  p-value: 4.471e-10
```

(d)

```
Coefficients:
              Estimate Std. Error t value Pr(>|t|)
(Intercept) -7.558e+01  1.562e+01  -4.839 0.001880 **
EAPR         8.271e-01  2.944e-01   2.809 0.026176 *
EGR          4.589e-01  1.280e-01   3.584 0.008925 **
IR           2.490e+00  8.674e-01   2.870 0.023979 *
Policy       6.373e-01  1.199e-01   5.482 0.000924 ***
LCR         -2.175e-01  6.578e-02  -3.308 0.013016 *
FER          1.365e-02  1.658e-03   8.235 7.57e-05 ***
CG          -5.737e-04  2.886e-04  -1.988 0.087158 .
VCR         -1.364e-05  2.056e-06  -6.633 0.000295 ***
---
Signif. codes:  0 '***' 0.001 '**' 0.01 '*' 0.05 '.' 0.1 ' ' 1

Residual standard error: 0.1811 on 7 degrees of freedom
Multiple R-squared:  0.9979,	Adjusted R-squared:  0.9956
F-statistic: 421.2 on 8 and 7 DF,  p-value: 1.082e-08
```

(e)

```
Coefficients:
              Estimate Std. Error t value Pr(>|t|)
(Intercept) -75.651820  53.221745  -1.421   0.1889
EAPR          0.993093   0.822030   1.208   0.2578
IR            3.950801   2.128182   1.856   0.0964 .
FT          -15.830488  10.303056  -1.536   0.1588
Policy        0.667655   0.401190   1.664   0.1304
FER           0.015332   0.004963   3.089   0.0129 *
CG           -0.006497   0.004862  -1.336   0.2143
---
Signif. codes:  0 '***' 0.001 '**' 0.01 '*' 0.05 '.' 0.1 ' ' 1

Residual standard error: 0.6683 on 9 degrees of freedom
Multiple R-squared:  0.9642,	Adjusted R-squared:  0.9403
F-statistic: 40.37 on 6 and 9 DF,  p-value: 5.252e-06
```

(f)

```
Coefficients:
            Estimate Std. Error t value Pr(>|t|)
(Intercept) -93.2324    18.3501  -5.081 0.000270 ***
EAPR          1.3089     0.3477   3.764 0.002701 **
FT           27.7808     5.2886   5.253 0.000203 ***
Policy        0.7443     0.2797   2.661 0.020741 *
---
Signif. codes:  0 '***' 0.001 '**' 0.01 '*' 0.05 '.' 0.1 ' ' 1

Residual standard error: 0.664 on 12 degrees of freedom
Multiple R-squared:  0.9109,	Adjusted R-squared:  0.8886
F-statistic: 40.89 on 3 and 12 DF,  p-value: 1.412e-06
```

Figure 17. Checking the significant relationship through the stepwise selection method: (**a**) Apgujeong Area, (**b**) Daechi Area, (**c**) Samsung Area, (**d**) Yeoksam Area, (**e**) Gaepo Area, (**f**) Suseo Area.

As shown in Figure 18, there were differences in the factors relevant to each local living zone. Compared to other factors, the economic growth rate, unemployment rate, interest rate, policy, land building regulation, and violent crime rate were found to be relatively low.

In conclusion, the factors influencing the cost of living in each region through regression analysis in R were the amount of foreign exchange reserves, number of criminal activities, interest rates, and policies, and the factors correlated with the price of living in each region through correlation analysis in Python included the economic participation rate of the youth, rate of application of the comprehensive real estate tax bill, and amount of foreign exchange reserves, but the research results confirmed that fluctuations in foreign currency reserves are closely related to real estate land prices. As explained in Section 4.3, below, we would like to examine the impact of land prices associated with fluctuations in foreign exchange reserves in combination with the current data.

4.3. Analysis of the Relationship between Foreign Exchange Reserves and Land Prices

Through the R program regression analysis and the correlation analysis of Python, it was confirmed in Sections 4.1 and 4.2 that the most relevant factor for the land prices is the foreign exchange reserves. Next, we sought to analyze the fluctuations in foreign currency reserves and the relationship with land prices from 2019 to the present, and to investigate how the influence is applied as it is.

Figure 19, below, shows the fluctuations in foreign exchange reserves from the first quarter of 2019 to the first quarter of 2020, and the average land price fluctuations in each region's living area. The foreign exchange reserves can be checked in parentheses next to the year; the unit is 100 million dollars, and the land price is also 100 million.

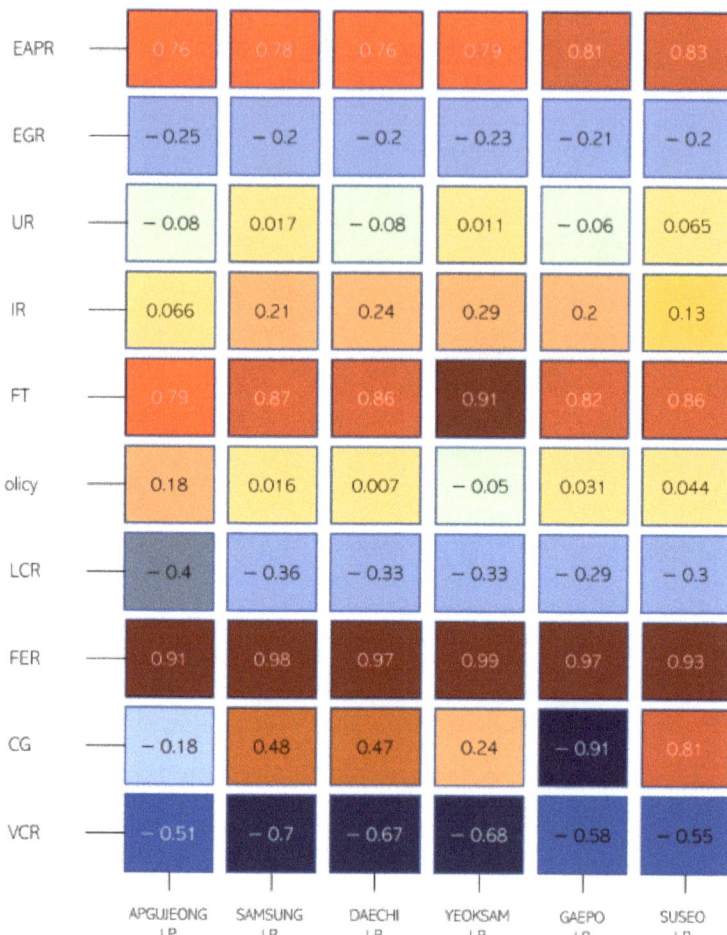

Figure 18. Relationship between real estate prices and variables.

The foreign currency reserve was set as an independent variable through a Python program. The representative apartment area in the living area of each region was set as the dependent variable. The results were then confirmed through correlation analysis and regression analysis. It was confirmed that, among the six regional living areas, the representative apartments in the regional living area of Samsung have a significant relationship with the fluctuation of foreign exchange reserves. The correlation was also confirmed. In addition, the fluctuation of foreign currency reserves was confirmed to be related to the land prices of each regional living area. Unfortunately, the real estate transaction is active, and it was set at 120 square yards, so there was not much data, and the relevance between foreign currency reserves and land prices increased. However, other studies confirming fluctuations in foreign exchange reserves and their relationship to the stock market have confirmed that an increase in the amount of currency has led to overinvestment in real estate and the stock market, leading to price increases [41,42]. Foreign exchange reserves in the first quarter of 2020 showed a decline due to the increase in the dollar due to the foreign exchange market stabilization measures and COVID19, but has been on the rise since. Korea's foreign exchange reserves at the end of December last year were $443.1 billion, an increase of $6.7 billion compared to November, indicating that securities will also have a significant increase in return on investment, and that real estate land prices will also rise significantly. This research also confirmed the data of 2019 using the data of 2015 to 2018, but for this research, it was also confirmed that the fluctuation of real estate land prices due to the fluctuation of foreign currency reserves has a correlation [42–44]. The result of this can be valid. Figure 20, below, shows the transactions for a representative apartment in 120 square yards in the Samsung area of Gangnam-gu, where the blue line denotes the quotes for the apartment. The red dot shows the actual transaction price. The green line shows the current price of the property, and the red line at the end is the speculation that the market price will rise due to the increase in foreign currency reserves.

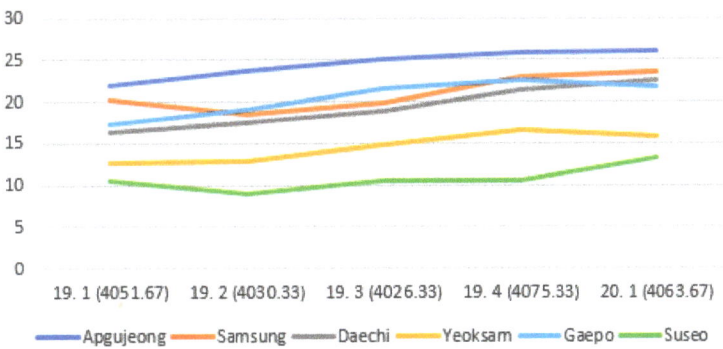

Figure 19. Changes in the land price of living areas in each region due to changes in the foreign exchange reserves.

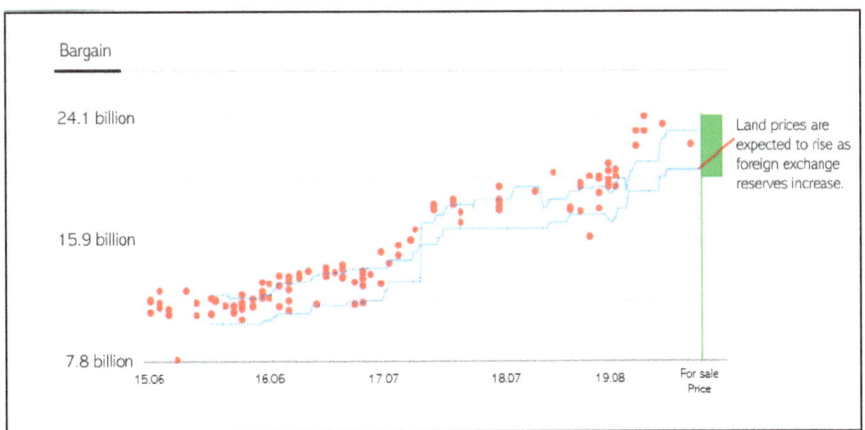

Figure 20. Prediction of changes in the market prices due to fluctuations in foreign exchange reserves.

5. Impact on Landscape Districts of Real Estate

In addition to the macroscopic and microscopic perspectives in the real estate market, the landscape district is also a desirable tool for the prediction of future land prices. Landscape districts are districts required for the preservation, management, and formation of landscapes, and they are determined by the National Land Planning and Utilization Act. According to their designated purpose, landscape districts are classified into natural landscapes, urban landscapes, and waterside landscape districts. The natural landscape district is necessary for the protection of mountainous and hilly areas, and for maintaining the natural scenery of the city. The urban landscape district is a district required for protecting and maintaining urban landscapes such as residential areas or centers, and it is a waterside landscape district and specialized landscape district. Finally the waterside landscape district is a district designed to protect and maintain the landscape around the main waterfront or buildings with great cultural conservation value.

There are four major factors influencing land price fluctuations in these landscape areas. First, the city planning ordinance can be changed. For example, the green belt in Haeundae-gu, Busan has recently been enhanced. Second is a case wherein changes are made through development projects such as residential land development projects. Third are the environmental factors which affect real estate or policies related to restrictions and business promotion related to the national landscape, such as the Second Framework Plan for Landscape Policy recently established in Korea. Lastly, due to factors such as capital inflow, there are various factors which can vary real estate prices, such as landscape districts.

Because these landscape districts were formed in order to preserve and manage landscapes, it was difficult for landowners to retain property rights; the release of the landscape districts could affect real estate prices because it attracts investment and creates jobs in the area. Nonetheless, with the release of the landscape district, industrial factors are becoming positive, but the analysis of environmental factors does not yield good results. Because the ecosystem elements in the area are destroyed, and because there is a risk of environmental damage, the current landscape policy is called the watch landscape district or highest altitude district in order to protect the environment and urban landscape in the residential area, or to prevent overcrowding. It is a situation which sets a minimum limit for the height of a building [45].

Therefore, the current landscape district development has a policy of preventing environmental damage; for want of a better word, it is called a multifunctional landscape, providing various functions to maintain the current environmental ecosystem services [46]. To put this into the real estate market, a smart city is to be built [47–49]. In the case of the current smart city construction in the Republic of Korea, construction is roughly divided into two areas. First, in the case of the Sejong Smart City, it is a policy promoted by the nation. Before the introduction of the Sejong Smart City, it was in a remote state. After focusing on artificial-intelligence–based cities, however, the building of elements of seven major innovations—such as mobility and healthcare—was sought to transform them into nature-friendly cities [50].

The second area is the Busan Eco-Delta City. Busan City plans to build a robot city unlike Sejong City: one that can be utilized in daily life. There was also an attempt to change to a waterfront city in the future based on teenage innovation. Overseas cases include Hangzhou, which decided to realize a paper-free society by using blockchain technology, and Toronto, which decided to improve the problem of major cities and build eco-friendly cities. The purpose of introducing smart city construction is to solve various urbanization problems and build a convenient, comfortable life. In addition, the land prices in the surrounding area are likely to increase with the introduction of smart cities [51,52].

Therefore, the method of introducing a smart city in Gangnam-gu, the target area of the current study, can be explained as follows. Of the six living areas in Gangnam-gu, the southern area of Gaepo area and the western area of Suseo area are currently limited to green belt development. Therefore, it is desirable to develop a smart city that can interact with real estate and landscape in this area. Through this, various uses such as welfare, transportation, and education will be created. In addition, it would be desirable to develop real estate and landscape by benchmarking the introduction of overseas smart cities in the region. Therefore, it is to realize self-driving public transportation or to establish a nature-friendly city through a paperless society. As a result, it is expected that through the introduction of smart cities, various effects such as a nature-friendly life and a satisfying life will be enjoyed. Therefore, it is considered that the introduction of a smart city is a way to make good use of the effect of interaction between landscape and real estate. Therefore, it is necessary to develop real estate and landscape based on the design plan for the introduction of smart cities in Korea through Figure 21 below [53].

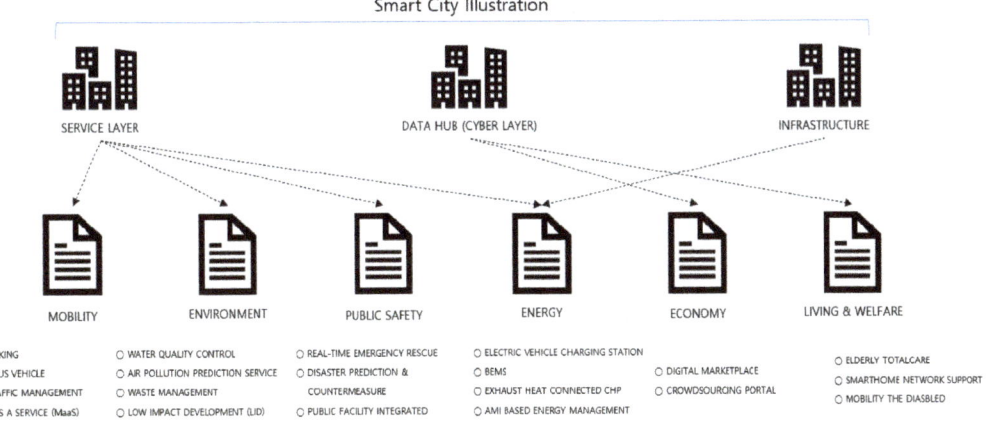

Figure 21. Smart city illustration.

6. Discussion

Recently, people's interest in the real estate market has increased [13,14]. Among them, what attracts attention is the exploration of the factors that cause changes in real estate land prices [19]. Various factors, such as transportation access, financial stability, and stocks exist as factors which can change the land prices [26,27,54,55], but in the current study, based on macro and micro factors—which are frequently used terms in the economy—we analysed which ones have a greater influence. In addition, the technologies used for real estate Big Data analysis include artificial neural network analysis, data mining, and machine learning, but in the current study, through regression analysis and correlation analysis, we investigated which factors are influential, and explained the correlation well. As a result, it was found that the fluctuation of foreign exchange holdings among macro factors exerts influence on real estate land prices, and it was found that future real estate prices also have an influence and explain the correlation well. In addition, it was confirmed that changes in foreign exchange holdings exert an influence on changes in land prices in China and Taiwan, as well as in Korea. Based on this, it can be seen that it is an effective method to predict future land prices through changes in foreign exchange reserves among macro and micro factors in real estate Big Data analysis.

In addition to the above-described factors, it can be confirmed that the factor of the landscape is also closely related to the real estate market. Since the landscape district is a district formed for the conservation and management of the landscape, there are positive aspects for industrial factors, but negative influences for environmental factors also exist.

In fact, in the Republic of Korea, Busan and Sejong are introducing smart cities to build a city, and technologies such as Blockchain, Big Data, and IoT are being used [36,37]. Therefore, in this paper, the factor that can interact in the landscape district and the real estate market is the establishment of a smart city. When the construction is completed, it is believed that this could also be a big factor in fluctuations in land prices.

7. Conclusions

In real estate, there are various variables in addition to the macro and micro factors discussed in the previous study as factors which change the land price. Therefore, it was not difficult to obtain statistical data related to land prices, and analysis sites related to this were also increased. As a representative method of real estate analysis, there is a method of grasping the current real estate market by grasping the trends of apartment sales prices and charter prices using past data, and the situation uses an analysis tool provided by real estate applications.

Therefore, in this paper, the focus was on finding out which factors of the past data have a significant influence on the change in land prices. In the case of factor data, the data from fiscal years 15 to 18 were used for the analysis, because the data was public up to a certain point, and as a result, it was confirmed that the change in foreign exchange reserves was the most influential factor. Subsequently, as a result of substituting the data for the year 19, it was confirmed that it had an influence on the land price. In addition, in order to check whether the landscape district correlates with the real estate market, we investigated the factors influencing price fluctuations; as a result, it was confirmed that the way to interact with real estate is the introduction of smart cities.

Since the current study focused on the living areas of Gangnam-gu, it was less accurate than expected. Therefore, in future studies, if the relationship between the ten factors and the land price is explained in more detail by an administrative unit, a more accurate result will be obtained. This is believed to be possible. In addition, 14 factors were explained, especially six micro factors, but since only two were used, we would like to find a way to convert the four data points that could not be used as data. Finally, after explaining the correlation between real estate and landscape districts, we came to the conclusion that the introduction of a smart city is the way to interact. Based on the case of smart city construction, we want to confirm the relationship with real estate land prices.

Author Contributions: Conceptualization, S.-H.L., J.-H.K. and J.-H.H.; Data curation, S.-H.L. and J.-H.K.; Formal analysis, J.-H.H.; Funding acquisition, J.-H.K.; Investigation, S.-H.L., J.-H.K. and J.-H.H.; Methodology, S.-H.L., J.-H.K. and J.-H.H.; Project administration, J.-H.K. and J.-H.H.; Resources, S.-H.L., J.-H.K. and J.-H.H.; Software, S.-H.L., J.-H.K. and J.-H.H.; Supervision, J.-H.K.; Validation, S.-H.L.; Visualization, S.-H.L.; Writing—original draft, S.-H.L., J.-H.K. and J.-H.H.; Writing—review and editing, J.-H.K. and J.-H.H. All authors have read and agreed to the published version of the manuscript.

Funding: This research received no external funding.

Institutional Review Board Statement: Not applicable.

Informed Consent Statement: Not applicable.

Data Availability Statement: Not applicable.

Conflicts of Interest: The authors declare no conflict of interest.

References

1. Mavrodiy, A. Factor Analysis of Real Estate Prices. EERC MA Paper. Master's Thesis, Kyiv School of Economics, National University of Kyiv-Mohyla, Kyiv, Ukraine, 2005; pp. 1–35.
2. Bork, L.; Møller, S. Housing price forecastability: A factor analysis. *Real Estate Econ.* **2018**, *46*, 582–611. [CrossRef]
3. Jang, S.H. *The History and Reality of the Concept of Land Disclosure. The Development of Korean Capitalism and Real Estate Speculation after Liberation*; Historical Criticism; The Institute for Korean Historical Studies: Seoul, Korea, 2004; Volume 66, pp. 55–78. (In Korean)
4. Ghosalkar, N.; Sudhir, N. Real estate value prediction using linear regression. In Proceedings of the 2018 Fourth International Conference on Computing Communication Control and Automation (ICCUBEA), Pune, India, 16–18 August 2018; pp. 1–5.
5. Jang, S.W. The real estate market and big data utilization plan. *Real Estate Focus* **2013**, *61*, 14–26. (In Korean)
6. Winson-Geideman, K.; Krause, A. Transformations in real estate research: The Big Data Revolution. In Proceedings of the 22nd Annual Pacific-Rim Real Estate Society Conference, Sunshine Coast, QLD, Australia, 17–20 January 2016; pp. 1–10.
7. Jeong, K.S.; Kim, S.W. *Real Estate Sector Big Data Utilization and Countermeasures, Real Estate Market Analysis and Prediction Model Development*; The Institute for Korean Historical Studies: Seoul, Korea, 2015; Volume 84, pp. 4–15. (In Korean)
8. Kauškale, L.; Ineta, G. Integrated approach of real estate market analysis in sustainable development context for decision making. *Procedia Eng.* **2017**, *172*, 505–512. [CrossRef]

9. Bareicheva, M.A.; Kubina, E.A.; Stepanova, N.R. Structural Analysis with Visualization Elements as a Factor in the Development of the Commercial Real Estate Market. In *IOP Conference Series: Earth and Environmental Science*; IOP Publishing: Bristol, UK, 2021; Volume 666.
10. Jeong, J.H. Real estate market reaction to real estate policy. *Real Estate J.* **2007**, *29*, 99–110. (In Korean)
11. Hyun, M.G.; Jeong, J.H. The correlation between the real estate market and the auction market and economic fluctuations. *Real Estate J.* **2015**, *60*, 86–100.
12. Li, L.; Chu, K.H. Prediction of real estate price variation based on economic parameters. In Proceedings of the 2017 International Conference on Applied System Innovation (ICASI), Sapporo, Japan, 13–17 May 2017.
13. Koo, M.S. *A Real Estate Market Analysis Method Using 3 Hours of Study and 30 Years*; The Korea Economic Daily I: Seoul, Korea, 2017; pp. 1–252. (In Korean)
14. Ok, J.A.; Jo, M.S. *Gyeonggi-Do Housing and Real Estate Big Data Analysis and Utilization System Research*; Policy Studies, Gyeonggi Research Institute: Suwon City, Korea, 2016; pp. 1–206. (In Korean)
15. Jo, M. *Searching for a New Paradigm in Housing Policy after the Global Financial Crisis*; Korea Intellectual Property Research Institute Book DB, Korea Intellectual Property Research Institute: Seoul, Korea, 2012; pp. 207–257. (In Korean)
16. Korea Land & Housing Corporation SEE: REAL, SEE: REAL Introduction. Available online: https://seereal.lh.or.kr/main.do (accessed on 28 March 2021).
17. Real Estate Statistics Information R-ONE. Available online: https://www.r-one.co.kr/ (accessed on 28 March 2021).
18. Real Estate Aptjin. Big Data Real Estate Friend. Available online: https://www.aptgin.com/ (accessed on 28 March 2021).
19. Perez-Rave, Z.I.; Correa-Morales, J.C.; Gonzalez-Echavariia, F. A machine learning approach to big data regression analysis of real estate prices for inferential and predictive purposes. *J. Prop. Res.* **2019**, *36*, 59–96. [CrossRef]
20. Pace, R.K.; Barry, R.; Gilley, O.W.; Sirmans, C.F. A method for spatial–temporal forecasting with an application to real estate prices. *Int. J. Forecast.* **2000**, *16*, 229–246. [CrossRef]
21. Damban, J.A.; Sigrist, F.; Furrer, R. Maximum likelihood estimation of spatially varying coefficient models for large data with an application to real estate price prediction. *Spat. Stat.* **2021**, *41*, 100470. [CrossRef]
22. Chaturvedi, A.; Gupta, A.; Rajpoot, V. Parameterized Comparison of Regularized Regression Models to Develop Models for Real Estate. In *IOP Conference Series: Materials Science and Engineering*; IOP Publishing: Bristol, UK, 2021; Volume 1099.
23. AI-Gbury, O.; Kurnaz, S. Real Estate Price Range Prediction Using Artificial Neural Network and Grey Wolf Optimizer. In Proceedings of the 2020 4th International Symposium on Multidisciplinary Studies and Innovative Technologies (ISMSIT), Istanbul, Turkey, 22–24 October 2020; pp. 1–5.
24. Khare, S.L.; Gourisaria, M.K.; Harshvardhan, G.M.; Joardar, S.; Singh, V. Real Estate Cost Estimation through Data Mining Techniques. In *IOP Conference Series: Materials Science and Engineering*; IOP Publishing: Bristol, UK, 2021; Volume 1099.
25. Sharma, N.; Arora, Y.; Makkar, P.; Sharma, V.; Gupta, H. Real Estate Price's Forecasting through Predictive Modelling. In *Machine Learning for Predictive Analysis*; Springer: Singapore, 2021; pp. 589–597.
26. Mohd, T.; Jamil, N.S.; Johari, N.; Abdullah, L.; Masrom, S. An Overview of Real Estate Modelling Techniques for House Price Prediction. In *Charting a Sustainable Future of ASEAN in Business and Social Sciences*; Springer: Berlin/Heidelberg, Germany, 2020; pp. 321–338.
27. Pai, P.F.; Wang, W.C. Using Machine Learning Models and Actual Transaction Data for Predicting Real Estate Prices. *Appl. Sci.* **2020**, *10*, 5832. [CrossRef]
28. Donner, H.; Eriksson, K.; Steep, M. Digital Cities: Real Estate Development Driven by Big Data. Working Paper. 2018. Available online: https://gpc.stanford.edu/publications/digital-cities-real-estate-development-driven-big-data (accessed on 28 March 2021).
29. Yakub, A.R.A.; Hishamuddin, M.; Ali, K.; Achu, R.B.A.J.; Folake, A.F. The Effect of Adopting Micro and Macro-Economic Variables on Real Estate Price Prediction Models Using ANN: A Systematic Literature. *J. Crit. Rev.* **2020**, *7*, 2020.
30. Gyourko, J.; Keim, D.B. What does the stock market tell us about real estate returns? *Real Estate Econ.* **1992**, *20*, 457–485. [CrossRef]
31. Hartmann, P. Real estate markets and macroprudential policy in Europe. *J. Money Credit Bank.* **2015**, *47*, 69–80. [CrossRef]
32. DiPasquale, D.; Wheaton, W.C. The markets for real estate assets and space: A conceptual framework. *Real Estate Econ.* **1992**, *20*, 181–198. [CrossRef]
33. Liu, Z.; Wang, P.; Zha, T. Land-price dynamics and macroeconomic fluctuations. *Econometrica* **2013**, *81*, 1147–1184.
34. Public Data Portal. Available online: https://www.data.go.kr/ (accessed on 28 March 2021).
35. National Tax Service. Comprehensive Real Estate Tax. Available online: https://www.nts.go.kr/ (accessed on 28 March 2021).
36. Seoul Living Area Plan. Local Living Area-Gangnam-gu. Available online: https://planning.seoul.go.kr/plan/map/getPlanMap.do (accessed on 28 March 2021).
37. National Police Agency. Police Crime Statistics. Available online: https://www.police.go.kr/www/open/publice/publice03_2018.jsp (accessed on 28 March 2021).
38. De Nadai, M.; Lepri, B. The economic value of neighborhoods: Predicting real estate prices from the urban environment. In Proceedings of the 2018 IEEE 5th International Conference on Data Science and Advanced Analytics (DSAA), Turin, Italy, 1–3 October 2018.
39. Holtermans, R.; Kok, N. On the value of environmental certification in the commercial real estate market. *Real Estate Econ.* **2019**, *47*, 685–722. [CrossRef]

40. Xue, C.; Ju, Y.; Li, S.; Zhou, Q.; Liu, Q. Research on Accurate House Price Analysis by Using GIS Technology and Transport Accessibility: A Case Study of Xi'an, China. *Symmetry* **2020**, *12*, 1329. [CrossRef]
41. Liu, C.; Zheng, Y.; Zhao, Q.; Wang, C. Financial stability and real estate price fluctuation in China. *Phys. A Stat. Mech. Appl.* **2020**, *540*, 122980. [CrossRef]
42. Shim, S.H. The effect of currency volume fluctuations on inflation and housing prices. *Hous. Res.* **2004**, *12*, 55–87. (In Korean)
43. Allen, F.; Hong, J.Y. Why are there large foreign exchange reserves? The case of South Korea. *Korean Soc. Sci. J.* **2011**, *38*, 1–33.
44. Ming, L.P.Y. Foreign Exchange Reserves, Foreign Exchange Rate Fluctuation and Monetary Policy Operation: The Case of Taiwan. *J. Finace* **2004**, *2*, 79–86.
45. Kim, K.H.; Jeon, S.S.; Irakoze, A.; Son, K.Y. A study of the green building benefits in apartment buildings according to real estate prices: Case of non-capital areas in South Korea. *Sustainability* **2020**, *12*, 2206. [CrossRef]
46. Fry, G.L. Multifunctional landscapes-towards transdisciplinary research. *Landsc. Urban Plan.* **2001**, *57*, 159–168. [CrossRef]
47. Lai, L.W.; Lorne, F.T. Sustainable urban renewal and built heritage conservation in a global real estate revolution. *Sustainability* **2019**, *11*, 850. [CrossRef]
48. Choi, H.O. Evolutionary Approach to Technology Innovation of Cadastre for Smart Land Management Policy. *Land* **2020**, *9*, 50. [CrossRef]
49. Kitchin, R. The real-time city? Big data and smart urbanism. *GeoJournal* **2014**, *79*, 1–14. [CrossRef]
50. Sejong Special Self-Governing City, Smart City. Available online: https://www.sejong.go.kr/kor/sub04_1405.do (accessed on 28 March 2021).
51. Rathore, M.M.; Paul, A.; Hong, W.H.; Seo, H.; Awan, I.; Saeed, S. Exploiting IoT and big data analytics: Defining smart digital city using real-time urban data. *Sustain. Cities Soc.* **2018**, *40*, 600–610. [CrossRef]
52. Ullah, F.; Al-Turjman, F. A conceptual framework for blockchain smart contract adoption to manage real estate deals in smart cities. *Neural Comput. Appl.* **2021**, 1–22. [CrossRef]
53. Presidential 4th Industrial Revolution Committee, Smart City Promotion Strategy. Available online: https://www.4th-ir.go.kr (accessed on 28 March 2021).
54. Ho, T.; Thanh, T.-D. Discovering Community Interests Approach to Topic Model with Time Factor and Clustering Methods. *J. Inf. Process. Syst.* **2021**, *17*, 163–177.
55. Lee, S.-H. Land Price Forecasting Research by Macro and Micro Factors and Real Estate Market Utilization Plan Research by Landscape Factors: Big Data Analysis Approach. Master's Thesis, Department of Data Informatics, Korea Maritime and Ocean University, Busan, Korea, 2021; pp. 1–50.

Article

Comparative Assessment of the Stability of AHP and FAHP Methods

Irina Vinogradova-Zinkevič [1], Valentinas Podvezko [2] and Edmundas Kazimeras Zavadskas [3,*]

[1] Department of Information Technologies, Vilnius Gediminas Technical University, Saulėtekio al. 11, 10223 Vilnius, Lithuania; irina.vinogradova-zinkevic@vilniustech.lt
[2] Department of Mathematical Statistics, Vilnius Gediminas Technical University, Saulėtekio al. 11, 10223 Vilnius, Lithuania; valentinas.podvezko@vilniustech.lt
[3] Laboratory of Operational Research, Institute of Sustainable Construction, Vilnius Gediminas Technical University, Saulėtekio al. 11, 10223 Vilnius, Lithuania
* Correspondence: edmundas.zavadskas@vilniustech.lt; Tel.: +37-0652-744-910

Citation: Vinogradova-Zinkevič, I.; Podvezko, V.; Zavadskas, E.K. Comparative Assessment of the Stability of AHP and FAHP Methods. *Symmetry* **2021**, *13*, 479. https://doi.org/10.3390/sym13030479

Academic Editor: José Carlos R. Alcantud

Received: 31 January 2021
Accepted: 9 March 2021
Published: 15 March 2021

Publisher's Note: MDPI stays neutral with regard to jurisdictional claims in published maps and institutional affiliations.

Copyright: © 2021 by the authors. Licensee MDPI, Basel, Switzerland. This article is an open access article distributed under the terms and conditions of the Creative Commons Attribution (CC BY) license (https://creativecommons.org/licenses/by/4.0/).

Abstract: Mathematical models describing physical, technical, economic, and other processes can be used to analyze these processes and predict their results, providing that these models are stable and their results are stable relative to the model parameters used. Small changes in the values of the model parameters correspond to small changes in the results. Multicriteria decision-making models need to check the results' stability against the models' main components: the values of the criteria weights and the elements of the decision matrix. In this article, we study the stability of models associated with the calculation of criteria weights. For the analysis, the most commonly used models are taken—the Analytic Hierarchy Process (AHP) method and the fuzzy Analytic Hierarchy Process (FAHP) method, in which fuzzy numbers are used under conditions of data uncertainty. Both mathematically well-based methods verify the consistency of the expert evaluations. The method of statistical simulation (Monte Carlo) is the basis for studying the results' stability. The study checks the experts' provided evaluations' consistency, calculates the criteria weights, and evaluates their relative errors after a slight change in the estimates of the pairwise comparisons of the criteria provided by the experts. The matrix of comparisons of the FAHP method is constructed based on the entire expert group's assessments. It estimates the boundaries of variance in the fuzzy criteria weights. This paper estimates the stability of the criteria' weights associated with the mathematical methods themselves and the experts' estimates. The results are useful to study the stability of specific MCDM methods when ranking alternatives.

Keywords: Analytic Hierarchy Process; fuzzy Analytic Hierarchy Process; symmetric and asymmetric fuzzy numbers; uncertainty; stability

1. Introduction

A mathematical model makes practical sense if its results are stable concerning the model parameters. If an insignificant variation in the values of the resulting characteristics of the model corresponds to slight variations in the model parameters. Components of Multicriteria Decision-Making (MCDM) models are represented by the criteria characterizing the process under evaluation, and these criteria' weights.

The criteria weights provide a quantitative estimation of the importance of the criteria. Given that the use of criteria weights in MCDM methods has an essential influence on the result of the evaluations and on the making of the proper decision, an investigation of the accuracy of such evaluations is interesting and important from both the theoretical and the practical point of view. This paper contains an investigation of the stability of the evaluations of the subjective weights of the criteria and the influence of data uncertainty upon the results.

Uncertainty of data may result from the evaluation of a subjective expert, the extent of the expert's interest, ambiguity, inaccuracy of measurements, or improperly applied methods. Various approaches, such as, in particular, fuzzy set theory and the methods of mathematical statistics, Boolean logic, logistic regression, Monte Carlo simulation, Bayesian networks, and neural networks, are used to evaluate the influence of the degree of uncertainty [1].

So-called subjective weights, obtained based on peer reviews, are most frequently applied in practice [2–6]. For that reason, the subjective evaluation carries an uncertainty in itself. Despite the experience and competence of the expert, the evaluations provided by the same expert may vary when solving complex problems with a large number of criteria. For example, if an expert fills in the same questionnaire several times at different times, these evaluations are usually different from each other.

There are various techniques applied in the evaluation of the weight criteria. The simplest methods are based on a ranking of the criteria depending on their significance and on the direct evaluation of the weights when the sum of the evaluations is equal to one or to 100%. The use of other scales with normalization of the results is also possible. More complex subjective methods for weight evaluation, like the AHP and FAHP, use mathematical theories and verify the consistency of the expert evaluations.

There is another approach to the quantitative evaluation of the importance of the criteria. This approach evaluates the structure of the data array—the criteria values for all the alternatives [3,7,8]. Methods like this are called objective. Objective weights are applied rarely in practice, and we disregard them in this paper. A combined evaluation of the weights, which is based on the integration of subjective and objective evaluations, is also possible [9–12].

Evans [13] related the concept of sensitivity analysis in decision-making theory to the stability of an optimal solution under variation of the model parameters and the accurate evaluation of the values of such parameters. The first significant papers in the sector of sensitivity analysis were written on the basis of using the concepts of sensitivity analysis in linear programming for the development of an optimal approach that could be applied to the classical problems of decision theory [13], and on using entropy and the least squares method [14].

Zhou et al. [15] suggested a method for the calculation of the entropy weights in the situation when the evaluation of the criteria might contain uncertainties such as, for example, interval values, and when it contains both uncertainties and incompleteness, for example, with the distribution of judgements. Wolters and Mareschal suggested three types of sensitivity analysis: (1) a fixed relation between the variation of the ranking and the variations of the alternatives based on certain criteria, (2) the influence exerted by specific variations of the points/criteria of the alternative, and (3) the minimum modification of the weights necessary to provide for the alternative to take first place [16]. The analysis was focused on and developed for the preference ranking organization method for enrichment evaluation (PROMETHEE) methods. Triantaphyllou and Sánchez [17] presented the methodology for the performance of sensitivity analysis of the weights of the decision-making criteria and the alternative efficiency values for the weighted sum model (WSM), the weighted product model (WPM), and the analytic hierarchy process (AHP) methods. Evaluation of the influence exerted by uncertainty in the SAW method was performed by Podvezko [18], who evaluated the ranges of weight intervals for the process criteria, the levels of matching and stability of the expert evaluations, and the influence of uncertainty on the ranking of the matched objects. The influence of weight variation upon the final result in the SAW method was studied by Zavadskas et al. [19], and sensitivity analysis of the SAW, TOPSIS, MOORA, and PROMETHEE methods was studied by Vinogradova [20]. Memariani et al. [21] and Alinezhad [22] studied the influence of the values of the decision matrix elements upon the results of the ranking. Moghassem [23] increased and decreased the weights of all the criteria by 5, 10, 15, and 20 percent in sensitivity analysis of the TOPSIS and VIKOR methods. Hsu et al. performed sensitivity analysis of the TOPSIS method by increasing the three maximum weights by 10% and decreasing the three minimum ones by 10% [24].

Erkut and Tarimcilar [25] suggested dividing the problems of the stability of the AHP method that are to be solved into two groups. The approach of group one assumes operations over the criteria proper, by means of calculating the alternative evaluation as the sum of the alternative evaluations multiplied by the correspondent weights, based on the criteria under evaluation. The problems in group two are solved as decision-making problems under conditions of uncertainty, with the uncertainty meaning that there are a number of possible states of the nature and only one of them can be transformed into a true state. The very meaning of state probability is directly related to the meaning of the uncertainty of the problem to be solved within the framework of risk evaluation. The authors of the paper follow the first approach to the problems, solving them graphically by creating the weight space, which is represented as all the possible combinations of the weights for the purposes of tier one of the hierarchy. Consequently, separating the weight space into sets, the spatial data can be generated from the space. Any of the alternatives possesses the highest evaluation ranking in every one of the subsets [25].

In his paper, Masuda [26] studied how variations of the entire columns of the decision-making matrix might influence the values of the alternative priorities. He suggested using the sensitivity coefficient of the finite vector of the alternative priorities for each of the column vectors in the decision matrix to show how significantly the values of the finite alternative priorities vary. Warren [27] studied in more detail the theoretical aspects of the AHP method related to the evaluation scale, the determination of the vector of eigenvalues, the issue of normalization of the weights, and so on. Mimović et al. [28] suggested an integrated application of the analytic hierarchy process (AHP) and Bayesian analysis. The Bayesian formula managed to increase the input data accuracy for the analytic hierarchy process. The AHP method was used in this paper for the representation of the objectivized input data for the Bayesian formula in situations in which statistical evaluations of the probability are not possible. In the same way, Wu et al. [29], who generated pairwise comparison matrices and verified their stability, also suggested one of the methods for verification of the stability of the AHP method. The paper by Aguarón et al. shows the development of the theoretical basis for improvement of the AHP matrix inconsistency, when the Row Geometric Mean (RGM) is used as the prioritization procedure and the Geometric Consistency Index (GCI) as the inconsistency measure [30].

A number of papers with a genuine use of the MCDM model have appeared recently in which the stability of results of the methods is studied. The paper by Chen et al. [31] evaluated the stability of the multicriteria weights by studying the GIS-based MCDM model, showing the influence of the variation of the criteria weights upon the model results in the spatial dimension and graphically. The weights were determined with the help of the AHP method and were varied from their initial values within limits of 20%. This range of variation for the initial weights was applied either to all the criteria or to each criterion, as required [31]. The paper by Deepa and Swamynathan [32] facilitated an improvement in the efficiency of internet networks through increasing their throughput capacity, by suggesting a mathematical model of a clustering protocol known as AETCP (a clustering protocol based on AHP-Entropy-TOPSIS). The mobile nodes were hierarchically organized into different clusters based on certain criteria. The integrated method for evaluation of the subjective and objective weights was applied to the evaluation of the mobile nodes. Later on, ranking of the sets of nodes was performed with the purpose selecting the nodes with the largest weight as the correspondent nodes of the cluster-head [32]. The paper by Zyoud and Fuchs-Hanusch [33] address a severe problem of a water deficit in the water supply networks. The FAHP method was used to evaluate the factors influencing the loss of water. The decision was made by diagnosing the loss-of-water risk index at the level of the pipes and the areas. The Fuzzy Synthetic Evaluation Technique (FSET) was used to evaluate the water loss index at the level of the water supply system, and Ordered Weighted Averaging (OWA) was used to aggregate individual values of the index applied to each area. A Monte Carlo simulation model was used to generate the final ranking of the areas. The results of this modeling provided sufficient stability from the point of view of the ranking of the investigated areas. Xue et al. [34] suggested a method for the evaluation of stability and safety in the construction of engineering facilities for a protective tunnel under a river using the AHP-entropy weight method and the ideal point evaluation model. The paper by Kumar et al. [35] contains an evaluation of the stability of the factor model for the environmental impact risk for materials (products/services) related to pharmaceutical drugs. The model sensitivity was checked in terms of the pro rata variation of the considered risk factor with respect to other factors, varying the weight value from 0.9 to 0.1; variations of inconsistencies were also observed for other risks. Evaluation of the supplier selection stability model was suggested by Stević et. al. [36] and executed by means of varying the weight and recording the variations in the ranking of the alternatives. The weights varied in a manner that on the increase of one criterion by a conditional unit (for example, 12%), the other criterion was, naturally, decreased correspondingly in order to satisfy the condition under which the sum of the values of all the criteria remained unchanged. Continuing with the topic of the estimation of supplier model quality, Stojić et al. [37] used the WASPAS method and suggested the calculation of the coefficient α to generate the number of relative values of the alternative; the coefficient depended on the weight parameter (α lay within the limits of 0 to 1, with increments of 0.1).

The generation of individual values of the criteria weights in the SWARA method was suggested by Zavadskas et al. [38]. The paper by Pamucar et al. [39] also evaluated the influence of the criteria (and the sub-criteria) upon the order of ranking of the alternatives, which were represented by suppliers, within the framework of the problem of increasing the service quality of third-party logistics providers. To process uncertain data under the procedure of group decision-making, the paper considered interval rough numbers (IRN) and the IRN-BWM (best worst method). The stability of the ranking of alternatives that was obtained was checked by varying the values of the coefficients of the linear combination and by the application of the operational competitiveness rankings analysis (OCRA) method [40]. Sensitivity analysis has also been used to confirm the stability of the final rankings of the results [41,42], or to verify and evaluate the feasibility of the optimal alternative [43], as well as to study the influence of the variation of the parameters and criteria weights upon the final results of ranking of the alternatives [44].

The stochastic approach to determining the uncertainty of the AHP weights has been used in different ways. Janssen [45] studied the sensitivity of the ranking of the alternatives using the effects table and compared this with the maximum evaluation of the decision-making person. The sensitivities of the rankings of alternatives to overall uncertainty in scores and priorities were analyzed using a Monte Carlo approach. Eskandari and Rabelo [46] followed another stochastic approach, and this gave these authors the opportunity to calculate the AHP weight dispersions, and to process their uncertain behavior with the help of a Monte Carlo simulation. An approach that applied fuzzy logic, an analytic hierarchy process, and a Monte Carlo simulation was used to solve the problem of the over-expenditure of funds within the framework of urban transit projects, to facilitate the effective planning of the future budget by the decision-making persons [47].

The stability of models related to calculations of subjective criteria weights is investigated in this paper. The most frequently used methods in the MCDM model—the analytic hierarchy process (AHP) method and the FAHP method, when fuzzy numbers are used under the conditions of data uncertainty—are taken for the analysis. The method of statistical simulation (Monte Carlo) is used in order to investigate the stability issues. The practical realization of the algorithm is written in the Python programming language. This paper's results can be used as an integral part of the study of the stability of MCDM methods in the ranking of alternatives.

2. Materials and Methods

2.1. Analytic Hierarchy Process (AHP) Method

The AHP method is the most frequently used in practice among all the subjective methods for the evaluation of criteria weights. The reason is that this method is mathematically substantiated, logically understandable, and allows the performance of a quantitative determination of the consistency of the evaluations provided by each of the experts. The experts compare all the possible pairs of criteria with each other. The pairwise comparison matrix $P = (p_{ij})$ is theoretically a ratio of unknown criteria weights: $p_{ij} = \frac{w_i}{w_j}$, $(i, j = 1, 2, \ldots, m)$, $p_{ij} = \frac{1}{p_{ji}}$, $p_{ii} = 1$, where m is the number of criteria. The element p_{ij} shows by how many times the i-th criterion is more important than the j-th one. The scale 1-3-5-7-9 suggested by the author of the method—Saaty [2]—is applied to the evaluation.

The criteria weights $\overline{w}$ are the normalized values of the eigenvector of the matrix P, corresponding to the largest eigenvalue λ_{max} of the matrix:

$$P\overline{w} = \lambda \overline{w} \tag{1}$$

The degree of consistency (internal consistency) of the expert evaluations determines the Consistency Index CI and the Consistency Ratio CR:

$$CI = \frac{\lambda_{max} - m}{m - 1}, \tag{2}$$

$$CR = \frac{CI}{RI}, \tag{3}$$

where RI is the average evaluation of the CI of the simulated matrices of the order of m [2]. The evaluations are considered to be consistent if the Consistency Ratio is such that $CR < 0.1$.

2.2. Fuzzy Analytic Hierarchy Process (FAHP) Method

In the case of weight calculations using the FAHP method, the experts evaluate the criteria using interval values. Therefore, the uncertainty is included in the evaluations themselves. Unlike the deterministic AHP case, each evaluation for triangular fuzzy numbers can be represented as (L, M, U). The most probable evaluation M corresponds to the evaluation provided by the AHP method. The number L shows the lowest possible boundary of the evaluation, and the number U the corresponding upper boundary [48].

The matrix $\widetilde{P}$ for the pairwise comparison of the criteria by the expert (or total evaluation by the entire group of experts) has the following representation:

$$\widetilde{P} = (\widetilde{p}_{ij}) = (L_{ij}, M_{ij}, U_{ij}) = \begin{pmatrix} (1,1,1) & (L_{12}, M_{12}, U_{12}) & \cdots & (L_{1m}, M_{1m}, U_{1m}) \\ (1/U_{12}, 1/M_{12}, 1/L_{12}) & (1,1,1) & \cdots & (L_{2m}, M_{2m}, U_{2m}) \\ \vdots & \vdots & \vdots & \vdots \\ (1/U_{1m}, 1/M_{1m}, 1/L_{1m}) & (1/U_{2m}, 1/M_{2m}, 1/L_{2m}) & \cdots & (1,1,1) \end{pmatrix}. \tag{4}$$

The symmetric fuzzy numbers with respect to the main diagonal are $\widetilde{p}_{ji} = \widetilde{p}_{ij}^{-1} = \left(\frac{1}{U_{ij}}, \frac{1}{M_{ij}}, \frac{1}{L_{ij}}\right)$; the main diagonal elements are $\widetilde{p}_{ii} = (1, 1, 1)$.

The Chang algorithm [49] is used for calculation of the criteria weights. The value $\widetilde{S}_i$, called the extension of the fuzzy synthesis, is calculated for the i-th criterion using the following formula:

$$\widetilde{S}_i = \sum_{j=1}^{m} \widetilde{p}_{ij} \otimes \left\{ \sum_{i=1}^{m} \sum_{j=1}^{m} \widetilde{p}_{ij} \right\}^{-1}; i = 1, \ldots, m \tag{5}$$

All the criteria are compared pairwise using the value $\tilde{S}_i$:

$$V\left(\tilde{S}_j \geq \tilde{S}_i\right) = \begin{cases} 1, & if\ M_j \geq M_i \\ \frac{L_i - U_j}{(M_j - U_j) - (M_i - L_i)}, & if\ L_i \leq U_j\ ,i = 1, \ldots, m;\ j = 1, \ldots, m \\ 0, & in\ other\ cases \end{cases} \quad (6)$$

The theory of the fuzzy numbers comparison is applied to the comparison of the values:

$$V_j = V\left(\tilde{S}_j \geq \tilde{S}_1, \tilde{S}_2, \ldots \tilde{S}_{j-1}, \tilde{S}_{j+1}, \ldots, \tilde{S}_m\right) = \min_{i \in \{1,\ldots,m; i \neq j\}} V\left(\tilde{S}_j \geq \tilde{S}_i\right),\ i = 1, \ldots, m. \quad (7)$$

The weight vector w_j of the criteria is calculated using the following formula:

$$w_j = \frac{V_j}{\sum_{j=1}^{m} V_j},\ j = 1, \ldots, m. \quad (8)$$

3. Stability Check for the AHP and FAHP Methods

The AHP and FAHP methods are applied in Multicriteria Decision-Making (MCDM) evaluations in order to determine the criteria weights. The AHP method is applied in the deterministic case when the significance (weight) of each of the criteria is determined with one number. In this case, each expert determines the criterion significance in the matrix of pairwise comparisons of the criteria with one number (taken from the Saaty scale: 1-3-5-7-9). The FAHP method is used in conditions of data uncertainty when interval fuzzy evaluations are used for the calculations. In this case, evaluations of the pairwise comparison of the criteria (that is, the values of the FAHP method matrix) are also represented by interval fuzzy numbers.

The criteria weights can be used in the MCDM model methods if the weight evaluation methods, that is, the AHP and FAHP methods, are stable (resistant) in relation to natural random variations of the evaluations. Considering that the value M of a triangular fuzzy number is matched with the most probabilistic evaluation of the AHP method, it would be of interest to perform a parallel investigation of stability for the AHP and FAHP methods. The references suggest more than 25 scales that can be used in order to form the triangular values of the triangular fuzzy numbers. The frequently applied symmetric and asymmetric scales of triangular fuzzy numbers are used in this paper.

The stability of the AHP method can be understood in two ways: the stability of just the method, which depends upon the essence of the method or its mathematical basis, and the stability of the results, that is, the values of the criteria weights depending upon the evaluations provided by the experts that vary due to the uncertainty inherent to their thinking processes.

Both stability options are studied in this paper.

3.1. Stability Check Algorithm for the AHP Method

The quantitative evaluation of the stability and the criterion for evaluating the stability depend upon the specific problem to be solved. Thus, for the evaluation of the stabilities of the method for the MCDM model, we can apply the percentage of loss as the best alternative to the leading position, the maximum inconsistencies of the evaluations of the method, the percentage of variation of the order for the ranking of the alternatives, etc. [20].

The stability δ is evaluated in this paper as the maximum relative error of the criteria weights:

$$\delta = \max_{1 \leq j \leq m; 1 \leq \xi \leq T} \frac{\left|\omega_j^{(\xi)} - \omega_j\right|}{\omega_j}, \quad (9)$$

where ω_j is the weight of the j-th criterion, $\omega_j^{(\xi)}$ is the weight of the j-th criterion obtained as the result of the simulation, ξ is the simulation number, $1 \le \xi \le T$, and T is the number of simulations.

The stability of the AHP method itself is understood as follows.

The Saaty scale for the AHP method applies only integer evaluation numbers p_{ij} from 1 to 9, showing by how many times one (the i-th) criterion is more important than the other (the j-th). With respect to the main diagonal, the symmetric evaluations are $1/p_{ij}$—where numbers that are less than 1 show by how many times the second (j-th) criterion is less important than the first (i-th) one. To check the stability of the AHP method itself, we expand the evaluation scale and assume that any real numbers can act as evaluations. That would allow variation in a random manner of the evaluations provided by each of the experts, using the method of statistical simulation (Monte Carlo) to simulate the evaluations within the limits of certain intervals, performing a consistency check of the evaluations each time, and recording the weight variation intervals. The statistical modeling method (Monte Carlo) allows reproducing a real situation on a computer many times. This cannot be replicated in practice, or implementation may require significant resources and time.

Why did Saaty suggest an integer number scale and not expand the scale to the set of real numbers? In the latter case, it would be sufficient to compare the importance of one criterion only (for example, the most important one) in relation to all the other criteria, that is, to fill in one column (or row) only. It would then immediately be possible to fill in all the remaining rows (or columns) of the matrix. The elements would be pro rata with the elements of the one filled-in column.

Considering that the criteria weights are related to the eigenvector of the comparison matrix, it is important to determine how small variations of the matrix elements affect the values of the eigenvector elements and, correspondingly, influence the values of the criteria weights—the normalized values of the eigenvector.

The stability check algorithm for the AHP method can be represented in the following manner.

Step 1. The matrix $P^{(k)}$ for pairwise comparison of the criteria of one of the experts ($k = 1$) is selected. The consistency of the evaluations ($CR < 0.1$) is verified. The criteria weights $\Omega = (\omega_j), j = 1, 2, \ldots, m$ are calculated.

Step 2. The percentage q of inconsistency $\hat{p}_{ij}^{(k)}$ of all the elements $p_{ij}^{(k)}$ ($i \ne j$) with the expert evaluations ($q = 5\%, q = 10\%$) is determined. Therefore, the random simulated values of the evaluations $p_{ij}^{(k)}$ vary within the following interval $\hat{p}_{ij}^{(k)} \in [p_{ij}^{(k)} - p_{ij}^{(k)} \frac{q}{100}, p_{ij}^{(k)} + p_{ij}^{(k)} \frac{q}{100}]$. The elements of the main diagonal remain unchanged: $p_{ii}^{(k)} = 1$.

We vary the values of the integer numbers only (the evaluations) $p_{ij}^{(k)} = 1, 2, \ldots, 9$ on both sides of the main diagonal. With respect to the main diagonal the symmetric elements are $p_{ji}^{(k)} = \frac{1}{p_{ij}^{(k)}}$.

Step 3. A sequence of random numbers ξ_r ($r = 1$) uniformly distributed within the interval $[0, 1]$ is selected using the method of statistical simulation (Monte Carlo). The random evaluation $\hat{p}_{ij}^{(k)}$ by the k-th expert with the q-th inconsistency is calculated; this belongs to the interval $[p_{ij}^{(k)} - p_{ij}^{(k)} \frac{q}{100}, p_{ij}^{(k)} + p_{ij}^{(k)} \frac{q}{100}]: \hat{p}_{ij}^{(k)} = p_{ij}^{(k)} - p_{ij}^{(k)} \frac{q}{100} + 2p_{ij}^{(k)} \frac{q}{100} \xi_r \in [p_{ij}^{(k)} - p_{ij}^{(k)} \frac{q}{100}, p_{ij}^{(k)} + p_{ij}^{(k)} \frac{q}{100}]$.

A new random number from the sequence ξ_r is used for each element $p_{ij}^{(k)}$ of the matrix.

Step 4. A random pairwise comparison matrix P is formed from the simulated elements $P = \| \hat{p}_{ij}^{(k)} \|$. The consistency of the evaluations ($CR < 0.1$) is verified. If the value of the consistency ratio for the evaluations is $CR \ge 0.1$, the matrix is discarded. The criteria weights $\Omega = (\omega_j^{(r)}), (r = 1)$ are calculated.

Step 5. New sequences of random numbers ξ_r ($r = 2, 3, \ldots, T$) are selected, where T is the number of repetitions (simulations). Steps 3 and 4 are repeated. The criteria weights $(\omega_j^{(r)})$, ($r = 2, 3, \ldots, T$) are calculated.

Step 6. The largest values of the relative errors of the criteria weights for every j-th criterion of the AHP method are calculated for every simulation ξ: $\delta_j^{(\xi)} = \frac{|\omega_j^{(\xi)} - \omega_j|}{\omega_j}$.

Step 7. The largest values of the relative errors $\delta_j^{(\xi)}$ of the criterion weight values for all the criteria are calculated for every simulation ξ: $\delta^\xi = \max_j \delta_j^{(\xi)}$.

Step 8. The largest value of the relative errors δ^ξ of the criteria weights for all the simulations ξ is taken as the AHP method error for the given matrix of comparison: $\delta = \max_\xi \delta^\xi$.

3.2. Stability Check Algorithm for the AHP Method Related to the Evaluations of the Experts

The stability of the results—the values of the criteria weights depending upon the psychological state of the experts and the incomplete certainty of their evaluations—is understood as follows.

We have repeatedly proved that one and the same expert provides ambiguous evaluations when performing comparative evaluations of the importance of the same criteria, and even when ranking their importance at different moments in time. Naturally, the logic of the expert's thinking process is not undergoing major changes at that time, and the evaluations provided by the expert do not differ significantly.

Therefore, we vary the evaluations provided by the experts using, naturally, the Saaty scale, varying their values by 1 (or 2), both towards an increase and towards a decrease of the values, while the comparative evaluations of the other criteria are also varied. However, internal inconsistency of the evaluations must not occur: the Consistency Ratio CR must be less than 0.1.

The stability check algorithm for the AHP method depending on the state and psychological condition of the experts can be represented in the following manner.

Step 1. The matrix $P^{(k)}$ for the pairwise comparison of the criteria of one of the experts ($k = 1$) is selected. Consistency of the evaluations ($CR < 0.1$) is verified. The criteria weights $\Omega = (\omega_j)$ are calculated, $j = 1, 2, \ldots, m$.

Step 2. A sequence of random numbers ξ_r ($r = 1$) uniformly distributed within the interval of [0, 1] is selected using the statistical simulation method (Monte Carlo). The values of all the evaluations of the experts—the elements $p_{ij}^{(k)}$ ($i \neq j$) of the matrix $P^{(k)}$ are varied (increased or decreased) by 1. To do that, if $0 \leq \xi_r <0.5$, the value increases. In the other case ($0.5 < \xi_r \leq 1$), the value decreases. In order to attain complete symmetry, we exclude the value of $\xi_r = 0.5$, that is, we do not vary the elements of the matrix. The two options have equal probability. If $p_{ij}^{(k)} = 1$, the value is always increased. If $p_{ij}^{(k)} = 9$, the value is decreased. The elements of the main diagonal remain unchanged: $p_{ii}^{(k)} = 1$. The symmetric elements with respect to the main diagonal are $p_{ji}^{(k)} = \frac{1}{p_{ij}^{(k)}}$. A new random number from the sequence ξ_r is used for each element $p_{ij}^{(k)}$ of the matrix.

Step 3. A random pairwise comparison matrix P is formed of the simulated elements $P = \| \hat{p}_{ij}^{(k)} \|$. Consistency of evaluations ($CR < 0.1$) is verified. If the value of the Consistency Ratio is $CR \geq 0.1$, the matrix is discarded. The criteria weights are calculated $\Omega = (\omega_j^{(r)})$, ($r = 1$).

Step 4. New sequences of random numbers ξ_r ($r = 2, 3, \ldots, T$), are selected, where T is the number of repetitions (simulations). Steps 2 and 3 are repeated. The criteria weights $(\omega_j^{(r)})$, ($r = 2, 3, \ldots, T$) are calculated.

Step 5. The relative errors of the values of the weight for each of the j-th criterion of the AHP method are calculated for every simulation ξ: $\delta_j^{(\xi)} = \frac{\left|\omega_j^{(\xi)} - \omega_j\right|}{\omega_j}$.

Step 6. The largest values of the relative errors $\delta_j^{(\xi)}$ of the criteria weights for all the criteria are calculated for every simulation ξ: $\delta^\xi = \max_j \delta_j^{(\xi)}$.

Step 7. We take the largest value of the relative errors δ^ξ of the criteria weights over all the simulations ξ, as the AHP method error for the given matrix of comparison: $\delta = \max_\xi \delta^\xi$.

3.3. Stability Check Algorithm for the FAHP Method

Various types of uncertainties influence the evaluation of the stability of the FAHP method. As in the deterministic case, the values of the elements of the criteria comparison matrix depend on the logic of the thinking of the experts, and their state at the moment of evaluation. Besides, the fuzzy method itself includes uncertainty in the evaluations—a triad of values is used instead of a one-point evaluation. It should also be kept in mind that the stability evaluation for the FAHP method refers solely to the weight evaluation algorithm used by us (4)–(8).

The stability check for the FAHP method for the calculation of the criteria weights can be represented in the form of the following steps.

Step 1. A fuzzy pairwise comparison matrix for the criteria is formed on the basis of the AHP matrix $M = (M_{ij})$: $\widetilde{P} = (\widetilde{p}_{ij}) = (L_{ij}, M_{ij}, U_{ij})$. The values L_{ij} and U_{ij} vary depending on the selected symmetric or asymmetric scale of the fuzzy number.

Step 2. The consistency of evaluations (CR < 0.1) of the matrix $M = (M_{ij})$ is verified. If the Consistency Ratio is CR $\geq$ 0.1, the pairwise comparison matrix is discarded.

Step 3. A sequence of random numbers ζ_r ($r = 1$), uniformly distributed within the interval of [0, 1], is selected using the statistical simulation method (Monte Carlo). The values of all the M_{ij} evaluations of the experts – the elements $(\widetilde{p}_{ij}) = (L_{ij}, M_{ij}, U_{ij})$ ($i \neq j$) of the matrix $\widetilde{P}$—are varied (increased or decreased) by 1. To do that, if $0 \leq \zeta_r <0.5$, the value increases. In the other case ($0.5 < \zeta_r \leq 1$), the value decreases. In order to attain complete symmetry, we exclude the value of $\zeta_r = 0.5$, that is, we do not vary the elements of the matrix. The two options have equal probability. If at least one of the numbers (L_{ij}, M_{ij}, U_{ij}) is equal to 1, the value is always increased. If at least one of the numbers (L_{ij}, M_{ij}, U_{ij}) is equal to 9, the value is decreased. The elements of the main diagonal remain unchanged: $(\widetilde{p}_{ii}) = (L_{ii}, M_{ii}, U_{ii}) = (1, 1, 1)$. The symmetric elements with respect to the main diagonal are $(\widetilde{p}_{ii}) = (L_{ii}, M_{ii}, U_{ii}) = \left(\frac{1}{\widetilde{p}_{ii}}\right) = \left(\frac{1}{U_{ii}}, \frac{1}{M_{ii}}, \frac{1}{L_{ii}}\right)$. A new random number from the sequence ζ_r is used for each element $\widetilde{p}_{ij}$ of the matrix.

The matrix $\widetilde{P}$ is formed from the values of the matrix $M = (M_{ij})$. The consistency of evaluation of the values of the matrix M (CR < 0.1) is verified. If the Consistency Ratio is CR $\geq$ 0.1, the pairwise comparison matrix is discarded and a new fuzzy matrix $\widetilde{P}$ is formed.

The criteria weights $\left(\Omega = \omega_j^{(r)}\right)$, ($r = 1$) are calculated.

Step 4. New sequences of random numbers ζ_r ($r = 2, 3, \ldots, T$) are selected, where T is the number of repetitions (simulations). Step 3 is repeated. The criteria weights ($\omega_j^{(r)}$), ($r = 2, 3, \ldots, T$) are calculated.

Step 5. The relative errors of the values of the weight for each of the j-th criterion of the AHP method are calculated for every simulation ξ: $\delta_j^{(\xi)} = \frac{\left|\omega_j^{(\xi)} - \omega_j\right|}{\omega_j}$.

Step 6. The largest values of the relative errors $\delta_j^{(\xi)}$ of the criteria weights for all the criteria are calculated for every simulation ξ: $\delta^\xi = \max_j \delta_j^{(\xi)}$.

Step 7. We take the largest value of the relative errors δ^ξ of the criteria weights over all the simulations ξ, as the FAHP method error for the given comparison matrix: $\delta = \max_\xi \delta^\xi$.

4. Results

This part illustrates the implementation of the above algorithms for checking the stability with several examples. For clarity, the algorithms for checking the stability of the AHP method will use the same pairwise comparison matrices. In the first case, to assess the stability of the methods, a 6×6 matrix with a good consistency index is taken, CI = 0.025, RI = 1.25, CR = 0.02 < 1. The weights of the criteria of the first matrix are 0.0873, 0.4246, 0.149, 0.2585, 0.0496, and 0.0311 (Table 1).

Table 1. The first pairwise comparison matrix (6 × 6).

	cr1	cr2	cr3	cr4	cr5	cr6
cr1	1.00	0.2	0.5	0.25	2.00	4.00
cr2	5.00	1.00	4.00	2.00	7.00	9.00
cr3	2.00	0.25	1.00	0.5	4.00	5.00
cr4	4.00	0.5	2.00	1.00	5.00	7.00
cr5	0.5	0.14	0.25	0.2	1.00	2.00
cr6	0.25	0.11	0.2	0.14	0.5	1.00

In the second case, to assess the stability of the first and second algorithms, a 6 × 6 matrix with a critical consistency index is taken, CI = 0.116, RI = 1.25, CR = 0.09 < 1 (Table 2). When the data of such a matrix change, even a small percentage of deviation can change the consistency of the data. The weights of the criteria of the second matrix are 0.3601, 0.1544, 0.2804, 0.0712, 0.0433, and 0.0905 (Table 2).

Table 2. The second pairwise comparison matrix (6 × 6).

	cr1	cr2	cr3	cr4	cr5	cr6
cr1	1.00	4.00	1.00	5.00	7.00	5.00
cr2	0.25	1.00	0.25	3.00	5.00	3.00
cr3	1.00	4.00	1.00	2.00	4.00	3.00
cr4	0.20	0.33	0.50	1,00	1.00	1.00
cr5	0.14	0.2	0.25	1.00	1.00	0.20
cr6	0.20	0.33	0.33	1.00	5.00	1.00

In all the above algorithms for checking stability, the value of the largest relative error $\delta^{\tilde{\zeta}}$ of the values of the criteria weights is taken. The stability of the method is established using different numbers of iterations: 100, 10,000, and 100,000. As with a small number of iterations the values of the largest relative errors $\delta^{\tilde{\zeta}}$ change with each new check, the check is carried out several times (ten attempts). From the values obtained from the ten attempts, an interval is established, that is, the smallest and the largest values of the largest relative errors $\delta_j^{(\zeta)}$ for each of the criteria calculated by formula (9).

4.1. Practical Application and Analysis of the Implementation of the First Algorithm for Checking the Stability

Using the first algorithm for checking the stability, a different percentage of deviation of all the elements is set. In the first case, the deviation is $q = 5\%$, while in the second $q = 10\%$. In each case, ten attempts are made to fix the interval of the largest relative errors.

In the first case, the matrix data with a good consistency index are used (Table 1). Table 3 shows the results of ten attempts to check the stability of the method, and their largest relative errors $\delta^{\tilde{\zeta}}$, with the number of iterations equal to 100 and 10% deviation, using the matrix of data from Table 1. The results show small $\delta^{\tilde{\zeta}}$ values for the largest relative errors with a deviation of all elements by 10%.

Table 3. The largest relative errors of the criteria weights δ^ζ, when checking the stability by the first algorithm, $q = 10\%$, 100 iterations, 10 repetitions, 1st matrix.

1	2	3	4	5	6	7	8	9	10
0.0527	0.0584	0.063	0.0813	0.0596	0.0745	0.0573	0.0641	0.0699	0.0653
0.0283	0.0443	0.0346	0.0351	0.0367	0.0398	0.0372	0.0502	0.0386	0.0382
0.057	0.0523	0.0644	0.0537	0.0638	0.0557	0.0671	0.0597	0.0651	0.0638
0.0511	0.0662	0.048	0.0456	0.053	0.0472	0.0441	0.0522	0.0588	0.0561
0.0746	0.0665	0.0645	0.0766	0.0665	0.0766	0.0524	0.0806	0.0565	0.0827
0.0611	0.0611	0.0707	0.0611	0.0836	0.0772	0.0836	0.0675	0.0675	0.074
100	100	100	100	100	100	100	100	100	100

During the checking process, the percentage of consistent matrices is fixed for the total number of simulated matrices. At 5% and 10% deviation and with the number of simulations from 100 to 100,000, all the matrices, that is, 100%, are consistent.

The intervals of the largest relative errors for different numbers of iterations are shown in Tables 4 and 5 (5% and 10% deviation, respectively). With an increase in the number of iterations, the range of values of the largest relative errors narrows. With a deviation q of 5%, the value of the relative errors δ^ζ is less than with a deviation of 10%.

Table 4. The interval of the largest relative errors of the criteria weights δ^ζ, when checking the stability by the first algorithm, $q = 5\%$, 10 repetitions, 1st matrix.

	100	10,000	100,000
cr1	0.0275–0.0401	0.0412–0.047	0.0447–0.0493
cr2	0.016–0.024	0.0252–0.0283	0.0287–0.0318
cr3	0.0262–0.0356	0.0376–0.0456	0.0436–0.047
cr4	0.0209–0.0333	0.0344–0.0414	0.0383–0.0414
cr5	0.0262–0.0423	0.0464–0.0544	0.0504–0.0544
cr6	0.0289–0.045	0.045–0.0547	0.0514–0.0579

Table 5. The interval of the largest relative errors of the criteria weights δ^ζ, when checking the stability by the first algorithm, $q = 10\%$, 10 repetitions, 1st matrix.

	100	10,000	100,000
cr1	0.0527–0.0813	0.0825–0.1031	0.0893–0.1054
cr2	0.0283–0.0502	0.0476–0.0546	0.0558–0.061
cr3	0.0523–0.0671	0.0792–0.0899	0.0866–0.1007
cr4	0.0441–0.0662	0.0696–0.0812	0.0774–0.0874
cr5	0.0524–0.0827	0.0907–0.1008	0.1048–0.1149
cr6	0.0611–0.0836	0.0932–0.1061	0.1029–0.1093

In both verification cases, the results show the stability of the method: $\delta = 0.0579$ (at 5% deviation) and $\delta = 0.1149$ (at 10% deviation).

A similar stability check is implemented with the data from the other matrix, for which data consistency is critical (Table 2). With the number of simulations equal to 100, the consistency interval is wider than with 10,000 and 100,000 simulations. In the general case, with a deviation of 5%, the percentage of consistent matrices ranges from 97% to 100%; with a deviation of 10%, the percentage of consistent matrices is, on average, 16% less and, more precisely, fluctuates in the range from 77% to 89% (Table 6).

Table 6. The percentage of consistent matrices when checking the stability of the first algorithm using the data of the second matrix (5%, 10% deviation).

Number of Cycles	5%	10%
100	97–100%	77–89%
10,000	98.55–98.88%	81.87–83.24%
100,000	98.62–98.71%	82.22–82.69%

The intervals for the largest relative errors for the different numbers of iterations are shown in Tables 7 and 8 (5% and 10% deviation, respectively). With a deviation of 5%, the value of the largest relative errors δ^ξ is less than with a deviation of 10%. In both verification cases, the results show the stability of the method: δ = 0.0531 (at 5% deviation) and δ = 0.116 (at 10% deviation).

Table 7. The interval of the largest relative errors of the criteria weights δ^ξ, when checking the stability by the first algorithm, q = 5%, 10 repetitions, 2nd matrix.

	100	10,000	100,000
cr1	0.0194–0.0283	0.0297–0.0342	0.0325–0.0375
cr2	0.0253–0.0369	0.0389–0.0427	0.0427–0.0466
cr3	0.0225–0.0285	0.0328–0.0389	0.0364–0.0396
cr4	0.0281–0.0435	0.0407–0.0492	0.0463–0.0506
cr5	0.0323–0.0462	0.0439–0.0508	0.0462–0.0531
cr6	0.0265–0.0486	0.0431–0.0508	0.0475–0.0519

Table 8. The interval of the largest relative errors of the criteria weights δ^ξ, when checking the stability by the first algorithm, q = 10%, 10 repetitions, 2nd matrix.

	100	10,000	100,000
cr1	0.0361–0.0594	0.0583–0.065	0.0628–0.0703
cr2	0.0505–0.0725	0.0771–0.0868	0.0842–0.0913
cr3	0.0481–0.0649	0.0674–0.0777	0.0717–0.0802
cr4	0.0562–0.0829	0.0885–0.0997	0.0969–0.1096
cr5	0.0577–0.0831	0.0855–0.1039	0.0993–0.1085
cr6	0.063–0.0917	0.0862–0.1083	0.1006–0.116

The results obtained for the largest relative errors of the second matrix differ a little from the results for the largest relative errors of the first matrix (Tables 4 and 5). Testing the AHP method with the first algorithm shows a good result.

4.2. Practical Application and Analysis of the Implementation of the Second Algorithm for Checking the Stability

Using the second algorithm for checking the stability, the elements of the pairwise comparison matrix are changed by one. The stability of the method is also set by the different numbers of iterations: 100, 10,000, and 100,000. The value of the relative errors δ^ξ of the values of the criteria weights is fixed. In each case, ten attempts are made to fix the range of the relative errors. In the first case, the matrix data with a good consistency index are used (Table 1). Table 9 shows the results of ten attempts to check the stability of the method, and the largest relative errors δ^ξ, with the number of iterations equal to 100, using the first matrix data (Table 1). The results show small δ^ξ values of the largest relative errors of the weights of the criteria. Comparing the results for the relative errors of the weights of the criteria (Table 10) with the results of the first algorithm (a deviation of 10%) (Table 3), the results have increased on average by 23%.

Table 9. The largest relative errors of the criteria weights δ^{ξ}, when checking the stability by the second algorithm, 100 iterations, 10 repetitions, 1st matrix.

1	2	3	4	5	6	7	8	9	10
0.4639	0.3723	0.3551	0.433	0.4089	0.394	0.4238	0.4261	0.4227	0.4135
0.2033	0.2061	0.2047	0.2143	0.2051	0.2268	0.2129	0.2179	0.2047	0.2235
0.4362	0.3799	0.3389	0.4081	0.3725	0.3839	0.4181	0.3926	0.4154	0.3846
0.3346	0.3149	0.3222	0.3095	0.3219	0.3292	0.3451	0.3493	0.3319	0.2967
0.3911	0.4335	0.4254	0.371	0.4415	0.4657	0.3609	0.4476	0.3871	0.3851
0.3762	0.2765	0.3023	0.3119	0.3087	0.3537	0.2797	0.3505	0.3151	0.3312
100	100	100	100	100	100	100	100	100	100

Table 10. The interval of the largest relative errors of the criteria weights δ^{ξ}, when checking the stability by the second algorithm, 10 repetitions, 1st matrix.

	100	10,000	100,000
cr1	0.3551–0.4639	0.4868–0.5052	0.5052
cr2	0.2033–0.2268	0.2275–0.2365	0.2365
cr3	0.3389–0.4362	0.4416–0.4577	0.455–0.4577
cr4	0.2967–0.3493	0.3563–0.3683	0.3683
cr5	0.3609–0.4657	0.4879–0.5121	0.5121
cr6	0.2765–0.3762	0.3794–0.4084	0.4084

Checking the consistency of the first matrix, the results of checking the second algorithm for the largest relative errors δ^{ξ} (Table 10) are less than with a 10% data deviation, but more than with a 5% deviation. With the number of iterations equal to 100,000, the intervals of the criteria are practically narrowed to one value.

When checking the consistency of the matrices using the first matrix, all the other generated matrices are consistent, in contrast to the second matrix, in which 55–70% of the matrices are inconsistent and discarded (Table 11).

Table 11. The percentage of consistent matrices when checking the stability by the second algorithm using the data of the first and second matrices.

Number of Cycles	First Matrix	Second Matrix
100	100%	30–45%
10,000	100%	35.29–36.83%
100,000	100%	35.78–36.357%

The largest relative error δ^{ξ} of the results for the second matrix is small (Table 12). The results turn out to be better than when using the first matrix and the same algorithm. This can be explained by the smaller number of consistent matrices used (30–45%).

Table 12. The interval of the largest relative errors of the criteria weights δ^{ξ}, when checking the stability by the second algorithm, 10 repetitions, 2nd matrix.

	100	10,000	100,000
cr1	0.1997–0.2591	0.2533–0.2694	0.2694–0.2694
cr2	0.215–0.2869	0.3089–0.3206	0.3206–0.3206
cr3	0.2282–0.3356	0.3434–0.347	0.347–0.347
cr4	0.4663–0.7051	0.7514–0.7739	0.7739–0.7739
cr5	0.2356–0.2771	0.2818–0.3048	0.3048–0.3048
cr6	0.2188–0.3083	0.3381–0.3746	0.3746–0.3746

In both verification cases, the results show the stability of the method: $\delta = 0.5121$ (using the first matrix) and $\delta = 0.7739$ (using the second matrix).

4.3. Practical Application and Analysis of the Implementation of the Third Algorithm for Checking the Stability

First, the step-by-step calculation of the weights of the original matrix using Chang's method will be illustrated for a better understanding of the stability check of the FAHP method. This paper uses a matrix with triangular fuzzy numbers, which will be formed from the AHP matrix. In many papers, the authors prefer to use symmetric triangular fuzzy numbers, such as {1: [1, 1, 1], 2: [1, 2, 3], 3: [2, 3, 4], 4: [3, 4, 5], 5: [4, 5, 6], 6: [5, 6, 7], 7: [6, 7, 8], 8: [7, 8, 9], 9: [8, 9, 9]}. There are also different modifications of this scale, for example, 1: [0, 1, 1] or 9: [7, 9, 9], and others. Ishizaka et al. [50] describe different modifications of these scales in paper. Chang himself used non-symmetric triangular fuzzy numbers in his paper [49]. This paper will use both symmetric and asymmetric scales (Tables 13 and 14). The scales used do not go beyond the AHP scale proposed by Saaty, in the range from 1 to 9, so in the case of "Equally important" and "Absolutely important", the symmetry of the triangle is broken (Table 13).

Table 13. Symmetrical scale of triangular fuzzy numbers.

Linguistic Characteristics of a Triangular Fuzzy Number	L	M	U
Equally important	1	1	1
Equally to moderately important	1	2	3
Moderately important	2	3	4
Weakly important	3	4	5
Important	4	5	6
Strongly important	5	6	7
Very important	6	7	8
Very strongly important	7	8	9
Absolutely important	8	9	9

Table 14. Asymmetrical scale of triangular fuzzy numbers.

Linguistic Characteristics of a Triangular Fuzzy Number	L	M	U
Equally important	1	1	1
Equally to moderately important	1	2	3
Moderately important	1	3	4
Weakly important	2	4	5
Important	3	5	6
Strongly important	4	6	7
Very important	5	7	8
Very strongly important	6	8	9
Absolutely important	7	9	9

In previous papers [51,52], it was noted that when forming a triangular fuzzy matrix from separate AHP matrices, the M value is located closer to U than to L, so the asymmetric triangular fuzzy scale is formed with a large distance from L to M (Table 14).

An important point in Chang's proposed method for calculating the criteria weights is the comparison of $\tilde{S}_i$, the extension of the fuzzy synthesis values (5). The essence of calculating the value of $V(\tilde{S}_j \geq \tilde{S}_i)$ is to find the ordinate of the intersection point of two triangular numbers (Figure 1). The triangles S_1 and S_2 do not intersect in the case when $L_1 > U_2$. Then, with further calculation, using the formulas (4)–(8), the criterion weight is zero. That is, if a triangle does not intersect with at least one of the subsequent triangles, its weight is zero. This case is possible if the distance between the values M_1 and M_2 is large, and the triangles themselves are narrow (the distance from L to M and from M to U is 1), as in the case of the symmetric scale from Table 13. To give a better explanation of the case of zero weights when using narrow symmetric triangles, we will illustrate it with an example.

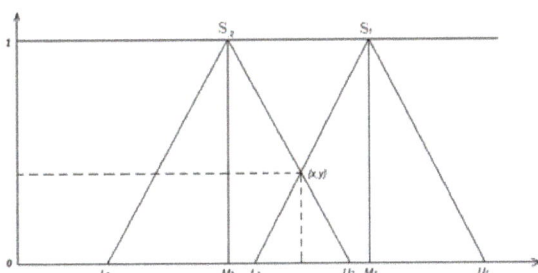

Figure 1. Illustration of the value of $V(\tilde{S}_2 \geq \tilde{S}_1)$.

In solving real problems, when forming a fuzzy matrix from several AHP matrices, the M values are most often averaged [49,51]. Chang's work uses triangular numbers where the M value does not exceed three [49].

In the following sections, symmetric and asymmetric triangular fuzzy numbers are used to form the AHP fuzzy matrix of pairwise comparisons. The implementation of the third algorithm will be illustrated using different matrices of pairwise comparisons, depending on the scale of the triangular fuzzy numbers used.

4.3.1. Using the Symmetric Scale for the Fuzzy Triangle

The fuzzy matrix (Table 15) is formed in such a way that the most likely estimate of M corresponds to the estimate of the AHP method. A 6×6 matrix with a good consistency index is used (Table 1). Fuzzy numbers replaces natural numbers, using the scales specified in Tables 13 and 14, The remaining matrix estimates are calculated using the formula (4).

Table 15. Pairwise comparison matrix using a symmetric triangular fuzzy numbers scale.

	1			2			3			4			5			6		
1	1	1	1	1/6	1/5	1/4	1/3	1/2	1	1/5	1/4	1/3	1	2	3	3	4	5
2	4	5	6	1	1	1	3	4	5	1	2	3	6	7	8	8	9	9
3	1	2	3	1/5	1/4	1/3	1	1	1	1/3	1/2	1	3	4	5	4	5	6
4	3	4	5	1/3	1/2	1	1	2	3	1	1	1	4	5	6	6	7	8
5	1/3	1/2	1	1/8	1/7	1/6	1/5	1/4	1/3	1/6	1/5	1/4	1	1	1	1	2	3
6	1/5	1/4	1/3	1/9	1/9	1/8	1/6	1/5	1/4	1/8	1/7	1/6	1/3	1/2	1	1	1	1

The matrix uses narrow symmetric triangular fuzzy numbers and a full scale of Saaty scores from 1 to 9. Systematically, we illustrate the calculation of weights using the Chang method.

Consider the summed values of $S_i = \sum_{i=1}^{m}\sum_{j=1}^{m} \tilde{p}_{ij}$ (Table 16). The values of the number L of the second and fourth criteria (S_2, S_4) are very different from the other values of the L criteria. Note that the L value of the second criterion is greater than the U values of the first, third, fifth, and sixth criteria, and the L value of the fourth criterion is greater than the U values of the first, fifth and sixth criteria.

Table 16. Summed values of S_i.

	L	M	U
S_1	5.70	7.95	10.58
S_2	23.00	28.00	32.00
S_3	9.53	12.75	16.33
S_4	15.33	19.50	24.00
S_5	2.83	4.09	5.75
S_6	1.94	2.20	2.88

Further normalization, proposed by Chang, increases the values of U (dividing their values by the sum of the L numbers) and decreases the values of L (dividing the values by the sum of the U numbers). The values of M are normalized by dividing all elements by their sum, so the sum of the normalized values of M by all criteria is 1 (Table 17).

Table 17. $\widetilde{S}_i$ the extension of the fuzzy synthesis.

	$\hat{L}$	$\hat{M}$	$\hat{U}$
$\widetilde{S}_1$	0.06	0.11	0.18
$\widetilde{S}_2$	0.25	0.38	0.55
$\widetilde{S}_3$	0.10	0.17	0.28
$\widetilde{S}_4$	0.17	0.26	0.41
$\widetilde{S}_5$	0.03	0.05	0.10
$\widetilde{S}_6$	0.02	0.03	0.05
Σ	0.64	1.00	1.57

For each i-th criterion, the value of $\widetilde{S}_i$—the extension of the fuzzy synthesis—is calculated using the formula (5), and the specified answers are rounded.

$$\widetilde{S}_1 = (5.7, 7.95, 10.58) \odot \left(\tfrac{1}{91.54}, \tfrac{1}{74.5}, \tfrac{1}{58.33}\right) = (0.06, 0.11, 0.18),$$
$$\widetilde{S}_2 = (23, 28, 32) \odot \left(\tfrac{1}{91.54}, \tfrac{1}{74.5}, \tfrac{1}{58.33}\right) = (0.25, 0.38, 0.55),$$
$$\widetilde{S}_3 = (9.53, 12.75, 16.33) \odot \left(\tfrac{1}{91.54}, \tfrac{1}{74.5}, \tfrac{1}{58.33}\right) = (0.1, 0.17, 0.28),$$
$$\widetilde{S}_4 = (15.33, 19.5, 24) \odot \left(\tfrac{1}{91.54}, \tfrac{1}{74.5}, \tfrac{1}{58.33}\right) = (0.17, 0.26, 0.41),$$
$$\widetilde{S}_5 = (2.83, 4.09, 5.75) \odot \left(\tfrac{1}{91.54}, \tfrac{1}{74.5}, \tfrac{1}{58.33}\right) = (0.03, 0.05, 0.1),$$
$$\widetilde{S}_6 = (1.94, 2.2, 2.88) \odot \left(\tfrac{1}{91.54}, \tfrac{1}{74.5}, \tfrac{1}{58.33}\right) = (0.02, 0.03, 0.05).$$

The normalized summed values of $\widetilde{S}_i$ are shown in Table 17. After normalization, the sum of the values of the triangular numbers is $0 < \Sigma \hat{L} < 1$, $\Sigma \hat{M} = 1$, and $\Sigma \hat{U} > 1$. Let us analyze how normalization changed the values of L and U, while expanding the values of the triangular numbers. Taking the example of the first criterion, the difference increased from $\tfrac{U_1}{L_1} = 1.85$ to $\tfrac{\hat{U}_1}{\hat{L}_1} = 3$. Unfortunately, normalization did not solve all the problems of the second and fourth criteria ($\hat{L}_2 > \hat{U}_1$, $\hat{L}_2 > \hat{U}_5$, $\hat{L}_2 > \hat{U}_6$, $\hat{L}_4 > \hat{U}_5$, $\hat{L}_4 > \hat{U}_6$). The inequalities show that the weights of the first, fifth, and sixth criteria will be zero. Further calculations will also show this.

To avoid this situation, it is recommended that, when using a narrow symmetric scale to fill in the matrix of pairwise comparisons, extreme/large values, such as (8, 9, 9), (7, 8, 9), and so on, are not used. Another possible way to avoid zero values is to use an asymmetric scale, which expands the triangle and the differences between the L and U values.

Then, using the extension of the fuzzy synthesis, all the criteria are compared in pairs using the formula (6):

$$V\left(\tilde{S}_1 \geq \tilde{S}_2\right) = 0, \ (\hat{L}_2 > \hat{U}_1),$$
$$V\left(\tilde{S}_1 \geq \tilde{S}_3\right) = \frac{0.1 - 0.18}{(0.11 - 0.18) - (0.17 - 0.1)} = 0.545,$$
$$V\left(\tilde{S}_1 \geq \tilde{S}_4\right) = \frac{0.17 - 0.18}{(0.11 - 0.18) - (0.26 - 0.17)} = 0.083,$$
$$V\left(\tilde{S}_1 \geq \tilde{S}_5\right) = 1, \ (\hat{M}_1 > \hat{M}_5),$$
$$V\left(\tilde{S}_1 \geq \tilde{S}_6\right) = 1, \ (\hat{M}_1 > \hat{M}_6).$$

$$V_1 = \min(0, \ 0.545, \ 0.083, \ 1, \ 1) = 0.$$

Then, a comparison is made in pairs of $\tilde{S}_2$ with all the other extensions of the fuzzy synthesis:

$$V\left(\tilde{S}_2 \geq \tilde{S}_1\right) = 1, \ (\hat{M}_2 > \hat{M}_1),$$
$$V\left(\tilde{S}_2 \geq \tilde{S}_3\right) = 1, \ (\hat{M}_2 > \hat{M}_3),$$
$$V\left(\tilde{S}_2 \geq \tilde{S}_4\right) = 1, \ (\hat{M}_2 > \hat{M}_4),$$
$$V\left(\tilde{S}_2 \geq \tilde{S}_5\right) = 1, \ (\hat{M}_2 > \hat{M}_5),$$
$$V\left(\tilde{S}_2 \geq \tilde{S}_6\right) = 1, \ (\hat{M}_2 > \hat{M}_6).$$

$$V_2 = \min(1, \ 1, \ 1, \ 1, \ 1) = 1.$$

Then, we carry out a pairwise comparison of $\tilde{S}_3$ with all the other values:

$$V\left(\tilde{S}_3 \geq \tilde{S}_1\right) = 1, \ (\hat{M}_3 > \hat{M}_1),$$
$$V\left(\tilde{S}_3 \geq \tilde{S}_2\right) = \frac{0.25 - 0.28}{(0.17 - 0.28) - (0.38 - 0.25)} = 0.123,$$
$$V\left(\tilde{S}_3 \geq \tilde{S}_4\right) = \frac{0.17 - 0.28}{(0.17 - 0.28) - (0.26 - 0.17)} = 0.554,$$
$$V\left(\tilde{S}_3 \geq \tilde{S}_5\right) = 1, \ (\hat{M}_3 > \hat{M}_5),$$
$$V\left(\tilde{S}_3 \geq \tilde{S}_6\right) = 1, \ (\hat{M}_3 > \hat{M}_6).$$

$$V_3 = \min(1, \ 0.123, \ 0.554, \ 1, \ 1) = 0.123.$$

Subsequent values V_4, V_5, and V_6 are calculated in the same way. The following values are obtained: $V_4 = \min(1, 0.584, 1, 1, 1) = 0.584$; $V_5 = \min(1, 0, 0.123, 0.584, 0) = 0$; $V_6 = \min(0, 0, 0, 0, 0.42) = 0$; The vector of non-normalized criteria weights is $V = (0, 1, 0.123, 0.584, 0, 0)$.

The vector of normalized criteria weights is obtained by applying formula (8): $w = (0, 0.586, 0.072, 0.342, 0, 0)$.

In our further study of the stability of the AHP fuzzy method, we use the matrix from Table 18, with a good consistency index (CR = 0.022).

Table 18. The third matrix of pairwise comparisons (6 × 6).

	cr1	cr2	cr3	cr4	cr5	cr6
cr1	1.00	0.33	0.50	2.00	1.00	2.00
cr2	3.00	1.00	1.00	2.00	2.00	3.00
cr3	2.00	1.00	1.00	2.00	1.00	2.00
cr4	0.50	0.50	0.50	1.00	0.50	1.00
cr5	1.00	0.50	1.00	2.00	1.00	2.00
cr6	0.50	0.33	0.50	1.00	0.50	1.00

Using the third algorithm, the stability of the method is also set by different numbers of iterations: 100, 10,000, and 100,000. The value of the largest relative errors $\delta^{\tilde{z}}$ of the values of the criteria weights is fixed. At least ten attempts are made to fix the interval of the largest relative errors, for non-zero values of the weights.

To analyze the stability with a symmetric scale of triangular numbers, we use the matrix presented in Table 18. When simulating an AHP matrix with 100 iterations, 60–70% of the subsequent matrices are consistent. The values of the weights of the initial fuzzy matrix criteria are 0.171, 0.288, 0.227, 0.071, 0.187, and 0.055. When calculating the criteria weights generated, and the matched pairwise comparison matrices, 70–80% of the matrices have zero weights, with the largest relative error being 1. The non-zero values of the weights and their largest relative errors are shown in Table 19. The results show a high maximum relative error $\delta = 0.9797$.

Table 19. The criteria weights of 5 matrices and the errors of the criteria weights when using a symmetric scale.

	ω	1	2	3	4	5	δ
cr1	0.1715	0.2351	0.2535	0.214	0.1745	0.1204	0.9028
cr2	0.2882	0.2484	0.302	0.3236	0.2673	0.3304	0.439
cr3	0.227	0.1666	0.1753	0.0792	0.2576	0.277	0.651
cr4	0.0715	0.0552	0.0236	0.1181	0.1325	0.0258	0.8532
cr5	0.1868	0.1888	0.1939	0.2295	0.1568	0.222	0.8285
cr6	0.0551	0.106	0.0518	0.0356	0.0113	0.0245	0.9797

In general, the results for the relative errors of the third algorithm (Table 19), using a symmetric scale of triangular numbers, are greater than those for the first and second algorithms.

4.3.2. Using the Asymmetric Scale for the Fuzzy Triangle

A fuzzy matrix using an asymmetric triangular scale is formed in the same way as a symmetric one, only using the scale from Table 14. The same 6 × 6 matrix with a good consistency index is used (Table 18). The values of the weights of the initial fuzzy matrix criteria are 0.171, 0.253, 0.208, 0.095, 0.179, and 0.093. In contrast to the symmetric scale, zero values of weights are extremely rare, 1–3%. The values of the criteria weights when using an asymmetric scale differ from the values obtained when using a symmetric one. However, the correlation coefficient of the weights obtained using symmetric and asymmetric scales is significant and is equal to 0.9987. The third matrix criteria weights were obtained using symmetric and asymmetric fuzzy scales from Tables 13 and 14, shown in Figure 2.

The last check step was implemented to avoid zero weights using a symmetric scale using a third matrix with scores not exceeding 3. The result showed that the correlation of weights when using symmetric and asymmetric scales is high. Small changes to the symmetric scale do not significantly affect the scores, but they avoid zero weights.

Analyzing the results of 15 repetitions (100 iterations) (Table 20), the values of the largest relative errors of the criteria weights of the second and fourth criteria are high, which means that the weights in some cases are more than doubled.

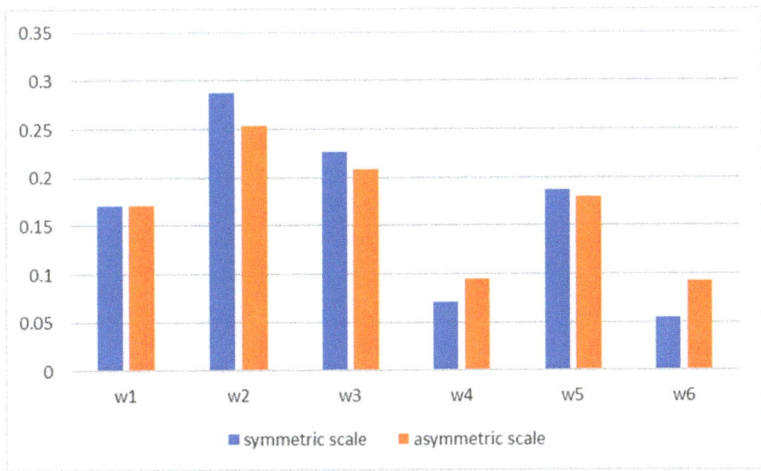

Figure 2. Comparison of the weights of the third matrix criteria using symmetric and asymmetric fuzzy scales.

Table 20. The largest relative errors of the criteria weights $\delta^{\tilde{c}}$, when checking the stability of the third algorithm, 100 iterations, 10 repetitions.

1	2	3	4	5	6	7	8	9	10
0.8933	0.7878	0.8397	0.9953	0.8933	0.6525	0.6052	0.6974	0.6496	0.7137
1.0924	1.1216	0.5863	1.0189	1.0446	0.6028	0.8377	0.6344	1.0367	0.5724
0.744	0.6998	0.7089	0.7983	0.7305	0.5985	0.6724	0.561	0.7166	0.6734
1.0571	0.8372	0.833	0.8002	0.8996	0.7833	0.6808	0.7526	0.8118	0.7294
0.891	0.6596	0.6372	0.768	0.891	0.6177	0.6831	0.5914	0.7144	0.6082
0.9636	0.7238	0.8619	0.9936	0.969	0.5921	0.8501	0.6585	0.7227	0.7013

The results of the relative error intervals for different numbers of iterations are presented in Table 21. As the number of iterations increases, the largest relative errors also increase. The weights increase and decrease by almost a factor of two. The largest changes are for the weight value of the second criterion, by almost four times.

Table 21. The third algorithm, the largest $\delta^{\tilde{c}}$ relative errors of the criteria weights, 10 repetitions.

	100	10,000	100,000
cr1	0.6052–0.9953	1–1.0641	1.0338–1.0641
cr2	0.5724–1.1216	2.3281–2.9479	2.9479
cr3	0.561–0.7983	1–1.0442	1.0442
cr4	0.6808–1.0571	1.333–1.8541	1.8541
cr5	0.5914–0.891	1–1.332	1.332
cr6	0.5921–0.9936	1.0	1.0

The use of an asymmetric scale of triangular numbers shows an improvement in the result compared to the results for the symmetric scale. There are practically no zero values of the weights, but even with a small fluctuation in the values of the matrix, the weights vary greatly. At the same time, the scale used in the AHP matrix varies from 1 to 4 or, respectively, fuzzy numbers from (1, 1, 1) to (3, 4, 5).

To further test the algorithm, the triangular values of fuzzy numbers are extended. We use the asymmetric scale from Table 22, in order to avoid zero weights for the criteria of the first matrix (Table 1).

Table 22. Asymmetrical scale of triangular fuzzy numbers.

Linguistic Characteristics of a Triangular Fuzzy Number	L	M	U
Equally important	1	1	3
Equally to moderately important	1	2	5
Moderately important	1	3	6
Weakly important	1	4	8
Important	2	5	8
Strongly important	2	6	9
Very important	5	7	9
Very strongly important	5	8	9
Absolutely important	7	9	9

The initial values of M are used from the first matrix, which has a high consistency score (Table 1). The weights of the criteria of the fuzzy matrix that is formed when using triangular fuzzy numbers with the new scale in Table 22 are 0.159, 0.286, 0.205, 0.247, 0.088, and 0.017.

Figure 3 shows a greater degree of consistency of weight estimates by the AHP and FAHP methods using Chang's algorithm. This result could not be predicted because Chang's algorithm uses both different rating scales and the theory of comparing fuzzy numbers. The most significant difference in the weights of the first-matrix criteria obtained by the AHP and FAHP methods is observed in the first-third criterion.

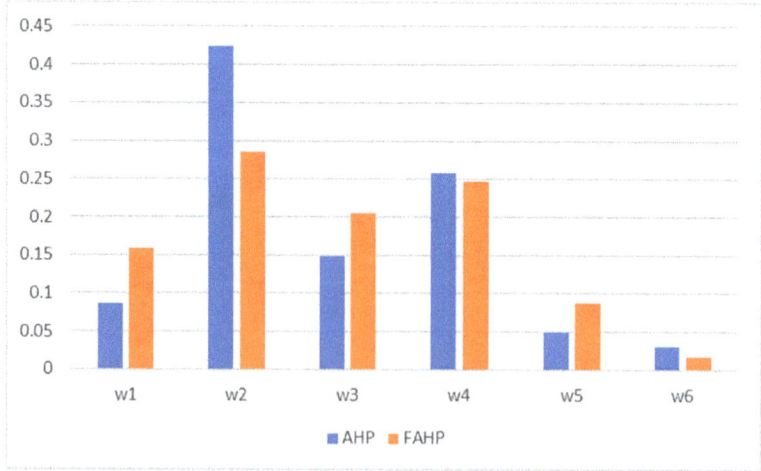

Figure 3. Comparison of the weights of the first matrix criteria using Analytic Hierarchy Process (AHP) and fuzzy Analytic Hierarchy Process (FAHP) methods.

An analysis of the values of $\delta^{\tilde{z}}$ for ten repetitions shows good results for the algorithm for criteria 1 to 5 (Table 23). The large relative error values for the sixth criterion are explained by the fact that the weight in the original matrix is not large ($\omega_6 = 0.017$).

Table 23. The third algorithm, δ^{ξ} the relative errors of the criteria weights, 100 iterations, 10 repetitions.

1	2	3	4	5	6	7	8	9	10
0.2421	0.273	0.3008	0.2018	0.2598	0.2718	0.2692	0.2421	0.2497	0.2522
0.1929	0.1782	0.1765	0.1852	0.1828	0.1695	0.181	0.1831	0.1824	0.1786
0.1594	0.1569	0.1559	0.1598	0.1525	0.153	0.1559	0.1506	0.153	0.1569
0.1561	0.1436	0.1468	0.1545	0.1395	0.1358	0.133	0.1553	0.1476	0.1521
0.5422	0.5217	0.5628	0.5514	0.5548	0.5434	0.5674	0.5776	0.5479	0.5947
4.3455	4.6545	4.0727	4.3697	4.0667	4.4788	4.0182	4.2788	3.9576	4.3212

When checking the stability of the algorithm with a large number of iterations, the result remains the same, but the interval is narrowed to one value (Table 24).

Table 24. The third algorithm, δ^{ξ} relative errors of the criteria weights, 10 repetitions.

	100	10,000	100,000
cr1	0.2018–0.3008	0.2957–0.3071	0.3071
cr2	0.1695–0.1929	0.1957–0.1992	0.1992
cr3	0.1506–0.1598	0.1618–0.1657	0.1657
cr4	0.133–0.1561	0.161–0.1675	0.1675
cr5	0.5217–0.5947	0.5959–0.6073	0.6073
cr6	3.9576–4.6545	4.5515–4.6606	4.6606

Despite the results for criterion 6 ($\delta = 4.6606$), the weight of which varies from 0.017 to 0.08, the method using the new scale for forming triangular numbers shows a good result, comparable to the results of algorithms 1 and 2.

5. Discussion

Using the results of calculations of MCDM methods to choose the best alternative and to make the right decision makes practical sense if the models used are stable with respect to possible minor fluctuations in the initial data. Experts play a significant, and often crucial, role in the preparation of these MCDM methods. They form a set of criteria that characterize the process being evaluated. The criteria weights are usually calculated on the basis of their estimates, and often experts evaluate the values of the criteria themselves. Experts' estimates are characterized by uncertainty. Therefore, when using MCDM methods, it is very important to investigate the influence of incomplete certainty about the data on the results of the calculations, and to assess the stability of the methods themselves.

The stability of MCDM models and the stability of the results depend both on the methods used and on the problem data themselves. Therefore, for each specific problem solved by MCDM, the use of methods for calculating the criteria weights and the specific methods for evaluating alternatives can be selected after checking these methods and the data for stability.

This paper should be considered as an integral part of the general task of studying the stability of MCDM models. For each specific MCDM method, it is necessary to investigate the stability of the weight estimates (this paper), as well as to evaluate the stability of the MCDM method itself. After that, the total error of the calculations can be estimated and the model with the smallest errors accepted.

A change often expresses the assessment of MCDM methods' stability in the ranking of alternatives. In solving specific problems using many possible MCDM methods, the method's result with the lowest degree of change of rang estimates is used.

Various methods can establish the weights of the criteria. Still, the AHP and FAHP methods' peculiarity is in checking the consistency of expert assessments, which allows controlling the correctness of filling out the questionnaire.

The AHP method, as a mathematical method, shows a high degree of stability. This is to be expected: the method is mathematically justified, the elements of the matrix of the pairwise comparison of the criteria are ideally the ratio of the unknown criteria weights, and the weights themselves are normalized values of the eigenvector of the matrix.

Issues related to changes in the criteria weights that depend on ambiguous expert assessments have not received sufficient attention in the scientific literature. An expert, when filling out the same questionnaire again, usually fills it out a little differently. The errors in the calculated weights of the AHP method described in the second algorithm, which are related to the estimates of the experts themselves and the logic of their thinking, are significantly higher than the errors in the mathematical method itself. That, too, was to be expected. Reducing or increasing the comparative estimates of the experts by one significantly changes the values of the components of the eigenvector and the values of the criteria weights. The relative error of the weights increases. When comparing one criterion with all the others, the expert should also remember his previous assessments of the other criteria. With a large number of criteria, this task is not simple and often the comparison matrix is contradictory, not consistent. The expert is forced to fill in a new matrix, and his new estimates, of course, differ significantly from the original ones, as do the weights of the criteria. The relative error is quite large. It is possible to recommend that experts, before filling out an AHP matrix, rank the criteria according to their significance and, when filling out the matrix, constantly take into account the ranking results.

The greatest problems arise when evaluating the stability of the FAHP method weights. This is mainly due to the Chang algorithm used. Checking the AHP fuzzy method shows non-unambiguous results when using different scales of triangular numbers. In the analysis of the algorithm proposed by Chang for calculating weights, the possibility of zero weights for the criteria is emphasized. This is due to the possible excess of the value of L over U ($L > U$), which occurs because of the narrow scale of triangular numbers. Chang's proposed algorithm includes normalization, which partially solves the problem of decreasing L and increasing U values, by expanding the triangular numbers and increasing the probability of an intersection of the $\widetilde{S}_i$ values. This paper proposed an asymmetric scale of triangular numbers, which excluded the appearance of zero weights. At the same time, the calculated fuzzy weights correlated well with the weights of the AHP method. In subsequent work, the authors plan to study in more detail the influence on the final result of the scale used for the triangular numbers and suggest other ways of normalization, to avoid zero values for the criteria weights. Chang's algorithm is also sensitive to large estimates from the Saaty scale (close to 9), in which case the criteria weights can take zero values.

The criteria weights calculated using the AHP and FAHP methods are naturally different, but as the average M values of the FAHP matrix coincide with the values of the AHP matrix, the weights of the two methods should correlate with each other. However, when some of the criteria weights are zero, there is no need to talk about compliance. The situation is "corrected" by the use of the asymmetric scale proposed in this article.

The order of significance of the criteria weights of the first matrix calculated by the AHP and FAHP methods coincided: (cr2 $\succ$ cr $\succ$ cr3 $\succ$ cr1 $\succ$ cr5 $\succ$ cr6). The correlation coefficient of the AHP weights (0.0873, 0.4246, 0.149, 0.2585, 0.0496, 0.0311) and the FAHP scales (0.159, 0.286, 0.205, 0.247, 0.088, 0.017) is large enough and equal to 0.8894.

A review of the scientific literature confirms the relevance of the problems studied in this paper. Despite the presence of papers that use a stability check for the AHP method, the results of the algorithms could not be compared because of different interpretations of the results. Noted that despite the widespread use of the FAHP method, little attention has been paid to checking its stability, so the results of this paper are of scientific interest.

The theory of interval numbers is a universal approach for solving many applied problems. The FAHP method is useful for solving problems using linguistic scales that cannot be written down in a single number. In this case, the sensitivity test of the FAHP method to select the scale of triangular numbers is recommended. Otherwise, the AHP method is recommended.

6. Conclusions

The stability of multicriteria MCDM methods is associated with the incomplete certainty of the data used for calculations.

This uncertainty is particularly evident when calculating the subjective weights of criteria based on expert assessments. Unstable estimates (ranking) in MCDM methods reduce the quality of the estimates and the reliability of the decision. The instability of the MCDM methods can result in an incorrect ranking of the evaluated alternatives, not the proper choice of the best option, inaccurate estimates of the criteria' significance, and the criteria weights' values in a particular situation and environment. Therefore, the problem investigated in this publication is relevant. The calculations show that the AHP method, as a mathematical method, is stable with respect to minor fluctuations in the elements of the comparison matrix. The transition from the Saaty scale integers 1-3-5-7-9 to close real numbers slightly changes the values of the weights. The relative error of the weight estimates that were insignificant varied between $\delta = 0.0531$ (at 5% deviation) and $\delta = 0.116$ (at 10% deviation).

The maximum relative error of the AHP method, related to the assessments of the experts themselves, the logic of their thinking, and psychology, is significantly greater than the error of AHP as a mathematical method. At the same time, changing the elements of the comparison matrix by units significantly affects the values of the eigenvector components of the matrix. The relative error of the estimates of the weights much higher and varied in the range $\delta = 0.5121$ to $\delta = 0.7739$.

The stability of the weights of the FAHP method is related not only to the factors listed above for the AHP method, but also to the use of Chang's algorithm for estimating weights. The calculations show that the algorithm itself is not universal, is not applicable for all matrices, and depends on the scale used for the estimates of the triangular numbers. If the evaluation scale is incorrectly selected, the weights may be zero for some matrices. The relative error of the FAHP method is significantly higher than that for the AHP method and varied from $\delta = 0.2421$ to $\delta = 0.9797$. It was anomalous ($\delta = 4.6606$) in the case of a very small weight for a criterion.

The proposed asymmetric FAHP scale significantly improved the results: it eliminated the appearance of zero weights for criteria, reduced the values of the maximum relative errors, and showed a high degree of correlation with the weights obtained by the AHP method.

Regarding the novelty and relevance of this paper, we can point to the study of the stability of the AHP method, which depends on the instability of the estimates of the experts themselves, and the analysis of the stability of the FAHP method, which was clearly insufficiently studied earlier. This paper can be used to analyze the stability of specific MCDM methods by ranking the alternatives.

Author Contributions: V.P., E.K.Z. and I.V.-Z. conceived the presented idea. V.P. and I.V.-Z. developed the theory. I.V.-Z. performed the computations. E.K.Z. supervised the findings of this paper. All authors discussed the results and contributed to the final manuscript. All authors have read and agreed to the published version of the manuscript.

Funding: This research received no external funding.

Institutional Review Board Statement: Not applicable.

Informed Consent Statement: Not applicable.

Conflicts of Interest: The authors declare no conflict of interest.

References

1. Erdoğan, A.; Zwick, P.D. Spatial decision making under determinism vs. uncertainty: A comparative multi-level approach to preference mapping. *Hacet. J. Math. Stat.* **2016**, *45*, 1. [CrossRef]
2. Saaty, T.L. *The Analytic Hierarchy Process*; McGraw-Hill: New York, NY, USA, 1980.
3. Hwang, C.L.; Yoon, K. *Multiple Attribute Decision-Making Methods and Applications*; A State of the Art Survey; Springer: Berlin/Heidelberg, Germany, 1981.
4. Keršulienė, V.; Zavadskas, E.K.; Turskis, Z. Selection of rational dispute resolution method by applying new step-wise weight assessment ratio analysis (SWARA). *J. Bus. Econ. Manag.* **2010**, *11*, 243–258. [CrossRef]
5. Podvezko, V.; Sivilevičius, H. The use of AHP and rank correlation methods for determining the significance of the interaction between the elements of a transport system having a strong influence on traffic safety. *Transport* **2013**, *28*, 389–403. [CrossRef]
6. Gudienė, N.; Banaitis, A.; Podvezko, V.; Banaitienė, N. Identification and evaluation of the critical success factors for construction projects in Lithuania: AHP approach. *J. Civ. Eng. Manag.* **2014**, *20*, 350–359. [CrossRef]
7. Kou, G.; Lin, C. A cosine maximization method for the priority vector derivation in AHP. *Eur. J. Oper. Res.* **2014**, *235*, 225–232. [CrossRef]
8. Zavadskas, E.K.; Podvezko, V. Integrated determination of objective criteria weights in MCDM. *Int. J. Inf. Technol. Decis. Mak.* **2016**, *15*, 267–283. [CrossRef]
9. Ustinovichius, L.; Zavadskas, E.K.; Podvezko, V. Application of a quantitative multiple criteria decision-making (MCDM–1) approach to the analysis of investments in construction. *Control Cybern.* **2007**, *36*, 251–268.
10. Ma, J.; Fan, Z.-P.; Huang, L.-H. A subjective and objective integrated approach to determine attribute weights. *Eur. J. Oper. Res.* **1999**, *112*, 397–404. [CrossRef]
11. Lazauskaitė, D.; Burinskienė, M.; Podvezko, V. Subjectively and objectively integrated assessment of the quality indices of the suburban residential environment. *Int. J. Strat. Prop. Manag.* **2015**, *19*, 297–308. [CrossRef]
12. Vinogradova, I.; Podvezko, V.; Zavadskas, E.K. The recalculation of the weights of criteria in MCDM methods using the bayes approach. *Symmetry* **2018**, *10*, 205. [CrossRef]
13. Evans, J.R. Sensitivity analysis in decision theory. *Decis. Sci.* **1984**, *15*, 239–247. [CrossRef]
14. Barron, H.; Schmidt, C.P. Sensitivity analysis of additive multiattribute value models. *Oper. Res.* **1988**, *36*, 122–127. [CrossRef]
15. Zhou, M.; Liu, X.-B.; Chen, Y.-W.; Qian, X.-F.; Yang, J.-B.; Wu, J. Assignment of attribute weights with belief distributions for MADM under uncertainties. *Knowl.-Based Syst.* **2020**, *189*, 105110. [CrossRef]
16. Wolters, W.; Mareschal, B. Novel types of sensitivity analysis for additive MCDM methods. *Eur. J. Oper. Res.* **1995**, *81*, 281–290. [CrossRef]
17. Triantaphyllou, E.; Sánchez, A. A sensitivity analysis approach for some deterministic multi-criteria decision-making methods. *Decis. Sci.* **1997**, *28*, 151–194. [CrossRef]
18. Podvezko, V. The comparative analysis of MCDA methods SAW and COPRAS. *Eng. Econ.* **2011**, *22*, 134–146. [CrossRef]
19. Zavadskas, E.K.; Turskis, Z.; Dejus, T.; Viteikiene, M. Sensitivity analysis of a simple additive weight method. *Int. J. Manag. Decis. Mak.* **2007**, *8*, 555. [CrossRef]
20. Vinogradova, I. Multi-attribute decision-making methods as a part of mathematical optimization. *Mathematics* **2019**, *7*, 915. [CrossRef]
21. Memariani, A.; Amini, A.; Alinezhad, A. Sensitivity analysis of simple additive weighting method (SAW): The results of change in the weight of one attribute on the final ranking of alternatives. *J. Ind. Eng.* **2009**, *4*, 13–18.
22. Alinezhad, A.; Sarrafha, K.; Amini, A. Sensitivity analysis of SAW technique: The impact of changing the decision-making matrix elements on the final ranking of alternatives. *Iran. J. Oper. Res.* **2014**, *5*, 82–94.
23. Moghassem, A.R. Comparison among two analytical methods of multi-criteria decision-making for appropriate spinning condition selection. *World Appl. Sci. J.* **2013**, *21*, 784–794.
24. Hsu, L.C.; Ou, S.L.; Ou, Y.C. A comprehensive performance evaluation and ranking methodology under a sustainable development perspective. *J. Bus. Econ. Manag.* **2015**, *16*, 74–92. [CrossRef]
25. Erkut, E.; Tarimcilar, M. On sensitivity analysis in the analytic hierarchy process. *IMA J. Math. Appl. Bus. Ind.* **1991**, *3*, 61–83. [CrossRef]
26. Masuda, T. Hierarchical sensitivity analysis of priority used in analytic hierarchy process. *Int. J. Syst. Sci.* **1990**, *21*, 415–427. [CrossRef]
27. Warren, L. *Uncertainties in the Analytic Hierarchy Process*; Command and Control Division Information Sciences Laboratory: Edinburgh, Australia, 2004.
28. Mimović, P.; Stankovic, J.; Milić, V.J. Decision-making under uncertainty—The integrated approach of the AHP and Bayesian analysis. *Ekon. Istraživanja* **2015**, *28*, 868–878. [CrossRef]
29. Wu, D.; Yang, Z.; Wang, N.; Li, C.; Yang, Y. An integrated multi-criteria decision-making model and AHP weighting uncertainty analysis for sustainability assessment of coal-fired power units. *Sustainability* **2018**, *10*, 1700. [CrossRef]
30. Aguarón, J.; Escobar, M.T.; Moreno-Jiménez, J.M. Reducing inconsistency measured by the geometric consistency index in the analytic hierarchy process. *Eur. J. Oper. Res.* **2021**, *288*, 576–583. [CrossRef]
31. Chen, Y.; Yu, J.; Khan, S. Spatial sensitivity analysis of multi-criteria weights in GIS-based land suitability evaluation. *Environ. Model. Softw.* **2010**, *25*, 1582–1591. [CrossRef]

32. Deepa, R.; Swamynathan, S. AHP-Entropy-TOPSIS based clustering protocol for mobile ad hoc networks. *Ad. Hoc. Sens. Wirel. Netw.* **2014**, *24*, 161–177.
33. Zyoud, S.H.; Fuchs-Hanusch, D. An integrated decision-making framework to appraise water losses in municipal water systems. *Int. J. Inf. Technol. Decis. Mak.* **2020**, *19*, 1–34. [CrossRef]
34. Xue, Y.; Li, X.; Qiu, D.; Ma, X.; Kong, F.; Qu, C.; Zhao, Y. Stability evaluation for the excavation face of shield tunnel across the Yangtze River by multi-factor analysis. *Geomech. Eng.* **2019**, *19*, 283–293. [CrossRef]
35. Kumar, A.; Zavadskas, E.K.; Mangla, S.K.; Agrawal, V.; Sharma, K.; Gupta, D. When risks need attention: Adoption of green supply chain initiatives in the pharmaceutical industry. *Int. J. Prod. Res.* **2019**, *57*, 3554–3576. [CrossRef]
36. Stević, Ž.; Vasiljević, M.; Puška, A.; Tanackov, I.; Junevičius, R.; Vesković, S. Evaluation of suppliers under uncertainty: A multiphase approach based on fuzzy AHP and fuzzy EDAS. *Transport* **2019**, *34*, 52–66. [CrossRef]
37. Stojic, G.; Stević, Ž.; Antuchevičienė, J.; Pamucar, D.; Vasiljević, M. A novel rough WASPAS approach for supplier selection in a company manufacturing PVC carpentry products. *Information* **2018**, *9*, 121. [CrossRef]
38. Zavadskas, E.K.; Stević, Ž.; Tanackov, I.; Prentkovskis, O. A novel multicriteria approach—Rough step-wise weight assessment ratio analysis method (R-SWARA) and its application in logistics. *Stud. Inform. Control* **2018**, *27*, 97–106. [CrossRef]
39. Pamucar, D.; Chatterjee, K.; Zavadskas, E.K. Assessment of third-party logistics provider using multi-criteria decision-making approach based on interval rough numbers. *Comput. Ind. Eng.* **2019**, *127*, 383–407. [CrossRef]
40. Madić, M.; Antucheviciene, J.; Radovanović, M.; Petković, D. Determination of manufacturing process conditions by using MCDM methods: Application in laser cutting. *Eng. Econ.* **2016**, *27*, 144–150. [CrossRef]
41. Salimi, A.H.; Noori, A.; Bonakdari, H.; Masoompour Samakosh, J.; Sharifi, E.; Hassanvand, M.; Gharabaghi, B.; Agharazi, M. Exploring the role of advertising types on improving the water consumption behavior: An application of integrated fuzzy AHP and fuzzy VIKOR method. *Sustainability* **2020**, *12*, 1232. [CrossRef]
42. Singh, S.; Olugu, E.U.; Musa, S.N.; Mahat, A.B.; Wong, K.Y. Strategy selection for sustainable manufacturing with integrated AHP-VIKOR method under interval-valued fuzzy environment. *Int. J. Adv. Manuf. Technol.* **2015**, *84*, 547–563. [CrossRef]
43. Wang, H.; Jiang, Z.; Zhang, H.; Wang, Y.; Yang, Y.; Li, Y. An integrated MCDM approach considering demands-matching for reverse logistics. *J. Clean. Prod.* **2019**, *208*, 199–210. [CrossRef]
44. Wen, Z.; Liao, H.; Zavadskas, E.K. MACONT: Mixed aggregation by comprehensive normalization technique for multi-criteria analysis. *Informatica* **2020**, *31*, 1–24. [CrossRef]
45. Porter, M.; Janssen, R. *Multiobjective Decision Support for Environmental Management*; Kluwer Academic Publisher: Dordrecht, The Netherlands, 1996.
46. Eskandari, H.; Rabelo, L. Handling uncertainty in the analytic hierarchy process: A stochastic approach. *Int. J. Inf. Technol. Decis. Mak.* **2007**, *6*, 177–189. [CrossRef]
47. Afzal, F.; Yunfei, S.; Junaid, D.; Hanif, M.S. Cost-risk contingency framework for managing cost overrun in metropolitan projects: Using fuzzy-AHP and simulation. *Int. J. Manag. Proj. Bus.* **2020**, *13*, 1121–1139. [CrossRef]
48. Zadeh, L.A. Fuzzy sets. *Inf. Control* **1965**, *8*, 338–353. [CrossRef]
49. Chang, D.-Y. Applications of the extent analysis method on fuzzy AHP. *Eur. J. Oper. Res.* **1996**, *95*, 649–655. [CrossRef]
50. Ishizaka, A.; Nguyen, N.H. Calibrated fuzzy AHP for current bank account selection. *Expert Syst. Appl.* **2013**, *40*, 3775–3783. [CrossRef]
51. Trinkūnienė, E.; Podvezko, V.; Zavadskas, E.K.; Jokšienė, I.; Vinogradova, I.; Trinkūnas, V. Evaluation of quality assurance in contractor contracts by multi-attribute decision-making methods. *Ekon. Istraživanja* **2017**, *30*, 1152–1180. [CrossRef]
52. Kurilovas, E.; Vinogradova, I.; Kubilinskiene, S. New MCEQLS fuzzy AHP methodology for evaluating learning repositories: A tool for technological development of economy. *Technol. Econ. Dev. Econ.* **2016**, *22*, 142–155. [CrossRef]

Article

Qualitative Rating of Lossy Compression for Aerial Imagery by Neutrosophic WASPAS Method

Romualdas Bausys * and Giruta Kazakeviciute-Januskeviciene

Department of Graphical Systems, Vilnius Gediminas Technical University, Sauletekio al. 11, LT-10223 Vilnius, Lithuania; giruta.kazakeviciute-januskeviciene@vgtu.lt
* Correspondence: romualdas.bausys@vgtu.lt

Citation: Bausys, R.; Kazakeviciute-Januskeviciene, G. Qualitative Rating of Lossy Compression for Aerial Imagery by Neutrosophic WASPAS Method. *Symmetry* **2021**, *13*, 273. https://doi.org/10.3390/sym13020273

Academic Editors: Zenonas Turskis, Jurgita Antuchevičienė and Edmundas Kazimieras Zavadskas
Received: 28 December 2020
Accepted: 2 February 2021
Published: 5 February 2021

Publisher's Note: MDPI stays neutral with regard to jurisdictional claims in published maps and institutional affiliations.

Copyright: © 2021 by the authors. Licensee MDPI, Basel, Switzerland. This article is an open access article distributed under the terms and conditions of the Creative Commons Attribution (CC BY) license (https://creativecommons.org/licenses/by/4.0/).

Abstract: The monitoring and management of consistently changing landscape patterns are accomplished through a large amount of remote sensing data using satellite images and aerial photography that requires lossy compression for effective storage and transmission. Lossy compression brings the necessity to evaluate the image quality to preserve the important and detailed visual features of the data. We proposed and verified a weighted combination of qualitative parameters for the multi-criteria decision-making (MCDM) framework to evaluate the quality of the compressed aerial images. The aerial imagery of different contents and resolutions was tested using the transform-based lossy compression algorithms. We formulated an MCDM problem dedicated to the rating of lossy compression algorithms, governed by the set of qualitative parameters of the images and visually acceptable lossy compression ratios. We performed the lossy compression algorithms' ranking with different compression ratios by their suitability for the aerial images using the neutrosophic weighted aggregated sum product assessment (WASPAS) method. The novelty of our methodology is the use of a weighted combination of different qualitative parameters for lossy compression estimation to get a more precise evaluation of the effect of lossy compression on the image content. Our methodology includes means of solving different subtasks, either by altering the weights or the set of aspects.

Keywords: aerial imagery; lossy compression; qualitative evaluation; MCDM; WASPAS; neutrosophic set

1. Introduction

The use of modern technologies increases the capabilities to explore the landscape using satellite images and aerial photography. Remote sensed data provide us with the information for studying and surveying the Earth and its bodies. The land cover patterns–vegetation, soil, rock, water, buildings, roads, and other elements–are continually changing due to anthropogenic impact and climate variations. The monitoring of land cover changes and use, and emergency management [1] is accomplished through a large amount of remote sensing data. These changes are related to urban planning [2], deforestation, biodiversity loss [3–5] and other causes, like natural disasters [6]. This amount of data requires compression for effective management–storage, transmission, view, manipulation, processing, etc. of the information. Uncompressed high-resolution images, containing remote sensing data, tend to fill the storage space ineffectively and require long transmission time. Effective data compression reduces the amount of data at the expense of their quality. Therefore, it is important to determine the balance between the quality of remote sensing data and the degree of compression.

Both lossy and lossless compression can be used for remote sensing imagery, reducing the amount of data with significantly different compression ratios. Lossless compression can be considered symmetric compression, which does not introduce the loss and distortions into information, so the compression ratios in most cases are low [7]. Higher compression ratios are achievable using lossy compression methods at the expense of image quality [7] as this type of compression is asymmetric (the original file does not match the decompressed file). For extremely large image files, lossy compression is the obvious solution. Simultaneously, it is essential to evaluate the quality of the compressed images to preserve the detailed and important visual features of the aerial images [8]. In this article, an image that is reconstructed after compression will be referred to as a compressed image.

The degree of image degradation during each lossy compression process depends on the compression algorithm, compression ratio, and the image itself. It is important to select the proper lossy compression format and compression quality for the appropriate aerial image to minimize the compression impact [8,9]. Different algorithms are used to save satellite images and aerial photography data into the lossy compression formats [10–12]. The majority of the popular compression algorithms for aerial imagery are wavelet-based [13]. The most used are the proprietary Enhanced Compression Wavelet (ECW) [14] and Joint Photographic Experts Group (JPEG2000) [15]. The Consultative Committee for Space Data Systems (CCSDS) is mostly used for real-time remote sensing data transmission [16]. The ICER (Progressive Wavelet Image Compressor) is used for onboard image compression by the NASA Mars Rovers [17]. The ECW method, in comparison to the proprietary wavelet-based method Multiresolution Seamless Image Database (MrSid), produces smaller and better quality images and in less time [18]. JPEG image compression is based on the discrete cosine transform (DCT) and is the most well-known and widely applied [19]. All these algorithms offer excellent compression performance, which is usually evaluated by efficiency and computational requirements [13]. There are works [13,19–21] devoted to the analysis of lossy compression performance comparing different algorithms at various conditions. We are interested in the compression efficiency as it relates to the ability to maintain the highest possible visual quality of the compressed aerial image by increasing the number of bits per pixel for data storage. Our analysis and selection of lossy compression for aerial images do not target the real-time applications, and the compression and decompression times are not a priority. Considering the peculiarities of the algorithms used for satellite and aerial images, we selected three of them for qualitative evaluation: ECW, JPEG2000, and JPEG. The CCSDS method, compared to ECW and JPEG2000, retains the lower qualitative result when reconstructing the original image after compression but is faster [13].

Continuous improvement of the current state-of-the-art lossy compression methods requires proper methods and methodologies for qualitative evaluation of lossy compression. Usually, the single objective metrics are used to examine images' lossy compression quality [9–13]. We think the related and weighted combination of different qualitative parameters can evaluate the influence of lossy compression on the image content more precisely. We proposed and verified a set of qualitative parameters evaluating the compressed aerial images using the MCDM framework. We formulated a new MCDM problem dedicated to the rating of lossy compression algorithms governed by appropriate qualitative parameters of compressed images and visually acceptable lossy compression for them. Herewith, we performed ranking for lossy compression algorithms with different compression ratios by their suitability for the different resolution aerial images. To ensure the stability of MCDM ranking results, we chose the direct weight determination and weighted aggregated sum product assessment (WASPAS) methods in the neutrosophic environment. These methods show great stability in solving various real-life problems. We created the original multi-criteria decision-making methodology for the qualitative selection of the aerial images' lossy compression, which also provides the means of solving different subtasks, either altering the weights or the set of aspects.

The article consists of five sections. Section 2 provides a summary of published papers on the qualitative assessment of compressed aerial images. Section 3 describes the general framework of the methodology, a set of alternatives and criteria for a multi-criteria task of the qualitative rating of aerial images' lossy compression, and defines the direct weight determination and MCDM neutrosophic WASPAS methods for data processing. Section 4 presents the set of selected aerial images, qualitative evaluation, the ranking of compression results of the set by the neutrosophic WASPAS-SVNS method, and discussion of the results. Concluding remarks and future directions are presented in Section 5.

2. Related Works

Qualitative assessment for compressed aerial images plays a vital role in identifying the quality of different features of interest after the compression like forests, marshes, shrubs, roads, buildings, water bodies, and others. The task is to identify the important visual features that were lost during lossy compression. The features can be characterized by generalizations like shape, size, density, color tone, texture [22,23]. Various land covers, like vegetation, sand, or water, have distinct textures and colors in the aerial images. Information on the change of the colors and textures can be calculated using global [20] and local [20,23] statistical parameters: first-order histogram-based global statistics, like standard deviation, mean, or second-order Grey Level Co-occurrence Matrix (GLCM)-based local statistics like contrast, homogeneity, entropy, and other. Textural or color changes can be evaluated without prior image processing, and compared to the other features like shape, size, density. The effect of lossy compression on the region color is usually calculated using statistics of the image color components before and after compression obtaining color components after image conversion to the appropriate color spaces [20]. Qualitative evaluation of color changes after compression can be performed using prior image processing—segmentation by color [24,25]—and comparing the quality of segmentation before and after compression, where the original image segmentation results serve as ground truth. The color RGB images of the remote sensing are obtained by assigning a specific multispectral band to each RGB channel. The obtained color of the object is the combination of radiometric resolution (RS), or the number of bits obtained for each band. The RS range depends on the possibility to collect values, based on the sensitivity and range of the instrumentation. As edge detection is closely related to the image density [26,27], the qualitative evaluation of edge detection after image compression can be used to assess the change of compressed and original image density. Segmentation, edge detection, morphological, and other image processing and analysis methods are applied to extract the regions of the image. After the image regions are separated, their shape and size can be evaluated. Mostly the general objective image quality assessment (IQA) metrics are used to evaluate the degradations of the compressed images: mean square error (MSE) [8,19], Peak Signal to Noise Ratio (PSNR) [8,9,13,19], Structural Similarity Index (SSIM) [8,19], multiscale SSIM (MS-SSIM) [8,19], Visual Information Fidelity (VIF) [19], etc. Some authors derived new methods to evaluate compression quality [28,29]. There were attempts to include more parameters for the comparative analysis and evaluation of the compression algorithms, including texture measures [20]. In [13,16,18], the authors included compression speed and compression ratios to evaluate the performance of appropriate algorithms. The change of land cover pattern after lossy compression influences the proper detection of distinct areas and their boundaries. The impact of lossy compression on the content of remote sensing images usually occurs at higher compression ratios and depends on the compression algorithms. In [30], the effect of lossy compression was evaluated for edge detection, segmentation [31,32], and classification [32,33]. The visual features' degradation in areal images compressed using lossy algorithms is related to the image content and resolution [34]. The effect of lossy compression on the processed result and quality of the compressed images can be evaluated using subjective metrics like Mean Opinion Score (MOS), but it is not always effective. Visual data in the relevant application areas can be collected, compressed for easier transmission, saving storage space, and later reviewed by the inspectors or processed by the appropriate methods [35]. In these cases, it should be useful to find the best solution for image lossy compression implementation in hardware.

We aim to manage the qualitative rating process of lossy compression by the set of qualitative parameters such as general image quality metrics, change of color (using first-order histogram-based statistics), change of texture (using second-order GLCM-based statistics), and subjective evaluation (using MOS). These qualitative parameters were applied both for the ranking of lossy compression algorithms and the decision making about the acceptable threshold of visual distortions in the lossy compressed image. A weighted combination of different qualitative parameters could be used to evaluate the effect of lossy compression on the image content more precisely. This approach also provides the possibilities to solve different subtasks, either altering the weights or the set of aspects.

The impact of the lossy compression process was analyzed using a set of qualitative parameters, considered as criteria in our multi-criteria decision-making methodology. The MCDM approach was successfully applied in a broad spectrum of image processing areas: improvement of edge detection [36] and segmentation [37] of images, selection of edge detection algorithms for satellite images [27]. The MCDM was used as an important technique in sustainability engineering [38,39], as a solution for various complex tasks based on the assessment of variants. Direct determination for qualitative parameters' weighting and WASPAS methods were chosen as efficient decision-making tools. These methods were not applied for the qualitative rating of lossy compression by a set of aspects before our research. WASPAS is capable of providing a higher accuracy result compared to the weighted product model (WPM), and the weighted sum model (WSM) methods as it is the combination of both methods [40].

3. Methods for the Methodology of the Selection of Lossy Compression Algorithms by Set of Qualitative Parameters

We apply the framework of multi-criteria decision-making for the evaluation of lossy compression algorithms. The problem formulation in the MCDM context is formalized by constructing the decision matrix. This matrix is defined by the criteria, placed in rows, and the alternatives are placed in columns. The first step in the selection of lossy compression algorithms is the definition of the set of qualitative parameters. The content change of the reconstructed aerial image after compression depends on the compression algorithm, compression ratio, image resolution, and image content itself. Image content is presented by pixel values, and after lossy compression, these values of the reconstructed image are altered. Herewith, the visual appearance of the features, like a forest, cropland, roads, buildings, water, is changing too. In this work, visual features are characterized by generalizations like texture, color tone, and luminance.

3.1. A Framework of the Methodology

The developed original MCDM methodology for the qualitative rating (selection) of lossy compression algorithms for aerial images includes seven essential stages:

- The selection and verification of a set of qualitative parameters for the change detection between the original and compressed aerial images as the criteria;
- The selection of a set of lossy compression algorithms with the appropriate compression ratios that are used for aerial image compression as the alternatives;
- The compression of the selected aerial images using the selected lossy compression algorithms with different compression ratios;
- The evaluation of the influence of lossy compression to the content of the aerial image using the set of qualitative parameters;
- Definition of the acceptable visible distortion threshold in the compressed image;
- The processing of the acquired data using MCDM neutrosophic WASPAS method;
- The ranking of the compression algorithms and their compression ratios by their qualitative suitability for the appropriate aerial images of different resolutions.

The generalized framework for the implementation of the methodology is presented in Figure 1.

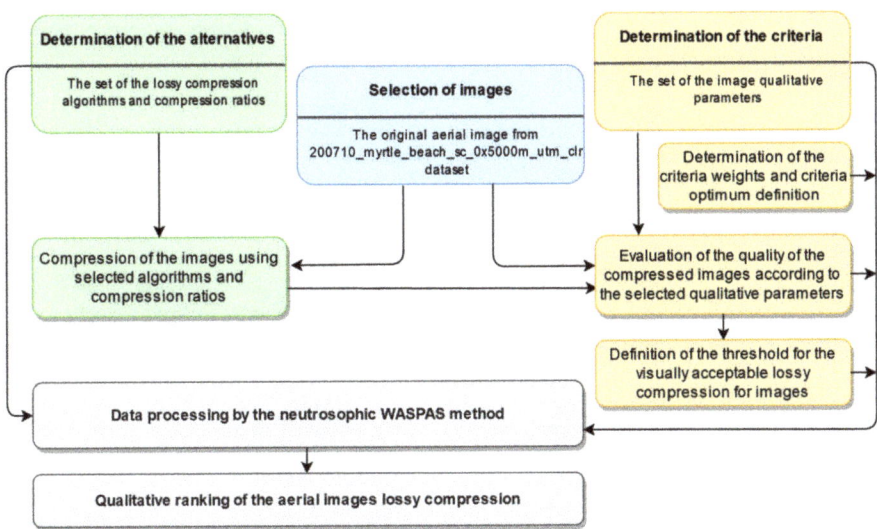

Figure 1. The framework for rating the lossy compression algorithms and their compression ratios by their qualitative suitability for the aerial images. Different colors present stages related to the data selection, lossy compression (alternatives), lossy compression evaluation by the qualitative parameters (criteria) and data processing for qualitative ranking of lossy compression.

The transform-based lossy compression algorithms—JPEG2000, ECW, and JPEG— were selected to implement our methodology. The algorithms were ranked by the amount of the distortions introduced to the aerial image, estimated using: (a) the supervised objective image quality measures; (b) subjective evaluation; (c) the change in the appropriate first-order statistical measures; (d) the change in the second-order statistical measures. The novelty of the approach is the use of a weighted combination of different qualitative parameters for lossy compression estimation compared to the estimation using only single objective image quality metrics. Thus, the effect of lossy compression on the image content can be evaluated more precisely. This also allows targeting different subtasks, either altering the weights or the set of aspects: the same approach can be used to assess the texture or color quality after the compression.

3.2. Lossy Compression Algorithms for Aerial Images

In this work, three lossy transform-based compression algorithms, namely, JPEG2000 [41], ECW [42,43], and JPEG [44], were selected as alternatives for MCDM methodology to evaluate them by compression efficiency. JPEG2000 is a still image (greyscale, color etc.) encoding and decoding system that defines both lossy and lossless compression techniques based on the discrete wavelet transform (DWT) method [45]. ECW is a proprietary lossy compression format based on the DWT method, targeted for satellite imagery and aerial photography [46]. JPEG is a commonly used image encoding and decoding system, using a lossy compression technique based on the DCT [47].

It has been stated [48] that the transform-based compression is less sensitive to changes in the statistical image properties, and the subjective image quality is preserved better. The proper lossy compression technique uses the image data decomposition to reduce the redundant information and maintain the quality of the image. The generalized scheme for lossy aerial image compression and decompression is presented in Figure 2. It consists of the reduction in redundancy, entropy coding, bit stream transmission, decoding, and data reconstruction. The typical encoder performs color space conversion and image decomposition, transformation, quantization and coding [49,50]. The decoder performs entropy decoding, dequantization, inverse transformation, and inverse color space conversion [49,50].

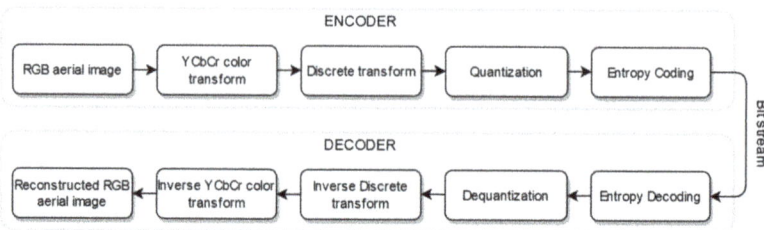

Figure 2. Basic procedures for aerial image transform-based lossy compression–decompression.

As shown in Figure 1, the encoder converts the original image into the bit stream. The encoded bit stream is received by the decoder, and the restored image is obtained. For the lossy compression system, the total data quantity of the original image is larger than the data quantity of the compressed image. The ratio between these images is called the compression ratio [7,51] and can be expressed as:

$$C_r = \frac{U_{size}}{C_{size}}, \qquad (1)$$

where U_{size}—uncompressed image size; C_{size}—the size of a compressed image file stored in a disk.

It must be noted that the compression ratio is calculated for the storage size, not the image data, so storing the same compressed image in the different storage formats will affect the compression ratio because of the additional data, introduced by the file format.

The aerial image is transformed from the spatial domain to the frequency domain at the decomposition stage. This process is usually lossless. The JPEG2000 and ECW algorithms use DWT to decompose an image into sub-images (sub-bands) of low-pass (approximate) and high-pass (detail) coefficients at different resolutions. The ECW algorithm exploits this decomposition during compression of images to maintain the quality close to the uncompressed imagery, and the quality at different compression ratios changes less compared to JPEG2000. The difference between JPEG2000 and ECW is the analysis and synthesis filters used for DWT. The JPEG uses a discrete cosine transform (DCT) to obtain the approximation blocks, representing the magnitude of the appropriate frequencies. DWT and DCT coefficients of the decomposed image are ordered by their impact, and coefficients contributing insignificant information to image content may be omitted. Properties like energy compaction, data decorrelation, computational speed characterize the discrete transforms and can be reused in data compression.

The quantization is an irreversible process in the lossy compression pipeline. It is a compromise between the quality of the image and the compression ratio. As the lower frequencies provide the most important part of the information in the image, there is a possibility to discard high-frequency components and reduce the amount of data considering the human eye is almost insensitive to the rapidly varying differences in brightness (high frequencies). In the JPEG pipeline, blocks containing high-frequency and thus low-importance coefficients that are close to zero are discarded to get an enhanced compression rate. The visually weighted quantization tables are exploited for the minimization of the perceptible loss of information. Considering that each sub-band has different importance based on the human perceptibility, the selection of the quantizer step-size can exploit the human visual system (HVS) model like DCT quantization tables in JPEG. The JPEG2000 uses a uniform scalar quantizer to quantize wavelet sub-band coefficients, for which the magnitudes are below the quantizer step-size. The sub-bands of each JPEG2000 image tile are further divided into non-overlapping blocks—the rectangular arrays for entropy coding. Similar to JPEG2000, the ECW quantization is adopted to the coefficients of separate wavelet sub-bands. The image compression is achieved after the quantization.

For the creation of the compressed bit stream, the JPEG2000 algorithm uses Embedded Block Coding with Optimized Truncation (EBCOT) that encompasses the arithmetic coding system. The entropy coder of JPEG uses Huffman coding. The encoded bit stream can be transmitted over communication channels or stored in repositories. The encoding procedure is lossless.

The compressed image is reconstructed via decoding, dequantization, and transformation, inverse DWT for JPEG2000/ECW and inverse DCT for JPEG. Finally, the color transform from YCbCr to the presentation color space is performed. The reconstructed aerial image is a close approximation of the original image, as distortions are introduced during lossy compression.

Since ECW is a proprietary algorithm, only the compression results can expose its peculiarities. The aerial images were compressed by the ECW algorithm using Global Mapper v20.0.1 software package [52] in our work.

3.3. Qualitative Parameters for Compressed Aerial Images

In aerial images, the different areas like grass, sand, vegetation, water, and others may be defined as regions of different textures. As the texture is defined by the local fluctuations of intensities or color brightness in an image, a human can discern the appropriate regions even in grayscale images by distinct textures. The region of rough texture is characterized by contrasting values of the neighboring pixels (e.g., forest canopy). The smooth region contains pixels of similar values (e.g., calm water) [27]. Texture characteristics are used in various application areas of remote sensing images like segmentation and classification [23,53,54]. The aerial images are rich not only in texture but also in color information. This information is used for edge detection, segmentation, classification, and other purposes [5,36,37].

The visual features depend on the image content since it is represented by the spatial arrangement and interrelationships of pixel values. The pixel-based approaches are widely used in change detection in remote sensing data [23,55]. Because of this, it is essential to evaluate the impact of lossy compression on the visual features of the aerial image content. Change detection of the texture and color characteristics can be evaluated by numerical pixel-based statistical measures [20,55]. The image does not require the prior processing to assess the statistical change of information after lossy compression and statistics are calculated for the compressed and the original image to find the differences.

There are different methods to calculate the texture features, like Gabor Filter [56], wavelet [57], Grey Level Co-occurrence Matrix (GLCM) [53–55]. The GLCM-based method is commonly used for texture analysis and discrimination using second-order histogram statistics. In [58], the authors proposed 14 statistics properties to describe the texture. There are five commonly used Haralic statistical measures (irrelative to each other) for texture analysis in remote sensing images: contrast, correlation, energy, entropy, and homogeneity [53,59]. The statistical texture measures are calculated using the probability matrix P of the GLCM method. The number of grey levels in the aerial image determines the dimensions of this matrix. The gray levels can be quantized with the cost of the reduction in the information [60]. Each element (i, j) of the probability matrix P defines the frequency of a pixel of the i grayscale intensity occurring at a specified distance d and direction θ adjacent to a pixel of a grayscale intensity j. Smaller distances are used for capturing local information [54].

In this research, we used five GLCM-based statistics to evaluate the distortions introduced into the grayscale image (Y channel of YCbCr color space) textures after lossy compression: contrast, correlation, homogeneity, energy, entropy.

The contrast [53,54,58] statistic measures the intensity contrast between each image pixel and its neighbor. This statistic presents the local variations in the image content and is defined by the equation:

$$Contrast = \sum_{i=0}^{N-1} \sum_{j=0}^{N-1} |i-j|^2 P(i,j), \qquad (2)$$

where P—the probability matrix, (i,j)—location of the current pixel.

The correlation [53,54,58] shows the link between a pixel and its neighbors. It also reflects texture similarity in the appropriate direction and will be high for the image regions with a linear structure. The correlation is expressed as:

$$Correlation = \sum_{i=0}^{N-1} \sum_{j=0}^{N-1} \frac{(i-\mu_i)(j-\mu_j)P(i,j)}{\sigma_i \sigma_j}, \qquad (3)$$

where μ_i, μ_j—the mean, σ_i, σ_j—the standard deviation.

The homogeneity [53,54,58] statistic reflects how close to the GLCM diagonal are distributed the elements of GLCM. Low contrast image exposes high values of homogeneity. This statistic is closely related to the change of the pixel intensity values in the image region. The homogeneity is calculated as:

$$Homogeneity = \sum_{i=0}^{N-1} \sum_{j=0}^{N-1} \frac{P(i,j)}{1+|i-j|}. \qquad (4)$$

The energy [53,54,58] statistic measures the uniformity. The less smooth the texture of the image is, the lower its energy value. The energy is computed as:

$$Energy = \sum_{i=0}^{N-1} \sum_{j=0}^{N-1} P^2(i,j). \qquad (5)$$

The entropy [53,54,58] measures the image information. The high entropy reflects the high complexity and disorder of the image textures. The smooth textures have low entropy values. The entropy statistic is computed as:

$$Entropy = -\sum_{i=0}^{N-1} \sum_{j=0}^{N-1} P(i,j) \log P(i,j). \qquad (6)$$

The effect of lossy compression on the image color is defined by first-order statistics—mean and standard deviation—of Cb and Cr color channels of YCbCr color space in our research. These histogram-based statistics are global as they do not localize image distortions in the spatial domain. The one-dimensional histogram is used to provide statistical information about the greyscale or color image or textures. The probability density function $p(i)$ can be calculated by dividing the values of intensity level histogram $h(i)$ by the number of image pixels $N \times M$ [61]:

$$p(i) = \frac{h(i)}{NM}, \qquad (7)$$

where $i = 0, 1, \ldots, G-1$, G—the number of image intensity levels.

The average intensity level of the image is defined by the mean statistics. The standard deviation defines the density of the image intensity dispersion around the mean.

Supervised quality metrics—PSNR, PSNR-HVS-M, SSIM, MS-SSIM—compare the distorted image with reference. We included subjective metrics alongside the commonly used supervised objective metrics to evaluate the quality of lossy aerial image compression.

Simple pixel-based differences metric—Peak Signal to Noise Ratio (PSNR) is usually used for assessment of image distortion after lossy compression. The PSNR is only an approximation to human visual perception. Peak signal to noise ratio between the original $Im(i,j)$ and compressed $Im'(i,j)$ images [62] is calculated as:

$$PSNR = 10 log_{10} \frac{2^B - 1}{\sqrt{MSE}}, \tag{8}$$

where *MSE*—the mean square error; *B*—the bits per sample.

The Mean Square Error (MSE) [62]:

$$MSE = \frac{1}{MN} \sum_{i=0}^{M-1} \sum_{j=0}^{N-1} (Im(i,j) - Im'(i,j))^2, \tag{9}$$

where *M* and *N*—the width and high of the aerial image, respectively.

For YCbCr color space, PSNR is computed as [62]:

$$PSNR_{YCbCr} = \frac{6PSNR_Y + PSNR_{Cb} + PSNR_{Cr}}{8}. \tag{10}$$

PSNR-HVS-M metric was designed to improve PSNR's performance [63,64], taking into account the HVS. The original and distorted images are divided into 8 × 8 non-overlapping blocks of pixels. The difference $\delta(i,j)$ between each distorted and original block of DCT coefficients is multiplied by a contrast masking metric (CM), and further, the result is weighted using coefficients of Contrast Sensitivity Function (CSF) [64]:

$$\delta_{PSNRHSVM}(i,j) = (\delta(i,j) \cdot CM(i,j)) \cdot CSF_{Cof}(i,j). \tag{11}$$

Then, the MSE in DCT domain [64]:

$$MSE_{PSNRHSVM}(i,j,I,J) = \frac{1}{MN} \sum_{I=1}^{M/8} \sum_{J=1}^{N/8} \left(\sum_{i=1}^{8} \sum_{j=1}^{8} (\delta_{PSNRHSVM}(i,j))^2 \right), \tag{12}$$

where (I, J)—the position of the 8 × 8 non-overlapping block in the image; (i, j)—the position of the pixel in the block.

PSNR-HVS-M is computed using Equation (8) and replacing MSE with $MSE_{PSNRHSVM}$. Values of PSNR and PSNR-HVS-M metrics are in the range $[0, +\infty]$ dB.

The Structural Similarity Index (SSIM) [65,66] shows the similarity between the two images—the original and reconstructed after compression. The changes of structural information are analyzed in the images using the structure *s*, luminance *l*, and contrast *c*. This HVS-based metric is usually applied to a luminance channel of images (Y channel of YCbCr color space). For *j*-th scale SSIM, the quality assessment is defined as [66]:

$$SSIM_j = \frac{1}{N_j} \sum_i c(x_{j,i}, y_{j,i}) s(x_{j,i}, y_{j,i}), \tag{13}$$

for $j = 1, \ldots, M-1$ and

$$SSIM_j = \frac{1}{N_j} \sum_i l(x_{j,i}, y_{j,i}) c(x_{j,i}, y_{j,i}) s(x_{j,i}, y_{j,i}), \tag{14}$$

for $j = M$. In (7) and (8), $x_{j,i}, y_{j,i}$ are *i*-th local image patches at the *j*-th scale that are extracted from *i*-th evaluation widow, and N_j—the number of the evaluation windows in the scale.

The overall multiscale SSIM is denoted as MS-SSIM [66] and is expressed by the equation:

$$MSSSIM = \prod_{j=1}^{M} (SSIM_j)^{\beta_j}, \tag{15}$$

where β_j—the values that are obtained through psychophysical measurements [56].

The values of SSIM and MS-SSIM metrics are in the range from [0, 1]. High image quality is indicated by the high score of SSIM, MS-SSIM, PSNR, and PSNR-HVS-M.

A subjective evaluation of the distorted image quality is based on human visual perception. This method is called the Mean Opinion Score (MOS) [62] and defines the average score of opinions. MOS is commonly used to assess the image quality in a broad spectrum of applications, including image compression. Human judgment is important, but the subjective method is time-consuming and can fail to evaluate high-resolution images because of the vast amount of the data present; it is almost impossible to perceive and estimate the small distortions. This method is reasonable to combine with objective methods.

These four groups of qualitative parameters are presented in Figure 3.

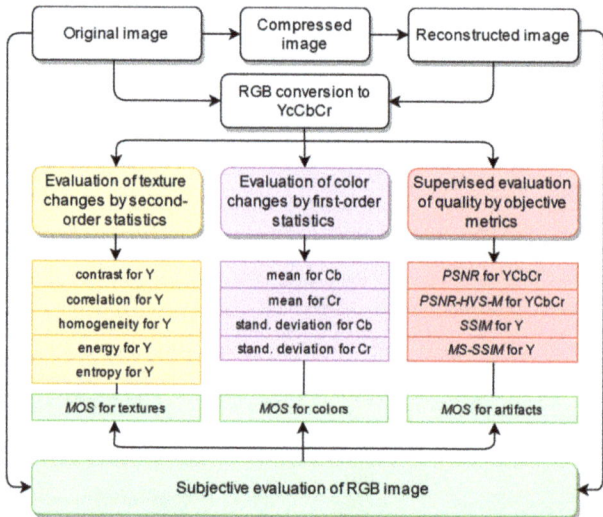

Figure 3. Qualitative parameters for the evaluation of the reconstructed aerial image after lossy compression. Different colors represent different groups of qualitative parameters.

They were used as criteria for the qualitative evaluation of aerial image lossy compression using MCDM methodology. The chosen combination of the different types of qualitative measurements can improve the qualitative assessment of the image reconstructed after lossy compression.

3.4. Evaluation of the Criteria Weights

One of the constituent parts of MCDM methods is the determination of criteria weights. The criteria weights were assessed using the subjective direct weight determination method. The majority of the present methods for the determination of criteria weights are based on the subjective expert judgment [67,68]. The direct weighting method of criteria importance was used in most cases. This widespread, while subjective, method has higher accuracy compared to the ranking method [68]. Using the criteria weights direct determination method, the sum of all the assessment weights of each expert must be equal to 100% or 1.0 [69–71].

The qualitative parameters—criteria—were provided for the experts to evaluate their importance. The calculation of the importance of a criterion $\overline{c}_i$ is calculated according to (16):

$$\overline{c}_i = \frac{\sum_{k=1}^{r} c_{ik}}{r} \qquad (16)$$

where c_{ik}—the estimation value of i criterion by k expert, and r is the number of experts.

The weights of the criteria are calculated using (17):

$$w_i = \frac{\sum_{k=1}^{r} c_{ik}}{\sum_{i=1}^{m} \sum_{k=1}^{r} c_{ik}} \quad (17)$$

where r is the number of experts, m—the number of criteria, c_{ik}—i criterion by k expert.

The assessment of the importance of qualitative parameters by experts and the calculated weight of each parameter are presented in Table 1.

Table 1. Evaluation of the importance of criteria and their weights.

Criteria of Images	Optimum	Experts					Average Criteria Values	Criteria Weights
		1st	2nd	3rd	4th	5th		
Change of Y contrast, C_1	min	2	3	2	2	2	2.2	0.022
Change of Y correlation, C_2	min	2	3	3	1	3	2.4	0.024
Change of Y homogeneity, C_3	min	2	3	4	4	3	3.2	0.032
Change of Y energy, C_4	min	9	10	8	8	9	8.8	0.088
Change of Y entropy, C_5	min	9	10	9	10	10	9.6	0.096
MOS for RGB image textures, C_6	max	7	8	8	8	9	8.0	0.080
Change of Cb mean, C_7	min	10	9	10	10	8	9.4	0.094
Change of Cr mean, C_8	min	9	9	8	9	10	9.0	0.090
Change of Cb standard deviation, C_9	min	5	3	5	4	3	4.0	0.040
Change of Cr standard deviation, C_{10}	min	3	3	4	4	2	3.2	0.032
MOS for RGB image colors, C_{11}	max	8	7	6	9	6	7.2	0.072
SSIM for Y component of YCbCr, C_{12}	max	8	6	6	6	7	6.6	0.066
MS-SSIM for Y component of YCbCr, C_{13}	max	8	7	7	6	9	7.4	0.074
PSNR for YCbCr image, C_{14}	max	6	5	4	5	5	5.0	0.050
PSNR-HVS-M for YCbCr image, C_{15}	max	5	6	8	6	7	6.4	0.064
MOS for RGB image artifacts, C_{16}	min	7	8	8	8	7	7.6	0.076

3.5. MCDM WASPAS Method for Data Processing and Evaluation

In the present research, WASPAS has been selected for the exploration of the problem related to the qualitative rating of aerial image lossy compression. The applications of the WASPAS method were presented in [67]. The WASPAS approach is used for the solution to a broad range MCDM problems. This method is popular due to stability and simplicity. WASPAS method initially was introduced in [72] and later was extended by single-valued neutrosophic sets (WASPAS-SVNS) [73]. Although this method has been already used to solve different MCDM tasks [74,75], we could not find any research where WASPAS was applied to assess the lossy compression in the satellite images.

WASPAS-SVNS approach can be decomposed into several steps [73] presented below:

1. For the construction of the decision matrix, we need to have the initial information that consists of the evaluations of lossy compression algorithms and compression ratios (as alternatives) according to the qualitative parameters of compressed aerial images (as criteria). When the decision matrix X is constructed, vector normalization is used to normalize the decision matrix X.

$$\widetilde{x}_{ij} = \frac{x_{ij}}{\sqrt{\sum_{i=1}^{m}(x_{ij})^2}} \quad (18)$$

Here, $x_{ij}, i = 1, \ldots m; j = 1, \ldots n$ is the value of the of jth variable for the ith ithalternative (criteria).

2. Then, the neutrosophication and calculation of the neutrosophic decision matrix $\widetilde{X}^n$ are performed. For the conversion between crisp normalized values $\widetilde{x}_{ij}$ and single-valued neutrosophic numbers (SVNNs), $\widetilde{X}^n$ is calculated. Elements of the neutrosophic decision matrix $\widetilde{X}^n$ are the single-valued neutrosophic numbers $\widetilde{x}_{ij}^n = (t_{ij}, i_{ij}, f_{ij})$, where t is the membership degree, i—the indeterminacy degree and f—the non-membership degree. The standard crisp-to-neutrosophic mapping will be applied in this study.

3. The first decision component that is based on the sum of the total relative importance of the ith alternative is calculated by the equation:

$$\widetilde{Q}_i^{(1)} = \sum_{j=1}^{L_{max}} \widetilde{x}_{+ij}^n \cdot w_{+j} + \left(\sum_{j=1}^{L_{min}} \widetilde{x}_{-ij}^n \cdot w_{-j} \right)^c \quad (19)$$

Here, the values $\widetilde{x}_{+ij}^n$ and w_{+j} are associated with the criteria which are maximized; consequently, $\widetilde{x}_{-ij}^n$ and w_{-j} correspond to the criteria which are minimized. The weight of criteria is an arbitrary positive real number, the amount of the maximized criteria is L_{max}, and the amount of the minimized criteria is L_{min}. For the single-valued neutrosophic numbers (SVNNs), the following algebra operations should be applied:

$$\widetilde{x}_1^n \oplus \widetilde{x}_2^n = (t_1 + t_2 - t_1 t_2, i_1 i_2, f_1 f_2) \quad (20)$$

$$\widetilde{x}_1^n \otimes \widetilde{x}_2^n = (t_1 t_2, i_1 + i_2 - i_1 i_2, f_1 + f_2 - f_1 f_2) \quad (21)$$

$$w \widetilde{x}_1^n = \left(1 - (1 - t_1)^w, i_1^w, f_1^w \right), w > 0 \quad (22)$$

$$\widetilde{x}_1^{nw} = \left(t_1^w, 1 - (1 - i_1)^w, 1 - (1 - f_1)^w \right), w > 0 \quad (23)$$

$$\widetilde{x}_1^{nc} = (f_1, 1 - i_1, t_1) \quad (24)$$

Here, $\widetilde{x}_1^n = (t_1, i_1, f_1)$ and $\widetilde{x}_2^n = (t_2, i_2, f_2)$.

4. The second decision component based on the product of total relative importance in the ith alternative is calculated by the equation:

$$\widetilde{Q}_i^{(2)} = \prod_{j=1}^{L_{max}} \left(\widetilde{x}_{+ij}^n \right)^{w_{+j}} \cdot \left(\prod_{j=1}^{L_{min}} \left(\widetilde{x}_{-ij}^n \right)^{w_{-j}} \right)^c \quad (25)$$

5. The following equation calculates the weighted criteria:

$$\widetilde{Q}_i = 0.5 \widetilde{Q}_i^{(1)} + 0.5 \widetilde{Q}_i^{(2)} \quad (26)$$

6. The final ranking of the alternatives is evaluated considering the descending order of the $S(\widetilde{Q}_i)$. This is a score function (further referred to as utility function) for deneutrosophication of the joint generalized criteria and is calculated as follows:

$$S(\widetilde{Q}_i) = \frac{3 + t_i - 2i_i - f_i}{4} \quad (27)$$

4. An MCDM Application for the Selection of Lossy Compression Algorithms and Discussion

In this section, we present the verification of the proposed methodology on the qualitative selection of lossy compression for the aerial images. The aerial images of different content and resolution were selected for the compression and the qualitative evaluation of their lossy compression. The set of qualitative parameters named criteria, encompass the general image quality assessment metrics, first-order color statistics, second-order texture statistics, and subjective evaluation. The influence of the lossy compression algorithms with different compression ratios to the aerial images' content was estimated using the set of criteria. The compression algorithms with appropriate compression ratios were ranked according to the qualitative degradation for corresponding compressed image using the neutrosophic WASPAS-SVNS method.

4.1. Compression of Aerial Images

Three lossy compression algorithms were selected for the initial experiment: JPEG200, ECW, JPEG. As the quality of the compressed image depends not only on the compression algorithm but also on the compression ratio, four compression ratios were selected for each algorithm named as follows: low (25:1), medium (50:1), high (75:1), very high (100:1). The influence of the compression ratios lower than 25:1 is negligible, as shown in [19,31,34]. Higher compression ratios deteriorated image quality significantly and were not estimated in this work. Larger intervals between compression ratios were chosen to make their effect on the content of an image more explicit. Each algorithm introduces unique artifacts to the image content that are more noticeable in the higher compression ratios.

The GLOBAL MAPPER software [46] was used for the ECW compression of the original aerial images. The RGB color *.tiff* image file saved as the *.ecw* image using Global Mapper changing the compression ratios. The *imwrite()* function from MATLAB was used for JPEG2000 and JPEG compression. The source images were obtained as TIFF images with lossless compression. The JPEG2000 compressed files were generated using the *imwrite* (... , "CompressionRatio", Value) function, altering *Value* for the target compression ratio. For JPEG compression *imwrite* (... , "Quality", Value) function was used, altering *Value* as the quality from 100 to 1 of the JPEG compressed file. The smaller the number, the more compression will be reached with the worse quality for the image. All other settings for the *imwrite()* function were set to default values. The experimental compression ratios were tailored and verified using Equation (1).

The content and resolution of the image also affect the result of the lossy compressed image. Relevant compression algorithms have different effects on image textures, colors, and luminance. Three high-resolution (1 pixel = 0.5 m) aerial images of different content were selected using Earth Explorer [76]. The aerial images used in the experiment (Figure 4) are "img1", "img2", and "img3" of the dataset *200710_myrtle_beach_sc_0x5000m_utm_clr*, saved as 3000 × 3000 24-bit TIFF images in RGB (8 bits for each band). The "img1" has more smooth textures with low spatial frequencies of intensity changes, and the large regions of different colors and intensities dominate in it. The "img2" is rich with similar rough textures with high spatial frequencies of intensity changes, and small regions occupy a slight part of the image. The "img3" has various types of textures, and a large number of regions differ in size, color, and intensity [27]. We have tested other images with similar textures and colors to verify objective qualitative parameters. Images were selected by the varying characteristic features (texture, color tone, luminance, number, and size of the objects) but not by the appropriate classes, as the aim is to verify the methodology.

For the other three images of different resolutions, the original images were reduced four times using the *impyramid()* MATLAB function. The reduced "img1", "img2", and "img3" will be referenced as "img4", "img5", and "img6" accordingly, with the resolution of 1 pixel = 2 m and the size of 750 × 750 pixels. The remote sensing images with higher spatial resolution have richer spatial textures as their pixels contain more information compared to low-resolution images. All six images of different structures were compressed using three different algorithms using four compression ratios. Figure 5 presents the cropped images "img1" and "img4" compressed using JPEG2000, ECW, and JPEG algorithms at a 100:1 compression ratio.

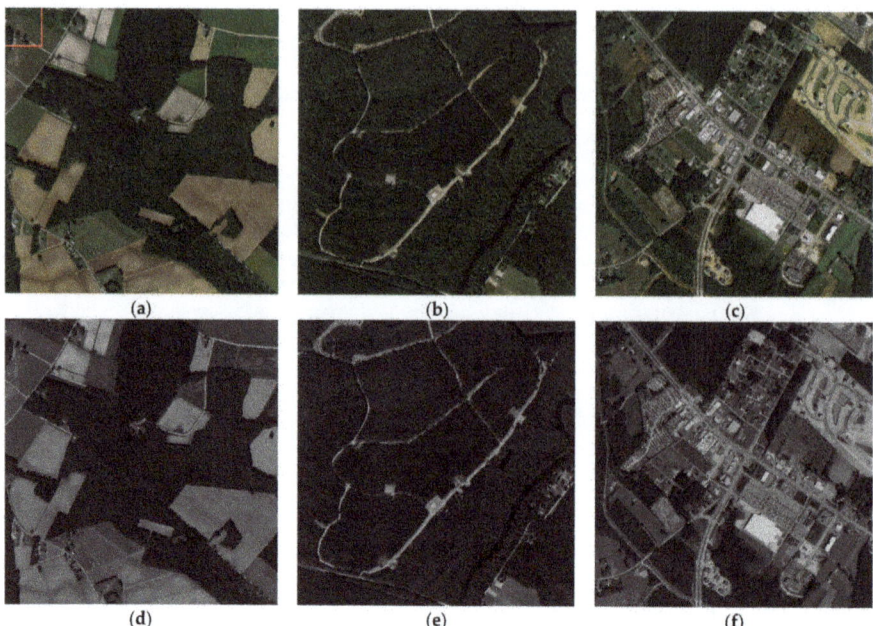

Figure 4. The original aerial images used in the experiment (Landsat-7 images courtesy of the U.S. Geological Survey): (**a**) "img1" in RGB. The red rectangular indicates a cropped region presented in Figure 5); (**b**) "img2" in RGB; (**c**) "img3" in RGB; dataset *200710_myrtle_beach_sc_0x5000m_utm_clr*. (**d**) "img1", component Y; (**e**) "img2", component Y; (**f**) "img3", component Y.

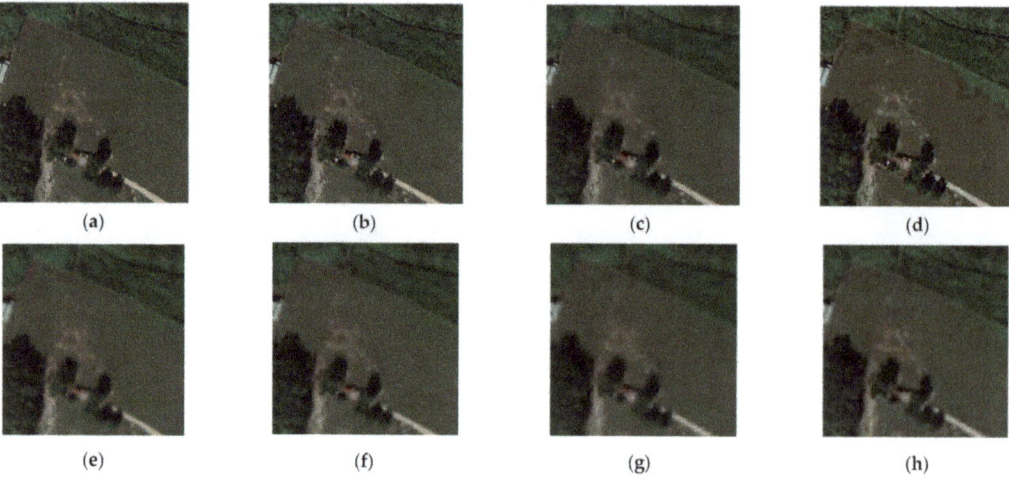

Figure 5. The same cropped region of the aerial images "img1" and "img4" compressed using different lossy compression algorithms at the compression ratio 100:1: (**a**) "img1", the original image; (**b**) "img1", Joint Photographic Experts Group (JPEG)2000 compression; (**c**) "img1", Enhanced Compression Wavelet (ECW) compression; (**d**) "img1", JPEG compression; (**e**) "img4", the reduced "img1"; (**f**) "img4", JPEG2000 compression; (**g**) "img4", ECW compression; (**h**) "img4", JPEG compression.

4.2. Qualitative Evaluation of Aerial Image Lossy Compression

The qualitative evaluation was performed using MATLAB. After lossy compression of images "img1", "img2", "img3", "img4", "img5", and "img6" all selected qualitative parameters were calculated and estimated using the original and reconstructed versions of the aerial images.

The first group of parameters—texture change of images after compression—includes the second-order statistics: contrast (Equation (2)), correlation (Equation (3)), homogeneity (Equation (4)), energy (Equation (5)), and entropy (Equation (6)). The GLCM-based statistics were calculated for the luminance component in the YCbCr space of the original and compressed images. The difference between them was used to evaluate texture changes. The size of the probability matrix P of the GLCM method was determined by the number of the original gray levels in the Y component. The smaller distances between the image pixel of interest and its neighboring pixel are used to capture local texture information. For 3000 × 3000 images with the resolution of 1 pixel = 0.5 m and for 750 × 750 images with resolution of 1 pixel = 2 m were taken different displacements (respectively, d = 1, 2, 3, 4, 5, 6, and d = 1) for six directions (θ = 0°, 45°, 90°, 135°, 180°, 225°, 270° and 315°) as the texture changes are to be assessed in the same area. The extra pixel in each direction is used to minimize the influence of pixel-shifting during image resizing. The mean of each GLCM's texture statistic was calculated to define final contrast, correlation, homogeneity, energy, and entropy measures used to evaluate changes after lossy compression. Calculated texture changes between the original and compressed images are presented in Figure 6a–e. The more significant difference between the qualitative parameters of textures of the original and distorted images, the higher impact of lossy compression was on the loss of image texture information. As seen from Figure 6a,e, changes of texture contrast and entropy commonly increase with increasing compression ratios for the selected algorithms. However, statistical changes in textures increase in the negative direction for correlation, homogeneity, and energy as the compression ratios increase (Figure 6b–d). Table 2 in the first five rows shows the same results for the calculated qualitative texture parameters, respectively, C_1, C_2, C_3, C_4, and C_5 but only for the "img1". The differences between the qualitative parameters of textures of the original and distorted images slightly decrease in some cases from the lower compression ratios to the higher as presented in Figure 6c,e, respectively, for homogeneity and entropy changes using ECW lossy compression from 75:1 to 100:1 compression ratios for "img5".

The second group of parameters—color change of images after compression—includes the first-order statistics: mean and standard deviation of Cb and Cr components. Calculated color changes between the original and the compressed images are presented in Figure 6g,h,i,j. The more significant the difference between the original and distorted images' qualitative color parameters, the higher the impact of lossy compression on the distortions of color information. Changes of chrominance (mean and standard deviation) commonly increase with increasing compression ratios for the selected algorithms. Rows from 7 to 10 in Table 2 show the calculated results of the qualitative texture parameters C_7, C_8, C_9, and C_{10} for the "img1". For JPEG lossy compression ratios from 75:1 to 100:1, the change of the mean for the Cb component considerably decreases for "img6", as presented in Figure 6g.

The third group of parameters—supervised objective IQA metrics—includes PSNR for YCbCr image (Equation (8)), PSNR-HVS-M for YCbCr image (Equation (10)), SSIM for Y component (Equations (13) and (14)), MS-SSIM for Y component (Equation (15)). The supervised objective quality metrics compare the compressed images with the original, and the better image quality is indicated by a higher score (Figure 6l–o). The same results of IQA metrics for the "img1" are presented in Table 2, rows 12 to 15, respectively, including criteria C_{12}, C_{13}, C_{14}, and C_{15}. IQA metrics decrease with increasing compression ratios for the selected algorithms for all images.

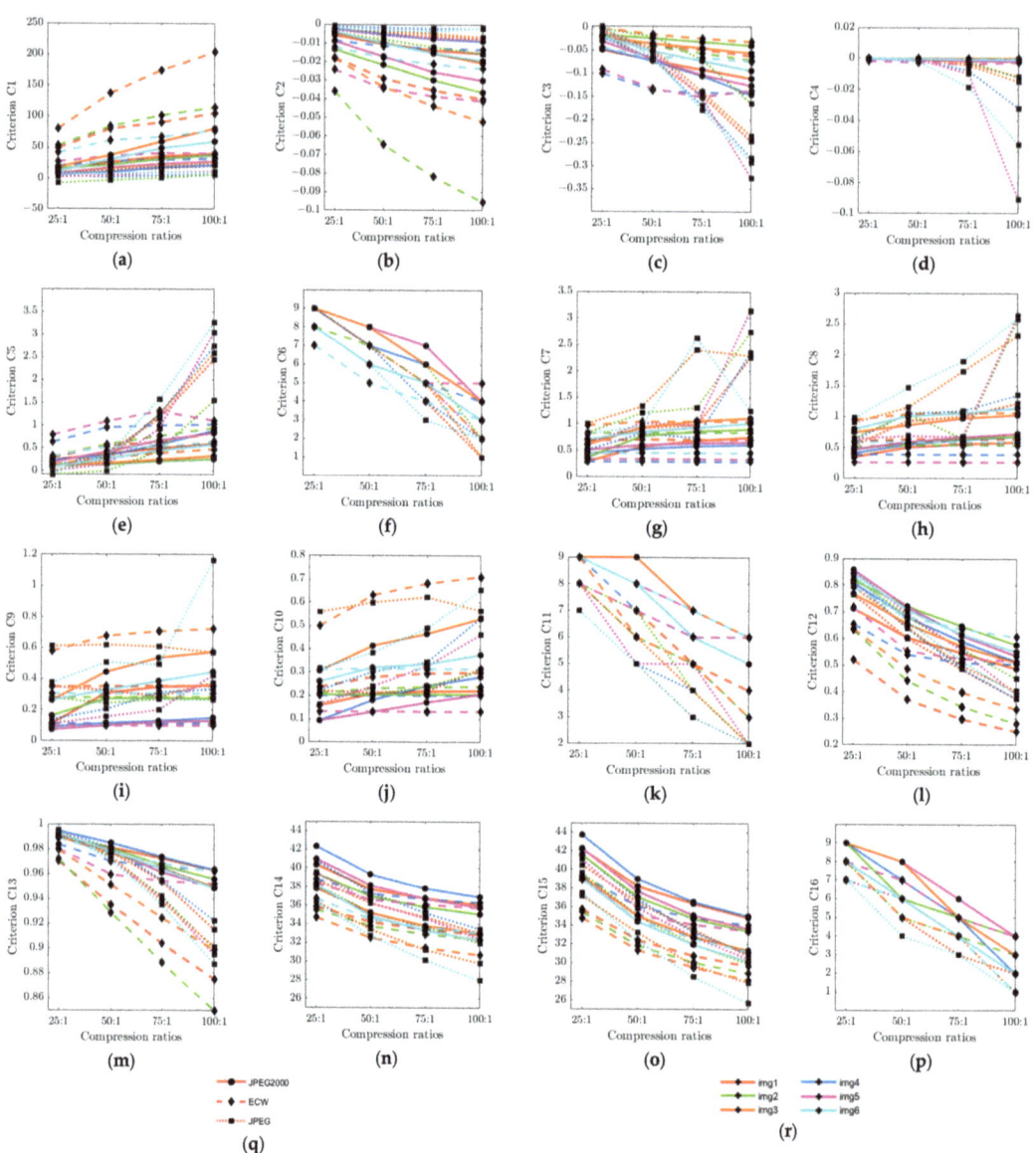

Figure 6. Influence of lossy compression with selected compression ratios to the quality of the reconstructed different aerial images after compression. Distinct colors represent aerial images "img1", "img2", "img3", "img4", "img5" and "img6". Different line types represent lossy compression algorithms JPEG2000, ECW, JPEG. Each figure shows the results of the selected qualitative parameter (criterion) for the six images compressed with different algorithms: (**a**) C_1—contrast change for Y component; (**b**) C_2—correlation change for Y component; (**c**) C_3—homogeneity change for Y component; (**d**) C_4—energy change for Y component; (**e**) C_5—entropy change for Y component; (**f**) C_6—MOS for RGB image texture; (**g**) C_7—change of the mean of Cb component; (**h**) C_8—change of the mean of Cr component; (**i**) C_9—change of the standard deviation of Cb component; (**j**) C_{10}—change of the standard deviation of Cr component; (**k**) C_{11}—MOS for RGB image colors; (**l**) C_{12}—SSIM for Y component; (**m**) C_{13}—MS-SSIM for Y component; (**n**) C_{14}—PSNR for YCbCr image; (**o**) C_{15}—PSNR-HVS-M for YCbCr image; (**p**) C_{16}—MOS for RGB image artifacts; (**q**) legends for marking the separate algorithms in each figure; (**r**) legends for marking the separate images in each figure.

Table 2. Impact of the lossy compression algorithms with relevant compression ratios to the aerial image "img1" content.

Qualitative Parameters (Criteria) of Images	Criteria Optimum	Compression Algorithm, Compression Ratio (Alternatives)														
		JPEG2000 25:1, A_1	ECW, 25:1, A_2	JPEG, 25:1, A_3	JPEG2000 50:1, A_4	ECW, 50:1, A_5	JPEG, 50:1, A_6	JPEG2000 75:1, A_7	ECW, 75:1, A_8	JPEG, 75:1, A_9	JPEG2000 100:1, A_{10}	ECW, 100:1, A_{11}	JPEG, 100:1, A_{12}	JPEG2000 A01, A_{13}	ECW-A02, A_{14}	JPEG-A03, A_{15}
Change of Y contrast, C_1	min	14.5651	48.7378	7.1548	26.0821	79.8598	12.1424	35.1855	89.8264	16.5589	39.4098	104.8575	21.0296	35.1855	79.8598	12.1424
Change of Y correlation, C_2	min	−0.0057	−0.0178	−0.0028	−0.0103	−0.0291	−0.0050	−0.0139	−0.0355	−0.0065	−0.0156	−0.0402	−0.0077	−0.0139	−0.0291	−0.0050
Change of Y homogeneity, C_3	min	−0.0483	−0.0180	−0.0164	−0.0722	−0.0395	−0.0708	−0.0917	−0.0477	−0.1475	−0.1109	−0.0619	−0.2465	−0.0917	−0.0395	−0.0708
Change of Y energy, C_4	min	−0.0001	−0.0001	−0.00004	−0.0002	−0.0002	−0.0006	−0.0003	−0.0002	−0.0033	−0.0004	−0.0004	−0.0118	−0.0003	−0.0002	−0.0006
Change of Y entropy, C_5	min	0.2388	0.2998	0.0773	0.3784	0.5623	0.3958	0.4936	0.6272	1.1482	0.5946	0.8330	2.4476	0.4936	0.5623	0.3958
MOS for RGB image textures, C_6	max	9	8	9	8	7	7	6	5	4	4	2	1	6	7	7
Change of Cb mean, C_7	min	0.2966	0.6955	0.6452	0.5759	0.7086	0.9265	0.6897	0.7065	0.9880	0.7523	0.7066	2.2541	0.7523	0.7065	0.9265
Change of Cr mean, C_8	min	0.3514	0.6056	0.5366	0.5097	0.6388	0.9350	0.5605	0.6429	1.0032	0.5920	0.6428	1.2186	0.5920	0.6429	0.9350
Change of Cb standard deviation, C_9	min	0.1128	0.3493	0.3522	0.3083	0.3524	0.3253	0.3483	0.3537	0.2878	0.3576	0.3538	0.3737	0.3576	0.3537	0.3253
Change of Cr standard deviation, C_{10}	min	0.1579	0.2374	0.2199	0.2089	0.2797	0.2130	0.2182	0.2955	0.2199	0.2207	0.2988	0.3151	0.2207	0.2955	0.2130
MOS for RGB image colors, C_{11}	max	9	8	8	8	7	5	7	5	3	6	4	2	6	5	5
SSIM for Y component of YCbCr, C_{12}	max	0.7125	0.5208	0.7647	0.6038	0.3720	0.6012	0.5460	0.2979	0.4854	0.4866	0.2509	0.3742	0.5460	0.3720	0.6012
MS-SSIM for Y component of YCbCr, C_{13}	max	0.9891	0.9704	0.9935	0.9811	0.9350	0.9773	0.9724	0.9037	0.9541	0.9632	0.8750	0.9149	0.9724	0.9350	0.9773
PSNR for YCbCr image, C_{14}	max	40.3640	35.8226	38.7328	37.7416	34.2080	36.2407	36.7678	33.4156	34.7346	36.0396	32.8686	32.9938	36.7678	34.2080	36.2407
PSNR-HVS-M for YCbCr image, C_{15}	max	42.1918	35.7247	40.4886	38.1932	32.4256	36.4482	36.3451	30.7566	33.5373	34.8503	29.6463	30.8029	36.3451	32.4256	36.4482
MOS for RGB image artifacts, C_{16}	min	9	8	8	6	5	5	5	4	3	4	3	2	5	5	5

The fourth group of parameters—subjective evaluations of RGB images after compression —includes MOS values in the range from 1 to 10 using a 10-point Likert scale [77] for the quality of image textures, colors, and artifacts after compression. The meaning of the qualitative parameters C_6, C_{11}, C_{16}, and a rating scale was explained to the 15 students of Information Technologies. They were provided with a questionnaire (see Appendix A) and an individual blank response table (Table 2), excluding all rows except the sixth, eleventh, and sixteenth. The respondents were asked to fill the response tables for the six images. The assessments' mean values were calculated and included as criteria C_6, C_{11}, and C_{16}. Estimated MOS values for textures, colors, general artifacts after lossy compression are presented in both Table 2 and Figure 6f,k,p.

The threshold for the acceptable visible distortions in aerial images reconstructed after each lossy compression was estimated visually by five experts from Vilnius Gediminas technical university, Department of Graphical systems with at least 15 years of experience in image processing. These experts also present their opinion concerning the image visual criteria weights considered in Section 3.4. The qualitative parameters from acceptable compression ratios for each algorithm and image were taken considering their groups—texture, color, IQA. Three threshold alternatives—JPEG2000-A01, ECW-A02, JPEG-A03—were constructed to evaluate acceptable visible distortions for each algorithm (Table 2, A_{13}, A_{14}, A_{15}). The threshold alternatives help to decide at which compression ratios of selected lossy compression algorithms are aerial images' distortions visually acceptable.

4.3. Ranking of Aerial Image Lossy Compression

After the alternatives were defined and qualitative criteria were calculated, the initial decision matrix for qualitative evaluation of the lossy compression of aerial images was formed. The example of the initial decision matrix for "img1" is presented in Table 2. As the matrix has negative values for the change of correlation, homogeneity, and energy, to make calculations consistent with WASPAS-SVNS, the rows with negative values were upshifted before the vector normalization. The obtained results by WASPAS-SVNS methodology described in Section 3.5 (steps 2–6) are presented in Table 3. The qualitative ranking of images' lossy compression was calculated using the utility function $S(\tilde{Q}_i)$ (Equation (27)). Figure 7 presents the ranking of lossy compression for high and low-resolution images. Ranking of compression algorithms based on their qualitative suitability for the images makes it difficult to decide which compression ratios of lossy compression are unacceptable for visual inspection. Qualitative ranking by estimating the threshold of acceptable visual distortions places the algorithms with their compression ratios in order of priority, excluding those whose distortions are greater than the subjectively determined quality threshold (Table 3, Figure 8).

Table 3. Qualitative ranking of aerial images' lossy compression.

No	Alternatives	Utility Function $S(\tilde{Q}_i)$						Rank by WASPAS					
		"img1"	"img2"	"img3"	"img4"	"img5"	"img6"	"img1"	"img2"	"img3"	"img4"	"img5"	"img6"
1	JPEG200025:1, A_1	0.7673	0.7554	0.7526	0.7578	0.7647	0.7472	1	1	1	1	1	1
2	ECW 25:1, A_2	0.7157	0.7161	0.7343	0.7372	0.7258	0.7380	4	5	2	3	5	2
3	JPEG25:1, A_3	0.7380	0.7410	0.7268	0.7387	0.7389	0.7327	2	2	4	2	2	4
4	JPEG200050:1, A_4	0.7243	0.7218	0.7263	0.7329	0.7387	0.7160	3	4	5	6	3	8
5	ECW 50:1, A_5	0.6820	0.6799	0.7060	0.7135	0.6829	0.7175	10	12	8	8	10	7
6	JPEG 50:1, A_6	0.6866	0.6994	0.6666	0.7007	0.7021	0.6820	8	8	12	10	8	11
7	JPEG200075:1, A_7	0.7049	0.7069	0.6970	0.7076	0.7072	0.6885	5	7	9	9	7	10
8	ECW 75:1, A_8	0.6645	0.6551	0.6942	0.6881	0.6601	0.7033	12	13	10	11	12	9
9	JPEG 75:1, A_9	0.6479	0.6835	0.6275	0.6632	0.6132	0.5651	13	10	14	14	14	14
10	JPEG2000100:1, A_{10}	0.6889	0.6918	0.6624	0.6785	0.6819	0.6612	7	9	13	13	11	13
11	ECW 100:1, A_{11}	0.6397	0.6285	0.6783	0.6880	0.6293	0.6754	14	14	11	12	13	12
12	JPEG100:1, A_{12}	0.5041	0.4853	0.4612	0.3991	0.4906	0.4856	15	15	15	15	15	15
13	JPEG2000-A01, A_{13}	0.7002	0.7079	0.7159	0.7329	0.7282	0.7248	6	6	7	7	4	6
14	ECW-A01, A_{14}	0.6787	0.6799	0.7324	0.7363	0.6987	0.7370	11	11	3	4	9	3
15	JPEG-A01, A_{15}	0.6866	0.7223	0.7261	0.7343	0.7199	0.7327	9	3	6	5	6	5

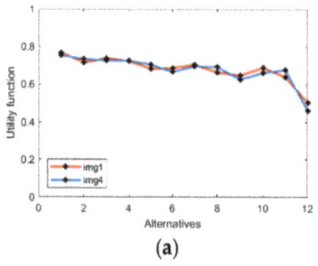 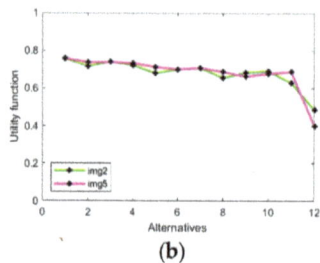 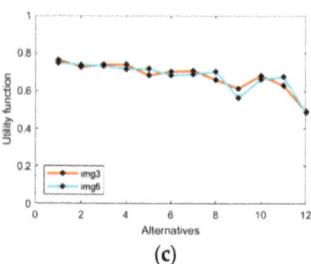

Figure 7. Qualitative ranking of the high- and low-resolution aerial images' lossy compression using the selected alternatives as 1 (A_1)—JPEG2000, 25:1; 2 (A_2)—ECW, 25:1; 3 (A_3)—JPEG, 25:1; 4 (A_4)—JPEG2000, 50:1; 5 (A_5)—ECW, 50:1; 6 (A_6)—JPEG, 50:1; 7 (A_7)—JPEG2000, 75:1; 8 (A_8)—ECW, 75:1; 9 (A_9)—JPEG, 75:1; 10 (A_{10})—JPEG2000, 100:1; 11 (A_{11})—ECW, 100:1; 12 (A_{12})—JPEG, 100:1: (**a**) "img1" and its reduced version "img4"; (**b**) "img2" and its reduced version "img5"; (**c**) "img3" and its reduced version "img6".

As presented in Table 3 and Figure 7a–c graphs, the ranking of algorithms with different compression ratios according to the qualitative suitability for the high-resolution images "img1" and "img2" do not coincide. The "img3" ranking differs more from the first two because its content has more features sensitive to the lossy compression, such as the different types of textures, many small regions of different colors and intensities. The best quality presents JPEG2000 25:1 compression for all high-resolution images (1st place in Table 3, row 1), and the worst—JPEG 100:1 (15th place in Table 3, row 12). The JPEG2000 algorithm maintains better image quality than ECW and JPEG at compression ratios 50:1, 75:1, 100:1 (Table 3, JPEG2000 alternatives at 1st, 4th, 7th, 10th rows) too. Considering the threshold alternative A_{13} for the JPEG2000 algorithm (Table 3, 13th row), a visually acceptable lossy compression for "img1" and "img2" was ranked above 6th place and for "img3" above 7th place. This corresponds to JPEG2000 compression lower than 100:1 for "img1" (Figure 8a) and lower than 75:1 for "img2" and "img3" (Figure 8e,f). ECW and JPEG algorithms were ranked worse than JPE2000 at all compression ratios. At lower compression ratios 25:1, 50:1, the JPEG algorithm (Table 3, JPEG alternatives at 3rd, 6th rows) was ranked higher than the ECW algorithm for "img1" and "img2". However, for "img3" can be seen the opposite tendency. At higher compression ratios 75:1, 100:1, the JPEG algorithm (Table 3, JPEG alternatives at 9th, 12th rows) was ranked worse than the ECW algorithm for "img1" and "img3". For "img2", JPEG 75:1 was ranked higher than ECW 75:1. Considering the threshold alternative A_{15} for the JPEG algorithm (Table 3, 15th row), a visually acceptable lossy compression for "img1" was ranked above 9th place, for "img2" above 3rd place, and for "img3" above 6th place. This corresponds to JPEG compression lower than 75:1 for "img1" (near to 50:1 and less, Figure 8a), lower than 50:1 for "img2" and "img3" (near to 25:1 and less Figure 8e,f). The ECW compression rating is presented in 2nd, 5th, 8th, 11th rows of Table 3. At lower compression ratios 25:1, 50:1, the ECW algorithm was rated worse than the JPEG algorithm for "img1" and "img2", but at very high—100:1—compression ratios was rated higher than JPEG2000. Considering the threshold alternative $A14$ for the ECW algorithm (Table 3, 14th row), a visually acceptable lossy compression for "img1" was ranked above 11th place, for "img2" above 12th place, and for "img3" above 3rd place. This corresponds to ECW compression lower than 75:1 for "img1" (near to 50:1 and less, Figure 8a), and lower than 50:1 for "img2" and "img3" (near to 25:1 and less, Figure 8e,f).

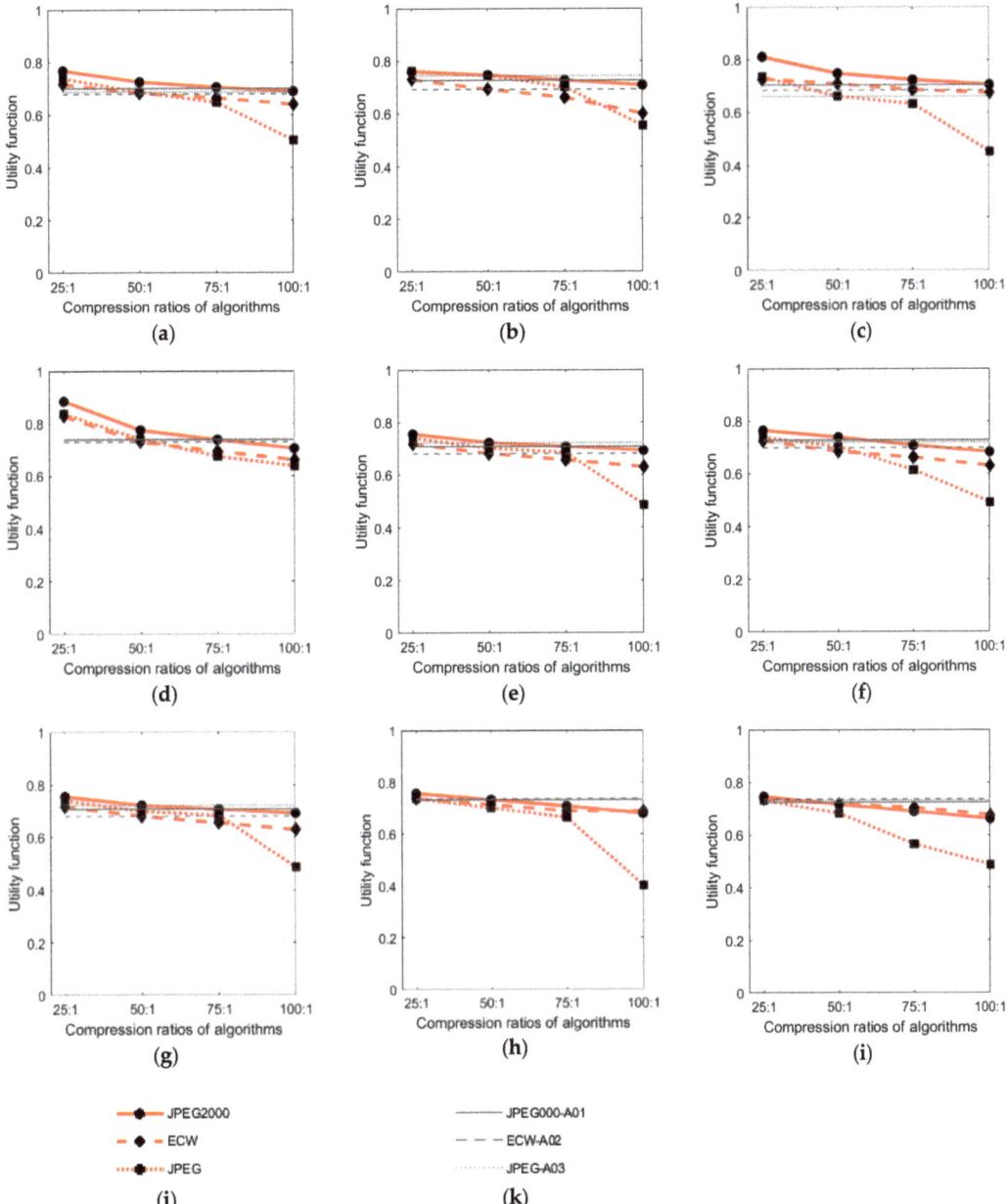

Figure 8. Qualitative ranking of lossy compression algorithms with selected compression ratios solving the full and partial tasks for aerial images: (**a**) "img1"—by all the selected qualitative parameters (**b**) "img1"—by the texture quality; (**c**) "img1"—by the color quality; (**d**) "img1"—by the general quality metrics; (**e**) "img2"—by the all selected qualitative parameters; (**f**) "img3"—by the all selected qualitative parameters; (**g**) "img4"—by the all selected qualitative parameters; (**h**) "img5"—by the all selected qualitative parameters; (**i**) "img6"—by the all selected qualitative parameters; (**j**) legends for marking the compression algorithms for each image; (**k**) legends for marking the thresholds of compression quality of separate algorithms for each image.

A similar ranking tendency is observed for the corresponding low-resolution images "img4", "img5", and "img6" (Figure 8), but the changes of images' content due to the reduced resolution made the influence on the rating of lossy compression. The best quality presents JPEG2000 25:1 compression for all low-resolution images (1st place–Table 3, row 1), and the worst—JPEG 100:1 (15th place—Table 3, row 12). The JPEG2000 algorithm maintains better quality than ECW and JPEG at compression ratios 50:1 and 75:1 for "img4" and "img5", but at 100:1 for "img5" is superior ECW compression (Table 3, JPEG2000 alternatives at 4th, 7th, 10th rows). ECW compression at compression ratios 50:1, 75:1, 100:1 is superior to JPEG2000 compression for "img6" too. Considering the threshold alternative A_{13} for the JPEG2000 algorithm, a visually acceptable lossy compression for "img4" was ranked above 7th place, for "img5" above 4th place, and "img6" above 6th place. This corresponds to JPEG2000 compression lower than 75:1 for "img4" and "img5" (near to 50:1 and less, Figure 8g,h), and lower than 50:1 for "img6". At higher compression ratios 75:1, 100:1, the ECW algorithm was ranked higher than the JPEG for the selected low-resolution images, but at low—25:1—compression ratios was ranked worse than JPEG for "img4" and "img5". Considering the threshold alternative A_{14} for the ECW algorithm, a visually acceptable lossy compression for "img4" was ranked above 4th place, for "img5" above 9th place, and "img6" above 3rd place. This corresponds to ECW compression lower than 50:1 for "img4", "img5," and "img6" (near to 25:1 and less, Figure 8g–i). A visually acceptable JPEG lossy compression for was ranked by $A15$ alternative for "img4" above 5th place, for "img5" above 6th place, and "img6" above 5th place. This corresponds to JPEG compression lower than 50:1 for "img4", "img5," and "img6" (for all images near to 25:1 and less, Figure 8g–i).

The effect of lossy compression on the image content can be evaluated more precisely by the set of qualitative parameters and by using the parameters of the texture, color, and IQA, different subtasks can be solved: the same approach can be used to assess the texture, color, and general quality after the image lossy compression. Figure 8 shows the qualitative suitability of JPEG2000, ECW, JPEG compression for "img1" solving the full (Figure 8a,e–i) and partial tasks (Figure 8b–d)). Figure 8 shows that the JPEG2000 lossy compression is superior to the lossy ECW and JPEG compression in texture (b), color features (c), and by IQA (d). The JPEG compression provides similar image quality to JPEG2000 in texture features only at low compression ratios. JPEG has a significant effect on color, except at low compression ratios. The ECW compression at high compression ratios negatively affects texture but has a low impact on color. By IQA, the JPEG and ECW compression have a similar effect on the "img1" content.

4.4. Discussion

The ranking of JPEG2000, JPEG and ECW algorithms with different compression ratios differs slightly according to the qualitative suitability for the high-resolution aerial images "img1", and "img2" (Table 3, Figure 7a,b) as both images have similar features of the content. The "img1" and "img2" have textures of the same RGB values and intensities, but rough textures dominate in the "img2", while smooth ones are more common in the "img1". Due to prevalence of rough textures, "img1" has the lower visually acceptable threshold of JPEG2000, JPEG and ECW lossy compression (Figure 8a) and the compression artifacts are barely visible in the compressed image, compared to other ones. The "img3" ranking, as well as the content, differs considerably comparing to the "img1" and "img2" (Table 3, Figure 7c). The "img3" contains more features, sensitive to the lossy compression, like textures with the high spatial frequencies (of intensity change) and a large number of small regions differing in size, color, and intensity.

The changes of the content in the images "img4", "img5", and "img6" due to the down sampling also influenced the ranking of lossy compression (Table 3, Figure 7a–c) and the visually acceptable threshold of lossy compression (Figure 8g–i). The low-resolution aerial images do not have the rich spatial textures of the high-resolution images, and their lossy compression artifacts are more noticeable. The "img6" has the highest visually acceptable threshold of JPEG2000, JPEG and ECW lossy compression (Figure 8i) compared to "img4" and "img5" (Figure 8g,h). After the image "img2" was down sampled to the "img5", the textured regions became smoother. As the textures in the "img1" are of dominating low spatial frequencies of intensity changes, then down sampling it to the "img4" exposes a smaller effect on the visual content of the image. Thus, the low-resolution images "img4" and "img5" were similarly affected by lossy compression, especially at higher compression ratios for JPEG (Figure 8g,h).

Each algorithm introduces unique artifacts and has a different effect on the aerial images of different resolutions and contents. The JPEG lossy compression has a high impact on the images' content with uniform and coarse (low spatial frequencies of intensity changes) textures. The "img1" and "img3" contains this type of textures, but "img3" was affected more by JPEG compression as it contains a large number of small, uniform regions. The JPEG2000 compression more affects images containing a large number of regions with textures of high spatial frequencies of intensity changes ("img2"), and especially with the small regions of different textures ("img3"). The ECW lossy compression has a higher effect on images rich with rough textures of high spatial frequencies of intensity changes ("img2"). The JPEG2000 and ECW compression have a similar effect for low-resolution images with textures of high spatial frequencies of intensity changes ("img5"), or with small regions with different textures ("img6"). The JPEG2000 has higher quality at higher compression ratios than JPEG as it does not expose visually distracting artifacts, especially in low frequency or uniform areas. The JPEG artifacts are more pronounced in the low-resolution images' content than they are in the high-resolution images. The smoothing artifacts are more noticeable in ECW high-resolution images than in JPEG2000, specifically in images with textures of high spatial frequencies of intensity changes. The ECW compression has a slightly lesser effect on the low-resolution images.

5. Conclusions and Future Work

We proposed the original multi-criteria decision-making methodology for the qualitative selection of the lossy compression for the aerial images based on their resolution and content. The transform-based lossy compression algorithms with the appropriate compression ratios were ranked by their suitability for aerial images using MCDM WASPAS-SVNS and direct criteria weights evaluation methods. The rating of lossy compression is governed by the set of qualitative parameters of images and visually acceptable lossy compression ratios.

Because of the need for the qualitative lossy compression for the effective storage and transmission of a large amount of remote sensing data, it is imperative to decide which algorithm and what compression ratio will be suitable for the selected image content and resolution. Since the image quality after lossy compression can be determined by various parameters, and they belong to the different groups that vary significantly, the weighted combination of different qualitative parameters should be used.

The visual features (e.g., a forest, cropland, roads, buildings, water) in an image can be characterized by generalizations like texture, color tone, and luminance. The information on the change of the colors and textures can be calculated using the first-order color statistics and second-order texture statistics, respectively. It is reasonable to include the often-used objective IQA metrics and subjective evaluation. Using the set of the verified groups of parameters and altering their weights, the effect of lossy compression on the image content can be evaluated more precisely compared to the estimation using only single objective image quality metrics.

The use of the set of the qualitative parameters for the texture, color, and IQA, can solve different subtasks: the same approach can be used to assess the texture, color, and general quality after the image lossy compression.

In the aerial imagery application context, it is useful to define the acceptable lossy compression ratio for the selected lossy compression algorithm. We concentrated on visual image inspection after data collection and compression for easier transmission and saving storage space. It should be useful to find the best solution for image lossy compression implementation in hardware in such cases. The threshold of acceptable visual distortions places the algorithms with their compression ratios in order of priority, excluding those whose distortions are greater than the subjectively determined quality threshold. The experimental results showed that the visually acceptable lossy compression for the high-resolution aerial images is: JPEG2000—lower than 100:1 for "img1" and lower than 75:1 for "img2" and "img3"; ECW and JPEG—lower than 75:1 for "img1" (near to 50:1 and less), lower than 50:1 for "img2" and "img3" (near to 25:1 and less). The visually acceptable lossy compression for the low-resolution aerial images is worse than for the high-resolution images: JPEG2000—lower than 75:1 for "img4" and "img5" (near to 50:1 and less), and lower than 50:1 for "img6"; ECW and JPEG—lower than 50:1 for "img4", "img5," and "img6" (near to 25:1 and less).

As the lossy compression quality is a complex task and needs to be investigated further, we are going to evaluate the lossy compression quality for the different classes of satellite images against the segmentation using the appropriate set of qualitative parameters.

Author Contributions: Conceptualization, R.B. and G.K.-J.; methodology, R.B., G.K.-J.; software, G.K.-J.; validation, R.B., G.K.-J.; formal analysis, R.B., G.K.-J.; investigation, G.K.-J.; resources, R.B., G.K.-J.; data curation, G.K.-J.; writing—original draft preparation, G.K.-J.; writing—review and editing, R.B., G.K.-J.; supervision, R.B; project administration, R.B. All authors have read and agreed to the published version of the manuscript.

Funding: The research received no external funding.

Institutional Review Board Statement: Not applicable.

Informed Consent Statement: Not applicable.

Data Availability Statement: Data sharing not applicable.

Conflicts of Interest: The authors declare no conflict of interest.

Appendix A

The questionnaire for the evaluation of the visual image quality after the relevant lossy compression:

- Evaluate the visual quality of compressed image textures according to the original image textures.
- Evaluate the visual quality of compressed image colors according to the original image colors.
- Evaluate a number of artifacts in the compressed image according to the original image.

References

1. ESA. *Sentinel-2 User Handbook*; ESA: Auckland, New Zealand, 2015; pp. 1–64.
2. Alam, A.; Bhat, M.S.; Maheen, M. Using Landsat satellite data for assessing the land use and land cover change in Kashmir valley. *GeoJournal* **2019**. [CrossRef]
3. Fonji, S.F.; Taff, G.N. Using satellite data to monitor land-use land-cover change in North-eastern Latvia. *SpringerPlus* **2014**, *3*. [CrossRef] [PubMed]
4. Tan, K.; Zhang, Y.; Wang, X.; Chen, Y. Object-Based Change Detection Using Multiple Classifiers and Multi-Scale Uncertainty Analysis. *Remote Sens.* **2019**, *11*. [CrossRef]
5. Falco, N.; Mura, M.D.; Bovolo, F.; Benediktsson, J.A.; Bruzzone, L. Change Detection in VHR Images Based on Morphological Attribute Profiles. *IEEE Geosci. Remote Sens. Lett.* **2013**. [CrossRef]
6. Debusscher, B.; Coillie, F. Object-Based Flood Analysis Using a Graph-Based Representation. *Remote Sens.* **2019**, *11*, 1883. [CrossRef]
7. Hussain, A.J.; Al-Fayadh, A.; Radi, N. Image compression techniques: A survey in lossless and lossy algorithms. *Neurocomputing* **2018**, *300*, 44–69. [CrossRef]
8. Faria, L.N.; Fonseca, L.M.G.; Costa, M.H.M. Performance Evaluation of Data Compression Systems Applied to Satellite Imagery. *J. Electr. Comput. Eng.* **2012**, *2012*. [CrossRef]
9. Hagag, A.; Fan, X.; El-Samie, F.E.A. Lossy compression of satellite images with low impact on vegetation features. *Multidimens. Syst. Signal Proces.* **2016**, *28*, 1717–1736. [CrossRef]

10. Christophe, E.; Thiebaut, C.; Latry, C. Compression Specification for Efficient Use of High Resolution Satellite data. *Int. Arch. Photogramm. Remote Sens. Spat. Inf. Sci.* **2008**, *XXXVII*, B4.
11. Hagag, A.; Hassan, E.S.; Amin, M.; El-Samie, F.E.A.; Fana, X. Satellite multispectral image compression based on removing sub-bands. *Optik* **2017**, *131*, 1023–1035. [CrossRef]
12. Ahujaa, S.L.; Bindub, M.H. High Resolution Satellite Image Compression using DCT and EZW. In Proceedings of the International Conference on Sustainable Computing in Science, Technology & Management, Jaipur, India, 26–28 January 2019. [CrossRef]
13. Indradjad, A.; Nasution, A.S.; Gunawan, H.; Widipaminto, A. A comparison of Satellite Image Compression methods in the Wavelet Domain. *IOP Conf. Ser. Earth Environ. Sci.* **2019**, *280*, 012031. [CrossRef]
14. Genitha, C.H.; Rajesh, R.K. A Technique for Multi-Spectral Satellite Image Compression Using EZW Algorithm. In Proceedings of the International Conference on Control, Instrumentation, Communication and Computational Technologies, Kumaracoil, India, 16–17 December 2016. [CrossRef]
15. Fiorucci, F.; Baruffa, G.; Frescura, F. Objective and subjective quality assessment between JPEG XR with overlap and JPEG 2000. *J. Vis. Commun. Image Represent.* **2012**, *23*, 835–844. [CrossRef]
16. Manthey, K. A New Real-Time Architecture for Image Compression Onboard Satellites based on CCSDS Image Data Compression. In Proceedings of the 4th International Conference on On-Board Payload Data Compression Workshop, Venice, Italy, 23–24 October 2014.
17. Kiely, A.B.; Klimesh, M. *The ICER Progressive Wavelet Image Compressor. Interplanetary Network Progress Report*; California Institute of Technology: Pasadena, CA, USA, 2003.
18. Bateson, L.; Mcintosh, R. *An Investigation into File Formats for the use and Delivery of Large Format Images*; British Geological Survey Internal Report; British Geological Survey: Nottingham, UK, 2004.
19. Simone, F.; Ticca, D.; Dufaux, F.; Ansorge, M.; Ebrahimi, T. A comparative study of color image compression standards using perceptually driven quality metrics. In Proceedings of the Conference on Applications of Digital Image Processing, San Diego, CA, USA, 10–14 August 2008; Volume XXXI, p. 7073. [CrossRef]
20. Matsuoka, R.; Sone, M.; Fukue, K.; Cho, K.; Shimoda, H. Quantitative analysis of image quality of lossy compression images. In Proceedings of the ISPRS Congress, Istanbul, Turkey, 12–26 July 2004.
21. Tao, D.; Di, S.; Guo, H.; Chen, Z.; Cappello, F. Z-checker: A framework for assessing lossy compression of scientific data. *Int. J. High Perform. Comput. Appl.* **2017**, 1–19. [CrossRef]
22. Johnson, B.A.; Jozdani, S.E. Identifying Generalizable Image Segmentation Parameters for Urban Land Cover Mapping through Meta-Analysis and Regression Tree Modeling. *Remote Sens.* **2018**, *10*, 73. [CrossRef]
23. Kupidura, P. The Comparison of Different Methods of Texture Analysis for Their Efficacy for Land Use Classification in Satellite Imagery. *Remote Sens.* **2019**, *11*, 1233. [CrossRef]
24. Sirmaçek, B.; Ünsalan, C. Road Detection from Remotely Sensed Images Using Color Features. In Proceedings of the 5th International Conference on Recent Advances in Space Technologies—RAST2011, Istanbul, Turkey, 9–11 June 2011. [CrossRef]
25. Kazakeviciute-Januskeviciene, G.; Janusonis, E.; Bausys, R.; Limba, T.; Kiskis, M. Assessment of the Segmentation of RGB Remote Sensing Images: A Subjective Approach. *Remote Sens.* **2020**, *12*, 4152. [CrossRef]
26. Fynn, I.E.M.; Campbell, J. Forest Fragmentation Analysis from Multiple Imaging Formats. *J. Landsc. Ecol.* **2019**, *12*. [CrossRef]
27. Bausys, R.; Kazakeviciute-Januskeviciene, G.; Cavallaro, F.; Usovaite, A. Algorithm Selection for Edge Detection in Satellite Images by Neutrosophic WASPAS Method. *Sustainability* **2020**, *12*, 548. [CrossRef]
28. Öztürk, E.; Mesut, A. Entropy Based Estimation Algorithm Using Split Images to Increase Compression Ratio. *Trakya Univ. J. Eng. Sci.* **2017**, *18*, 31–41.
29. Cheon, M.; Lee, J.S. Ambiguity-based evaluation of objective quality metrics for image compression. In Proceedings of the Eighth International Conference on Quality of Multimedia Experience, Lisbon, Portugal, 6–8 June 2016. [CrossRef]
30. Hagara, M.; Ondráček, O.; Kubinec, P.; Stojanović, R. Detecting edges with sub-pixel precision in JPEG images. In Proceedings of the 27th International Conference Radioelektronika, Brno, Czech Republic, 19–20 April 2017. [CrossRef]
31. Zabala, A.; Cea, C.; Pons, X. Segmentation and thematic classification of color orthophotos over non-compressed and JPEG 2000 compressed images. *Int. J. Appl. Earth Observ. Geoinf.* **2012**, *15*, 92–104. [CrossRef]
32. Ales, M.; Kokalj, Z.; Ostir, K. The Effect of Lossy Image Compression on Object Based Image Classification—WORLDVIEW-2 Case Study. *Int. Arch. Photogramm. Remote Sens. Spat. Inf. Sci.* **2012**, *3819*, 187–192. [CrossRef]
33. Elkholy, M.; Hosny, M.M.; El-Habrouk, H.M.F. Studying the effect of lossy compression and image fusion on image classification. *Alexandria Eng. J.* **2019**, *58*, 143–149. [CrossRef]
34. Hayati, A.K.; Dyatmika, H.S. The Effect of JPEG2000 Compression on Remote Sensing Data of Different Spatial Resolutions. *Int. J. Remote Sens. Earth Sci.* **2017**, *2*, 111–118. [CrossRef]
35. Ham, Y.; Han, K.; Lin, J.; Golparvar-Fard, M. Visual monitoring of civil infrastructure systems via camera-equipped Unmanned Aerial Vehicles (UAVs): A review of related works. *Vis. Eng.* **2016**, *4*. [CrossRef]
36. Li, R.; Han, D.; Dezert, J.; Yang, Y. A novel edge detector for color images based on MCDM with evidential reasoning. In Proceedings of the 2017 20th International Conference on Information Fusion, Xi'an, China, 10–13 July 2017.
37. Khelifi, L.; Mignotte, M. A Multi-Objective Approach Based on TOPSIS to Solve the Image Segmentation Combination Problem. In Proceedings of the 2016 23rd International Conference on Pattern Recognition, Cancun, Mexico, 4–8 December 2016. [CrossRef]

38. Stojčić, M.; Zavadskas, E.K.; Pamučar, D.; Stević, Ž; Mardani, A. Application of MCDM Methods in Sustainability Engineering: A Literature Review 2008–2018. *Symmetry* **2019**, *11*, 350. [CrossRef]
39. Wang, W.M.; Peng, H.H. A Fuzzy Multi-Criteria Evaluation Framework for Urban Sustainable Development. *Mathematics* **2020**, *8*, 330. [CrossRef]
40. Guitouni, A.; Martel, J.-M. Tentative guidelines to help choosing an appropriate MCDA method. *Eur. J. Oper. Res.* **1998**, *109*, 501–521. [CrossRef]
41. Skodras, A.; Christopoulos, C.; Ebrahimi, T. The JPEG 2000 still image compression standard. *IEEE Signal Process. Mag.* **2001**, *18*, 36–58. [CrossRef]
42. Ueffing, C. *Wavelet Based ECW Image Compression. Photogrammetric Week 01*; Wichmann Verlag: Heidelberg, Germany, 2001.
43. Mallat, S.A. *Wavelet Tour of Signal Processing*, 3rd ed.; Academic Press: Cambridge, MA, USA, 2009.
44. Wallace, G.K. The JPEG Still Picture Compression Standard. *Commun. ACM* **1991**, *34*, 31–44. [CrossRef]
45. Overview of JPEG. 2000. Available online: https://jpeg.org/jpeg2000/ (accessed on 21 January 2021).
46. *Compression White Paper. Using and Distributing ECW V2.0 Wavelet Compressed Imagery*; Earth Resource Mapping Pty Ltd.: Perth, Australia, 2012; pp. 2–27.
47. Overview of JPEG. Available online: https://jpeg.org/jpeg/index.html (accessed on 21 January 2021).
48. Sonka, M.; Hlavac, V.; Boyle, R. *Image Processing, Analysis, and Machine Vision*, 4th ed.; Cengage Learning: Boston, MA, USA, 2014.
49. Gonzalea, R.C.; Woods, R.E. *Digital Image Processing*, 2nd ed.; Prentice Hall: Upper Saddle River, NJ, USA, 2004.
50. Hilles, S.M.S.; Hossain, M.A. Classification on Image Compression Methods: Review Paper. *Int. J. Data Sci. Res.* **2018**, *1*, 1–7.
51. Lam, K.W.; Li, Z.; Yuan, X. Effects of Jpeg Compression on the Accuracy of Digital Terrain Models Automatically Derived from Digital Aerial Images. *Photogramm. Rec.* **2001**, *17*. [CrossRef]
52. Blue Marble Geographics. Available online: https://www.bluemarblegeo.com/products/global-mapper.php (accessed on 8 June 2020).
53. Dawwd, S. GLCM Based Parallel Texture Segmentation using A Multicore Processor. *Int. Arab J. Inf. Technol.* **2019**, *16*, 8–16.
54. Inthiyaz, S.; Madhav, B.T.P.; Kishore, P.V.V. Flower image segmentation with PCA fused colored covariance and gabor texture features based level sets. *Ain Shams Eng. J.* **2018**, *9*, 3277–3291. [CrossRef]
55. Janalipour, M.; Taleai, M. Building change detection after earthquake using multi-criteria decision analysis based on extracted information from high spatial resolution satellite images. *Int. J. Remote Sens.* **2017**, *38*, 82–99. [CrossRef]
56. Yang, F.; Lishman, R. Land Cover Change Detection Using Gabor Filter Texture. In Proceedings of the 3rd International Workshop on Texture Analysis and Synthesis, Nice, France, 17–18 December 2003; pp. 113–118.
57. Chen, Y.; Cao, Z. Change Detection of Multispectral Remote-Sensing Images Using Stationary Wavelet Transforms and Integrated Active Contours. *Int. J. Remote Sens.* **2013**, *34*, 8817–8837. [CrossRef]
58. Haralick, M.; Shanmugam, K.; Dinstein, I. Textural Features for Image Classification. *IEEE Trans. Syst. Man Cybern.* **1973**, *SMC-3*, 610–621. [CrossRef]
59. Zheng, S.; Zheng, J.; Shi, M.; Guo, B.; Sen, B.; Sun, Z.; Jia, X.; Li, X. Classification of cultivated Chinese medicinal plants based on fractal theory and gray level co-occurrence matrix textures. *J. Remote Sens.* **2014**, *18*, 868–886. [CrossRef]
60. Abdulrahman, A.-J. Performance evaluation of cross-diagonal texture matrix method of texture analysis. *Pattern Recogn.* **2001**, *34*, 171–180. [CrossRef]
61. Wood, E.M.; Pidgeon, A.M.; Radeloff, V.C.; Keuler, N.S. Image Texture Predicts Avian Density and Species Richness. *PLoS ONE* **2013**, *8*. [CrossRef]
62. Performance Evaluation of Learning based Image Coding Solutions and Quality Metrics. Coding of Still Pictures, ISO/IEC JTC 1/SC 29/WG 1 (ITU-T SG16). In Proceedings of the 85th JPEG Meeting, San Jose, CA, USA, 2–8 November 2019.
63. Ponomarenko, N.; Silvestri, F.; Egiazarian, K.; Carli, M.; Astola, J.; Lukin, V. On between-coefficient contrast masking of DCT basis functions. In Proceedings of the Third International Workshop on Video Processing and Quality Metrics, Scottsdale, AZ, USA, 25–26 January 2007; Available online: http://hdl.handle.net/11590/175246 (accessed on 29 June 2020).
64. Tong, Y.; Konik, H.; Cheikh, F.; Tremeau, A. Full Reference Image Quality Assessment Based on Saliency Map Analysis. *J. Imaging Sci. Technol.* **2010**, *54*, 503–514. [CrossRef]
65. Wang, Z.; Simoncelli, E.P.; Bovik, A.C. Multi-scale structural similarity for image quality assessment. In Proceedings of the IEEE Asilomar Conference on Signals, Systems and Computers, Pacific Grove, CA, USA, 9–12 November 2003; Volume 2, pp. 1398–1402. [CrossRef]
66. Wang, Z.; Li, Q. Information content weighting for perceptual image quality assessment. *IEEE Trans. Image Process.* **2011**, *20*, 1185–1198. [CrossRef]
67. Mardani, A.; Nilashi, M.; Zakuan, N.; Loganathan, N.; Soheilirad, S.; Saman, M.Z.M.; Ibrahimb, O. A systematic review and meta-Analysis of SWARA and WASPAS methods: Theory and applications with recent fuzzy developments. *Appl. Soft Comput.* **2017**, *57*, 265–292. [CrossRef]
68. Kendall, M.G. *Rank Correlation Methods*, 4th ed.; Hafner Press: New York, NY, USA, 1970.
69. Ginevicius, R.; Podvezko, V. Objective and subjective approaches determining the criterion weights in multicriteria models. *Transp. Telecommun.* **2005**, *6*, 133–137.
70. Zavadskas, E.K.; Podvezko, V. Integrated Determination of Objective Criteria Weights in MCDM. *Int. J. Inf. Technol. Decis. Mak.* **2016**, *15*, 267–283. [CrossRef]

71. Zavadskas, E.K.; Ustinovichius, L.; Turskis, Z.; Shevchenko, G. Application of Verbal Methods to Multi Attribute Comparative Analysis of Investments Risk Alternatives in Construction. *Comput. Model. New Technol.* **2008**, *12*, 30–37.
72. Zavadskas, E.K.; Turskis, Z.; Antucheviciene, J.; Zakarevicius, A. Optimization of weighted aggregated sum product assessment. *Elektron. Elektrotech.* **2012**, *122*, 3–6. [CrossRef]
73. Zavadskas, E.K.; Bausys, R.; Lazauskas, M. Sustainable assessment of alternative sites for the construction of a waste incineration plant by applying WASPAS method with single-valued neutrosophic set. *Sustainability* **2015**, *7*, 15923–15936. [CrossRef]
74. Bausys, R.; Cavallaro, F.; Semenas, R. Application of sustainability principles for harsh environment exploration by autonomous robot. *Sustainability* **2019**, *11*, 2518. [CrossRef]
75. Zavadskas, E.K.; Bausys, R.; Mazonaviciute, I. Safety evaluation methodology of urban public parks by multi-criteria decision making. *Landsc. Urban Plan.* **2019**, *189*, 372–381. [CrossRef]
76. Earth Explorer. Available online: https://earthexplorer.usgs.gov/ (accessed on 2 March 2020).
77. Likert Scale. Available online: https://www.britannica.com/topic/Likert-Scale (accessed on 29 June 2020).

Article
Global Sensitivity Analysis of Quantiles: New Importance Measure Based on Superquantiles and Subquantiles

Zdeněk Kala

Department of Structural Mechanics, Faculty of Civil Engineering, Brno University of Technology, 602 00 Brno, Czech Republic; kala.z@fce.vutbr.cz

Abstract: The article introduces quantile deviation l as a new sensitivity measure based on the difference between superquantile and subquantile. New global sensitivity indices based on the square of l are presented. The proposed sensitivity indices are compared with quantile-oriented sensitivity indices subordinated to contrasts and classical Sobol sensitivity indices. The comparison is performed in a case study using a non-linear mathematical function, the output of which represents the elastic resistance of a slender steel member under compression. The steel member has random imperfections that reduce its load-carrying capacity. The member length is a deterministic parameter that significantly changes the sensitivity of the output resistance to the random effects of input imperfections. The comparison of the results of three types of global sensitivity analyses shows the rationality of the new quantile-oriented sensitivity indices, which have good properties similar to classical Sobol indices. Sensitivity indices subordinated to contrasts are the least comprehensible because they exhibit the strongest interaction effects between inputs. However, using total indices, all three types of sensitivity analyses lead to approximately the same conclusions. The similarity of the results of two quantile-oriented and Sobol sensitivity analysis confirms that Sobol sensitivity analysis is empathetic to the structural reliability and that the variance is one of the important characteristics significantly influencing the low quantile of resistance.

Keywords: sensitivity analysis; buckling; reliability; safety; quantile; superquantile; subquantile; civil engineering; limit states

Citation: Kala, Z. Global Sensitivity Analysis of Quantiles: New Importance Measure Based on Superquantiles and Subquantiles. *Symmetry* **2021**, *13*, 263. https://doi.org/10.3390/sym13020263

Academic Editors: Edmundas Kazimieras Zavadskas, Jurgita Antuchevičienė and Zenonas Turskis

Received: 21 January 2021
Accepted: 31 January 2021
Published: 4 February 2021

Publisher's Note: MDPI stays neutral with regard to jurisdictional claims in published maps and institutional affiliations.

Copyright: © 2021 by the author. Licensee MDPI, Basel, Switzerland. This article is an open access article distributed under the terms and conditions of the Creative Commons Attribution (CC BY) license (https://creativecommons.org/licenses/by/4.0/).

1. Introduction

Traditional sensitivity analysis (SA) methods are focused on model output [1]. SA is a computational procedure that divides and quantifies the uncertainty of input variables according to their influence on the uncertainty of the output of the mathematical model. Variance-based SA (generally called Sobol SA) introduces uncertainty as variance and decomposes the variance of the output of the model or system into portions that can be attributed to inputs or sets of inputs [2,3]. Sobol SA is very popular; the principles of the method are often mentioned [4–8] and many articles have applied Sobol SA in their research [9–13].

In a more general form, SA can be defined as the study of how the output of a system is related to, and is influenced by, its inputs. In practical applications, research does not usually end with obtaining the output as a random variable or histogram, but other specific point estimates, such as quantiles, are needed. However, what influences the variance may or may not have the same influence on the quantile.

1.1. A Brief Review of Sensitivity Analysis in Civil Engineering

SA is a multidisciplinary science and, therefore, review articles focused purely on SA have a multidisciplinary character [14–19]. Only approximately 2.5% of all articles on SA are focused on civil engineering. In civil engineering, publications related to SA have a growing trend, but are not as progressive as traditional engineering topics, such as buckling; see Figure 1.

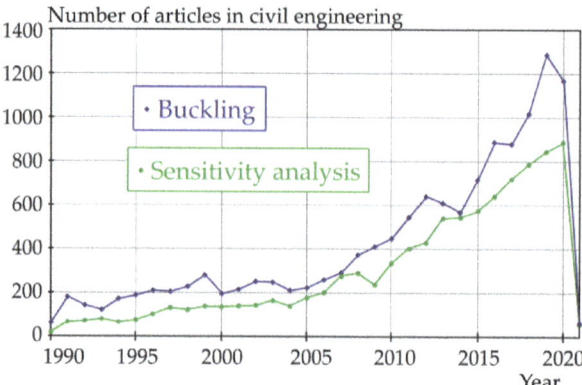

Figure 1. Number of publications in civil engineering Web of Science categories (Web of Science core collection database, 29 January 2021) on the topic "sensitivity analysis "and "buckling".

In civil engineering, SA is focused on the stability of steel frames [20], deflection of concrete beams with correlated inputs [21], multiple-criteria decision-making (MCDM) [22], structural response to stochastic dynamic loads [23], rheological properties of asphalt [24], thermal performance of facades [25], strength of reinforced concrete beams [26], use of machines during the construction of tunnels [27], stress-based topology of structural frames [28], seismic response of steel plate shear walls [29], deformation of retaining walls [30], multiple-attribute decision making (MADM) [31], efficiency of the operations of transportation companies [32], unbalanced bidding prices in construction projects [33], shear buckling strength [34], reliability index β of steel girders [35], system reliability [36], seismic response and fragility of transmission toners [37], shear strength of corrugated web panels [38], inelastic response of conical shells [39], fatigue limit state [40], corrosion depth [41], building-specific seismic loss [42], vibration response of train–bridge coupled systems [43], shear strength of reinforced concrete beam–column joints [44], forecasts of groundwater levels [45], equivalent rock strength [46], vertical displacement and maximum axial force of piles [47], regional-scale subsurface flow [48], ultimate limit state of cross-beam structures [49], serviceability limit state of structures [50], deflection of steel frames [51], stability of observatory central detectors [52], bearing deformation and pylon ductility of bridges [53], load-carrying capacity of masonry arch bridges [54], free torsional vibration frequencies of thin-walled beams [55], stress and displacement of pipelines [56], fatigue dynamic reliability of structural members [57], deflection of roof truss structures [58], etc. Studies are performed using very different SA methods, which are not always chosen solely for purpose, but are subject to different paradigms that define what and how it should be investigated. Many studies apply only one type of SA, although more than one suitable SA method can be used. Some of the applied methods are traditional, e.g., applications of derivations [25,28], applications of Sobol SA [42,46] or application of the Borgonovo method [30], but highly specific and original SA methods [23,54], which are difficult or even impossible to compare with conventional methods [1], are also being developed.

In civil engineering, SA objectives are usually focused on the optimization of the properties of structures, design characteristics of structures or processes associated with construction activities. One of the important features of any structure is its reliability.

1.2. Reliability-Oriented Sensitivity Analysis

In civil engineering, structural reliability is assessed using the well-developed concept of limit states [59,60], which clearly defines the design quantiles of resistance and the effect of load action. Regarding the ultimate limit state, a load-bearing structure is considered reliable if the high quantile of load action is smaller than the low quantile of resistance [61].

A comparative study [61] showed large differences between four reliability-oriented sensitivity analyses (ROSA) and additional four SA used in reliability analysis. The conclusions [61] showed that a common platform that clearly translates the correlation between indices and their information value is absent in ROSA methods.

A reliability-oriented SA concept based on design quantiles was introduced in [62]. SA was performed using the total indices of the design quantiles of resistance and load without having to evaluate the SA of failure probability. This saves the computational costs of numerically demanding models. Mirroring the concept of limit states into the principles of SA brings the results of sensitivity studies closer to the engineering practice, reduces computational costs and expands the possibilities of modelers.

This article builds on [62] by introducing more general quadratic forms of quantile-oriented sensitivity indices, which are compared with quantile-oriented sensitivity indices subordinated to contrasts [63]. Two SAs are compared with the classical Sobol SA in a case study using a non-linear function of the elastic static resistance of a compressed steel structural member. The advantages and disadvantages of all three methods are described and discussed.

2. Quantile-Oriented and Sobol Global Sensitivity Indices

From a black box perspective, any model may be regarded as a function $R = g(X)$, where X is a vector of M uncertain model inputs $\{X_1, X_2,... X_M\}$, and R is a one-dimensional model output. The uncertain model inputs are considered as statistically independent random variables. This incurs no loss of generality, because mutual relations are created through the computational model on the path to the output.

Three types of global SA (in short SA) are used: Q indices, K indices and Sobol indices. All three types of SA have the ability to measure sensitivity across the input space (i.e., they are global methods), are capable of dealing with non-linear responses, and can quantify the influence of interactions in a non-additive systems. The first two SAs [62,63] are quantile-oriented, the third is the classical Sobol SA [2,3]. Both quantile-oriented SAs can study structural reliability, the assessment of which is based on limit states and design quantiles. The reason for including Sobol SA is its orientation on variance, which is an important, but not the only, part of reliability analysis.

2.1. Linear Form of Quantile-Oriented Sensitivity Indices—Contrast Q Indices

Sensitivity indices subordinated to contrasts associated with quantiles [63] (in short, Contrast Q indices) are based on linear contrast functions. The contrast function ψ associated with the α-quantile of output R can be expressed using parameter θ as

$$\psi(\theta) = E(\psi(R,\theta)) = E((R-\theta)(\alpha - 1_{R<\theta})), \tag{1}$$

where R is a scalar. Equation (16) attains its minimum if the argument θ has a value of α-quantile of R, see Equation (2)

$$\theta^* = \underset{\theta}{\text{Argmin }} \psi(\theta) = \underset{\theta}{\text{Argmin }} E((R-\theta)(\alpha - 1_{R<\theta})), \tag{2}$$

where θ^* is the α-quantile of R. The minimum of Equation (1) can be expressed using θ^* as

$$\min_{\theta} \psi(\theta) = \psi(\theta^*) = E((R-\theta^*)(\alpha - 1_{R<\theta^*})) = l \cdot \alpha \cdot (1-\alpha), \tag{3}$$

where l is the absolute difference (distance) between the mean value of the population below the α-quantile θ^* and mean value of the population above the α-quantile θ^*. Let l be the quantile deviation. The quantile deviation l is the difference between superquantile $E(R\mid R \geq \theta^*)$ and subquantile $E(R\mid R < \theta^*)$

$$l = \frac{1}{1-\alpha}\underbrace{\int_{\theta^*}^{\infty} r \cdot f(r)dr}_{Superquantile} - \frac{1}{\alpha}\underbrace{\int_{-\infty}^{\theta^*} r \cdot f(r)dr}_{Subquantile} = \frac{1}{1-\alpha}\underbrace{\int_{\theta^*}^{\infty} |r - \theta^*| \cdot f(r)dr}_{l_2} + \frac{1}{\alpha}\underbrace{\int_{-\infty}^{\theta^*} |r - \theta^*| \cdot f(r)dr}_{l_1}, \qquad (4)$$

where $l = l_1 + l_2$. l_1 is the mean absolute deviation from θ^* below θ^*, l_2 is the mean absolute deviation from θ^* above the quantile θ^* (in short quantile deviation l), and $f(r)$ is the probability density function (pdf) of the model output.

The introduction of superquantile and subquantile in Equation (4) introduces quantile deviation l as a new quantile sensitivity measure.

It can be noted that superquantiles are fundamental building blocks for estimates of risk in finance [64] and engineering [65]. In finance, the superquantile has various names, such as expected tail loss [66], conditional value-at-risk (CVaR) [67–70] or tail value-at-risk [71], average value at risk [72], expected shortfall [73,74]. Subquantile is not such a widespread concept.

In the context of SA, l was first introduced as a new sensitivity measure in [62]. A property of the quantile deviation l is that it is expressed in the same unit as the data. The quantile deviation l is a robust statistic, which, compared with the standard deviation, is more resilient to outliers in a dataset. This is due to the fact that in the case of standard deviation, i.e., the square root of variance, the distances from the mean are squared, so that large deviations are weighted more and can, therefore, be strongly influenced by outliers. Regarding quantile deviation l, the deviations of a small number of outliers are inconsequential.

With regard to random sampling, the quantile deviation l of a finite observation of size N with values r_j can be estimated as

$$l \approx \frac{1}{N_2}\underbrace{\sum_{j:r_j \geq \theta^*} r_j}_{Superquantile} - \frac{1}{N_1}\underbrace{\sum_{j:r_j < \theta^*} r_j}_{Subquantile} = \frac{1}{N_2}\underbrace{\sum_{j:r_j \geq \theta^*} |r_j - \theta^*|}_{l_2} + \frac{1}{N_1}\underbrace{\sum_{j:r_j < \theta^*} |r_j - \theta^*|}_{l_1}, \qquad (5)$$

where N_1 is the total number of observations below the α-quantile, $N_2 = N - N_1$ is the total number of observations above the α-quantile, where α-quantile θ^* can be estimated so that $\alpha \cdot N$ observations are smaller than θ^* and $(1-\alpha) \cdot N$ observations are greater than θ^*.

Figures 2 and 3 depict examples of symmetric and asymmetric probability density functions (pdfs), where the value of l is expressed as the distance between the centres of gravity of the green and yellow areas. All probability density functions (pdfs) have mean value $\mu_R = 0$ and standard deviation $\sigma_R = 1$. Figure 2a depicts the Uniform probability density function (pdf). Figures 2b and 3a,b depict a four-parameter Hermite pdf, where the third and fourth parameters are skewness and kurtosis.

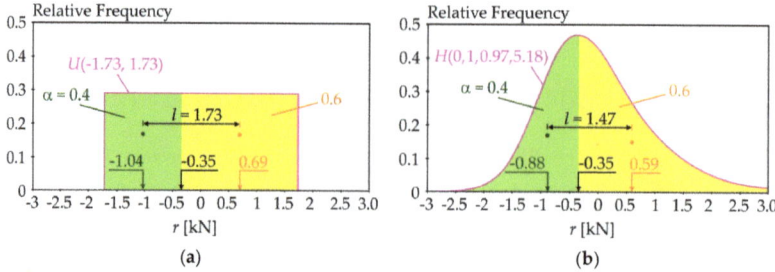

Figure 2. Quantile deviation l of 0.4-quantile of: (a) Uniform symmetric pdf; (b) Hermite asymmetric pdf.

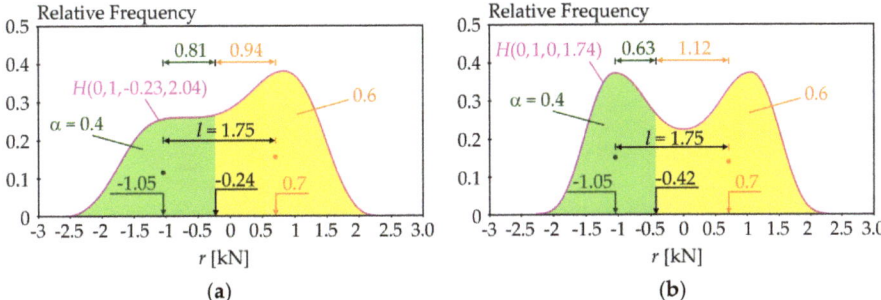

Figure 3. Quantile deviation l of 0.4-quantile of: (**a**) Hermite asymmetric pdf; (**b**) Hermite symmetric pdf.

By modifying Equation (3), quantile deviation l can be computed using the probability density function according to Equation (6)

$$l = \frac{1}{\alpha \cdot (1-\alpha)} \psi(\theta^*) = \frac{1}{\alpha \cdot (1-\alpha)} E((R - \theta^*)(\alpha - 1_{R<\theta^*})), \quad (6)$$

where the value of $\alpha \cdot (1-\alpha)$ is constant. The first-order contrast Q_i index defined in [63] has a form that can be rewritten using the quantile deviation l as Equation (7)

$$Q_i = \frac{\min_\theta \psi(\theta) - E\left(\min_\theta E(\psi(R,\theta)|X_i)\right)}{\min_\theta \psi(\theta)} = \frac{l \cdot \alpha \cdot (1-\alpha) - E((l|X_i) \cdot \alpha \cdot (1-\alpha))}{l \cdot \alpha \cdot (1-\alpha)} = \frac{l - E(l|X_i)}{l}, \quad (7)$$

where the mean value $E(\cdot)$ is considered over all likely values of X_i. The new form of the contrast index Q_i is

$$Q_i = \frac{l - E(l|X_i)}{l}. \quad (8)$$

In a general model, fixing X_i can change all the statistical characteristics of output R. Only the changes in l caused by changes in X_i are important for the value of index Q_i; see Equation (8). What statistical characteristics does l depend on? The quantile deviation l is not dependent on μ_R. Changes in l would hypothetically depend only on changes in σ_R provided that the shape of the pdf does not change (e.g., still Gaussian output in additive model with Gaussian inputs). However, this cannot be generally assumed.

Figure 2 shows an example where changing the shape of the pdf causes a change in l from $l = 1.73$ to $l = 1.47$ when $\mu_R = 1$ and $\sigma_R = 1$ is considered. Analogously, changing the shape of the pdf can change σ_R, but not l. Figure 3 shows an example where changing the pdf shape does not cause a change in l when $\mu_R = 1$ and $\sigma_R = 1$ is considered. Therefore, changing the shape of the pdf may or may not affect l. The skewness and kurtosis may or may not affect l. In general, l does not depend on the change of μ_R itself, but depends on the pdf shape where the influence of moments acts in combinations, which can have a greater or lesser influence on l depending on the specific model type. These questions are examined in more detail in the case study presented in Chapter 5.

The second-order α-quantile contrast index Q_{ij} is derived similarly by fixing of pairs X_i, X_j

$$Q_{ij} = \frac{l - E(l|X_i, X_j)}{l} - Q_i - Q_j, \quad (9)$$

where $E(\cdot)$ is considered across all X_i and X_j. The third-order sensitivity index Q_{ijk} is computed analogously

$$Q_{ijk} = \frac{l - E(l|X_i, X_j, X_k)}{l} - Q_i - Q_j - Q_k - Q_{ij} - Q_{ik} - Q_{jk}. \quad (10)$$

Statistically independent input random variables are considered. The sum of all indices must be equal to one

$$\sum_i Q_i + \sum_i \sum_{j>i} Q_{ij} + \sum_i \sum_{j>i} \sum_{k>j} Q_{ijk} + \ldots + Q_{123\ldots M} = 1. \tag{11}$$

The total index Q_{Ti} can be written as

$$Q_{Ti} = 1 - \frac{l - E(l|X_{\sim i})}{l}, \tag{12}$$

where the second term in the numerator contains the conditional quantile deviation l evaluated for input random variable X_i and fixed variables $(X_1, X_2, \ldots, X_{i-1}, X_{i+1}, \ldots, X_M)$.

Contrast Q indices expressed using the quantile deviation l are the same as the indices based on contrasts defined in [63], but are obtained in a different way. Contrast Q indices can also be written in an asymptotic form [62] (p. 15), which is based on measuring the distance between an α-quantile θ^* and the mean value μ of the model output $l \approx \pm(\theta^* - \mu)$, but limited to only large and small quantiles.

The contrast Q indices described in this chapter use quantile deviation l in linear form.

2.2. Quadratic Form of Quantile-Oriented Sensitivity Indices—K Indices

New sensitivity indices focused on quantiles can be obtained using the square of the quantile deviation l. The basic concept of this quadratic form of quantile-oriented sensitivity analysis was introduced in [62] (p. 16). Unlike contrast Q indices, the sensitivity measure is expressed in the same unit as the variance. The decomposition of l^2 can be performed in a similar manner to the decomposition of the variance in Sobol sensitivity indices [62]. The asymptotic form of these indices has been denoted as QE indices [62].

The first-order K_i index can be written as

$$K_i = \frac{l^2 - E(l^2|X_i)}{l^2}. \tag{13}$$

The second-order index K_{ij} is computed similarly with fixing of pairs X_i, X_j

$$K_{ij} = \frac{l^2 - E(l^2|X_i, X_j)}{l^2} - K_i - K_j. \tag{14}$$

The third-order sensitivity index K_{ijk} is computed analogously

$$K_{ijk} = \frac{l^2 - E(l^2|X_i, X_j, X_k)}{l^2} - K_i - K_j - K_k - K_{ij} - K_{ik} - K_{jk}. \tag{15}$$

The other higher-order indices are obtained similarly. Statistically independent input random variables are considered. The sum of all indices must be equal to one

$$\sum_i K_i + \sum_i \sum_{j>i} K_{ij} + \sum_i \sum_{j>i} \sum_{k>j} K_{ijk} + \ldots + K_{123\ldots M} = 1. \tag{16}$$

The total index K_{Ti} can be written as

$$K_{Ti} = 1 - \frac{l^2 - E(l^2|X_{\sim i})}{l^2}, \tag{17}$$

where the second term in the numerator contains the conditional parameter l^2 evaluated for input random variable X_i and fixed variables $(X_1, X_2, \ldots, X_{i-1}, X_{i+1}, \ldots, X_M)$. Equations (13)–(17) can be used for all quantiles, i.e., they are not limited to small and large quantiles.

2.3. Sobol Sensitivity Indices—Sobol Indices

Sobol variance-based sensitivity analysis is the most frequently used SA method [2,3]. Sobol SA is based on the decomposition of the variance of the model output. Sobol SA estimates the degree of variance that each parameter contributes to the model output, including interaction effects. The first-order S_i index can be written as

$$S_i = \frac{V(R) - E(V(R|X_i))}{V(R)}, \quad (18)$$

where $E(\cdot)$ is considered across all X_i. The total effect index S_{Ti}, which measures first and higher-order effects (interactions) of variable X_i, is another popular variance-based measure [1]

$$S_i = \frac{V(R) - E(V(R|X_{\sim i}))}{V(R)}, \quad (19)$$

where the second term in the numerator contains the conditional variance evaluated for input random variable X_i and fixed variables $(X_1, X_2, \ldots, X_{i-1}, X_{i+1}, \ldots, X_M)$.

Sobol SA is dependent only on the variance. The similarity of the results of Sobol SA and quantile-oriented SA can be sought in connection with the degree of the influence of the variance on the quantile.

3. Resistance of Steel Member under Compression

Most forms of civil engineering structures are designed using European unified design rules [75]—Eurocodes. The limit state is the structural condition past which it no longer satisfies the pertinent design criteria [76]. Limit state design requires the structure to satisfy two fundamental conditions: the ultimate limit state (strength and stability) and the serviceability limit state (deflection, cracking, vibration).

The aim of the case study presented in this article is to analyse the static resistance (load-carrying capacity) of a slender steel member, which is limited by the strength of the material and stability. The resistance R is a random variable that depends on material and geometrical characteristics, which are generally random variables. A structure is considered to satisfy the ultimate limit state criterion if the random realization of the external load action is less than the low (design) quantile of load-carrying capacity R_d. Standard [59] enables the determination of design value R_d as 0.1 percentile [77–81].

The stochastic model of ultimate limit state of a hot-rolled steel member under longitudinal compression load action F is shown in Figure 4a. Biaxially symmetrical cross section HEA 180 of steel grade S235 is considered; see Figure 4b.

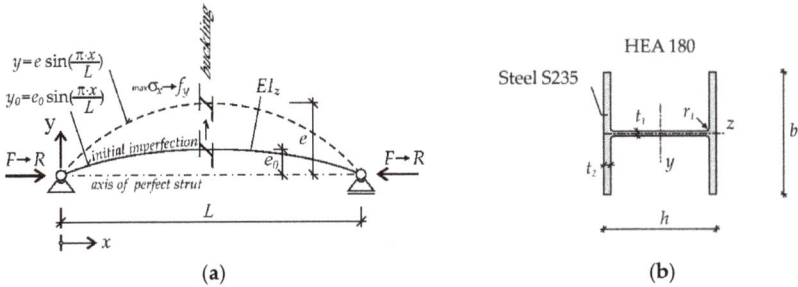

Figure 4. Static model: (**a**) steel member under compression; (**b**) Cross-section HEA 180.

The resistance of the steel structural member shown in Figure 4a was derived in [82] using the equation $e = e_0/(1 - F/F_{cr})$, where F_{cr} is Euler's critical load. Increasing the external load action F increases the compressive stress σ_x until the yield strength f_y is attained in the middle of the span in the lower (extremely compressed) part of the cross-section; see Figure 4a. Hooke's law with Young's modulus E is considered. The dependence of σ_x on F is non-linear if $e_0 > 0$, where $F < F_{cr}$. The elastic resistance R (unit Newton) is the maximum load action F; a higher value of force F would cause overstressing and structural failure. The resistance R can be computed using the response function [82]

$$R = \frac{Q \cdot A + F_{cr} \cdot W_z - \sqrt{Q^2 \cdot A^2 + 2 \cdot A \cdot F_{cr} \cdot W_z \cdot (|e_0| \cdot F_{cr} - f_y \cdot W_z) + F_{cr}^2 \cdot W_z^2}}{2 \cdot W_z}, \quad (20)$$

where

$$Q = F_{cr} \cdot |e_0| + f_y \cdot W_z, \quad (21)$$

$$A = 2 \cdot b \cdot t_2 + t_1 \cdot (h - 2t_2), \quad (22)$$

$$F_{cr} = \pi^2 E I_z / L^2, \quad (23)$$

$$I_z = 2 \cdot t_2 \cdot b^3 / 12 + (h - 2t_2) \cdot t_1^3 / 12, \quad (24)$$

$$W_z = 2 \cdot I_z / b, \quad (25)$$

where e_0 is the amplitude of initial axis curvature, L is the member length, h is the cross-sectional height, b is the cross-sectional width, t_1 is the web thickness and t_2 is the flange thickness. These variables are used to further compute the following variables: A is cross-sectional area and I_z is second moment of area around axis z.

It can be noted that e_0 is the amplitude of pure geometrical imperfection with an idealized shape according to the elastic critical buckling mode [83]. Amplitude e_0 is not an equivalent geometrical imperfection [84–86], which would replace the influence of other imperfections, such as the residual stress. In Equation (20), the influence of residual stress is neglected.

The member length L is a deterministic parameter. Equation (20) is a non-linear, non-monotonic function for $R > 0$ that has the typical elastic resistance properties of a compressed member with initial material and geometrical imperfections with the exception of residual stress. Although R is a vector quantity, the direction is still horizontal; see Figure 4a) and only the magnitude is a random variable. Thus, in this article, the resistance R is examined as a scalar model output.

The material and geometrical characteristics of hot-rolled steel beams have been studied experimentally [87,88]. Studies [82,89–91] have confirmed that the variance of t_1 and h have a minimal influence on R. Therefore, these variables can be considered as deterministic with values $t_1 = 6$ mm and $h = 171$ mm. The input random variables are listed in Table 1. All random variables are statistically independent of each other.

Table 1. Input random variables.

Characteristic	Index	Symbol	Mean Value μ	Standard Deviation σ
Yield strength	1	f_y	297.3 MPa	16.8 MPa
Young's modulus	2	E	210 GPa	10 GPa
Imperfection	3	e_0	0	$L/1960$
Flange thickness	4	t_2	9.5 mm	0.436 mm
Flange width	5	b	180 mm	1.776 mm

All random variables have Gauss pdf, but with the condition $f_y > 0$, $E > 0$, $t_2 > 0$ and $b > 0$. However, negative realizations of random variables f_y, E, t_2 and b practically never occur if the LHS method [92,93] is used with no more than tens of millions of runs. Theoretically, if $f_y \to 0$ then $R \to 0$ (due to no stress), if $E \to 0$ then $R \to 0$ (due to zero stiffness), if $e_0 \to 0$

then $R \to F_{cr}$ or $R \to f_y \cdot A$ (pure buckling for high L or simple compression for low L), if $L \to 0$ then $R \to f_y \cdot A$ (simple compression).

4. Results of Sensitivity Analysis

The member length L is a deterministic parameter that changes step-by-step as $L = 0.001, 0.424, 0.849, \ldots, 6.366$ m. The step value is $L_0/10$, where $L_0 = 4.244$ m is the length of the member with non-dimensional slenderness [94] $\bar{\lambda} = 1.0$. The common non-dimensional slenderness of a strut in an efficient structural system is around one, but struts usually do not have non-dimensional slenderness higher than two [95]. The slenderness is directly proportional to the length. It is possible, for the presented case study, to write the transformation $L = \bar{\lambda} \cdot L_0$, which makes it easier to understand the lengths.

All three types of SA are based on double-nested-loop algorithms. Estimation of indices was software-based by implementing randomized Latin Hypercube Sampling-based Monte Carlo simulation (LHS) algorithms [92,93], which have been tuned for sensitivity assessments [78,80]. Using LHS runs, the outer loop is repeated 2000 times to estimate the arithmetic mean $E(\cdot)$ of the samples (l, l^2 or variance), which are estimated using an inner loop algorithm. The inner loop is repeated 4 million times (4 million LHS runs) to compute statistics (l, l^2 or variance) with some random realizations fixed by the outer loop.

The subject of interest for the two quantile-oriented SA is the 0.001-quantile θ^* of R. The estimate l quantifies the population distribution around the 0.001-quantile θ^*, where 0.001-quantile θ^* is estimated as the 4000th smallest value in the set of four million LHS runs ordered from smallest to largest [78,80].

The estimates of the unconditional characteristics in the denominators of the indices are computed using four million runs of the LHS method. Higher-order indices are estimated similarly.

The same set of (pseudo-) random numbers is used in each member length L, hereby ensuring that sampling and numerical errors do not swamp the statistics being sought [96,97].

Figures 5–8 show contrast Q indices, K indices and Sobol indices for four selected member lengths corresponding to non-dimensional slenderness values $\bar{\lambda} = 0, 0.5, 1, 1.5$. The outer coloured ring displays 31 sensitivity indices, and the inner white-grey pie chart shows the representation of member lengths of first-order indices (white area of the chart) and higher-order indices (grey areas).

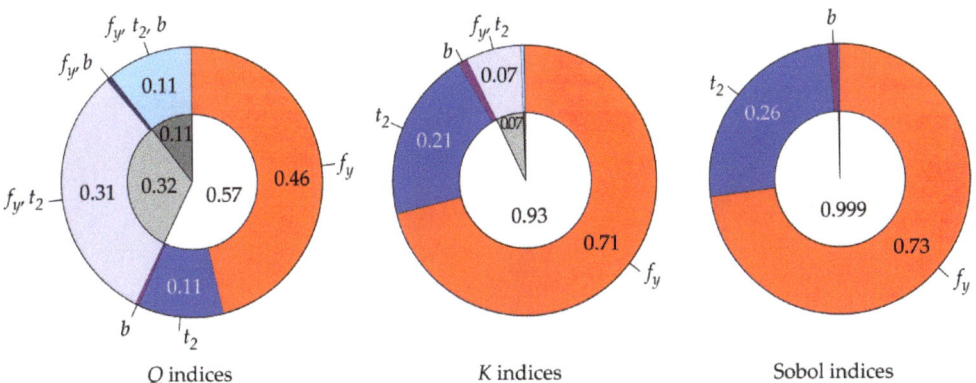

Figure 5. Comparison of three types of sensitivity analysis (SA) for $L = 0$ m ($\bar{\lambda} = 0$).

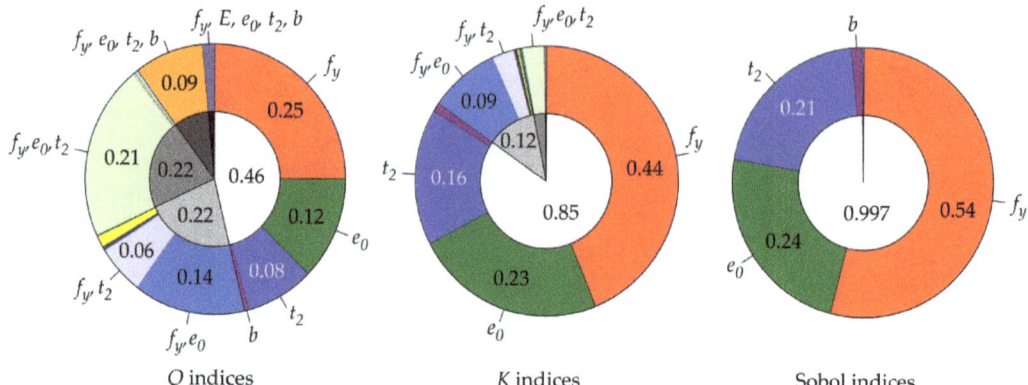

Figure 6. Comparison of three types of SA for $L = 2.122$ m ($\bar{\lambda} = 0.5$).

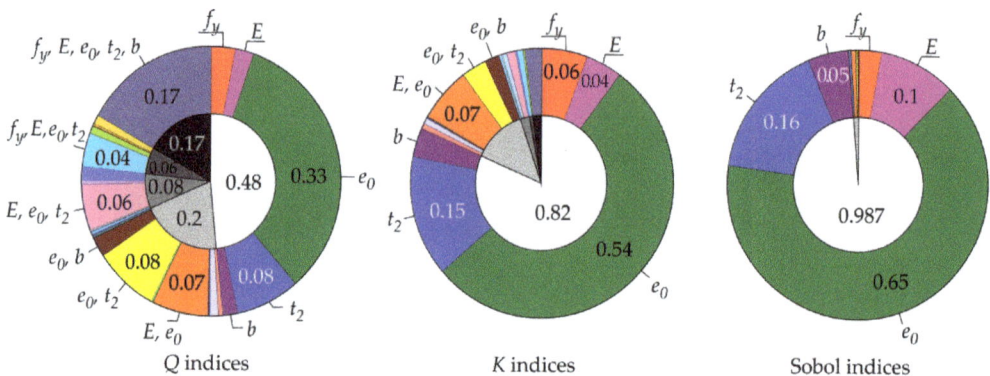

Figure 7. Comparison of three types of SA for $L = 4.244$ m ($\bar{\lambda} = 1.0$).

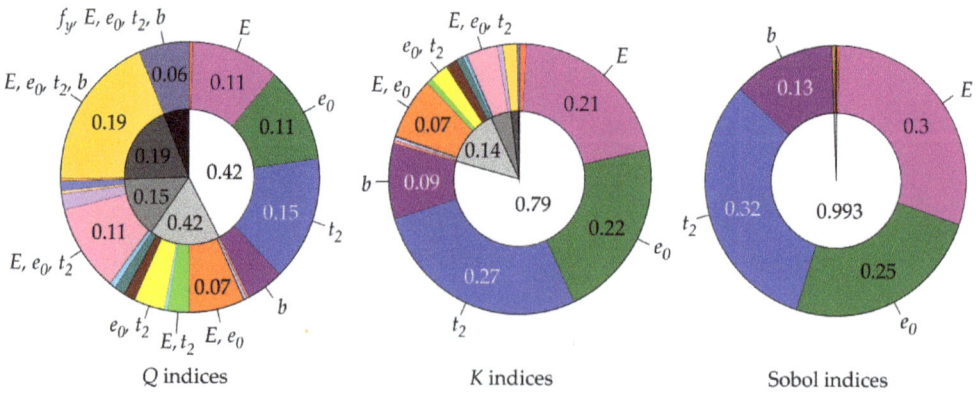

Figure 8. Comparison of three types of SA for $L = 6.366$ m ($\bar{\lambda} = 1.5$).

The results in Figures 5–8 show that Sobol indices have the largest proportion of first-order sensitivity indices; see the white area in the inner circles in Figures 5–8. Small higher-order indices make Sobol first-order indices transparent without the need to evaluate total indices. Unfortunately, Sobol indices are not quantile-oriented.

The new quantile-oriented K indices also have a relatively small proportion of higher-order indices (grey areas in the inner circles), and thus approach Sobol indices with their properties. Q indices have the lowest proportion of first-order sensitivity indices and a high proportion of higher-order indices (interaction effects), which makes the results less comprehensible, and the evaluation of total indices is then necessary.

Figures 9 and 10 display the plots of all thirty-one Q indices vs. member length L. A finer step is used in places where the curves change course faster.

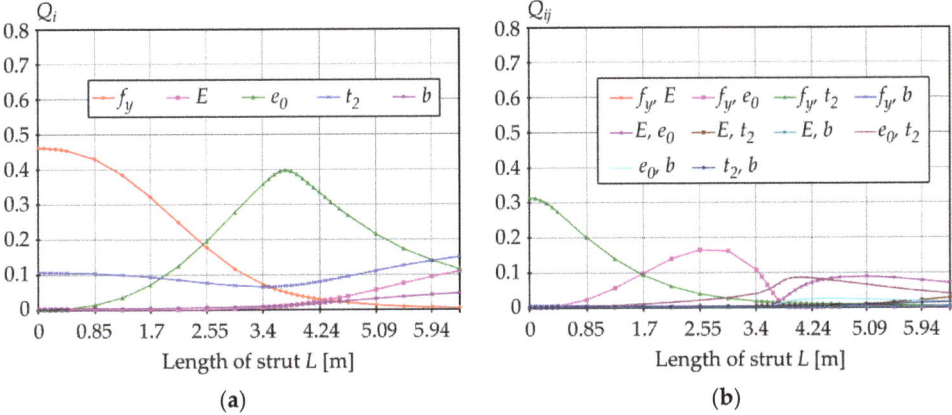

Figure 9. Q indices: (**a**) first-order sensitivity indices; (**b**) second-order sensitivity indices.

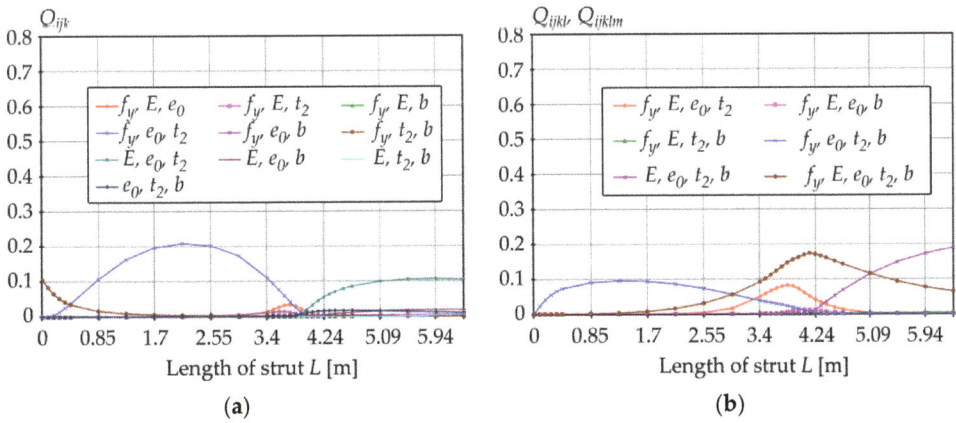

Figure 10. Q indices: (**a**) third-order sensitivity indices; (**b**) fourth- and fifth-order sensitivity indices.

As for Q indices, the clear influence of individual variables on the 0.001-quantile of R is evident only after the evaluation of total indices, see Figure 11. The yield strength f_y is dominant for low values of L (low slenderness), imperfection e_0 is dominant for intermediate lengths L (intermediate slenderness), Young's modulus and flange thickness gain dominance in the case of long members (high slenderness).

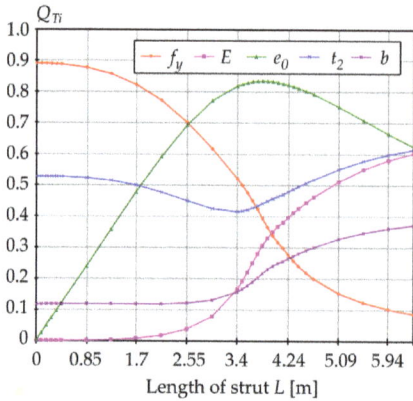

Figure 11. Q indices: total indices.

Figures 12 and 13 display the plots of all thirty-one K indices vs. member length, with the proportion of higher-order sensitivity indices being relatively small. The total K_T indices shown in Figure 14 provide very similar (but not the same) information as the first-order K_i indices depicted in Figure 12.

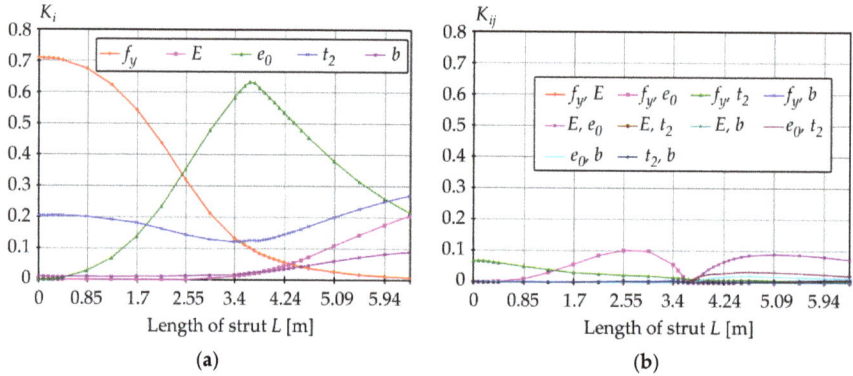

Figure 12. K indices: (**a**) first-order sensitivity indices; (**b**) second-order sensitivity indices.

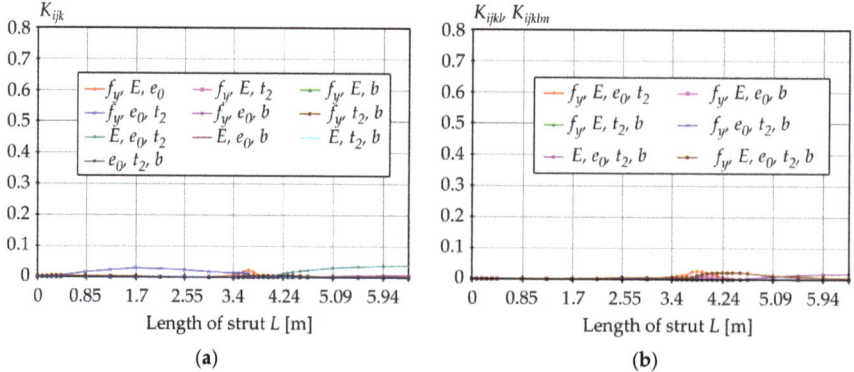

Figure 13. K indices: (**a**) third-order sensitivity indices; (**b**) fourth- and fifth-order sensitivity indices.

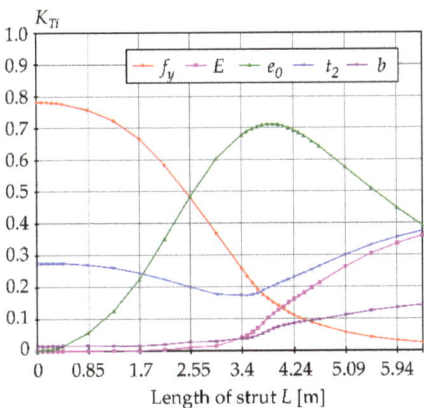

Figure 14. K indices: total indices.

Figure 15a shows Sobol first-order sensitivity indices. Sobol higher-order sensitivity indices are not shown because they are practically zero. The total indices shown in Figure 15b provide practically the same information as Sobol first-order sensitivity indices S_i.

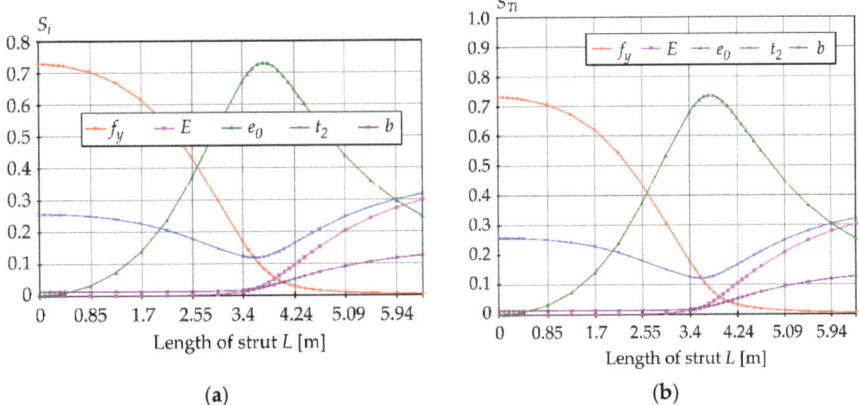

Figure 15. Sobol indices: (**a**) first-order sensitivity indices; (**b**) total indices.

Examples of percentage differences between first-order indices are as follows. The yield strength has the greatest influence for $L = 0$ m, with Q_1 being 37% smaller than S_1, and K_1 being 3% smaller than S_1. Imperfection e_0 has the greatest influence for $L \approx 3.8$ m, with Q_3 being 46% smaller than S_3, and K_3 being 16% smaller than S_3. K_i indices are closer to S_i indices (compared to Q_i indices).

The percentage differences between total indices are as follows. The yield strength has the greatest influence for $L = 0$ m, with Q_{T1} being 22% greater than S_{T1}, and K_{T1} being 7% greater than S_{T1}. Imperfection e_0 has the greatest influence for $L \approx 3.8$ m, with Q_{T3} being 13% greater than S_{T3} and K_{T3} being 3% smaller than S_{T3}. K_{Ti} indices are closer to S_{Ti} indices (compared to Q_{Ti} indices).

A comparison of the results of all three types of SA shows that the conclusions are very similar, despite being reached in a different way. The new K indices with their properties approach Sobol indices due to quadratic measures of sensitivity using l^2, which behaves similarly to variance σ_R^2.

5. Static Dependencies between l and σ_R and Other Connections

Quantile-oriented sensitivity indices are based on the quantile deviation l or its square l^2 while Sobol sensitivity indices are based on variance σ_R^2. The subject of interest of both quantile-oriented SA is the 0.001-quantile of R.

To better understand the essence of the computation of sensitivity indices, screening of statistics l and σ_R is performed when X_i is fixed. The aim is to identify similarities and differences between l and σ_R, rather than to accurately quantify sensitivity using Equations (8), (13) and (18). Samples $\sigma_R \mid X_i$ and $l \mid X_i$ are plotted for 400 LHS runs of X_i, otherwise the solution is the same as in the previous chapter. Skewness $a_R \mid X_i$ and kurtosis $k_R \mid X_i$ are added for selected samples, see Figures 16–21.

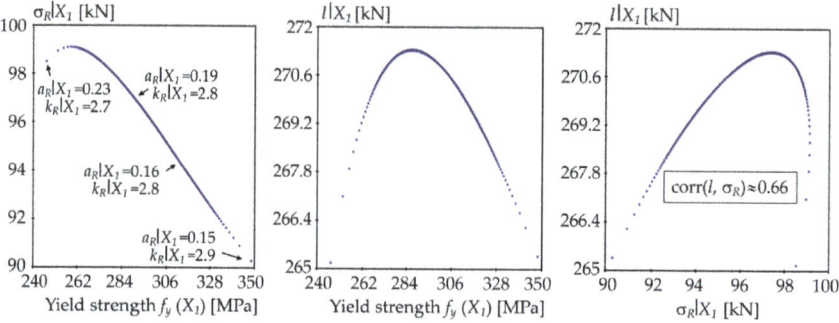

Figure 16. Samples of $\sigma_R \mid X_1$ and $l \mid X_1$ for $L = 4.244$ m ($\overline{\lambda} = 1.0$).

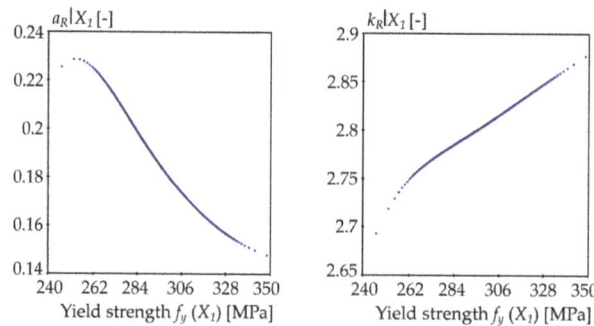

Figure 17. Samples of skewness $a_R \mid X_3$ and kurtosis $k_R \mid X_3$ for $L = 4.244$ m ($\overline{\lambda} = 1.0$).

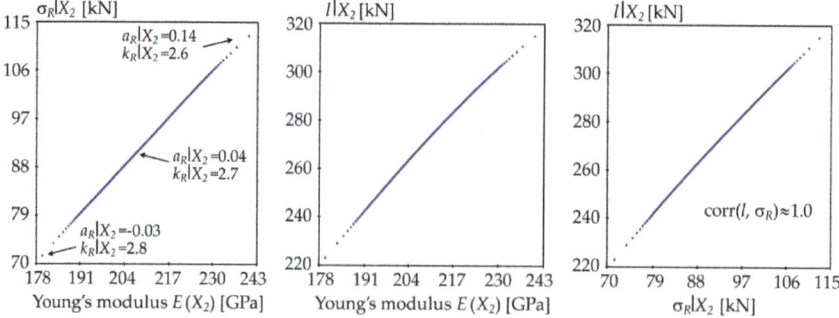

Figure 18. Samples of $\sigma_R \mid X_2$ and $l \mid X_2$ for $L = 4.244$ m ($\overline{\lambda} = 1.0$).

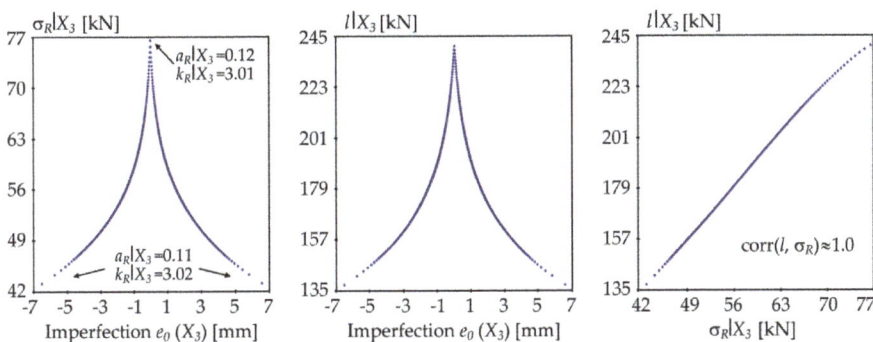

Figure 19. Samples of $\sigma_R \mid X_3$ and $l \mid X_3$ for $L = 4.244$ m ($\bar{\lambda} = 1.0$).

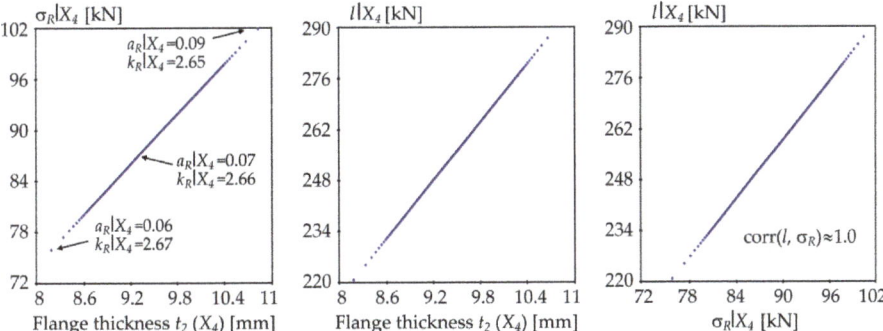

Figure 20. Samples of $\sigma_R \mid X_4$ and $l \mid X_4$ for $L = 4.244$ m ($\bar{\lambda} = 1.0$).

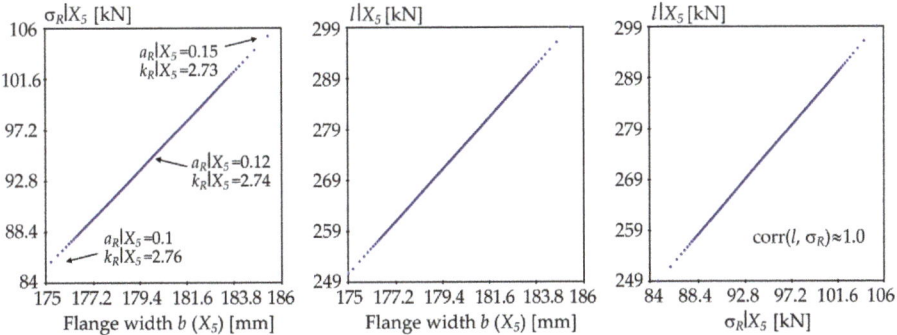

Figure 21. Samples of $\sigma_R \mid X_5$ and $l \mid X_5$ for $L = 4.244$ m ($\bar{\lambda} = 1.0$).

The samples in Figure 19 are symmetric due to the symmetric shape of the probability distribution (Gauss pdf) of input variable e_0 with a mean value of zero. Only the absolute value of this variable is applied in Equation (20). The output R is not monotonically dependent on e_0. The practical consequence is that in the case of an even number of LHS runs, it is sufficient to compute the nested loop in Equations (8), (13) and (18) only once for the positive value of random realization e_0, because the solution is the same for a negative value. This reduces the computational cost of estimating indices Q_3, K_3 and S_3 by half.

The smaller the estimated $\sigma_R \mid X_i$, the more fixing of X_i reduces the uncertainty of the output in terms of variance, which measures change around μ_R. The smaller the estimated $l \mid X_i$, the more the fixing of X_i reduces the uncertainty of the output in terms of parameter l, which measures change around θ. Imperfection e_0 (X_3) has the greatest influence in both cases, see low values on the vertical axes in Figure 19.

In all cases, the dependence $l \mid X_i$ vs. $\sigma_R \mid X_i$ is approximately linear with the exception of the concave course on the right in Figure 16. Pearson correlation coefficient between 400 samples $l \mid X_i$ vs. $\sigma_R \mid X_i$ is approximately 0.66. The concave course and lower correlation (compared to other variables) is due to the conflicting influences of σ_R, a_R and k_R. By approximating R using the Hermite distribution $R \sim H(\mu_R, \sigma_R, a_R, k_R)$, the effects of μ_R, σ_R, a_R and k_R on l can be observed separately as follows: change in μ_R has no influence on l, increasing σ_R increases l, increasing a_R decreases l, increasing k_R increases l, assuming small values of changes.

The influence of X_1 is interesting. Figure 16, on the left, shows that with increasing X_1, $\sigma_R \mid X_1$ has an approximately decreasing plot, with the exception of the beginning on the left. Figure 17 shows that $a_R \mid X_1$ has an approximately decreasing course, $k_R \mid X_1$ has an increasing course. At the beginning on the left, increasing X_1 causes an increase in $\sigma_R \mid X_1$, $k_R \mid X_1$ and $a_R \mid X_1$, which, taken together, increases $l \mid X_1$ due to the dominance of the joint effect of $\sigma_R \mid X_1$, $k_R \mid X_1$ and $a_R \mid X_1$. The region where $\sigma_R \mid X_1$ starts decreasing but l still increases is interesting. Although the standard deviation is an important output characteristic, a change in the input variable can have a stronger influence on the quantile through skewness and kurtosis. At the opposite end (right), increasing X_1 causes a decrease in $\sigma_R \mid X_1$, a decrease in $a_R \mid X_1$ and an increase in $k_R \mid X_1$, which together reduces $l \mid X_1$, because the decreasing sole effect of $\sigma_R \mid X_1$ is dominant. The whole course of $l \mid X_1$ vs. X_1 is shown in Figure 16 in the middle. The example shows the combined effect of standard deviation, skewness and kurtosis on the quantile deviation l, which is the core of the computation of quantile-oriented sensitivity indices Q_i and K_i.

For other variables X_2, X_3, X_4 and X_5 the range of $\sigma_R \mid X_i$ is significantly larger than that of $\sigma_R \mid X_1$ (99.1 − 90.3 = 8.8 MPa) and $\sigma_R \mid X_i$ has a crucial influence on $l \mid X_i$. Hence, the dependences $l \mid X_i$ vs. $\sigma_R \mid X_i$, $i = 2, 3, 4, 5$ are approximately linear.

6. Discussion

Low quantiles represent a significant part of the analysis of reliability of load-bearing structures. SA of design quantiles can be used wherever reliability can be judged by comparing two statistically independent variables.

Both types of quantile-oriented sensitivity analysis identified a very similar sensitivity order to Sobol SA. Identical identification of probabilistically insignificant variables can serve to reliably decrease the dimension of random design space by introducing non-influential variables as deterministic. On the contrary, the probability distribution of dominant variables should be identified with the greatest possible accuracy.

In all cases, the most important output information is the sensitivity order obtained using total indices. Total indices identify approximately the same sensitivity order for all types of SA; see Figures 11, 14 and 15b. Sobol total indices can be a good proxy of quantile-oriented total indices in cases where changes in the quantile are primarily influenced by changes in the variance and less by the shape of the probability distribution of the output variable R. It can be noted that although the case of strong discrepancy between quantile-oriented indices and Sobol indices has not yet been observed, some atypical (in practice, less real) tasks have not yet been solved, e.g., Sobol SA with strong interaction effects or SA of quantiles close to the mean.

Quantile-oriented contrast Q indices are based on the quantile deviation l, which is the absolute distance of two average values of the population below and above the quantile; see Equations (4)–(6). Quantile deviation l has the same unit and is similar to σ_R, because it measures the variability of the population around the quantile. Quantile deviation l has good resistance to outlier values around the quantile. When X_i changes deterministically, the quantile deviation l is found to change, but not always monotonically, despite a monotonic variation in the standard deviation σ_R. The correlation between l and σ_R may or may not be strong even though a dependence exists; see Figure 16.

By applying the quantile deviation l as a new measure of sensitivity, contrast Q indices defined by Fort [63] can be rewritten in a new form; see Equations (8)–(12). By substituting l with l^2, Q indices can be rewritten as the new K indices, which are based on the decomposition of l^2, similarly to the way Sobol indices are based on the decomposition of variance; see Equations (13)–(17).

Contrast Q indices have an unpleasantly relatively high proportion of higher-order indices (interaction effects), which makes it difficult to interpret SA results. The new K indices have characteristics close to Sobol indices because they have a smaller proportion of interaction effects than Q indices. Although K and Sobol indices are similar, they are not the same because the key variable l depends not only on the variance but also on the shape of the distribution (variance, skewness, kurtosis).

The comparison of contrast Q indices, K indices and Sobol indices was performed using a non-linear function R, which includes both non-linear and non-monotonic effects of five input variables X_i on the output. In the case study, four input variables X_i, i = 2, 3, 4, 5 have approximately linear dependence $l\,|\,X_i$ vs. $\sigma_R\,|\,X_i$, where l and σ_R are computed for fixed X_i while the other $X_{\sim i}$ are considered as random. However, this does not apply to input variable X_1 (yield strength f_y), which leads to a non-linear concave dependence $l\,|\,X_i$ vs. $\sigma_R\,|\,X_i$. The example shows the strong influence of the shape of the distribution (skewness and kurtosis) on the quantile deviation l as one of the causes leading to differences in K indices from Sobol indices.

The findings presented here correlate very well with the results of SA of a beam under bending exposed to lateral-torsional buckling, where contrast Q indices and Sobol indices identified very similar sensitivity rank of input random variables [78,80].

Although other types of quantile-oriented sensitivity indices exist [98–100], they are not of a global type with the sum of all indices equal to one, so they were not used in this paper, because mutual comparison would be difficult.

The K indices and Q indices presented here are as computationally demanding as the sensitivity indices derived in [62], but with the advantage that they are not limited to small and large quantiles. For small 0.001-quantile, the estimates of asymptotic QE indices [62] are practically the same as the results published in this article; therefore, the asymptotic form [62] does not provide any immediately apparent application advantage when the Monte Carlo method is applied.

It can be noted that civil engineering has numerous reliability tasks in which interactions can be a significant part of the design of structural members or systems, see e.g., [101–105]. Another goal of SA may be the examination of the design quantiles of these tasks.

7. Conclusions

Low and high quantiles represent a significant part of the analysis of reliability, not only in the design of building structures. The sensitivity analysis of the resistance R of the steel strut showed significant similarities and differences between both types of quantile-oriented sensitivity analysis (SA) and classical Sobol SA.

The quantile deviation l was defined as the difference between superquantile and subquantile. New global sensitivity measures based on the quantile deviation l of model output were introduced. The quantile deviation l measures the statistical variability around the quantile similarly to how standard deviation measures the statistical variability around the mean value. By using l to the first power, it is possible to rewrite quantile-oriented sensitivity indices subordinated to contrasts (Q indices) in a new form. The obtained results of the presented case study established that Q indices are the least comprehensible because they exhibit the strongest interaction effects between inputs. The results of Sobol SA are clear; however, they are not directly oriented to design quantiles and reliability.

With this motivation in mind, new quantile-oriented sensitivity indices (K indices) are expressed in this paper with sensitivity measure l^2 expressed in the same unit as variance, thus approaching Sobol sensitivity indices with their properties. l^2 has a significance similar to variance, but around quantile. The unit consistency between K indices and Sobol indices makes K indices attractive in stochastic models, where more parameters (goals) of the probability distribution of the model output need to be analysed. Overall, the new K indices can be considered effective in solving the effect of input random variables on design quantiles.

The case study based on a non-linear and non-monotonic function showed that all three types of SA give very similar conclusions when total indices are evaluated. Although Sobol SA is based on the decomposition of only the variance of the model output, its conclusions are in good agreement with the conclusions of both quantile-oriented SA. The case study showed that the correlation between quantile deviation l and standard deviation σ_R may or may not be strong. Although l correlates with σ_R, l is also related to the shape of the probability distribution.

In general, it is always better to prioritize quantile-oriented types of global SA, which measure the statistical variability around a quantile (e.g., quantile deviation l) rather than around a mean value (variance), for quantile-based reliability analysis.

Funding: The work has been supported and prepared within the project namely "Probability oriented global sensitivity measures of structural reliability" of The Czech Science Foundation (GACR, https://gacr.cz/) no. 20-01734S, Czechia.

Institutional Review Board Statement: Not applicable.

Informed Consent Statement: Not applicable.

Data Availability Statement: Not applicable.

Conflicts of Interest: The author declares no conflict of interest.

References

1. Saltelli, A.; Ratto, M.; Andres, T.; Campolongo, F.; Cariboni, J.; Gatelli, D.; Saisana, M.; Tarantola, S. *Global Sensitivity Analysis: The Primer*; John Wiley & Sons: West Sussex, UK, 2008.
2. Sobol, I.M. Sensitivity Estimates for Non-linear Mathematical Models. *Math. Model. Comput. Exp.* **1993**, *1*, 407–414.
3. Sobol, I.M. Global Sensitivity Indices for Nonlinear Mathematical Models and Their Monte Carlo Estimates. *Math. Comput. Simul.* **2001**, *55*, 271–280. [CrossRef]
4. Gödel, M.; Fischer, R.; Köster, G. Sensitivity Analysis for Microscopic Crowd Simulation. *Algorithms* **2020**, *13*, 162. [CrossRef]
5. Gao, P.; Li, J.; Zhai, J.; Tao, Y.; Han, Q. A Novel Optimization Layout Method for Clamps in a Pipeline System. *Appl. Sci.* **2020**, *10*, 390. [CrossRef]
6. Gatel, L.; Lauvernet, C.; Carluer, N.; Weill, S.; Paniconi, C. Sobol Global Sensitivity Analysis of a Coupled Surface/Subsurface Water Flow and Reactive Solute Transfer Model on a Real Hillslope. *Water* **2020**, *12*, 121. [CrossRef]
7. Prikaziuk, E.; van der Tol, C. Global Sensitivity Analysis of the SCOPE Model in Sentinel-3 Bands: Thermal Domain Focus. *Remote Sens.* **2019**, *11*, 2424. [CrossRef]
8. Dimov, I.; Georgieva, R. Monte Carlo Algorithms for Evaluating Sobol' Sensitivity Indices. *Math. Comput. Simul.* **2010**, *81*, 506–514. [CrossRef]
9. Gamannossi, A.; Amerini, A.; Mazzei, L.; Bacci, T.; Poggiali, M.; Andreini, A. Uncertainty Quantification of Film Cooling Performance of an Industrial Gas Turbine Vane. *Entropy* **2020**, *22*, 16. [CrossRef] [PubMed]
10. Xu, N.; Luo, J.; Zuo, J.; Hu, X.; Dong, J.; Wu, T.; Wu, S.; Liu, H. Accurate Suitability Evaluation of Large-Scale Roof Greening Based on RS and GIS Methods. *Sustainability* **2020**, *12*, 4375. [CrossRef]
11. Islam, A.B.M.; Karadoğan, E. Analysis of One-Dimensional Ivshin–Pence Shape Memory Alloy Constitutive Model for Sensitivity and Uncertainty. *Materials* **2020**, *13*, 1482. [CrossRef] [PubMed]
12. Mattei, A.; Goblet, P.; Barbecot, F.; Guillon, S.; Coquet, Y.; Wang, S. Can Soil Hydraulic Parameters be Estimated from the Stable Isotope Composition of Pore Water from a Single Soil Profile? *Water* **2020**, *12*, 393. [CrossRef]
13. Akbari, S.; Mahmood, S.M.; Ghaedi, H.; Al-Hajri, S. A New Empirical Model for Viscosity of Sulfonated Polyacrylamide Polymers. *Polymers* **2019**, *11*, 1046. [CrossRef] [PubMed]
14. Koo, H.; Iwanaga, T.; Croke, B.F.W.; Jakeman, A.J.; Yang, J.; Wang, H.-H.; Sun, X.; Lü, G.; Li, X.; Yue, T.; et al. Position Paper: Sensitivity Analysis of Spatially Distributed Environmental Models- a Pragmatic Framework for the Exploration of Uncertainty Sources. *Environ. Model. Softw.* **2020**, *134*, 104857. [CrossRef]

15. Douglas-Smith, D.; Iwanaga, T.; Croke, B.F.W.; Jakeman, A.J. Title. Certain Trends in Uncertainty and Sensitivity Analysis: An Overview of Software Tools and Techniques. *Environ. Model. Softw.* **2020**, *124*, 104588. [CrossRef]
16. Norton, J. An Introduction to Sensitivity Assessment of Simulation Models. *Environ. Model. Softw.* **2015**, *69*, 166–174. [CrossRef]
17. Wei, P.; Lu, Z.; Song, J. Variable Importance Analysis: A Comprehensive Review. *Reliab. Eng. Syst. Saf.* **2015**, *142*, 399–432. [CrossRef]
18. Razavi, S.; Gupta, H.V. What Do We Mean by Sensitivity Analysis? The Need for Comprehensive Characterization of "Global" Sensitivity in Earth and Environmental Systems Models. *Water Resour. Res.* **2015**, *51*, 3070–3092. [CrossRef]
19. Borgonovo, E.; Plischke, E. Sensitivity Analysis: A Review of Recent Advances. *Eur. J. Oper. Res.* **2016**, *248*, 869–887. [CrossRef]
20. Ma, T.; Xu, L. Story-Based Stability of Multistory Steel Semibraced and Unbraced Frames with Semirigid Connections. *J. Struct. Eng.* **2021**, *147*, 04020304. [CrossRef]
21. Pan, L.; Novák, L.; Lehký, D.; Novák, D.; Cao, M. Neural Network Ensemble-based Sensitivity Analysis in Structural Engineering: Comparison of Selected Methods and the Influence of Statistical Correlation. *Comput. Struct.* **2021**, *242*, 106376. [CrossRef]
22. Antucheviciene, J.; Kala, Z.; Marzouk, M.; Vaidogas, E.R. Solving Civil Engineering Problems by Means of Fuzzy and Stochastic MCDM Methods: Current State and Future Research. *Math. Probl. Eng.* **2015**, *2015*, 362579. [CrossRef]
23. Su, C.; Xian, J.; Huang, H. An Iterative Equivalent Linearization Approach for Stochastic Sensitivity Analysis of Hysteretic Systems Under Seismic Excitations Based on Explicit Time-domain Method. *Comput. Struct.* **2021**, *242*, 106396. [CrossRef]
24. Bi, Y.; Wu, S.; Pei, J.; Wen, Y.; Li, R. Correlation Analysis Between Aging Behavior and Rheological Indices of Asphalt Binder. *Constr. Build. Mater.* **2020**, *264*, 120176. [CrossRef]
25. Gelesz, A.; Catto Lucchino, E.; Goia, F.; Serra, V.; Reith, A. Characteristics That Matter in a Climate Facade: A Sensitivity Analysis with Building Energy Simulation Tools. *Energy Build.* **2020**, *229*, 110467. [CrossRef]
26. Naderpour, H.; Haji, M.; Mirrashid, M. Shear Capacity Estimation of FRP-reinforced Concrete Beams Using Computational Intelligence. *Structures* **2020**, *28*, 321–328. [CrossRef]
27. Khetwal, A.; Rostami, J.; Nelson, P.P. Investigating the Impact of TBM Downtimes on Utilization Factor Based on Sensitivity Analysis. *Tunn. Undergr. Space Technol.* **2020**, *106*, 103586. [CrossRef]
28. Changizi, N.; Warn, G.P. Stochastic Stress-based Topology Optimization of Structural Frames Based upon the Second Deviatoric Stress Invariant. *Eng. Struct.* **2020**, *224*, 111186. [CrossRef]
29. Farahbakhshtooli, A.; Bhowmick, A.K. Seismic Collapse Assessment of Stiffened Steel Plate Shear Walls using FEMA P695 Methodology. *Eng. Struct.* **2019**, *200*, 109714. [CrossRef]
30. He, L.; Liu, Y.; Bi, S.; Wang, L.; Broggi, M.; Beer, M. Estimation of Failure Probability in Braced Excavation using Bayesian Networks with Integrated Model Updating. *Undergr. Space* **2020**, *5*, 315–323. [CrossRef]
31. Zolfani, S.H.; Yazdani, M.; Zavadskas, E.K.; Hasheminasab, H. Prospective Madm and Sensitivity Analysis of the Experts Based on Causal Layered Analysis (CLA). *Econ. Manag.* **2020**, *23*, 208–223.
32. Radović, D.; Stević, Ž.; Pamučar, D.; Zavadskas, E.K.; Badi, I.; Antuchevičiene, J.; Turskis, Z. Measuring Performance in Transportation Companies in Developing Countries: A Novel Rough ARAS Model. *Symmetry* **2018**, *10*, 434. [CrossRef]
33. Su, L.; Wang, T.; Li, H.; Chao, Y.; Wang, L. Multi-criteria Decision Making for Identification of Unbalanced Bidding. *J. Civ. Eng. Manag.* **2020**, *26*, 43–52. [CrossRef]
34. Fortan, M.; Ferraz, G.; Lauwens, K.; Molkens, T.; Rossi, B. Shear Buckling of Stainless Steel Plate Girders with Non-rigid end Posts. *J. Constr. Steel Res.* **2020**, *172*, 106211. [CrossRef]
35. Leblouba, M.; Tabsh, S.W.; Barakat, S. Reliability-based Design of Corrugated web Steel Girders in Shear as per AASHTO LRFD. *J. Constr. Steel Res* **2020**, *169*, 106013. [CrossRef]
36. Rykov, V.; Kozyrev, D. On the Reliability Function of a Double Redundant System with General Repair Time Distribution. *Appl. Stoch. Models Bus. Ind.* **2019**, *35*, 191–197. [CrossRef]
37. Pan, H.; Tian, L.; Fu, X.; Li, H. Sensitivities of the Seismic Response and Fragility Estimate of a Transmission Tower to Structural and Ground Motion Uncertainties. *J. Constr. Steel Res.* **2020**, *167*, 105941. [CrossRef]
38. Leblouba, M.; Barakat, S.; Al-Saadon, Z. Shear Behavior of Corrugated Web Panels and Sensitivity Analysis. *J. Constr. Steel Res.* **2018**, *151*, 94–107. [CrossRef]
39. Lellep, J.; Puman, E. Plastic response of conical shells with stiffeners to blast loading. *Acta Comment. Univ. Tartu. Math.* **2020**, *24*, 5–18. [CrossRef]
40. Kala, Z. Estimating probability of fatigue failure of steel structures. *Acta Comment. Univ. Tartu. Math.* **2019**, *23*, 245–254. [CrossRef]
41. Strieška, M.; Koteš, P. Sensitivity of Dose-response Function for Carbon Steel under Various Conditions in Slovakia. *Transp. Res. Procedia* **2019**, *40*, 912–919. [CrossRef]
42. Cremen, G.; Baker, J.W. Variance-based Sensitivity Analyses and Uncertainty Quantification for FEMA P-58 Consequence Predictions. *Earthq. Eng. Struct. Dyn.* **2020**, in press. [CrossRef]
43. Liu, X.; Jiang, L.; Lai, Z.; Xiang, P.; Chen, Y. Sensitivity and Dynamic Analysis of Train-bridge Coupled System with Multiple Random Factors. *Eng. Struct.* **2020**, *221*, 111083. [CrossRef]
44. Feng, D.-C.; Fu, B. Shear Strength of Internal Reinforced Concrete Beam-Column Joints: Intelligent Modeling Approach and Sensitivity Analysis. *Adv. Civ. Eng.* **2020**, *2020*, 8850417. [CrossRef]
45. Amaranto, A.; Pianosi, F.; Solomatine, D.; Corzo, G.; Muñoz-Arriola, F. Sensitivity Analysis of Data-driven Groundwater Forecasts to Hydroclimatic Controls in Irrigated Croplands. *J. Hydrol.* **2020**, *587*, 124957. [CrossRef]

46. Štefaňák, J.; Kala, Z.; Miča, L.; Norkus, A. Global Sensitivity Analysis for Transformation of Hoek-Brown Failure Criterion for Rock Mass. *J. Civ. Eng. Manag.* **2018**, *24*, 390–398. [CrossRef]
47. Shao, D.; Jiang, G.; Zong, C.; Xing, Y.; Zheng, Z.; Lv, S. Global Sensitivity Analysis of Behavior of Energy Pile under Thermo-mechanical Loads. *Soils Found.* **2021**, in press. [CrossRef]
48. Erdal, D.; Xiao, S.; Nowak, W.; Cirpka, O.A. Sampling Behavioral Model Parameters for Ensemble-based Sensitivity Analysis using Gaussian Process Eemulation and Active Subspaces. *Stoch. Environ. Res. Risk Assess.* **2020**, *34*, 1813–1830. [CrossRef]
49. Yurchenko, V.; Peleshko, I. Searching for Optimal Pre-Stressing of Steel Bar Structures Based on Sensitivity Analysis. *Arch. Civ. Eng.* **2020**, *66*, 525–540.
50. Liu, F.; Wei, P.; Zhou, C.; Yue, Z. Reliability and Reliability Sensitivity Analysis of Structure by Combining Adaptive Linked Importance Sampling and Kriging Reliability Method. *Chin. J. Aeronaut.* **2020**, *33*, 1218–1227. [CrossRef]
51. Javidan, M.M.; Kim, J. Variance-based Global Sensitivity Analysis for Fuzzy Random Structural Systems. *Comput. Aided Civ. Infrastruct. Eng.* **2019**, *34*, 602–615. [CrossRef]
52. Wan, H.-P.; Zheng, Y.; Luo, Y.; Yang, C.; Xu, X. Comprehensive Sensitivity Analysis of Rotational Stability of a Super-deep Underground Spherical Structure Considering Uncertainty. *Adv. Struct. Eng.* **2021**, *24*, 65–78. [CrossRef]
53. Zhong, J.; Wan, H.-P.; Yuan, W.; He, M.; Ren, W.-X. Risk-informed Sensitivity Analysis and Optimization of Seismic Mitigation Strategy using Gaussian Process Surrogate Model. *Soil Dyn. Earthq. Eng.* **2020**, *138*, 106284. [CrossRef]
54. Vokál, M.; Drahorád, M. Sensitivity Analysis of Input Parameters for Load Carrying Capacity of Masonry Arch Bridges. *Acta Polytech.* **2020**, *60*, 349–358. [CrossRef]
55. Szymczak, C.; Kujawa, M. Sensitivity Analysis of Free Torsional Vibration Frequencies of Thin-walled Laminated Beams Under Axial Load. *Contin. Mech. Thermodyn.* **2020**, *32*, 1347–1356. [CrossRef]
56. Yang, K.; Xue, B.; Fang, H.; Du, X.; Li, B.; Chen, J. Mechanical Sensitivity Analysis of Pipe-liner Composite Structure Under Multi-field Coupling. *Structures* **2021**, *29*, 484–493. [CrossRef]
57. Guo, Q.; Liu, Y.; Liu, X.; Chen, B.; Yao, Q. Fatigue Dynamic Reliability and Global Sensitivity Analysis of Double Random Vibration System Based on Kriging Model. *Inverse Probl. Sci. Eng.* **2020**, *28*, 1648–1667. [CrossRef]
58. Song, S.; Wang, L. A Novel Global Sensitivity Measure Based on Probability Weighted Moments. *Symmetry* **2021**, *13*, 90. [CrossRef]
59. European Committee for Standardization (CEN). *EN 1990:2002: Eurocode—Basis of Structural Design*; European Committee for Standardization: Brussels, Belgium, 2002.
60. Joint Committee on Structural Safety (JCSS). Probabilistic Model Code. Available online: https://www.jcss-lc.org/ (accessed on 25 January 2021).
61. Kala, Z. Sensitivity Analysis in Probabilistic Structural Design: A Comparison of Selected Techniques. *Sustainability* **2020**, *12*, 4788. [CrossRef]
62. Kala, Z. From Probabilistic to Quantile-oriented Sensitivity Analysis: New Indices of Design Quantiles. *Symmetry* **2020**, *12*, 1720. [CrossRef]
63. Fort, J.C.; Klein, T.; Rachdi, N. New Sensitivity Analysis Subordinated to a Contrast. *Commun. Stat. Theory Methods* **2016**, *45*, 4349–4364. [CrossRef]
64. Rockafellar, R.T.; Uryasev, S. Conditional Value-at-risk for General Loss Distributions. *J. Bank. Financ.* **2002**, *26*, 1443–1471. [CrossRef]
65. Tyrrell Rockafellar, R.; Royset, J.O. Engineering Decisions under Risk Averseness. *ASCE-ASME J. Risk Uncertain. Eng. Syst. Part A Civ. Eng.* **2015**, *1*, 04015003. [CrossRef]
66. Airouss, M.; Tahiri, M.; Lahlou, A.; Hassouni, A. Advanced Expected Tail Loss Measurement and Quantification for the Moroccan All Shares Index Portfolio. *Mathematics* **2018**, *6*, 38. [CrossRef]
67. Rockafellar, R.T.; Royset, J.O. Superquantile/CVaR Risk Measures: Second-order Theory. *Ann. Oper. Res.* **2018**, *262*, 3–28. [CrossRef]
68. Mafusalov, A.; Uryasev, S. CVaR (Superquantile) Norm: Stochastic Case. *Eur. J. Oper. Res.* **2016**, *249*, 200–208. [CrossRef]
69. Hunjra, A.I.; Alawi, S.M.; Colombage, S.; Sahito, U.; Hanif, M. Portfolio Construction by Using Different Risk Models: A Comparison among Diverse Economic Scenarios. *Risks* **2020**, *8*, 126. [CrossRef]
70. Bosch-Badia, M.-T.; Montllor-Serrats, J.; Tarrazon-Rodon, M.-A. Risk Analysis through the Half-Normal Distribution. *Mathematics* **2020**, *8*, 2080. [CrossRef]
71. Norton, M.; Khokhlov, V.; Uryasev, S. Calculating CVaR and bPOE for Common Probability Distributions with Application to Portfolio Optimization and Density Estimation. *Ann. Oper. Res.* **2019**, 1–35. [CrossRef]
72. Kouri, D.P. Spectral Risk Measures: The Risk Quadrangle and Optimal Approximation. *Math. Program.* **2019**, *174*, 525–552. [CrossRef]
73. Golodnikov, A.; Kuzmenko, V.; Uryasev, S. CVaR Regression Based on the Relation between CVaR and Mixed-Quantile Quadrangles. *J. Risk Financ. Manag.* **2019**, *12*, 107. [CrossRef]
74. Jiménez, I.; Mora-Valencia, A.; Ñíguez, T.-M.; Perote, J. Portfolio Risk Assessment under Dynamic (Equi)Correlation and Semi-Nonparametric Estimation: An Application to Cryptocurrencies. *Mathematics* **2020**, *8*, 2110. [CrossRef]
75. Sedlacek, G.; Müller, C. The European Standard Family and its Basis. *J. Constr. Steel Res.* **2006**, *62*, 522–548. [CrossRef]
76. Sedlacek, G.; Stangenberg, H. Design Philosophy of Eurocodes—Background Information. *J. Constr. Steel Res.* **2000**, *54*, 173–190. [CrossRef]
77. Jönsson, J.; Müller, M.S.; Gamst, C.; Valeš, J.; Kala, Z. Investigation of European Flexural and Lateral Torsional Buckling Interaction. *J. Constr. Steel Res.* **2019**, *156*, 105–121. [CrossRef]
78. Kala, Z. Quantile-oriented Global Sensitivity Analysis of Design Resistance. *J. Civ. Eng. Manag.* **2019**, *25*, 297–305. [CrossRef]

79. Kala, Z.; Valeš, J.; Jönsson, L. Random Fields of Initial out of Straightness Leading to Column Buckling. *J. Civ. Eng. Manag.* **2017**, *23*, 902–913. [CrossRef]
80. Kala, Z. Quantile-based Versus Sobol Sensitivity Analysis in Limit State Design. *Structures* **2020**, *28*, 2424–2430. [CrossRef]
81. Kala, Z.; Valeš, J. Sensitivity Assessment and Lateral-torsional Buckling Design of I-beams Using Solid Finite Elements. *J. Constr. Steel Res.* **2017**, *139*, 110–122. [CrossRef]
82. Kala, Z. Sensitivity Assessment of Steel Members Under Compression. *Eng. Struct.* **2009**, *31*, 1344–1348. [CrossRef]
83. Yang, X.; Xiang, Y.; Luo, Y.-F.; Guo, X.-N.; Liu, J. Axial Compression Capacity of Steel Circular Tube with Large Initial Curvature: Column Curve and Application in Structural Assessment. *J. Constr. Steel Res.* **2021**, *177*, 106481. [CrossRef]
84. Mercier, C.; Khelil, A.; Khamisi, A.; Al Mahmoud, F.; Boissiere, R.; Pamies, A. Analysis of the Global and Local Imperfection of Structural Members and Frames. *J. Civ. Eng. Manag.* **2019**, *25*, 805–818. [CrossRef]
85. Agüero, A.; Baláž, I.; Koleková, Y.; Martin, P. Assessment of in-Plane Behavior of Metal Compressed Members with Equivalent Geometrical Imperfection. *Appl. Sci.* **2020**, *10*, 8174. [CrossRef]
86. Agüero, A.; Baláž, I.; Koleková, Y. New Method for Metal Beams Sensitive to Lateral Torsional Buckling with an Equivalent Geometrical UGLI Imperfection. *Structures* **2021**, *29*, 1445–1462. [CrossRef]
87. Melcher, J.; Kala, Z.; Holický, M.; Fajkus, M.; Rozlívka, L. Design Characteristics of Structural Steels Based on Statistical Analysis of Metallurgical Products. *J. Constr. Steel Res.* **2004**, *60*, 795–808. [CrossRef]
88. Kala, Z.; Melcher, J.; Puklický, L. Material and Geometrical Characteristics of Structural Steels Based on Statistical Analysis of Metallurgical Products. *J. Civ. Eng. Manag.* **2009**, *15*, 299–307. [CrossRef]
89. Kala, Z. Global Sensitivity Analysis in Stability Problems of Steel Frame Structures. *J. Civ. Eng. Manag.* **2016**, *22*, 417–424. [CrossRef]
90. Kala, Z. Geometrically Non-linear Finite Element Reliability Analysis of Steel Plane Frames with Initial Imperfections. *J. Civ. Eng. Manag.* **2012**, *18*, 81–90. [CrossRef]
91. Kala, Z. Sensitivity Analysis of Steel Plane Frames with Initial Imperfections. *Eng. Struct.* **2011**, *33*, 2342–2349. [CrossRef]
92. McKey, M.D.; Beckman, R.J.; Conover, W.J. Comparison of the Three Methods for Selecting Values of Input Variables in the Analysis of Output from a Computer Code. *Technometrics* **1979**, *21*, 239–245.
93. Iman, R.C.; Conover, W.J. Small Sample Sensitivity Analysis Techniques for Computer Models with an Application to Risk Assessment. *Commun. Stat. Theory Methods* **1980**, *9*, 1749–1842. [CrossRef]
94. European Committee for Standardization (CEN). *EN 1993-1-9. Eurocode3: Design of Steel Structures, Part 1–1: General Rules and Rules for Buildings*; European Standards: Brussels, Belgium, 2005.
95. Galambos, T.V. *Guide to Stability Design Criteria for Metal Structures*, 5th ed.; Wiley: Hoboken, NJ, USA, 1998; 911p.
96. Ahammed, M.; Melchers, R.E. Gradient and Parameter Sensitivity Estimation for Systems Evaluated Using Monte Carlo Analysis. *Reliab. Eng. Syst. Saf.* **2006**, *91*, 594–601. [CrossRef]
97. Rubinstein, R.Y. *Simulation and the Monte Carlo Method*; John Wiley & Sons: New York, NY, USA, 1981.
98. Volk-Makarewicz, W.M.; Heidergott, B.F. Sensitivity Analysis of Quantiles. *AEnorm* **2012**, *20*, 26–31.
99. Heidergott, B.F.; Volk-Makarewicz, W.M. A Measure-valued Differentiation Approach to Sensitivities of Quantiles. *Math. Oper. Res.* **2016**, *41*, 293–317. [CrossRef]
100. Kucherenko, S.; Song, S.; Wang, L. Quantile Based Global Sensitivity Measures. *Reliab. Eng. Syst. Saf.* **2019**, *185*, 35–48253. [CrossRef]
101. Koteš, P.; Vavruš, M.; Jošt, J.; Prokop, J. Strengthening of Concrete Column by Using the Wrapper Layer of Fibre Reinforced Concrete. *Materials* **2020**, *13*, 5432. [CrossRef]
102. Kmet, S.; Tomko, M.; Soltys, R.; Rovnak, M.; Demjan, I. Complex Failure Analysis of a Cable-roofed Stadium Structure Based on Diagnostics and Tests. *Eng. Fail. Anal.* **2019**, *103*, 443–461. [CrossRef]
103. Norkus, A.; Martinkus, V. Experimental Study on Bearing Resistance of Short Displacement Pile Groups in Dense Sands. *J. Civ. Eng. Manag.* **2019**, *25*, 551–558. [CrossRef]
104. Agüero, A.; Baláž, I.; Koleková, Y.; Moroczová, L. New Interaction Formula for the Plastic Resistance of I- and H-sections under Combinations of Bending Moments $M_{y,Ed}$, $M_{z,Ed}$ and Bimoment B_{Ed}. *Structures* **2021**, *29*, 577–585. [CrossRef]
105. Kaklauskas, G.; Ramanauskas, R.; Ng, P.-L. Predicting Crack Spacing of Reinforced Concrete Tension Members Using Strain Compliance Approach with Debonding. *J. Civ. Eng. Manag.* **2019**, *25*, 420–430. [CrossRef]

Article

Improving the Results of the Earned Value Management Technique Using Artificial Neural Networks in Construction Projects

Amirhossein Balali [1], Alireza Valipour [1,*], Jurgita Antucheviciene [2] and Jonas Šaparauskas [2]

1. Department of Civil Engineering, Shiraz Branch, Islamic Azad University, Shiraz 5-71993, Iran; a.balali@iaushiraz.ac.ir
2. Department of Construction Management and Real Estate, Vilnius Gediminas Technical University, LT-10223 Vilnius, Lithuania; jurgita.antucheviciene@vgtu.lt (J.A.); jonas.saparauskas@vgtu.lt (J.Š.)
* Correspondence: vali@iaushiraz.ac.ir; Tel.: +98-9177914214

Received: 9 October 2020; Accepted: 19 October 2020; Published: 21 October 2020

Abstract: The cost, time and scope of a construction project are key parameters for its success. Thus, predicting these indices is indispensable. Correct and accurate prediction of cost throughout the progress of a project gives project managers the chance to identify projects that need revision in their schedules in order to result in the maximum benefit. The aim of this study is to minimize the shortcomings of the Earned Value Management (EVM) method using an Artificial Neural Network (ANN) and multiple regression analysis in order to predict project cost indices more precisely. A total of 50 road construction projects in Fars Province, Iran, were selected for analysis in this research. An ANN model was used to predict the projects' cost performance indices, thereby creating a more accurate symmetry between the predicted and actual cost by considering factors that influence project success. The input data of the ANN model were analysed in MATLAB software. A multiple regression model was also used as another analytical tool to validate the outcome of the ANN. The results showed that the ANN model resulted in a lower Mean Squared Error (MSE) and a greater correlation coefficient than both the traditional EVM model and the multiple regression model.

Keywords: symmetry; earned value management (EVM); artificial neural networks (ANNs); multiple regression analysis; road industry

1. Introduction

The number of road construction projects is increasing dramatically every year. Although project management is being more expertly implemented, there are still problems associated with cost overruns in projects [1]. One of the factors that increases the capital output ratio for a country's economy is cost overrun. Estimating the cost of projects has always been a crucial, demanding and sophisticated challenge [2,3]. Cost estimation is a process in which the total cost of a project is predicted based on the existing information [4]. Generally, cost estimation is conducted in order to set the initial budget of a project, which will ideally produce symmetry between the initial estimation and the subsequent actual cost [1]. Cost estimation presents some difficulties, such as the initial information required, the small number of databases available for road construction project costs, the low efficiency of existing cost estimation methods and the existence of uncertainties [5].

Earned Value Management (EVM) is a tool to help with controlling the progress of a project. EVM is able to illustrate the current status of projects, as well as measuring current variances [6]. To assess the progress of projects, EVM exploits three constraints: time, scope and cost. Moreover, EVM is able to predict the future parameters of projects, including the final cost, based on existing data [7–9]. This comprehensive management approach has been widely used in numerous studies and in different fields [10–14].

Artificial Neural Networks (ANNs) are an effective tool that imitates the human mind for application in various problems [15]. The first application of ANNs in construction activities took place in the late 1980s [16]. Adeli (2001) published the first scientific article regarding the use of ANNs in the construction industry [17]. ANNs are widely used in various stages of a project, including design, construction, maintenance, renovation and destruction [18]. Some examples of the use of ANNs are presented in the following.

Albino and Garavelli (1998) applied a neural network in order to rank subcontractors in construction firms [19]. Leung et al. (2001) exploited ANNs to predict the hoisting times of tower cranes [20]. Cheung et al. (2006) forecasted the performance of projects using neural networks [21]. Vouk et al. (2011) analyzed the economy of wastewater systems using neural networks [22]. Mucenski et al. (2013) estimated the recycling capacity of multistorey buildings using ANNs [23]. Chaphalkar et al. (2015) used a multilayer perceptron neural network in order to forecast the outcome of construction dispute claims [24]. Golanaraghi et al. (2019) predicted formwork labor productivity using an ANN [25]. Tijanic et al. (2019) used an ANN in order to predict costs in road construction [26]. Readers are referred to References [27–36] for further uses of ANNs for various applications in the construction industry, as well as in other fields of science.

Cost, time and quality are the three components of success in a construction project. In other words, a project in which construction is finished within the predicted cost, to the required quality and within the forecasted time can be called a successful project [37]. The cost of construction projects usually deviates from the initial estimation due to a variety of factors [38]. In other words, the costs in construction projects do not usually remain the same as they were predicted to be before the construction phase. Cost increases are normal, as can be seen in most projects [39]. According to the available literature, not many projects are finished within the forecasted cost. A lot of construction projects face both delays and cost overruns [40]. Flyvbejerg et al. illustrated that cost underestimation happens dramatically more frequently than cost overestimation [41]. Iran is a developing country, and cost overruns are common in such countries. For instance, Heravi and Mohammadian (2019) investigated 72 construction projects in Iran based on both their documentation and their actual performance. They concluded that larger projects faced higher cost overruns and delays [42]. Although EVM is able to illustrate the degree to which delays and cost shortages exist in a project on the basis of the project's previous data, it cannot provide an accurate prediction of the future status of the project [8,9].

EVM results are obtained during and after the implementation phase. Thus, having the ability to predict the future situation of the project during the implementation phase could be very useful for project managers. The novelty of this study is in using an ANN, a tool that possesses the ability to learn from existing data in order to effectively predict the future status, in order to obtain more precise future predictions [25]. In this way, hazardous situations are less likely to happen, as they will have been forecasted before their occurrence. There are few previous research studies that have attempted to address the deficiency of the earned value management system in accurately predicting a project's future status. Moreover, as mentioned before, construction projects usually face time and cost overruns, making it a permanent issue for all project managers [37]. For instance, Moura et al. conducted a research study and concluded that construction projects experienced cost overruns of 20.4% to 44.7% in comparison to the initial cost estimation [43]. Thus, the significance of this study is in enabling project managers to use ANNs instead of the traditional EVM method in order to predict a project's future status more accurately and to fill the mentioned gaps in the body of knowledge. In the current study, we chose to investigate road construction projects in Fars Province, Iran, as a case study. The findings of this study will help road construction industry members to predict cost indices more precisely in their projects.

2. Methodology

The methodology of the current study was determined according to the research aim. The main purpose of this research was to improve the prediction of the traditional EVM system in Fars road construction projects using an artificial neural network, as well as comparing it with a multiple regression model. The abovementioned main aim can be divided into three stages. Firstly, factors affecting the earned value of Fars road construction projects were determined using the existing literature. An artificial neural network was built in MATLAB, and the identified factors were introduced to the ANN model. In the next stage, the identified factors were prioritized in MATLAB using the ANN model. Finally, multiple regression was used as the analyzing tool, and the obtained results were compared with the ANN model. The abovementioned stages are summarized in Figure 1.

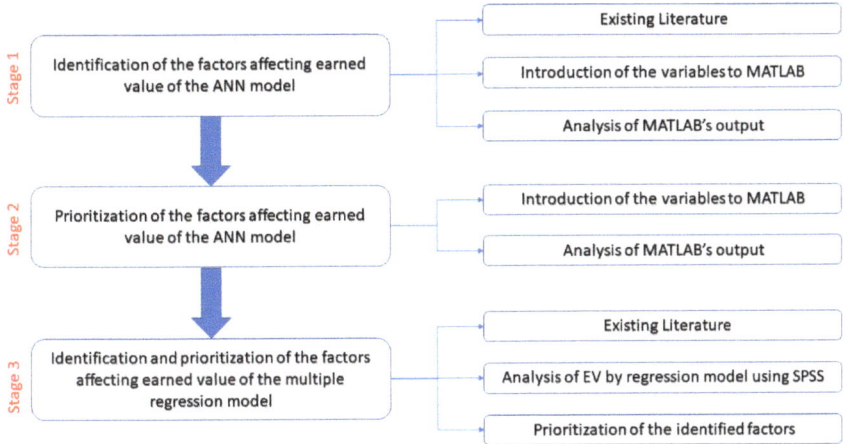

Figure 1. Research methodology according to the study aim.

2.1. Predicting Earned Value Using Artificial Neural Network

Intelligent dynamic systems, such as ANNs, have been under researchers' focus recently [44–51]. ANNs are able to identify the relationship among data by analyzing them and to then exploit this relationship in further analyses [52]. In fact, these computational intelligence-based systems attempt to model the neurosynaptic structure of the brain and are able to contribute to estimation, prediction and categorization problems effectively [53]. Generally, ANNs consist of three layers, namely, the input, hidden and output layers. Each of the abovementioned layers possesses its own neurons. It is important to mention that the number of hidden layers may be more than one according to the problem. In the current study, a multilayer perceptron network was used.

2.1.1. Input Data

Variables affecting the status of the project must be identified in order to investigate its future status. In fact, these variables are the input data of the artificial neural network. In this study, 14 factors affecting a project's success were identified by investigating the existing literature, including books, journal papers and documents from the Fars State Road Administration. Due to the high sensitivity of this paper's topic, the authors were not able to reduce the abovementioned number of factors. Some of the variables possessed numerical values, such as inflation rate. The inflation rate was derived from the Central Bank of Iran. However, there were variables that were not numerical, such as the qualification of the project management team. The abovementioned data were then quantified by scoring the variables from 1 to 5, where 1 and 5 stand for the worst and best status of a variable, respectively. In order to make it clearer, the qualitative status of a variable and its corresponding quantitative value are illustrated in Table 1. Ten questionnaires were filled out by experts for each project. Thus, 500 questionnaires were used for data gathering.

Table 1. Qualitive status of a variable and its corresponding value for analysis.

Qualitive Status	Quantitative Value
Critical	1
Very unsuitable	2
Unsuitable	3
Suitable	4
Very Suitable	5

Using Microsoft Project files of the studied projects, the Cost Performance Index (*CPI*) of each project was extracted. Then, using Microsoft Excel, Mean Squared Error (*MSE*) was calculated. This error was used to compare the results of the ANN, multiple regression and the traditional EVM method. The BOX-COX method was used in order to normalize data using SPSS software. Then, the obtained data were exported to MATLAB software for further stages. *CPI* and *MSE* formulas are presented as follows [1,8,54,55]:

$$MSE = \frac{\sum (desired\ output - predicted\ output)2}{no\ of\ data} \quad (1)$$

$$CPI = \frac{BCWP}{ACWP} \quad (2)$$

where *BCWP* and *ACWP* stand for the actual cost of the work performed and the budgeted cost of the work performed, respectively.

2.1.2. Architecture of the Network

In this stage, the network's architecture must be determined. In order to do so, the number of input, hidden and output layers should be specified [15]. In this study, an MLP (Multilayer perceptron) network is used in which the output of each layer is considered the input vector for the next layer. Each layer's neurons have connections with the previous layer's neurons. Each neuron's duty is to calculate the net layer's weight and pass data through a function called the transfer function. Sigmoid Tangent is regarded as one of the most useful functions in this case and has been widely used by experts [56–61]. Thus, the abovementioned function was used as the transfer function. The final network in this research constitutes a multilayer perceptron neural network with 14 input variables in an input layer, a hidden layer and an output layer. The schematic structure of the designed neural network is illustrated in Figure 2.

2.2. Determination and Prioritization of Factors Using ANN

After training the network, output coefficients of introduced variables can be extracted from MATLAB software. As the artificial neural network considers all the introduced factors important, the prioritization of factors is conducted according to the coefficients.

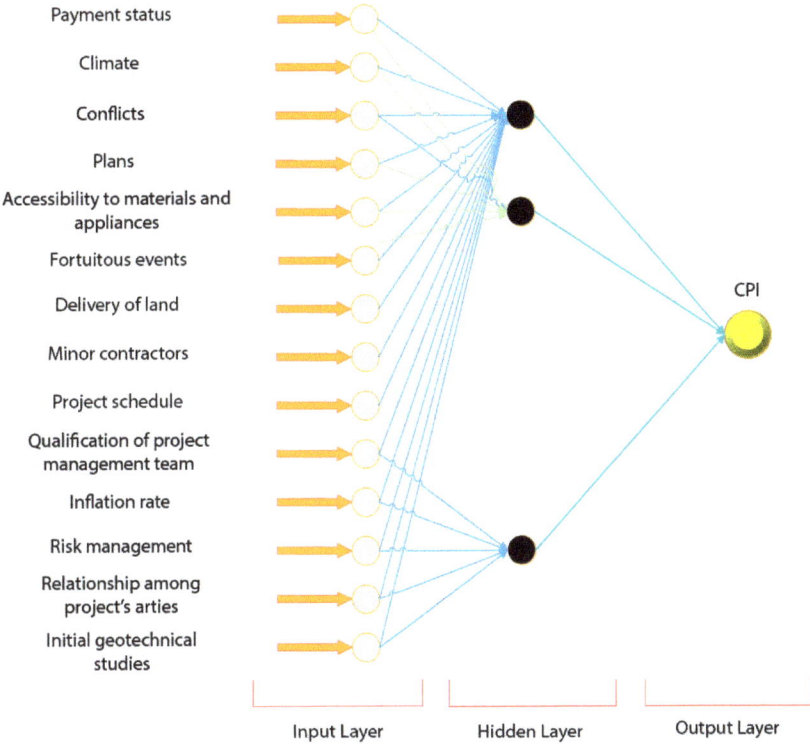

Figure 2. Schematic structure of the Artificial Neural Network (ANN).

2.3. Earned Value Prediction Using Multiple Regression Method

The correlation among dependent and independent variables can be determined using the multiple regression method [62]. There are four methods to enter input data into the model. These methods are the entering method (direct method), backward method, forward method and step-wise method [63]. In this study, the direct entering method was selected to be exploited. The linear relationship among the variables is illustrated below:

$$y_i = b_0 + b_1 x_{i1} + \cdots + b_p x_{ip} + e_i \qquad (3)$$

where p is the number of predictions, b_j is the value of the jth coefficient, x_{ij} is the ith value of the jth prediction, and e_i is the error of the ith value. Furthermore, the matrix form of the model is presented as follows:

$$Y = X\beta + \varepsilon \qquad (4)$$

where β is the vector of regression coefficients, ε is the matrix of fitting errors, Y is the vector of the dependent variable, and X is the matrix of independent variables.

In order to determine and rank factors affecting the earned value of the studied projects, outputs of SPSS analyses were used. Variables with a significance of less than 0.05 were selected as effective factors. Furthermore, according to their significance value, variables were prioritized.

Finally, the ANN and the multiple regression model were compared according to the correlation coefficient and mean squared error of each model. The model possessing the higher correlation coefficient, as well as the lower MSE, was introduced as the preferable model [64].

2.4. Data Collection

In order to collect data, information regarding 50 road construction projects in Fars Province was extracted from documents. Then, besides other literature sources, data were turned into matrices and analyzed. As all factors affecting the cost of the abovementioned projects had to be considered, 14 factors were finally selected.

3. Results and Discussion

3.1. Predicting Earned Value Using Artificial Neural Network

3.1.1. Gathering the MLP Network's Data

Data regarding road construction projects in Fars Province from 2010 to 2020 were gathered by conducting a vast study on documents from Fars Road Administration. Then, data were turned into matrices. In order to determine the best pattern of network input, all the probable factors affecting the cost of projects were determined. Thus, as input, 14 neurons were formed. These neurons were the identified factors, namely, "Payment status (F1)", "Climate (F2)", "Conflicts (F3)", "Plans (F4)", "Accessibility of materials and appliances (F5)", "Fortuitous events (F6)", "Delivery of land (F7)", "Minor contractors (F8)", "Project schedule (F9)", "Qualification of project management team (F10)", "Inflation rate (F11)", "Risk management (F12)", "Relationship among project's parties (F13)" and "Initial geotechnical studies (F14)". Moreover, the output layer of the ANN was determined, i.e., the cost performance index of the projects.

3.1.2. Normalizing Data

Using SPSS software, data were normalized in a range between −1 and 1. It seems necessary to mention that the ANN's output can be returned to the initial format using the reverse algorithm. Normalized data are illustrated in Table 2.

Table 2. Normalized ANN input data.

Project No.	F1	F2	F3	F4	F5	F6	F7	F8	F9	F10	F11	F12	F13	F14
1	0.70	0.90	0.50	0.50	0.63	0.63	0.63	0.70	0.50	0.70	0.21	0.70	0.70	0.70
2	0.30	0.90	0.10	0.70	0.90	0.63	0.37	0.50	0.90	0.90	0.61	0.30	0.90	0.70
3	0.70	0.63	0.10	0.70	0.63	0.90	0.10	0.90	0.90	0.70	0.31	0.70	0.70	0.90
4	0.30	0.10	0.30	0.50	0.37	0.37	0.63	0.50	0.70	0.30	0.49	0.50	0.50	0.90
5	0.10	0.37	0.70	0.10	0.10	0.63	0.37	0.90	0.90	0.70	0.31	0.70	0.70	0.70
6	0.10	0.10	0.70	0.50	0.37	0.63	0.37	0.90	0.30	0.50	0.49	0.50	0.30	0.90
7	0.70	0.63	0.30	0.70	0.37	0.37	0.63	0.30	0.10	0.30	0.39	0.10	0.50	0.30
8	0.70	0.37	0.90	0.30	0.90	0.10	0.90	0.10	0.10	0.70	0.39	0.30	0.70	0.30
9	0.50	0.10	0.10	0.50	0.37	0.90	0.63	0.30	0.70	0.70	0.90	0.50	0.90	0.70
10	0.50	0.37	0.70	0.10	0.37	0.63	0.10	0.50	0.10	0.70	0.39	0.70	0.30	0.70
11	0.10	0.37	0.10	0.90	0.90	0.37	0.63	0.50	0.90	0.90	0.49	0.70	0.50	0.70
12	0.50	0.10	0.30	0.70	0.10	0.37	0.10	0.30	0.90	0.70	0.31	0.30	0.50	0.50
13	0.10	0.90	0.10	0.70	0.63	0.63	0.63	0.50	0.30	0.70	0.31	0.90	0.10	0.50
14	0.70	0.63	0.70	0.90	0.10	0.37	0.63	0.10	0.50	0.90	0.49	0.30	0.30	0.90
15	0.50	0.37	0.70	0.30	0.37	0.90	0.37	0.70	0.50	0.50	0.49	0.90	0.10	0.10
16	0.70	0.10	0.50	0.90	0.90	0.37	0.37	0.90	0.90	0.50	0.49	0.30	0.70	0.70
17	0.50	0.37	0.50	0.90	0.63	0.90	0.10	0.50	0.10	0.50	0.77	0.30	0.10	0.10
18	0.90	0.90	0.50	0.30	0.10	0.63	0.90	0.90	0.70	0.90	0.49	0.50	0.70	0.30
19	0.30	0.37	0.50	0.70	0.63	0.63	0.90	0.90	0.50	0.50	0.77	0.30	0.50	0.10
20	0.90	0.37	0.70	0.30	0.37	0.90	0.37	0.50	0.70	0.30	0.19	0.70	0.30	0.90
21	0.70	0.90	0.50	0.90	0.63	0.63	0.90	0.70	0.30	0.30	0.31	0.10	0.10	0.70
22	0.70	0.37	0.70	0.50	0.63	0.63	0.90	0.10	0.50	0.70	0.12	0.90	0.70	0.30
23	0.90	0.90	0.50	0.50	0.63	0.37	0.90	0.90	0.50	0.90	0.39	0.70	0.50	0.50
24	0.90	0.37	0.70	0.70	0.63	0.63	0.63	0.70	0.90	0.90	0.39	0.90	0.50	0.50
25	0.90	0.37	0.50	0.30	0.90	0.90	0.37	0.70	0.70	0.30	0.49	0.50	0.70	0.30

Table 2. Cont.

Project No.	F1	F2	F3	F4	F5	F6	F7	F8	F9	F10	F11	F12	F13	F14
26	0.90	0.90	0.50	0.90	0.63	0.63	0.90	0.90	0.30	0.70	0.19	0.50	0.50	0.50
27	0.10	0.10	0.50	0.70	0.63	0.63	0.37	0.30	0.50	0.70	0.49	0.70	0.90	0.50
28	0.10	0.63	0.50	0.70	0.10	0.63	0.37	0.90	0.70	0.10	0.10	0.30	0.50	0.50
29	0.50	0.63	0.90	0.30	0.90	0.90	0.90	0.50	0.30	0.50	0.10	0.50	0.70	0.10
30	0.10	0.37	0.30	0.50	0.37	0.63	0.37	0.10	0.50	0.50	0.49	0.30	0.90	0.30
31	0.50	0.10	0.70	0.70	0.63	0.37	0.90	0.70	0.30	0.30	0.61	0.30	0.10	0.90
32	0.50	0.37	0.30	0.30	0.37	0.90	0.90	0.50	0.70	0.30	0.49	0.10	0.30	0.50
33	0.10	0.63	0.50	0.70	0.10	0.90	0.10	0.90	0.90	0.30	0.16	0.50	0.30	0.10
34	0.50	0.37	0.50	0.50	0.90	0.63	0.63	0.70	0.30	0.90	0.49	0.30	0.90	0.50
35	0.90	0.10	0.10	0.50	0.63	0.37	0.63	0.70	0.70	0.70	0.12	0.90	0.50	0.70
36	0.30	0.37	0.70	0.70	0.37	0.90	0.63	0.30	0.70	0.50	0.49	0.50	0.50	0.10
37	0.10	0.63	0.10	0.50	0.90	0.37	0.37	0.70	0.30	0.50	0.90	0.90	0.90	0.30
38	0.30	0.90	0.30	0.90	0.63	0.63	0.63	0.50	0.70	0.70	0.39	0.70	0.90	0.10
39	0.30	0.90	0.50	0.50	0.37	0.90	0.63	0.90	0.30	0.50	0.31	0.10	0.10	0.30
40	0.70	0.10	0.50	0.10	0.90	0.90	0.37	0.90	0.90	0.70	0.49	0.90	0.50	0.30
41	0.70	0.63	0.30	0.50	0.37	0.63	0.90	0.50	0.70	0.30	0.78	0.30	0.70	0.50
42	0.30	0.90	0.50	0.30	0.10	0.63	0.10	0.50	0.30	0.30	0.78	0.50	0.10	0.30
43	0.70	0.10	0.10	0.30	0.37	0.90	0.63	0.10	0.70	0.30	0.49	0.70	0.70	0.90
44	0.50	0.37	0.90	0.70	0.63	0.90	0.37	0.50	0.30	0.30	0.39	0.10	0.50	0.50
45	0.30	0.37	0.10	0.30	0.37	0.63	0.63	0.90	0.50	0.70	0.10	0.70	0.50	0.90
46	0.90	0.63	0.70	0.10	0.37	0.37	0.63	0.90	0.70	0.50	0.39	0.50	0.30	0.10
47	0.30	0.37	0.10	0.50	0.37	0.90	0.63	0.50	0.70	0.10	0.21	0.30	0.70	0.50
48	0.10	0.37	0.30	0.50	0.63	0.37	0.37	0.30	0.90	0.90	0.49	0.30	0.90	0.30
49	0.90	0.37	0.30	0.70	0.37	0.90	0.37	0.50	0.70	0.90	0.31	0.30	0.90	0.50
50	0.10	0.63	0.10	0.30	0.90	0.63	0.90	0.30	0.50	0.70	0.90	0.70	0.50	0.10

3.1.3. Determining Hidden Layers of ANN

It is best for the number of hidden layers to be as low as possible. One hidden layer is initially considered for an ANN. Then, after training the ANN, the number of layers will be increased if the output is not suitable. Furthermore, there are a number of functions that can be used to produce the network's outcome. In this study, the Sigmoid Tangent function was exploited. The network introduced into MATLAB software included 14 neurons in its input layer and 3 neurons in its hidden layer. The structure of the network is illustrated in Figure 3.

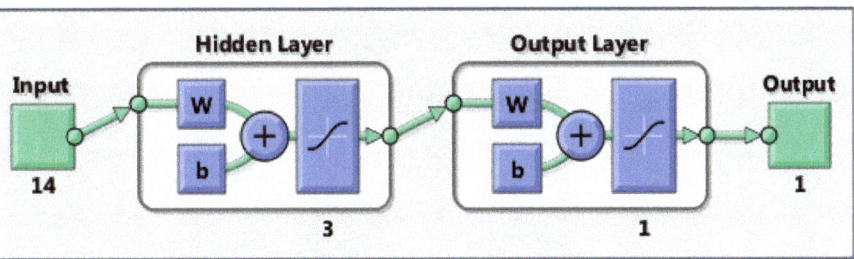

Figure 3. ANN introduced into MATLAB.

3.1.4. Training of the ANN

The introduced network in this study is an MLP network with back propagation error. The selected training function for the network was the Levenberg–Marquardt function due to its ability to converge fast. The transfer function was selected by trial and error, until the MSE reached the lowest value in both the training set and testing set. The data set was randomly divided into three groups. Seventy percent of the data was used for acquisition of the network, fifteen percent was used for testing the data, and fifteen percent was used for validation. The settings of the training ANN in MATLAB are demonstrated in Figure 4. The number of epochs was selected as 1000. As a result, the network reached its lowest acquisition error after 15 epochs. The network's gradient function performance, MSE graph and regression graphs are shown in Figures 5–7, respectively.

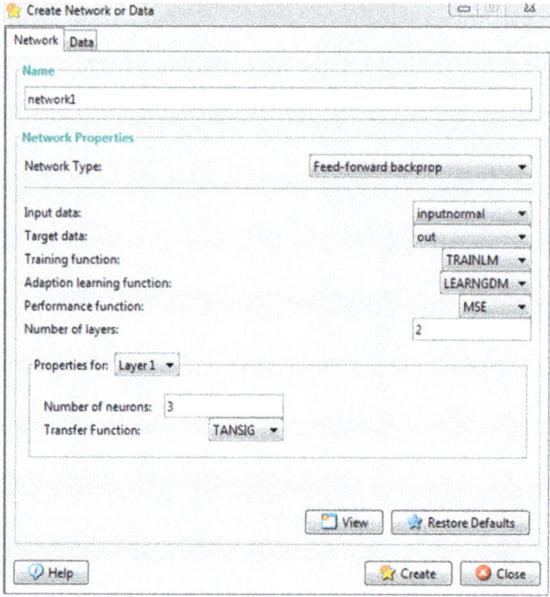

Figure 4. Settings of the training ANN in MATLAB.

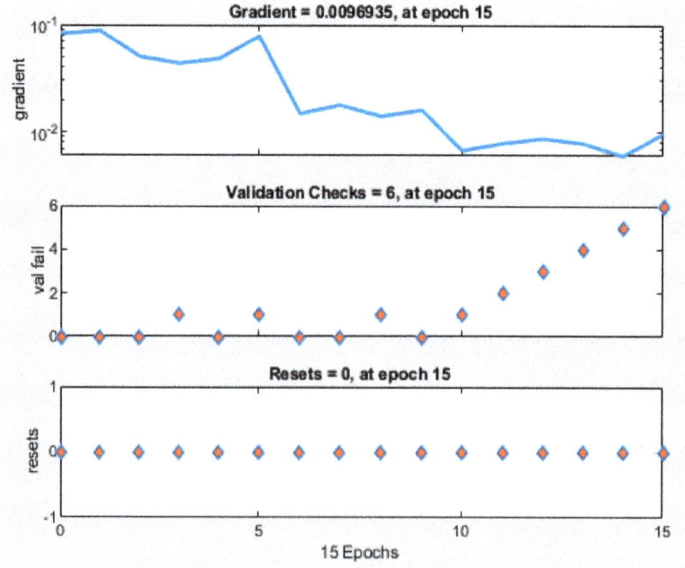

Figure 5. ANN's gradient function performance.

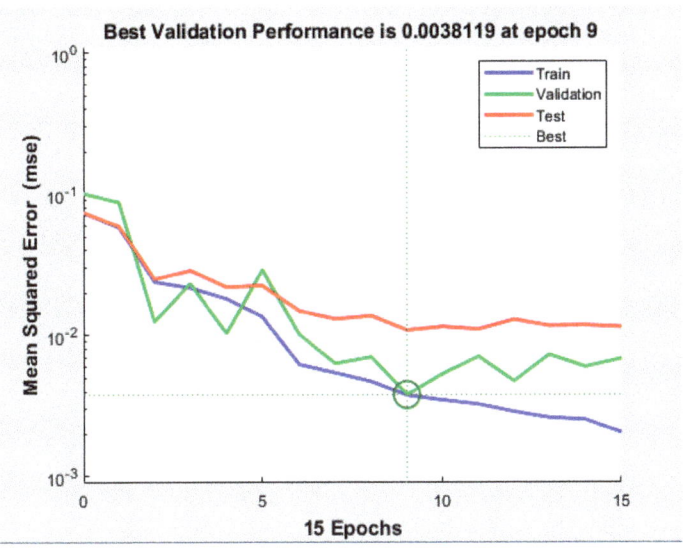

Figure 6. Mean Squared Error (MSE) graph of the trained ANN.

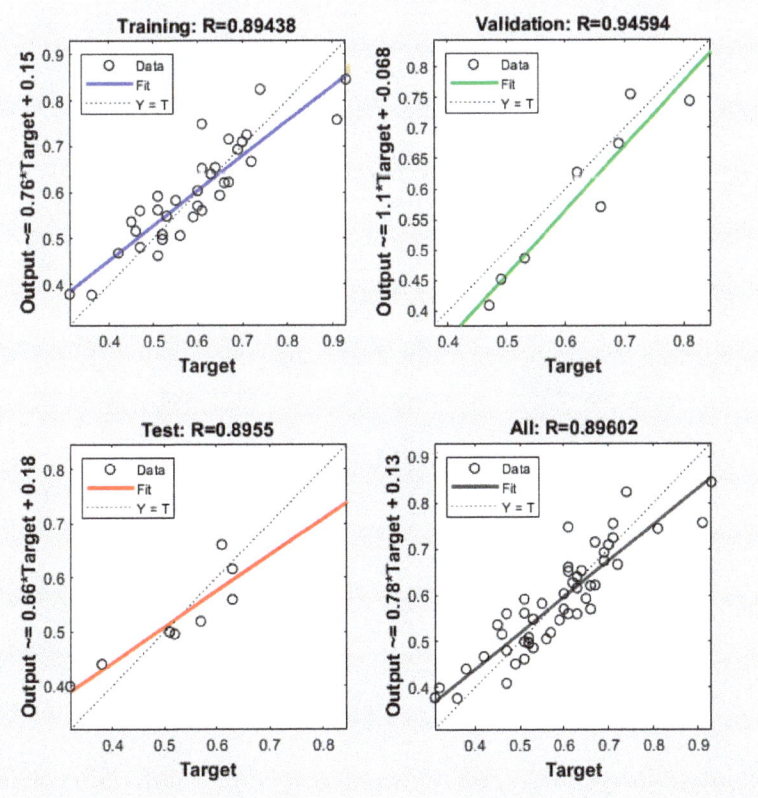

Figure 7. ANN's regression graphs.

As a sample, one of the studied project's Status Curve (S-Curve) was drawn using the trained ANN and was compared with the traditional EVM's S-Curve. Improvement of the S-Curve is clearly seen in the figures below. Figures 8 and 9 illustrate the traditional model and ANN's S-Curves, respectively.

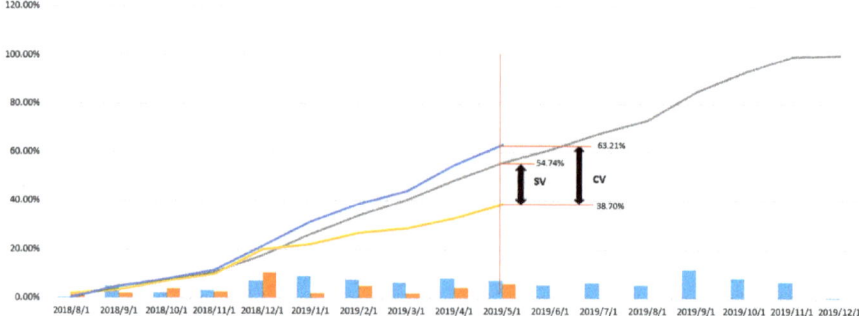

Figure 8. Sample project's S-Curve according to the traditional Earned Value Management (EVM) model.

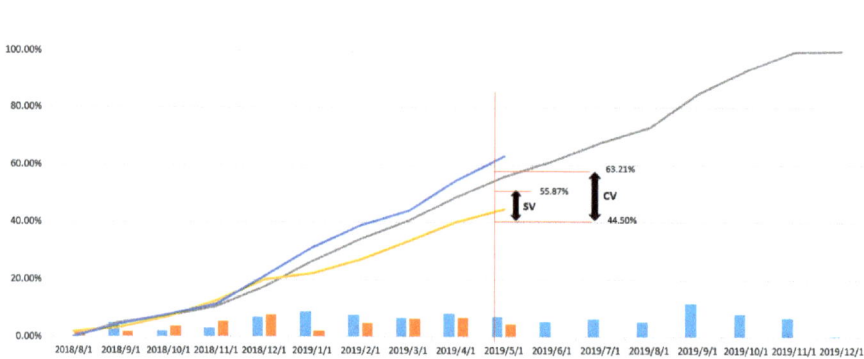

Figure 9. Sample project's S-Curve according to the ANN model.

3.2. Determination and Prioritization of Factors Affecting Earned Value in the ANN

After training of the ANN in MATLAB, each variable is given a unique coefficient. Coefficients for the identified factors are illustrated in Table 3.

According to the factors' coefficients, the ANN's function to predict the aim is obtained as follows:

$$
\begin{aligned}
n = (0.81)F1 &+ (0.65)F2 - (0.58)F3 + (0.42)F4 + (0.4)F5 + (0.38)F6 - (0.33)F7 \\
&+ (0.24)F8 + (0.21)F9 + (0.2)F10 + (0.14)F11 + (0.12)F12 \\
&+ (0.1)F13 - (0.017)F14
\end{aligned}
\tag{5}
$$

Then, the final equation is obtained as follows:

$$CPI = tan\,sig(n) = \frac{2}{1 + exp(-2n)} \tag{6}$$

Table 3. Prioritization and importance coefficients of the study factors using ANN.

Priority	Sign	Factor	Factor's Coefficient
1	F1	Project Schedule	0.81
2	F2	Payment status	0.65
3	F3	Inflation rate	−0.58
4	F4	Fortuitous events	0.42
5	F5	Qualification of project management team	0.4
6	F6	Delivery of land	0.38
7	F7	Conflicts	−0.33
8	F8	Climate	0.24
9	F9	Minor contractors	0.21
10	F10	Plans	0.20
11	F11	Relationship among project's parties	0.14
12	F12	Risk management	0.12
13	F13	Accessibility of materials and appliances	0.1
14	F14	Initial geotechnical studies	−0.017

3.3. Determination and Prioritization of Factors Affecting Earned Value Using Multiple Regression Method and Comparison with the ANN Model for Data Validation

3.3.1. Investigating the Condition of Using Multiple Regression Analysis

In this stage, SPSS software was exploited. The first condition if using linear regression is having normal data of earned value. Thus, a Kolmogorov–Smirnov test was conducted on the data in order to determine whether they were normal. The results illustrated that the data were not normal. Table 4 and Figure 10 illustrate the information regarding the abovementioned test.

Table 4. Kolmogorov–Smirnov test for initial data.

	Tests of Normality		
	Kolmogorov–Smirnov		
	Statistic	df	Sig.
CPI	0.519	51	0.000

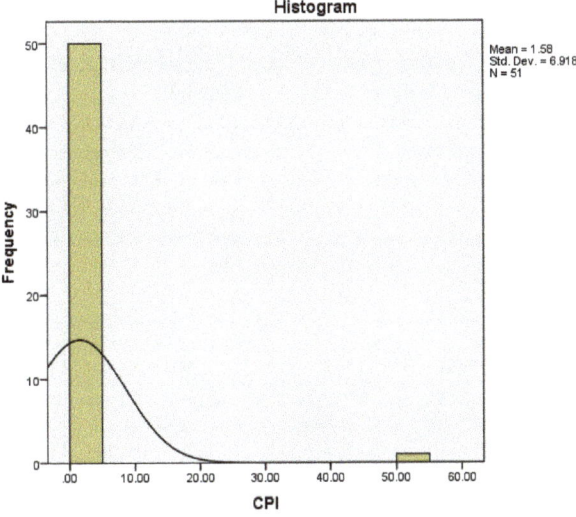

Figure 10. Normalization test histogram.

3.3.2. Analysis of Multiple Regression Model

Data analysis was conducted in order to validate the ANN results by comparing them with the multiple regression results. The correlation coefficient and determination coefficient of this study's fitted multiple regression were 0.864 and 0.747, respectively. This means that about 74% of the dependent variable's variance is determined according to the model's independent variables. Information regarding the mentioned coefficients and the model analysis results is illustrated in Tables 5 and 6, respectively.

Table 5. Determination and correlation coefficients of the multiple regression model.

Model	R	R Square	Adjusted R Square
1	0.864	0.747	0.646

Table 6. Multiple regression model's results.

Factor	Sign	Unstandardized Coefficients B	Unstandardized Coefficients Std. Error	Sig	Standardized Coefficients β
(Constant)		−4.999	1.154	0.000	
Payment status	F2	0.155	0.065	0.022	0.230
Climate	F8	0.098	0.098	0.324	0.105
Conflicts	F7	0.201	0.084	0.023	0.254
Plans	F10	0.263	0.081	0.003	0.321
Accessibility of materials and appliances	F13	−0.031	0.105	0.766	−0.032
Fortuitous events	F4	−0.031	0.113	0.784	−0.026
Delivery of land	F6	0.062	0.096	0.523	0.062
Minor contractors	F9	0.208	0.072	0.007	0.283
Project schedule	F1	0.238	0.084	0.008	0.311
Qualification of project management team	F5	0.060	0.089	0.505	0.072
Inflation rate	F3	−0.029	0.014	0.040	−0.206
Risk management	F12	0.259	0.081	0.003	0.333
Relationship among project's parties	F11	0.222	0.082	0.011	0.297
Initial geotechnical studies	F14	0.061	0.072	0.400	0.085

In Table 6, B and β stand for unstandardized coefficients and standardized coefficients, respectively. Although it is easier to write the multiple regression model's equation using unstandardized coefficients, using standardized coefficients enables researchers to compare variables more easily. In other words, a higher value of the coefficient means that the variable can predict the outcome more effectively. According to the results, "Risk management", "Plans", "Project schedule", "Relationship among project's parties" and "Conflicts" are the most important factors.

In this study, an artificial neural network model for road construction projects was used in order to improve the prediction of the earned value. Moreover, a multiple regression model was used to validate the ANN results. The ANN and multiple regression models' calculated mean squared errors and the real values of projects are illustrated in Table 7. As it is easily seen, both the ANN model and the multiple regression model possess low errors. Moreover, the ANN model not only had the lowest error, but also possessed the most effective prediction coefficient.

Table 7. Comparison of the ANN and multiple regression models.

MSE	R	Model
0.0152	0.727	Traditional EVM
0.00206	0.896	ANN
0.012	0.864	Multiple regression

4. Conclusions

Perceptron neural networks, especially multilayer perceptron networks, are considered to be some of the best neural networks. In this study, it was observed that these networks were able to perform a non-linear mapping with desirable accuracy by selecting a suitable number of layers and neurons. As these neural networks possess the two main features of experimental data-based learning and parallel generalization ability, they are highly suitable for sophisticated systems that are impossible or difficult to model. Artificial neural networks are more accurate in comparison to other methods due to their usage of proven mathematical formulas possessing the lowest possible errors. One of the aspects that limit the usage of artificial neural networks is the difficulty faced when training them. These networks produce better results when they receive a large group of data. However, adjusting the parameters of network training is a difficult task that requires experience and a lot of trial and error. Furthermore, convergence to an incorrect answer, keeping internal information instead of learning it, and requiring a lot of time for training are other difficulties associated with using artificial neural networks.

In this research, two different models, i.e., an artificial neural network model and a multiple regression model, were designed and analyzed in order to improve the traditional earned value management system. The latter model was used as a validation test for the ANN model. Road construction projects in Fars Province, Iran, between 2010 and 2020 were investigated as a case study. Fourteen factors affecting the earned value of these projects were identified. According to the ANN results, "Project plan", "Payment status", "Inflation rate", "Fortuitous events" and "Qualification of project management team" with coefficients of 0.81, 0.65, −0.58, 0.42 and 0.4 were the top five influencing factors, respectively. On the other hand, according to the multiple regression model results, "Risk management", "Plans", "Project schedule", "Relationship among project's parties" and "Conflicts" with standardized coefficients of 0.333, 0.321, 0.311, 0.297 and 0.254, respectively, were the most important factors. A comparison of the two models illustrated that both models result in better results in comparison to the traditional EVM method. Moreover, the ANN model with an MSE of 0.00206 and an R value of 0.896 was selected as the best model.

The methods used in this study could also be used to tackle other problems in the construction industry. The results obtained in this study will help road construction industry members to predict the earned value of future projects more precisely. ANN models are highly recommended by the authors for use in other construction problems. Furthermore, it is suggested that prospective researchers focus on more complex construction projects in order to investigate the performance criteria more deeply [65].

Author Contributions: A.B.: Conceptualization, Methodology, Software, Investigation, Writing—Original draft; A.V.: Methodology, Visualization, Validation, Investigation, Writing—Reviewing and Editing, Supervision; J.A.: Writing—Reviewing and Editing, Supervision; J.Š.: Writing—Reviewing and Editing. All authors have read and agreed to the published version of the manuscript.

Funding: This research received no external funding.

Conflicts of Interest: The authors declare no conflict of interest. The funders had no role in the design of the study; in the collection, analyses, or interpretation of data; in the writing of the manuscript, or in the decision to publish the results.

References

1. Mahalakshmi, G.; Rajasekaran, C. Early cost estimation of highway projects in India using artificial neural network. In *Sustainable Construction and Building Materials Lecture Notes in Civil Engineering*; Das, B., Neithalath, N., Eds.; Springer: Singapore, 2019; Volume 25, pp. 659–672.
2. Wideman, R.M. *Cost Control of Capital Projects and the Project Cost Management System Requirements: A Handbook for Owners, Architects, Engineers, and All Those Involved in Project Management of Constructed Facilities*; AEW Services, BiTech Publishers: Richmond, BC, Canada, 1995.
3. Al-Zwainy, F.M.; Aidan, I.A.-A. Forecasting the cost of structure of infrastructure projects utilizing artificial neural network model (highway projects as case study). *Indian J. Sci. Technol.* **2017**, *10*, 1–12. [CrossRef]

4. Turochy, R.E.; Hoel, L.A.; Doty, R.S. *Highway Project Cost Estimating Methods Used in the Planning Stage of Project Development*; Virginia Transportation Research Council: Charlottesville, VA, USA, 2001.
5. Sodikov, J. Cost estimation of highway projects in developing countries: Artificial neural network approach. *J. East. Asia Soc. Transp. Stud.* **2005**, *6*, 1036–1047.
6. Czernigowska, A. Earned value method as a tool for project control. *Bud. Archit.* **2008**, *3*, 15–32.
7. Anbari, F.T. Earned value project management method and extensions. *Proj. Manag. J.* **2003**, *34*, 12–23. [CrossRef]
8. Koke, B.; Moehler, R.C. Earned Green Value Management for Project Management: A systematic review. *J. Clean. Prod.* **2019**, *230*, 180–197. [CrossRef]
9. Bryde, D.; Unterhitzenberger, C.; Joby, R. Conditions of success for earned value analysis in projects. *Int. J. Proj. Manag.* **2018**, *36*, 474–484. [CrossRef]
10. Colin, J.; Vanhoucke, M. A comparison of the performance of various project control methods using earned value management systems. *Expert Syst. Appl.* **2015**, *42*, 3159–3175. [CrossRef]
11. Kerkhove, L.-P.; Vanhoucke, M. Extensions of earned value management: Using the earned incentive metric to improve signal quality. *Int. J. Proj. Manag.* **2017**, *35*, 148–168. [CrossRef]
12. Abdi, A.; Taghipour, S.; Khamooshi, H. A model to control environmental performance of project execution process based on greenhouse gas emissions using earned value management. *Int. J. Proj. Manag.* **2018**, *36*, 397–413. [CrossRef]
13. Sutrisna, M.; Pellicer, E.; Torres-Machi, C.; Picornell, M. Exploring earned value management in the Spanish construction industry as a pathway to competitive advantage. *Int. J. Constr. Manag.* **2020**, *20*, 1–12. [CrossRef]
14. De Andrade, P.A.; Martens, A.; Vanhoucke, M. Using real project schedule data to compare earned schedule and earned duration management project time forecasting capabilities. *Autom. Constr.* **2019**, *99*, 68–78. [CrossRef]
15. Kulkarni, P.; Londhe, S.; Deo, M. Artificial neural networks for construction management: A review. *J. Soft Comput. Civ. Eng.* **2017**, *1*, 70–88.
16. Adeli, H.; Yeh, C. Perceptron learning in engineering design. *Comput. Aided Civ. Infrastruct. Eng.* **1989**, *4*, 247–256. [CrossRef]
17. Adeli, H. Neural networks in civil engineering: 1989–2000. *Comput. Aided Civ. Infrastruct. Eng.* **2001**, *16*, 126–142. [CrossRef]
18. Peško, I.; Mučenski, V.; Šešlija, M.; Radović, N.; Vujkov, A.; Bibić, D.; Krklješ, M. Estimation of costs and durations of construction of urban roads using ANN and SVM. *Complexity* **2017**, *2017*, 2450370. [CrossRef]
19. Albino, V.; Garavelli, A.C. A neural network application to subcontractor rating in construction firms. *Int. J. Proj. Manag.* **1998**, *16*, 9–14. [CrossRef]
20. Leung, A.W.; Tam, C.; Liu, D. Comparative study of artificial neural networks and multiple regression analysis for predicting hoisting times of tower cranes. *Build. Environ.* **2001**, *36*, 457–467. [CrossRef]
21. Cheung, S.O.; Wong, P.S.P.; Fung, A.S.; Coffey, W. Predicting project performance through neural networks. *Int. J. Proj. Manag.* **2006**, *24*, 207–215. [CrossRef]
22. Vouk, D.; Malus, D.; Halkijevic, I. Neural networks in economic analyses of wastewater systems. *Expert Syst. Appl.* **2011**, *38*, 10031–10035. [CrossRef]
23. Mučenski, V.; Trivunić, M.; Ćirović, G.; Peško, I.; Dražić, J. Estimation of recycling capacity of multi-storey building structures using artificial neural networks. *Acta Polytech. Hung.* **2013**, *10*, 175–192.
24. Chaphalkar, N.; Iyer, K.; Patil, S.K. Prediction of outcome of construction dispute claims using multilayer perceptron neural network model. *Int. J. Proj. Manag.* **2015**, *33*, 1827–1835. [CrossRef]
25. Golnaraghi, S.; Zangenehmadar, Z.; Moselhi, O.; Alkass, S. Application of artificial neural network (s) in predicting formwork labour productivity. *Adv. Civ. Eng.* **2019**, *2019*, 5972620. [CrossRef]
26. Tijanić, K.; Car-Pušić, D.; Šperac, M. Cost estimation in road construction using artificial neural network. *Neural Comput. Appl.* **2020**, *32*, 9343–9355. [CrossRef]
27. Casilari-Perez, E.; García-Lagos, F. A comprehensive study on the use of artificial neural networks in wearable fall detection systems. *Expert Syst. Appl.* **2019**, *138*, 112811. [CrossRef]
28. Kim, H.-J.; Jo, N.-O.; Shin, K.-S. Optimization of cluster-based evolutionary undersampling for the artificial neural networks in corporate bankruptcy prediction. *Expert Syst. Appl.* **2016**, *59*, 226–234. [CrossRef]
29. Kocadagli, O.; Langari, R. Classification of EEG signals for epileptic seizures using hybrid artificial neural networks based wavelet transforms and fuzzy relations. *Expert Syst. Appl.* **2017**, *88*, 419–434. [CrossRef]

30. Kwon, H.-B.; Lee, J.; Davis, K.N.W. Neural network modeling for a two-stage production process with versatile variables: Predictive analysis for above-average performance. *Expert Syst. Appl.* **2018**, *100*, 120–130. [CrossRef]
31. Bandara, K.; Bergmeir, C.; Smyl, S. Forecasting across time series databases using recurrent neural networks on groups of similar series: A clustering approach. *Expert Syst. Appl.* **2020**, *140*, 112896. [CrossRef]
32. Yazdani-Chamzini, A.; Zavadskas, E.K.; Antucheviciene, J.; Bausys, R. A model for shovel capital cost estimation, using a hybrid model of multivariate regression and neural networks. *Symmetry* **2017**, *9*, 298. [CrossRef]
33. Juszczyk, M.; Leśniak, A. Modelling construction site cost index based on neural network ensembles. *Symmetry* **2019**, *11*, 411. [CrossRef]
34. AlHares, E.F.T.; Budayan, C. Estimation at completion simulation using the potential of soft computing models: Case study of construction engineering projects. *Symmetry* **2019**, *11*, 190. [CrossRef]
35. Juszczyk, M.; Zima, K.; Lelek, W. Forecasting of sports fields construction costs aided by ensembles of neural networks. *J. Civ. Eng. Manag.* **2019**, *25*, 715–729. [CrossRef]
36. Shan, M.; Le, Y.; Yiu, K.T.; Chan, A.P.; Hu, Y.; Zhou, Y. Assessing collusion risks in managing construction projects using artificial neural network. *Technol. Econ. Dev. Econ.* **2018**, *24*, 2003–2025. [CrossRef]
37. Tadewos, S.G.; Patel, D. Factors influencing time and cost overruns in road construction projects: Addis Ababa, Ethiopian scenario. *Int. Res. J. Eng. Technol.* **2018**, *5*, 177–180.
38. Ökmen, Ö.; Öztaş, A. Construction cost analysis under uncertainty with correlated cost risk analysis model. *Constr. Manag. Econ.* **2010**, *28*, 203–212. [CrossRef]
39. Plebankiewicz, E. Model of predicting cost overrun in construction projects. *Sustainability* **2018**, *10*, 4387. [CrossRef]
40. Habibi, M.; Kermanshachi, S.; Safapour, E. Engineering, procurement and construction cost and schedule performance leading indicators: State-of-the-art review. In Proceedings of the Construction Research Congres, New Orleans, LA, USA, 2–4 April 2018; pp. 2–4.
41. Flyvbjerg, B.; Holm, M.S.; Buhl, S. *Cost Underestimation in Public Works Projects: Error or Lie?* Aalborg University, Department of Development and Planning: Aalborg, Denmark, 2004.
42. Heravi, G.; Mohammadian, M. Investigating cost overruns and delay in urban construction projects in Iran. *Int. J. Constr. Manag.* **2019**, 1–11. [CrossRef]
43. Moura, H.M.P.; Teixeira, J.M.C.; Pires, B. Dealing with cost and time in the Portuguese construction industry. In Proceedings of the CIB World Building Congress, Cape Town, South Africa, 14–17 May 2007; pp. 1252–1265.
44. Bai, S.; Fang, G.; Zhou, J. Construction of three-dimensional extrusion limit diagram for magnesium alloy using artificial neural network and its validation. *J. Mater. Process Technol.* **2020**, *275*, 116361. [CrossRef]
45. Nov, P.; Peansupap, V. Using artificial neural network for selecting type of subcontractor relationships in construction project. *Eng. J.* **2020**, *24*, 73–88. [CrossRef]
46. Jang, H.-S.; Shuli, X.; So, S.-Y. Analysis the compressive strength of flue gas desulfurization gypsum using artificial neural network. *J. Nanosci. Nanotechnol.* **2020**, *20*, 485–490. [CrossRef] [PubMed]
47. Ghanizadeh, A.R.; Abbaslou, H.; Amlashi, A.T.; Alidoust, P. Modeling of bentonite/sepiolite plastic concrete compressive strength using artificial neural network and support vector machine. *Front. Struct. Civ. Eng.* **2019**, *13*, 215–239. [CrossRef]
48. Chesnokov, A.; Mikhailov, V.; Dolmatov, I. Evaluation of adverse factors acting on a pre-stressed wire rope structure by means of artificial neural network. In Proceedings of the 1st International Conference on Control Systems, Mathematical Modelling, Automation and Energy Efficiency (SUMMA), Lipetsk, Russia, 20–22 November 2019; pp. 500–504.
49. Hammoudi, A.; Moussaceb, K.; Belebchouche, C.; Dahmoune, F. Comparison of artificial neural network (ANN) and response surface methodology (RSM) prediction in compressive strength of recycled concrete aggregates. *Constr. Build. Mater.* **2019**, *209*, 425–436. [CrossRef]
50. Roh, Y.; Choi, E.; Choi, Y. An artificial neural network based phrase network construction method for structuring facility error types. *J. Internet Comput. Serv.* **2018**, *19*, 21–29.
51. Johnson, J.; Hossain-McKenzie, S.; Bui, U.; Etigowni, S.; Davis, K.; Zonouz, S. Improving power system neural network construction using modal analysis. In Proceedings of the 19th International Conference on Intelligent System Application to Power Systems (ISAP), San Antonio, TX, USA, 17–20 September 2017; pp. 1–6.

52. Veelenturf, L.P. *Analysis and Applications of Artificial Neural Networks*; Prentice-Hall, Inc.: Upper Saddle River, NJ, USA, 1995.
53. Beale, M.H.; Hagan, M.T.; Demuth, H.B. *Neural Network Toolbox*; User's Guide MathWorks: Natick, MA, USA, 2010; Volume 2, pp. 77–81.
54. McRoberts, R.E.; Næsset, E.; Gobakken, T.; Chirici, G.; Condés, S.; Hou, Z.; Saarela, S.; Chen, Q.; Ståhl, G.; Walters, B.F. Assessing components of the model-based mean square error estimator for remote sensing assisted forest applications. *Can. J. For. Res.* **2018**, *48*, 642–649. [CrossRef]
55. Vanhoucke, M. *Measuring Time: Improving Project Performance Using Earned Value Management*; Springer Science & Business Media: Berlin/Heidelberg, Germany, 2009; Volume 136.
56. Zadeh, M.R.; Amin, S.; Khalili, D.; Singh, V.P. Daily outflow prediction by multi layer perceptron with logistic sigmoid and tangent sigmoid activation functions. *Water Resour. Manag.* **2010**, *24*, 2673–2688. [CrossRef]
57. Datta, D.; Agarwal, S.; Kumar, V.; Raj, M.; Ray, B.; Banerjee, A. Design of current mode sigmoid function and hyperbolic tangent function. In Proceedings of the International Symposium on VLSI Design and Test, Sapporo, Japan, 26–29 May 2019; pp. 47–60.
58. Namin, A.H.; Leboeuf, K.; Muscedere, R.; Wu, H.; Ahmadi, M. Efficient hardware implementation of the hyperbolic tangent sigmoid function. In Proceedings of the IEEE International Symposium on Circuits and Systems, Taipei, Taiwan, 24–27 May 2009; pp. 2117–2120.
59. Leboeuf, K.; Namin, A.H.; Muscedere, R.; Wu, H.; Ahmadi, M. High speed VLSI implementation of the hyperbolic tangent sigmoid function. In Proceedings of the Third International Conference on Convergence and Hybrid Information Technology, Busan, Korea, 11–13 November 2008; pp. 1070–1073.
60. Lin, C.-W.; Wang, J.-S. A digital circuit design of hyperbolic tangent sigmoid function for neural networks. In Proceedings of the IEEE International Symposium on Circuits and Systems, Seattle, WA, USA, 18–21 May 2008; pp. 856–859.
61. Koyuncu, I. Implementation of high speed tangent sigmoid transfer function approximations for artificial neural network applications on FPGA. *Adv. Electr. Comput. Eng.* **2018**, *18*, 79–86. [CrossRef]
62. Asiltürk, I.; Çunkaş, M. Modeling and prediction of surface roughness in turning operations using artificial neural network and multiple regression method. *Expert Syst. Appl.* **2011**, *38*, 5826–5832. [CrossRef]
63. Gao, Y.; Cowling, M. *Introduction to Panel Data, Multiple Regression Method, and Principal Components Analysis Using Stata: Study on the Determinants of Executive Compensation—A Behavioral Approach Using Evidence from Chinese Listed Firms*; SAGE Publications: Thousand Oaks, CA, USA, 2019.
64. Yilmaz, I.; Kaynar, O. Multiple regression, ANN (RBF, MLP) and ANFIS models for prediction of swell potential of clayey soils. *Expert Syst. Appl.* **2011**, *38*, 5958–5966. [CrossRef]
65. Stumpe, F.; Katina, P.F. Multi-objective multi-customer project network: Visualising interdependencies and influences. *Int. J. Syst. Syst. Eng.* **2019**, *9*, 139–166. [CrossRef]

Publisher's Note: MDPI stays neutral with regard to jurisdictional claims in published maps and institutional affiliations.

© 2020 by the authors. Licensee MDPI, Basel, Switzerland. This article is an open access article distributed under the terms and conditions of the Creative Commons Attribution (CC BY) license (http://creativecommons.org/licenses/by/4.0/).

Article

Adaptation of a Cost Overrun Risk Prediction Model to the Type of Construction Facility

Edyta Plebankiewicz * and Damian Wieczorek

Department of Construction Management Cracow University of Technology, Warszawska 24, 31-155 Kraków, Poland; dwieczorek@L7.pk.edu.pl
* Correspondence: eplebank@L7.pk.edu.pl; Tel.: +48-12-628-23-30

Received: 5 October 2020; Accepted: 15 October 2020; Published: 20 October 2020

Abstract: To assess the risk of project cost overrun, it is necessary to consider large amounts of symmetric and asymmetric data. This paper proposes a cost overrun risk prediction model, the structure of which is based on the fuzzy inference model of Mamdani. The model consists of numerous inputs and one output (multi-input-single-output (MISO)), based on processes running consecutively in three blocks (the fuzzy block, the interference block, and the block of sharpening the representative output value). The input variables of the model include the share of element costs in the building costs (SE), predicted changes in the number of works (WC), and expected changes in the unit price (PC). For the input variable SE, it is proposed to adjust the fuzzy set shapes to the type of building object. Single-family residential buildings, multi-family residential buildings, office buildings, highways, expressways, and sports fields were analyzed. The initial variable is the value of the risk of exceeding the costs of a given element of a construction investment project (R). In all, 27 rules were assumed in the interference block. Considering the possibility of applying sharpening methods in the cost overrun risk prediction model, the following defuzzification methods were investigated: the first of maxima, middle of maxima, and last of maxima method, the center of gravity method, and the bisector area method. Considering the advantages and disadvantages, the authors assumed that the correct and basic defuzzification method in the cost overrun risk prediction model was the center of gravity method. In order to check the correctness of the assumption made at the stage of designing the rule database, result diagrams were generated for the relationships between the variable (R) and the input variables of individual types of buildings. The results obtained confirm the correctness of the assumed assumptions and allow to consider the input variable (SE), adjusted individually to the model for each type of construction object, as crucial in the context of the impact on the output value of the output variable (R).

Keywords: cost overrun; construction project; fuzzy sets

1. Introduction

Cost overruns in construction projects are a common phenomenon, occurring in different market and legal conditions and, unfortunately, often negatively influencing the achievement of project goals. Numerous research results indicate the scale of this problem. For instance, Love et al. [1] analyzed cost overruns from 276 construction and engineering projects. The research revealed a mean cost overrun of 12.22%. According to research performed by Andrić et al. [2] on cost overruns in infrastructure projects in Asia, the mean value of cost overrun is 26.24%. Senouci et al. [3] in their study on the increase in term cost in 122 construction contracts in Qatari showed that 54% had their costs increased and 72% their deadlines increased. Larsen et al. [4] established that more than half of Malaysian construction projects (55%) experienced cost overruns.

Different types of construction investments can be specified in various stages of their implementation, and these are characterized by different technological, organizational, and economic specificities. When determining the risk of cost overruns, this specificity and different symmetry and asymmetry data must be taken into account. However, when attempting to determine the risk of exceeding the costs of a given element of a facility, one should consider, for instance, the share of a given element in the total cost of the facility, the risk of changes in the number of works, as well as exposure of a given type of works to changes in the unit price, including the price of construction materials [5].

In the literature, various approaches have been described to estimate the real costs of construction projects, including the value of cost overrun. The novelty of the proposed methodology is the assumption of the analysis of individual works included in the project, which allows for a more detailed analysis of the cost overrun risk. The model takes into account the impact of three elements on the risk of cost overrun for a given construction work, which are input variables, namely share of element costs in the building costs (SE), predicted changes in the number of works (WC), and expected changes in the unit price (PC). For each of the variables, a fuzzy interpretation was proposed. The first variable depends on the type of the building and is therefore the most difficult to describe. The authors decided to analyze different types of buildings in the context of determining for each of the them a fuzzy interpretation of the linguistic input variable SE. This can greatly simplify the use of the model in practice.

The aim of the paper is to present a model allowing to assess the risk of exceeding the costs of individual stages of a construction project, adapted to various construction investments.

2. Literature Review

The problem often discussed in the literature are the factors influencing cost overruns in construction projects. According to [2], the main reasons of cost overruns are the increasing cost of resources (labor, materials, machinery), changes in design specifications, land acquisition and resettlement as well as changes in currency exchange. Chen and Hu [6] identified the following main reasons of cost overruns: delay in construction period, engineering quantity increase, and lack of technical skill and experience. Cantarelli et al. [7] investigated the causes of cost overruns in construction projects and categorized them into four main explanations for cost overruns, i.e., technical, economic, psychological, and political. Specific examples of factors were identified for each of these categories. The results of research performed by Phama et al. [8] show that four factors—risks, resources, incompetence of parties, and components, transportation, and machinery cost—are important. Firm policies, project policies, and poor collaboration of parties are not very important for cost overrun. Shaikh [9] identified five main factors as common in causing time and cost overrun in megaprojects in Pakistan. These main factors are financial issues, weather conditions, political approach, design changes, and owner interference. In [10], the authors concluded that the most significant cost overrun factors are schedule delay (47%), improper planning and scheduling (47%), frequent design changes (45%), frequent changes to the scope of work (43%), and inaccurate time and cost estimates of the project (42%). In [11], the authors identified 44 factors affecting cost overrun. Of these, 11 have a decisive influence. Sohu et al. [12] identified nine major causes of cost overrun from professionals working with contractors in highway projects in Pakistan. Catalão et al. [13] presented a methodology using the existing methods but taking into account political, legal, regulatory, and economic determinants. The analysis suggests that these factors have been underestimated in the literature but are of great importance in understanding cost overruns.

Many authors draw attention to the complexity of cost overruns, emphasizing that the factors causing overrun can only be understood by looking at the whole project system in which it occurs and how several variables dynamically interact with each other [14]. The relationships between the different characteristics of the project and cost overrun were studied, for example, in [15–20]. Many authors also analyze the generating process of cost overruns along the various phases of the project life cycle [21–23].

Another extremely important issue is the possibility of predicting the risk of cost overruns and the amount of such overruns. The risk of cost overruns is dynamic, interdependent, complex, subjective, and fuzzy, especially in large and complex projects [24]. This is the reason why many researchers have attempted to apply fuzzy set theory to solve problems related to cost overrun. Sharma and Goyal [25] proposed a fuzzy-based model to estimate the risk magnitude of the same factors influencing cost overrun. Fuzzy sets were also applied by Marzouk and Amin [26], Knight and Robinson-Fayek [27], and Plebankiewicz [5].

Ghazal and Hammad [28] proposed a Knowledge Discovery in Databases (KDD) model, which may supplement the traditional estimation methods and provide more reliable final cost forecasting to overcome the cost overrun problem. In [29], the authors developed a method for estimating the impact of project management maturity (PMM) on project performance. The proposed method uses Bayesian networks to formalize the knowledge of project management experts and to extract knowledge from a database of previous projects. The operation of the method is shown using the example of a large project in the oil and gas industry.

Other approaches used for the analysis of cost overrun problems include statistical methods, such as multiple regression analysis (MRA) [30], a regression and ANN models [31], and case-based reasoning (CBR) [32,33].

3. Concept of a Cost Overrun Risk Prediction Model

3.1. Main Assumptions of the Model

The construction of the cost overrun risk prediction model was based on the fuzzy inference model of Mamdani. This model has been frequently used in the field of construction management, for instance, to build fuzzy risk inference models, in the context of assessing:

- exceeding the time and cost of construction investments [34],
- exceeding the time, cost, and impact on quality and other technical considerations in the implementation of construction projects [35,36],
- occupational risks on construction sites [37],
- level of safety of construction workers [38],
- technological, financial, political, environmental, and legal risk factors in the life cycle of buildings [39],
- technological risk factors for old buildings [40].

A cost overrun risk prediction model is a model with multiple inputs and one output (multi-input-single-output (MISO)), based on processes that run sequentially in three blocks (the fuzzy block, the interference block, and the block of sharpening the representative output value). Share of element costs in the building costs (SE), predicted changes in the number of works (WC), and expected changes in the unit price (PC) are the input variables of the model. The database of 27 individually designed rules supports the inference process in the interference block, and the level of risk of exceeding the costs of a given element of a construction project (R) is an output variable (y).

To construct a cost overrun risk prediction model, the authors decided to choose the theory of possibilities and fuzzy logic, because the risk is related to the so-called measurable uncertainty. Its measurable character results also from the fact that the risk is quantifiable and can be directly translated into the size of parameters necessary, for example, to determine the value of the risk of cost overrun. In practice, it often happens that an expert who evaluates risk does not have a sufficient number of historical data to perform statistical research that would result in a probabilistic distribution, and thus determines subjectively the size of parameters necessary for risk assessment.

3.2. Block of Fuzzification

The input variables, namely share of element costs in the building costs (SE), predicted changes in the number of works (WC), and expected changes in the unit price (PC), are described with appropriate linguistic terms (fuzzy sets) in the consideration spaces on the so-called universes X_1, X_2, and X_3. The domain (range of arguments) of the universes was determined as a percentage within the interval

[0; 100%] for each input variable, with the model using the decimal notation corresponding to the interval [0; 1]. In defining the X consideration spaces, for all variables described by the linguistic terms "high", "average", and "low", it was assumed that the adjacent fuzzy sets (representing consecutive linguistic terms) would overlap. According to Hovde and Moser [41], only this modelling of the linguistic terms for the input variables gives a favorable effect in the inference process.

Table 1 represents the fuzzy sets for the linguistic terms $L(X_2)$ and $L(X_3)$, that is, for the input variables WC and PC. For the description of linguistic terms, membership functions with line graphs were used (triangular functions and classes Γ and L). The qualitative definition of fuzzy sets was based on the selection of appropriate types of membership functions. The quantitative definition was performed on the basis of the selection of the values of parameters characterizing the functional curves, which made it possible to precisely determine the degrees of membership of individual fuzzy sets. Degrees of membership for fuzzy sets are described in Table 1 (in the last column) by means of four numbers $\{\alpha_1, \alpha_2, \alpha_3, \alpha_4\}$. These parameters indicate, respectively, the intervals of achieving the value of membership degree 1.0 $\{\alpha_2, \alpha_3\}$ and the left or right width of the distribution of the membership function to the value of the membership degree 0.0 $\{\alpha_1, \alpha_4\}$. It was assumed that linguistic values for both input variables (WC and PC) would remain unchanged regardless of the type of the building object.

Table 1. Fuzzy interpretations of the linguistic input variables "predicted changes in the number of works" (WC) or expected changes in the unit price (PC).

Fuzzy Set of Linguistic Values for WC or PC		Description of the Variables x_2 or x_3	Fuzzy Evaluation of Membership $\mu(x_2)$ or $\mu(x_3)$
High	Hi	About or above 75.0%	(0.5; 0.75; 1.0; 1.0)
Average	Av	About 50.0%	(0.25; 0.5; 0.5; 075)
Low	Lo	About or below 25.0%	(0.0; 0.0; 0.25; 0.5)

The data presented in Table 1 correspond to the graphic interpretation of fuzzy sets of linguistic values for WC and PC, which is illustrated in Figure 1.

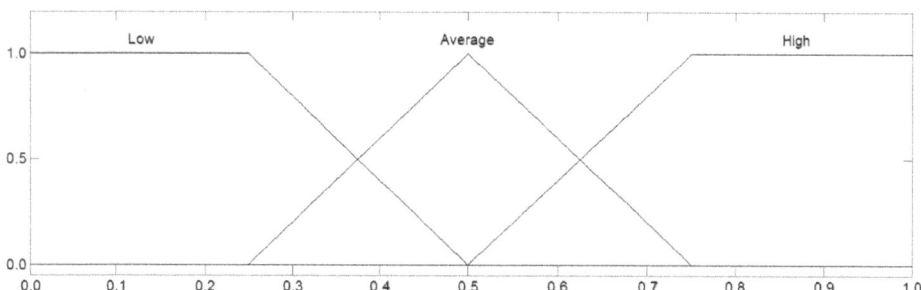

Figure 1. Linguistic terms of the input variables WC and PC.

Input variable: share of element costs in the building costs (SE) should be subject to the process of adjusting the shapes of fuzzy sets described by the linguistic terms "high", "average", and "low" individually, depending on the type of the building object. The authors decided to analyze the following types of building objects in the context of determining the parameters denoting the intervals of attaining the value of the membership degree of 1.0 and the left or right width of the distribution of the membership function to the value of the membership degree 0.0. The following types of buildings were analyzed:

- single-family residential buildings,
- multi-family residential buildings,

- office buildings,
- highways and expressways,
- sports fields.

Each of the buildings was divided according to cost elements following the tables of billing elements for an average of five buildings of each type. Table 2 presents the range of cost elements for cubature facilities, highways and expressways, as well as sports fields.

Table 2. Range of cost elements for individual buildings.

Type of Building	Cost Elements
Cubature facilities (single- and multi-family residential buildings, office buildings)	Earthworks, foundations (including walls and insulation of the ground floor of the building), ground walls, ceilings, stairs, partition walls, roof (construction and covering), sleepers and canals inside the building, insulation of the ground, plaster and interior cladding, windows and doors, painting work, floors (with layer), facades with works outside the building, water and sewage installations, central heating installations and electrical installations.
Highways and expressways	Preparatory works, earthworks, drainage of road body, substructures, surfaces, finishing works, traffic safety equipment, street and road elements and other works.
Sports fields	Site preparation and earthworks, substructures, sports surfaces, landscaping and equipment.

For each building object, based on the data from an average of five objects, the average percentage of each cost component was determined. Then, the values of quartiles Q1 and Q3 and the median were calculated using statistical measures. The results are presented in Table 3.

Table 3. Values of statistical measures for cost elements of building objects.

Type of Building	Quartile Q1	Median	Quartile Q3
Single-family residential buildings	3	6	9
Multi-family residential buildings	3	5	8
Office buildings	2	5	8
Highways and expressways	2	6	21
Sports fields	6	18	51

It should be noted that the research sample (five objects) is relatively small. However, it can be concluded that for standard material and technological solutions, the deviations from the results obtained for a given type of building are small. In the case of non-standard solutions, the share of component costs should be modified, taking into account the specificity of a given building object.

On the basis of the data presented in Table 3, a fuzzy interpretation of the linguistic input variable SE for each of the buildings was proposed. It was assumed that for fuzzy sets:

- "high"—description of the variable would relate to the value "about or above quartile Q3",
- "average"—description of the variable would relate to the value "about median",
- "low"—description of the variable would relate to the value "about or below quartile Q1".

Table 4 depicts a fuzzy interpretation of the linguistic input variable SE for all types of buildings.

Table 4. Fuzzy interpretation of the linguistic input variable share of element costs in the building costs (SE).

Fuzzy Set of Linguistic Values for SE		Description of the Variable x_1	Fuzzy Evaluation of Membership $\mu(x_1)$
Single-family residential buildings			
High	Hi	About or above 9.0%	(0.06; 0.09; 1.0; 1.0)
Average	Av	About 6.0%	(0.0; 0.06; 0.06; 0.09)
Low	Lo	About or below 3.0%	(0.0; 0.0; 0.03; 0.06)
Multi-family residential buildings			
High	Hi	About or above 8.0%	(0.05; 0.08; 1.0; 1.0)
Average	Av	About 5.0%	(0.0; 0.05; 0.05; 0.08)
Low	Lo	About or below 3.0%	(0.0; 0.0; 0.03; 0.05)
Office buildings			
High	Hi	About or above 8.0%	(0.05; 0.08; 1.0; 1.0)
Average	Av	About 5.0%	(0.0; 0.05; 0.05; 0.08)
Low	Lo	About or below 2.0%	(0.0; 0.0; 0.02; 0.05)
Highways and expressways			
High	Hi	About or above 21.0%	(0.06; 0.21; 1.0; 1.0)
Average	Av	About 6.0%	(0.0; 0.06; 0.06; 0.21)
Low	Lo	About or below 2.0%	(0.0; 0.0; 0.02; 0.06)
Sports fields			
High	Hi	About or above 51.0%	(0.08; 0.51; 1.0; 1.0)
Average	Av	About 8.0%	(0.0; 0.08; 0.08; 0.51)
Low	Lo	About or below 6.0%	(0.0; 0.0; 0.06; 0.08)

In Figures 2–6, graphical interpretations of the input variable consideration space are presented for the subsequent types of buildings subjected to analysis. These interpretations accurately reproduce the fuzzy sets for linguistic terms "high", "average", and "low", which are described in Table 4.

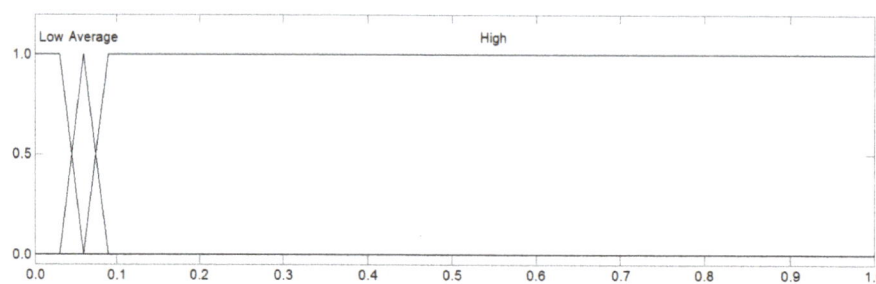

Figure 2. Linguistic terms of the input variable SE for single-family residential buildings.

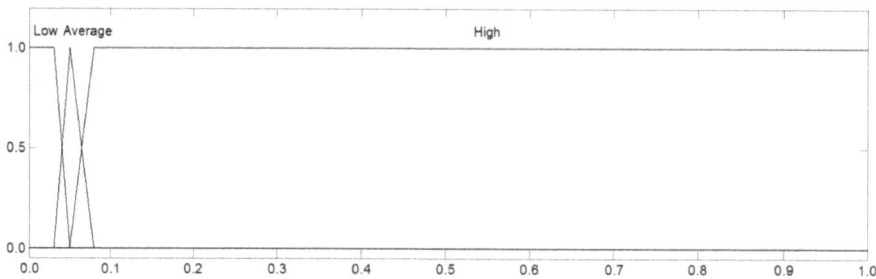

Figure 3. Linguistic terms of the input variable SE for multi-family residential buildings.

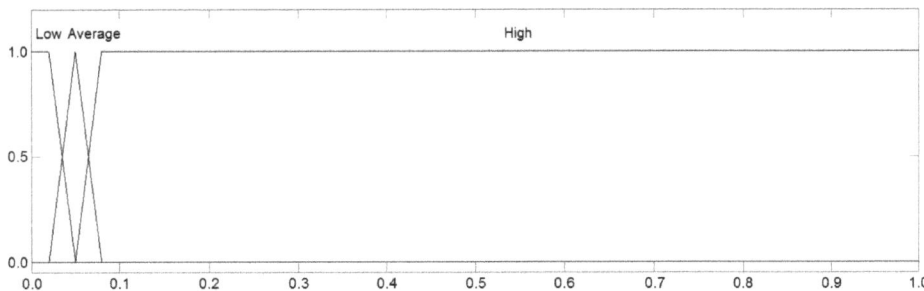

Figure 4. Linguistic terms of the input variable SE for office buildings.

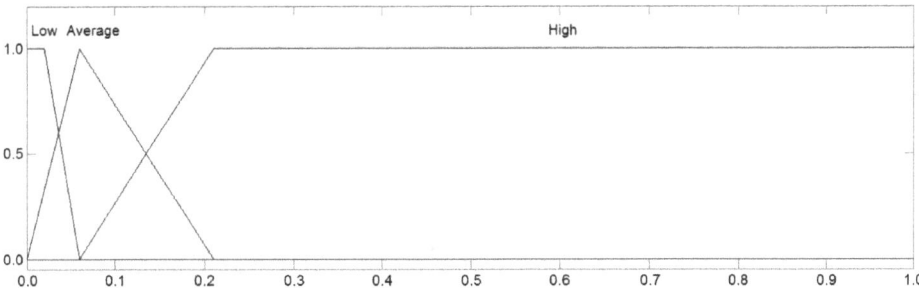

Figure 5. Linguistic terms of the input variable SE for highways and expressways.

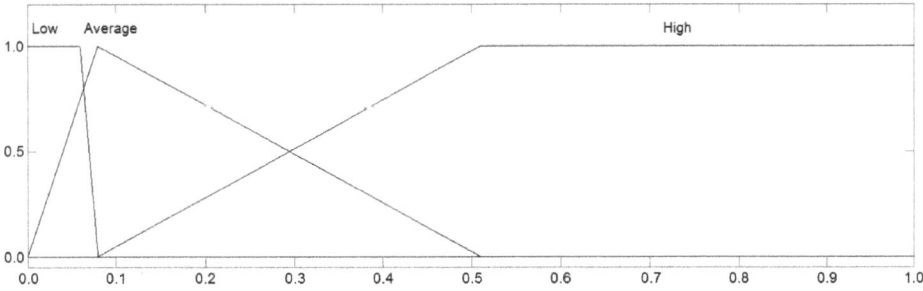

Figure 6. Linguistic terms of the input variable SE for sports fields.

3.3. Block of Inference

In the inference block in the fuzzy inference model of Mamdani of the MISO type, the resulting membership function is calculated for the output variable $\mu(y)$. Its calculation is based on the values of the degree of membership of the sharp input variables $\mu(x_1)$, $\mu(x_2)$, and $\mu(x_3)$ for individual fuzzy sets of linguistic values. The resulting function often has a complex shape and its calculation is done by the so-called inference (inference process). The inference block consists of two basic elements, namely the rule base and the inference mechanism, the operation of which is based on the three following consecutive mathematical operations: aggregation of simple premises, implications of fuzzy inference rules, and aggregation of conclusions of all rules.

The designed base of rules in the cost overrun risk prediction model has a conjunctive form due to the logical conjunction "and" used in conditional sentences, which combines all three simple premises. he model proposes five result conclusions that inform about the size of the calculated risk of cost overruns, i.e., "very low" (Vl), "quite low" (Ql), "average" (Av), "quite high" (Qh), and "very high" (Vh).

For the purpose of developing the rule base, the authors assumed that with an increase in the share of element costs in the building costs (SE), predicted changes in the number of works (WC), and expected changes in the unit price (PC), the value of the risk level of exceeding the costs of a given element in the construction project (R) will naturally and smoothly increase. For this purpose, it was decided to examine the quantities of the products of all combinations of input variables in a set of all 27 possible rules, and then to assign the results to five possible result conclusions on the assumption that the minimum quantities correspond to the "very low" conclusion, the maximum—to the "very high" conclusion, and the intermediate—to the "quite low", "average", and "quite high" conclusions, respectively and proportionally. The following weights were assumed for the linguistic input variables SE, WC, and PC: 1 for "low", 2 for "average", and 3 for "high". Table 5 illustrates the rule base of the inference block consisting of 27 rules, for which equal degrees of fuzzy relationship validity are assumed to be 1.0.

In the interference block, the processes of premise aggregation and rule conclusion aggregation are performed. Aggregation of simple premises consists in calculating the degree of belonging (truthfulness) of the fuzzy rule created by these premises. Due to the fact that in the conditional sentences the logical conjunction "and" was used, which in fuzzy logic is represented by the concept of intersection (product) of the fuzzy sets, the operation of premise aggregation was reduced to searching for the value of the degree of membership to the fuzzy relationship (F_R). This value was determined by applying the Mamdani fuzzy implication rule (T-norm), calculated according to the following formula:

$$T_M = min(\mu(x_1), \mu(x_2), \mu(x_3)) \tag{1}$$

The final stage of the inference block is the aggregation of the conclusions of all running fuzzy rules (the so-called output aggregation). This procedure consists of summing up the conclusions of activated rules that are responsible for the shape of the resulting membership function $\mu(y)$. According to the calculation algorithm, the first step is to define separately the modified membership functions of the fuzzy sets of the output variable for the rules involved in the inference, and then sum up these fuzzy sets based on one of the formulas for S-norm. In the cost overrun risk prediction model, the basic S-norm is the following formula of Mamdani:

$$S_M = max(\mu(x_1), \mu(x_2), \mu(x_3)) \tag{2}$$

Output variable (y) is described in space (universe) Y. The scope of the Y universe was determined as a percentage [0; 100%]. As in the case of all input variables, the record of the argument domain in the decimal interval was adopted [0; 1]. Sets correspond to the resultant conclusions in the rule database ("very low", "quite low", "average", "quite high", and "very high").

Fuzzy sets for the final result conclusions ("very low" and "very high") and the intermediate internal conclusion ("average") were attempted to be parameterized in such a way that the membership function graphs did not interpenetrate, but were continuous in the full scope of the Y universe. For internal relative conclusions ("quite low" and "quite high"), the same procedure was followed, where the fuzzy sets were entered symmetrically between the extreme (final) and internal (intermediate) conclusions. The parameterization was performed in such a way that the adjacent fuzzy sets overlapped with the membership degree for intermediate elements equal to $\mu(0.2) = \mu(0.4) = \mu(0.6) = \mu(0.8) = 0.5$. Table 6 presents sets of linguistic terms L(Y) for the output variable (y). The membership of all fuzzy sets was defined as in the case of the input variables, that is, using four numbers $\{\alpha_1, \alpha_2, \alpha_3, \alpha_4\}$.

Figure 7 presents a graphic interpretation of the consideration space of the output variable (y), which is represented by the fuzzy sets of all five result conclusions, described in Table 6.

Table 5. Rule base of the inference block.

Rule No.	If (SE) LV	If (SE) Weight	And (WC) LV	And (WC) Weight	And (PC) LV	And (PC) Weight	Then (R) Product	Then (R) Concl.
1	Lo	1	Lo	1	Lo	1	1	Vl
2	Lo	1	Lo	1	Av	2	2	Vl
3	Lo	1	Lo	1	Hi	3	3	Ql
4	Lo	1	Av	2	Lo	1	2	Vl
5	Lo	1	Av	2	Av	2	4	Ql
6	Lo	1	Av	2	Hi	3	6	Av
7	Lo	1	Hi	3	Lo	1	3	Ql
8	Lo	1	Hi	3	Av	2	6	Av
9	Lo	1	Hi	3	Hi	3	9	Qh
10	Av	2	Lo	1	Lo	1	2	Vl
11	Av	2	Lo	1	Av	2	4	Ql
12	Av	2	Lo	1	Hi	3	6	Av
13	Av	2	Av	2	Lo	1	4	Ql
14	Av	2	Av	2	Av	2	8	Av
15	Av	2	Av	2	Hi	3	12	Qh
16	Av	2	Hi	3	Lo	1	6	Av
17	Av	2	Hi	3	Av	2	12	Qh
18	Av	2	Hi	3	Hi	3	18	Vh
19	Hi	3	Lo	1	Lo	1	3	Ql
20	Hi	3	Lo	1	Av	2	6	Av
21	Hi	3	Lo	1	Hi	3	9	Qh
22	Hi	3	Av	2	Lo	1	6	Av
23	Hi	3	Av	2	Av	2	12	Qh
24	Hi	3	Av	2	Hi	3	18	Vh
25	Hi	3	Hi	3	Lo	1	9	Qh
26	Hi	3	Hi	3	Av	2	18	Vh
27	Hi	3	Hi	3	Hi	3	27	Vh

where LV—fuzzy set of linguistic values (fuzzy sets in accordance with Tables 1 and 4), Concl—resulting conclusion for the output variable risk of exceeding the costs of a given element of a construction investment project (R). Vl, very low; Ql, quite low, Av, average; Qh, quite high; Vh, very high.

Table 6. Fuzzy interpretation of the linguistic output variable R.

Fuzzy Set of Linguistic Values for R		Description of the Variable y	Fuzzy Evaluation of Membership $\mu(y)$
Very high	Vh	About or above 0.9	(0.7; 0.9; 1.0; 1.0)
Quite high	Qh	About 0.7	(0.5; 0.7; 0.7; 0.9)
Average	Av	About 0.5	(0.3; 0.5; 0.5; 0.7)
Quite low	Ql	About 0.3	(0.1; 0.3; 0.3; 0.5)
Very low	Vl	About or below 0.1	(0.0; 0.0; 0.1; 0.3)

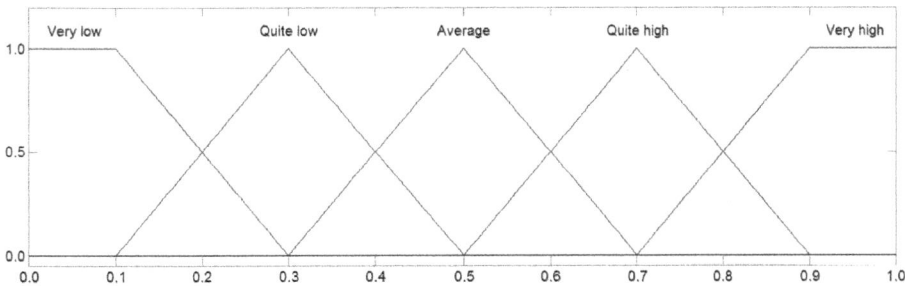

Figure 7. Linguistic terms of the output variable R.

3.4. Block of Defuzzification

The defuzzification process is a mathematical operation performed on the resultant membership function shape (the resulting fuzzy set) obtained after aggregating the conclusions of all inference rules. This operation aims to determine one sharp value of the variable (y) that will appropriately represent the output fuzzy set and indicate unambiguously the result conclusion.

Considering the possibility of using sharpening methods in the cost overrun risk prediction model, the following defuzzification methods were investigated: the first of maxima, middle of maxima, and last of maxima method, the center of gravity method, and the bisector area method. The advantages and disadvantages, as well as the conditions for the application of individual methods, were highlighted. The suggestions and observations contained in [42] were especially taken into account, according to which the methods of maxima:

- are not able to implement the assumption adopted for the purposes of building the rule base, that with the increase in the share of element costs in the building costs (SE), predicted changes in the number of works (WC), and expected changes in the unit price (PC), the value of the risk level of exceeding the costs of a given element of the construction investment (R) will naturally and smoothly increase,
- result in sharp values, which will not in every case adequately represent the output fuzzy set, which is caused by the impact on the sharp result of only the most activated fuzzy set of the output variable.

Figure 8 confirms the observations described above with regard to the use of the last of maxima defuzzification method. On the left, there is the result surface for the output variable (R) due to the influence of the input variables PC and SE. The result surface is analogous for the set of input variables WC and SE. On the right, the same result area is shown, but in terms of the input variables PC and WC.

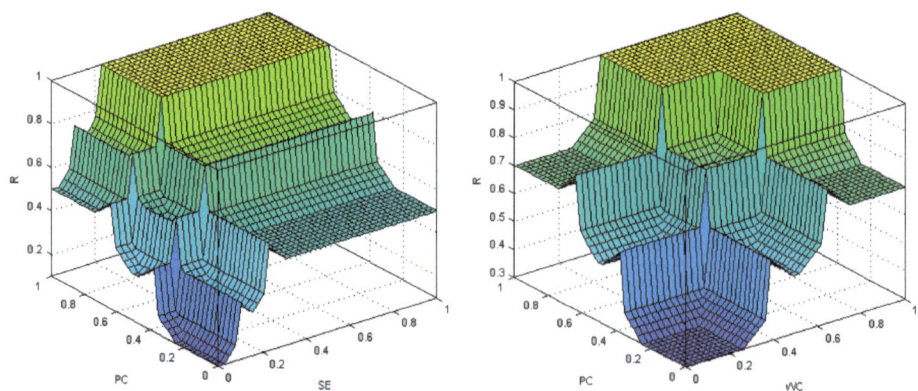

Figure 8. Result area in terms of input variables PC and SE (**left**) and PC and WC (**right**)—last of maxima defuzzification method.

Taking into account the above observations, it was assumed that the proper and basic defuzzification method in the cost overrun risk prediction model would be the center of gravity method.

4. Discussion

A cost overrun risk prediction model was developed for each type of construction site separately using the "Fuzzy Logic Designer" application that is available in the MATLAB R2013a software package (The MathWorks, Inc., Natick, MA, USA) for scientific and engineering calculations.

In order to investigate the correctness of the assumption made at the design stage of the rule base (i.e., that as the share of element costs in the building costs (SE), predicted changes in the number of works (WC) and expected changes in the unit price (PC) increase, the value of the risk level of exceeding the costs of a given element of the construction project (R) will increase naturally and smoothly) and also to examine the impact of the change of the membership function for the input variable (i.e., share of element costs in the building costs (SE) for individual types of building objects on the value of the results obtained for the output variable (R)), the following result diagrams were generated for the relationships between the variable R and the input variables:

- diagrams of the result area for the output variable (R) due to the influence of the input variables PC and SE in the cross-section, when WC = 0.5, and WC and SE in the cross-section, when PC = 0.5,
- diagrams of the result area for the output variable (R) taking into account the set of input variables PC and WC in the cross-section, when SE = 0.5,
- flat diagrams of the resultant curves for the output variable (R) due to the influence of PC input variables in the cross-section, when WC = SE = 0.5, WC in the cross-section, when PC = SE = 0.5, and SE in the cross-section, when PC = WC = 0.5.

The following figures show flat and spatial diagrams for the relationships between the output variable (R) and the input variables (SE, WC, and PC) for all types of buildings under analysis (single- and multi-family residential buildings, office buildings, highways and expressways, and sports fields). Figure 9 shows the result area for the output variable (R) in terms of PC and WC variables (left diagram) and the relationship between the output variable (R) and the PC input variable (right diagram). It should be noted that both the result areas as well as dependencies on the output variable (R) are analogous for each type of building object because, in the cost overrun risk prediction model, it was assumed that PC and WC input variables would remain the same for all buildings.

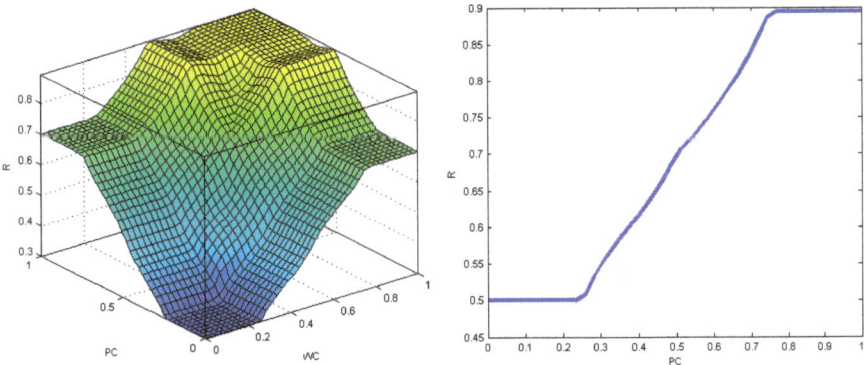

Figure 9. The result area for the output variable (R) in terms of the PC and WC variables in the cross-section, when SE = 0.5 (**left** diagram), and the relationship between the output variable (R) and the input variable PC in the cross-section, when WC = SE = 0.5 (**right** diagram).

Figures 10–14 show the result area for the output variable (R) in terms of the variables PC and SE (diagrams on the left, respectively) and the relationships between the output variable (R) and the input variable SE (diagrams on the right, respectively). It should be noted that both the result area and the dependencies with respect to the output variable (R) are analogous for the set of input variables WC and SE.

Diagrams of the result areas and of the relationship between the output variable (R) and the input variables confirm the correctness of the assumptions made when designing the rule base of the cost overrun risk prediction model. Figures 9–14 indicate unequivocally that with an increase in the share of element costs in the building costs (SE), predicted changes in the number of works (WC), and expected changes in the unit price (PC), the value of the risk level of exceeding the costs of a given element of a construction investment (R) increases naturally and smoothly.

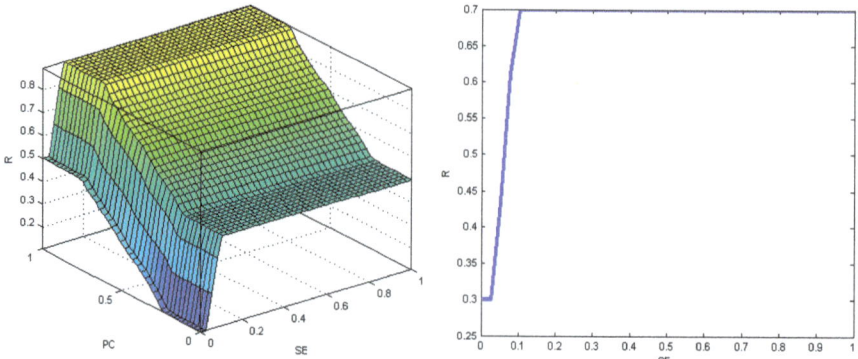

Figure 10. The result area for the output variable (R) in terms of the PC and SE variables in the cross-section, when WC = 0.5 (**left** diagram), and the relationship between the output variable (R) and the input variable SE in the cross-section, when WC = PC = 0.5 (**right** diagram)—single-family residential buildings.

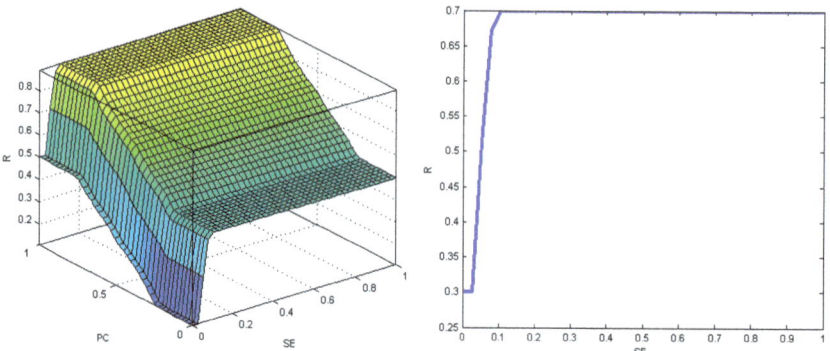

Figure 11. The result area for the output variable (R) in terms of the PC and SE variables in the cross-section, when WC = 0.5 (**left** diagram), and the relationship between the output variable (R) and the input variable SE in the cross-section, when WC = PC = 0.5 (**right** diagram)—multi-family residential buildings.

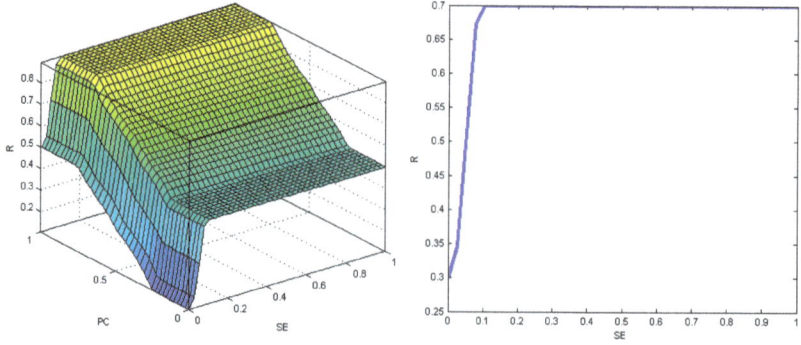

Figure 12. The result area for the output variable (R) in terms of the PC and SE variables in the cross-section, when WC = 0.5 (**left** diagram), and the relationship between the output variable (R) and the input variable SE in the cross-section, when WC = PC = 0.5 (**right** diagram)—office buildings.

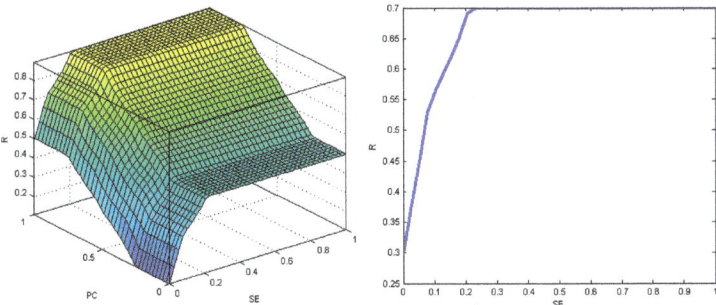

Figure 13. The result area for the output variable (R) in terms of the PC and SE variables in the cross-section, when WC = 0.5 (**left** diagram), and the relationship between the output variable (R) and the input variable SE in the cross-section, when WC = PC = 0.5 (**right** diagram)—highways and expressways.

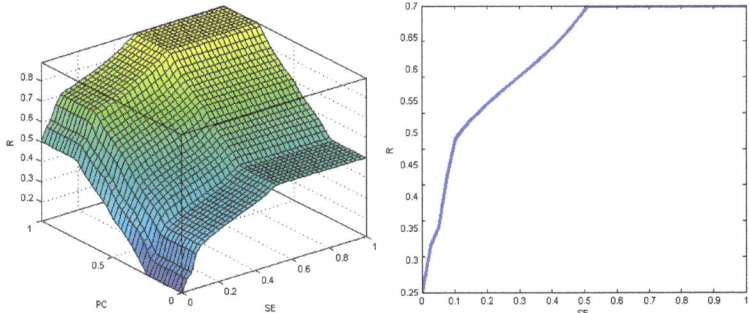

Figure 14. The result area for the output variable (R) in terms of the PC and SE variables in the cross-section, when WC = 0.5 (**left** diagram), and the relationship between the output variable (R) and the input variable SE in the cross-section, when WC = PC = 0.5 (**right** diagram)—sports.

In contrast, the diagrams of the dependence between the output variable (R) and the input variable SE in the cross-section were superimposed on Figure 15 when WC = PC = 0.5 for all five types of construction objects.

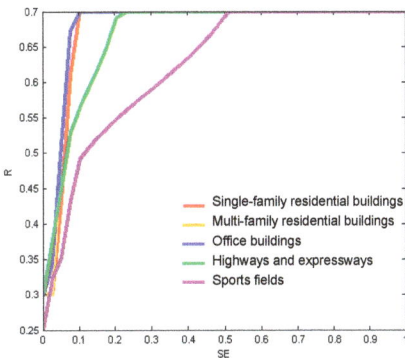

Figure 15. The diagrams of the dependence between the output variable (R) and the input variable SE for all five types of construction objects.

From the comparison of flat dependence diagrams (Figure 15), the input variable share of element costs in the building costs (SE), adjusted individually to the model for each building type, should be considered crucial in the context of the impact on the result value of the output variable (R). The lower the membership for the values of the arguments of the X1 universe domain for the linguistic terms "average" and "high" of the SE variable, the more the resulting value of the risk of construction investment cost overrun (R) increases for the arguments of the X1 variable universe with smaller values—the SE interval approximately [0.1; 0.3]. This conclusion is confirmed in particular by the comparison of the course of the result curves for office buildings (blue line) and sports fields (purple line).

5. Conclusions

The phenomenon of exceeding planned investment costs is often encountered in the construction industry, and the determination of the risk associated with it may be of key importance for achieving the objectives of the project. This paper discusses a cost overrun risk prediction model, the development of which was based on the fuzzy inference model of Mamdani. The model input variables include the following: share of element costs in the building costs (SE), predicted changes in the number of works (WC), and expected changes in the unit price (PC). The basic problem is to adjust the shape of the fuzzy sets for a given input SE to the type of building object. The paper proposes a shape for cubature buildings (residential and office ones), highways and expressways, and sports fields.

In order to check the correctness of the assumption made of the rule database, result diagrams were generated for the relationships between the variable R and the input variables of individual types of buildings. The obtained results confirm the correctness of the assumptions. With an increase in input variables, the value of the risk level of exceeding the costs increases naturally and smoothly. The results prove that the input variable SE, adjusted individually to the model for each type of construction object, is crucial in the context of influencing the output value. The lower the membership for the values of the arguments of the X1 universe domain for the linguistic terms "average" and "high" of the SE variable, the more the resulting value of the risk of construction investment cost overrun (R) increases for the arguments of the X1 variable universe with smaller values.

The model requires further research, both in terms of the input data taken into account and the diversity of the analyzed construction projects. Further testing of the model on actual construction projects will confirm its usefulness in determining the risk of cost overruns.

Author Contributions: E.P. carried out a review of the literature concerning the introduction part. E.P. and D.W. described all assumptions of the cost overrun risk prediction model. D.W. prepared all figures and tables. E.P. and D.W. discussed the results, drew conclusions. All authors have read and agreed to the published version of the manuscript.

Funding: This research received no external funding.

Conflicts of Interest: The authors declare no conflict of interest.

References

1. Love, P.E.D.; Wang, X.; Sing, C.; Tiong, R.L.K. Determining the Probability of Cost Overruns. *J. Constr. Eng. Manag.* **2013**, *139*, 321–330. [CrossRef]
2. Andrić, J.M.; Mahamadu, A.; Wang, J.; Zou, P.X.W.; Zhong, R. The cost performance and causes of overruns in infrastructure development projects in Asia. *J. Civ. Eng. Manag.* **2019**, *25*, 203–214. [CrossRef]
3. Senouci, A.; Ismail, A.; Eldin, N. Time Delay and Cost Overrun in Qatari Public Construction Projects. *Procedia Eng.* **2016**, *164*, 368–375. [CrossRef]
4. Larsen, J.K.; Shen, G.Q.; Lindhard, S.M.; Ditlev, T. Factors Affecting Schedule Delay, Cost Overrun, and Quality Level in Public Construction Projects. *J. Manag. Eng.* **2016**, *32*, 04015032. [CrossRef]
5. Plebankiewicz, E. Model of predicting cost overrun in construction projects. *Sustainability* **2018**, *10*, 4387. [CrossRef]
6. Chen, Y.; Hu, Z. Exploring the properties of cost overrun risk propagation network (CORPN) for promoting cost management. *J. Civ. Eng. Manag.* **2019**, *25*, 1–18. [CrossRef]

7. Cantarelli, C.C.; Flyvbjerg, B.; Molin, J.E.E.; van Wee, B. Cost Overruns in Large-Scale Transportation Infrastructure Projects: Explanations and their Theoretical Embeddedness. *Eur. J. Transp. Infrastruct. Res.* **2010**, *10*, 21.
8. Phama, H.; Luub, T.-V.; Kimc, S.-Y.; Viend, D.-T. Assessing the Impact of Cost Overrun Causes in Transmission Lines Construction Projects. *Ksce J. Civ. Eng.* **2020**, *24*, 1029–1036. [CrossRef]
9. Shaikh, F.A. Financial Mismanagement: A Leading Cause of Time and Cost Overrun in Mega Construction Projects in Pakistan. *Eng. Technol. Appl. Sci. Res.* **2020**, *10*, 5247–5250.
10. Gunduz, M.; Maki, O.L. Assessing the risk perception of cost overrun through importance rating. *Technol. Econ. Dev. Econ.* **2018**, *24*, 1829–1844. [CrossRef]
11. El-Kholy, A.M. Predicting Cost Overrun in Construction Projects. *Int. J. Constr. Eng. Manag.* **2015**, *4*, 95–105.
12. Sohu, S.; Abdullah, A.H.; Nagapan, S.; Rind, T.A.; Jhatial, A.A. Controlling Measures for Cost Overrun Causes in Highway Projects of Sindh Province Engineering. *Technol. Appl. Sci. Res.* **2019**, *9*, 4276–4280.
13. Catalão, F.P.; Cruz, C.O.; Sarmento, J.M. The determinants of cost deviations and overruns in transport projects, an endogenous models approach. *Transp. Policy* **2019**, *74*, 224–238. [CrossRef]
14. Ahiaga-Dagbui, D.D.; Gordon, R.; Love, P.E.D.; Smith, S.D.; Ackermann, F. Toward a Systemic View to Cost Overrun Causation in Infrastructure Projects: A Review and Implications for Research. *Proj. Manag. J.* **2017**, *48*, 88–98. [CrossRef]
15. Huo, T.; Ren, H.; Cai, W.; Shen, G.Q.; Liu, B.; Zhu, M.; Wu, H. Measurement and dependence analysis of cost overruns in megatransport infrastructure projects: Case study in Hong Kong. *J. Constr. Eng. Manag.* **2018**, *144*, 05018001. [CrossRef]
16. França, A.; Haddad, A. Causes of Construction Projects Cost Overrun in Brazil. *Int. J. Sustain. Constr. Eng. Technol.* **2018**, *9*, 69–83. [CrossRef]
17. Johnson, J. Comparing the Effects of ABC and BIM in Construction Projects and Choose the Best Solution to Minimise the Delay and Cost Overrun Using MADMA. *PM World J.* **2019**, *8*, 1–18.
18. Keng, T.C.; Mansor, N.; Ching, Y.K. An Exploration of Cost Overrun in Building Construction Projects. *Glob. Bus. Manag. Res. Int. J.* **2018**, *10*, 638–646.
19. Mahamid, I. Study of relationship between cost overrun and labour productivity in road construction projects. *Int. J. Product. Qual. Manag.* **2018**, *24*, 143–164. [CrossRef]
20. Akinradewo, O.; Aghimien, D.; Aigbavboa, C. Comparative Analysis of Cost Overrun on Road Construction Projects Executed by Indigenous and Expatriate Contractors. In Proceedings of the International Conference on Industrial Engineering and Operations Management, Dubai, United Arab Emirates, 10–12 March 2020.
21. Cavalieri, M.; Cristaudo, R.; Guccio, C. On the magnitude of cost overruns throughout the project life-cycle: An assessment for the Italian transport infrastructure projects. *Transp. Policy* **2019**, *79*, 21–36. [CrossRef]
22. Derakhshanalavijeh, R.; Teixeira, J.M.C. Cost overrun in construction projects in developing countries, Gas-Oil industry of Iran as a case study. *J. Civ. Eng. Manag.* **2017**, *23*, 125–136. [CrossRef]
23. Cantarelli, C.C.; Molin, E.J.E.; van Wee, B.; Flyvbjerg, B. Characteristics of cost overruns for Dutch transport infrastructure projects and the importance of the decision to build and project phases. *Transp. Policy* **2012**, *22*, 49–56. [CrossRef]
24. Islam, M.S.; Nepal, M.P.; Skitmore, M.; Kabir, G. A knowledge-based expert system to assess power plant project cost overrun risks. *Expert Syst. Appl.* **2019**, *136*, 12–32.
25. Sharma, S.; Goyal, P.K. Fuzzy assessment of the risk factors causing cost overrun in construction industry. *Evol. Intell.* **2019**, 1–13. [CrossRef]
26. Marzouk, M.; Amin, A. Predicting Construction materials prices using fuzzy logic and neural networks. *J. Constr. Eng. Manag.* **2013**, *139*, 1190–1198. [CrossRef]
27. Knight, K.; Robinson-Fayek, A. Use of fuzzy logic of predicting design cost overruns on building projects. *J. Constr. Eng. Manag.* **2002**, *128*, 503–512. [CrossRef]
28. Ghazal, M.M.; Hammad, A.M. Data Acquisition Model for Analyzing Cost Overrun in Construction Projects using KDD. In Proceedings of the International Conference on Industrial Engineering and Operations Management, Bandung, Indonesia, 6–8 March 2018; pp. 2255–2266.
29. Sanchez, F.; Bonjour, E.; Micaelli, J.-P.; Monticolo, D. An Approach Based on Bayesian Network for Improving Project Management Maturity: An Application to Reduce Cost Overrun Risks in Engineering Projects. *Comput. Ind.* **2020**, *119*, 103227. [CrossRef]

30. Abu Hammad, A.A.; Ali, S.M.A.; Sweis, G.J.; Basher, A. Prediction Model for Construction Cost and Duration in Jordan. *Jordan J. Civ. Eng.* **2008**, *2*, 250–266.
31. Juszczyk, M.; Leśniak, A.; Zima, K. ANN based approach for estimation of construction costs of sports fields. *Complexity* **2018**, *2018*, 7952434. [CrossRef]
32. Ji, S.H.; Park, M.; Lee, H.S. Cost Estimation Model for Building Projects Using Case-Based Reasoning. *Can. J. Civ. Eng.* **2011**, *38*, 570–581. [CrossRef]
33. Leśniak, A.; Zima, K. Cost Calculation of Construction Projects Including Sustainability Factors Using the Case Based Reasoning (CBR) Method. *Sustainability* **2018**, *10*, 1608. [CrossRef]
34. Ibadov, N.; Kulejewski, J. The assessment of construction project risks with the use of fuzzy sets theory. *Tech. Trans.* **2014**, *1-B*, 175–182.
35. Nieto-Morote, A.; Ruz-Vila, F. A fuzzy approach to construction project risk assessment. *Int. J. Proj. Manag.* **2011**, *29*, 220–231. [CrossRef]
36. Tavakolan, M.; Mohammadi, A. Construction risk management framework using fuzzy sets and failure mode and effect analysis. In Proceedings of the 51st ASC Annual International Conference, The Associated Schools of Construction, College Station, TX, USA, 22–25 April 2015.
37. Debnath, J.; Biswas, A.; Sivan, P.; Sen, K.N.; Sahu, S. Fuzzy inference model for assessing occupational risks in construction sites. *Int. J. Ind. Ergon.* **2016**, *55*, 114–128. [CrossRef]
38. Othman, M.H.H.; Arbaiy, N.; Lah, M.S.C.; Lin, P.C. Mean-Variance Model With Fuzzy Random Data. *J. Crit. Rev.* **2020**, *7*, 1347–1352.
39. Plebankiewicz, E.; Wieczorek, D. Rozmyta ocena ryzyka w cyklu życia obiektów budowlanych. *Mater. Bud.* **2016**, *6*, 59–61. [CrossRef]
40. Konior, J. Technical assessment of old buildings by fuzzy approach. *Arch. Civil. Eng.* **2019**, *65*, 130–141. [CrossRef]
41. Hovde, P.J.; Moser, K. *Performance based Methods for Service Life Prediction*; State of the Art Reports; CIB Report; Trondheim Publication: Trondheim, Norway, 2004; p. 294.
42. Wieczorek, D. Fuzzy risk assessment in the life cycle of building object—Selection of the right defuzzification method. In *AIP Conference Proceedings*; AIP Publishing: Melville, NY, USA, 2018; Volume 1978, p. 240005.

Publisher's Note: MDPI stays neutral with regard to jurisdictional claims in published maps and institutional affiliations.

© 2020 by the authors. Licensee MDPI, Basel, Switzerland. This article is an open access article distributed under the terms and conditions of the Creative Commons Attribution (CC BY) license (http://creativecommons.org/licenses/by/4.0/).

Article

From Probabilistic to Quantile-Oriented Sensitivity Analysis: New Indices of Design Quantiles

Zdeněk Kala

Department of Structural Mechanics, Faculty of Civil Engineering, Brno University of Technology, 602 00 Brno, Czech Republic; kala.z@fce.vutbr.cz

Received: 28 September 2020; Accepted: 15 October 2020; Published: 19 October 2020

Abstract: In structural reliability analysis, sensitivity analysis (SA) can be used to measure how an input variable influences the failure probability P_f of a structure. Although the reliability is usually expressed via P_f, Eurocode building design standards assess the reliability using design quantiles of resistance and load. The presented case study showed that quantile-oriented SA can provide the same sensitivity ranking as P_f-oriented SA or local SA based on P_f derivatives. The first two SAs are global, so the input variables are ranked based on total sensitivity indices subordinated to contrasts. The presented studies were performed for P_f ranging from 9.35×10^{-8} to $1\text{--}1.51 \times 10^{-8}$. The use of quantile-oriented global SA can be significant in engineering tasks, especially for very small P_f. The proposed concept provided an opportunity to go much further. Left-right symmetry of contrast functions and sensitivity indices were observed. The article presents a new view of contrasts associated with quantiles as the distance between the average value of the population before and after the quantile. This distance has symmetric hyperbola asymptotes for small and large quantiles of any probability distribution. Following this idea, new quantile-oriented sensitivity indices based on measuring the distance between a quantile and the average value of the model output are formulated in this article.

Keywords: sensitivity analysis; reliability; failure probability; quantile; civil engineering; limit states; mathematical model; uncertainty

1. Introduction

The reliability of building structures is influenced by inherent uncertainties associated with the material properties, geometry, and structural load variables to which the reliability measure is sensitive [1]. A common measure of reliability is the failure probability P_f, which is estimated using stochastic models [2]. Failure occurs when the load action is greater than the resistance. In this respect, the key issue is the identification of the significance of input random variables with regard to P_f.

Reliability-oriented sensitivity analysis (ROSA) consists of computing the sensitivity ranking of input variables ranked according to the amount of influence each has on P_f. It is argued that sensitivity analysis (SA) should be used "in tandem" with uncertainty analysis and the latter should precede the former in practical applications [3]. This can encumber the entire computational process, especially in cases of very small P_f.

Alternatively, the assessment of reliability can be performed by comparing the design quantiles of load and resistance [4,5]. A structure is reliable if the design resistance is greater than the design load action. One might ask, if the reliability assessment based on P_f can be replaced by a reliability assessment based on design quantiles, can the SA of P_f be replaced by the SA of design quantiles? For this purpose, new types of sensitivity indices oriented to both design quantiles and P_f can be investigated in engineering applications.

In civil engineering, classical Sobol SA (SSA) [6,7] is applied in the research of structural responses [8–16] or responses in geotechnical applications [17,18]. SSA is attractive for a number of reasons, e.g., it measures sensitivity across the whole input space (i.e., it is a global method), and it is capable of dealing with non-linear responses, as well as measuring the effect of interactions in non-additive models. However, SSA is based on the decomposition of variance of the model output, without a direct reference (only with partial empathy) to reliability [19].

Sobol indices in the context of ROSA can be derived as in [20], by introducing the binary random variable 1 (failure) or 0 (success) as the quantity of interest [21], where the basis of this transformation is the importance measure between P_f and conditional P_f defined in [22]. Indices can be derived in different variants, depending on whether the square of the importance measure [20] or the absolute value of the importance measure [23,24] is considered, but only the variant [20] after Sobol is based on decomposition, with the sum of all indices equal to one.

Both classical Sobol indices [6,7] and Sobol indices in the context of ROSA [20] are a subset of sensitivity indices subordinated to contrasts [25] (in short, Fort contrast indices). The general idea of Fort contrast indices [25] is that the importance of an input variable may vary, depending on what the quantity of interest is. Fort contrast indices define different types of indices based on a common platform, thus providing new perspectives on solving reliability tasks of different types.

It can be shown that Sobol indices in the context of ROSA [20] are Fort contrast indices [25] associated with P_f (referred to as contrast P_f indices in this article). Furthermore, it can be shown that the classical Sobol indices [6,7] are Fort contrast indices [25] associated with variance. In general, the type of Fort contrast index [25] varies, according to the type of contrast used. Contrast functions permit the estimation of various parameters associated with a probability distribution. By changing the contrast, SA can change its key quantity of interest. The contrast may or may not be reliability-oriented.

Fort contrast indices can be considered as global since they are based on changes of the key quantity of interest (P_f, α-quantile, variance, etc.) with regard to the variability of the inputs over their entire distribution ranges and they provide the interaction effect between different input variables. On the other hand, contrast functions account for the variability of the inputs regionally, according to the type of key quantity of interest, e.g., changes around the mean value are important for variance, changes around the quantile are important for the quantile, etc.

Standard [4] establishes the basis that sets out the way in which Eurocodes can be used for structural design. Although the concept of the probability-based assessment of structural reliability has been known about for a long time [5], new types of quantile-oriented SA have not yet been examined, in the context of structural reliability, at an appropriate depth. It can be expected that many of the reliability principles applied in [4] can be applied symmetrically in ROSA using new types of sensitivity indices to find new relationships. The introduced ROSA may be connected to decision-oriented methods [26] in areas of civil engineering, where decision-making under uncertainty is presently uncommon.

2. Probability-Based Assessment of Structural Reliability

Let the reliability of building structures be a one-dimensional random variable Z:

$$Z = g(X) = g(X_1, X_2, \ldots, X_M), \tag{1}$$

where $X_1, X_2, \ldots, X_M$ are random variables employed for its computation. The classical theory of structural reliability [27] expresses Equation (1) as a limit state using two statistically independent random variables, the load effect (action F), and the load-carrying capacity of the structure (resistance R).

$$Z = R - F \geq 0 \tag{2}$$

The variable that unambiguously quantifies reliability or unreliability is the probability that inequality (2) will not be satisfied. If Z is normally distributed, reliability index β is given as

$$\beta = \frac{\mu_Z}{\sigma_Z}, \quad (3)$$

where μ_Z is the mean value of Z and σ_Z is its standard deviation. By modifying Equation (3), we can express $\mu_Z - \beta \cdot \sigma_Z = 0$. The failure probability P_f can then be expressed as

$$P_f = P(Z < 0) = P(Z < \mu_Z - \beta \cdot \sigma_Z) = \Phi_U(-\beta), \quad (4)$$

where $\Phi_U(\cdot)$ is the cumulative distribution function of the normalized Gaussian probability density function (pdf). Reliability is defined as $P_s = (1 - P_f)$. For other distributions of Z, β is merely a conventional measure of reliability. Equation (3) can be modified for normally distributed Z, F, and R as

$$\beta = \frac{\mu_Z}{\sigma_Z} = \frac{\mu_R - \mu_F}{\sqrt{\sigma_R^2 + \sigma_F^2}} = \frac{\mu_R - \mu_F}{\frac{\sigma_R^2}{\sqrt{\sigma_R^2 + \sigma_F^2}} + \frac{\sigma_F^2}{\sqrt{\sigma_R^2 + \sigma_F^2}}} = \frac{\mu_R - \mu_F}{\alpha_R \cdot \sigma_R + \alpha_F \cdot \sigma_F}, \quad (5)$$

where α_F and α_R are values of the first-order reliability method (FORM) sensitivity factors.

$$\alpha_R = \frac{\sigma_R}{\sqrt{\sigma_R^2 + \sigma_F^2}}, \quad \alpha_F = \frac{\sigma_F}{\sqrt{\sigma_R^2 + \sigma_F^2}}, \text{ with } |\alpha| \leq 1 \quad (6)$$

It can be noted that Sobol's first-order indices are equal to the squares of α_F and α_R: $S_F = \alpha_F^2$ and $S_R = \alpha_R^2$, respectively [19]. By applying α_F and α_R according to Equation (6), Equation (5) can be written with formally separated random variables as

$$\mu_F + \alpha_F \cdot \beta \cdot \sigma_F = \mu_R - \alpha_R \cdot \beta \cdot \sigma_R. \quad (7)$$

Equation (7) is a function of the four statistical characteristics of μ_F, σ_F, μ_R, and σ_R, from which β, α_F, and α_R are computed. The left side in Equation (7) is the design load F_d (upper quantile) and the right side is the design resistance R_d (lower quantile).

Standard [4] verifies the reliability by comparing the obtained reliability index β with the target reliability index β_d, according to the equation $\beta \geq \beta_d$, which transforms Equation (7) into the design condition of reliability:

$$\mu_F + \alpha_F \cdot \beta_d \cdot \sigma_F \leq \mu_R - \alpha_R \cdot \beta_d \cdot \sigma_R, \quad (8)$$

where α_F and α_R may be considered as 0.7 and 0.8, respectively [4].

3. Sensitivity Analysis

In structural reliability, the key quantities of interest are the failure probability P_f and the design quantiles F_d and R_d. In order to analyse the reliability, ROSA must be focused on the same key quantity of interest: P_f, F_d, and R_d. Local and global types of ROSA are applied in this article.

3.1. Local ROSA

The partial derivative $\delta P_f / \delta \mu_{xi}$ with respect to the mean value μ of the input variable X_i presents a classical measure of change in P_f (see, e.g., [28–32]). The derivative-based approach has the advantage of being very efficient in terms of the computation time. There are two main disadvantages of using the derivative as an indicator of sensitivity.

The first disadvantage is that the derivative measures only change at the point (local SA) where it is numerically realized. If the algorithms on the computer are of the "black-box" type, then only a numerical evaluation of the derivative is possible. The second disadvantage is that a large absolute value of the derivative does not necessarily mean a large influence of the input on the output if the distribution range of the input variable is small compared to other variables.

A better proportional degree of sensitivity is obtained when the derivative is multiplied by the standard deviation σ_{X_i} of the input variable.

$$D_i = \frac{\partial P_f}{\partial \mu_{X_i}} \sigma_{X_i} \tag{9}$$

The advantage of using Equation (9) is the inclusion of σ_{X_i} and the possibility of introducing a correlation between the input random variables. A limitation of the derivative-based approach occurs when the analysed variable is of an unknown linearity.

Regarding quantiles, the use of partial derivatives as an indicator of sensitivity analogously to Equation (9) is not offered. For example, for the additive model $X_1 + X_2$, the derivative of the quantile with respect to the mean value is always equal to one. Conversely, in non-additive models, the derivative of the quantile with respect to the mean value may give very high or low values, and thus, the derivative of the quantile does not appear to be a useful measure of sensitivity.

3.2. Global ROSA

Global ROSA can be computed using Fort contrast indices [25], which implicitly depend on parameters associated with the probability distribution. In engineering applications, it is primarily the probability P_f [33,34], the design quantiles F_d and R_d [35], or the median [36].

Sensitivity indices subordinated to contrasts associated with probability (in short, contrast P_f indices) are based on quadratic-type contrast functions [25]. However, contrast P_f indices can be defined more easily based on the probability of failure and the conditional probabilities of failure [19]. A formula that does not require the evaluation of contrast functions can be used for practical computation. For practical use, the first-order probability contrast index C_i can be rewritten in the form of [19]

$$C_i = \frac{P_f(1-P_f) - E\big((P_f|X_i)(1-P_f|X_i)\big)}{P_f(1-P_f)}. \tag{10}$$

The sensitivity index C_i measures, on average, the effect of fixing X_i on P_f, where $P_f = P(Z < 0)$ is the failure probability and $P_f|X_i = P((Z|X_i) < 0)$ is the conditional failure probability. The mean value $E[\cdot]$ is taken over X_i. In Equation (10), the term $P_f(1 - P_f)$ is derived for probability estimator $\theta^* = \text{Argmin } \psi(\theta) = P_f$ from the minimum of contrast $\min_\theta \psi(\theta)$:

$$\min_\theta \psi(\theta) = \min_\theta E(\psi(Z,\theta)) = \min_\theta E(1_{Z<0} - \theta)^2 = V(1_{Z<0}) = P_f(1-P_f), \tag{11}$$

where $V(1_{Z<0})$ is the variance in the case where there are only two outcomes of 0 and 1, with one having a probability of P_f. The largest variance occurs if $P_f = 0.5$, with each outcome given an equal chance. The contrast function $\psi(\theta) = E(1_{Z<0} - \theta)^2$ vs. θ is convex and symmetrical in the interval across the vertical axis θ^*. The plot of $P_f(1 - P_f)$ vs. P_f is a concave function with left-right symmetry. The contrast for conditional probability is expressed in a similar manner as $(P_f|X_i)(1 - P_f|X_i)$.

The second-order sensitivity index C_{ij} is computed similarly:

$$C_{ij} = \frac{P_f(1-P_f) - E\big((P_f|X_i,X_j)(1-P_f|X_i,X_j)\big)}{P_f(1-P_f)} - C_i - C_j, \tag{12}$$

where $P_f|X_i,X_j = P((Z|X_i,X_j) < 0)$ is the conditional failure probability for fixed X_i and X_j. $E[\cdot]$ is taken over X_i and X_j. The index C_{ij} measures the joint effect of X_i and X_j on P_f minus the first-order effects of the same factors. The third-order sensitivity index C_{ijk} is computed similarly:

$$C_{ijk} = \frac{P_f(1-P_f) - E((P_f|X_i,X_j,X_k)(1-P_f|X_i,X_j,X_k))}{P_f(1-P_f)} - C_i - C_j - C_k - C_{ij} - C_{ik} - C_{jk}, \quad (13)$$

where $P_f|X_i,X_j,X_k = P((Z|X_i,X_j,X_k) < 0)$ is the conditional failure probability for fixed triples X_i, X_j, and X_k. The other indices are computed analogously. All input random variables are considered statistically independent. The sum of all indices must be equal to one:

$$\sum_i C_i + \sum_i \sum_{j>i} C_{ij} + \sum_i \sum_{j>i} \sum_{k>j} C_{ijk} + \ldots + C_{123\ldots M} = 1. \quad (14)$$

Contrast P_f indices can also be derived by rewriting Sobol indices in the context of ROSA [21]. Estimating all sensitivity indices in Equation (14) can be highly computationally challenging and difficult to evaluate. For a large number of input variables, it may be better to analyse the effects of input variables using the total effect index (in short, the total index) C_{Ti}.

$$C_{Ti} = 1 - \frac{P_f(1-P_f) - E((P_f|X_{\sim i})(1-P_f|X_{\sim i}))}{P_f(1-P_f)} \quad (15)$$

$P_f|X_{\sim i} = P((Z|X_{\sim i}) < 0)$ is the conditional failure probability evaluated for a input random variable X_i and fixed variables $(X_1, X_2, \ldots, X_{i-1}, X_{i+1}, \ldots, X_M)$. The total index C_{Ti} measures the contribution of input variable X_i, including all of the effects caused by its interactions, of any order, with any other input variable. The total index C_{Ti} can also be computed if all sensitivity indices in Equation (14) are computed. For example, C_{T1} for $M = 3$ can be written as $C_{T1} = C_1 + C_{12} + C_{13} + C_{123}$.

The structural reliability can also be assessed using design quantiles (see, e.g., [37]). Sensitivity indices subordinated to contrasts associated with the α-quantile [25] (in short, contrast Q indices) are based on contrast functions of the linear type. The contrast function ψ associated with the α-quantile can be written with parameter θ as [25]

$$\psi(\theta) = E(\psi(Y, \theta)) = E((Y - \theta)(\alpha - 1_{Y<\theta})), \quad (16)$$

where Y is scalar (here, F or R). Equation (16) reaches the minimum if the argument θ is the α-quantile estimator θ^* (here, F_d or R_d). The plot of contrast function $\psi(\theta)$ vs. θ is convex and, with some exceptions, asymmetric.

Equation (16) is not quadratic like the contrast associated with P_f, because the distance $(Y - \theta)$ is considered linear. The first-order contrast Q index is defined, on the basis of Equation (16), as

$$Q_i = \frac{\min_\theta \psi(\theta) - E(\min_\theta E(\psi(Y, \theta)|X_i))}{\min_\theta \psi(\theta)}, \quad (17)$$

where the first term in the numerator (and denominator) is the contrast computed for the estimator of α-quantile $\theta^* = \text{Argmin } \psi(\theta)$. The second term in the numerator is computed analogously, but with the provision that X_i is fixed. $E[\cdot]$ is taken over X_i.

The second-order α-quantile contrast index Q_{ij} is computed analogously, but with the fixing of pairs X_i and X_j:

$$Q_{ij} = \frac{\min_\theta \psi(\theta) - E\left(\min_\theta E(\psi(Y,\theta)|X_i,X_j)\right)}{\min_\theta \psi(\theta)} - Q_i - Q_j. \tag{18}$$

The third-order sensitivity index Q_{ijk} is computed similarly:

$$Q_{ijk} = \frac{\min_\theta \psi(\theta) - E\left(\min_\theta E(\psi(Y,\theta)|X_i,X_j,X_k)\right)}{\min_\theta \psi(\theta)} - Q_i - Q_j - Q_k - Q_{ij} - Q_{ik} - Q_{jk}. \tag{19}$$

All input random variables are considered statistically independent. The sum of all indices must be equal to one:

$$\sum_i Q_i + \sum_i \sum_{j>i} Q_{ij} + \sum_i \sum_{j>i} \sum_{k>j} Q_{ijk} + \ldots + Q_{123\ldots M} = 1. \tag{20}$$

The total index Q_{Ti} can be written analogously to Equation (15) as:

$$Q_{Ti} = 1 - \frac{\min_\theta \psi(\theta) - E\left(\min_\theta E(\psi(Y,\theta)|X_{\sim i})\right)}{\min_\theta \psi(\theta)}, \tag{21}$$

where the second term in the numerator contains the conditional contrast evaluated for input random variable X_i and fixed variables $(X_1, X_2, \ldots, X_{i-1}, X_{i+1}, \ldots, X_M)$. Equation (21) is analogous to Equation (15), but for the quantile.

3.3. Specific Properties of Contrasts Associated with Quantiles

Can contrast indices Q be estimated more easily, without having to evaluate the contrast function from Equation (16)? Let us study Equation (16) using a simple case study, where Y has a Gaussian pdf:

$$\phi(y, \mu, \sigma) = \frac{1}{\sigma\sqrt{2\pi}} e^{-\frac{(y-\mu)^2}{2\sigma}}. \tag{22}$$

Figure 1 depicts an example of the evaluation of the contrast function for the 0.4-quantile of the normalized Gaussian pdf—$Y \sim N(0, 1)$—where the 0.4-quantile is $\theta^* \approx -0.253$. The estimation of contrast function $\psi(\theta^*)$ is based on the dichotomy of the pdf into two parts, separated by the α-quantile.

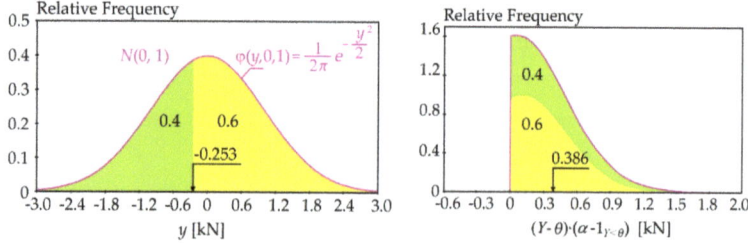

Figure 1. Example of the evaluation of Equation (16) for the 0.4-quantile of the Gaussian pdf.

The value of the contrast function in Equation (16) is $\psi(-0.253) = E((Y-(-0.253))(0.4-1_{Y<-0.253}))$ = 0.386, where the weight 0.6 favors the minority population over the 0.4-quantile and the weight 0.4 puts the majority population after the 0.4-quantile at a disadvantage. In this specific example, it can be observed that the function $\psi(\theta^*)$ vs. θ^* has an $N(0, 1)$ course and therefore, $\psi(-0.253) = \phi(-0.253,$

0, 1) = 0.386. In the case of the general Gaussian pdf $Y \sim N(\mu, \sigma^2)$, function $\psi(\theta^*)$ can be written in a specific form:

$$\psi(\theta^*) = \sigma^2 \cdot \phi(\theta^*, \mu, \sigma) = \frac{\sigma}{\sqrt{2\pi}} e^{-\frac{(\theta^*-\mu)^2}{2\sigma}}. \qquad (23)$$

Equation (23) can only be used for estimates of contrast Q indices if Y has a Gaussian pdf; otherwise, Equation (23) has the form of an approximate relation. Another form of the sensitivity indices in Equation (20) derived from Equation (23) would be very practical; however, the conditional Gaussian pdf of Y, Gaussian pdf of $Y|X_i$, etc., makes the use of Equation (23) problematic in black box tasks, where skewness and kurtosis can have non-Gaussian values.

Due to the left-right symmetry of the Gaussian pdf in Figure 1, the same contrast function value can be obtained for the 0.6-quantile (see Figure 2).

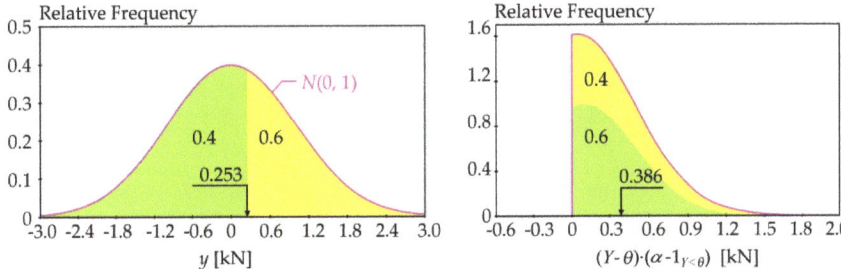

Figure 2. Example of the evaluation of Equation (16) for the 0.6-quantile of the Gaussian pdf.

The following approach is more powerful. The value of contrast function $\psi(\theta^*)$ can be expressed using the centers of gravity of the green and yellow areas (see Figure 3).

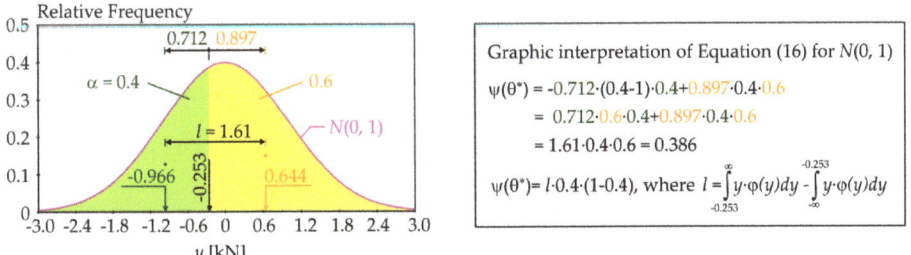

Figure 3. Graphical representation of the contrast in Equation (16) for the 0.4-quantile of $N(0, 1)$.

In the specific case of $Y \sim N(0, 1)$, the dependence between l and θ^* is a hyperbola $l^2 - (\theta^*)^2 \approx 1.6^2$ with asymptotes $l = \pm \theta^*$ (see Figure 4). In a more general case of $Y \sim N(\mu, \sigma^2)$, the dependence between l and θ^* is a hyperbola $l^2 - (\theta^* - \mu)^2 \approx \sigma^2 \cdot 1.6^2$ with asymptotes $l = \pm(\theta^* - \mu)$. The intersection of two asymptotes is at the center of symmetry of the hyperbola, which is the mean value $\mu = E(Y)$. The skewness and kurtosis (departure from the Gaussian pdf) lead to asymmetric and symmetric deviations from this hyperbola, but asymptotes of such a curve remain $l = \pm(\theta^* - \mu)$. Figure 4 illustrates an example with the so-called Hermite pdf with a mean value of 0, standard deviation of 1, skewness of 0.9, and kurtosis of 2.9. Although deviations from the hyperbola are significant around the mean value, the dependence l vs. θ^* approaches the asymptotes $l = \pm(\theta^* - \mu)$ in the regions of design quantiles (see Figure 4b). The observation can be generalized to any pdf or histogram of Y.

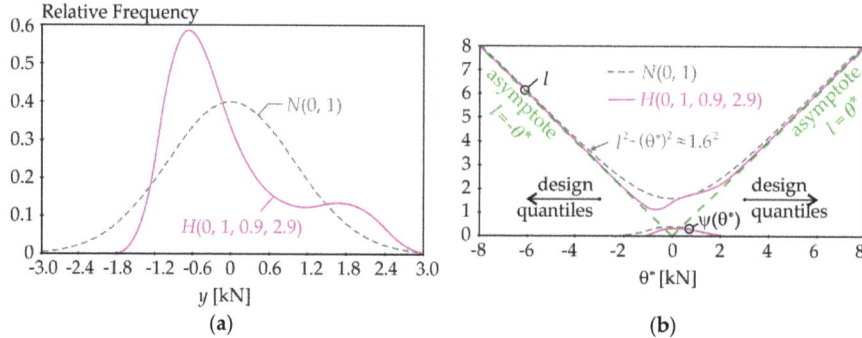

Figure 4. Plot of parameter l and function $\psi(\theta^*)$ vs. the α-quantile θ^*: (**a**) The Gaussian and non-Gaussian pdf; (**b**) The same asymptotes of hyperbolic and non-hyperbolic function.

For any pdf of $f(y)$ of Y, an alternative form of the contrast function to Equation (16) can be derived in a new form:

$$\psi(\theta^*) = l \cdot \alpha \cdot (1-\alpha), \qquad (24)$$

where l is the distance of the centers of gravity of the two areas before and after the α-quantile (see the example in Figure 3). Sensitivity indices reflect change around the α-quantile estimator θ^* using l while α is constant. Equation (24) is general for any pdf and offers new possibilities for evaluating contrast via l.

$$l = \int_{\theta^*}^{\infty} y \cdot f(y) dy - \int_{-\infty}^{\theta^*} y \cdot f(y) dy \qquad (25)$$

In general, SSA is relevant to the mean value of Y, while the SA of the quantile (QSA) is relevant to the α-quantile of Y. However, in many cases, there is a strong similarity between the conclusions of QSA and SSA if all or at least the total sensitivity indices are examined. It can be shown in a simple example of $Y = X_1 + X_2$ that $\text{corr}(Q(Y|X_i), E(Y|X_i)) \approx 1$, where $Q(Y|X_i)$ is the conditional α-quantile and $E(Y|X_i)$ is the conditional mean value. Changing X_i causes synchronous changes in the α-quantile $Q(Y|X_i)$ and mean value $E(Y|X_i)$.

Although contrasts are of a different type, similarities between the results of QSA and SSA have been observed in the task of SA of the resistance of a building load-bearing element [35]. Other numerical illustrations of contrast Q indices are presented in [38,39].

4. Case Study of the Ultimate Limit State

Probability-based reliability analysis considers a stochastic model of an ultimate limit state of a bar under tension (see Figure 5a). The structural member is safe when the sum of loads is less than the relevant resistance.

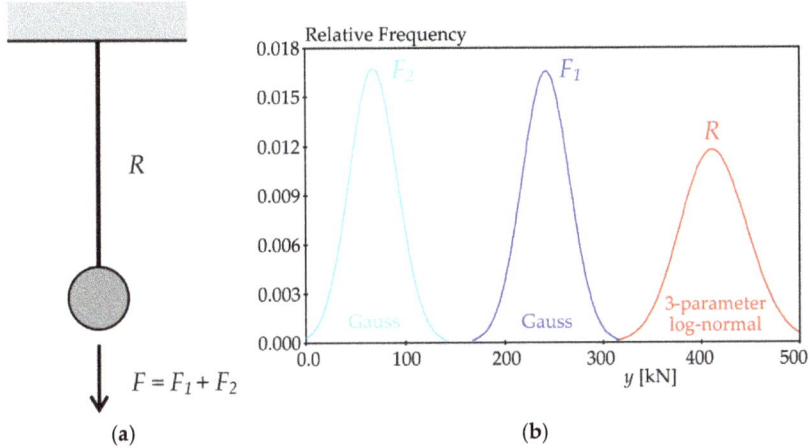

Figure 5. Static model: (**a**) Bar under tension and (**b**) probability density functions of R, F_1, and F_2 for $\mu_P = 0$.

The bar is loaded by two statistically independent forces F_1 and F_2, both of which have a Gaussian pdf (see Figure 5b and Table 1). Parameter μ_P changes the mean value of the axial load of the bar, while the standard deviation of F is constant. The resulting force $F = F_1 + F_2$ has a Gaussian pdf with a mean value of $\mu_F = \mu_{F_1} + \mu_{F_2} = 309.56$ kN $+ \mu_P$ and standard deviation $\sigma_F = (\sigma_{F_1}^2 + \sigma_{F_2}^2)^{0.5} = 33.94$ kN.

Table 1. The input random variables on the load action side.

Characteristic	Index	Symbol	Mean Value μ (kN)	Standard Deviation σ
Load Action	1	F_1	$241.4 + 0.5 \mu_P$	24.14 kN
Load Action	2	F_2	$68.16 + 0.5 \cdot \mu_P$	23.86 kN

The stochastic computational model for the evaluation of the static resistance R is a function of three statistically independent random variables: The yield strength f_y; plate thickness t; and plate width b [40]:

$$R = f_y \cdot t \cdot b, \tag{26}$$

where $t \cdot b$ is the cross-sectional area. The resistance R is a function of material and geometric characteristics f_y, t, and b, whose random variabilities are considered according to the results of experimental research [41,42]. Random variables f_y, t, and b are statistically independent and are introduced with Gaussian pdfs (see Table 2).

Table 2. The input random variables on the resistance side.

Characteristic	Index	Symbol	Mean Value μ	Standard Deviation σ
Yield strength	3	f_y	412.68 MPa	27.941 MPa
Thickness	4	t	10 mm	0.46 mm
Width	5	b	100 mm	1 mm

The arithmetic mean μ_R, standard deviation σ_R, and standard skewness a_R of resistance R can be expressed using equations (see [40]), based on arithmetic means μ_{f_y}, μ_t, and μ_b and standard deviations σ_{f_y}, σ_t, and σ_b presented in Table 2.

The mean value of R can be written as

$$\mu_R = \mu_{fy} \cdot \mu_t \cdot \mu_b. \tag{27}$$

The standard deviation of R can be written as

$$\sigma_R = \sqrt{\mu_{fy}^2 \cdot \left(\mu_t^2 \cdot \sigma_b^2 + \sigma_t^2 \cdot \left(\mu_b^2 + \sigma_b^2\right)\right) + \mu_t^2 \cdot \sigma_{fy}^2 \cdot \left(\mu_b^2 + \sigma_b^2\right) + \sigma_{fy}^2 \cdot \sigma_t^2 \cdot \left(\mu_b^2 + \sigma_b^2\right)}. \tag{28}$$

The standard skewness of R can be written as

$$a_R = 6 \cdot \frac{\mu_R}{\sigma_R^3} \cdot \left(\mu_{fy}^2 \cdot \sigma_t^2 \cdot \sigma_b^2 + \sigma_{fy}^2 \cdot \mu_t^2 \cdot \sigma_b^2 + \sigma_{fy}^2 \cdot \sigma_t^2 \cdot \mu_b^2 + 4 \cdot \sigma_{fy}^2 \cdot \sigma_t^2 \cdot \sigma_b^2\right). \tag{29}$$

For example, for input random variables from Table 2, we can write μ_R = 412.68 kN, σ_R = 34.057 kN, and a_R = 0.111.

Goodness-of-fit and comparison tests [40] have shown that probabilities down to 1×10^{-19} are estimated relatively accurately using the approximation of probability density R by a three-parameter lognormal pdf with parameters μ_R, σ_R, and a_R. This approximation is also suitable when one variable in Equation (26) is fixed. Fixing two variables leads to R with a Gaussian pdf with parameters μ_R and σ_R.

In SA, the failure probability $P_f = P(Z < 0) = P(R < F)$ can be computed using distributions F (Gaussian) and R (three-parameter lognormal or Gaussian) as the integral:

$$P_f = \int_{-\infty}^{\infty} \Phi_R(y) \varphi_F(y) dy, \tag{30}$$

where $\varphi_F(y)$ is the pdf of load action, $\Phi_R(y)$ is the distribution function of resistance, and y denotes a general point of the force (the observed variable) with the unit of Newton. The integration in Equation (30) is performed in the case study numerically using Simpson's rule, with more than ten thousand integration steps over the interval $[\mu_Z - 10\sigma_Z, \mu_Z + 10\sigma_Z]$.

5. Computation of Sensitivity Indices

The aim of SA in the presented case study is to assess the influence of input quantities F_1, F_2, f_y, t, and b on the failure probability P_f or design quantiles F_d and R_d.

The numerical parameter of the case study is μ_P, which changes with the step $\Delta\mu_P$ = 10 kN. Although μ_P is the computation parameter, sensitivity indices are preferably plotted, depending on P_f, because P_f has a clear relevance to reliability. The transformation of μ_P to P_f is expressed using Equation (30) (see Figure 6a).

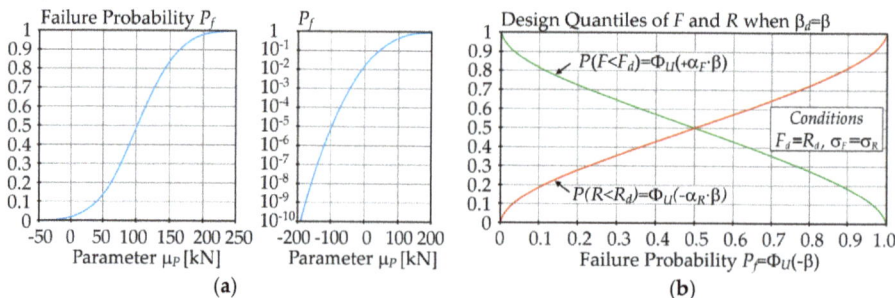

Figure 6. Probability of design α-quantiles vs. failure probability P_f: (**a**) μ_P vs. P_f; (**b**) P_f vs. α-quantiles.

In practice, the procedure is as follows: The value of μ_P is selected, the sensitivity indices and P_f are computed, and the indices vs. P_f are then plotted. If the design quantiles are the key quantities of interest, then the dependency between P_f and the probabilities of the design quantiles can be considered, according to Figure 6b.

In Figure 6b, the probability of design quantiles F_d and R_d is considered under the condition $F_d = R_d$ in Equation (7) and $\sigma_F = \sigma_R$. Perfect biaxial symmetry of the curves in Figure 6b is only observed for perfect $\sigma_F = \sigma_R$; otherwise, the curve of the variable with the smaller standard deviation has a steeper slope. In the case study, for $\beta = 3.8$ ($P_f = 7.2 \times 10^{-5}$), $P(F < F_d) = 0.9963$, and $P(R < R_d) = 0.0036$, where $F_d = R_d = 321.01$ kN ($\mu_F = 229.97$ kN, $\mu_R = 412.68$ kN, and $\sigma_F = 33.94$ kN $\approx \sigma_R = 34.057$ kN).

5.1. Local ROSA—Sensitivity Indices Based on Derivatives

Figure 7a shows the partial derivatives of P_f with respect to the mean values μ_{xi}. Although the partial derivative of P_f with respect to μ_t has the greatest value, t is not the most influential input variable in terms of the absolute change of P_f due to the uncertainty (variance) of the input variable t. A better measure of sensitivity is obtained by multiplying the partial derivatives by the standard deviations of the respective input variables (see Figure 7b). Ranking according to D_i gives the sensitivity ranking of input variables as f_y, F_1, F_2, t, and b.

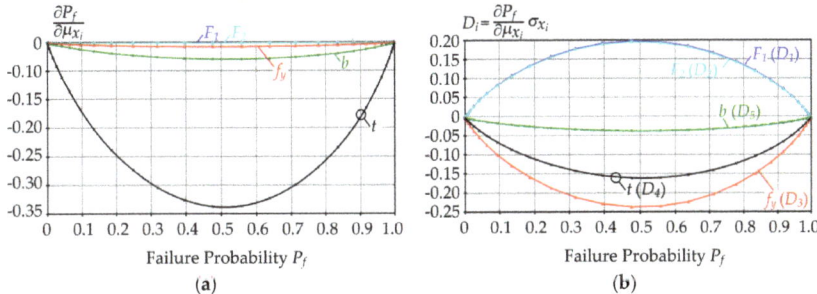

Figure 7. Derivative-based local SA of failure probability P_f: (a) Derivatives; (b) Sensitivity index D_i.

The plots in Figure 7 are approximately symmetrical about the vertical axis, but not perfectly symmetrical. The small amount of asymmetry is due to the small skewness of resistance R in Equation (1) (see Equation (29)). Perfect symmetry of the curves would occur if F and R had zero skewness (symmetric pdfs of both F and R).

A small amount of asymmetry is graphically visible upon mirroring the solid curves to the dashed curves (see Figure 8). The dashed curves are artificial, showing the left-right asymmetry of the solid curves.

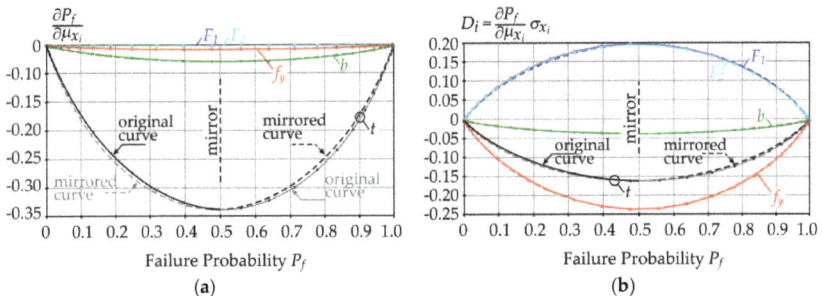

Figure 8. Derivative-based local SA of failure probability P_f: (a) Derivatives; (b) Sensitivity index D_i.

In Figure 8a, the dashed curves are lower than the solid curves on the left side of the graph. On the right side of the graph, the opposite is true. The same is observed in Figure 8b. A small amount of asymmetry occurs due to the small positive skewness of R. If R had a (theoretically) negative skewness, then the dashed curves would be higher than the solid curves on the left sides of each graph, and the opposite would be true on the right sides of the graphs.

5.2. Global ROSA—Contrast P_f Indices

For the case study, contrast P_f indices are depicted in Figures 9–13. All contrast P_f indices were computed numerically using Equation (30) for the interval $P_f \in [9.35 \times 10^{-8}, 1\text{–}1.51 \times 10^{-8}]$.

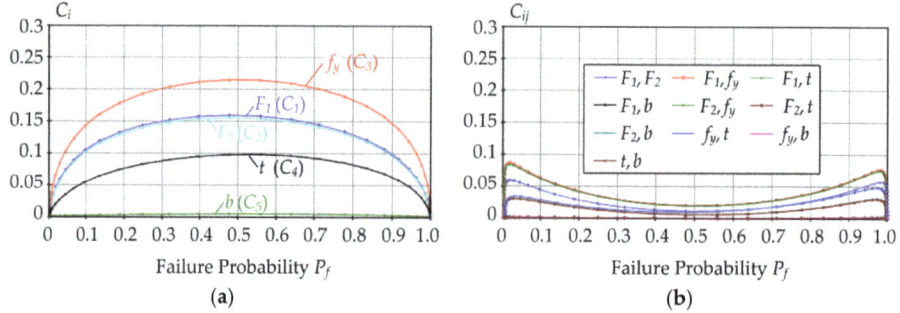

Figure 9. (a) First-order contrast P_f indices and (b) second-order contrast P_f indices.

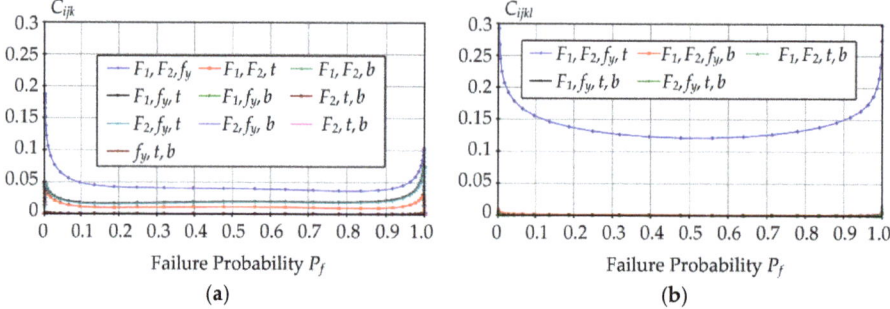

Figure 10. (a) Third-order contrast P_f indices and (b) fourth-order contrast P_f indices.

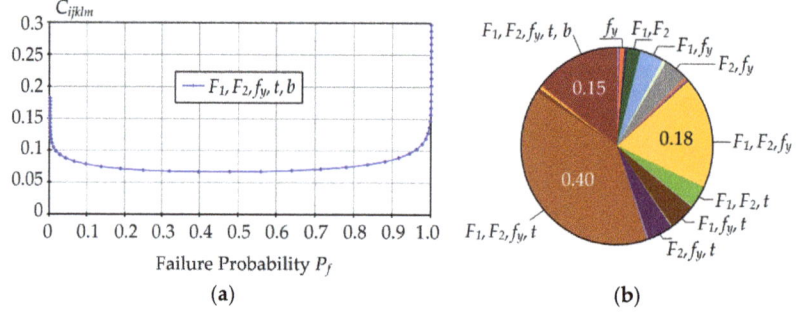

Figure 11. (a) Fifth-order contrast P_f indices and (b) all-order contrast P_f indices for $P_f = 7.2 \times 10^{-5}$.

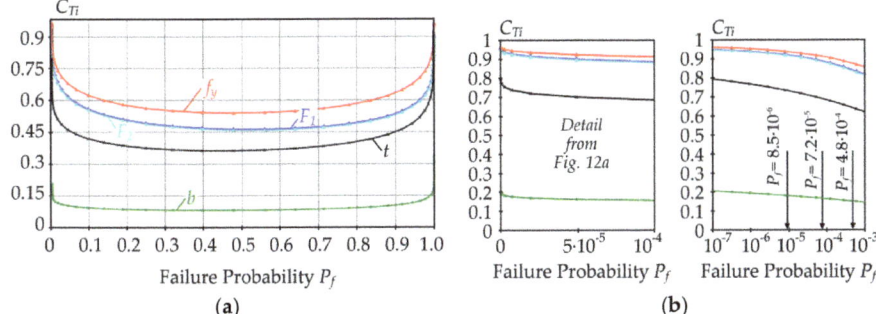

Figure 12. Total contrast P_f indices: (**a**) All P_f and (**b**) low P_f.

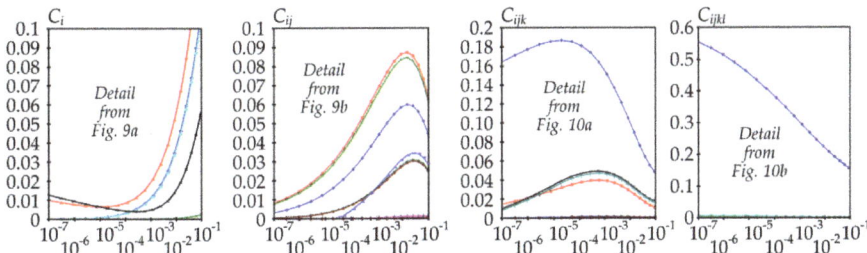

Figure 13. Details of contrast P_f indices for low P_f.

In the interval $P_f \in [0.1, 0.9]$, the plot of C_i is a concave function with approximately left-right symmetry. The sum of indices $C_1 + C_2$ is the same as what would have been obtained had we introduced only one random variable for F with a Gaussian pdf with a mean value of $\mu_F = 309.56$ kN $+\mu_P$ and standard deviation of $\sigma_F = 33.94$ kN: $C_2 + C_1 = C_F$. The sum of indices $C_3 + C_4 + C_5$ is the same as what would have been obtained had we introduced only one random variable for R with a three-parameter lognormal pdf with parameters $\mu_R = 412.68$ kN, $\sigma_R = 34.057$ kN, and $a_R = 0.111$: $C_3 + C_4 + C_5 = C_R$.

The slight asymmetry of the indices is of the same type as was described in the previous chapter for indices D_i. For example, for $P_f = 0.3$, indices C_1, C_2, and C_{12} (load action) have slightly smaller values and indices C_3, C_4, C_5, C_{34}, C_{35}, C_{45}, and C_{345} (resistance) have slightly higher values, compared to the perfect symmetry. For the other indices, there is a mix of both influences.

In the interval $P_f \in [0.1, 0.9]$, the first-, fourth-, and fifth-order indices generally have higher values than the second- and third-order indices.

In civil engineering, the target values of P_f for reliability classes RC1, RC2, and RC3 taken from [4] are 8.5×10^{-6}, 7.2×10^{-5}, and 4.8×10^{-4} (also see [19]). Figure 11b shows the contribution of all 31 indices for target value $P_f = 7.2 \times 10^{-5}$. First-order indices are represented minimally, where $\sum S_i = 0.017$. On the contrary, the representation of higher-order indices is significant, especially those related to f_y, F_1, and F_2 (see Figure 11b).

In Figure 11, f_y occurs in all significant parts of the graph, but the same is true for F_1 or F_2. Determining the order of importance of input variables using 31 indices can be difficult. The use of total indices C_{Ti} is more practical. Input variables are ranked based on C_{Ti} as f_y, F_1, F_2, t, and b (see Figure 12). This is the same ranking as was found using index D_i (Figure 7b).

Figure 12b shows the total sensitivity indices for small P_f, which are relevant for the design of building structures. Figure 13 shows the local extremes of some sensitivity indices in the interval of small P_f. Interestingly, the sensitivity indices of small P_f have plots that are not obvious (cannot be extrapolated) from the plots in the interval $P_f \in [0.1, 0.9]$. Similar local extremes as in Figure 13 were not observed for D_i in Figure 7.

5.3. Global ROSA—Contrast Q Indices

In the case study, contrast Q indices were estimated using the Latin Hypercube Sampling (LHS) method [43,44], according to the procedure in [35]. Indices Q_i were estimated from Equation (17) using double-nested-loop computation. In the outer loop, $E[\cdot]$ was computed using one thousand runs of the LHS method. In the nested loop, conditional contrast values were computed using four million runs of the LHS method. The unconditional contrast value in the denominator was computed using four million runs of the LHS method. Higher-order indices were estimated similarly.

The target value $P_f = 7.2 \times 10^{-5}$ is considered according to [4]. In Equation (7), the design value of resistance R_d is considered as the 0.0036-quantile and the design load value F_d is considered as the 0.9963-quantile (see Figure 6). Sensitivity analysis is performed for R with a three-parameter lognormal pdf when no or one variable in Equation (26) is fixed; otherwise, a Gaussian pdf is used in the stochastic model.

It can be noted that standard design quantiles $F_d = R_d = 321.01$ kN computed using Equation (7) consider F and R with a Gaussian pdf. However, the design resistance value computed using a three-parameter lognormal pdf (stochastic model) is 325.00 kN. The small difference is because the skewness $a_R = 0.111$ was neglected in Equation (7).

The SA results of the 0.9963-quantile of F are depicted in Figure 14a. Input random variables for F are considered according to Table 1, where the value of μ_P for $P_f = 7.2 \times 10^{-5}$ is $\mu_P = -79.592$ kN. Input random variables for R are considered according to Table 2. The results of SA of the 0.0036-quantile of R are depicted in Figure 14b.

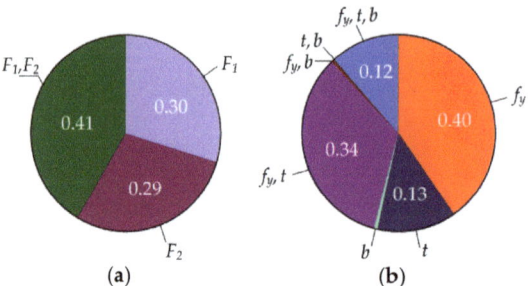

Figure 14. Contrast Q indices: (**a**) 0.9963-quantile of F and (**b**) 0.0036-quantile of R.

By computing total indices $Q_{T1} = 0.71$, $Q_{T2} = 0.70$ and $Q_{T3} = 0.86$, $Q_{T4} = 0.59$, and $Q_{T5} = 0.13$, the order of importance of input variables can be determined as F_1 and F_2 and f_y, t, and b. Variables F and R have the same weight in Equation (2) and therefore, the order of importance of all five input variables can be determined as f_y, F_1, F_2, t, and b, based on the estimates of all Q_{Ti}.

This is a typical example of how the ranking of input parameters based on total indices can give reliable results. The results are satisfactory, although ROSA is not evaluated directly using P_f; it is "only" based on the SA of design quantiles R_d and F_d.

In the presented study, the results for other values of the α-quantile are the same as in Figure 14. In practice, this means that the change in μ_P (generally a change in μ_F) is not reflected in the results of contrast Q indices.

6. New Sensitivity Indices of Small and Large Design Quantiles

6.1. The Asymptotic Form of Contrast Q Indices for Small and Large Quantiles

For small and large (design) quantiles, contrast Q indices can be rewritten using Equation (24) and the asymptotes of hyperbolic functions described in Chapter 3.3. The first-order contrast Q index can be rewritten as

$$Q_i = \frac{l \cdot \alpha \cdot (1-\alpha) - E((l|X_i) \cdot \alpha \cdot (1-\alpha))}{l \cdot \alpha \cdot (1-\alpha)} = \frac{l - E(l|X_i)}{l}. \tag{31}$$

By substituting the hyperbolic function $l^2 - (\theta^* - \mu)^2 = \sigma^2 \cdot l_0^2$ for l, we can obtain an approximate relation for Q_i:

$$Q_i \approx \frac{\sqrt{V(Y) \cdot l_0 + (Q(Y) - E(Y))^2} - E\left(\sqrt{V(Y|X_i) \cdot (l_0|X_i) + (Q(Y|X_i) - E(Y|X_i))^2}\right)}{\sqrt{V(Y) \cdot l_0 + (Q(Y) - E(Y))^2}}, \tag{32}$$

where $Q(Y) = \theta^*$, $E(Y) = \mu$, and $V(Y) = \sigma^2$. The non-dimensional parameter l_0 can be calculated from Equation (25) as $l_0 = l^2/\sigma^2$ at the point $\theta^* = \mu$. However, the precise value of l_0 is not important if $|Q(Y)-E(Y)|$ is large and l_0 does not affect the asymptotes. By substituting the hyperbolic functions with their asymptotes, Equation (31) can be simplified as

$$Q_i = \frac{l - E(l|X_i)}{l} \approx \frac{|Q(Y) - E(Y)| - E(|Q(Y|X_i) - E(Y|X_i)|)}{|Q(Y) - E(Y)|}. \tag{33}$$

Using asymptotes, the index is independent of variance and l_0. The second-order probability Q index can be rewritten analogously:

$$Q_{ij} \approx \frac{|Q(Y) - E(Y)| - E(|Q(Y|X_i, X_j) - E(Y|X_i, X_j)|)}{|Q(Y) - E(Y)|} - Q_i - Q_j. \tag{34}$$

The third-order probability Q index can be rewritten analogously:

$$Q_{ijk} \approx \frac{|Q(Y) - E(Y)| - E(|Q(Y|X_i, X_j, X_k) - E(Y|X_i, X_j, X_k)|)}{|Q(Y) - E(Y)|} - Q_i - Q_j - Q_k - Q_{ij} - Q_{ik} - Q_{jk} \tag{35}$$

Equations (33)–(35) represent an asymptotic form of contrast Q indices that can be used for SAs of low and high quantiles. Higher-order contrast Q indices can be rewritten analogously. The sum of all indices thus estimated is equal to one.

In civil engineering, the design quantile of resistance tends to be less than the 0.01-quantile and the design quantile of resistance tends to be greater than the 0.99-quantile [4]. The asymptotic form of contrast Q indices reveals the degree of sensitivity as the distance between the quantile and the average value.

In the case study presented here, the use of Equation (33)–(35) leads to practically the same results as shown in Figure 14b, but only when low and high quantiles are analysed; otherwise, the formulas cannot be used. The computation of indices eliminates the repeated evaluation of contrast functions in the second loop.

6.2. New Quantile-Oriented Sensitivity Indices for Small and Large Quantiles: QE Indices

In Equation (33) to (35), replacing the absolute values with squares $(Q(Y) - E(Y))^2$, $(Q(Y|X_i) - E(Y|X_i))^2$, etc., leads to new sensitivity indices, which we denote as QE indices. The new first-order quantile-oriented index is defined as

$$K_i = \frac{(Q(Y) - E(Y))^2 - E\left((Q(Y|X_i) - E(Y|X_i))^2\right)}{(Q(Y) - E(Y))^2}. \tag{36}$$

The new second-order QE index is defined as

$$K_{ij} = \frac{(Q(Y) - E(Y))^2 - E\left((Q(Y|X_i, X_j) - E(Y|X_i, X_j))^2\right)}{(Q(Y) - E(Y))^2} - K_i - K_j. \tag{37}$$

The new third-order QE index is defined as

$$K_{ijk} = 1 - \frac{E\left((Q(Y|X_i, X_j, X_k) - E(Y|X_i, X_j, X_k))^2\right)}{(Q(Y) - E(Y))^2} - K_i - K_j - K_k - K_{ij} - K_{ik} - K_{jk}. \tag{38}$$

Sensitivity indices K_i, K_{ij}, and K_{ijk} were formulated via analogies to Equations (33)–(35) and were tested by numerical experiments using linear and non-linear Y functions and LHS simulations. Only low and high quantiles can be studied. The sum of the indices of all orders was equal to one in all cases. The total index K_{Ti} can be formulated analogously to Equation (21).

The new sensitivity indices can be explained using an analogy to Sobol sensitivity indices. The classical Sobol's first-order sensitivity index has the form

$$S_i = \frac{V(Y) - E(V(Y|X_i))}{V(Y)}. \tag{39}$$

Equation (36) can be interpreted using Equation (39). The key idea is to introduce l^2 as a variance. Equation (36) can be rewritten analogously to Equation (39) in the form

$$K_i = \frac{l^2 - E\left((l|X_i)^2\right)}{l^2}, \tag{40}$$

where l is the standard deviation of the "artificial" two-point probability mass function (pmf) having left-right symmetry around quantile $Q(Y)$ (see Figure 15). Half of the population is mirrored behind the quantile $Q(Y)$ and replaced by a dot on each side of $Q(Y)$. In SA, only low and high quantiles of Y can be analysed, indicating high l and low σ_Y in unconditional and conditional pdfs.

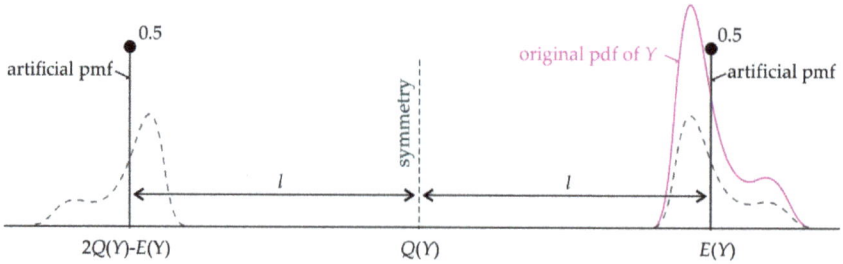

Figure 15. Introduction of l as the standard deviation of the two-point probability mass function.

Let $\mu_P = -79.592$ kN ($P_f = 7.2 \times 10^{-5}$). In the case study, QE indices were obtained on the load action side as $K_1 = 0.50$, $K_2 = 0.49$, and $K_{12} = 0.01$ and on the resistance side as $K_3 = 0.65$, $K_4 = 0.25$, $K_5 = 0.01$, $K_{34} = 0.08$, $K_{35} = 0.00$, $K_{45} = 0.00$, and $K_{345} = 0.01$ (see Figure 16). By computing the total indices $Q_{T1} = 0.51$, $Q_{T2} = 0.50$ and $Q_{T3} = 0.74$, $Q_{T4} = 0.34$, and $Q_{T5} = 0.02$, the order of importance of input variables can be determined as F_1 and F_2 and f_y, t, and b. The sensitivity ranking based on all five Q_{Ti} is f_y, F_1, F_2, t, and b.

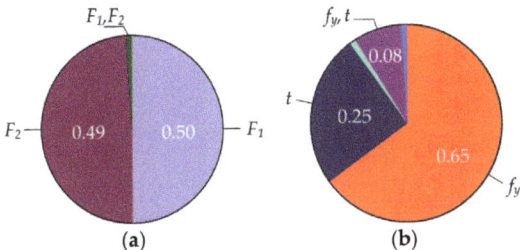

Figure 16. Contrast QE indices: (a) 0.9963-quantile of F ad (b) 0.0036-quantile of R.

7. Discussion

In the case study, input variables were listed in decreasing order of sensitivity as f_y, F_1, F_2, t, and b. Although the values of sensitivity indices of the different ROSA types vary, each ROSA gives the same sensitivity ranking:

- $Q_{T3} = 0.86 > Q_{T1} = 0.71 > Q_{T2} = 0.70 > Q_{T4} = 0.59 > Q_{T5} = 0.13$;
- $C_{T3} = 0.92 < C_{T1} = 0.892 < C_{T2} = 0.887 < C_{T4} = 0.69 < C_{T5} = 0.16$;
- $|D_3| = 1.64 \times 10^{-4} > |D_1| = 1.52 \times 10^{-4} > |D_2| = 1.50 \times 10^{-4} > |D_4| = 1.02 \times 10^{-4} > |D_5| = 0.21 \times 10^{-4}$;
- $K_{T3} = 0.74 > K_{T1} = 0.51 > K_{T2} = 0.50 > K_{T4} = 0.34 > K_{T5} = 0.02$.

These results were obtained for $P_f = 7.2 \times 10^{-5}$ and the corresponding design quantiles (see previous sections). Contrast Q and P_f indices of higher-orders have a significant share in both types of ROSA; therefore, key information is provided by total indices. Regarding the sensitivity ranking, the total indices of design quantiles are a good proxy of the total indices of P_f. However, the result cannot be generalized beyond the Gaussian (or approximately Gaussian) design reliability conditions.

The proposed SA concept is applicable in tasks where the reliability can be assessed by comparing two α-quantiles of two statistically independent variables analogous to R and F (see Equation (2)). The pdfs of R and F should be close to Gaussian (see Equation (8)), with condition $\sigma_F \approx \sigma_R$. Then, ROSA can be effectively evaluated using the SA of design quantiles R_d and F_d, without having to analyse either P_f or the interactions between R and F. This is advantageous because estimates of contrast Q indices are usually numerically easier than estimates of contrast P_f indices, especially for small values of P_f.

For inequalities $\sigma_F \neq \sigma_R$, the total indices of design quantiles should be corrected using weights based on the sensitivity factors α_F and α_R from Equation (6). For example, if $\sigma_F \to 0$, then $\alpha_F \to 0$ and $\alpha_R \to 1$. When the influence of input variables on the load action side approaches zero, the reliability is only influenced by the variables on the resistance side. In the presented case study, the corrections of Q_{Ti} indices are as follows: $\alpha_F \cdot Q_{T1}$, $\alpha_F \cdot Q_{T2}$, $\alpha_R \cdot Q_{T3}$, $\alpha_R \cdot Q_{T4}$, and $\alpha_R \cdot Q_{T5}$. The correction of indices K_{Ti} can be performed similarly. If $\sigma_F = \sigma_R$, corrections are not necessary because $\alpha_F = \alpha_F = 0.7071$. Initial studies have shown the rationality of this approach; however, further analysis is necessary. Corrections of indices C_{Ti} are not performed. If $\sigma_F \to 0$, then C_{Ti} of the variables on the load action side approaches zero naturally. If an extreme value distribution is used, such as a Gumbel or Weibull pdf [45,46], then the proposed concept cannot be used.

Contrast Q indices are based on measuring the fluctuations around the quantile, which is the distance l between the average value of the population before and after the quantile (see Figure 3). For low and high quantiles, contrast Q indices can be rewritten using asymptotes $l = \pm\theta^*$ of hyperbolic functions (see Figure 4). Although contrast Q indices do not have an analogy to the variance decomposition offered by Sobol's indices through the Hoeffding theorem, studies of contrasts in applications [35,36] show some similarities between contrast Q indices and Sobol's indices. The new QE indices and Sobol's indices have formulas based on the squares of the distances from the average value and therefore, their comparison may be interesting in further work.

It can be noted that QE indices K_i, K_{ij}, and K_{ijk} give significant values of first-order indices K_i (compared to Q_i) and relatively small values of higher-order indices, which is also a property observed in Sobol's indices in the case study [35]. QE indices are based on quadratic measures of sensitivity like Sobol, but associated with quantiles. This domain deserves much more work in order to make QE indices a useful and practical tool.

All of the presented techniques are appropriate for SA of the stochastic model type considered in this article. For a general model, an important criterion is also the ease with which the SA can be performed. The most fundamental aspect of sensitivity techniques is local SA based on partial derivatives for computing the rate of change in P_f with respect to a given input parameter. Although the sensitivity ranking determined on the basis of D_i is the same as from C_{Ti}, Q_{Ti}, or K_{Ti}, this conclusion cannot be generalized, and D_i is not suitable for application in every task. The one-at-a-time techniques are only valid for small variabilities in parameter values or linear computation models; otherwise, the partials must be recalculated for each change in the base-case scenario. In contrast, contrast-based SA does not have these limitations because computational models can generally be non-linear and sensitivity indices take into account the variability of inputs throughout their distribution range and provide interaction effects between different input variables.

The results of ROSA can be compared with traditional SA techniques, such as the correlation between input X_i and output Z. Spearman's rank correlation coefficients are computed using one million LHS runs as corr(X_1, Z) = −0.49, corr(X_2, Z) = −0.48, corr(X_3, Z) = 0.56, corr(X_4, Z) = 0.38, and corr(X_5, Z) = 0.08. The second traditional SA technique is SSA. Sobol's first-order indices S_i are computed according to Equation (39), using double-nested-loop computation [35], whereas the inner loop has four million runs and the outer loop ten thousand runs. The model output is Z. The values of S_i are $S_1 = 0.25$, $S_2 = 0.24$, $S_3 = 0.34$, $S_4 = 0.16$, and $S_5 = 0.01$. Sobol's higher-order sensitivity indices are negligible. Both the correlation and SSA give the same sensitivity ranking as ROSA: f_y, F_1, F_2, t, and b. The case study shows that the normalization of the newly proposed indices K_{Ti} leads to the classical S_i, i.e., $K_{Ti}/2.11 \approx S_i$. Although correlations and Sobol's indices are commonly used in SA of the limit states of structures, neither is directly reliability-oriented [19]. Further analysis of the relationship between the new QE indices and traditional Sobol indices is needed because it can provide new insights into the use of SSA in reliability tasks.

The dominance of the yield strength is an important finding for static tensile tests of steel specimens in the laboratory. In structural systems, the slender members under compression may be influenced by other initial imperfections, such as bow and out-of-plumb imperfections [9,10]. In a general steel structure, these imperfections can change the order of importance of the input random variables.

Symmetry is an important part of sensitivity indices and contrast functions (see, e.g., Equation (11) or Equation (24)). Reliability $P_{\sim f} = (1 - P_f)$ or unreliability P_f leads to the same contrast P_f indices, because $P_f(1 - P_f) = P_{\sim f}(1 - P_{\sim f})$. In the case study, the plots of the sensitivity indices were slightly asymmetric due to the small values of skewness of R. The plots of sensitivity indices vs. P_f would be perfectly symmetric in the case of a perfectly symmetric pdf of R and F, with zero skewness.

In the presented study, conclusions were made using SA subordinated to a contrast [25] and SA based on partial derivatives of P_f and new types of QE indices. Other types of SA of P_f like [47] or SA of the quantile [48] have not been studied. Numerous other types of sensitivity measures exist, such as [49–59], and it cannot be expected that the conclusions would be confirmed using any sensitivity index. The advantage of SA subordinated to a contrast is the use of a single platform (contrast) for the analysis of different parameters associated with a probability distribution.

8. Conclusions

This article has examined the relationships between the principles of semi-probabilistic reliability assessment of building structures according to the EN1990 standard and reliability-oriented sensitivity analysis (ROSA). The probability distributions of load and resistance close to Gaussian have been considered.

The article proposes new tools for performing ROSA. It has been shown that ROSA can be credibly evaluated using total indices of quantiles of resistance and load action, without the need to study the failure probability. ROSA of design quantiles gives the same sensitivity ranking as the two types of ROSA oriented to failure probability. Although this conclusion has been established based on one case study, the initial results suggest the possibility of using quantile-oriented ROSA in structural reliability studies. It should be interesting to develop a general approach for determining how to combine the various known indices, and in what order, in order to tackle a reliability task.

New quantile-oriented sensitivity indices denoted as QE indices have been formulated in the article. The first study showed that the distance between the quantile and the average value can be a very interesting measure of sensitivity, with the possibility of further development.

The apparent efforts to develop new types of sensitivity analyses show that the scientific community is still looking for the right combination of computational methods to solve specific problems. An important problem in structural reliability analysis is how to reduce the failure probability. Research focused on design quantities complements the development of failure probability estimation methods.

In engineering applications, the inclusion of quantile-oriented sensitivity analysis among the tools for assessing the effects of input variables on reliability makes it possible to effectively reduce the computational cost of sensitivity analysis of reliability with numerically demanding models. An example is the sensitivity analysis of design quantiles of numerous load cases, where the design quantile of the resistance of a structure only needs to be analysed once. It is worth noting that the specification of which parameters constantly appear close to the top of the list with the order of sensitivity is more important than the actual ranking. In practice, we can neglect the discrepancy between rankings for less important variables because these variables have a minimal or no effect on the reliability of structures.

Funding: The work has been supported and prepared within the project named "Influence of material properties of stainless steels on reliability of bridge structures" of The Czech Science Foundation (GACR, https://gacr.cz/), No. 20-00761S, Czechia.

Conflicts of Interest: The author declares no conflict of interest.

References

1. Ditlevsen, O.; Madsen, H. *Structural Reliability Methods*; John Wiley & Sons Inc.: New York, NY, USA, 1996.
2. Au, S.-K.; Wang, Y. *Engineering Risk Assessment with Subset Simulation*; Wiley: New York, NY, USA, 2014.
3. Antucheviciene, J.; Kala, Z.; Marzouk, M.; Vaidogas, E.R. Solving civil engineering problems by means of fuzzy and stochastic MCDM methods: Current state and future research. *Math. Probl. Eng.* **2015**, *2015*, 362579. [CrossRef]
4. European Committee for Standardization. *EN 1990:2002: Eurocode—Basis of Structural Design*; European Committee for Standardization: Brussels, Belgium, 2002.
5. Joint Committee on Structural Safety (JCSS). Probabilistic Model Code. Available online: https://www.jcss-lc.org/ (accessed on 15 May 2020).
6. Sobol, I.M. Sensitivity estimates for non-linear mathematical models. *Math. Model. Comput. Exp.* **1993**, *1*, 407–414.

7. Sobol, I.M. Global sensitivity indices for nonlinear mathematical models and their Monte Carlo estimates. *Math. Comput. Simul.* **2001**, *55*, 271–280. [CrossRef]
8. Kala, Z. Sensitivity assessment of steel members under compression. *Eng. Struct.* **2009**, *31*, 1344–1348. [CrossRef]
9. Kala, Z. Sensitivity analysis of steel plane frames with initial imperfections. *Eng. Struct.* **2011**, *33*, 2342–2349. [CrossRef]
10. Kala, Z. Global sensitivity analysis in stability problems of steel frame structures. *J. Civ. Eng. Manag.* **2016**, *22*, 417–424. [CrossRef]
11. Kala, Z.; Valeš, J. Global sensitivity analysis of lateral-torsional buckling resistance based on finite element simulations. *Eng. Struct.* **2017**, *134*, 37–47. [CrossRef]
12. Xiao, S.; Lu, Z.; Wang, P. Global sensitivity analysis based on distance correlation for structural systems with multivariate output. *Eng. Struct.* **2018**, *167*, 74–83. [CrossRef]
13. Zamanian, S.; Hur, J.; Shafieezadeh, A. Significant variables for leakage and collapse of buried concrete sewer pipes: A global sensitivity analysis via Bayesian additive regression trees and Sobol' indices. *Struct. Infrastruct. Eng.* **2020**, 1–13. [CrossRef]
14. Carneiro, G.D.; Antonio, C.C. Sobol' indices as dimension reduction technique in evolutionary-based reliability assessment. *Eng. Comput. Swans.* **2020**, *37*, 368–398. [CrossRef]
15. El Kahi, E.; Deck, O.; Khouri, M.; Mehdizadeh, R.; Rahme, P. Simplified probabilistic evaluation of the variability of soil-structure interaction parameters on the elastic transmission of ground movements. *Eng. Struct.* **2020**, *213*, 110554. [CrossRef]
16. Jafari, M.; Akbari, K. Global sensitivity analysis approaches applied to parameter selection for numerical model-updating of structures. *Eng. Comput.* **2019**, *36*, 1282–1304. [CrossRef]
17. Štefaňák, J.; Kala, Z.; Miča, L.; Norkus, A. Global sensitivity analysis for transformation of Hoek-Brown failure criterion for rock mass. *J. Civ. Eng. Manag.* **2018**, *24*, 390–398. [CrossRef]
18. Xu, Z.X.; Zhou, X.P.; Qian, Q.H. The uncertainty importance measure of slope stability based on the moment-independent method. *Stoch. Environ. Res. Risk Assess.* **2020**, *34*, 51–65. [CrossRef]
19. Kala, Z. Sensitivity Analysis in Probabilistic Structural Design: A Comparison of Selected Techniques. *Sustainability* **2020**, *12*, 4788. [CrossRef]
20. Wei, P.; Lu, Z.; Hao, W.; Feng, J.; Wang, B. Efficient sampling methods for global reliability sensitivity analysis. *Comput. Phys. Commun.* **2012**, *183*, 1728–1743. [CrossRef]
21. Li, L.; Lu, Z.; Feng, J.; Wang, B. Moment-independent importance measure of basic variable and its state dependent parameter solution. *Struct. Saf.* **2012**, *38*, 40–47. [CrossRef]
22. Cui, L.; Lu, Z.; Fhao, X. Moment-independent importance measure of basic random variable and its probability density evolution solution. *Sci. China Technol. Sci.* **2010**, *53*, 1138–1145. [CrossRef]
23. Xiao, S.; Lu, Z. Structural reliability sensitivity analysis based on classification of model output. *Aerosp. Sci. Technol.* **2017**, *71*, 52–61. [CrossRef]
24. Ling, C.; Lu, Z.; Cheng, K.; Sun, B. An efficient method for estimating global reliability sensitivity indices. *Probabilistic Eng. Mech.* **2019**, *56*, 35–49. [CrossRef]
25. Fort, J.C.; Klein, T.; Rachdi, N. New sensitivity analysis subordinated to a contrast. *Commun. Stat. Theory Methods* **2016**, *45*, 4349–4364. [CrossRef]
26. Zavadskas, E.K.; Antucheviciene, J.; Vilutiene, T.; Adeli, H. Sustainable decision-making in civil engineering, construction and building technology. *Sustainability* **2018**, *10*, 14. [CrossRef]
27. Freudenthal, A.M. Safety and the probability of structural failure. *Trans. ASCE* **1956**, *121*, 1337–1375.
28. Melchers, R.E.; Ahammed, M. A fast-approximate method for parameter sensitivity estimation in Monte Carlo structural reliability. *Comput. Struct.* **2004**, *82*, 55–61. [CrossRef]
29. Ahammed, M.; Melchers, R.E. Gradient and parameter sensitivity estimation for systems evaluated using Monte Carlo analysis. *Reliab. Eng. Syst. Safe.* **2006**, *91*, 594–601. [CrossRef]
30. Millwater, H. Universal properties of kernel functions for probabilistic sensitivity analysis. *Probabilistic Eng. Mech.* **2009**, *24*, 89–99. [CrossRef]
31. Wang, P.; Lu, Z.; Tang, Z. A derivative based sensitivity measure of failure probability in the presence of epistemic and aleatory uncertainties. *Comput. Math. Appl.* **2013**, *65*, 89–101. [CrossRef]
32. Zhang, X.; Liu, J.; Yan, Y.; Pandey, M. An effective approach for reliability-based sensitivity analysis with the principle of Maximum entropy and fractional moments. *Entropy* **2019**, *21*, 649. [CrossRef]

33. Kala, Z. Global sensitivity analysis of reliability of structural bridge system. *Eng. Struct.* **2019**, *194*, 36–45. [CrossRef]
34. Kala, Z. Estimating probability of fatigue failure of steel structures. *Acta Comment. Univ. Tartu. Math.* **2019**, *23*, 245–254. [CrossRef]
35. Kala, Z. Quantile-oriented global sensitivity analysis of design resistance. *J. Civ. Eng. Manag.* **2019**, *25*, 297–305. [CrossRef]
36. Kala, Z. Benchmark of goal oriented sensitivity analysis methods using Ishigami function. *Int. J. Math. Comput. Methods* **2018**, *3*, 43–50.
37. Jönsson, J.; Müller, M.S.; Gamst, C.; Valeš, J.; Kala, Z. Investigation of European flexural and lateral torsional buckling interaction. *J. Constr. Steel Res.* **2019**, *156*, 105–121. [CrossRef]
38. Browne, T.; Fort, J.-C.; Iooss, B.; Le Gratiet, L. Estimate of quantile-oriented sensitivity indices. *HAL* **2017**, hal-01450891.
39. Maume-Deschamps, V.; Niang, I. Estimation of quantile oriented sensitivity indices. *Stat. Probab. Lett.* **2018**, *134*, 122–127. [CrossRef]
40. Kala, Z. Limit states of structures and global sensitivity analysis based on Cramér-von Mises distance. *Int. J. Mech.* **2020**, *14*, 107–118.
41. Melcher, J.; Kala, Z.; Holický, M.; Fajkus, M.; Rozlívka, L. Design characteristics of structural steels based on statistical analysis of metallurgical products. *J. Constr. Steel Res.* **2004**, *60*, 795–808. [CrossRef]
42. Kala, Z.; Melcher, J.; Puklický, L. Material and geometrical characteristics of structural steels based on statistical analysis of metallurgical products. *J. Civ. Eng. Manag.* **2009**, *15*, 299–307. [CrossRef]
43. McKey, M.D.; Beckman, R.J.; Conover, W.J. Comparison of the three methods for selecting values of input variables in the analysis of output from a computer code. *Technometrics* **1979**, *21*, 239–245.
44. Iman, R.C.; Conover, W.J. Small sample sensitivity analysis techniques for computer models with an application to risk assessment. *Commun. Stat. Theory Methods* **1980**, *9*, 1749–1842. [CrossRef]
45. Nadarajah, S.; Pogány, T.K. On the characteristic functions for extreme value distributions. *Extremes* **2013**, *16*, 27–38. [CrossRef]
46. Keshtegar, B.; Gholampour, A.; Ozbakkaloglu, T.; Zhu, S.-P.; Trung, N.-T. Reliability analysis of FRP-confined concrete at ultimate using conjugate search direction method. *Polymers* **2020**, *12*, 707. [CrossRef] [PubMed]
47. Shi, Y.; Lu, Z.; Zhao, L. Global sensitivity analysis of the failure probability upper bound to random and fuzzy inputs. *Int. J. Fuzzy Syst.* **2019**, *21*, 454–467. [CrossRef]
48. Kucherenko, S.; Song, S.; Wang, L. Quantile based global sensitivity measures. *Reliab. Eng. Syst. Saf.* **2019**, *185*, 35–48253. [CrossRef]
49. Saltelli, A.; Ratto, M.; Andres, T.; Campolongo, F.; Cariboni, J.; Gatelli, D.; Saisana, M.; Tarantola, S. *Global Sensitivity Analysis: The Primer*; John Wiley & Sons: West Sussex, UK, 2008.
50. Rykov, V.; Kozyrev, D. On the reliability function of a double redundant system with general repair time distribution. *Appl. Stoch. Models Bus. Ind.* **2019**, *35*, 191–197. [CrossRef]
51. Shahnewaz, M.; Islam, M.S.; Tannert, T.; Alam, M.S. Flange-notched wood I-joists reinforced with OSB collars: Experimental investigation and sensitivity analysis. *Structures* **2019**, *19*, 490–498. [CrossRef]
52. Douglas-Smith, D.; Iwanaga, T.; Croke, B.F.W.; Jakeman, A.J. Certain trends in uncertainty and sensitivity analysis: An overview of software tools and techniques. *Environ. Model. Softw.* **2020**, *124*, 104588. [CrossRef]
53. Kaklauskas, A.; Zavadskas, E.K.; Radzeviciene, A.; Ubarte, I.; Podviezko, A.; Podvezko, V.; Kuzminske, A.; Banaitis, A.; Binkyte, A.; Bucinskas, V. Quality of city life multiple criteria analysis. *Cities* **2018**, *72 Pt A*, 82–93. [CrossRef]
54. Lellep, J.; Puman, E. Plastic response of conical shells with stiffeners to blast loading. *Acta Comment. Univ. Tartu. Math.* **2020**, *24*, 5–18.
55. Medina, Y.; Muñoz, E. A Simple time-varying sensitivity analysis (TVSA) for assessment of temporal variability of hydrological processes. *Water* **2020**, *12*, 2463. [CrossRef]
56. Mohebby, F. Function estimation in inverse heat transfer problems based on parameter estimation approach. *Energies* **2020**, *13*, 4410. [CrossRef]
57. Strauss, A.; Moser, T.; Honeger, C.; Spyridis, P.; Frangopol, D.M. Likelihood of impact events in transport networks considering road conditions, traffic and routing elements properties. *J. Civ. Eng. Manag.* **2020**, *26*, 95–112. [CrossRef]

58. Su, L.; Wang, T.; Li, H.; Cao, Y.; Wang, L. Multi-criteria decision making for identification of unbalanced bidding. *J. Civ. Eng. Manag.* **2020**, *26*, 43–52. [CrossRef]
59. Szymczak, C.; Kujawa, M. Sensitivity analysis of free torsional vibration frequencies of thin-walled laminated beams under axial load. *Contin. Mech. Thermodyn.* **2020**, *32*, 1347–1356. [CrossRef]

Publisher's Note: MDPI stays neutral with regard to jurisdictional claims in published maps and institutional affiliations.

© 2020 by the author. Licensee MDPI, Basel, Switzerland. This article is an open access article distributed under the terms and conditions of the Creative Commons Attribution (CC BY) license (http://creativecommons.org/licenses/by/4.0/).

Article

Appropriate Feature Set and Window Parameters Selection for Efficient Motion Intent Characterization towards Intelligently Smart EMG-PR System

Mojisola Grace Asogbon [1,2,†], Oluwarotimi Williams Samuel [1,2,†], Yanbing Jiang [1,2], Lin Wang [1], Yanjuan Geng [1,2], Arun Kumar Sangaiah [3], Shixiong Chen [1,2], Peng Fang [1,2] and Guanglin Li [1,2,4,*]

1. CAS Key Laboratory of Human-Machine Intelligence-Synergy Systems, Shenzhen Institutes of Advanced Technology (SIAT), Chinese Academy of Sciences (CAS), Shenzhen 518055, China; grace@siat.ac.cn (M.G.A.); samuel@siat.ac.cn (O.W.S.); yb.jiang@siat.ac.cn (Y.J.); lin.wang1@siat.ac.cn (L.W.); yj.geng@siat.ac.cn (Y.G.); sx.chen@siat.ac.cn (S.C.); peng.fang@siat.ac.cn (P.F.)
2. Shenzhen College of Advanced Technology, University of Chinese Academy of Sciences, Shenzhen 518055, China
3. School of Computing Science and Engineering, VIT University, Vellore 632014, Tamil Nadu, India; sarunkumar@vit.ac.in
4. SIAT Branch, Shenzhen Institute of Artificial Intelligence and Robotics for Society, CAS, Shenzhen 518055, China
* Correspondence: gl.li@siat.ac.cn
† These authors contributed equally to this work.

Received: 13 September 2020; Accepted: 12 October 2020; Published: 16 October 2020

Abstract: The constantly rising number of limb stroke survivors and amputees has motivated the development of intelligent prosthetic/rehabilitation devices for their arm function restoration. The device often integrates a pattern recognition (PR) algorithm that decodes amputees' limb movement intent from electromyogram (EMG) signals, characterized by neural information and symmetric distribution. However, the control performance of the prostheses mostly rely on the interrelations among multiple dynamic factors of feature set, windowing parameters, and signal conditioning that have rarely been jointly investigated to date. This study systematically investigated the interaction effects of these dynamic factors on the performance of EMG-PR system towards constructing optimal parameters for accurately robust movement intent decoding in the context of prosthetic control. In this regard, the interaction effects of various features across window lengths (50 ms~300 ms), increments (50 ms~125 ms), robustness to external interferences and sensor channels (2 ch~6 ch), were examined using EMG signals obtained from twelve subjects through a symmetrical movement elicitation protocol. Compared to single features, multiple features consistently achieved minimum decoding error below 10% across optimal windowing parameters of 250 ms/100 ms. Also, the multiple features showed high robustness to additive noise with obvious trade-offs between accuracy and computation time. Consequently, our findings may provide proper insight for appropriate parameter selection in the context of robust PR-based control strategy for intelligent rehabilitation device.

Keywords: rehabilitation device; electromyogram; symmetry; window parameters; feature extraction; pattern recognition

1. Introduction

Individuals with limb amputation or congenital limb deficits or stroke often have difficulty in performing simple and complex daily life activities that involve the use of their upper extremity (UE). They often depend on the healthy part of their body to compensate for a lost limb, which can greatly affect body posture and symmetry alignment. They also experience phantom limb sensation (which is usually painful), fatigue, and depression among others, which can cause emotional and psychological damage. In addition, majority of individuals with UE disability normally feel inferior or perhaps rejected in the society because they can hardly cope with certain physical daily life activities [1–3].

Re-integrating this category of persons into the society would require the development of a smart and intelligent rehabilitation robotic system [2–5]. Such intelligent robotic system normally incorporate less computational control algorithms that operate on symmetric principle and attract low memory and processor requirement, thus, aiding the realization of portable rehabilitation device that could be worn by amputees to help restore their arm functions [3–6]. Notably, such symmetrical principle play a significant role when it comes to the dynamics of controlling the prosthetic device during activities of daily living [7]. At the forefront of this technology is the pattern recognition based prostheses that seamlessly decode multiple patterns of targeted limb movements from measured bioelectrical data and provide multiple degrees of freedom arm function in an intuitive fashion [1,3,4]. Typically, the pattern recognition strategy involves extraction of highly informative feature sets from the measured surface electromyogram (sEMG) data, which are applied to a machine learning model for limb movement intent decoding.

Afterwards, the deciphered movement intents are coded into control commands that drives the intelligently smart prostheses in a way similar to the natural human arm [6–10]. The pattern recognition based control strategy consist of sequentially connected phases in which the machine learning algorithm and feature extraction phases are well-thought-out as important with the latter being the most significant. Hence, the feature extraction approach adopted would either potentially improve or degrade the overall performance of device, and it has been proven by several previous studies [5,11,12]. In other words, developing an intelligently smart pattern recognition based prostheses would require the integration of appropriate feature extraction technique. Moreover, extracting features from segmented sEMG data as against the entire length of measured data would expedite the response rate of the prosthetic device in real-life applications, and the sliding window segmentation technique has been widely employed due to its dense decision stream attribute [13]. Integral elements of the sliding window segmentation scheme includes the window length and increment parameters, which would normally influence the characteristics of the extracted feature set (in terms of stability and accuracy) [12,13]. These parameters have direct impact on the extracted features and as well influence the characteristics of the prostheses controller in terms of its delay, since the delay is a function of the computation time associated with the extracted features [14,15]. Therefore, the overall effect of the feature extraction scheme and windowing parameters should not be underestimated if the goal is to realize an intelligently smart prostheses that would be clinically viable. Towards addressing the above highlighted problem, Menon et al. examined the effect of sliding window segmentation on classification accuracy using sEMG data measured from different groups of participants (able-bodied, partial hand and transhumeral participants). They found that the impact of window length on classification performance does not depend on the number of electrodes channels irrespective of the participants group. It was also discovered that the window increment has no direct effect on the classification accuracy regardless of the window length, number of electrode channels considered and the amputation status of participants, [16]. Meanwhile, in the Englehart and Hudgins study, they demonstrated the relationship between the analysis window length and classification error and it was realized that the mean classification error increase with short window length [13]. Smith et al. in their work investigated the relationship between window length, classification accuracy and controller delay and their result showed that the choice of window length is an important factor that could, either improve or degrade the performance of pattern recognition based prostheses control [14]. Other researchers demonstrated that to realize acceptable accuracy with reasonable controller delay, window lengths in the range of 100 ms~125 ms should be considered and that the controller delay in real-time operation should be lower than 200 ms. Also, window lengths between the range of 100 ms~300 ms [12], and 300 ms~400 ms [13] were previously recommended [17–21]. However, no singular study has considered investigating the interrelation effects amongst classification accuracy, computation time, robustness to external noise, and number of electrode channels, across different window parameters and multiple feature sets for EMG-Pattern recognition (EMG-PR) systems. In other words, it is unclear how these multiple dynamic factors would influence movement intent decoding, which represent an essential control input for intelligently smart EMG-PR based prostheses. Additionally, investigations on the tradeoff amongst these factors across combinations of window parameters and feature sets has seldom been considered particularly when using sEMG recordings from amputees for movement intent decoding, thus, constituting a core research gap in the field of intelligently smart prostheses.

In this study, we systematically investigated the interrelations and impact of various windowing parameters on a range of feature sets when applied to decode multiple-patterns of targeted limb movement intents across amputees (who are the final users of the prosthetic device) and healthy subjects. Afterwards, the performance evaluation of the extracted features were carried out with respect to classification error, computation time, robustness to external noise and number of recording channels, in the context of machine learning based EMG-PR movement intent classifier.

Interestingly, the experiment and analyses were conducted using sEMG data acquired from both able-bodied-subjects, transradial, and transhumeral amputees, which would ensure the potential application of the study outcomes in clinical and commercial settings. The main contributions of this study are in three folds:

1. Towards providing a standard guideline that would aid the development of intelligently intuitive and symmetric prosthesis for upper limb amputees, this study systematically investigated the interrelations of multiple dynamic factors (windowing parameters, signal conditioning, and feature sets) on the movement intent decoding performance of EMG-PR system based on Linear Discriminant Analysis (LDA). It is worth noting that this issue has rarely been investigated to date.
2. A framework for optimal feature set and windowing parameter (window length and increment) construction in context of movement intent decoding was established. This enables the identification of features with low computation and high discrimination capability alongside their corresponding windowing parameters for both amputees and healthy subjects.
3. Further, the tradeoff between the decoding accuracy of a range of feature sets and their computational complexity across a combination of window parameters was examined with the aim of triggering positive development in the field of smart prosthetic control system and other pattern recognition-based systems that focus on providing smart healthcare services.

In summary, the outcomes of this study are capable of providing researchers and developers with proper insight on how to best select features and/or windowing parameters to achieve optimal movement intent decoding in EMG pattern recognition systems. Furthermore, it may spur potential advancement in smart prosthetic control system and other areas that employs pattern recognition based concept for the provision of smart healthcare services [22–24].

2. Materials and Methods

The EMG-PR framework, adopted in this study, is shown in Figure 1. The process begins with the acquisition of the EMG signals, followed by the preprocessing of the signals to remove motion artifacts and power line interference. The resulting filtered EMG signal is segmented using a sliding analysis window technique. This step is often recommended to improve the efficiency of the subsequent processes which typical involves feature extraction and classification. Thereafter, each feature extraction method, considered in this study, is extracted from the analysis window, and the classifier is employed to decode the motion intent based on the extracted features.

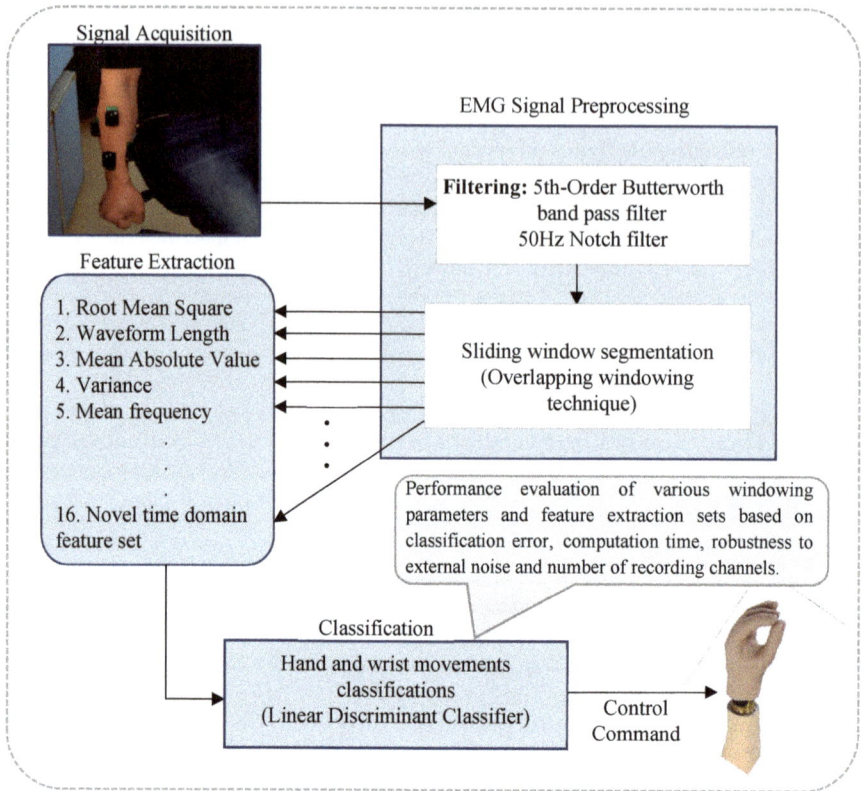

Figure 1. The block diagram of the electromyogram based pattern recognition control model.

2.1. Participant Information

In this study, a total of twelve subjects participated in the sEMG data measurement experiments. Five out of the recruited participants are fully-limbed subjects also referred to as able-bodied subjects while the remaining seven are arm amputees. Their ages range between 20~28 years and they all right-hand dominated. For the seven amputees, five of them had transradial amputation while the other two had transhumeral amputation. Prior to their inclusion in the study, their residual limbs were carefully examined to ensure appropriate conformity with the study objectives. Firstly, their residual limb muscles were carefully checked to ensure that they had no neuromuscular disorder. Secondly, the amputees were asked to perform a number targeted limb movements in a random sequence during which the myoelectric activities of their residual muscles were visualized, and afterwards certifies as being okay. Meanwhile, the amputees all have unilateral amputation with three of them having core experience in the usage of myoelectrically driven prostheses. Prior to the commencement of this experiment, the subjects were made to understand the aim of study, and they all consented and gave permission for the publication of their photographs/data for scientific purposes. Afterwards, the study protocol was approved by the Shenzhen Institutes of Advanced Technology Institutional Review Board, Chinese Academy of Sciences, China.

2.2. EMG Data Measurement

The commonly utilized sEMG data recording device known as Trigno wireless recording system (Developed by Delsys Inc., a company based in Boston, MA, USA) was employed for the acquisition of the required sEMG signals. To determine the number of needed sEMG electrodes, we firstly examined different electrode configurations that involved the placement of 4~8 sensors on the forearm region. Afterwards, we realized that a total of six sensors would be sufficient to acquire high-quality recordings from which multiple-patterns of targeted limb movements could be adequately decoded. Each of the sensor contains 4 silver-bars that integrates three-axis accelerometer to capture arm dynamics and mechanomyogram signals. Meanwhile, the six sensors were configured to measure only sEMG without capturing the eighteen-channel mechanomyogram data, since we are only interested in analyzing the participants' limb movement intent from the sEMG signals. Although, there are other EMG measurement devices, but we decided to use the Trigno wireless recording system because it easy to use, it allows the recorded signals to be visualized in real-time which enables us to assess the signal quality, and it has wireless capability, that does not constrain the subjects during the experiment.

Haven determined the electrode configurations, the placement of the sensors was preceded by palpation of the remaining arm muscles in the amputee subjects to locate their belly and length as indicated in previous studies [24,25]. Afterwards, the sensors were placed over the skin area underlying the identified arm muscles in a symmetrical manner across both arms with the aid of adhesive (Figure 2a). That is, two out of the six sEMG sensors were placed on the extensor and flexor arm muscles while the remaining four sensors were positioned about 2–3 cm around the elbow crease as shown in Figure 2a,b. Notably, the symmetrical concept adopted in placing the electrode across both arms would enable the participant's intact arm to guide the amputated arm in adequately eliciting their movement intent during the experiment, which would lead to the recording of EMG signals with high neural information for movement intent decoding (Figure 2a). Prior to the sensor placement, the sensor sites mapped out on the participants' skin surface were thoroughly wiped using alcohol pads that takes off dry-dermis and skin-oil, which may affect the recorded signal's quality. For participants with unduly dry skin, the skin cells were extricated via tapping of the site with medical tapes to guarantee good electrode-skin contact. After ensuring proper electrode placement and good experimental condition, the subjects were presented with an audio prompt to guide them in performing all the classes of targeted upper-limb movements in a sequential order that includes: wrist movements (wrist flexion/extension/pronation/supination), hand movements (hand close/open) as shown in Figure 2c.

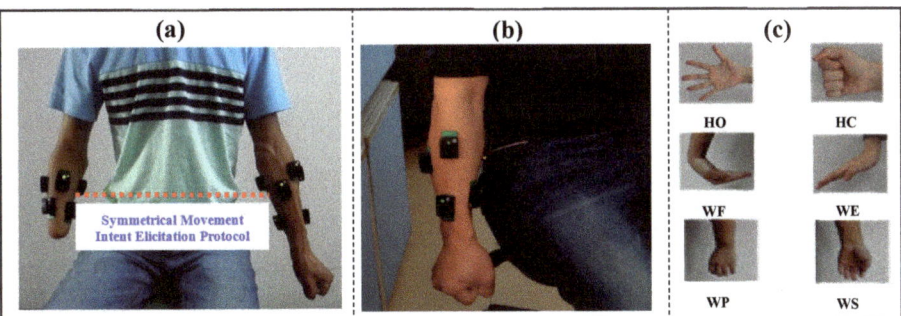

Figure 2. Pre-experimental settings showing the placement of surface EMG electrodes on the residual limb of a representative amputee and healthy subject's limb alongside the active limb movement classes considered in the study. (**a**) Symmetrical placement of the wireless EMG signal sensors on the intact and amputated arm muscles of a representative amputee, (**b**) EMG electrode placement on the forearm of a representative healthy subject, (**c**) The classes of active targeted limb movements considered in the study. Note that: HO, HC, WF, WE, WP, WS, denotes hand open, hand close, wrist flexion, wrist extension, wrist pronation, and wrist supination, respectively.

Following the audio prompt, the subjects were required to perform muscle contractions conforming to the above described classes of targeted arm movements in which each movement was maintained for 5 s. And a rest session of 5 s was introduced between two consecutive classes of active movements to prevent the subjects from having fatigue. Meanwhile, each movement class got repeated five times, leading to 25 s of active EMG signal recordings and 20 s of rest session per experimental trial.

2.3. Preprocessing of the Measure sEMG Data

The sEMG data were obtained during the experimental sessions at a sampling frequency of 1024 Hz, and then stored for further processing. The raw signals were firstly filtered using a 5th-Order Butterworth band pass filter designed with frequency in the range of 20 Hz~500 Hz to enable the extraction of useful components of the signals. Also, power line interferences were eliminated from the filtered signal using 50 Hz notch filter. It should be noted that recorded sEMG signals for all the subjects were preprocessed and analyzed offline using MATLAB version R2017b (Mathworks, Natick, MA, USA) programming tool.

Considering each class of movement, the recorded myoelectric signal is made up of five trials. With a careful observation, the signals were partitioned into contraction/non-contraction segments for each class of targeted movement. To accomplish this task, signals from channels that have clear muscular activities, with respect to the baseline, were visually chosen and combined to obtain an average data stream, which would be needed in the subsequent stage. This process was realized based on the onset and offset times of each muscular activity from a representative channel that is applied to the signals of the other 5 channels.

2.4. Windowing Technique

The EMG data segmentation is one of the important processes used to improve the performance and response time of EMG based pattern recognition control strategy and in this study, overlapping window technique introduced by [13] was adopted to segment the EMG signal into different analysis window. This technique is associated with windowing parameters (length and window increment), where a part of the new analysis window data overlaps with the current window data, and all analysis windows increase with processing time as shown in Figure 3.

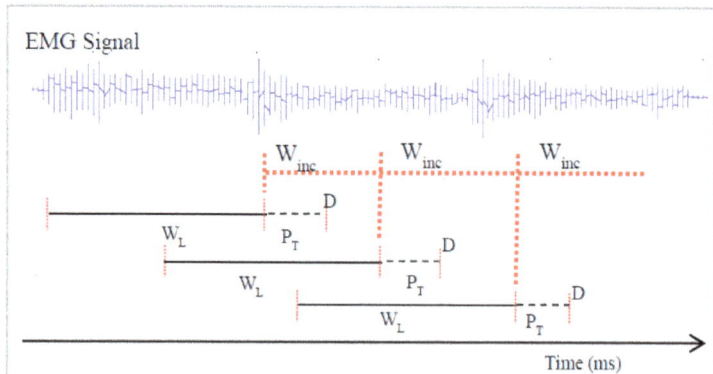

Figure 3. The framework of the overlapping windowing technique for the extraction of feature sets. Note: W_L denotes window length, W_{inc} denotes window increment and P_T represent the processing time.

The processing time is the time require to extract feature sets and the classification algorithm to decode the motion intent. It is worth noting that the window increment is usually shorter than the window length, ideally it is equivalent to the processing time [14]. According to Englehart and

Hudgins [13], a longer window length allows more features to be extracted, resulting in higher classification accuracy, but results in a slower response time of the prosthetic controller, while classification performance reduces with shorter window length but with a faster controller response.

Considering the fact that the utilized windowing parameters would influence the extracted feature characteristics, it is important to determine the optimal windowing parameters that will result in the extraction of accurately robust feature set for multi-class limb movement intent decoding [14,17]. Although, different combinations of windowing parameters have been reported in previous studies with little or no justification in the selection of these parameters. Hence, overlapping analysis window technique with combination of window lengths raging between 100 ms~300 ms and increments from 50 ms–125 ms were examined in this study as shown in Table 1.

Table 1. The combinations of window lengths and increments considered.

S/No.	Window Lengths	Window Increments			
1	100	50	75	-	-
2	150	50	75	100	125
3	200	50	75	100	125
4	250	50	75	100	125
5	300	50	75	100	125

2.5. Feature Extraction Procedure

In this study, a total of sixteen feature extraction methods (including two feature sets proposed previously by our research group) that have been applied for characterizing multi-classes of targeted limb movement intent were selected from four functional EMG feature groups namely: time-domain, frequency-domain, time-series domain, and the statistical features. Furthermore, four feature sets are based on EMG signal amplitude, five are based on nonlinear complexity and frequency information, two are based on time-series modelling, and the remaining five are based on combination of feature sets (Table 2).

Table 2. Time-frequency based features adopted for EMG signal characterization.

Feature Extraction Methods		
S/N	Features Description	Mathematical Expression
1	Root Mean Square (RMS): It is modeled as amplitude modulated Gaussian random process whose relates to constant force and non-fatiguing contraction [11,26].	$\sqrt{\frac{1}{k}\sum_{n=1}^{k} x_n^2}$
2	Waveform Length (WL): This is the aggregate length of the EMG waveform in an analysis window [27,28].	$\sum_{n=1}^{k-1}[f(|x_{n+1} - x_n|)]$
3	Mean Absolute Value (MAV): is an average of absolute value of the EMG signal in an analysis time window [12,27].	$\frac{1}{k}\sum_{n=1}^{k}|x_n|$
4	Variance (VAR): measures the power of the EMG signal [12,29].	$\frac{1}{N-1}\sum_{k=1}^{N} x^2 k$
5	Mean Frequency (MNF): is this feature is calculated as the sum of product of the EMG power spectrum and frequency divided by the total sum of spectrum intensity [27,30].	$\sum_{j=1}^{m} \sum f_j P_j / \sum_{j=1}^{m} \sum P_j$
6	PSR: Power Spectral Ratio(PSR)as ratio between the energy P0 which is nearby the maximum value of the EMG power spectrum and the energy P which is the whole energy of the EMG power spectrum: [31]	$\frac{P_0}{P} : \sum_{j=f0-n}^{f0+n} P_j / \sum_{j=-\infty}^{\infty} P_j$

Table 2. Cont.

	Feature Extraction Methods	
S/N	Features Description	Mathematical Expression
7	TTP: Total Power (TTP): computes the total EMG signal power spectrum: [30,32]	$\sum_{j=1}^{M} P_j \;:\; SMO$
8	PKF: Peak Frequency (PKF): this is a frequency at which the maximal power take place [32]	$PKF = \max(P_j), \; j = 1, \ldots, M$
9	Median Frequency (MDF): is a frequency at which the spectrum is divided into two regions with equal amplitude [27]	$\sum_{j=1}^{MDF} P_j = \sum_{j=MDF}^{M} P_j = \frac{1}{2} \sum_{j=1}^{M} P_j$
10	4th order Autoregressive Coefficient (AR4): The feature model the signal by previous data point of the EMG signal and as well gives information about the state of muscle contraction [24,27,28].	$\sum_{n=1}^{k} a_n x_{k-i} + e_k, \; a_n = 4$
11	6th order Autoregressive Coefficient (AR6): [11,12,29].	$\sum_{n=1}^{k} a_n x_{k-i} + e_k, \; a_n = 6$
12	TD2: Summation of Square root (ASS) and absolute value of Summation of exponent root and Mean (ASM) of the data in a given analysis window [6]	$ASS = \left\lvert \sum_{n=1}^{k} (x_n)^{1/2} \right\rvert, \; ASM = \left\lvert \frac{\sum_{n=1}^{k} (x_n)^{exp}}{k} \right\rvert$
13	Time Domain Power Spectral Descriptor (TD-PSD): this feature sets estimate a set of power spectrum characteristics directly from the time-domain: [33,34]	$f_1 = \log(m_0), \; f_2 = \log(m_0 - m_2)$ $f_3 = \log(m_0 - m_4), \; f_5 = \frac{m_2}{\sqrt{m_0 m_4}}, \; f_6 = \log\left(\frac{\sum_{j=0}^{N-1} \lvert \Delta x \rvert}{\sum_{j=0}^{N-1} \lvert \Delta^2 x \rvert}\right)$
14	Four time Domain and AR6 (TDAR6): Combination of RMS and AR6 [23,24,26,27]	RMS and AR6
15	Five time Domain and AR6 (TD5AR6): combination of MAV, RMS, WL, ZC, SSC and AR6 (ZC: Zero Crossing, SSC: Slope Sign Change) [11,12,26–29,35]	MAV, RMS, WL, ZC, SSC, AR6 $ZC = \sum_{n=2}^{k-1}[f(x_n - x_{n-1}) * (x_n - x_{n+1})]$ $SSC = \sum_{n=1}^{k-1}[\operatorname{sgn}(x_n * x_{n+1}) \cap (x_n - x_{n+1}) \geq Thr.]$
16	Novel Time Domain Feature Set (NTDFS), that combined neuromuscular information for adequate characterization of EMG signal patterns even in the presence of co-founding factors [36]	$SISx_n = \sum_{n=0}^{N-1} x[n]^2, \; normRSdx_1 = \frac{1}{N} \sum_{n=0}^{N-1} dx_1[n]^2, \; normRSDx_2 = \frac{1}{N} \sum_{n=0}^{N-1} dx_2[n]^2, \; normLogDet. = norm(e^{\frac{1}{N} \sum_{n=0}^{N-1} \log(x[n])})$, mMSR, and mASM

It should be noted that features from the above described categories were considered to adequately account for all possible types of meaningful information associated with EMG signal classification [5]. Meanwhile, the accuracy, computational complexity, and robustness of the feature extraction methods were systematically investigated for each combination of window length and increment presented in Table 1 using a number of evaluation metrics described in the Section 2.6.

2.6. Evaluation Metrics

To effectively evaluate the performance of the feature extraction methods, in terms of characterizing multiple-classes of movement intents in the context of EMG-PR system, four different metrics were utilized which are described as follows.

1. The commonly applied metric know as classification error (CE) which represent the number of non-correctly identified samples over the sum of all samples (Equation (1)) was utilized to evaluate the classification accuracy of the feature extracted methods:

$$CE = \frac{\text{Number of incorrectly classified samples}}{\text{Total number of testing samples}} * 100 \qquad (1)$$

2. The F1_score was utilized to further validate the performance of the extracted feature sets. This metric was computed as the weighted average of precision and recall (Equations (2) and (3)) [37]. Basically, the F1_score reveals the performance of the classifier in classifying the data points of a particular feature set compared to others,

$$\text{Precision} = \frac{TP}{TP+FP} \text{ , Recall} = \frac{TP}{TP+FN} \qquad (2)$$

$$F1_{score} = \frac{2 * \text{Recall} * \text{Precision}}{\text{Recall} + \text{Precision}} \qquad (3)$$

where TP is the count of true positives, TN is the count of true negatives, FP represent number of false positives, and FN is the number of false negatives obtained from a confusion matrix. It is worth noting that F1_score reaches its best value at 1 and worst at 0.

3. In principle, the computation time of a feature set would generally influence the response time of the microprocessor-based controller embedded in the prosthesis socket [15]. In this regard, the computation time of each extracted feature set presented in Table 2 was investigated by adopting the formulae in Equation (4) that was proposed by Weir and Farell [15],

$$D = \frac{1}{2}W_L + \frac{1}{2}W_{inc} + P_T \qquad (4)$$

where D is the delay, W_L is the window length, W_{inc} is the window increment and P_T is the signal processing time. It should be noted that the configuration of the system utilized for this study is Microsoft window 7 professional with 64-bit operating system, Intel(R) Core(TM) i7 processor with processing speed of 3.6 GHz and 8 GB random access memory.

4. In the context of EMG-based pattern recognition system, an ideal feature extraction method would normally be influenced/affected by unwanted disturbances that may degrade the decoding of the user's intended limb movement. Therefore, it is important to quantify the robustness of a feature in other to guarantee that the features would be consistently stable when applied in real-life applications. In this regard, the stability index (S_{Index}) metrics adopted in a previous study [38], which is defined by Equation (5) was applied to examine the robustness of the feature extraction methods in the presence of noise,

$$S_{Index} = \frac{\frac{1}{N}\sum_{i=1}^{N} CA_i}{\left[\frac{1}{N-1}\sum_{i=1}^{N}\left(CA_i - \frac{1}{N}\sum_{i=1}^{N} CA_i\right)^2\right]^{\frac{\alpha}{2}}} \qquad (5)$$

where the numerator is the average classification performance, the denominator is the scaled standard deviation, α is the scaled value and is set to 0.1 and N is the sample size. The value of α was chosen after many trials.

2.7. Machine Learning Classification Technique

To decode the subjects' limb movement intent from the constructed feature matrix, two machine learning based classification algorithms including support vector machine (SVM) and linear discriminant analysis (LDA) were utilized. Meanwhile, five-fold cross validation technique was employed for the partitioning of the extracted feature matrix into training and testing sets. The rationale behind considering these classification schemes is that their performances are relatively good, especially when considering multi-class problems [1,10,36]. Therefore, we built an SVM classifiers driven by radial basis function, and compared its classification performance with that of the LDA classifiers. Notably, we found that SVM achieved an overall accuracy that is slightly lower in comparison to the LDA. Meanwhile, the LDA classification scheme runs much faster than its SVM counterpart. Also due to its relatively simple structure, and easy implemented in real-time, it was adopted in the current study [6,8,10].

3. Results

3.1. Analysis of the Feature Sets Based on Classification Error across Windowing Parameters

In this section, the properties of the different extracted feature sets were studied in terms of their classification error (CE) across combinations of window lengths and increments (Table 1) for movement intent decoding based on the LDA algorithm. The obtained results across subjects and movement classes is presented using the Heatmap plot shown in Figure 4. This analysis shows the average CE across subjects (amputees and able-bodied subjects) and movement classes, where the columns represent the different extracted features and the rows denote the combinations of windowing parameters utilized in this study.

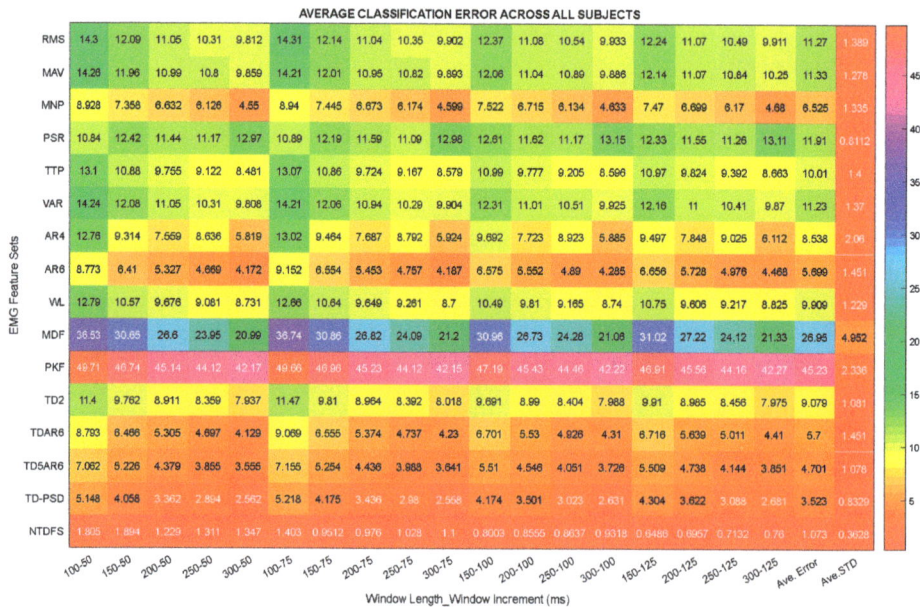

Figure 4. Heatmap plot of classification error across combinations of window lengths and increments.

It is worth noting that preliminary analysis showed that the symmetrical movement intent elicitation experiment protocol (Figure 2a) adopted in this study was helpful in aiding the amputee subjects perform seven of the pre-defined classes of movements with their amputated limbs. Meanwhile, all the results presented in this study are based on the recordings from the amputated limb, and not both limbs.

From Figure 4, it could be observed that the PKF and MDF features achieved the lowest classification performances with an average CE value of 45.23 ± 4.95% and 26.95 ± 2.33% while the NTDFS, TD-PSD, and TD5AR6 recorded an average CE of 1.07 ± 0.35%, 3.52 ± 0.83%, and 4.70 ± 1.08%, respectively, which were much better than the other feature extracted methods.

In summary, by critically analyzing the results shown in Figure 4, it was found that keeping the window length constant and varying the increment parameter does not meaningfully influence the classification performance of the extracted feature sets. On the other hand, varying the window length with a relatively constant increment would have more influence on the classification performance of the extracted feature sets. For instance, considering the RMS feature, when the increment parameter is fixed at 50ms, average decoding errors of 14.05%, 12.34%, 11.46%, and 10.35% were recorded for 150 ms, 200 ms, 250 ms, and 300 ms window lengths, respectively. Meanwhile, when the window length was kept constant at 200 ms, average decoding errors of 11.46%, 11.50%, 11.60%, 11.55% were obtained for 50 ms, 75 ms, 100 ms, and 125 ms increments, respectively. Overall it could be deduced that most features achieved the least CE at window increment of 100 ms, hence the subsequent analysis were conducted using a window increment of 100 ms.

3.2. Analysis of the Feature Sets Based on Computation Time across Windowing Parameters

In this section, the characteristics of the feature sets were further studied based on their computation time (CT) across different combination of window lengths and increments, and the analysis was done based on sEMG data from both category of subjects, as shown in the Heatmap plot presented in Figure 5. The columns represent all the considered features extraction methods while the rows depicts the different combination of window lengths and window increments.

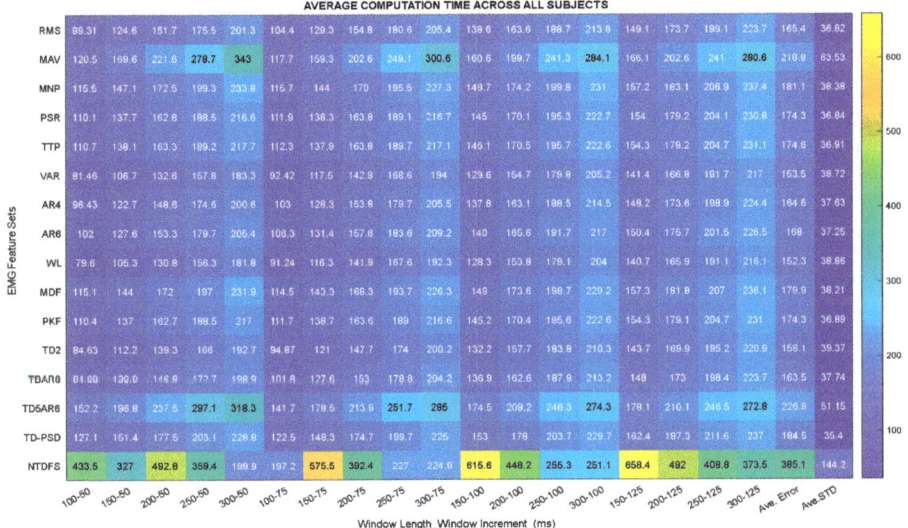

Figure 5. Heatmap plot of Computation time across combinations of window lengths and increments.

By closely analyzing the CT of each feature extraction method across different combinations of window lengths and increments (Figure 5), it could be seen that WL and TD2 features achieved the smallest CT of approximately 152.3 ms and 158.1 ms, while NTDFS and TD5AR6 features recorded relatively higher average CT of 385.1 ms and 226.9 ms, respectively. One possible explanation for the high computation time recorded by the NTDFS and TD5AR6 descriptors may be because they both consist of a combination of features, thus, leading to a correspondingly higher dimension compared to the other feature extraction methods.

Fundamentally, the higher the dimension of the extracted feature set, the more the computation time. In summary, it was observed that the smaller the difference between the window length and increment, the lesser the computation time, which would lead to the realization of a prosthesis controller with relatively faster response time. On the contrary, the larger the difference between the window length and its increment, the more the computation time, leading to a prosthesis controller with slower response time although it would result in higher classification performance. Hence, such tradeoff could be taking into consideration by prostheses manufacturers. Importantly, this phenomenon has rarely been reported till date and this phenomenon could be observed with the other feature extraction methods investigated in this study.

3.3. Analysis of the Feature Sets' Data Point Characterization Using F1-Score Metric

In this section, the performance of the feature sets in terms of data point characterization were also examined by computing the F1-score values for both the amputees and able-bodied subjects across all the movement classes and the obtained results are presented in Tables 3 and 4 as follows using window length ranging from 150 to 300 ms with 100 ms increment. It could be seen from the results presented in Table 3 that the NTDFS, TD-PSD, and TD5AR6 features achieved relatively high F1-scores of approximately 0.99 ± 0.003%, 0.97 ± 0.005%, and 0.96 ± 0.005%, respectively, as against the PKF and MDF features that recorded the lowest accuracy of 0.58 ± 0.03%, and 0.72 ± 0.04%, across subjects.

Table 3. Average motion classification accuracies based on F1_score metric for able-bodied subject.

S/No.	Feature Sets	150	200	250	300	Mean ± SD
1	RMS	0.8829	0.8978	0.9046	0.9096	0.8987 ± 0.0116
2	MAV	0.8862	0.8978	0.9039	0.9103	0.8995 ± 0.0103
3	MNP	0.9167	0.9269	0.9343	0.9392	0.9293 ± 0.0098
4	PSR	0.8750	0.8843	0.8877	0.8647	0.8779 ± 0.0103
5	TTP	0.8955	0.9089	0.9157	0.9228	0.9107 ± 0.0116
6	VAR	0.8837	0.8985	0.9039	0.9099	0.8990 ± 0.0112
7	AR4	0.8813	0.9086	0.9204	0.9324	0.9107 ± 0.0219
8	AR6	0.9253	0.9387	0.9477	0.9550	0.9417 ± 0.0128
9	WL	0.9053	0.9131	0.9204	0.9242	0.9157 ± 0.0084
10	MDF	0.6654	0.7083	0.7384	0.7759	0.7220 ± 0.0468
11	PKF	0.4987	0.5109	0.5223	0.5376	0.5174 ± 0.0165
12	TD2	0.9014	0.9093	0.9171	0.9220	0.9124 ± 0.0090
13	TDAR6	0.9229	0.9394	0.9456	0.9546	0.9406 ± 0.0133
14	TD5AR6	0.9390	0.9517	0.9586	0.9619	0.9528 ± 0.0101
15	TD-PSD	0.9559	0.9657	0.9714	0.9753	0.9671 ± 0.0084
16	NTDFS	0.9904	0.9934	0.9952	0.9964	0.9938 ± 0.0026

Table 4. Average motion classification accuracies based on F1_score metric for amputee subject.

S/No.	Feature Sets	150	200	250	300	Mean ± SD
1	RMS	0.8816	0.8912	0.8948	0.9014	0.8922 ± 0.0083
2	MAV	0.8852	0.8931	0.8979	0.9034	0.8949 ± 0.0077
3	MNP	0.9366	0.9422	0.9461	0.9497	0.9436 ± 0.0056
4	PSR	0.8761	0.8870	0.8919	0.8755	0.8826 ± 0.0081
5	TTP	0.8958	0.9057	0.9097	0.9143	0.9064 ± 0.0079
6	VAR	0.8819	0.8919	0.8960	0.9013	0.8928 ± 0.0082
7	AR4	0.9262	0.9384	0.9458	0.9514	0.9405 ± 0.0109
8	AR6	0.9065	0.9198	0.9287	0.9346	0.9224 ± 0.0122
9	WL	0.9100	0.9100	0.9200	0.9200	0.9150 ± 0.0058
10	MDF	0.6703	0.7199	0.7415	0.7671	0.7247 ± 0.0411
11	PKF	0.5495	0.5743	0.5835	0.6141	0.5804 ± 0.0267
12	TD2	0.9123	0.9184	0.9221	0.9256	0.9196 ± 0.0057
13	TDAR6	0.9449	0.9517	0.9559	0.9604	0.9532 ± 0.0066
14	TD5AR6	0.9516	0.9583	0.9612	0.9643	0.9589 ± 0.0054
15	TD-PSD	0.9622	0.9656	0.9694	0.9730	0.9676 ± 0.0047
16	NTDFS	0.9830	0.9863	0.9877	0.9895	0.9866 ± 0.0028

Also for the amputee subjects, similar trend was observed regarding the features performance with no significant differences across the varying window lengths. Taking a closer look at the F1-score results for both the able-bodied subjects and amputees, it could be seen that the abled-bodied subjects recorded relatively higher values, basically because the amputees had limited residual muscle and could not provide sufficient EMG information for accurate decoding of their targeted limb movement intents. This phenomenon has also been verified by a number of previous studies [14,16]. Overall, the characteristics of the feature extraction methods based on the F1-score metric is also found to be consistent with the previous two metrics, which further confirms the validity of our findings, thus far.

3.4. Effect of Disturbance on the Feature Set Performance

The robustness of the individual feature extraction methods were examined by introducing specific amount of random noise into the sEMG signals and then using each of the selected feature extraction methods to characterize the participants' limb movement intents. Thus, a statistically driven stability index ($S_{\_Index}$) metric defined in Section 2.6 (Equation (5)) was utilized to evaluate the robustness of the feature sets considered and the obtained results for the able-bodied and amputee subjects were presented in Figures 6 and 7 respectively.

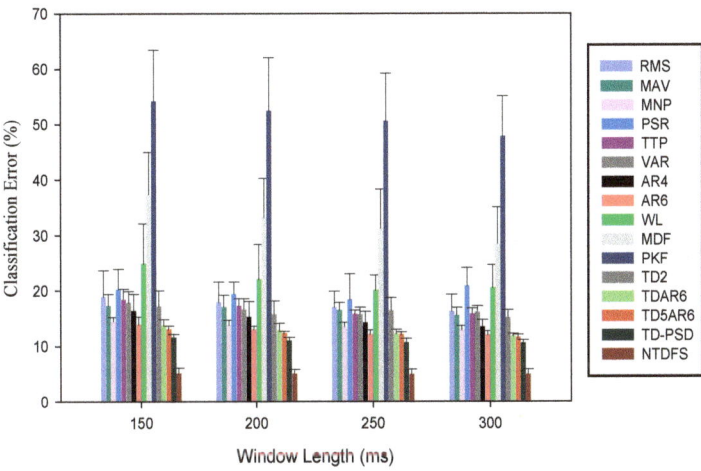

Figure 6. Mean classification error of the features in terms of their robustness to external noise across varying window length at window increment of 100 ms for abled-bodied subjects.

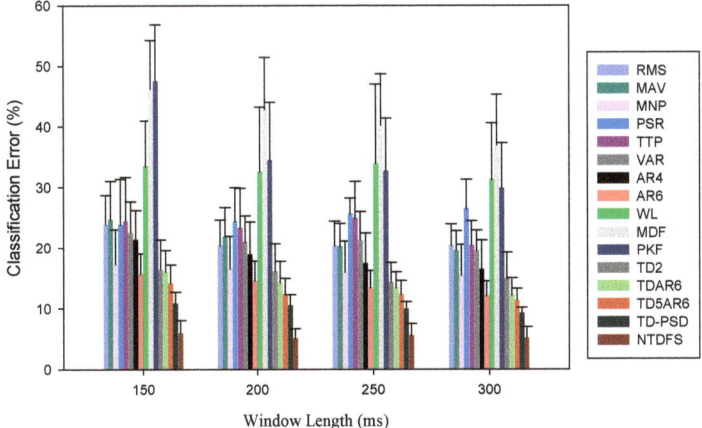

Figure 7. Mean classification error of the features in terms of their robustness to external NOISE across varying window length at window increment of 100 ms for amputee subjects.

From the result illustrated in Figures 6 and 7, it could be seen that the CE of the feature sets decreased with increase in window length, which is consistent with previous results. Furthermore, the results show that multi-features are more robust to disturbance compared to single features. As the noise was introduced, NTDFS feature recorded the least CE values ranging between 4.19%~5.94% for both able-bodied and amputee subjects, correspondingly across window lengths (150 ms~300 ms) compared to other feature sets. Meanwhile, the PKF and MDF are mostly affected by the noise, thus recording CE between 47.51%~54.14%, and 46.30%~37.41%, respectively, indicating high-level of instability in the presence of noise.

Additionally, the standard error bars in Figure 6 were observed to be relatively lower than those in Figure 7 across subjects and window lengths, thus, indicating that the able-bodied subjects' data resulted in a better S_{Index} compared to the amputee subjects. In other words, the amputee subjects are more susceptible to the disturbance compared to the able-bodied subjects. Since the amputee subjects are the end-user of the myoelectric device, there is a need to employ a robust feature sets that could enhance movement intent decoding task needed for the EMG-PR control system regardless of the windowing parameters adopted.

3.5. The Effect of Number of Channels on the Feature Sets across Windowing Parameters

Finally, we investigated the influence of the number of electrode channels on limb movement intent classification across window length (150 ms~300 ms) with a window increment of 100 ms for all the feature sets using sEMG recordings from 2, 4, and 6 channels, and the obtained results are presented in Figure 8a–f for both the able-bodied and amputee subjects. Figure 8a,b represent the classification performances of all the features using two channels. Therefore, the CE of all the feature sets (except PKF) decreased with increasing window length and this trend was consistent with the other results obtained when sEMG recordings from 4 and 6 channels were utilized (Figure 8c–f) for both able-bodied and amputee subjects. In other word, the CE reduces with increasing window length and number of channels regardless of the kind of feature set employed.

In like manner, the classification performances of the feature extraction methods were again observed to be better for the able-bodied subjects compared to the amputee subjects (Figure 8a–f) when sEMG recordings from the same number of electrode channels were utilized. In other words, it could be seen that the PKF (able-bodied: 65.65 ± 1.58%, amputee: 72.90 ± 0.72%) and MDF (able-bodied: 52.65 ± 3.02%, amputee: 56.21 ± 3.21%) features recorded the highest CE values for 2-channel sEMG recordings regardless of the type of participants, while the NTDF (able-bodied: 4.05 ± 0.83%, amputee: 6.15 ± 1.54%) and TD-PSD (able-bodied: 16.54 ± 1.78%, amputee: 22.81 ± 2.55%) features achieved the least CE values.

In similar trend, the same phenomenon was observed for 4-channels and 6-channels sEMG recording though with slight decrease in CE values. In general, utilizing sEMG recordings from 6-channels achieved the lowest CE for all the feature sets. Hence, such variability indicate that the number channels utilized may influence the classification performance of EMG-PR classifiers. It is important to note that the computation time of all the features across varying window length increases with increasing number of electrode channels, indicating a trade-off between number of electrode channels and computation time.

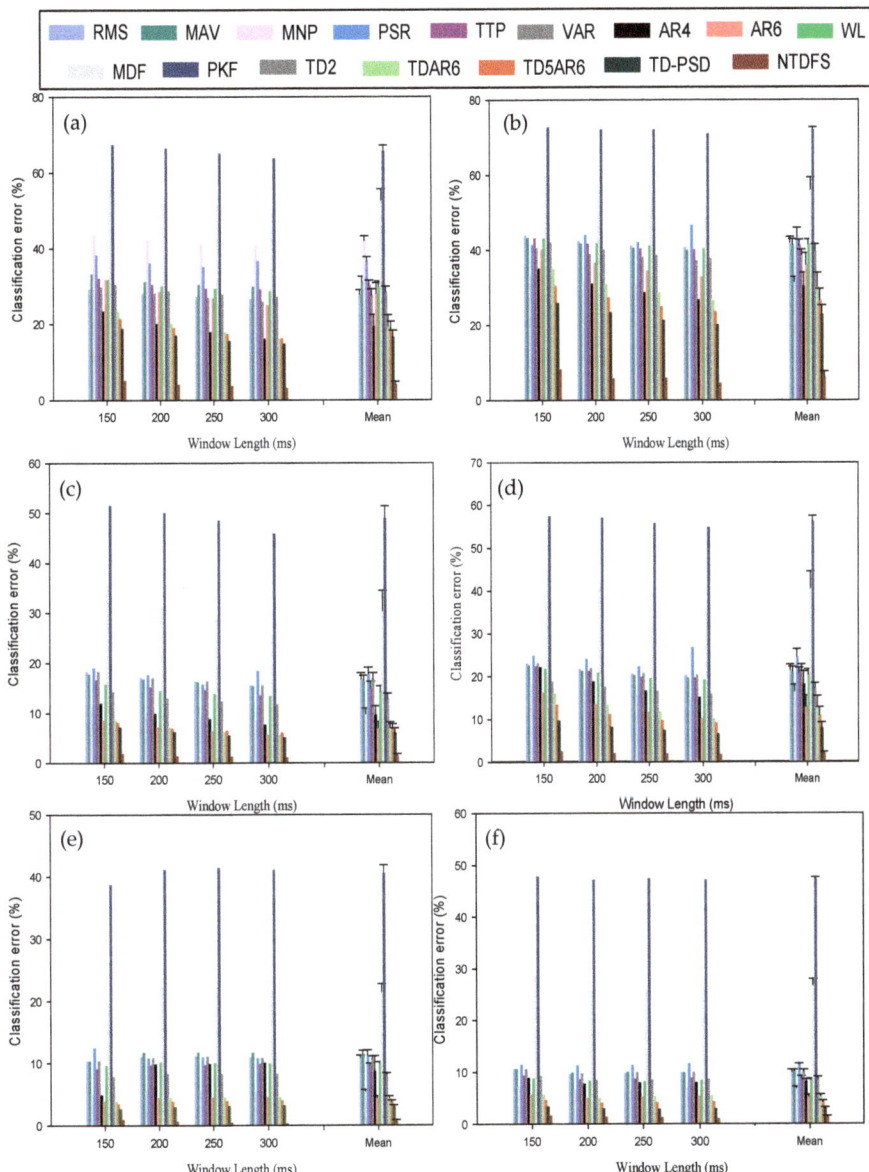

Figure 8. Mean classification error across varying window length at window increment of 100 ms for (**a**) 2-channel recording of able-bodied subjects; (**b**) 2-channel recording of amputee subjects (**c**) 4-channel recording of able-bodied subjects; (**d**) 4-channel recording of amputee subjects (**e**) 6-channel recording of able-bodied subjects (**f**) 6-channel recording of amputee subjects.

4. Discussion

A detailed analysis of the experimental results obtained from this study revealed that multiple factors, including windowing parameters, choice of feature sets, and number of electrode channels would influence the overall performance of myoelectric pattern recognition system that adopts linear discriminant analysis classifier. A few previous works recognized the need for such study and they had attempted to investigate the effect of window length and increment on myoelectric controller delay though in the context of limited factors [12–14,16,38]. Remarkably, this study considered additional critical factors by investigating the effect and interactions amongst windowing parameters and feature sets with respect to classification error, computational time, robustness to noise and number of electrode channels on the overall performance of pattern recognition system. Investigation on the interaction of these factors towards realizing a consistently stable and accurate EMG-PR scheme for multi-class movement intent decoding has rarely been considered till date. It is worth noting that this investigation may be adopted in other fields of study [39,40].

More precisely, the results presented in Figure 4 demonstrate the effect of windowing parameters (window length and window increment) on the sixteen feature sets and their resultant influence on the classification performance of the EMG-PR classifier across movement classes and subjects. In general, for all the considered feature sets, the classification error reduces as the window length increases, however we found that window increment do not have direct effect on the classification performance which corroborate the findings from a previous study [14]. Additionally, the multi-feature sets of NTDFS, TD-PSD, and TD5AR6 achieved the minimum average classification errors and deviations of $1.07 \pm 0.36\%$, $3.52 \pm 0.83\%$, and $4.70 \pm 1.07\%$, across subjects compared to the single features selected from the four EMG feature functional groups presented in Table 2. One possible reason for the improved performance observed for the multiple feature sets of NTDFS, TD-PSD, and TD5AR6 should be because they integrate neuromuscular information from multiple dimensions, thereby aggregating rich set of information for the movement intent decoding tasks compared to the other single features. From the perspective of the single feature set, AR6 and MNP were observed to have achieved better performance than other single features by recording classification error as low as $5.70 \pm 1.45\%$, and $6.52 \pm 1.33\%$, respectively. One core benefit of this findings is that the classification performance of EMG-PR system can be improved by using a combination of features from the four EMG feature functional groups presented in Table 2, rather than considering single feature set. Therefore, this findings corroborates the report of a previous study [39].

Generally, the least classification error across features was achieved at window length of 300 ms and increment of 100 ms and it could be seen that window increment do not have direct influence on the classification performance. Most features recorded the least classification error at window increment of 100 ms hence it was adopted for subsequent results presented in this study. Analysis of computation time of the feature sets across varying window length and increments was also reported in Figure 5. Here, we observed from the result that the multi-features attracts high computation time, compared to the single features. From the angle of computational complexity, the multiple NTDFS feature set that recorded the lowest movement intent decoding error was observed to have had the highest average computation time (385.1 ms) followed by the TD5AR6 multiple feature (226.9 ms). In addition, increasing the analysis window length resulted to corresponding increase in computation time, indicating a trade-off between classification performance and computation time. Therefore, this further provided us with the insight that it may be beneficial to consider features with relatively lower classification error and slightly higher computation time if the goal is to achieve a classifier with high performance in terms of accuracy that could also output its decision within a reasonable time-frame.

The performances of the feature sets were examined across varying window length of 150 ms–300 ms at a window increment 100 ms based on the feature data points in the feature space using F1-score metric, and the outcome was presented in Tables 3 and 4 for both able-bodied and amputee subjects. From detailed analysis based on EMG recordings from both categories of subjects (amputees and able-bodied individuals), it was observed that the NTDFS and TD-PSD (multiple features) recorded the highest accuracies as against the PKF and MDF (single features) that recorded the lowest accuracies. Also, Tables 3 and 4 showed that there is no significant difference in the classification accuracy across the varying window length, while the F1-score results were consistent with the results presented in Figure 1, thereby further supporting our findings.

Furthermore, we investigated the performances of the feature sets in the presence of a disturbance, by introducing random noise into the EMG recording signal and the features' performances were evaluated using the stability index metric across subjects and window lengths (150 ms–300 ms) as shown in Figures 6 and 7. In this investigation, we found that the multi features, such as NTDFS, TD-PSD, and TD5AR6 recorded the least classification error, while PKF, MDF, and WL features recorded the highest classification error for both able-bodied and amputee subjects. Interestingly, this result further proves that multi features would be more robust to external interferences (noise) compared to the single features irrespective of the windowing parameters considered. Also, we observed that the effect of the introduced noise was much obvious on the sEMG recordings of the amputees compared to the able-bodied, which could be attributed to the fact that the residual arm muscles of the amputees may produce less-rich information than those of the able-bodied subjects in an ideal situation. Therefore, considering the fact that amputees are the end-users of the myoelectric device, there is need to employ a robust feature sets that will help to enhance classification performance of EMG-PR control system regardless of the windowing parameters adopted.

Lastly, we examined the effect of the number of channels on the extracted features across varying window parameters and we found that the classification error of the features reduces with increasing number of channels for both able-bodied and amputee subjects. (Figure 8a–f). In similar trends with other results, the multi-features outperformed the single features when 2-channels, 4-channels and 6-channels were considered. Finally, by critically analyzing of our results, we discovered that when classification error, computation time, and number of electrodes were considered together, most feature sets achieved good classification performance with optimal windowing parameters of 250 ms/100 ms. Also, discoveries from this study through the systematic approach adopted can facilitate positive development in other areas where optimal features and machine learning driven approaches are required [41–50]. Last, one limitation of the current work is that the EMG pattern recognition system for movement intent decoding was analyzed in an off-line mode, and we hope to conduct online and real-time analysis in our future work. By doing so, it would further broaden the applicability of the current study in real-life applications.

5. Conclusions

In developing intelligent multifunctional prostheses where symmetrical limb motion intent elicitation protocol was adopted, this study systematically investigated the characteristics of a range of features across varying windowing parameters when applied for movement intent decoding in the context of pattern recognition system,. The interrelation and impact of different windowing parameters on the performances of the feature sets were extensively explored with respect to accuracy, computation complexity, robustness to additive random noise and number of electrode channels. From the experimental results, we found that a combination of features mostly achieved high classification performance with correspondingly higher computation time compared with their individual counterparts (single features) that had lower computation time and high classification error. Interestingly, this phenomenon explains the trade-off that exist between accuracy and controller delay in the practical use of upper limb prosthesis in real-life applications. Furthermore, we discovered that the combinations of features are more robust to noise, compared to single features, and with lesser channels they can still achieved relative good classification performance across varying windowing parameters regardless of the subject category. Particularly, NTDFS, TD-PSD, and TD5AR6 features exhibited consistent stability, robustness, and accuracy across all the windowing parameters for both, able-bodied and amputee subjects compared to the other features. Findings from this study would provide researchers and engineers with a framework for proper selection of appropriate feature set, windowing parameters, and signal conditioning, required to develop a computationally efficient PR-based control strategy for intelligently smart prostheses and other PR based systems aimed at providing smart health care services.

Author Contributions: Conceptualization, M.G.A., and O.W.S., investigation, M.G.A., and O.W.S., methodology, M.G.A. and O.W.S.; software, M.G.A.; validation, M.G.A.; subjects recruitment, L.W.; data collection, O.W.S., Y.G., and Y.J. data analysis, M.G.A., and O.W.S.; data interpretation, M.G.A., and O.W.S.; writing—original draft preparation, M.G.A.; writing—review and editing, O.W.S., S.C., P.F., A.K.S., and G.L.; supervision, G.L.; funding acquisition, G.L. All authors have read and agreed to the published version of the manuscript.

Funding: The research work was supported in part by the National Natural Science Foundation of China under Grants (#U1613222, #81850410557, #U1913601, #8201101443, #5061773364), CAS President's International Fellowship Initiative Grant (#2019PB0036), Shenzhen Science and Technology Program (#SGLH20180625142402055), the Shenzhen Governmental Basic Research Grant (#JCYJ20160331185848286), the International Collaboration Program, Natural Science Foundation of Guangdong Province (2019A050510029), the Natural Science Foundation of Guangdong Province (2018A030313065), the Science, Technology and Innovation Commission of Shenzhen Municipality Fund (JCYJ20170818163445670), and the Shenzhen Institute of Artificial Intelligence and Robotics for Society.

Acknowledgments: Mojisola G. Asogbon Samuel sincerely appreciate the support of the Chinese Government Scholarship (CSC) in the pursuit of a Ph.D. degree at the University of Chinese Academy of Sciences, Beijing, China.

Conflicts of Interest: The authors declare no conflict of interest.

References

1. Samuel, O.W.; Asogbon, M.G.; Geng, Y.; Al-Timemy, A.H.; Pirbhulal, S.; Ji, N.; Chen, S.; Fang, P.; Li, G. Intelligent EMG pattern recognition control method for upper-limb multifunctional prostheses: Advances, current challenges, and future prospects. *IEEE Access* **2019**, *7*, 10150–10165. [CrossRef]
2. Geng, Y.; Ouyang, Y.; Samuel, O.W.; Chen, S.; Lu, X.; Lin, C.; Li, G. A robust sparse representation based pattern recognition approach for myoelectric control. *IEEE Access* **2018**, *6*, 38326–38335. [CrossRef]
3. Khokhlova, M.; Migniot, C.; Morozov, A.; Sushkova, O.; Dipanda, A. Normal and pathological gait classification LSTM model. *Artif. Intell. Med.* **2019**, *94*, 54–66. [CrossRef] [PubMed]
4. Amsüss, S.; Goebel, P.M.; Jiang, N.; Graimann, B.; Paredes, L.; Farina, D. Self-correcting pattern recognition system of surface EMG signals for upper limb prosthesis control. *IEEE Trans. Biomed. Eng.* **2014**, *61*, 1167–1176. [CrossRef] [PubMed]
5. Phinyomark, A.; Khushaba, R.N.; Scheme, E. Feature extraction and selection for myoelectric control based on wearable EMG sensors. *Sensors* **2018**, *18*, 1615. [CrossRef] [PubMed]
6. Samuel, O.W.; Zhou, H.; Li, X.; Wang, H.; Zhang, H.; Sangaiah, A.K.; Li, G. Pattern recognition of electromyography signals based on novel time domain features for amputees' limb motion classification. *Comput. Electr. Eng.* **2018**, *67*, 646–655. [CrossRef]
7. Bi, M. Control of Robot Arm Motion Using Trapezoid Fuzzy Two-Degree-of-Freedom PID Algorithm. *Symmetry* **2020**, *12*, 665. [CrossRef]
8. Samuel, O.W.; Fang, P.; Chen, S.; Geng, Y.; Li, G. Activity recognition based on pattern recognition of myoelectric signals for rehabilitation. In *Handbook of Large-Scale Distributed Computing in Smart Healthcare*; Springer: Cham, Switzerland, 2017; pp. 427–442.
9. Rohm, M.; Schneiders, M.; Müller, C.; Kreilinger, A.; Kaiser, V.; Müller-Putz, G.R.; Rupp, R. Hybrid brain–computer interfaces and hybrid neuroprostheses for restoration of upper limb functions in individuals with high-level spinal cord injury. *Artif. Intell. Med.* **2013**, *59*, 133–142. [CrossRef]
10. Moloudi, M.; Mazinan, A.H. Controlling disturbances of islanding in a gas power plant via fuzzy-based neural network approach with a focus on load-shedding system. *Complex Intell. Syst.* **2019**, *5*, 79–89. [CrossRef]
11. Samuel, O.W.; Li, X.; Geng, Y.; Asogbon, M.G.; Fang, P.; Huang, Z.; Li, G. Resolving the adverse impact of mobility on myoelectric pattern recognition in upper-limb multifunctional prostheses. *Comput. Biol. Med.* **2017**, *90*, 76–87. [CrossRef]
12. Zardoshti-Kermani, M.; Wheeler, B.C.; Badie, K.; Hashemi, R.M. EMG feature evaluation for movement control of upper extremity prostheses. *IEEE Trans. Rehabil. Eng.* **1995**, *3*, 324–333. [CrossRef]
13. Englehart, K.; Hudgins, B. A robust, real-time control scheme for multifunction myoelectric control. *IEEE Trans. Biomed. Eng.* **2003**, *50*, 848–854. [CrossRef] [PubMed]
14. Smith, L.H.; Hargrove, L.J.; Lock, B.A.; Kuiken, T.A. Determining the optimal window length for pattern recognition-based myoelectric control: Balancing the competing effects of classification error and controller delay. *IEEE Trans. Neural Syst. Rehabil. Eng.* **2011**, *19*, 186–192. [CrossRef] [PubMed]

15. Li, G.; Schultz, A.E.; Kuiken, T.A. Quantifying pattern recognition based myoelectric control of multifunctional transradial prostheses. *IEEE Trans. Neural Syst. Rehabil. Eng.* **2010**, *18*, 185–192. [PubMed]
16. Menon, R.; Di, C.G.; Lakany, H.; Petropoulakis, L.; Conway, B.A.; Soraghan, J.J. Study on interaction between temporal and spatial information in classification of EMG signals for myoelectric prostheses. *IEEE Trans. Neural Syst. Rehabil. Eng.* **2011**, *25*, 1832–1842. [CrossRef] [PubMed]
17. Farrell, T.R. Analysis window induced controller delay for multifunctional prostheses. *Invol. Myoelectric Controls Symp.* **2008**, *2008*, 225–228.
18. Farrell, T.R.; Weir, R.F. The optimal controller delay for myoelectric prostheses. *IEEE Trans. Neural Syst. Rehabil. Eng.* **2007**, *15*, 111–118. [CrossRef]
19. Graupe, D.; Salahi, J.; Kohn, K.H. Multifunctional prosthesis and orthosis control via microcomputer identification of temporal pattern differences in single-site myoelectric signals. *J. Biomed. Eng.* **1982**, *4*, 17–22. [CrossRef]
20. Graupe, D.; Salahi, J.; Zhang, D. Stochastic analysis of myoelectric temporal signatures for multifunctional single-site activation of prostheses and orthoses. *J. Biomed. Eng.* **1985**, *7*, 18–29. [CrossRef]
21. Hefftner, G.; Zucchini, W.; Jaros, G.G. The electromyogram (EMG) as a control signal for functional neuromuscular stimulation. I. Autoregressive modeling as a means of EMG signature discrimination. *IEEE Trans. Biomed. Eng.* **1988**, *35*, 230–237. [CrossRef]
22. Li, X.; Zhuo, Q.; Zhang, X.; Samuel, O.W.; Xia, Z.; Zhang, X.; Fang, P.; Li, G. FMG-based body motion registration using piezoelectret sensors. In Proceedings of the 2016 38th Annual International Conference of the IEEE Engineering in Medicine and Biology Society, Orlando, FL, USA, 16–20 August 2016; pp. 4626–4629.
23. Samuel, O.W.; Asogbon, G.M.; Sangaiah, A.K.; Fang, P.; Li, G. An integrated decision support system based on ANN and Fuzzy_AHP for heart failure risk prediction. *Expert Syst. Appl.* **2017**, *68*, 163–172. [CrossRef]
24. Naderpour, H.; Mirrashid, M. Moment capacity estimation of spirally reinforced concrete columns using ANFIS. *Complex Intell. Syst.* **2020**, *6*, 97–107. [CrossRef]
25. Rainoldi, A.; Melchiorri, G.; Caruso, I. A method for positioning electrodes during surface EMG recordings in lower limb muscles. *J. Neurosci. Methods* **2004**, *134*, 37–43. [CrossRef]
26. Kim, K.S.; Choi, H.H.; Moon, C.S.; Mun, C.W. Comparison of k-nearest neighbor, quadratic discriminant and linear discriminant analysis in classification of electromyogram signals based on the wrist-motion directions. *Curr. Appl. Phys.* **2011**, *11*, 740–745. [CrossRef]
27. Oskoei, M.A.; Hu, H. Support vector machine-based classification scheme for myoelectric control applied to upper limb. *IEEE Trans. Biomed. Eng.* **2008**, *55*, 1956–1965. [CrossRef] [PubMed]
28. Hudgins, B.; Parker, P.; Scott, R.N. A new strategy for multifunction myoelectric control. *IEEE Trans. Biomed. Eng.* **2003**, *40*, 82–94. [CrossRef] [PubMed]
29. Park, S.H.; Lee, S.P. EMG pattern recognition based on artificial intelligence techniques. *IEEE Trans. Rehabil. Eng.* **1998**, *6*, 400–405. [CrossRef]
30. Du, S.; Vuskovic, M. Temporal vs. spectral approach to feature extraction from prehensile EMG signals. In Proceedings of the 2004 IEEE International Conference on Information Reuse and Integration, Las Vegas, NV, USA, 8–10 November 2004; pp. 344–350.
31. Qingju, Z.; Zhizeng, L. Wavelet de-noising of electromyography. In Proceedings of the 2006 International Conference on Mechatronics and Automation 2006, Luoyang, Henan, China, 25–28 June 2006; pp. 1553–1558.
32. Biopac Systems, Inc. Application Note 118: EMG Frequency Signal Analysis. Available online: http://www.biopac.com/Manuals/app_pdf/app118.pdf (accessed on 23 April 2020).
33. Al-Timemy, A.H.; Khushaba, R.N.; Bugmann, G.; Escudero, J. Improving the performance against force variation of EMG controlled multifunctional upper-limb prostheses for transradial amputees. *IEEE Trans. Neural Syst. Rehabil. Eng.* **2015**, *24*, 650–661. [CrossRef]
34. Khushaba, R.N.; Takruri, M.; Miro, J.V.; Kodagoda, S. Towards limb position invariant myoelectric pattern recognition using time-dependent spectral features. *Neural Netw.* **2014**, *55*, 42–58. [CrossRef] [PubMed]
35. Philipson, L. The Electromyographic Signal Used for Control of Upper Extremity Prostheses and for Quantification of Motor Blockade during Epidural Anaesthesia. Ph.D. Dissertation, Linköping University, Linköping, Sweden, 1987.

36. Samuel, O.W.; Asogbon, M.G.; Geng, Y.; Chen, S.; Feng, P.; Chuang, L.; Wang, L.; Li, G. A novel time-domain descriptor for improved prediction of upper limb movement intent in EMG-PR system. In Proceedings of the 2018 40th Annual International Conference of the IEEE Engineering in Medicine and Biology Society, Honolulu, HI, USA, 18–21 July 2018; pp. 3513–3516.
37. Samuel, O.W.; Yang, B.; Geng, Y.; Asogbon, M.G.; Pirbhulal, S.; Mzurikwao, D.; Idowu, O.P.; Ogundele, T.J.; Li, X.; Chen, S.; et al. A new technique for the prediction of heart failure risk driven by hierarchical neighborhood component-based learning and adaptive multi-layer networks. *Future Gener. Comput. Syst.* **2020**, *110*, 781–794. [CrossRef]
38. Tkach, D.; Huang, H.; Kuiken, T.A. Study of stability of time-domain features for electromyographic pattern recognition. *J. Neuroeng. Rehabil.* **2010**, *7*, 21. [CrossRef] [PubMed]
39. Geng, Y.; Samuel, O.W.; Wei, Y.; Li, G. Improving the robustness of real-time myoelectric pattern recognition against arm position changes in transradial amputees. *Biomed Res. Int.* **2017**, *2017*, 5090454. [CrossRef]
40. Zhang, X.; Li, X.; Samuel, O.W.; Huang, Z.; Fang, P.; Li, G. Improving the robustness of electromyogram-pattern recognition for prosthetic control by a postprocessing strategy. *Front. Neurorobotics* **2017**, *11*, 51. [CrossRef]
41. Samuel, O.W.; Li, X.; Fang, P.; Li, G. Examining the effect of subjects' mobility on upper-limb motion identification based on EMG-pattern recognition. In Proceedings of the 2016 Asia-Pacific Conference on Intelligent Robot Systems, Tokyo, Japan, 20–22 July 2016; pp. 137–141.
42. Zhang, J.; Williams, S.O.; Wang, H. Intelligent computing system based on pattern recognition and data mining algorithms. *Sustain. Comput. Inform. Syst.* **2018**, *20*, 192–202. [CrossRef]
43. Li, J.; Fong, S.; Wong, R.K.; Millham, R.; Wong, K.K. Elitist binary wolf search algorithm for heuristic feature selection in high-dimensional bioinformatics datasets. *Sci. Rep.* **2018**, *7*, 1–4. [CrossRef]
44. Aborokbah, M.M.; Al-Mutairi, S.; Sangaiah, A.K.; Samuel, O.W. Adaptive context aware decision computing paradigm for intensive health care delivery in smart cities—A case analysis. *Sustain. Cities Soc.* **2018**, *41*, 919–924. [CrossRef]
45. Wei, L.; Wan, S.; Guo, J.; Wong, K.K. A novel hierarchical selective ensemble classifier with bioinformatics application. *Artif. Intell. Med.* **2017**, *83*, 82–90. [CrossRef]
46. Ferreri, F.; Ponz, D.; Vollero, L.; Guerra, A.; Di, P.G.; Petrichella, S.; Benvenuto, A.; Tombini, M.; Rossini, L.; Denaro, L.; et al. Does an intraneural interface short-term implant for robotic hand control modulate sensorimotor cortical integration? An EEG-TMS co-registration study on a human amputee. *Restor. Neurol. Neurosci.* **2014**, *32*, 281–292. [CrossRef] [PubMed]
47. Asogbon, M.G.; Samuel, O.W.; Geng, Y.; Oluwagbemi, O.; Ning, J.; Chen, S.; Ganesh, N.; Feng, P.; Li, G. Towards resolving the co-existing impacts of multiple dynamic factors on the performance of EMG-pattern recognition based prostheses. *Comput. Methods Programs Biomed.* **2020**, *184*, 105278. [CrossRef] [PubMed]
48. Ma, C.; Lin, C.; Samuel, O.W.; Xu, L.; Li, G. Continuous estimation of upper limb joint angle from sEMG signals based on SCA-LSTM deep learning approach. *Biomed. Signal Process. Control* **2020**, *61*, 102024. [CrossRef]
49. Samuel, O.W.; Asogbon, M.G.; Geng, Y.; Rusydi, M.I.; Mzurikwao, Z.B.; Chen, S.; Feng, P.; Li, G. Characterizing Multiple Patterns of Motor Intent Using Spatial-Temporal Information for Intuitively Active Motor Training in Stroke Survivors. In Proceedings of the 2020 42nd Annual International Conference of the IEEE Engineering in Medicine & Biology Society (EMBC), Montreal, QC, Canada, 20–24 July 2020; pp. 3831–3834.
50. Asogbon, M.G.; Samuel, O.W.; Geng, Y.; Chen, S.; Mzurikwao, D.; Fang, P.; Li, G. Effect of window conditioning parameters on the classification performance and stability of EMG-based feature extraction methods. In Proceedings of the 2018 IEEE International Conference on Cyborg and Bionic Systems (CBS), Shenzhen, China, 25–27 October 2018; pp. 576–580.

Publisher's Note: MDPI stays neutral with regard to jurisdictional claims in published maps and institutional affiliations.

© 2020 by the authors. Licensee MDPI, Basel, Switzerland. This article is an open access article distributed under the terms and conditions of the Creative Commons Attribution (CC BY) license (http://creativecommons.org/licenses/by/4.0/).

Article

VASMA Weighting: Survey-Based Criteria Weighting Methodology that Combines ENTROPY and WASPAS-SVNS to Reflect the Psychometric Features of the VAS Scales

Ingrida Lescauskiene [1], Romualdas Bausys [1,*], Edmundas Kazimieras Zavadskas [2] and Birute Juodagalviene [1]

1. Department of Graphical Systems, Vilnius Gediminas Technical University, Sauletekio al. 11, LT-10223 Vilnius, Lithuania; ingrida.lescauskiene@vgtu.lt (I.L.); birute.juodagalviene@vgtu.lt (B.J.)
2. Department of Construction Management and Real Estate, Vilnius Gediminas Technical University, Sauletekio al. 11, LT-10223 Vilnius, Lithuania; edmundas.zavadskas@vgtu.lt
* Correspondence: romualdas.bausys@vgtu.lt

Received: 2 September 2020; Accepted: 29 September 2020; Published: 6 October 2020

Abstract: Data symmetry and asymmetry might cause difficulties in various areas including criteria weighting approaches. Preference elicitation is an integral part of the multicriteria decision-making process. Weighting approaches differ in terms of accuracy, ease of use, complexity, and theoretical foundations. When the opinions of the wider audience are needed, electronic surveys with the matrix questions consisting of the visual analogue scales (VAS) might be employed as the easily understandable data collection tool. The novel criteria weighting technique VASMA weighting (VAS Matrix for the criteria weighting) is presented in this paper. It respects the psychometric features of the VAS scales and analyzes the uncertainties caused by the survey-based preference elicitation. VASMA weighting integrates WASPAS-SVNS for the determination of the subjective weights and Shannon entropy for the calculation of the objective weights. Numerical example analyzing the importance of the criteria that affect parents' decisions regarding the choice of the kindergarten institution was performed as the practical application. Comparison of the VASMA weighting and the direct rating (DR) methodologies was done. It revealed that VASMA weighting is able to overcome the main disadvantages of the DR technique—the high biases of the collected data and the low variation of the criteria weights.

Keywords: visual analogue scales (VAS); criteria weighting; matrix question; survey; WASPAS-SVNS; entropy; direct rating

1. Introduction

Criteria weighting is an integral part of the multicriteria decision making (MCDM) models, that are widely applied in economics [1], service quality [2], talent identification process [3], robotics [4], healthcare [5], social studies [6], and other areas. Differences in the preference elicitations methodologies, transparency of the evaluation process, diversity of the opinions, and the competence of the decision-makers (DM) are the important factors affecting the final values of the criteria weights [7]. People participating in the decision-making processes tend to have not only a different understanding of the problem addressed but also to the factors associated with it. Moreover, the increasing interest in public participation activities enlightened differences between expert evaluations and public opinion [8]. Community involvement in the decision-making processes is particularly important when social, educational, environmental, and economic issues are addressed [9]. Non-symmetry in the reflection of the public opinion might cause not only inaccuracies in the preference elicitation results but also the repulsive reactions to the decisions based on them. In these circumstances, the increased interest in the criteria weighting approaches that respect opinions of the wider audience was recently observed.

1.1. Survey-Based Data Collection

Face-to-face interviews and workshops are the most common practices to collect opinions of the target groups. When it is impossible or too expensive to interview respondents through the direct meeting, online surveys might be especially helpful [10,11]. However, survey-based preference elicitation should be carefully organized, since criteria weighting results might be meaningfully affected by the survey structure, construction of the questions, or even by the visual means of the measurement scales. When contrasting unrelated questions are assessed, different survey items should be presented on separate pages [12,13]. If the respondents are asked to give ratings concerning the different aspects of a single latent variable, all the survey items should be intentionally presented on the same (web) page [14]. This particular way to present multiple, related items is called semantic differentials [15].

Semantic differentials are typically expressed as the matrix questions, where preferences are presented on the matrix side, and the response scale is presented on the top of it. Due to the ability to place multiple estimates on a single page, these structures are commonly used to collect public opinions on the quality, satisfaction, and the importance of the analyzed items [14]. Moreover, since humans are much better at making comparative judgments than the absolute ones [16,17], matrix questions might be valuable to increase the accuracy of the direct weighting techniques.

1.2. Matrix Questions and the Response Scales

Matrix questions are usually constructed when several questions about a similar idea should be assessed using the chosen measurement scale. Likert-type scales are typically expressed as the set of radio buttons, representing five or more discrete categories dedicated to revealing respondents' current state, feelings, or traits [18]. Since Likert-type scales are easily understandable, they are frequently met in the online surveys. However, the ambiguous number of response categories is the important disadvantage of these scales. Moreover, intervals between values cannot be presumed to be equal, and the biases induced by the ordinal data points might cause adversative effects on the calculations of the statistical measures like mean, covariance, correlations, or the reliability coefficients [19].

Issues inherent from the Likert-type measurement increased scientists' interests in the alternative scales [17]. Research on the historical origin of the semantic differentials revealed that they were initially made from the continuous scales, also known as the visual analogue scales (VAS). A VAS is typically presented as a horizontal line, anchored with two verbal descriptors at the extremes. A respondent indicates his opinion by placing a marker at the most appropriate point. Since VAS uses a line continuum to measure latent traits and to obtain data measurements, they are able to present weighting results without the constraints raised by the limited number of the response categories [20,21]. Fine-grained responses aid in reducing measurement error for both the value-based and the rank-based valuations. Since VAS scales produce interval-level measurement data, they are also better suited for statistical and mathematical algorithms [22].

VAS matrix is a set of the VAS scales placed in a single question. Since twofold data like the importance value and the ranking information can be gathered from a single VAS matrix, it might be successfully exploited for the preference elicitation tasks [23]. Besides, the high degree of details in the VAS scales is exceptionally beneficial when small differences can be detected between the evaluated subjects [24]. For instance, if 13 criteria ought to be assessed on the 7-point Likert scales, criteria of the different importance might fall into the same category making them indistinguishable from one another (Figure 1).

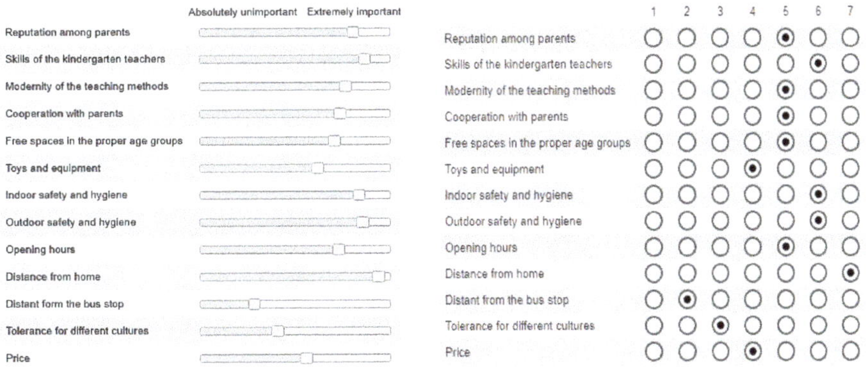

Figure 1. Matrix questions where the same set of criteria is assessed with the visual analogue scales (VAS) matrix (a) and with 7-point Likert-scales (b).

As can be seen, VAS scales are highly sensitive to the respondent's opinion. Due to this sensitivity, VAS scales are widely applied in medical studies and other areas where small differences might be significant.

1.3. Uncertainty of the Collected Data

VAS scales are easy to understand, administer, and score when implemented in online surveys [25]. Survey-based weighting processes are typically accompanied by the biases of the evaluators and the uncertainty of the experimental conditions. End-aversion bias and the positive skew are also the companions of the VAS scales [26]. End-aversion bias refers to the respondents' reluctance to use extreme categories such as "extremely important" or "absolutely unimportant". It does not affect the mean values of the respondent group, but it reduces the variance of the recorded scores [27]. Positive skew refers to the data distribution situation when the responses are not evenly distributed over the range of the scale but show a positive skew towards the favorable end [28].

Both the end-aversion bias and the positive skew suppose that data points belonging to the different ranges of the VAS scales should be treated unequally. Cautious attitude toward the psychometric features of the response scales and the uncertainty of the collected data is required to ensure the accuracy of the criteria weighting results. A new preference elicitation technique that uses the VAS Matrix for the survey-based data collection and employs the appropriate data processing approach to reduce the uncertainties of the collected data is going to be presented in this paper.

2. Criteria Weighting Approaches

Determination of the criteria weights is an important step of the decision-making processes related to the current state of the economic, social, or environmental aspects [5,29]. Since there is no unique classification of the criteria weighting methods, preference elicitation can be divided into statistical and algebraic, direct and indirect, subjective and objective, compensatory and non-compensatory techniques [30].

2.1. Subjective and Objective Techniques

Subjective, objective, and integrated approaches are widely used for preference elicitation. Subjective weights are determined solely according to the preference of the decision-makers. This type of preference elicitation is mostly based on pairwise comparison methods like AHP (Analytic Hierarchy Process) [31], DEMATEL (Decision-making Trial and Evaluation Laboratory) [32], SWARA

(Step-Wise Weight Assessment Ratio Analysis) [33], or PIPRECIA (Pivot Pairwise Relative Criteria Importance Assessment) [34]. Objective weights are typically applied then the influence of the individual decision-makers should be reduced. The most well-known objective weighting approaches are the entropy method [35], CRITIC (Criteria Importance Through Intercriteria Correlation) [36], FANMA methods [37].

Since the subjective judgments are noticeably affected by the knowledge and experience of the decision-makers, most of the time, weights determined by subjective approaches neglect the objective information [38]. The integrated preference elicitation approaches can be used to achieve the more accurate values of the criteria weights [39]. These approaches focus on the principle of integrating the subjective weights based on the expert's opinion and the information gathered from the criteria data in a mathematical form. For instance, Wang and Lee [40] proposed to integrate objective weights calculated by Shannon's entropy [35] and the subjective weights determined directly by the decision-makers. Saad et al. [41] proposed to weight the criteria combining the Fuzzy Shannon entropy and the subjective weights calculated as the averages of the direct valuations gathered from three decision-makers. The integrated approach that combines objective and subjective weights calculated from the same survey data will be presented in this paper.

2.2. Direct Weighting Approaches

Most of the currently used subjective approaches are based on the opinions of the specially trained experts [39]. Subjective weights calculation from the survey data is much rarer.

Theoretically, the VAS matrix might be exploited to collect data for the preference elicitation based on the pairwise comparisons. PIPRECIA-E [34] is an example of the pairwise comparison technique that might be used to obtain the attitudes of the respondents that were not specially trained for the criteria weighting. However, it should be mentioned that pairwise comparison is highly sensitive to the data loss caused by the respondent's unwillingness to assess all the criteria. Since a high level of the missing data is normally generated in the survey-based preference elicitation, application of the pairwise comparisons techniques might be especially challenging. Due to the nature of the pairwise comparison, responses, where at least one criterion is not weighed, should be omitted. Such a data cleaning procedure drastically reduces the number of responses; therefore, it might be an important disadvantage of its exploitation for the survey-based criteria weighting.

Direct weighting techniques are the most commonly used for online preference elicitation. In the direct methods, the decision-maker compares criteria by using a ratio scale, whereas, in indirect methods, criteria weights are calculated based on the preferences of the decision-maker [30]. Direct weighting approaches like the SWING [42], SMARTS [43], SMARTER [43], direct rating [44], and the point allocation [44] were recently used in a survey-based preference elicitation [9,45,46].

SWING method implies the construction of the extreme hypothetical scenarios, where initially a hypothetical worst-case scenario is presented, and then the criterion that might be enhanced to improve the overall situation the most is identified as the most important criterion which gets 100 points. All other criteria are weighted in a similar manner and get the point values less than 100 points.

In SMART (Simple Multi-Attribute Rating Technique) the order of the criteria importance is determined primarily and then, starting from the least important criterion, the relative importance of the criteria is assigned in the ascending order. SMARTS and SMARTER are elaborated versions of SMART [43]. SMARTS imply the procedure for determining criteria weights by comparing criteria with the best and the worst criterion from a defined set of criteria. SMARTER (SMART Exploiting Ranks) uses the centroid method to determine criteria weights [47].

Point allocation (PA) and direct rating (DR) are two relatively simple techniques that have lots in common but produce systematically different weighting results [44]. Decision-makers are asked to allocate 100 points among the analyzed criteria when the PA is applied. In the DR methodology, each object is separately assessed on a scale from 0 to 100. Since DR weights do not add up to 1 (100%), they should be normalized at the final stage of the preference elicitation. Direct rating is highly recommended when the performance evaluation relies on a large number of the criteria and when a respondent does not feel comfortable using complex weighting methods. Moreover, the weights elicited by DR are more reliable than those elicited by PA [44]. However, a little variation of the averaged weights is repeatedly identified as the downside of the straightforward DR technique [48].

2.3. VAS Matrix for the Criteria Weighting

VAS matrix can be used as the data collection tool in the survey-based decision. For instance, VAS scales are implemented in the SEIQoL methodology, which is widely used to nominate, weight, and rate different aspects of life quality [49]. SEIQoL with a direct weighting technique (SEIQoL-DW) is an interview-based tool that involves the interviewer to manage the evaluation process. The respondents are asked to nominate the five most important areas of their life (domains) in these semistructured interviews. For the evaluation of the importance of these domains, point allocation weighting is applied. Vertical VAS matrix with five adjacent VAS scales is used to assess the current functioning in the chosen domains. Finally, five separate indexes are calculated summing up the products of the functioning level and the relative weights.

Such a methodology is widely applied in various studies [50]. However, experiments with the SEIQoL-DW revealed that looking at the VAS matrix respondents comprehends the task as the assessment of the domain importance rather than the scoring of their functioning at the research moment [49].

Burckhardt et al. [46] proposed to employ VAS scales and the direct weighting for both the scoring and the weighting of the chosen domains. He also excluded the interviewer from the experiment and used a self-explanatory paper questionnaire to collect the data. In total, 100 participants were involved in this research. Since the averaged values of the VAS based DR technique showed a tendency toward the low variability of the domain weights, the usefulness of the improved methodology was highly questioned. Nevertheless, it must be noted that neither the subjectivity of the respondents nor the psychometric features of the VAS scales were analyzed in the domain importance assessments. We strongly believe that these aspects should be cautiously analyzed when the survey-based criteria weighting is performed.

3. VASMA Weighting Methodology

VASMA weighting (VAS Matrix for criteria weighting) is an easy to apply survey-based criteria weighting technique. It employs WASPAS-SVNS for the determination of the subjective weights and analyzes information entropy for the determination of the objective weights. VASMA weighting is constructed to decrease the uncertainties noticed in the survey-based criteria evaluation preserving the simplicity of the DR alike data collection. The overall VASMA weighting methodology is presented in Figure 2.

Answers provided by the respondents of the online survey are extracted from the survey database and saved in the data matrix R consisting of the values r_{nl}:

$$R = \begin{bmatrix} r_{11} & r_{12} & \cdots & r_{1l} \\ r_{21} & r_{22} & \cdots & r_{2l} \\ \vdots & \vdots & \ddots & \vdots \\ r_{n1} & r_{n2} & \cdots & r_{nl} \end{bmatrix}, \quad (1)$$

Here $l = 1, 2, \ldots L$ denote the number of the criteria and $n = 1, 2, \ldots N$ denote the number of the respondents.

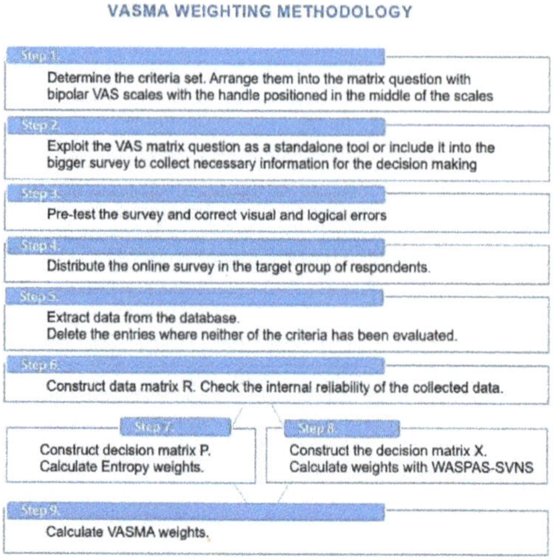

VASMA WEIGHTING METHODOLOGY

Step 1. Determine the criteria set. Arrange them into the matrix question with bipolar VAS scales with the handle positioned in the middle of the scales

Step 2. Exploit the VAS matrix question as a standalone tool or include it into the bigger survey to collect necessary information for the decision making

Step 3. Pre-test the survey and correct visual and logical errors

Step 4. Distribute the online survey in the target group of respondents.

Step 5. Extract data from the database. Delete the entries where neither of the criteria has been evaluated.

Step 6. Construct data matrix R. Check the internal reliability of the collected data.

Step 7. Construct decision matrix P. Calculate Entropy weights.

Step 8. Construct the decision matrix X. Calculate weights with WASPAS-SVNS

Step 9. Calculate VASMA weights.

Figure 2. VASMA weighting methodology.

All the evaluations are automatically transformed from the VAS scales to the integer numbers. The linguistic value at the negative anchor ("Absolutely unimportant") is determined as 1, and the linguistic value at the positive anchor ("Extremely important") is determined as 100. Other values are calculated as the distance between these two values. If the respondent n did not move a marker from the default position and left it in the middle of the VAS scales, we assume that he did not express his opinion on the specific criterion l, therefore the $r_{nl} = 0$. Finally, the simple data cleaning procedure must be done deleting the entries where the respondent n did not evaluate either of the criteria l.

Data saved in the matrix R is later exploited to construct two different matrixes P and X. Decision matrix P is used to calculate the entropy weights; the decision matrix X is constructed to calculate subjective weights via the WASPAS-SVNS approach. The matrixes R and X and their usage for the VASMA weighting will be explicitly described in the following subsections.

3.1. Entropy Weights Calculation

In most of the survey-based research, respondent characteristics are assumed to be constant across respondents. This assumption should be critically accepted since it is just hypothetically possible that all the respondents would be able to read and interpret survey items unanimously. Since such uncertainty might meaningfully affect the quantity of information in the responses, VASMA weighting is constructed in a specific way, ensuring that valuations providing different amounts of information would be treated differently [51]. In 2016, Friesner et al. [52] made an extensive analysis of how entropy-based information theory might be applied to evaluate survey items with multiple-choice responses. A similar methodology is going to be applied to calculate entropy weights and to deal with the ambiguity among respondents.

3.1.1. Construction of the Decision Matrix

Data from the data matrix R should be transformed into the decision matrix P, where p_{kl} is the proportion of response k for the criteria l:

$$P = \begin{bmatrix} p_{11} & \cdots & p_{1l} \\ \vdots & \ddots & \vdots \\ p_{k1} & \cdots & p_{kl} \end{bmatrix}. \tag{2}$$

For each of the possible responses k, p_{kl} is calculated by Equation (3):

$$p_{kl} = \frac{\sum_{i=1}^{N} D_{kli}}{N}, \text{ for each } k = 1, 2, \ldots 100. \tag{3}$$

Here N is the number of the non-zero assessments for the criterion l. D_{kl} is a binary indicator that gives a value of 1 if the respondent n gave the response k for the criteria l, otherwise $D_{kl} = 0$. Consistent with most statistical principles, the proportions of the responses should follow three rules: $0 \leq p_{kl} \leq 1$ and $\sum_{k=1}^{K} p_{kl} = 1$ and $p_{kl} \log_2(p_{kl}) = 0$ when $p_{kl} = 0$.

3.1.2. The Degree of the Information Entropy

Information entropy $E_l(p)$ is calculated for each of the p_{kl} elements and aggregated through the set of possible responses:

$$E_l(p) = -\sum_{k=1}^{K} p_{kl} \log_2(p_{kl}). \tag{4}$$

Normalization of the $E_l(p)$ is performed dividing the $E_l(p)$ by the maximum entropy attainable over the L possible survey items. For every value k entropy is maximized when $p_k = \frac{1}{k}$. Therefore, the normalized entropy is calculated by Equation (5):

$$\widetilde{E}_l(p) = -\frac{E_l(p)}{\log_2\left(\frac{1}{k}\right)}; l = 1, 2, \ldots L, \ 0 \leq \widetilde{E}_l(p) \leq 1. \tag{5}$$

3.1.3. The Entropy Weights

Finally, the entropy weights W_l are calculated as the level of change in each criterion l:

$$W_l = 1 - \widetilde{E}_l(p); l = 1, 2, \ldots L, \ 0 \leq W_l \leq 1. \tag{6}$$

By focusing on the distribution of responses, the entropy measure simultaneously encompasses measures of central tendency and the data variability.

3.2. WASPAS-SVNS for the Calculation of Subjective Weights

The uncertainty caused by the psychometric features of the VAS scales is going to be reduced, employing the Weighted Aggregated Sum Product Assessment extended by single-valued neutrosophic sets (WASPAS-SVNS). WASPAS was initially presented by Zavadskas et al. [53] and later extended by single-valued neutrosophic sets (WASPAS-SVNS) that are the extension of the intuitionistic fuzzy sets. WASPAS and its modifications are widely used for various multicriteria decision-making tasks [29,54–56]. We believe that WASPAS-SVNS also might be valuable to deal with the uncertainty caused by the end aversion and the positive skew of the VAS based preference elicitation. To the best of our knowledge, there is not any research where WASPAS would be applied in the criteria weighting process.

3.2.1. Construction of the Decision Matrix

Decision matrix X, where x_{ij} is the number of mth variable and l is the number of the criteria ($i = 1, 2, \ldots m$; $j = 1, 2, \ldots l$) has to be constructed prior to the other steps of the WASPAS-SVNS approach:

$$X = \begin{bmatrix} x_{11} & x_{12} & \cdots & x_{1l} \\ x_{21} & x_{22} & \cdots & x_{2l} \\ \vdots & \vdots & \ddots & \vdots \\ x_{m1} & x_{m2} & \cdots & x_{ml} \end{bmatrix}. \tag{7}$$

Six variables m are determined to assess each of the preferences l. Five variables analyze the nominal aspects of the collected data, and the sixth of them examines the ordinal information extracted from the matrix R.

Nominal variables. Nominal variable for the criterion l is expressed as the frequency of the values r_{nl} belonging to the predefined interval $[a,b]$. D_{nl} is a binary indicator that gives a value of 1 if $r_{nl} \in [a,b]$. Otherwise, $D_{nl} = 0$. Nominal variables V1–V5 for each of the criteria l are determined as the matrix X elements x_{ml} via the Equation (8).

$$x_{ml} = \frac{\sum_{n=1}^{N} D_{nl}}{N_l}, \text{ for each m} = 1, 2, \ldots, 5; \quad (8)$$

here N is the total number of the respondents participated in the survey, N_l is the amount of the non-zero assessments r_{nl} for the criterion l.

Ranges $[a,b]$ for the nominal variables V1–V5 were determined based on the medical research where VAS scales are widely used in pain studies. The physical manifestation of the pain is measured as the linear distance in the VAS scales of 100 mm length. It was revealed that VAS ratings of 0–4 mm might be considered as no pain; 5–44 mm—mild pain; 45–74 mm—moderate pain; 75–100 mm—severe pain, and 100 mm means the worst imaginable pain [57]. Similar intervals were determined as the five importance groups of the VAS scales (Table 1).

Table 1. Variables and their weights determined for the WASPAS-SVNS criteria weighting.

Data Type	Variable Name	Variable Description	SMART Weight	Normalized Weight	Optimum
Nominal values	V1	Frequency of the r_{nl} values $\subset$ [1–10]	90	0.161	Min
	V2	Frequency of the r_{nl} values $\subset$ [11–49]	50	0.089	Min
	V3	Frequency of the r_{nl} values $\subset$ [50–74]	10	0.018	Max
	V4	Frequency of the r_{nl} values $\subset$ [75–94]	30	0.054	Max
	V5	Frequency of the r_{nl} values $\subset$ [95–100]	100	0.179	Max
Ordinal values	V6	Overanking level	280	0.500	Max

Ordinal variable. VAS matrix provides a possibility to rank the several latent criteria visually. Scientific research proved that respondents actively use this feature and increase the precision of their answers. For instance, if the pointer of the VAS scales presenting the criterion l is moved to the right side more comparing with the others (Figure 1), it can be understood as criterion l is the most important for the respondent n. This concept can be used to determine the new variable called Overanking level (OVL). The OVL level for the criterion l is calculated individually for all the respondents n by the following algorithm:

$$\text{Let } OVL_{nl} = 0; \ j = 1 \text{ and } C_{nl} = r_{nl}. \quad (9)$$

While $j \leq l$:

$$\text{if } (C_{nl} > r_{nj}) \text{ and } (r_{nj} \neq 0), \ OVL_{nl} = OVL_{nl} + 1, \quad (10)$$

$$j = j + 1. \quad (11)$$

Return OVL_{nl}

The ordinal variable V6 of the criterion l (Table 1) is calculated as the average of the OVL_{nl} aggregated through the total amount of respondents:

$$x_{6l} = \frac{\sum_{n=1}^{N} OVL_{nl}}{N_l}, \quad (12)$$

here N_l is the amount of the non-zero values r_{nl} for the criterion l.

The final set of the predefined variables and their optimums for the MCDM process is presented in Table 1.

3.2.2. The Weighting of the Predefined Variables

Three experts working as the data analysts were introduced with the different aspects of the VAS matrix. Then they were asked to weight all the variables according to the SMARTS methodology. At first, all the experts found a consensus that both the cardinal and ordinal information is equally important for the final decision, therefore the sum of the weights for the variables V1–V5 should be equal to the variable V6.

At the next step, experts ranked all the cardinal variables according to their importance for the criteria weighting and the psychometric features of the VAS scales. Due to the positive skew that can be typically observed in the VAS based valuations, the lowest importance was set to the preference valuations where $r_{nl} \in [50 - 74]$. The highest importance was determined for the VAS values when $r_{nl} \in [95 - 100]$. Due to the tendency towards the positive assessment, critical opinions encountered in the variables V1 and V2 were considered more important than the positive ones (V3, V4). The final ranking order of the nominal variables was determined as V3 < V4 < V2 < V1 < V5. The relative scores were assigned to V4, V2, and V1 considering their trade-off to the variables V3 and V5.

3.2.3. Preference elicitation by the WASPAS-SVNS Approach

The WASPAS-SVNS approach can be deconstructed into several steps [54]:

1. Construction of the decision matrix X where x_{ij} ($i = 1, 2, \ldots m$; $j = 1, 2, \ldots, n$) is the value of the of jth variable for the ith ithalternative (criteria).
2. Vector normalization of the element $\widetilde{x}_{ij}$:

$$\widetilde{x}_{ij} = \frac{x_{ij}}{\sqrt{\sum_{i=1}^{m}(x_{ij})^2}},$$ (13)

3. The neutrosophication and calculation of the neutrosophic decision matrix $\widetilde{X}^n$. Matrix $\widetilde{X}^n$ is composed of the single-valued neutrosophic numbers $\widetilde{x}_{ij}^n = (t_{ij}, i_{ij}, f_{ij})$, where t means the membership degree, I is indeterminacy degree, and f is a non-membership degree. Standard conversion between crisp normalized values $\widetilde{x}_{ij}$ and neutrosophic numbers $\widetilde{x}_{ij}^n$ was applied [29].

4. Calculation of the first decision component $\widetilde{Q}_i^{(1)}$ is done by formula:

$$\widetilde{Q}_i^{(1)} = \sum_{j=1}^{L_{max}} \widetilde{x}_{+ij}^n \cdot w_{+j} + \left(\sum_{j=1}^{L_{min}} \widetilde{x}_{-ij}^n \cdot w_{-j}\right)^c.$$ (14)

The sum of the total relative importance of the ith alternative is used to calculate $\widetilde{Q}_i^{(1)}$. The $\widetilde{x}_{+ij}^n$ and w_{+j} are the values related with the criteria that should be maximized; $\widetilde{x}_{-ij}^n$ and w_{-j} are associated to the criteria that should be minimized. Criteria weights w_{+j} and w_{-j} are the arbitrary positive real numbers, L_{max} and L_{min} are the amount of the maximized and minimized criteria. The following algebra operations should be applied for the single-valued neutrosophic numbers:

$$\widetilde{x}_1^n \oplus \widetilde{x}_2^n = (t_1 + t_2 - t_1 t_2, i_1 i_2, f_1 f_2),$$ (15)

$$\widetilde{x}_1^n \otimes \widetilde{x}_2^n = (t_1 t_2, i_1 + i_2 - i_1 i_2, f_1 + f_2 - f_1 f_2),$$ (16)

$$w\widetilde{x}_1^n = \left(1 - (1 - t_1)^w, i_1^w, f_1^w\right), w > 0,$$ (17)

$$\widetilde{x}_1^{nw} = \left(t_1^w, 1-(1-i_1)^w, 1-(1-f_1)^w\right), w > 0, \tag{18}$$

$$\widetilde{x}_1^{nc} = (f_1, 1-i_1, t_1), \tag{19}$$

here $\widetilde{x}_1^n = (t_1, i_1, f_1)$ and $\widetilde{x}_2^n = (t_2, i_2, f_2)$.

5. Calculation of the second decision component $\widetilde{Q}_i^{(2)}$ is done by the formula:

$$\widetilde{Q}_i^{(2)} = \prod_{j=1}^{L_{max}} \left(\widetilde{x}_{+ij}^n\right)^{w_{+j}} \cdot \left(\prod_{j=1}^{L_{min}} \left(\widetilde{x}_{-ij}^n\right)^{w_{-j}}\right)^c. \tag{20}$$

$\widetilde{Q}_i^{(2)}$ value is based on the product of total relative importance in the ith alternative

6. Joint generalized criteria is computed by:

$$\widetilde{Q}_i = 0.5\widetilde{Q}_i^{(1)} + 0.5\widetilde{Q}_i^{(2)}. \tag{21}$$

7. The final weights of the criteria importance are determined considering the descending order of the score function $S(\widetilde{Q}_i)$, which is used for the deneutrosophication of the joint generalized criteria:

$$S(\widetilde{Q}_i) = \frac{3 + t_i - 2i_i - f_i}{4}. \tag{22}$$

3.3. VASMA Weights

VASMA weights w_j are calculated as the combination of the entropy weights W_j and the WASPAS-SVNS weights S_j:

$$w_j = \frac{S_j W_j}{\sum_{j=1}^l S_j W_j}. \tag{23}$$

here $j = 1, 2 \ldots, l$ is the index of the analyzed criterion.

4. Numeric Example

Children's care always has been the focus of governmental institutions since early childhood education is recognized as the basis for lifelong learning and development. Nowadays, kindergartens not only provide childcare but also perform protective, emotional, socializing, and educational functions [58]. Since parent's contribution to their child's education is increasingly growing, parental opinion and understanding of the kindergarten quality is becoming an important topic. Besides, a clear understanding of parents' opinions might help public authorities not only to improve the provision of services but also to ensure proper distribution of the public investments. Since organizing of the parental meetings is a time-consuming and human-intensive process, online surveys are the easiest way to find out what parents think.

4.1. Survey Construction and Distribution

The online survey consisting of 15 separate questions was prepared to find out parents' opinions on the quality of state kindergartens operating in Vilnius (capital of Lithuania). VAS Matrix was placed as the sixth question, where respondents were asked to indicate how important the analyzed criteria are for the search of the most suitable kindergarten for their children. Thirteen criteria adapted from the research of Malović [58] were presented in the VAS matrix. Continuous bipolar VAS scales with the single tick mark at the center of the scales were used. The anchors were named as "*Extremely important*" and "*Absolutely unimportant*" (Figure 1). All the texts were provided in Lithuanian, which is the national language of most of the respondents. The target audience was reached through the parents' groups already existing in the social networks. The survey took place just before the start of the new school year (at the end of August 2019). Since the survey had to be completed online, respondents were free to choose at what time of day to conduct the survey.

A total of 133 individuals completed the online survey. The results of three respondents were excluded from further study because they did not move any of the sliders in the VAS matrix. The demographic profile of all the rest of the respondents is presented in Table 2.

Table 2. Demographic profile of the respondents.

Variable	Category	(%)
Gender	Female	97.69
	Male	2.31
Age	24–28	16.5
	29–34	49.4
	35–40	29.8
	41–older	4.3
Degree of study	Secondary	4.3
	Professional	6.1
	Bachelor	43.3
	Masters	43.9
	Doctor	1.2
	Another option	1.2
Language spoken at home	Lithuanian	82.68
	Polish	3.94
	Russian	11.81
	English	1.57

4.2. Data Extraction from the Survey Database

Data collected with the VAS matrix was automatically converted to the data matrix R, where columns denote the set of criteria, and rows denote the ID of the respondent (Table 3). Records where $r_{nl} = 0$ depict situations when neither of the VAS markers were moved from their default position. We assumed these cases as non-response values.

Table 3. Criteria assessments converted from the VAS matrix to the data matrix R.

ID	C1	C2	C3	C4	C5	C6	C7	C8	C9	C10	C11	C12	C13
1	100	98	99	100	100	58	82	81	93	100	7	19	0
2	91	95	71	0	95	0	97	98	37	97	13	21	10
3	30	69	64	65	0	68	65	68	69	90	13	83	78
4	73	97	0	0	71	93	86	90	60	80	5	84	0
5	0	0	0	11	0	21	0	0	0	0	0	0	92
...	...	...	...	...	...	...	...	...	...	...	...	...	...
126	33	95	96	88	93	74	82	94	7	98	51	0	8
127	71	0	13	20	100	0	0	0	4	98	5	3	49
128	97	100	100	100	0	64	77	0	84	83	1	0	0
129	76	94	34	97	0	0	0	76	80	95	5	30	96
130	99	97	95	97	97	3	4	4	10	5	6	7	6

Descriptive statistics of the data collected via the preference elicitation process performed by the VAS Matrix are presented in Table 4. None of the criteria were assessed by all of the 130 respondents analyzed in the study.

Table 4. Descriptive statistics of the criteria weighting performed by the VAS Matrix.

No.	Criteria Descriptions	Count of Responses	Mean	SD	Median	Cronbach's Alfa
C1	Reputation among parents	117	78.26	24.94	88	0.9381
C2	Skills of the kindergarten teachers	112	82.16	21.44	90	0.9199
C3	Modernity of the teaching methods	104	76.70	26.64	86.5	0.9256
C4	Cooperation with parents	109	77.08	26.41	88	0.9266
C5	Free spaces in the proper age groups	102	74.25	28.50	85	0.9486
C6	Toys and equipment	100	71.19	27.00	79	0.9217
C7	Indoor safety and hygiene	106	78.30	24.01	85	0.9167
C8	Outdoor safety and hygiene	108	79.04	23.11	85	0.9189
C9	Opening hours	113	76.19	25.71	82	0.9311
C10	Distance from home	119	83.83	22.72	93	0.9435
C11	Distance from the bus stop	103	36.73	36.59	18	0.9493
C12	Tolerance for different cultures	81	49.89	38.88	52	0.9491
C13	Price	83	61.17	36.01	78	0.9494

4.3. Reliability of the Collected Data

Analysis of the collected data also revealed that only a quarter (27.16%) of the respondents moved all 13 sliders provided in the VAS matrix. It means that three-quarters of the respondents evaluated less than 13 criteria during the experiment. Since all the responses where single and more criteria are assessed contribute in the construction of the data matrix R (Equation (1)), it is necessary to make sure that the data collected during the survey can be trusted.

Both the Cronbach's Alpha and the Split-Half techniques (with Spearman and Brown correction) were employed to determine the internal reliability of the collected data. The calculated value for the *Split-Half technique* was 0.9772, and the total *Cronbach's Alpha* reliability coefficient was 0.9861 (Table 4). It means that the overall internal reliability of the collected data is very high. Cronbach's Alpha for all the 13 criteria also showed very high reliability (0.9189 to 0.9494). It is assumed that internal data reliability is appropriate if the value of the Alpha coefficient/ is at least 0.7.

4.4. Calculation of the Entropy Weights

The objective part of the VASMA weights was calculated applying the principles of the information entropy. Decision matrix P, where columns denote the set of criteria and rows denote the possible values k of the VAS scales ($k = 1 \ldots 100$) was constructed from the data matrix R (Table 3).

Values p_{kl} presented in Table 5 describe the proportion of responses k for the analyzed criterion l ($0 \leq p_{kl} \leq 1$ and $\sum_{k=1}^{100} p_{kl} = 1$). The calculation of the entropy weights presented in Table 6 is explicitly described in Section 3.2.

Table 5. Decision matrix P for the entropy weighting.

k	C1	C2	C3	C4	C5	C6	C7	C8	C9	C10	C11	C12	C13
1	0.009	0.009	0.010	0.009	0.020	0.010	0.009	0.009	0.018	0.000	0.058	0.049	0.048
2	0.000	0.000	0.000	0.000	0.000	0.000	0.000	0.009	0.000	0.000	0.010	0.025	0.012
3	0.000	0.009	0.010	0.000	0.000	0.030	0.009	0.000	0.018	0.000	0.058	0.074	0.000
4	0.000	0.000	0.000	0.009	0.000	0.000	0.009	0.009	0.009	0.000	0.049	0.049	0.000
5	0.026	0.000	0.019	0.000	0.000	0.000	0.000	0.000	0.000	0.017	0.097	0.012	0.012
...	...	...	...	...	...	...	...	...	...	...	...	...	...
95	0.034	0.045	0.038	0.018	0.029	0.020	0.028	0.009	0.035	0.059	0.039	0.049	0.036
96	0.051	0.036	0.038	0.055	0.059	0.010	0.028	0.083	0.018	0.143	0.010	0.025	0.084
97	0.026	0.054	0.067	0.073	0.039	0.040	0.085	0.037	0.053	0.092	0.010	0.025	0.048
98	0.060	0.143	0.087	0.064	0.039	0.050	0.113	0.065	0.062	0.067	0.029	0.037	0.036
99	0.077	0.071	0.048	0.064	0.029	0.020	0.038	0.046	0.035	0.034	0.000	0.000	0.000
100	0.043	0.027	0.029	0.037	0.069	0.020	0.009	0.019	0.018	0.050	0.010	0.025	0.024

Table 6. Entropy weights calculated from the survey data.

	C1	C2	C3	C4	C5	C6	C7	C8	C9	C10	C11	C12	C13
$\bar{E}_l(p)$	0.7886	0.7395	0.7935	0.7935	0.7828	0.8173	0.7660	0.7641	0.7768	0.7082	0.7813	0.7777	0.7654
W_l	0.2114	0.2605	0.2065 *	0.2065 *	0.2172	0.1827	0.2340	0.2359	0.2232	0.2918	0.2187	0.2223	0.2346
Rank	10	2	11	12	9	13	5	3	6	1	8	7	4

* The more precise weight value for the criterion C3 is 0.20652 and for the criterion C4 is 0.20648.

4.5. Calculation of the WASPAS-SVNS Weights

The subjective part of the VASMA weights was calculated as the MCDM task where WASPAS-SVNS is involved for the preference elicitation. Decision matrix X (Table 7), where columns denote variables V1–V6 and rows denote the analyzed preferences, was also constructed from the data matrix R (Table 3). Construction of the decision matrix X and the variables V1–V6 are explicitly described in the Section 3.2.

Table 7. Decision matrix X for the WASPAS-SVNS criteria weighting.

	C1	C2	C3	C4	C5	C6	C7	C8	C9	C10	C11	C12	C13
V1	3.42	1.79	5.77	2.75	4.90	5.00	3.77	3.70	6.19	4.20	39.81	29.63	16.87
V2	8.55	6.25	7.69	12.84	14.71	15.00	7.55	4.63	6.19	4.20	25.24	19.75	20.48
V3	17.09	16.96	21.15	13.76	11.76	19.00	18.87	20.37	17.70	9.24	6.80	8.64	7.23
V4	41.88	37.50	34.62	39.45	42.16	45.00	39.62	45.37	47.79	37.82	18.45	25.93	32.53
V5	29.06	37.50	30.77	31.19	26.47	16.00	30.19	25.93	22.12	44.54	9.71	16.05	22.89
V6	4.69	5.82	5.12	5.19	4.76	3.95	5.27	5.29	4.75	6.08	1.99	3.12	4.15

WASPAS-SVNS weights calculated as the score function for deneutrosophication of the joint generalized criteria are presented in Table 8.

Table 8. WASPAS-SVNS weights calculated from the survey data.

	C1	C2	C3	C4	C5	C6	C7	C8	C9	C10	C11	C12	C13
$S(\tilde{Q}_i)$	0.8492	0.8843	0.8239	0.8402	0.803	0.7935	0.8477	0.8565	0.8205	0.8596	0.3971	0.5381	0.6889
Rank	4	1	7	6	9	10	5	3	8	2	13	12	11

4.6. Calculation of the VASMA Weights

VASMA weights were calculated from the entropy weights W_j and the subjective weights $S(\tilde{Q}_i)$ by the Equation (23). The final VASMA weights and their ranks are presented in Table 9.

Table 9. Final VASMA weights.

No.	Criteria Description	VASMA Weight	Rank
C1	Reputation among parents	0.0789	6
C2	Skills of the kindergarten teachers	0.1013	2
C3	Modernity of the teaching methods	0.0748	9
C4	Cooperation with parents	0.0762	8
C5	Free spaces in the proper age groups	0.0767	7
C6	Toys and equipment	0.0637	11
C7	Indoor safety and hygiene	0.0872	4
C8	Outdoor safety and hygiene	0.0888	3
C9	Opening hours	0.0805	5
C10	Distance from home	0.1102	1
C11	Distance from the bus stop	0.0382	13
C12	Tolerance for different cultures	0.0526	12
C13	Price	0.0710	10

As can be seen, Distance from home (C10) and the Skills of the kindergarten teachers (C2) were detected as the most important aspects of the kindergarten selection process in Vilnius. Tolerance for different cultures (C12) and the Distance from the bus stop (C11) were identified as the least important criteria.

5. Results and Discussion

VAS matrix is a set of the VAS scales placed in a single question. Since multiple data like the importance value and the ranking information can be gathered from a single survey question, the VAS matrix might be successfully exploited for the survey-based criteria weighting tasks. However, biases of the respondents and the psychometric features of the VAS scales should be carefully treated to avoid uncertainties in the preference elicitation results.

Scatterplots of the two criteria with the highest mean value and with the lowest mean value were generated to illustrate the tendencies in the data collected with the VAS matrix (Figure 3). Analysis of the data distribution shows that the majority of estimates are in the range of 60–100. This is in line with the research showing that direct weighting performed with the Likert-scales or the VAS-scales shows a tendency towards the positive skew of the collected data. On the cognitive side, this may also suppose that parents have a tendency to say that most of the analyzed aspects are important for assessing the quality of kindergartens.

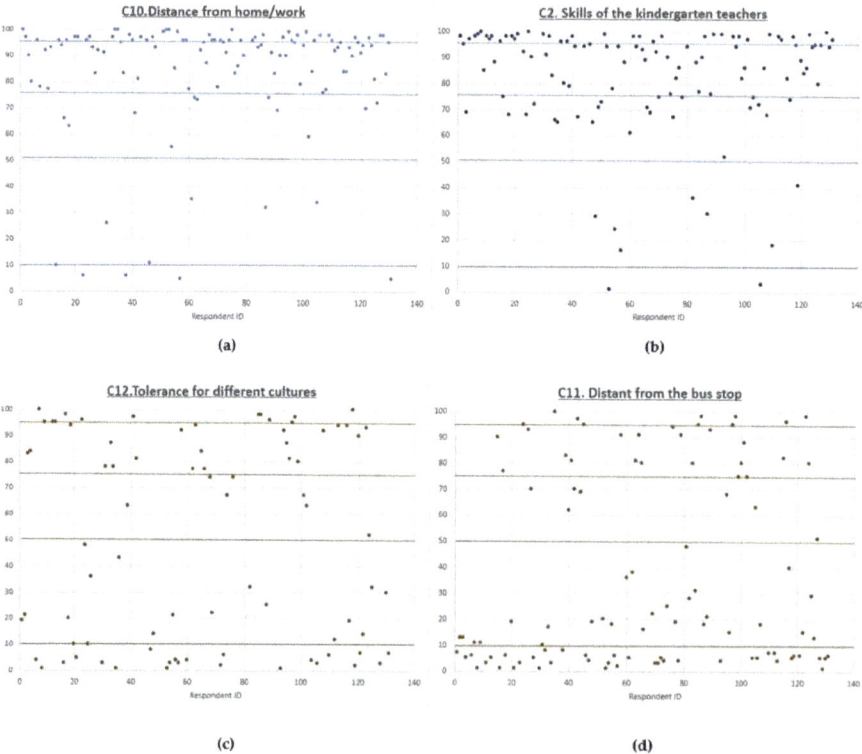

Figure 3. Scatterplots of the VAS values for the criteria that were determined as the most important (**a,b**), and the least important (**c,d**). Lines determines intervals for the five importance groups: (0–10)—not important at all, (10–50)—unimportant, (50–75)—important, (75–95)—very important, (95–100)–extremely important.

It is also noteworthy to observe that assessments ranging from 40 to 60 were hardly ever provided by the respondents. It might be related to the design of the VAS scales, where the default position of the marker is placed in the middle between the two linguistic anchors. A non-moved marker can be understood either as the non-response situation, or as the cognitive answer that the criteria is neither important nor unimportant (value = 50). To prevent the uncertainties caused by the erroneous interpretation, we consider this situation as the missing data.

In the numerical example presented in this paper, missing data is noticed in 72.84% of the answers. The accuracy of the survey results is usually sought to be improved by ensuring an appropriate sample of the responses. However, recently the significant decrease in the response rate of the online polls can be noticed [59]. In these circumstances, the opinion of each respondent becomes increasingly important. Pairwise comparison approaches like AHP or SWARA are not able to deal with the missing data, but it is not an issue for the VASMA weighting. On the contrary, VASMA weighting exploits the non-response values to achieve the greater accuracy of the preference elicitation results.

5.1. Comparison of the Direct Rating and VASMA Weights

Direct weighting approaches like point allocation, direct rating, SMART, and SMARTER might be considered as the simplest criteria elicitation methods [48]. Direct rating (DR) is probably the easiest of them since criteria weights are assessed by purely asking the respondents to assign absolute values of the criteria. Since DR does not require any prior learning on the preference elicitation process, it might also be easily applied for the survey-based criteria weighting [9]. However, two important disadvantages are recurrently associated with the direct rating methodology: the high potential for biased information [46] and the tendency towards the low variance of the criteria weights [9,44]. A comparison of the DR and VASMA approaches was performed to reveal how the data processing technique integrated into the VASMA weighting methodology affects both the variability and the accuracy of the criteria weights. Both the direct rating and the VASMA weighting techniques employ VAS Matrix as the data collection technique, but the distinctive data processing procedures. While DR simply calculates the averages of the criteria weights proposed by the respondents, VASMA calculates both the subjective and objective weights for the preference elicitation. The criteria weights calculated with the direct rating and VASMA weighting approaches are compared in Figure 4.

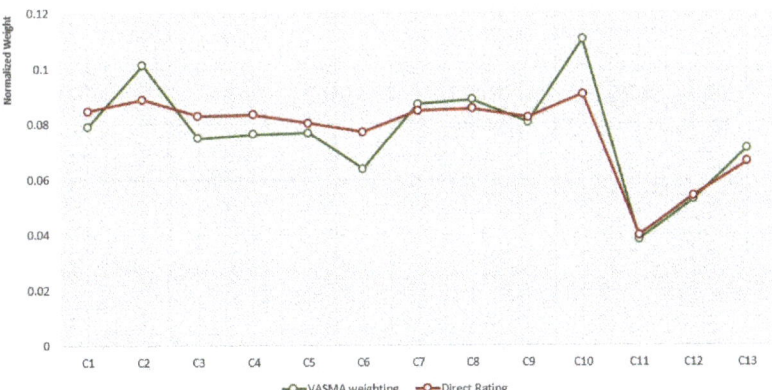

Figure 4. VASMA weighting and the direct rating comparison.

Results presented in Figure 4 support the idea that DR is typically associated with the low variation of the criteria weights. DR weights calculated for the criteria C1–C10 slightly vary in the interval (0.0770, 0.0906), while the range of the VASMA weights is much wider (0.0637, 0.1104). Respect for the psychometric properties of the VAS scales and the awareness on the uncertainty of the collected data showed that VASMA weighting demonstrates the positive effect for both the equal weighting and the high bias issues that are the vast disadvantages of the DR technique.

5.2. Sensitivity Analysis

The sensitivity analysis was performed to study the consistency of the obtained ranking. Ranks of the two direct weighting techniques (point allocation and direct rating) and VASMA weighting were determined and compared (Figure 5). Two popular direct weighting techniques SMART and SWING were not included in the comparison because of the methodological differences in the data collection procedure [9].

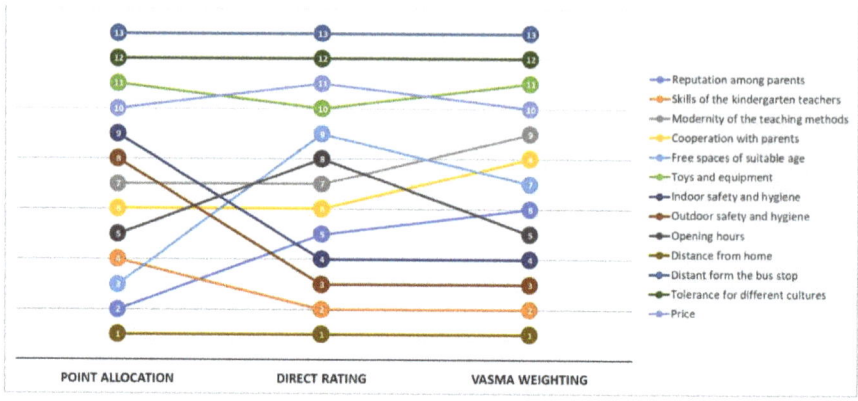

Figure 5. Criteria rank comparison for the different preference elicitation methods.

A comparison of the criteria ranks reveals differences between the point allocation (PA), direct rating (DR), and the VASMA weighting approaches (Figure 5). Due to the different direct weighting methodologies, PA and DR techniques give significantly different results. Greater stability can be observed between the criteria ranks determined by the direct rating and the VASMA weighting approaches. However, the weight values calculated by the DR and VASMA weighting techniques noticeably differ. Since a little variation of the weight values is repeatedly identified as the downside of the straightforward DR technique, VASMA weighting can be chosen as the solution to this issue. Results presented in the Figure 4 prove that the variance of the weighting values for the criterions C10 (Distance from home), C2 (Skills of kindergarten teachers), C8 (Outdoor safety and hygiene), and C7 (Indoor safety and hygiene) are considerably wider when the novel preference elicitation technique VASMA weighting is applied.

6. Conclusions

Criteria weighting is an integral part of the multicriteria decision-making process. When the opinions of the wider audience are needed, electronic surveys may be successfully employed to collect data for the preference elicitation procedure. Since both the psychologists and psychometricians agree that humans are much better at making comparative judgments than at making absolute judgments, visual analogue scales (VAS) have been proposed as the affective data collection tool for the assessment of the respondents' traits. However, survey-based criteria weighting processes are typically accompanied by the biases of the evaluators and the uncertainty of the experimental conditions. Besides, end-aversion bias and the positive skew are also the companions of the VAS based preference elicitation. The novel criteria weighting technique VASMA weighting respects the psychometric features of the VAS scales and analyzes the uncertainties caused by the survey-based criteria weighting. It is achieved by integrating the WASPAS-SVNS multicriteria decision making approach for the determination of the subjective weights and Shannon entropy for the calculation of the objective weights.

A numerical example analyzing the importance of the criteria that affect parents' decisions regarding the choice of the kindergarten institution was performed to reveal the practicalities of the proposed methodology. The experiment presented in this paper revealed that the data processing technique integrated into the VASMA weighting methodology is able to overcome the main disadvantages of the direct rating technique—the high biases of the collected data and the low variation of the criteria weights.

In the future, it would be interesting to analyze why the last three criterions presented in the VAS matrix got significantly lower weights than the rest of them. Is it an accidental situation, or is it associated with their position in the VAS Matrix? An optimal number of the criteria that can be weighted with the VASMA weighting methodology also should be analyzed in the future. It would be also interesting to disclose how the number of respondents and their homogeneity affects VASMA weighting values.

Author Contributions: Conceptualization, I.L., E.K.Z., R.B. and B.J.; methodology, I.L., E.K.Z., R.B. and B.J.; software, I.L.; validation, I.L., E.K.Z., R.B. and B.J.; formal analysis, I.L. and R.B.; investigation, I.L. and B.J.; resources, I.L. and B.J.; data curation, I.L.; writing—original draft preparation, I.L. and B.J.; writing—review and editing, I.L., E.K.Z., R.B. and B.J.; visualization, I.L.; supervision, R.B.; project administration, I.L. and R.B. All authors have read and agreed to the published version of the manuscript.

Funding: This research received no external funding.

Conflicts of Interest: The authors declare no conflict of interest.

References

1. He, T.; Zhang, S.; Wei, G.; Wang, R.; Wu, J.; Wei, C. CODAS method for 2-tuple linguistic Pythagorean fuzzy multiple attribute group decision making and its application to financial management performance assessment. *Technol. Econ. Dev. Econ.* **2020**, *26*, 920–932. [CrossRef]
2. Mishra, A.R.; Rani, P.; Pardasani, K.R.; Mardani, A.; Stević, Ž.; Pamučar, D. A novel entropy and divergence measures with multi-criteria service quality assessment using interval-valued intuitionistic fuzzy TODIM method. *Soft Comput.* **2020**, *24*, 11641–11661. [CrossRef]
3. Lai, Y.; Ishizaka, A. The application of multicriteria decision analysis methods into talent identification process: A social psychological perspective. *J. Bus. Res.* **2019**, *109*, 637–647. [CrossRef]
4. Semenas, R.; Bausys, R. Modelling of Autonomous Search and Rescue Missions by Interval-Valued Neutrosophic WASPAS Framework. *Symmetry* **2020**, *12*, 162. [CrossRef]
5. Stević, Ž.; Pamučar, D.; Puška, A.; Chatterjee, P. Sustainable supplier selection in healthcare industries using a new MCDM method: Measurement of alternatives and ranking according to Compromise solution (MARCOS). *Comput. Ind. Eng.* **2020**, *140*, 106231. [CrossRef]
6. Lo, W.C.; Lu, C.H.; Chou, Y.C. Application of Multicriteria Decision Making and Multi-Objective Planning Methods for Evaluating Metropolitan Parks in Terms of Budget and Benefits. *Mathematics* **2020**, *8*, 1304. [CrossRef]
7. Shukla, V.; Auriol, G. Methodology for determining stakeholders' criteria weights in system engineering. In Proceedings of the Poster Workshop at the 2013 Complex Systems Design and Management Conference, Paris, France, 4 December 2013; CSDM: Paris, France, 2013; pp. 1–12. Available online: http://ceur-ws.org/Vol-1085/02-paper.pdf (accessed on 30 August 2020).
8. Metzger, M.J.; Flanagin, A.J. Credibility and trust of information in online environments: The use of cognitive heuristics. *J. Pragmat.* **2013**, *59 Pt B*, 210–220. [CrossRef]
9. Aubert, A.H.; Esculier, F.; Lienert, J. Recommendations for online elicitation of swing weights from citizens in environmental decision-making. *Oper. Res. Perspect.* **2020**, *7*, 100156. [CrossRef]
10. Saris, W.E.; Gallhofer, I.N. *Design, Evaluation, and Analysis of Questionnaires for Survey Research*; John Wiley & Sons: New York, NY, USA, 2014.
11. Molléri, J.S.; Petersen, K.; Mendes, E. An empirically evaluated checklist for surveys in software engineering. *Inform. Softw. Technol.* **2020**, *119*, 106240. [CrossRef]

12. Sudman, S.; Bradburn, N.M.; Schwarz, N. *Thinking about Answers: The Application of Cognitive Processes to Survey Methodology*; Jossey-Bass: New York, NY, USA, 1996.
13. Reips, U.D. Standards for Internet-based experimenting. *Exp. Psychol.* **2002**, *49*, 243–256. [CrossRef]
14. Dillman, D.A.; Smyth, J.D.; Christian, L.M. *Internet, Mail, and Mixed-Mode Surveys: The Tailored Design Method*, 3rd ed.; John Wiley & Sons, Inc.: Hoboken, NJ, USA, 2009.
15. Osgood, C.E.; Suci, G.J.; Tannenbaum, P.H. *The Measurement of Meaning*; University of Illinois Press: Urbana, IL, USA, 1957.
16. Laming, D. *Understanding Human Motivation: What Makes People Tick*; Blackwells: Malden, MA, USA, 2004. [CrossRef]
17. Sung, Y.T.; Wu, J.S. The Visual Analogue Scale for Rating, Ranking and Paired-Comparison (VAS-RRP): A new technique for psychological measurement. *Behav. Res. Methods* **2018**, *50*, 1694–1715. [CrossRef] [PubMed]
18. Likert, R. A technique for the measurement of attitudes. *Arch. Psychol.* **1932**, *22*, 140–155. Available online: https://psycnet.apa.org/record/1933-01885-001 (accessed on 30 August 2020).
19. Chang, R.; Little, T. Innovations for Evaluation Research: Multiform Protocols, Visual Analog Scaling, and the Retrospective Pretest–Posttest Design. *Eval. Health Prof.* **2018**, *41*, 246–269. [CrossRef] [PubMed]
20. Musangu, L.M.; Kekwaletswe, R.M. Comparison of likert scale with visual analogue scale for strategic information systems planning measurements: A preliminary study. In Proceedings of the IADIS International Conference Information Systems, Lisbon, Portugal, 17–19 July 2012; Nunes, M.B., Isaias, P., Powell, P., Eds.; IADIS: Lisbon, Portugal, 2012; pp. 108–115. Available online: http://www.iadisportal.org/digital-library/comparison-of-likert-scale-with-visual-analogue-scale-for-strategic-information-systems-planning-measurements-a-preliminary-study (accessed on 30 August 2020).
21. Kuhlmann, T.; Dantlgraber, M.; Reips, U. Investigating measurement equivalence of visual analogue scales and Likert-type scales in Internet-based personality questionnaires. *Behav. Res. Methods* **2017**, *49*, 2173–2181. [CrossRef] [PubMed]
22. Reips, U.-D.; Funke, F. Interval-level measurement with visual analogue scales in Internet-based research: VAS Generator. *Behav. Res. Methods* **2008**, *40*, 699–704. [CrossRef] [PubMed]
23. Stanley, N.; Jenkins, S. Watch what I do: Using graphical input controls in web surveys. In *The Challenges of a Changing World, Proceedings of the Fifth International Conference of the Association for Survey Computing, Southampton, UK, 12–14 September 2007*; ASC: Berkeley, CA, USA, 2007; pp. 81–92.
24. Funke, F.; Reips, U.-D. Why semantic differentials in web-based research should be made from visual analogue scales and not from 5-point scales. *Field Methods* **2012**, *24*, 310–327. [CrossRef]
25. Yusoff, R.; Janor, R.M. Generation of an Interval Metric Scale to Measure Attitude. *SAGE Open* **2014**, *4*, 1–16. [CrossRef]
26. Rashidi, A.A.; Anis, A.H.; Marra, C.A. Do visual analogue scale (VAS) derived standard gamble (SG) utilities agree with Health Utilities Index utilities? A comparison of patient and community preferences for health status in rheumatoid arthritis patients. *Health Qual. Life Outcomes* **2006**, *4*, 25. [CrossRef]
27. Schmitt, D.P.; Allik, J. Simultaneous Administration of the Rosenberg Self-Esteem Scale in 53 Nations: Exploring the Universal and Culture-Specific Features of Global Self-Esteem. *J. Personal. Soc. Psychol.* **2005**, *89*, 623–642. [CrossRef]
28. Streiner, D.L.; Norman, G.R.; Cairney, J. *Health Measurement Scales: A Practical Guide to Their Development and Use*, 5th ed.; Oxford University Press: Oxford, UK, 2014.
29. Zavadskas, E.K.; Bausys, R.; Mazonaviciute, I. Safety evaluation methodology of urban public parks by multicriteria decision making. *Landsc. Urban Plan.* **2019**, *189*, 372–381. [CrossRef]
30. Pamučar, D.; Stević, Ž.; Sremac, S. A new model for determining weight coefficients of criteria in MCDM models: Full consistency method (FUCOM). *Symmetry* **2018**, *10*, 393. [CrossRef]
31. Saaty, T.L. A scaling method for priorities in hierarchical structures. *J. Math. Psychol.* **1977**, *15*, 234–281. [CrossRef]
32. Gabus, A.; Fontela, E. *World Problems an Invitation to Further Thought within the Framework of DEMATEL*; Battelle Geneva Research Centre: Geneva, Switzerland, 1972; pp. 1–8.
33. Kersuliene, V.; Zavadskas, E.K.; Turskis, Z. Selection of rational dispute resolution method by applying new step-wise weight assessment ratio analysis (SWARA). *J. Bus. Econ. Manag.* **2010**, *11*, 243–258. [CrossRef]

34. Stanujkic, D.; Zavadskas, E.K.; Karabasevic, D.; Smarandache, F.; Turskis, Z. The use of the pivot pairwise relative criteria importance assessment method for determining the weights of criteria. *Rom. J. Econ. Forecast* **2017**, *20*, 116–133. [CrossRef]
35. Shannon, C.E.; Weaver, W. *The Mathematical Theory of Communication*; University Illinois Press: Urbana, IL, USA, 1963.
36. Diakoulaki, D.; Mavrotas, G.; Papayannakis, L. Determining objective weights in multiple criteria problems: The CRITIC method. *Comput. Oper. Res.* **1995**, *22*, 763–770. [CrossRef]
37. Srdjevic, B.; Medeiros, Y.; Srđevic, Z.; Schaer, M. Evaluating management strategies in Paraguacu river basin by analytic hierarchy process. In Proceedings of the First Biennial Meeting of the International Environmental Modeling and Software Society, Lugano, Switzerland, 1 July 2002; pp. 42–47.
38. Odu, G. Weighting methods for multicriteria decision making technique. *J. Appl. Sci. Environ. Manag.* **2019**, *23*, 1449–1457. [CrossRef]
39. Vinogradova, I.; Podvezko, V.; Zavadskas, E.K. The recalculation of the weights of criteria in MCDM methods using the bayes approach. *Symmetry* **2018**, *10*, 205. [CrossRef]
40. Wang, T.C.; Lee, H.D. Developing a fuzzy TOPSIS approach based on subjective weights and objective weights. *Expert Syst. Appl.* **2009**, *36*, 8980–8985. [CrossRef]
41. Md Saad, R.; Ahmad, M.Z.; Abu, M.S.; Jusoh, M.S. Hamming Distance Method with Subjective and Objective Weights for Personnel Selection. *Sci. World J.* **2014**, *2014*, 865495. [CrossRef]
42. Von Winterfeldt, D.; Edwards, W. *Decision Analysis and Behavioral Research*; Cambridge University Press: Cambridge, UK, 1986.
43. Edwards, W.; Barron, F.H. SMARTS and SMARTER: Improved simple methods for multiattribute utility measurement. *Organ. Behav. Hum. Decis.* **1994**, *60*, 306–325. [CrossRef]
44. Bottomley, P.; Doyle, J.; Green, R. Testing the Reliability of Weight Elicitation Methods: Direct Rating versus Point Allocation. *J. Mark. Res.* **2000**, *37*, 508–513. [CrossRef]
45. Van Til, J.A.; Dolan, J.G.; Stiggelbout, A.M.; Groothuis, K.C.; Ijzerman, M.J. The use of multi-criteria decision analysis weight elicitation techniques in patients with mild cognitive impairment: A pilot study. *Patient* **2008**, *1*, 127–135. [CrossRef]
46. Burckhardt, M.; Fleischer, S.; Berg, A. Agreement between the Schedule for the Evaluation of Individual Quality of Life-Direct Weighting (SEIQoL-DW) interview and a paper-administered adaption. *BMC Med. Res. Methodol.* **2020**, *20*, 80. [CrossRef] [PubMed]
47. Mustajoki, J.; Hämäläinen, R.P.; Salo, A. Decision Support by Interval SMART/SWING—Incorporating Imprecision in the SMART and SWING Methods. *Decis. Sci.* **2005**, *36*, 317–339. [CrossRef]
48. Németh, B.; Molnár, A.; Bozóki, S.; Wijaya, K.; Inotai, A.; Campbell, J.D.; Kaló, Z. Comparison of weighting methods used in multicriteria decision analysis frameworks in healthcare with focus on low-and middle-income countries. *J. Comp. Eff. Res.* **2019**, *8*, 195–204. [CrossRef] [PubMed]
49. Stiggelbout, A.M.; de Vogel-Voogt, E.; Noordijk, E.M.; Vliet Vlieland, T.P. Individual quality of life: Adaptive conjoint analysis as an alternative for direct weighting? *Qual. Life Res.* **2008**, *17*, 641–649. [CrossRef] [PubMed]
50. Hamidou, Z.; Baumstarck, K.; Chinot, O.; Barlesi, F.; Salas, S.; Leroy, T.; Auquier, P. Domains of quality of life freely expressed by cancer patients and their caregivers: Contribution of the SEIQoL. *Health Qual. Life Outcomes* **2017**, *15*, 99. [CrossRef]
51. Dahl, F.; Osteras, N. Quantifying information content in survey data by entropy. *Entropy* **2010**, *12*, 161–163. [CrossRef]
52. Friesner, D.; Valente, F.; Bozman, C.S. Using Entropy-Based Information Theory to Evaluate Survey Research. *J. Mark. Dev. Compet.* **2016**, *10*, 32–48.
53. Zavadskas, E.K.; Turskis, Z.; Antucheviciene, J.; Zakarevicius, A. Optimization of Weighted Aggregated Sum Product Assessment. *Electron. Elektrotech.* **2012**, *6*, 3–6. [CrossRef]
54. Bausys, R.; Kazakeviciute-Januskeviciene, G.; Cavallaro, F.; Usovaite, A. Algorithm Selection for Edge Detection in Satellite Images by Neutrosophic WASPAS Method. *Sustainability* **2020**, *12*, 548. [CrossRef]
55. Mardani, A.; Saraji, M.K.; Mishra, A.R.; Rani, P. A novel extended approach under hesitant fuzzy sets to design a framework for assessing the key challenges of digital health interventions adoption during the COVID-19 outbreak. *Appl. Soft Comput.* **2020**, *96*, 106613. [CrossRef] [PubMed]

56. Baušys, R.; Juodagalvienė, B.; Žiūrienė, R.; Pankrašovaitė, I.; Kamarauskas, J.; Usovaitė, A.; Gaižauskas, D. The residence plot selection model for family house in Vilnius by neutrosophic WASPAS method. *Int. J. Strateg. Prop. Manag.* **2020**, *24*, 182–196. [CrossRef]
57. Altaim, A.A.; LeRoux, A.A. The use of box-counting method in the interpretation of Visual Analogue Scale scores. *JAPER* **2019**, *9*, 1–6.
58. Malović, M.; Malović, S. Parents' perspective on the quality of kindergarten. *Res. Pedagog.* **2017**, *7*, 200–220. [CrossRef]
59. Beullens, K.; Loosveldt, G.; Vandenplas, C.; Stoop, I. Response rates in the European Social Survey: Increasing, decreasing, or a matter of fieldwork efforts? *Surv. Methods Insights Field* **2018**. Available online: https://surveyinsights.org/?p=9673 (accessed on 30 August 2020). [CrossRef]

© 2020 by the authors. Licensee MDPI, Basel, Switzerland. This article is an open access article distributed under the terms and conditions of the Creative Commons Attribution (CC BY) license (http://creativecommons.org/licenses/by/4.0/).

Article

A New Model for Determining the EOQ under Changing Price Parameters and Reordering Time

Tetyana Nestorenko [1], Mangirdas Morkunas [2], Jana Peliova [3], Artiom Volkov [4], Tomas Balezentis [4,*] and Dalia Streimkiene [4,*]

[1] Department of Economics, Entrepreneurship and Finance, Faculty of the Humanities and Economics, Berdyansk State Pedagogical University, 4 Shmidt Str., 71112 Berdyansk, Ukraine; tetyana.nestorenko@bdpu.org.ua
[2] Department of Business, Faculty of Economics and Business Administration, Vilnius University, Sauletekio av. 9, 10222 Vilnius, Lithuania; mangirdas.morkunas@evaf.vu.lt
[3] Faculty of National Economy, University of Economics in Bratislava, Dolnozemska cesta 1, 85235 Bratislava, Slovakia; jana.peliova@euba.sk
[4] Division of Farm and Enterprise Economics, Lithuanian Institute of Agrarian Economics, A. Vivulskio Str. 4A., 03221 Vilnius, Lithuania; artiom.volkov@laei.lt
* Correspondence: tomas.balezentis@laei.lt (T.B.); dalia.streimikiene@lei.lt (D.S.)

Received: 29 July 2020; Accepted: 11 September 2020; Published: 14 September 2020

Abstract: The present study deals with the modification of Wilson's formulation by taking into account changes in the supply chain represented by the parameters of the model, namely varying delivery costs and price of goods stored. The four different models are presented. The proposed models avoid the main drawbacks of Wilson's formulation—the constant price and reordering time—and discuss the case where varying parameters are used alongside discounting. The proposed models render lower costs under particular settings.

Keywords: EOQ; Wilson's formulation; lot size; reordering time

---

1. Introduction

Sustainable business decisions require taking into account a wide range of factors and methodologies [1–4]. Therefore, a number of models have been proposed for efficient inventory management. In 1913, Harris introduced an economic order quantity concept to solve this problem in the form of a static formula (and started static inventory management models vein).

However, typical static economic order quantity (EOQ) models [5,6] do not satisfy practitioners because of their incapacity to consider changing consumer demand, requiring constant orders in equal periods of time [7]. Unpredictable and constantly changing demands, affecting the size and frequency of orders, lead to situations in which classical inventory management models become unfit for solving practical inventory management problems and motivate a search for new or modified alternatives. In the last decade, we observed increased scientific interest in solving this problem. Firstly, Sana [8] proposed an EOQ model for perishable goods reacting to retail price changes, although practical implementation is restricted by neglecting the minimizing effect of a negative power function of price, which generates high sensibility in consumer's demand. Later, Dobson et al. [9] proposed that perishable goods, with the demand rate as a linearly decreasing function of the age of the products, act similarly to nonperishable goods with the unit holding cost equal to the ratio of contribution margin to lifetime. In their model, they obtain traditional nonperishable Economic Order Quantity (EOQ)-like lower and upper bounds on the cycle length and the profit and show that they lead to near-optimal results for typical examples, like grocery items. Zeng et al. [10] formulate an extension to Wilson's model varying quantity of order and different ordering periods. Their model generates a substantial economic effect when a significant change in consumer demand is noticed and (or) a long period of planning the logistics process must be ensured.

Conventional models for inventory management with uncertain demand, such as variations of Harris formulation [11–13], Markov equation-based ones [14,15], and Wilson's formulation [16–19] are designed to minimize the expected costs of replenishment and stock-outs. They assume that complete satisfaction of uncertain and hardly predictable demand is too expensive or even deemed impossible. All these models are designed under the constant order quantity principle, where the size of the following order is based on the objective to minimize the whole cost of a company's inventory management.

The problem of economic order quantity (EOQ) is quite well-known and has been widely discussed in the scientific literature [20–24]. Determination of the EOQ has a particular importance in trade and retail activities. The optimal ordering plan allows for the companies to achieve smooth operation and competitive advantage [25–27].

In the context of steady economic growth, the EOQ models assuming steady demand for perishable consumer goods are suitable for determining the lot size [28–30]. There has been research on the EOQ with respect to the credit market [31] and stock dynamic sizing optimization under the Logistic 4.0 environment for material management of a very high-speed train [32].

However, the fluctuations in the demand and lead time have not been taken into account. Indeed, such fluctuations become more important during disruptions of the supply chains (e.g., due to pandemic events). The emergence of trade barriers requires retailers to reconsider the optimal lot size. This issue is further aggravated by fluctuations in the market prices of particular products. Indeed, the crisis affects the consumer behavior and demand for particular goods [33–35]. The changes in demand are reflected by the prices of the products retailed [36,37]. Therefore, one needs to adjust decisions to order and store goods. Even without facing serious crisis, changes in pricing occur over time in terms of both retail market and storage costs. Thus, a mathematical model capable of determining the optimal economic order quantity under varying reordering time and price parameters is obvious. Although there has been a wide range of models proposed for determining the lot sizes (Table 1), none of them are able to handle the varying stock quantity based on varying price and reordering time.

Table 1. Overview of the existing economic order quantity (EOQ) models.

No.	Reference	Model
1.	Sebatjane & Adetunji [38].	Costs per cycle are multiplied by the number of cycles. Discounting is not applied.
2.	Khan, Jaber & Bonney, M. [39]	Optimal order quantity in the presence of defective items in the order and with various options for defect detection: no implications to changing price parameters of an order are provided.
3.	Birbil, Ş. İ., Bülbül, K., Frenk, H., & Mulder, H. M. [40]	The demand and unit price are assumed to be constant.
4.	Taleizadeh, A. A. [41]	Divided payments are considered assuming constant parameters of the model.
5.	Molamohamadi, Z., Arshizadeh, R., Ismail, N., & Azizi, A. [42]	The delay of payment is allowed (it may be considered as a proxy for changing price parameters of the order). The objective is optimizing trade credit terms rather than the lot size.

Table 1. Cont.

No.	Reference	Model
6.	El-Kassar, A. N., Salameh, M., & Bitar, M. [43]	The model allows for identifying faulty intermediate consumption items rather than determining the optimal lot size.
7.	Tungalag, N., Erdenebat, M., & Enkhbat, R. [44]	EOQ extended with the Euler–Lagrange equation without varying price parameters.
8.	Jaggi, C. K., & Mittal, M. [45]	EOQ model with a focus on the lot size with regards to defected items and deterioration time.
9.	Elyasi, M., Khoshalhan, F., & Khanmirzaee, M. [46]	The EOQ model with constant price and lead time.
10.	Widyadana, G. A., Cárdenas-Barrón, L. E., & Wee, H. M. [47]	The model for deteriorating items.
11.	Shanshan, L. & Yong, H. [1]	Focus on mitigating effects of an already occurred stock out.
12.	Inprasit, T. & Tanachutiwat, S. [48]	A combination of machine learning and neural networks for determining a reordering point but not an EOQ.

This paper presents a model for determining the optimal lot size with fluctuating price building on the classical Wilson's formulation following extensions by Slesarenko and Nestorenko [49] and by Zeng et al. [10]. The proposed model optimizes the discounted costs of all orders rather than the costs per order. Due to this fundamental difference, our model is more relevant to economic decision making and ensures symmetry in the decision process. Presenting practical application of models with different parameters, we also show how this model performs in real-life situations.

2. The Proposed Model of Lot Management with Time-Variant Cost Parameters

Inventory management is understood as the definition of optimal controllable parameters (time between deliveries t_s (time set up) and q (quantity, or optimal order size)) of logistics processes, at which the minimum total costs (TC) for the purchase, delivery, and storage of goods is achieved for a certain planned time interval [0, T]. If the uncontrollable parameters of the logistics process (purchase price p, delivery cost c_s, (cost set up) daily demand μ, and daily interest rate i ($r = i/100\%$) are known and constant throughout the entire planning interval, this problem can be solved by using Wilson economic-mathematical model EOQ (Economic Order Quantity):

$$TC(t_s) = pD + \frac{c_s T}{t_s} + \frac{1}{2}c_h D t_s \tag{1}$$

where D is the demand for the period (time interval) [0, T] ($D = \mu T$) and c_h is the cost of storing a unit of goods per day (holding cost).

The optimal time between deliveries (t_{so}) and optimal order quantity (q_o) are found according to the Wilson formula:

$$t_{so} = t_w = \sqrt{\frac{2c_s T}{c_h D}} \tag{2}$$

$$q_o = \mu t_{so} \tag{3}$$

Slesarenko and Nestorenko [49], and Nestorenko et al. [50] proposed the modified EOQ model:

$$TC(t_s) = (c_s + p\mu t_s)\frac{(1+r)^{t_s}\left((1+r)^T - 1\right)}{(1+r)^{t_s} - 1} \tag{4}$$

The optimal time between deliveries is found by the following formula:

$$t_{so} = \sqrt{\frac{2c_s}{rp\mu}} \tag{5}$$

The formula coincides with Wilson's Formula (2) if the storage cost is expressed as a percentage of the unit price ($c_h = p\mu$).

If the parameters of the logistic process change, the optimal solution is recalculated using Wilson's Formula (5), taking into account the changes. Based on the available information, it is possible to build forecasts for further economic processes of behavior. The use of this information in economic and mathematical models leads to an increase in their adequacy and accuracy.

Zeng et al. [10] proposed models of inventory management that allow for determining the optimal values of parameters in the case when it is known that daily demand has a linear trend ($\mu(t) = \mu + \omega t$, $t \in [0, T]$). To find those parameters, it is necessary to use Wilson's Formula (5), replacing the constant value of daily demand μ with the arithmetic mean of daily demand $\bar{\mu}$ for the planning period $[0, T]$ ($\bar{\mu} = \mu + 0.5\omega T$).

We further construct economic and mathematical models of inventory management that allow for determining the values of optimal controlled parameters in the case when it is known that uncontrolled cost parameters (delivery cost and/or price) have uniform relative trends ($c_s(t) = c_s(1 + \rho_c)^t$, $p(t) = p(1 + \rho_p)^t$, $t \in [0, T]$).

Model 1. *The inventory management model with a simultaneous equal percentage change in the costs of delivery and prices (inflationary model).*

In the EOQ model, the uncontrollable cost parameters as the cost of delivery ($c_s = const$) and price ($p = const$) for the period $[0, T]$ will be replaced by the assumption that the cost of delivery and the price simultaneously change uniformly with equal percentage change ($c_s(t) = c_s(1 + \rho)^t$, $p(t) = p(1 + \rho)^t$, $t \in [0, T]$). It is an inflationary process when $\rho > 0$ and a deflationary one when $\rho < 0$.

The logistics process of purchasing, delivering, and storing goods with constant time between deliveries can be described by the following formula:

$$TC(t_s) = (c_s + p\mu t_s)(1 + r)^{nt_s} + \left(c_s(1 + \rho)^{t_s} + p(1 + \rho)^{t_s}\mu t_s\right)(1 + r)^{(n-1)t_s} + \cdots \\ + \left(c_s(1 + \rho)^{(n-1)t_s} + p(1 + \rho)^{(n-1)t_s}\mu t_s\right)(1 + r)^{t_s} \tag{6}$$

where n is the number of deliveries of consignments of goods for the period $[0, T]$ ($n = T/t_s$). Replacing it, we get the following:

$$(1 + r)^{jt_s} = e^{\ln(1+r)jt_s}, \; (1 + \rho)^{jt_s} = e^{\ln(1+\rho)jt_s}, \; j = \overline{1, n}$$

After performing arithmetic transformations, we get the following:

$$TC(t_s) = (c_s + p\mu t_s)e^{\ln(1+r)T}\left(1 + e^{(\ln(1+\rho) - \ln(1+r))t_s} + \cdots + e^{(n-1)(\ln(1+\rho) - \ln(1+r))t_s}\right) \tag{7}$$

Using the formula for the sum of the first members of a geometric progression, we get the formula for total costs:

$$TC(t_s) = (c_s + p\mu t_s)\frac{(e^{\ln(1+r) - \ln(1+\rho)})^T - 1)e^{\ln(1+\rho)T}}{e^{(\ln(1+r) - \ln(1+\rho))t_s} - 1} \tag{8}$$

The minimum total cost is obtained as follows:

$$\frac{dTC(t_s)}{dt_s} = p\mu \frac{(e^{(\ln(1+r)-\ln(1+\rho))T}-1)e^{\ln(1+\rho)T}}{e^{(\ln(1+r)-\ln(1+\rho))t_s}-1} - (\ln(1+r))$$
$$- \ln(1+\rho))(c_s + p\mu t_s) \frac{e^{(\ln(1+r)-\ln(1+\rho))t_s}(e^{(\ln(1+r)-\ln(1+\rho))T}-1)e^{\ln(1+\rho)T}}{\left(e^{(\ln(1+r)-\ln(1+\rho))t_s}-1\right)^2} \quad (9)$$
$$= 0$$

After transformations, the equation is as follows:

$$e^{(\ln(1+r)-\ln(1+\rho))t_s} - 1 = (\ln(1+r)-\ln(1+\rho))\left(\frac{c_s}{p\mu} + t_s\right) \quad (10)$$

The optimal time between deliveries of consignments of goods t_{so} is found from solving the nonlinear Equation (10). In order to find an approximate solution to Equation (10), we use the first three terms of the Maclaurin series [51] of the expansion of the function $y = e^x \approx 1 + x + 0.5x^2$ and the first term of the Maclaurin series of the expansion of the function $y = \ln(1+r) \approx r$.

$$t_{so} = t_s = \sqrt{\frac{2c_s}{(r-\rho)p\mu}} \quad (11)$$

Therefore, to determine the optimal time between deliveries of consignments of goods t_{so}, one can use Wilson's Formula (5), replacing r with the difference $r - \rho$.

Let $\alpha = \ln(1+\rho)/\ln(1+r) \approx \rho/r$. Then, Equation (11) can be written as follows:

$$t_{so} = \frac{t_w}{\sqrt{1-\alpha}} \quad (12)$$

The dependence of the optimal time between deliveries of consignments of goods t_{so} on α is shown in Figure 1. When $\alpha \geq \alpha_{max} = 1 - \frac{t_w^2}{T^2}$, it is necessary to purchase in the volume $q_o = \mu T$ and to deliver the goods once for the entire planning period of the logistic process. When $\alpha \leq \alpha_{min} = 1 - t_w^2$, it is necessary to purchase and deliver goods every day in the amount of $q_o = \mu$. When $\alpha_{min} < \alpha < \alpha_{max}$, it is necessary to purchase and deliver goods in $t_{so} = \frac{t_w}{\sqrt{1-\alpha}}$ days and in volume $q_o = \frac{\mu t_w}{\sqrt{1-\alpha}} = \frac{q_w}{\sqrt{1-\alpha}}$.

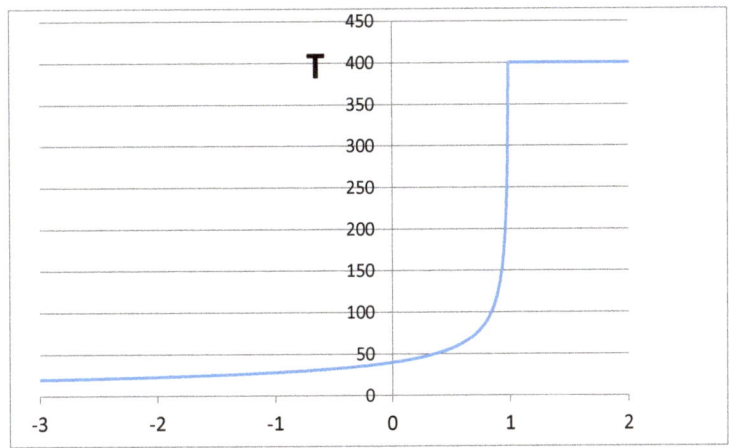

Figure 1. Dependence of the optimal time between deliveries of consignments of goods t_{so} on α.

Change in the dependence of total costs $TC(t_s, \alpha)$ on the time between deliveries of consignments of goods t_s for different values of α as well as the dependence of the minimum total costs $TC(t_{so}, \alpha)$ on the optimal time between deliveries of consignments of goods t_{so} for different values of α (black line and black squares) are shown in Figure 2.

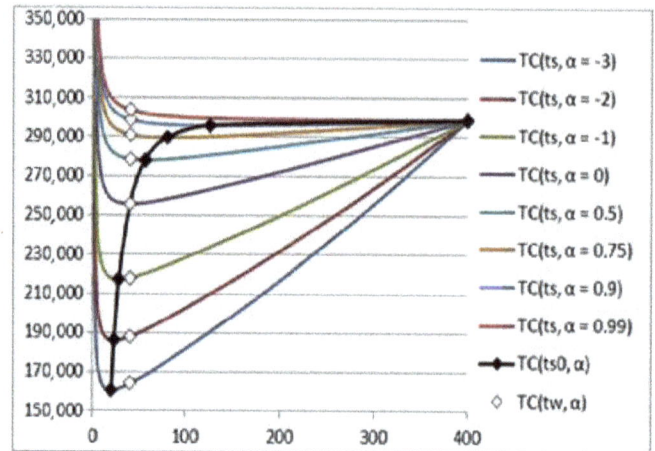

Figure 2. Dependence of total costs $TC(t_s, \alpha)$ on the time between deliveries of consignments of goods t_s for different α values; dependence of the minimum total costs $TC(t_{so}, \alpha)$ on the optimal time between deliveries of consignments of goods t_{so} for different values α; and the value of the total costs $TC(t_w, \alpha)$ for the time between deliveries of the consignment t_w for different α values.

Note: If we determine the values of the controlled parameters at i moment ($i = 1, 2, 3 \ldots$) of decision-making according to Wilson's Formula (5), we get the same time between deliveries equal to t_w:

$$t_{si} = \sqrt{\frac{2c_s(1+\rho)^{t_{si}}}{rp(1+\rho)^{t_{si}}\mu}} = \sqrt{\frac{2c_s}{rp\mu}} = t_w, \ i = 1, 2, 3 \ldots \quad (13)$$

This option on making decision is not optimal (differs from (11)). The result of using this option for different values of α (white squares) is also shown in Figure 2

Model 2. *The inventory management model with the percentage change in the cost of delivery.*

In the EOQ model, the assumption about constancy of the uncontrolled parameter delivery cost ($c_s = const$) for the period $[0, T]$ is replaced by the assumption in which the delivery cost changes uniformly according to the regularity $c_s(t) = c_s(1 + \rho_c)^t$, $t \in [0, T]$. If $\rho_c > 0$, there is an increase in the cost of delivery; if $\rho_c < 0$, there is a decrease.

Then, the logistics process of purchasing, delivering, and storing goods with constant time between deliveries can be described by the following formula:

$$TC(t_s) = (c_s + p\mu t_s)(1+r)^{nt_s} + \left(c_s(1+\rho_c)^{t_s} + p\mu t_s\right)(1+r)^{(n-1)t_s} + \cdots$$
$$+ \left(c_s(1+\rho_c)^{(n-1)t_s} + p\mu t_s\right)(1+r)^{t_s} \quad (14)$$

where n is the number of deliveries of consignments of goods for the period $[0, T]$ ($n = T/t_s$).

Replacing it, we get the following:

$$(1+r)^{jt_s} = e^{\ln(1+r)jt_s}, \ (1+\rho_c)^{jt_s} = e^{\ln(1+\rho_c)jt_s}, \ j = \overline{1, n}$$

After performing arithmetic transformations, we get the following:

$$TC(t_s) = e^{\ln(1+r)T}(c_s(1 + e^{(\ln(1+\rho_c)-\ln(1+r))t_s} + \cdots + e^{(n-1)(\ln(1+\rho_c)-\ln(1+r))t_s}) \\ + p\mu t_s(1 + e^{-\ln(1+r)t_s} + \cdots + e^{-\ln(1+r)(n-1)t_s})) \quad (15)$$

Using the formula for the sum of the first members of a geometric progression, we get the formula for total costs:

$$TC(t_s) = c_s \frac{e^{(\ln(1+r)-\ln(1+\rho_c))t_s}\left(e^{\ln(1+r)T} - e^{\ln(1+\rho_c)T}\right)}{e^{(\ln(1+r)-\ln(1+\rho_c))t_s} - 1} + p\mu t_s \frac{e^{\ln(1+r)t_s}\left(e^{\ln(1+r)T} - 1\right)}{e^{\ln(1+r)t_s} - 1} \quad (16)$$

The minimum total costs is as follows:

$$\frac{dTC(t_s)}{dt_s} = p\mu \frac{e^{\ln(1+r)t_s}\left(e^{\ln(1+r)T}-1\right)}{e^{\ln(1+r)t_s}-1} - \ln(1+r)p\mu t_s \frac{e^{\ln(1+r)t_s}\left(e^{\ln(1+r)T}-1\right)}{\left(e^{\ln(1+r)t_s}-1\right)^2} \\ - c_s \frac{(\ln(1+r)-\ln(1+\rho_c))e^{(\ln(1+r)-\ln(1+\rho_c))t_s}\left(e^{\ln(1+r)T}-e^{\ln(1+\rho_c)T}\right)}{\left(e^{(\ln(1+r)-\ln(1+\rho_c))t_s}-1\right)^2} = 0 \quad (17)$$

After transformations, the equation is as follows:

$$e^{\ln(1+r)t_s} - 1 - \ln(1+r)t_s \\ = \frac{c_s}{p\mu} \frac{(\ln(1+r)-\ln(1+\rho_c))\left(e^{\ln(1+r)t_s}-1\right)^2}{e^{\ln(1+\rho_c)}\left(e^{(\ln(1+r)-\ln(1+\rho_c))t_s}-1\right)^2} \frac{\left(e^{\ln(1+r)T}-e^{\ln(1+\rho_c)T}\right)}{\left(e^{\ln(1+r)T}-1\right)} \quad (18)$$

In model 2, the optimal time between deliveries of consignments of goods t_{so} is also found from the solution of the nonlinear Equation (18). In order to find an approximate solution of Equation (18), we use the first three terms of the Maclaurin series of the expansion of the function $y = e^x \approx 1 + x + 0.5x^2$ and the first term of the Maclaurin series of the expansion of the function $y = \ln(1+r) \approx r$.

$$t_{so} = t_s = \sqrt{\frac{2c_s(1+\rho_c)^{\frac{1}{2}T}}{r p \mu}} \quad (19)$$

Consequently, to determine the optimal time between deliveries of consignments of goods t_{so}, one can use Wilson's Formula (5), replacing the constant value of the delivery cost c_s with the geometric mean of the delivery cost $\bar{c_s}$ for the planning period $[0, T]$ ($\bar{c_s} = \sqrt{c_s c_s (1+\rho_c)^T} = c_s(1+\rho_c)^{\frac{1}{2}T}$).

$$t_{so} = (1+\rho_c)^{\frac{1}{4}T} t_w \quad (20)$$

Let $\alpha_c = \ln(1+\rho_c)/\ln(1+r)$; then Equation (20) can be represented in this form:

$$t_{so} = (1+r)^{\frac{1}{4}\alpha_c T} t_w \quad (21)$$

The dependence of the optimal time between deliveries of consignments of goods t_{so} on α_c is shown in Figure 3.

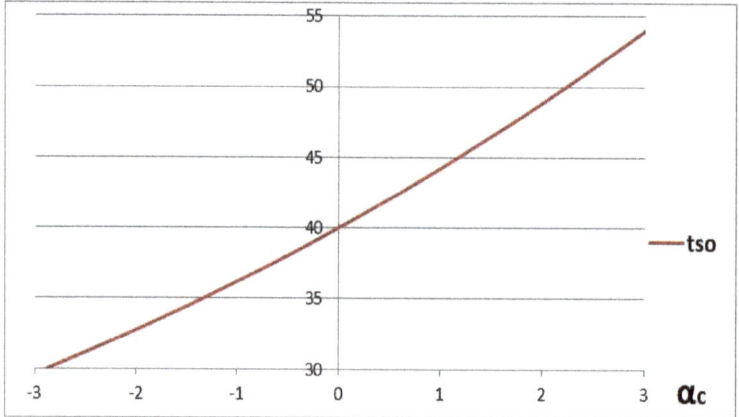

Figure 3. The dependence of optimal time between deliveries of consignments of goods t_{so} on α_c.

The change in the dependence of total costs $TC(t_s, \alpha_c)$ on the time between deliveries of consignments of goods t_s for different α_c values as well as the dependence of the minimum total costs $TC(t_{so}, \alpha_c)$ on the optimal time between deliveries of consignments of goods t_{so} for different α_c values (black line and black squares) are shown in Figure 4.

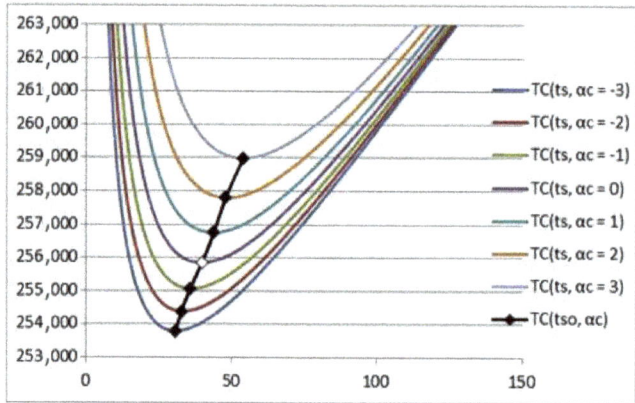

Figure 4. The dependence of total costs $TC(t_s, \alpha_c)$ on the time between deliveries of consignments of goods t_s for different α_c values and the dependence of the minimum total costs $TC(t_{so}, \alpha_c)$ on the optimal time between deliveries of consignments of goods t_{so} for different α_c values (black line and black squares).

Model 3. *Inventory management model with a percentage change in the price of goods.*

In the EOQ model, the assumption of the constancy of the uncontrollable parameter of the product price ($p = const$) for the period $[0, T]$ is replaced by the assumption that the price of the product changes uniformly according to the order that $p(t) = c_p(1 + \rho_p)^t$, $t \in [0, T]$). If $\rho_p > 0$, there is an increase in the price of goods, and if $\rho_p < 0$, there is a decrease.

To construct model 3, we will use the results from constructing model 1 (8) and model 2 (16). We represent the change (increase/decrease) in the price as a combination of two processes—the change (increase/decrease) in the price and delivery cost (model 1) and the simultaneous change (decrease/increase) in the delivery cost (model 2) by the same number of times. A change in the price and delivery cost, according to model 1, will lead to the replacement of $\ln(1+r)$ to $\ln(1+r) - \ln(1+\rho_p)$ in Formula (16) and will be multiplied by $e^{\ln(1+\rho_p)T}$. To compensate for the change in the cost of delivery, according to model 2, we make a replacement $1 + \rho_c = 1/(1+\rho_p)$:

$$TC(t_s) = c_s \frac{e^{\ln(1+r)t_s}\left(e^{\ln(1+r)T} - 1\right)}{e^{\ln(1+r)t_s} - 1} + p\mu t_s \frac{e^{(\ln(1+r) - \ln(1+\rho_p))t_s}\left(e^{(\ln(1+r) - \ln(1+\rho_p))T} - 1\right)e^{\ln(1+\rho_p)T}}{e^{(\ln(1+r) - \ln(1+\rho_p))t_s} - 1} \tag{22}$$

The minimum total cost is found as follows:

$$\frac{dTC(t_s)}{dt_s} = -c_s \frac{\ln(1+r)e^{\ln(1+r)t_s}\left(e^{\ln(1+r)T} - 1\right)}{\left(e^{\ln(1+r)t_s} - 1\right)^2} + p\mu \frac{e^{(\ln(1+r) - \ln(1+\rho_p))t_s}\left(e^{(\ln(1+r) - \ln(1+\rho_p))T} - 1\right)e^{\ln(1+\rho_p)T}}{e^{(\ln(1+r) - \ln(1+\rho_p))t_s} - 1} - p\mu t_s \frac{(\ln(1+r) - \ln(1+\rho_p))e^{(\ln(1+r) - \ln(1+\rho_p))t_s}\left(e^{(\ln(1+r) - \ln(1+\rho_p))T} - 1\right)e^{\ln(1+\rho_p)T}}{\left(e^{(\ln(1+r) - \ln(1+\rho_p))t_s} - 1\right)^2} = 0 \tag{23}$$

After transformations, the equation is as follows:

$$\frac{e^{(\ln(1+r) - \ln(1+\rho_p))t_s} - 1 - (\ln(1+r) - \ln(1+\rho_p))t_s}{\left(e^{\ln(1+r)t_s} - 1\right)^2 \left(e^{(\ln(1+r) - \ln(1+\rho_p))T} - 1\right)e^{\ln(1+\rho_p)T}} = \frac{c_s}{p\mu} \frac{\ln(1+r)e^{\ln(1+\rho_p)t_s}\left(e^{(\ln(1+r) - \ln(1+\rho_p))t_s} - 1\right)^2 \left(e^{\ln(1+r)T} - 1\right)}{\left(e^{\ln(1+r)t_s} - 1\right)^2 \left(e^{(\ln(1+r) - \ln(1+\rho_p))T} - 1\right)e^{\ln(1+\rho_p)T}} \tag{24}$$

We repeat the previously mentioned procedure: the optimal time between deliveries of consignments of goods t_{so} is found from the solution of the nonlinear Equation (24). In order to find an approximate solution of Equation (24), we use the first three terms of the Maclaurin series of the expansion of the function $y = e^x \approx 1 + x + 0.5x^2$ and the first term of the Maclaurin series of the expansion of the function $y = \ln(1+r) \approx r$.

$$t_s = \sqrt{\frac{2c_s}{(r - \rho_p)pe^{\frac{1}{2}\ln(1+\rho_p)T}\mu}} \tag{25}$$

Consequently, to determine the optimal time between deliveries of consignments of goods t_{so}, one can use Wilson's Formula (5), replacing r by the difference $r - \rho$ and the constant value of the price of goods p with the geometric mean of the price of goods $\bar{p}$ for the planning period $[0, T]$ ($\bar{p} = \sqrt{pp(1+\rho_p)^T} = p(1+\rho_p)^{\frac{1}{2}T}$).
Let $\alpha_p = \ln(1+\rho_p)/\ln(1+r)$; then Equation (25) can be represented as follows:

$$t_{so} = \frac{t_w}{(1+\rho_p)^{\frac{1}{4}T}\sqrt{1-\alpha_p}} \tag{26}$$

or

$$t_{so} = \frac{t_w}{(1+r)^{\frac{1}{4}\alpha_p T}\sqrt{1-\alpha_p}} \tag{27}$$

The dependence of the optimal time between deliveries of consignments of goods t_{so} on $α_c$ is shown in Figure 5.

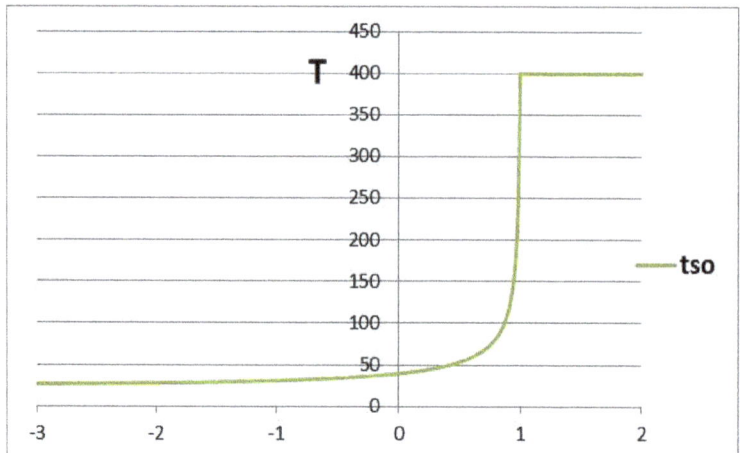

Figure 5. The dependence of the optimal time between deliveries of consignments of goods t_{so} on $α_c$.

The change in the dependence of total costs $TC(t_s, α_p)$ on the time between deliveries of consignments of goods t_s for different $α_p$ values as well as the dependence of the minimum total costs $TC(t_{so}, α_p)$ on the optimal time between deliveries of consignments of goods t_{so} for different $α_p$ values (black line and black squares) are shown in Figure 6.

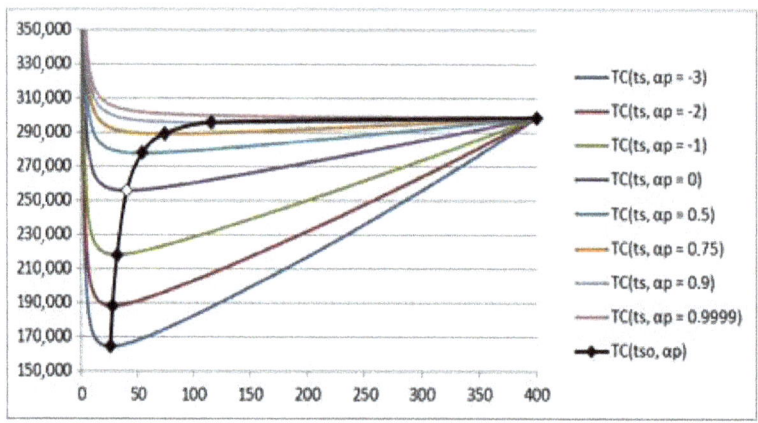

Figure 6. The dependence of total costs $TC(t_s, α_p)$ on the time between deliveries of consignments of goods t_s for different $α_p$ values and the dependence of the minimum total costs $TC(t_{so}, α_p)$ on the optimal time between deliveries of consignments of goods t_{so} for different $α_p$ values (black line and black squares).

Model 4. *Inventory management model with a different percentage change in the price of goods.*

In the EOQ model, the assumption of the constancy of the uncontrollable parameter of the product price ($p = const$) for the period $[0, T]$ is replaced by the assumption that the price of the product changes uniformly according to the order that $p(t) = c_p(1 + \rho_p)^t$, $t \in [0, T]$). If $\rho_p > 0$, there is an increase in the price of goods, and if $\rho_p < 0$, there is a decrease.

To construct model 4, we will use the results from constructing model 1 (8) and model 2 (16). We represent the change (increase/decrease) in the price as a combination of two processes—the change (increase/decrease) in the price and delivery cost (model 1) and the simultaneous change (decrease/increase) in the delivery cost by a certain number of times. A change in the price and delivery cost, according to model 1, will lead to the replacement of $\ln(1 + r)$ to $\ln(1 + r) - \ln(1 + \rho_p)$ in Formula (16) and will be multiplied by $e^{\ln(1+\rho_p)T}$. The change in the cost of delivery, according to model 2, we will receive by replacement of $1 + \rho_c = (1 + \rho_c)/(1 + \rho_p)$:

$$TC(t_s) = c_s \frac{e^{(\ln(1+r)-\ln(1+\rho_c))t_s}\left(e^{(\ln(1+r)-\ln(1+\rho_c))T} - 1\right)e^{\ln(1+\rho_c)T}}{e^{(\ln(1+r)-\ln(1+\rho_c))t_s} - 1}$$
$$+ p\mu t_s \frac{e^{(\ln(1+r)-\ln(1+\rho_p))t_s}\left(e^{(\ln(1+r)-\ln(1+\rho_p))T} - 1\right)e^{\ln(1+\rho_p)T}}{e^{(\ln(1+r)-\ln(1+\rho_p))t_s} - 1} \quad (28)$$

The minimum total costs are found as follows:

$$\frac{dTC(t_s)}{dt_s}$$
$$= p\mu \frac{e^{(\ln(1+r)-\ln(1+\rho_p))t_s}\left(e^{(\ln(1+r)-\ln(1+\rho_p))T}-1\right)e^{\ln(1+\rho_p)T}}{e^{(\ln(1+r)-\ln(1+\rho_p))t_s}-1}$$
$$- c_s \frac{(\ln(1+r)-\ln(1+\rho_c))e^{(\ln(1+r)-\ln(1+\rho_c))t_s}\left(e^{(\ln(1+r)-\ln(1+\rho_c))T}-1\right)e^{\ln(1+\rho_c)T}}{\left(e^{(\ln(1+r)-\ln(1+\rho_c))t_s}-1\right)^2} \quad (29)$$
$$p\mu t_s \frac{(\ln(1+r)-\ln(1+\rho_p))e^{(\ln(1+r)-\ln(1+\rho_p))t_s}\left(e^{(\ln(1+r)-\ln(1+\rho_p))T}-1\right)e^{\ln(1+\rho_p)T}}{\left(e^{(\ln(1+r)-\ln(1+\rho_p))t_s}-1\right)^2} = 0$$

After transformations, the equation appears as follows:

$$e^{(\ln(1+r)-\ln(1+\rho_p))t_s} - 1 - \left(\ln(1+r) - \ln(1+\rho_p)\right)t_s$$
$$= \frac{c_s}{p\mu} \frac{(\ln(1+r)-\ln(1+\rho_c))e^{(\ln(1+\rho_p)-\ln(1+\rho_c))t_s}\left(e^{(\ln(1+r)-\ln(1+\rho_p))t_s}-1\right)^2\left(e^{\ln(1+r)T}-e^{\ln(1+\rho_c)T}\right)}{\left(e^{(\ln(1+r)-\ln(1+\rho_c))t_s}-1\right)^2\left(e^{\ln(1+r)T}-e^{\ln(\rho_p)T}\right)} \quad (30)$$

The optimal time between deliveries of consignments of goods t_{so} is found from the solution of the nonlinear Equation (30). In order to find an approximate solution of Equation (30), we use the first three terms of the Maclaurin series of the expansion of the function $y = e^x \approx 1 + x + 0.5x^2$ and the first term of the Maclaurin series of the expansion of the function $y = \ln(1 + r) \approx r$.

$$t_{so} = t_s = \sqrt{\frac{2c_s(1+\rho_c)^{\frac{1}{2}T}}{(r-\rho_p)p(1+\rho_p)^{\frac{1}{2}T}\mu}} \quad (31)$$

Consequently, to determine the optimal time between deliveries of consignments of goods t_{so}, one can use Wilson's Formula (5), replacing r by the difference $r - \rho$ and the constant value of the price of goods p with the geometric mean of the price of goods $\bar{p}$ for the planning period $[0, T]$ ($\bar{p} = \sqrt{pp(1+\rho_p)^T} = p(1+\rho_p)^{\frac{1}{2}T}$) and the constant value of the product price c_s by geometric mean value of the product price $\bar{c_s}$ for the planning period $[0, T]$ ($\bar{c_s} = \sqrt{c_s c_s(1+\rho_c)^T} = c_s(1+\rho_c)^{\frac{1}{2}T}$).

Let $\alpha_p = \ln(1+\rho_p)/\ln(1+r)$ and $\alpha_c = \ln(1+\rho_c)/\ln(1+r)$; then Equation (31) can be represented as follows:

$$t_{so} = \frac{(1+\rho_c)^{\frac{1}{4}T}}{(1+\rho_p)^{\frac{1}{4}T}} \frac{t_w}{\sqrt{1-\alpha_p}} \quad (32)$$

or

$$t_{so} = (1+r)^{\frac{1}{4}(\alpha_c - \alpha_p)T} \frac{t_w}{\sqrt{1 - \alpha_p}} \qquad (33)$$

The dependence of the optimal time between deliveries of consignments of goods t_{so} on α_c and α_p is shown in Figure 7.

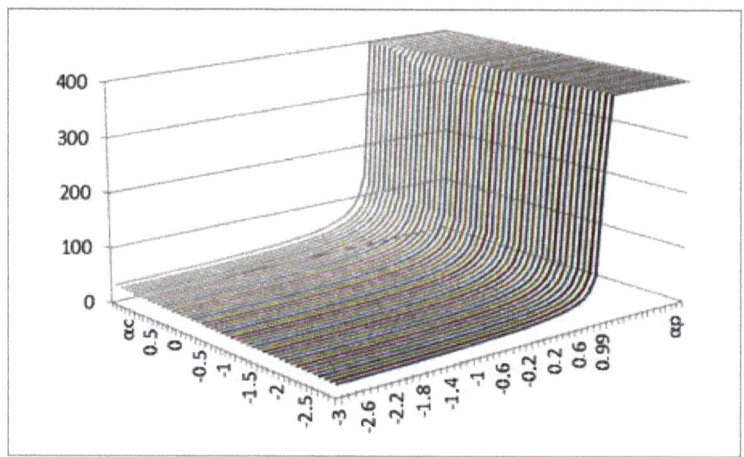

Figure 7. The dependence of the optimal time between deliveries of consignments of goods t_{so} on α_c and α_p.

The change in the dependence of the total costs $TC(t_s, \alpha_c = -3, \alpha_p)$ with a decrease in the cost of delivery ($\alpha_c = -3$) on the time between deliveries of consignments of goods t_s at different α_p values as well as the dependence of the minimum total costs $TC(t_{so}, \alpha_c = -3, \alpha_p)$ on the optimal time between deliveries of consignments of goods t_{so} for different α_p values (black line and black squares) are shown in Figure 8.

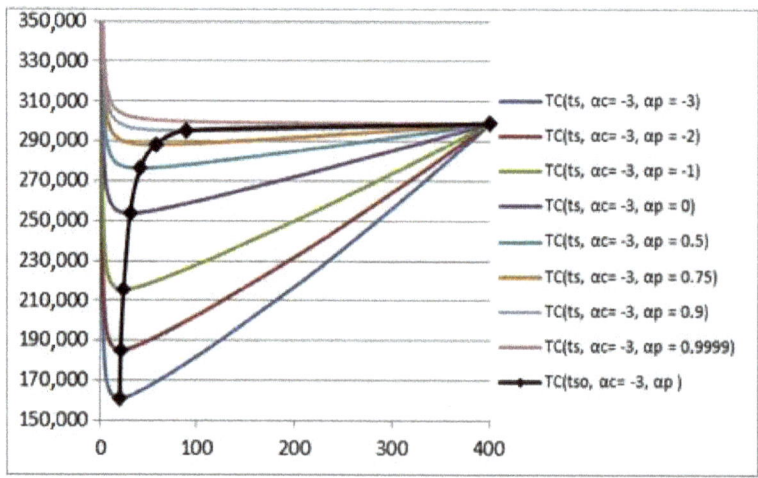

Figure 8. The dependence of the total costs $TC(t_s, \alpha_c = -3, \alpha_p)$ with a decrease in the cost of delivery ($\alpha_c = -3$) on the time between deliveries of consignments of goods t_s at different α_p values and the dependence of the minimum total costs $TC(t_{so}, \alpha_c = -3, \alpha_p)$ on the optimal time between deliveries of consignments of goods t_{so} for different α_p values (black line and black squares).

The change in the dependence of total costs $TC(t_s, \alpha_c = 0, \alpha_p)$ at constant delivery cost ($\alpha_c = 0$) on the time between deliveries of consignments of goods t_s for different α_p values as well as the dependence of the minimum total costs $TC(t_{so}, \alpha_c = 0, \alpha_p)$ on the optimal time between deliveries of consignments of goods t_{so} for different α_p values (black line and black squares) are shown in Figure 6.

The change in the dependence of total costs $TC(t_s, \alpha_c = 3, \alpha_p)$ with an increase in the cost of delivery ($\alpha_c = 3$) on the time between deliveries of consignments of goods t_s for different α_p values as well as the dependence of the minimum total costs $TC(t_{so}, \alpha_c = 3, \alpha_p)$ on the optimal time between deliveries of consignments of goods t_{so} for different α_p values (black line and black squares) are shown in Figure 9.

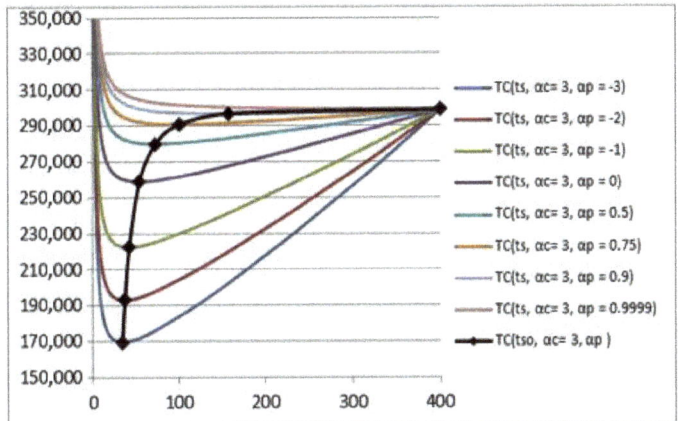

Figure 9. The dependence of total costs $TC(t_s, \alpha_c = 3, \alpha_p)$ with an increase in the cost of delivery ($\alpha_c = 3$) on the time between deliveries of consignments of goods t_s for different α_p values and the dependence of the minimum total costs $TC(t_{so}, \alpha_c = 3, \alpha_p)$ on the optimal time between deliveries of consignments of goods t_{so} for different α_p values (black line and black squares).

Model 4 is a generalization of models 1–3:

for $\alpha_c = \alpha_p$ we obtain model 1;
for $\alpha_p = 0$ we obtain model 2; and
for $\alpha_c = 0$ we obtain model 3.

Further, we provide some examples of the differences that arise when using models 1–4 and the modified EOQ model.

3. Empirical illustration

Model 1

If at the beginning of the period [0, T], uncontrollable parameters of the logistic process such as T = 400 days, r = 0.001, and μ = 25 units/day are known and the cost of delivery and the price increases equally during the period [0, T] with ρ = 0.00075, then the growth pattern will be $c_s(t) = 400 * 1.00075^t$, $p(t) = 20 * 1.00075^t$, $t \in [0, T](\alpha = 0.75)$.

When using the EOQ model, excluding the increase in delivery costs and prices, the time between deliveries will be the following:

$$t_w = \sqrt{\frac{2 * 400}{0.001 * 20 * 25}} = 40 \text{ days}$$

The total purchase, delivery, and storage costs for 400 days are as follows:

$$TC_w = (400 + 20 * 25 * 40) * 1.001^{400} + (400 * 1.00075^{40} + 20 * 1.00075^{40} * 25 * 40) * 1.001^{360} + \cdots + \left(400 * 1.00075^{360} + 20 * 1.00075^{360} * 25 * 40\right) * 1.001^{40} =$$
$$290911 \text{ EUR}$$

When applying model 1, the time between deliveries is found by Formula (12):

$$t_{so} = \frac{40}{\sqrt{1 - 0.75}} = 80 \text{ days}$$

The total purchase, delivery, and storage costs for 400 days are as follows:

$$TC_o = (400 + 20 * 25 * 80) * 1.001^{400} + (400 * 1.00075^{80} + 20 * 1.00075^{80} * 25 * 80) * 1.001^{320} + \cdots + (400 * 1.00075^{320} + 20 * 1.00075^{320} * 25 * 80) * 1.001^{80} =$$
$$289600 \text{ EUR}$$

The savings will be as follows:

$$\Delta TC = 290911 - 289600 = 1311 \text{ EUR}$$

If the cost of delivery and the price decrease equally during the period [0, T] with $\rho = -0.003$, the growth pattern has the following form: $c_s(t) = 400 * 0.997^t$, $p(t) = 20 * 0.997^t$, $t \in [0, T]$ ($\alpha = -3$).

When using the EOQ model, excluding the reduction in delivery costs and prices, the time between deliveries will be $t_w = 40$ days.

The total purchase, delivery, and storage costs for 400 days are as follows:

$$TC_w = (400 + 20 * 25 * 40) * 1.001^{400} + (400 * 0.997^{40} + 20 * 0.997^{40} * 25 * 40) * 1.001^{360} + \cdots + (400 * 0.997^{360} + 20 * 0.997^{360} * 25 * 40) * 1.001^{40} = 164156 \text{ EUR}$$

When applying model 1, the time between deliveries is found by Formula (12):

$$t_{so} = \frac{40}{\sqrt{1 + 3}} = 20 \text{ days}$$

The total purchase, delivery, and storage costs for 400 days are as follows:

$$TC_o = (400 + 20 * 25 * 20) * 1.001^{400} + (400 * 0.997^{20} + 20 * 0.997^{20} * 25 * 20) * 1.001^{380} + \cdots + (400 * 0.997^{380} + 20 * 0.997^{380} * 25 * 20) * 1.001^{20} = 160934 \text{ EUR}$$

The savings will be as follows:

$$\Delta TC = 164156 - 160934 = 3222 \text{ EUR}$$

Model 2

If at the beginning of the period [0, T] uncontrollable parameters of the logistic process such as T = 400 days, r = 0.001, µ = 25 units/day, and p = 20 EUR/unit are known and the cost of delivery increases during the period [0, T] with $\rho = 0.00075$, then the growth pattern will be $c_s(t) = 400 * 1.0023^t$, $t \in [0, T]$ ($\alpha_c = 2.3$).

When using the EOQ model, excluding the increase in delivery costs, the time between deliveries will be $t_w = 40$ days.

The total purchase, delivery, and storage costs for 400 days are as follows:

$$TC_w = (400 + 20 * 25 * 40) * 1.001^{400} + (400 * 1.0022^{40} + 20 * 25 * 40) *$$
$$1.001^{360} + \cdots + (400 * 1.0022^{360} + 20 * 25 * 40) * 1.001^{40} = 258365 \text{ EUR}$$

When applying model 2, the time between deliveries is found by Formula (20):

$$t_{so} = 1.0023^{100} * 40 = 50 \text{ days}$$

The total purchase, delivery, and storage costs for 400 days are as follows:

$$TC_o = (400 + 20 * 25 * 50) * 1.001^{400} + (400 * 1.0022^{50} + 20 * 25 * 50) *$$
$$1.001^{350} + \cdots + (400 * 1.0022^{320} + 20 * 25 * 50) * 1.001^{50} = 258068 \text{ EUR}$$

The savings will be as follows:

$$\Delta TC = 258365 - 258068 = 297 \text{EUR}$$

If the cost of delivery decreases during the period $[0, T]$ with $\rho_c = -0.0018$, the growth pattern has the form $c_s(t) = 400 * 0.9982^t$, $t \in [0, T]$ ($\alpha_c = -1.8$).

When using the EOQ model, excluding delivery cost reduction, the time between deliveries will be $t_w = 40$ days.

The total purchase, delivery, and storage costs for 400 days are as follows:

$$TC_w = (400 + 20 * 25 * 40) * 1.001^{400} + (400 * 0.9982^{40} + 20 * 25 * 40) *$$
$$1.001^{360} + \cdots + (400 * 0.9982^{360} + 20 * 25 * 40) * 1.001^{40} = 254627 \text{ EUR}$$

When applying model 2, the time between deliveries is found by Formula (20):

$$t_{so} = 0.9982^{100} * 40 = 33 \text{ days}$$

The total purchase, delivery, and storage costs for 400 days are as follows:

$$TC_o = (400 + 20 * 25 * 33) * 1.001^{400} + (400 * 0.9982^{33} + 20 * 25 * 33)$$
$$*1.001^{367} + \cdots + (400 * 0.9982^{367} + 20 * 25 * 33) * 1.001^{33} = 254513 \text{ EUR}$$

The savings will be as follows:

$$\Delta TC = 254627 - 254513 = 114 \text{ EUR.}$$

Model 3

If at the beginning of the period $[0, T]$ uncontrollable parameters of the logistic process such as T = 400 days, r = 0.001, µ = 25 units/day, and c_s = 25EUR are known and the price increases during the period $[0, T]$ with $\rho_p = 0.000786$, then the growth pattern will be $p(t) = 20 * 1.000786^t$, $t \in [0, T]$ ($\alpha_p = 0.786$).

When using the EOQ model without considering the price increase, the time between deliveries will be $t_w = 40$ days.

The total purchase, delivery, and storage costs for 400 days are as follows:

$$TC_w = (400 + 20 * 25 * 40) * 1.001^{400} + (400 + 20 * 1.000786^{40} * 25 * 40) *$$
$$1.001^{360} + \cdots + (400 + 20 * 1.000786^{360} * 25 * 40) * 1.001^{40} = 292146 \text{ EUR}$$

237

When applying model 3, the time between deliveries is found by Formula (26):

$$t_{so} = \frac{40}{1.000786^{100} \sqrt{1-0.786}} = 80 \text{ days}$$

The total purchase, delivery, and storage costs for 400 days are as follows:

$$TC_o = (400 + 20 * 25 * 80) * 1.001^{400} + (400 + 20 * 1.000786^{80} * 25 * 80) *$$
$$1.001^{320} + \cdots + (400 + 20 * 1.000786^{320} * 25 * 80) * 1.001^{80} = 290915 \text{ EUR}$$

The savings will be as follows:

$$\Delta TC = 292146 - 290915 = 1331 \text{ EUR}$$

If the price decreases during the period $[0, T]$ with $\rho_p = -0.003$, the growth pattern has the form $p(t) = 20 * 0.997^t$, $t \in [0, T]$ ($\alpha_p = -3$).
With the EOQ model, excluding price reductions, the time between deliveries will be $t_w = 40$ days.
The total purchase, delivery, and storage costs for 400 days are as follows:

$$TC_w = (400 + 20 * 25 * 40) * 1.001^{400} + (400 + 20 * 0.997^{40} * 25 * 40) * 1.001^{360} +$$
$$\cdots + (400 + 20 * 0.997^{360} * 25 * 40) * 1.001^{40} = 165954 \text{ EUR}$$

When applying model 3, the time between deliveries is found by Formula (26):

$$t_{so} = \frac{40}{0.997^{100} \sqrt{1+3}} = 25 \text{ days}$$

The total purchase, delivery, and storage costs for 400 days are as follows:

$$TC_o = (400 + 20 * 25 * 25) * 1.001^{400} + (400 + 20 * 0.997^{25} * 25 * 25) * 1.001^{375} +$$
$$\cdots + (400 + 20 * 0.997^{375} * 25 * 25) * 1.001^{25} = 164244 \text{ EUR}$$

The savings will be as follows:

$$\Delta TC = 165954 - 164244 = 1730 \text{ EUR}$$

Model 4

If at the beginning of the period $[0, T]$ uncontrollable parameters of the logistic process such as T = 400 days, r = 0.001, and µ = 25 units/day are known and the cost of delivery and the price increase during the period $[0, T]$ with $\rho_c = 0.003$, $\rho_p = 0.00075$, then the growth pattern will be $c_s(t) = 400 * 1.003^t$, $p(t) = 20 * 1.00075^t$, $t \in [0, T]$ ($\alpha_c = 3$, $\alpha_p = 0.75$).
When using the EOQ model, excluding the increase in delivery costs and prices, the time between deliveries will be $t_w = 40$ days.
The total purchase, delivery, and storage costs for 400 days are as follows:

$$TC_w = (400 + 20 * 25 * 40) * 1.001^{400} + (400 * 1.003^{40} + 20 * 1.00075^{40} * 25 *$$
$$40) * 1.001^{360} + \cdots + (400 * 1.003^{360} + 20 * 1.00075^{360} * 25 * 40) * 1.001^{40}$$
$$= 294083 \text{ EUR}$$

When applying model 4, the time between deliveries is found by Formula (32):

$$t_{so} = \frac{1.003^{100}}{1.00075^{100}} \frac{40}{\sqrt{1-0.75}} = 100 \text{ days}$$

The total purchase, delivery, and storage costs for 400 days are as follows:

$$TC_0 = (400 + 20 * 25 * 100) * 1.001^{400} + (400 * 1.003^{100} + 20 * 1.00075^{100} * 25 * 80) * 1.001^{300} + \cdots + (400 * 1.003^{300} + 20 * 1.00075^{300} * 25 * 80) * 1.001^{100} = $$
$$290748 \text{ EUR}$$

The savings will be as follows:

$$\Delta TC = 294083 - 290748 = 3335 \text{ EUR}$$

If the cost of delivery decreases and the price increases during the period $[0, T]$ with $\rho_c = -0.0039$, $\rho_p = 0.00075$, the growth pattern has the form $c_s(t) = 400 * 0.9961^t$, $p(t) = 20 * 1.00075^t$, $t \in [0, T]$ ($\alpha_c = -3.9$, $\alpha_p = 0.75$).

When using the EOQ model, excluding the reduction in delivery costs and the increase in prices, the time between deliveries will be $t_w = 40$ days.

The total purchase, delivery, and storage costs for 400 days are as follows:

$$TC_w = (400 + 20 * 25 * 40) * 1.001^{400} + (400 * 0.9961^{40} + 20 * 1.00075^{40} * 25 * 40) * 1.001^{360} + \cdots + (400 * 0.9961^{360} + 20 * 1.00075^{360} * 25 * 40) * 1.001^{40} = $$
$$288180 \text{ EUR}$$

When applying model 4, the time between deliveries is found by Formula (32):

$$t_{so} = \frac{0.9961^{100}}{1.00075^{100}} \frac{40}{\sqrt{1 - 0.75}} = 50 \text{ days}$$

The total purchase, delivery, and storage costs for 400 days are as follows:

$$TC_o = (400 + 20 * 25 * 50) * 1.001^{400} + (400 * 0.9961^{50} + 20 * 1.00075^{50} * 25 * 50) * 1.001^{350} + \cdots + (400 * 0.9961^{350} + 20 * 1.00075^{350} * 25 * 50) * 1.001^{50} = $$
$$288015 \text{ EUR}$$

The savings will be as follows:

$$\Delta TC = 288180 - 288015 = 165 \text{ EUR}$$

If the cost of delivery increases and the price decreases during the period $[0, T]$ with $\rho_c = 0.002$, $\rho_p = -0.003$, the growth pattern has the form $c_s(t) = 400 * 1.002^t$, $p(t) = 20 * 0.997^t$, $t \in [0, T]$ ($\alpha_c = 2$, $\alpha_p = -3$).

When using the EOQ model, excluding the increase in the cost of delivery and the decrease in the price, the time between deliveries will be $t_w = 40$ days.

The total purchase, delivery, and storage costs for 400 days are as follows:

$$TC_w = (400 + 20 * 25 * 40) * 1.001^{400} + (400 * 1.002^{40} + 20 * 0.997^{40} * 25 * 40) * 1.001^{360} + \cdots + (400 * 1.002^{360} + 20 * 0.997^{360} * 25 * 40) * 1.001^{40} = $$
$$168249 \text{ EUR}$$

When applying model 4, the time between deliveries is found by Formula (32):

$$t_{so} = \frac{1.002^{100}}{0.997^{100}} \frac{40}{\sqrt{1 + 3}} = 33 \text{ days}$$

The total purchase, delivery, and storage costs for 400 days are as follows:

$$TC_0 = (400 + 20 * 25 * 33) * 1.001^{400} + (400 * 1.002^{33} + 20 * 0.997^{33} * 25 * 33)*$$
$$1.001^{367} + \cdots + (400 * 1.002^{367} + 20 * 0.997^{367} * 25 * 33) * 1.001^{33} =$$
$$167620 \text{ EUR}$$

The savings will be as follows:

$$\Delta TC = 168249 - 167620 = 629 \text{ EUR}$$

If uncontrollable parameters of the logistic process such as T = 400 days, r = 0.001, and μ = 25 units/day are known at the beginning of the period [0, T] and the cost of delivery and the price are reduced during the period [0, T] with $\rho_c = -0.001$, $\rho_p = -0.003$, then the growth pattern will be: $c_s(t) = 400 * 0.999^t$, $p(t) = 20 * 0.997^t$, $t \in [0, T]$ ($\alpha_c = -1$, $\alpha_p = -3$).

When using the EOQ model, excluding the reduction in delivery costs and prices, the time between deliveries will be $t_w = 40$ days.

The total purchase, delivery and storage costs for 400 days are as follows:

$$TC_w = (400 + 20 * 25 * 40) * 1.001^{400} + (400 * 0.999^{40} + 20 * 0.997^{40} * 25 * 40)*$$
$$1.001^{360} + \cdots + (400 * 0.999^{360} + 20 * 0.997^{360} * 25 * 40) * 1.001^{40} =$$
$$165335 \text{ EUR}$$

When applying model 4, the time between deliveries is found by Formula (32):

$$t_{so} = \frac{0.999^{100}}{0.997^{100}} \frac{40}{\sqrt{1+3}} = 25 \text{ days}$$

The total purchase, delivery, and storage costs for 400 days are as follows:

$$TC_o = (400 + 20 * 25 * 25) * 1.001^{400} + (400 * 0.999^{25} + 20 * 0.997^{25} * 25 * 25)*$$
$$1.001^{375} + \cdots + (400 * 0.999^{375} + 20 * 0.997^{375} * 25 * 25) * 1.001^{25} =$$
$$163141 \text{ EUR}$$

The savings will be as follows:

$$\Delta TC = 165335 - 163141 = 2194 \text{ EUR}$$

4. Conclusions

There is an abundance of EOQ models based on Wilson's formulation. Although differing in purpose, application type, or calculation principles and providing quite precise predictions for a demand per selected time interval, all these models contain the same drawback. Being based on a logic of calculating costs per one order and multiplying it by number of orders, they all fail to meet the current needs of business environments in order to be applied in practice.

We propose the modification of EOQ based on a different calculation technique which shows significant savings in warehouses costs under particular conditions.

From the proposed models, the most significant savings were observed using the 2nd variation of the first proposed model and accounted for approximately 2% of all inventory costs. The highest potential for application in practice shows the first and second variations of a fourth model due to the ability to cope with the most uncontrolled variables as the retail sector is characterized by constant shifts in demand and supply which are reflected in prices in a nonlinear manner [52]. The savings in this case would amount to 0.4% when the price of stored goods increases under particular conditions (first variation of a fourth model) and to 1.3% when price decreases (second variation of a fourth model) under researched conditions.

The limitations of our proposed models are comprised of delivery costs and price for goods to be described by uniform trend. Thus, in the future, the model could be extended to investigate the inventory management where exogenous parameters do not follow any uniform trend.

Author Contributions: Conceptualization, T.N. and J.P.; methodology, T.N. and M.M.; formal analysis, T.N. and A.V.; resources, D.S. and T.B.; writing—original draft preparation, T.N., A.V., and M.M.; writing—review and editing, T.B. and D.S. All authors have read and agreed to the published version of the manuscript.

Funding: This research received no external funding.

Conflicts of Interest: The authors declare no conflict of interest.

References

1. Shanshan, L.; Yong, H. Dynamic mitigation strategy for stock-out based on joint compensation and procurement. *J. Southeast Univ.* **2019**, *35*, 509–515. [CrossRef]
2. Rostamzadeh, R.; Esmaeili, A.; Shahriyari Nia, A.; Saparauskas, J.; Keshavarz Ghorabaee, M.K. A fuzzy ARAS method for supply chain management performance measurement in SMEs under uncertainty. *Transform. Bus. Econ.* **2017**, *16*, 319–348.
3. Liu, M.; Feng, M.; Wong, C.Y. Flexible service policies for a Markov inventory system with two demand classes. *Int. J. Prod. Econ.* **2014**, *151*, 180–185. [CrossRef]
4. Brokesova, Z.; Deck, C.; Peliova, J. *An Experimental Comparison of News Vending and Price Gouging*; Working Paper; Chapman University, Economic Science Institute: Orange, CA, USA, 2020.
5. De Matteis, J.J.; Mendoza, A.G. An economic lot-sizing technique. *IBM Syst. J.* **1968**, *7*, 30–46. [CrossRef]
6. Silver, E.A.; Meal, H.C. A heuristic for selecting lot size quantities for the case of a deter-ministic time—Varying demand rate and discrete opportunities for replenishment. *Prod. Inventory Manag.* **1973**, *14*, 64–74.
7. Sterligova, A.N. O suguboi praktichnosti formuli Wilsona. *Logist. Sist.* **2005**, *4*, 42–52.
8. Sana, S.S. Price-sensitive demand for perishable items–an EOQ model. *Appl. Math. Comput.* **2011**, *217*, 6248–6259.
9. Dobson, G.; Pinker, E.J.; Yildiz, O. An EOQ model for perishable goods with age-dependent demand rate. *Eur. J. Oper. Res.* **2017**, *257*, 84–88. [CrossRef]
10. Zeng, S.; Nestorenko, O.; Nestorenko, T.; Morkūnas, M.; Volkov, A.; Baležentis, T.; Zhang, C. EOQ for perishable goods: Modification of Wilson's model for food retailers. *Technol. Econ. Dev. Econ.* **2019**, *25*, 1413–1432. [CrossRef]
11. Cárdenas-Barrón, L.E.; Chung, K.J.; Treviño-Garza, G. Celebrating a century of the economic order quantity model in honor of Ford Whitman Harris. *Int. J. Prod. Econ.* **2014**, *155*, 1–7. [CrossRef]
12. Nobil, A.H.; Taleizadeh, A.A. A single machine EPQ inventory model for a multi-product imperfect production system with rework process and auction. *Int. J. Adv. Logist.* **2016**, *5*, 141–152. [CrossRef]
13. Budd, J.K.; Taylor, P.G. Bounds for the solution to the single-period inventory model with compound renewal process input: An application to setting credit card limits. *Eur. J. Oper. Res.* **2019**, *274*, 1012–1018. [CrossRef]
14. Boute, R.N.; Disney, S.M.; Lambrecht, M.R.; Van Houdt, B. An integrated production and inventory model to dampen upstream demand variability in the supply chain. *Eur. J. Oper. Res.* **2007**, *178*, 121–142. [CrossRef]
15. Broyles, J.R.; Cochran, J.K.; Montgomery, D.C. A statistical Markov chain approximation of transient hospital inpatient inventory. *Eur. J. Oper. Res.* **2010**, *207*, 1645–1657. [CrossRef]
16. Wilson, R.H. A scientific routine for stock control. *Harv. Bus. Rev.* **1934**, *13*, 116–129.
17. Schwartz, J.D.; Wang, W.; Rivera, D.E. Simulation-based optimization of process control policies for inventory management in supply chains. *Automatica* **2006**, *42*, 1311–1320. [CrossRef]
18. Sarkar, B. A production-inventory model with probabilistic deterioration in two-echelon supply chain management. *Appl. Math. Model.* **2013**, *37*, 3138–3151. [CrossRef]
19. Manna, A.K.; Dey, J.K.; Mondal, S.K. Imperfect production inventory model with produc-tion rate dependent defective rate and advertisement dependent demand. *Comput. Ind. Eng.* **2017**, *104*, 9–22. [CrossRef]
20. Chang, H.C. Fuzzy opportunity cost for EOQ model with quality improvement investment. *Int. J. Syst. Sci.* **2003**, *34*, 395–402. [CrossRef]

21. Cárdenas-Barrón, L.E.; Wee, H.M.; Blos, M.F. Solving the vendor–buyer integrated inventory system with arithmetic–geometric inequality. *Math. Comput. Model.* **2011**, *53*, 991–997. [CrossRef]
22. Agarwal, S. Economic order quantity model: A review. *VSRD Int. J. Mech. Civ. Automob. Prod. Eng.* **2014**, *4*, 233–236.
23. Kozlovskaya, N.; Pakhomova, N.; Richter, K. *Complete Solution of the Extended EOQ Repair and Waste Disposal Model with Switching Costs*; No. 376; European University Viadrina Frankfurt: Frankfurt, Germany, 2015.
24. Sebatjane, M.; Adetunji, O. Economic order quantity model for growing items with incremental quantity discounts. *J. Ind. Eng. Int.* **2019**, *15*, 545–556. [CrossRef]
25. Ouyang, L.Y.; Yang, C.T.; Chan, Y.L.; Cárdenas-Barrón, L.E. A comprehensive extension of the optimal replenishment decisions under two levels of trade credit policy depending on the order quantity. *Appl. Math. Comput.* **2013**, *224*, 268–277. [CrossRef]
26. Chen, S.C.; Cárdenas-Barrón, L.E.; Teng, J.T. Retailer's economic order quantity when the supplier offers conditionally permissible delay in payments link to order quantity. *Int. J. Prod. Econ.* **2014**, *155*, 284–291. [CrossRef]
27. Afshar-Nadjafi, B.; Mashatzadeghan, H.; Khamseh, A. Time-dependent demand and utility-sensitive sale price in a retailing system. *J. Retail. Consum. Serv.* **2016**, *32*, 171–174. [CrossRef]
28. Bhunia, A.K.; Maiti, M. An inventory model of deteriorating items with lot-size dependent replenishment cost and a linear trend in demand. *Appl. Math. Model.* **1999**, *23*, 301–308. [CrossRef]
29. Tu, Y.M.; Lu, C.W. The Influence of Lot Size on Production Performance in Wafer Fabrication Based on Simulation. *Procedia Eng.* **2017**, *174*, 135–144. [CrossRef]
30. Sinha, A.K.; Anand, A. LOT SIZING PROBLEM FOR FAST MOVING PERISHABLE PRODUCT: MODELING AND SOLUTION APPROACH. *Int. J. Ind. Eng.* **2018**, *25*, 757–778.
31. Mahata, G.C.; De, S.K. An EOQ inventory system of ameliorating items for price dependent demand rate under retailer partial trade credit policy. *Opsearch* **2016**, *53*, 889–916. [CrossRef]
32. Di Nardo, M.; Clericuzio, M.; Murino, T.; Sepe, C. An Economic Order Quantity Stochastic Dynamic Optimization Model in a Logistic 4.0 Environment. *Sustainability* **2020**, *12*, 4075. [CrossRef]
33. Bolton, L.E.; Warlop, L.; Alba, J.W. Consumer perceptions of price (un) fairness. *J. Consum. Res.* **2003**, *29*, 474–491. [CrossRef]
34. Omarov, E. Trade Marketing as an Element of Managing Consumer Behaviour during Crisis. Тези доповідей міжнародної науково-практичної конференції"Економічний розвиток і спадщина Семена Кузнеця" 31 травня–1 червня2018 р = Abstracts of the international scientific-practical conference "Economic Development and Heritage of Semyon Kuznets" 31 May–1 June 2018. Available online: http://www.skced.hneu.edu.ua/files/tez_konferencii_simon_kuznets_14_05_18.pdf (accessed on 13 April 2020).
35. Andersen, A.L.; Hansen, E.T.; Johannesen, N.; Sheridan, A. Consumer Responses to the COVID-19 Crisis: Evidence from Bank Account Transaction Data. Available online: https://www.nielsjohannesen.net/wp-content/uploads/AHJS2020-Corona.pdf (accessed on 23 June 2020).
36. Lin, Q.; Xiao, Y.; Zheng, J. Selecting the Supply Chain Financing Mode under Price-Sensitive Demand: Confirmed Warehouse Financing vs. Trade Credit. *J. Ind. Manag. Optim.* **2017**, *13*. [CrossRef]
37. Govind, A.; Luke, R.; Pisa, N. Investigating stock-outs in Johannesburg's warehouse retail liquor sector. *J. Transp. Supply Chain Manag.* **2017**, *11*, 1–11. [CrossRef]
38. Sebatjane, M.; Adetunji, O. Economic order quantity model for growing items with imperfect quality. *Oper. Res. Perspect.* **2019**, *6*, 100088. [CrossRef]
39. Khan, M.; Jaber, M.Y.; Bonney, M. An economic order quantity (EOQ) for items with imperfect quality and inspection errors. *Int. J. Prod. Econ.* **2011**, *133*, 113–118. [CrossRef]
40. Birbil, Ş.İ.; Bülbül, K.; Frenk, H.; Mulder, H.M. On EOQ cost models with arbitrary purchase and transportation costs. *J. Ind. Manag. Optim.* **2014**, *11*, 1211–1245.
41. Taleizadeh, A.A. An economic order quantity model for deteriorating item in a purchasing system with multiple prepayments. *Appl. Math. Model.* **2014**, *38*, 5357–5366. [CrossRef]
42. Molamohamadi, Z.; Arshizadeh, R.; Ismail, N.; Azizi, A. An Economic Order Quantity Model with Completely Backordering and Nondecreasing Demand under Two-Level Trade Credit. *Adv. Decis. Sci.* **2014**, *2014*, 1–11. [CrossRef]
43. El-Kassar, A.N.; Salameh, M.; Bitar, M. EPQ model with imperfect quality raw material. *Math. Balk.* **2012**, *26*, 123–132.

44. Tungalag, N.; Erdenebat, M.; Enkhbat, R. A Note on Economic Order Quantity Model. *iBusiness* **2017**, *9*, 74. [CrossRef]
45. Jaggi, C.K.; Mittal, M. Economic order quantity model for deteriorating items with imperfect quality. *Investig. Oper.* **2011**, *32*, 107–113.
46. Elyasi, M.; Khoshalhan, F.; Khanmirzaee, M. Modified economic order quantity (EOQ) model for items with imperfect quality: Game-theoretical approaches. *Int. J. Ind. Eng. Comput.* **2014**, *5*, 211–222. [CrossRef]
47. Widyadana, G.A.; Cárdenas-Barrón, L.E.; Wee, H.M. Economic order quantity model for deteriorating items with planned backorder level. *Math. Comput. Model.* **2011**, *54*, 1569–1575. [CrossRef]
48. Inprasit, T.; Tanachutiwat, S. Reordering Point Determination Using Machine Learning Technique for Inventory Management. In Proceedings of the 2018 International Conference on Engineering, Applied Sciences, and Technology (ICEAST), Phuket, Thailand, 4–7 July 2018; IEEE: Piscataway, NJ, USA; pp. 1–4.
49. Slesarenko, A.; Nestorenko, A. Development of analytical models of optimizing an enterprise's logistics information system supplies. *East. Eur. J. Enterp. Technol.* **2014**, *5*, 61–66.
50. Nestorenko, O.; Péliová, J.; Nestorenko, T. Economic and mathematical models of inventory management with deficit and with proportional to waiting time the penal sanctions. Knowledge and skills for sustainable development: The role of Economics, Business, Management and Related Disciplines. EDAMBA-2017. In Proceedings of the International Scientific Conference for Doctoral Students and Post-Doctoral Scholars, University of Economics in Bratislava, Bratislava, Slovakia, 4–6 April 2017; pp. 351–359. Available online: https://edamba.euba.sk/www_write/files/archive/edamba2017proceedings.pdf (accessed on 13 April 2020).
51. Weisstein, E.W. *CRC Concise Encyclopedia of Mathematics*, 2nd ed.; Chapman & Hall/CRC: Boca Raton, FL, USA, 2003.
52. Chang, H.J.; Yan, R.N.; Eckman, M. Moderating effects of situational characteristics on impulse buying. *Int. J. Retail Distrib. Manag.* **2014**, *55*, 481–492. [CrossRef]

© 2020 by the authors. Licensee MDPI, Basel, Switzerland. This article is an open access article distributed under the terms and conditions of the Creative Commons Attribution (CC BY) license (http://creativecommons.org/licenses/by/4.0/).

Article

Preliminary Results in Testing of a Novel Asymmetric Underactuated Robotic Hand Exoskeleton for Motor Impairment Rehabilitation

Flaviu Ionuț Birouaș [1,†], Radu Cătălin Țarcă [1,*,†], Simona Dzitac [2,†] and Ioan Dzitac [3,4,*,†]

1. Mechatronics Department, University of Oradea, 410086 Oradea, Romania; fbirouas@uoradea.ro
2. Energetics Department, University of Oradea, 410086 Oradea, Romania; simona@dzitac.ro
3. Mathematics and Computer Science Department, Aurel Vlaicu University of Arad, 310130 Arad, Romania
4. Economic Sciences Department, Agora University of Oradea, 410526 Oradea, Romania
* Correspondence: rtarca@uoradea.ro (R.C.Ț.); idzitac@univagora.ro (I.D.)
† All the authors contributed equally to this work.

Received: 6 August 2020; Accepted: 3 September 2020; Published: 7 September 2020

Abstract: Robotic exoskeletons are a trending topic in both robotics and rehabilitation therapy. The research presented in this paper is a summary of robotic exoskeleton development and testing for a human hand, having application in motor rehabilitation treatment. The mechanical design of the robotic hand exoskeleton implements a novel asymmetric underactuated system and takes into consideration a number of advantages and disadvantages that arose in the literature in previous mechanical design, regarding hand exoskeleton design and also aspects related to the symmetric and asymmetric geometry and behavior of the biological hand. The technology used for the manufacturing and prototyping of the mechanical design is 3D printing. A comprehensive study of the exoskeleton has been done with and without the wearer's hand in the exoskeleton, where multiple feedback sources are used to determine symmetric and asymmetric behaviors related to torque, position, trajectory, and laws of motion. Observations collected during the experimental testing proved to be valuable information in the field of augmenting the human body with robotic devices.

Keywords: asymmetric underactuated; rehabilitation; robotic exoskeleton; symmetric and asymmetric trajectory; Bowden cable; video processing data

1. Introduction

This paper presents research and advances in the field of medical robotics, with a focus on data analysis of the symmetrical and asymmetrical mechanical behavior of the human hand during motor therapy rehabilitation using a novel robotic exoskeleton. As seen in numerous works regarding rigid exoskeleton applications for the human hand [1,2], there are a wide range of applications in this field that include medical [3–5], military, aerospace [6], and industrial uses. The need to augment the human body is driven by recent advances in technology [7,8] and the increasing automation of daily living [9]. Robotic exoskeletons as sometimes seen in movies have transitioned from the science fiction realm to real world applications due to recent advances [10] in a number of multidisciplinary fields such as mechatronics, artificial intelligence, bioengineering, medical robotics, and many more. Robotic exoskeletons continue to advance [11] and soon will become a big part in our daily lives, be it for medical rehabilitation, motor assistance for elder citizens, enhanced strength for military operations, or safer and easier work conditions in the modern factory environment. These types of robotic systems are slowly becoming an integral part of society [12], as a result, human–robot interfacing needs to be researched and understood in detail in order to improve the user experience, efficiency, and design of these devices. The human body is one of the most complex systems to attach to and augment with robotic devices [13–15]. The biomechanical nature of the human body contains both symmetric as well as asymmetric elements from a geometric point of view [16,17] and also generates symmetric and asymmetric trajectories and behaviors [18,19].

This paper aims to develop a new concept of a rigid robotic exoskeleton that adapts to the symmetric and asymmetric geometry and behavior of the human hand for research purposes in the field of medical robotics. The developed exoskeleton can also potentially be derived and optimized for a series of applications in areas other than medical rehabilitation such as the areas mentioned above.

The goal of the developed device is to provide an improved quality of life for people who suffer from motor impairment disability. The presented work discusses the development and research of a rigid robotic exoskeleton for rehabilitation therapy, mainly for people who had suffered a cerebrovascular accident, also known as stroke. The research data presented covers the development of a new concept of a rigid robotic hand exoskeleton and the symmetrical and asymmetrical behavior of the robot–human interaction during functional testing. The system integration and testing carried out are presented in a comprehensive study based on data generated from video processing software and sensors.

2. Materials and Methods

2.1. General Considerations

Taking into consideration a multitude of existing developed robotic hand exoskeletons, there are a few design factors that need to be taken into account. There are a number of structural designs that can be implemented in order to transmit motion to human fingers. These designs can be divided into three types, one of which is based on rigid structures that implement classical mechanical actuation. The second one is based on soft robotics [20,21], a new field of robotics that uses various types of soft actuators [22–25], and the third type, is based on hybrid actuation, which implements a combination of rigid, soft, and compliant [26] actuation systems [24,27–29]. In this paper, the structural type used belongs in the rigid structure category. This type of construction using a rigid exoskeleton implies that some parts must be customized for each wearer [30], in other words, a good design would permit interchangeable components to be easily swapped out and reconfigured. One alternative for customizing for each wearer is to use standard sizes similar to clothing and footwear. Having a kit of standardized sizes of elements for the fingers and palm region can speed up the process of configuring the exoskeleton for the wearer.

The device's level of complexity is increased due to the asymmetric distribution of the fingers since each finger has a unique set of anthropometric dimensions. Not only does each finger have unique anthropometric dimensions, but also the phalanges have unique anthropometric dimensions for each of the subjects, following a Fibonacci dimensional ratio [31–33]. As seen in Figure 1, a visual rendering of the human hand mechanical model is presented, where the asymmetric nature of the human hand can be observed. The phalange area represents the finger segments that comprise the thumb, index, middle, ring, and little finger. The blue segments represent the phalanges of the fingers, while the red segments represent the joints of the fingers, where the cylindrical joints have one degree of mobility (DOM) (comprised of 1 rotation) and the universal joint has two DOM (comprised of two rotations).

Considering a variety of mechanical designs present in this field of research [34], there are a few distinct constructive types that stand out. A solution with direct matching of the finger joint centers (DMFJC) was developed by Chiri et al. [6] which can be observed in Figure 2a. This type of design is a good type of construction due to its behavioral similarities to the biomechanics of the human hand. A limitation for this design is that the direct matching of the joints is possible on the Distal Interphalangeal (DIP) and Proximal Interphalangeal (PIP) joints, but mechanically it cannot be implemented on the Metacarpophalangeal (MCP) joint due to the hand anatomy. For the MCP joint, there are a number of other solutions that rely on more complex mechanisms to obtain an actuated or underactuated movement. The example shown in Figure 2a is an implementation of an underactuated MCP joint using a rotation translation mechanism controlled by a single actuator.

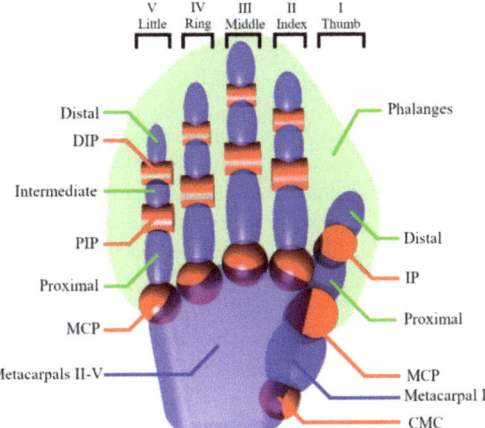

Figure 1. Proximal Interphalangeal (PIP), Distal Interphalangeal (DIP) and Metacarpophalangeal (MCP) connected to Metacarpals I joint have one axis of rotation, while the MCPs connected to Metacarpals II-V and Carpo-Metacarpal (CMC) joints have two axes of rotation.

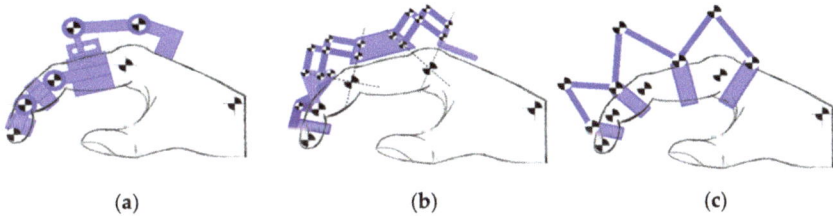

Figure 2. (a) Direct matching of the finger joint centers by Chiri et al. (b) Linkages for remote center of rotation (Shields et al.). (c) Underactuated redundant linkage (Wege et al.).

A significant issue that is critical to an exoskeleton mechanical structure is the orthotic shell. One of the most crucial dimensional characteristics is the thickness in the lateral areas of the fingers that is coaxial to the finger joints. This dimension is highly dependent on the wearer and the hand anthropometrics. In other words, a wearer that has thinner and longer fingers will have more space between the fingers, which will permit the mounting of an exoskeleton. In comparison, a wearer that has thicker and shorter fingers will have less space between the fingers, thus resulting in the need for a thinner orthotic shell. The finger segments of the exoskeleton must be designed in such a way as to not hinder the natural motion of the finger or even produce discomfort.

Another type of construction, developed by Shields et al. [35], implements a more complex structure based on a mechanism with linkages for remote center of rotation (LRCR), as seen in Figure 2b. Although it seems like a bulky design, considering the large and complex mechanism, it has the considerable advantage of saving a lot of space between the fingers, an essential factor to take into account when designing the orthotic shell of the exoskeleton fingers.

The hand compliance is also an important factor, so to produce a flexion and extension motion of the biological fingers some designer such as Wege et al. [36] utilized an underactuated mechanism for all joints by implementing an underactuated redundant linkage (URL) structure as seen in Figure 2c. The size of the mechanism is considerably larger than the one implementing a mechanism with the direct matching of the joints. While this design does not have the precise control of each phalange individually as the mechanism with LRCR structure [35], it has the advantages that it can be operated using fewer actuators and can provide a more natural movement of the wearer's hand due to its underactuated mechanism and the compliance of the biological hand.

2.2. Cable Drive Transmission

Cable-driven transmission in the literature of mechanics can refer to more than one type of mechanical transmission [37,38]. In this paper, two types of cable transmission are used, namely pulley-cable transmission [39] and Bowden cable transmission [40]. A Bowden cable is a type of flexible cable used in applications where there is a need to transmit mechanical force or energy, implementing the movement of an inner cable relative to a hollow outer cable housing known as a sheath. In the area of robotics, this form of actuation is usually applied for remote actuation of a robotic joint; force is delivered to the remote joint by means of mechanical displacement between the cable and the outer sheath.

The main factors influencing the cable efficiency are the normal forces on the cable, which are determined by cable tension or preload, the friction coefficients resulting between material combinations, and velocity of the inner wire. Friction between the internal cable and the external sheath usually has an impact on the entire assembly efficiency. Losses and inefficiencies of the Bowden transmission are mainly a result of the complex and non-linear friction phenomena. As described by Kaneko [41], Coulomb friction, viscous friction, stiction, and stick-slip may occur in Bowden cable transmission systems.

The main geometric parameter influencing friction between the sheath and the cable is the total wrap angle of the cable system, illustrated in Figure 3c. A simplified representation of the friction losses of a Bowden cables system can be represented by analogy to sliding a cable over a fixed cylinder at a constant velocity, as indicated in Figure 3a. For this simplified representation, the friction can be expressed by using the expression [42]:

$$\frac{F_{in}}{F_{out}} = e^{-\mu\theta} \tag{1}$$

where:

1. F_{in}/F_{out} is the ratio of input to output forces,
2. μ is the kinetic coefficient of friction between sheath and cable,
3. θ is the total wrap angle.

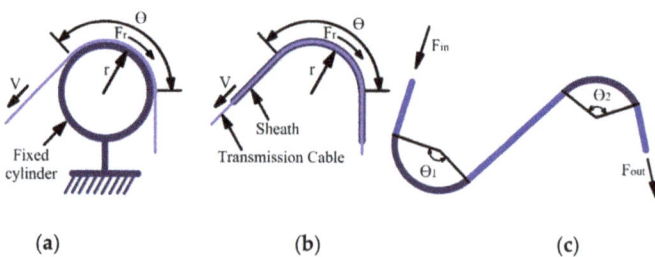

Figure 3. (a) Simplified equivalent representation of friction in a bowden transmission. (b) Representation of friction in a Bowden transmission. (c) Total wrap angle θ of the cable system.

The total wrap angle θ of the cable system represented in Figure 3c is defined by the equation [43]:

$$\theta = \theta_1 + \theta_2 = \sum_{i=1}^{n} \theta_i \tag{2}$$

In Figure 4, a model for determining the cable tensions at any point along the mechanism of the Bowden cable system is presented. A model based on Coulomb friction is considered since the system does not use lubricants, and the device can be generally considered on a macro scale. The current version of the prototype is designed to develop speeds and torques higher than needed for rehabilitation purposes. As a result, the frictions generated in the system are not a major challenge for the closed-loop control system [44]. However, at some later point in the project's development and optimization, other friction models may be required. Later optimizations such as reducing the scale of the actuation system may require a more thorough study regarding multiple or even more precise friction models [45,46]. For the current research, the work of Kaneko [41] is considered as the starting point for the Bowden cable transmission mechanism model. The normal force originating from the curved sheath creates friction force between the sheath and the cable. The friction force that appears in the mechanism has a nonlinear tension distribution along the wire. The equations that describe this phenomenon can be expressed using the following equations [41]:

$$T(p) = \begin{cases} T_{in} \exp\left(-\frac{<\mu>}{R} p \cdot sign(v)\right) & (p < L_1) \\ T_0 & (L_1 \leq p) \end{cases} \quad (3)$$

$$sign(v) = \begin{cases} 1 & (v \geq 0) \\ -1 & (v < 0) \end{cases} \quad (4)$$

$$L_1 = \min\{p \in T(p) = T_0\} \quad (5)$$

$$\begin{aligned} T_{in} &= T(p = 0) \\ T_{out} &= T(p = L) \end{aligned} \quad (6)$$

where:

1. $T(p)$ represents the tension of the cable at position p,
2. μ is the kinetic friction coefficient between sheath and cable,
3. θ is the summation of the bent angle of each segment,
4. v (noted as ξ in some works) is the velocity of the cable relative to the sheath,
5. dy is the angle subtended by the arc of length dx,
6. R is the radius of the sheath curvature,
7. T_0 tendon preload,
8. L is the total length of the sheath,
9. T_{out} output tension,
10. T_{in} input tension.

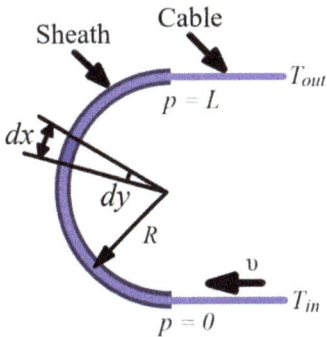

Figure 4. Cable tension model parameters of the Bowden cable system.

Numerous studies focus on determining and compensating the friction in a Bowden system. One method utilizes closed-loop feedback of the output tension [47–49]. The compensation is done by monitoring the stress of the cable on the output side, controlling the actuator in such a way that the output tension follows the reference set point. Other studies utilize position-based impedance feedback [41,50,51] combined with a decrease of pre-tension with a slack prevention actuation mechanism to reduce the effect of the friction [52]. For this paper, the friction compensation method relies on the position and current feedback of the system as described in a previous paper [44].

3. Results

3.1. Mechanical Concept

After observing several mechanical designs, it was determined that the links that comprise the exoskeleton segments corresponding to the finger phalanges do not need to be controlled individually [36]. A better solution is to rely on the body's natural compliance while actuating the exoskeleton. This structure, in turn, generates a natural asymmetric law of motion of the fingers that otherwise would be more difficult to recreate by directly controlling the individual links. As seen in anthropometric studies [53], the human hand's law of motion can have drastic differences from one person to another. According to the asymmetric law of motion, the flexion trajectory and extension trajectory are not symmetrical. As a result, an underactuated [54] mechanical structure is considered in developing the robotic exoskeleton presented and studied in this paper. One actuator is considered for each finger. In Figure 5a representation of the mechanism is given for one finger.

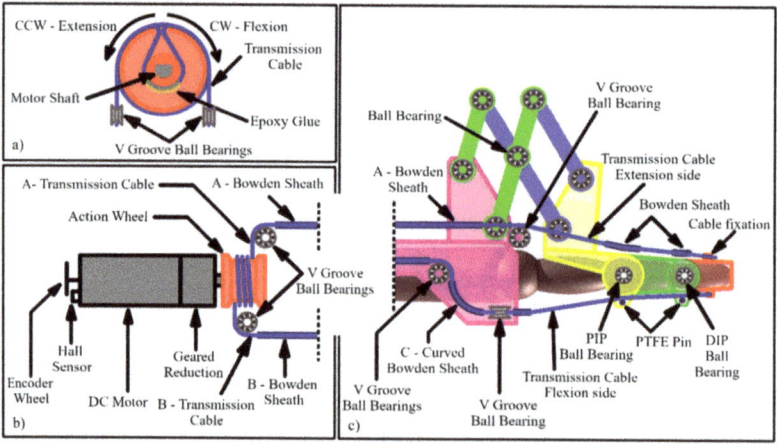

Figure 5. Finger actuation mechanism concept. (**a**) Action wheel wire mounting, rotation to translation conversion mechanism, front view. (**b**) Rotation to translation conversion mechanism, top view. (**c**) Cable transmission in the orthotic shell, lateral view.

The actuation is done using a DC motor mounted with a 31:1 ratio gearbox reduction. Position and displacement feedback are achieved using a Hall effect-based quadrature encoder [44]. The motion is transmitted from the motor output shaft (after the gearbox) to the finger, using a mixed transmission mechanism that contains cable-pulley transmission segments and Bowden cable transmission segments, also referred to as tendon-sheath transmission. The angle of the sheath curvature is fixed. As seen in Figure 5a,b, the motor actuates the action wheel, which in turn produces a symmetrical push/pull movement on the transmission cable that is guided further via ball bearing pulleys.

As represented in Figure 5a, the direction of the action wheel rotation produces a pulling motion on one end of the cable, while on the other, it creates a symmetrically pushing motion. The two ends of the wire are connected further in the mechanism; one end noted as A—Transmission Cable in Figure 5, is guided over the finger to produce the extension movement when tensioned. At the other end, the cable noted as B—Transmission Cable is guided under the finger to provide the flexion movement when tensioned. Most of the direction and angle changes of the translation of the cable is done by implementing ball bearing pulleys. The exception is the region between the two bearings from the flexion side of the cable, noted as C—Curved Bowden Sheath in Figure 5c; here a fixed Bowden sheath is used to guide the cable.

3.2. Mechanical Design

The mechanical design of the system is done using CATIA V5 R18. The assembly follows the concept described earlier in the paper. The mechanical concept is applied on all four fingers and taking into consideration a series of anthropometric measurements gathered in previous work [53]. The assembly of the system can be seen in Figure 6 where the distribution of the Bowden cable system can be observed.

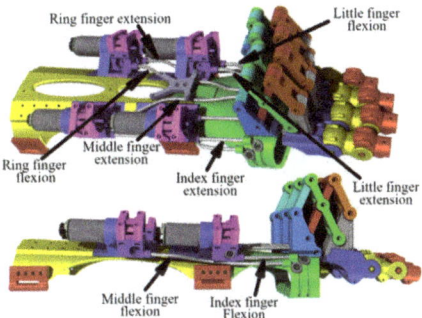

Figure 6. Mechanical design of the exoskeleton and the distribution of the Bowden cable transmission.

3.3. Manufacturing

The prototype is manufactured using 3D printing technology. In this case, the FDM (fused filament manufacturing) is the preferred 3D printing method. The material used for all parts is standard PLA (polylactic acid). The reason for choosing this material is the fact that it is biodegradable, eco-friendly, and it is easy to use in almost all 3D printers.

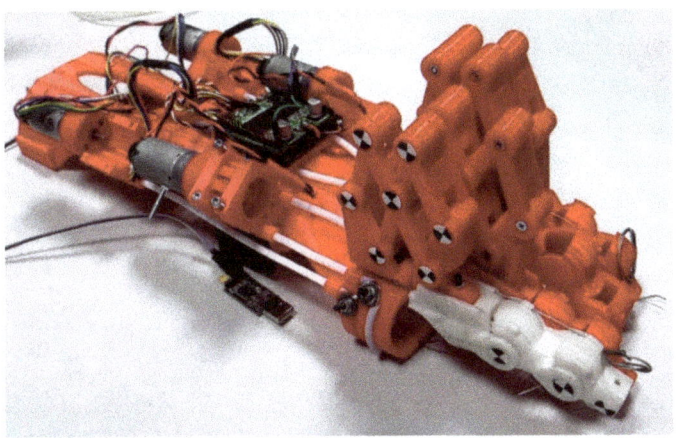

Figure 7. 3D-manufactured parts of the exoskeleton assembly.

The manufactured and assembled exoskeleton parts, as seen in Figure 7, were made on three separate 3D printers, two of which were Makerbot clones, while the third was a Whanhao i3 Plus. As with any prototyping process, the design had several iterations due to the optimization of the mechanical design.

3.4. Experimental Testing

Testing was carried out using measurements provided by the exoskeleton electronics and by video processing and recognition software. Electronics used for the exoskeleton were specifically designed and manufactured for this application. The data provided by the on-board electronics (as described in previous work) [44] were transferred via RS232 communication protocol onto a PC. The video recognition software was applied to determine trajectories and laws of motion of key points on the exoskeleton. A high-speed camera is required to capture the fast movement of the mechanical components. In the experimental section of this paper, a camera with 240 frames per second was used to capture the video data. The motion of one exoskeleton finger was studied with and without the operator's hand in the device.

3.4.1. Exoskeleton Testing without Wearer's Hand

The mechanical behavior of the exoskeleton was analyzed using Kinovea video processing software. The trajectories of key points were tracked via a high frame-rate camera for determining the workspace of the exoskeleton finger. The procedure used to capture and process the video via Kinovea software was described in a previous paper where the software was used to study and determine the anthropometric parameters of the human hand [53]. In Figure 8a the key points and their notations are illustrated. After studying the mechanical behavior of the system, it was observed that the joints rarely moved simultaneously in relation to one another; this phenomenon is simply explained by the friction differences from one joint to another and the friction variable of the cable on the contact guiding surface. As a result of this phenomenon, the joints of the exoskeleton will move sequentially one joint at a time. This phenomenon does not constitute a disadvantage since it offers a good indication for the positions where the system encounters greater frictions and it can be traced back to optimize the mechanism.

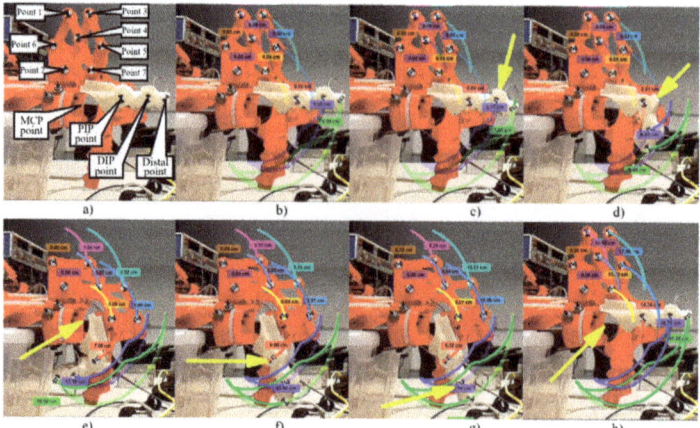

Figure 8. Joint phase steps of one flexion/extension cycle. (**a**) Key points and their notations. (**b**) Initial state of the exoskeleton. (**c**) The first phase of actuation—DIP joint flexion movement (**d**) The second phase of actuation—PIP joint flexion movement. (**e**) The third phase of actuation—MCP joint flexion movement. (**f**) The first phase of actuation—PIP joint extension movement. (**g**) The second phase of actuation—PIP joint extension movement. (**h**) The third phase of actuation—MCP joint extension movement.

In Figure 8 the phases of a flexion/extension cycle are detailed. In Figure 8c, it is observed that in the first phase of the finger actuation, the DIP joint is the first to move. The movement of the PIP joint, as seen in Figure 8d, characterizes the second phase. The third phase is the rotation of the MCP remote point, as seen in Figure 8e. The behavior observed is as expected, since the DIP and PIP joints each have two ball bearings, while the MCP remote center of rotation utilizes a more complex mechanism with multiple joints that will inherently encounter more significant friction forces. Based on the same logic, the extension's phase steps will be dependent on each joint's friction. As seen in Figure 8f, the first joint in the sequence to move is the PIP joint, followed by the DIP, as seen in Figure 8g. The final movement is again the MCP remote center of rotation, as seen in Figure 8h. An essential aspect to point out is that although the order of the joint movements for this cycle of flexion/extension is as expected, the system is still an underactuated mechanism. Given the right conditions, the order of the joint movements will not always be the same. Small variations of friction from the joints or cable can result in a different order in the joint movements, producing an asymmetric trajectory cycle during flexion/extension exercises. The next step in the analysis is generating the trajectory of the key points and the exoskeleton's workspace. Based on the captured motion of the key points over several flexion/extension exercises, the workspace seen in Figure 9 is generated.

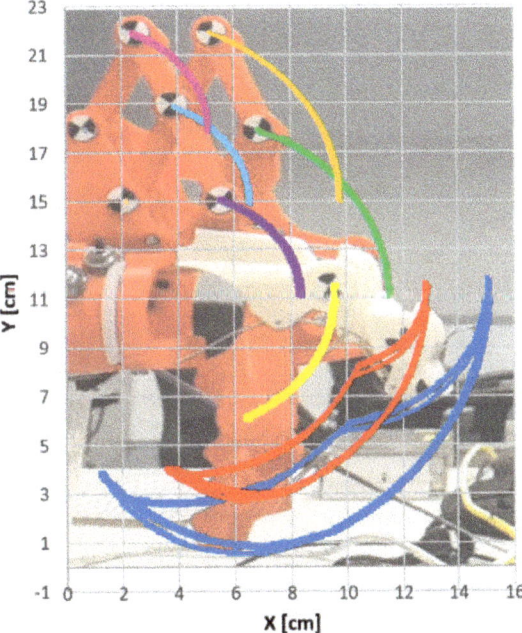

Figure 9. Exoskeleton key point asymmetric trajectory cycle and workspace analysis without operator's hand.

A more detailed analysis of the mechanical behavior is illustrated in Figure 10a, where the processed video data is used to generate a graphical representation of the laws of motion for each key point on the X and Y-axis.

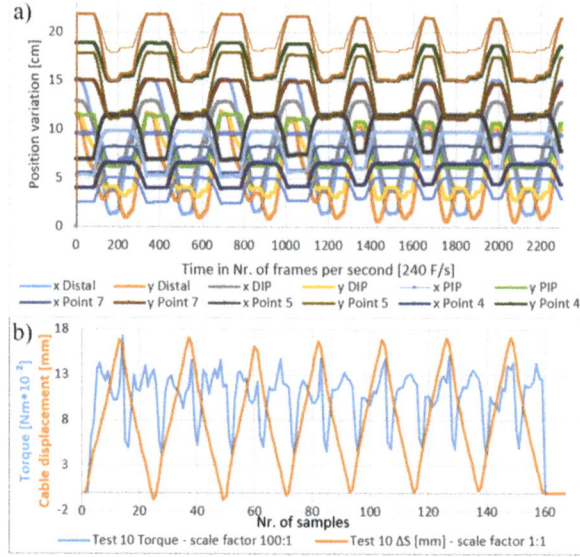

Figure 10. (a) Graphical representation of the law of motion of each key point when the wearer's hand is not mounted on the exoskeleton. (b) Influence of the joints' actuation order on the law of motion and torque.

The chosen example for generating the graph in Figure 10a, confirms that not all flexion/extension cycles have the same order of actuation of the joints when the human hand is not interfaced in the exoskeleton. It is observed that the first four cycles follow the sequence of steps described in Figure 8, while the next three cycles show a noticeable difference, which is the result of a different order of the joints' actuation. The difference is at the flexion part of the cycle, where the first four cycles follow the order DIP, PIP for flexion, and then MCP, while the remaining cycles follow the order DIP, MPC, and then PIP. This change in the joints' order of actuation is also observed in torque, as seen in Figure 10b, where the torque is significantly smaller after the change in the joints' actuation order.

3.4.2. Exoskeleton Testing with Wearer's Hand

Similar to previous tests, a trajectory was determined for the key measurement points. In this test, the human hand is interfaced with the exoskeleton. The generated path can be observed in Figure 11, where seven flexion/extension cycles were used to generate the data. An important observation is that, compared with the previous experiments, the mechanical behavior, such as the order of joint actuation, has changed. The first thing that was noticed is that the trajectory of the key points has changed in a way that the flexion/extension exercises tend to produce a more symmetrical pattern with the wearer's hand in the exoskeleton. While experimenting without the wearer's hand in the exoskeleton, the joint actuation was generally done one joint at a time. With the wearer's hand in the exoskeleton, the joints are actuated simultaneously, most of the time. This behavior is due to the reaction forces and friction forces introduced in the system by the biological finger, and its interactions with the exoskeleton's orthotic shell. In Figure 12a detailed graphical representation of the law of motion of the key points with the operator's hand in the exoskeleton is presented.

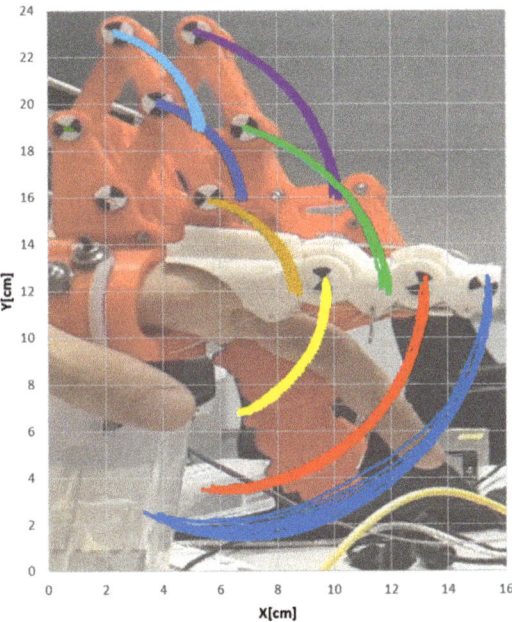

Figure 11. Exoskeleton key point trajectory analysis with operator's hand.

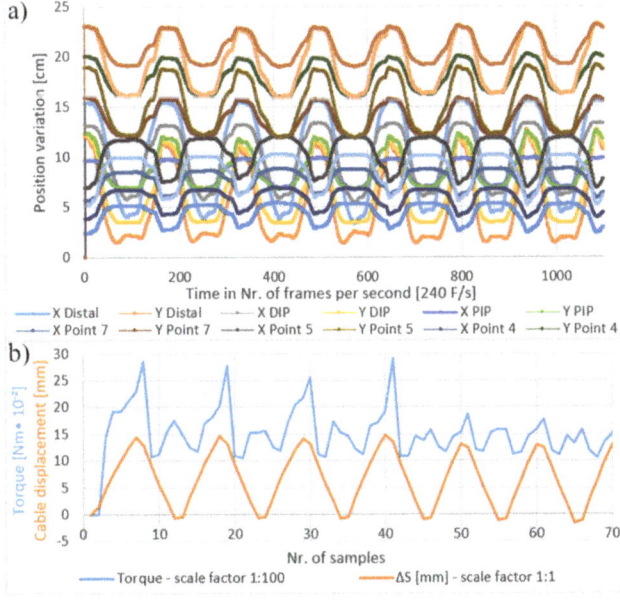

Figure 12. (a) Graphical representation of each key point's law of motion, while the operator's hand is mounted. (b) Torque variations as resulted from operator finger alignment in the exoskeleton.

A comparison of the cable displacement and torque is made for the seven cycles of flexion/extension, as seen in Figure 12b. Another interesting phenomenon that appeared in this experiment is that the torque values measured decreased after a random number of cycles, as seen in Figure 12b;

this phenomenon was investigated further to determine the cause. After extensive experimenting and comparing the data, it was observed that this phenomenon happens in almost every experiment iteration with the wearer's hand in the exoskeleton.

As seen in Figure 13, the torque and also cable displacement start to display a more regular pattern after 200 measurement samples. Extensive testing concluded that the decrease in torque occurs due to the finger self-alignment in the orthotic shell after several flexion/extension cycles. Although the mechanism functions, the biological articulation of the finger and the mechanical joints of the exoskeleton do not match perfectly at the start of exercise, due to coaxial offsets. This phenomenon produces an asymmetric behavior at the start of the exercises and after the biological and mechanical axis auto-align, the behavior tends to become symmetrical. This logical explanation corresponds to the irregular behavior of the system at the beginning and during the first flexion/extension cycles.

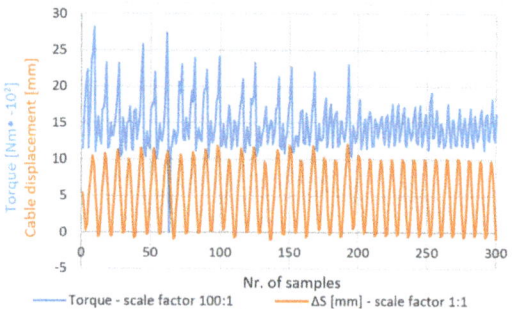

Figure 13. Torque and cable displacement stabilization due to the biological finger self-alignment in the orthotic shell of the exoskeleton.

4. Discussion

The proposed new exoskeleton design has been developed, starting from a thorough analysis of existing exoskeletons. The device is aimed at solving the mechanical problem in a way that adapts to the geometrical and behavioral parameters of the biological hand. The analysis of a variety of designs based on a rigid mechanical structure present in this field of research [1,4,5,20,27,28,45], showed some remarkably distinct types of construction. The solution developed by Chiri et al. [6], considering the direct matching of the finger joint centers, is a good one, due to its compliance with the asymmetric behavior of the human hand's biomechanics. A limitation for this design appears at the MCP joint, where direct matching of the joint cannot be implemented due to the hand anatomy. In most designs of hand exoskeletons, the DIP and PIP joints are easy to actuate via an exoskeleton mechanism, while the MCP joint presents a bigger challenge to actuate properly. For the MCP joint, there are several alternative solutions, based on more complex mechanisms for generating actuated or underactuated movement. Another type of construction, developed by Shields et al. [35], implements a more complex structure based on a mechanism with linkages for remote centers of rotation. Although it seems like a bulky design, considering the large and complex mechanism, it has a huge advantage considering that it saves a lot of space between the fingers, an important design factor in developing a compliant orthotic shell for the exoskeleton fingers. Comparing the design proposed in this work to the actual state of the art in the field, a series of advantages and disadvantages can be identified. In the first place, it has to be mentioned that the device presented in the paper benefits from the advantages offered by an underactuated mechanism, as a result of a low number of actuators. Another advantage of the proposed device is due to the fact that the actuators are not placed on the fingers' orthotic shell. Therefore, this device has the ability to present easily changeable components based on the person's anthropological measurements. Another advantage resides in a more compact design for DIP and PIP joints, compared to other underactuated models (as well as some fully-actuated models) such as those of Shields et al. [35], Wege et al. [36], and Zhang et al. [55]. One can mention, among advantages, that the proposed design offers a specified center of rotation for the MPC joint, in contrast to the solutions proposed by Chiri et al. [6]. It can be said that the current design can offer a natural movement of the wearer's hand, compared to other fully-actuated exoskeleton models, such as those presented in Zhang et al. [55], where each joint is independently actuated, thus involving a highly complicated control algorithm, due to the fact that the exoskeleton does not adapt very well to different anthropological dimensions and behaviors. On the other hand, one can mention as disadvantages the lack of certainty for each of the joints' positions, which obviously is a negative characteristic. Even though numerous advantages of the designed device are evident, a notable disadvantage is still present in this solution: the mechanism with the remote center of rotation implemented on the MPC joint is still a relatively large one. Further research has to be undertaken to optimize the device's dimensions. It was noted that the new exoskeleton adapts itself to the wearer's fingers, thus producing a compliant actuation, because of the underactuated mechanism implemented in the exoskeleton design. A notable difference in testing the exoskeleton with and without the wearer's hand is that while the device is being used with the wearer's hand, it produces trajectories that tend to be symmetrical between flexion and extension cycles. In contrast, in testing without the hand, the exoskeleton tends to produce asymmetrical flexion/extension cycles.

5. Conclusions

Based on the research results presented in this paper, the functionality of the proposed robotic exoskeleton device is tested and studied. Observations such as mechanical symmetrical and asymmetrical behavior determined in this paper will further benefit research regarding the augmentation of the human body with robotic exoskeletons. The study presented contains valuable data and observations that can be used not only for medical rehabilitation applications, but can potentially extend to other areas of application such as civil use, industrial or home environment, or even military and aerospace applications. Even though the study presented in this paper consists of only initial tests of the exoskeleton prototype, the system proved itself to be a good platform for experimental research. As for the development level of the device, it can be approximated that the device is still a prototype. The final aim of the project is to develop an adequate design for a commercial product. There is plenty of space for future research regarding optimization, such as, for example, size reduction, implementation of soft actuating systems, compliant systems, or hybrid systems, as well as studies related to robustness and device resilience [56]. In future research, we plan to extend the device's functionality, adding upgrades, including more feedback sources and integration of electromyography (EMG) signals with human brain interfaces to monitor rehabilitation progress during automated occupational therapy procedures. Other future updates are oriented towards increasing the device's autonomy in familiar environments, considering integrating elements such as batteries, internal data storage, wireless communication, and easy-to-use user interface software. Although the friction model related to the actuating system presented in the paper is a good starting point in research related to the proposed device, friction compensation control and optimization are broad subjects in themselves [45,46]. They deserve a dedicated and complete study, which may be taken into account in future developments of this project.

Author Contributions: Conceptualization, F.I.B. and R.C.Ț.; methodology, R.C.Ț. and I.D.; video processing, I.D. and S.D.; investigation, I.D. and R.C.Ț.; validation, S.D.; design of the CAD model, F.I.B and R.C.Ț.; formal analysis, R.C.Ț.; data curation, S.D.; writing—original draft preparation, F.I.B.; writing—review and editing, S.D. and I.D.; review, proofreading and improvements of the paper, I.D. and S.D.; resources and materials F.I.B.; visualization, S.D. and I.D.; supervision and project administration, R.C.Ț. All authors have read and agreed to the published version of the manuscript.

Funding: This research received no external funding. And the article processing charge (APC) is supported by Cercetare Dezvoltare Agora (R&D center of Agora University of Oradea).

Acknowledgments: The authors would like to thank the Ph D School of Engineering Sciences—University of Oradea, Romania, for providing technical support and access to online academic databases.

Conflicts of Interest: The authors declare no conflict of interest.

References

1. Cortese, M.; Cempini, M.; De Almeida Ribeiro, P.R.; Soekadar, S.R.; Carrozza, M.C.; Vitiello, N. A Mechatronic System for Robot-Mediated Hand Telerehabilitation. *IEEE ASME Trans. Mechatron.* **2015**, *20*, 1753–1764. [CrossRef]
2. Crawford, A.L.; Perez-Gracia, A. Design of a Robotic Hand and Simple EMG Input Controller with a Biologically-Inspired Parallel Actuation System for Prosthetic Applications. In Proceedings of the 1st IEEE International Conference on Applied Bionics and Biomechanics, Venice, Italy, 14–16 October 2010; pp. 1–8.
3. Nathan, D.E.; Johnson, M.J.; McGuire, J.R. Design and validation of low-cost assistive glove for hand assessment and therapy during activity of daily living-focused robotic stroke therapy. *J. Rehabil. Res. Dev.* **2009**, *46*, 587. [CrossRef] [PubMed]
4. Sandoval, G.O.; Juan, J.V.; Ignacio, H.A.; Otniel, P.R.; Tripicchio, P.; Hernandez-Ramos, M.; Flores Cuautle, A.; Avizzano, C. Design and development of a hand exoskeleton robot for active and passive rehabilitation. *Int. J. Adv. Robot. Syst.* **2016**, *13*. [CrossRef]
5. Durairajah, V.; Gobee, S.; Rauf, W.; Ngie, K.S.; Lim, J.H.A. Design and development of low cost hand exoskeleton for rehabilitation. *IFMBE Proc.* **2018**, *67*, 107–110. [CrossRef]
6. Chiri, T.A.; Giovacchini, F.; Roccella, S.; Vitiello, N.; Catti, E.; Vecchi, F.C. *HANDEXOS: Towards a Support Device for Hand Activities and Elepresence*; ESA: Paris, France, 2008.
7. Conti, R.; Saccares, L.; Giovacchini, F.; Crea, S.; Vitiello, N. IUVO: A Spin-Off Company on Wearable Robotics Technologies. In *Biosystems and Biorobotics*; Springer International Publishing: Berlin, Germany, 2020; Volume 25, pp. 3–7.
8. Gorgey, A.S. Robotic exoskeletons: The current pros and cons. *World J. Orthop.* **2018**, *9*, 112–119. [CrossRef]
9. Liu, Y.; Ouyang, D.; Liu, Y.; Chen, R. A Novel Approach Based on Time Cluster for Activity Recognition of Daily Living in Smart Homes. *Symmetry* **2017**, *9*, 212. [CrossRef]
10. Spence, P.R.; Westerman, D.; Edwards, C.; Edwards, A. Welcoming Our Robot Overlords: Initial Expectations About Interaction With a Robot. *Commun. Res. Rep.* **2014**, *31*, 272–280. [CrossRef]
11. Gull, M.A.; Bai, S.; Bak, T. A Review on Design of Upper Limb Exoskeletons. *Robotics* **2020**, *9*, 16. [CrossRef]
12. Pons, L.; Papers, S. Inclusive Robotics for a Better Society. In Proceedings of the Selected Papers from INBOTS Conference 2018, Pisa, Italy, 16–18 October 2018; Springer International Publishing: Cham, Switzerland, 2020; Volume 25, ISBN 9783030240738.
13. Herr, H. Robotics for Human Augmentation Science AAAS. Available online: https://www.sciencemag.org/journals/robotics/human-augmentation (accessed on 2 July 2020).
14. Carbone, G.; Rossi, C.; Savino, S. Performance Comparison Between Federica Hand and Larm Hand. *Int. J. Adv. Robot. Syst.* **2015**, *12*, 90. [CrossRef]
15. Antonio Zappatore, G.; Reina Politecnico di Bari, G.; Zappatore, G.A.; Reina, G.; Messina, A. Analysis of a Highly Underactuated Robotic Hand. *Artic. Int. J. Mech. Control.* **2017**, *18*, 20.
16. Held, L.I.J.; Held, L.I.J. Symmetry and asymmetry. In *Quirks of Human Anatomy*; Cambridge University Press: Cambridge, UK, 2010; pp. 17–32.
17. Feigin, V.L.; Nichols, E.; Alam, T.; Bannick, M.S.; Beghi, E.; Blake, N.; Culpepper, W.J.; Dorsey, E.R.; Elbaz, A.; Ellenbogen, R.G.; et al. Global, regional, and national burden of neurological disorders, 1990–2016: A systematic analysis for the Global Burden of Disease Study 2016. *Lancet Neurol.* **2019**, *459*–480. [CrossRef]
18. Van Dongen, S. Human Bodily Asymmetry Relates to Behavioral Lateralization and May not Reliably Reflect Developmental Instability. *Symmetry* **2018**, *10*, 117. [CrossRef]
19. Crivellato, E.; Ribatti, D. Body symmetry and asymmetry in early Greek anatomical reasoning. *Clin. Anat.* **2008**, *21*, 279–282. [CrossRef] [PubMed]
20. Gul, J.Z.; Sajid, M.; Rehman, M.M.; Siddiqui, G.U.; Shah, I.; Kim, K.H.; Lee, J.W.; Choi, K.H. 3D printing for soft robotics–a review. *Sci. Technol. Adv. Mater.* **2018**, *19*, 243–262. [CrossRef]
21. Zhou, X.; Majidi, C.; O'Reilly, O.M. Soft hands: An analysis of some gripping mechanisms in soft robot design. *Int. J. Solids Struct.* **2015**, *64*, 155–165. [CrossRef]
22. Marchese, A.D.; Katzschmann, R.K.; Rus, D. A Recipe for Soft Fluidic Elastomer Robots. *Soft Robot.* **2015**, *2*, 7–25. [CrossRef]

23. Rus, D.; Tolley, M.T. Design, fabrication and control of soft robots. *Nature* **2015**, *521*, 467–475. [CrossRef]
24. Jacob Rosen, P.W.F. *Wearable Robotics*; Elsevier: Amsterdam, The Netherlands, 2020.
25. Shahid, T.; Gouwanda, D.; Nurzaman, S.G.; Gopalai, A.A. Moving toward Soft Robotics: A Decade Review of the Design of Hand Exoskeletons. *Biomimetics* **2018**, *3*, 17. [CrossRef]
26. Cao, L.; Dolovich, A.T.; Schwab, A.L.; Herder, J.L.; Zhang, W. Toward a Unified Design Approach for Both Compliant Mechanisms and Rigid-Body Mechanisms: Module Optimization. *J. Mech. Des. Trans. ASME* **2015**, *137*. [CrossRef]
27. Zheng, Y.; Cao, L.; Qian, Z.; Chen, A.; Zhang, W. Topology optimization of a fully compliant prosthetic finger: Design and testing. In Proceedings of the IEEE RAS and EMBS International Conference on Biomedical Robotics and Biomechatronics, Singapore, 26–29 June 2016; IEEE Computer Society: Washington, DC, USA, 2016; pp. 1029–1034.
28. Rose, C.G.; O'Malley, M.K. Hybrid Rigid-Soft Hand Exoskeleton to Assist Functional Dexterity. *IEEE Robot. Autom. Lett.* **2019**, *4*, 73–80. [CrossRef]
29. Li, M.; He, B.; Liang, Z.; Zhao, C.-G.; Chen, J.; Zhuo, Y.; Xu, G.; Xie, J.; Althoefer, K. An Attention-Controlled Hand Exoskeleton for the Rehabilitation of Finger Extension and Flexion Using a Rigid-Soft Combined Mechanism. *Front. Neurorobot.* **2019**, *13*, 34. [CrossRef] [PubMed]
30. Eguren, D.; Cestari, M.; Luu, T.P.; Kilicarslan, A.; Steele, A.; Contreras-Vidal, J.L. Design of a customizable, modular pediatric exoskeleton for rehabilitation and mobility. In Proceedings of the International Conference on Systems, Man and Cybernetics (IEEE), Bari, Italy, 6–9 October 2019; Institute of Electrical and Electronics Engineers Inc.: Piscataway, NJ, USA, 2019; pp. 2411–2416.
31. Park, A.E.; Fernandez, J.J.; Schmedders, K.; Cohen, M.S. The Fibonacci sequence: Relationship to the human hand. *J. Hand Surg. Am.* **2003**, *28*, 157–160. [CrossRef] [PubMed]
32. Hutchison, A.L.; Hutchison, R.L. Fibonacci, Littler, and the Hand: A Brief Review. *Hand* **2010**, *5*, 364–368. [CrossRef] [PubMed]
33. Flatt, A.E. Fibonacci: His Numbers and Our Hands. *Bayl. Univ. Med. Cent. Proc.* **1998**, *11*, 119–122. [CrossRef]
34. Birouas, F.; Nilgesz, A.; Avram, F.; Mihalca, V.O. A review regarding hand exoskeleton technologies for rehabilitation. *Recent Innov. Mechatron.* **2018**, *5*. [CrossRef]
35. Shields, B.L.; Main, J.A.; Peterson, S.W.; Strauss, A.M. An anthropomorphic hand exoskeleton to prevent astronaut hand fatigue during extravehicular activities. *IEEE Trans. Syst. Man Cybern.* **1997**, *27*, 668–673. [CrossRef]
36. Wege, A.; Kondak, K.; Hommel, G. Mechanical Design and Motion Control of a Hand Exoskeleton for Rehabilitation. *Proc. IEEE Int. Conf. Mechatron. Autom.* **2005**, *1*, 155–159.
37. *New Trends in Mechanism and Machine Science*; Wenger, P., Flores, P., Eds.; Mechanisms and Machine Science; Springer International Publishing: Cham, Switzerland, 2017; Volume 43, ISBN 978-3-319-44155-9.
38. Yang, K.; Yang, G.; Chen, S.L.; Wang, Y.; Zhang, C.; Fang, Z.; Zheng, T.; Wang, C. Study on stiffness-oriented cable tension distribution for a symmetrical cable-driven mechanism. *Symmetry* **2019**, *11*, 1158. [CrossRef]
39. Liang, Y.; Du, Z.; Wang, W.; Sun, L. A Novel Position Compensation Scheme for Cable-Pulley Mechanisms Used in Laparoscopic Surgical Robots. *Sensors* **2017**, *17*, 2257. [CrossRef]
40. Goiriena, A.; Retolaza, I.; Cenitagoya, A.; Martinez, F.; Riafio, S.; Landaluze, J. Analysis of bowden cable transmission performance for orthosis applications. In Proceedings of the IEEE 2009 International Conference on Mechatronics (ICM 2009), Malaga, Spain, 26–29 June 2009.
41. Makoto Kaneko, T.; Yamashita, K.T. Basic considerations on transmission characteristics for tendon drive robots. In Proceedings of the Fifth International Conference of Advacend Robot. Robots Unstructured Environ, Bello Horizonte, Brazil, 2–6 December 1991. [CrossRef]
42. Schiele, A.; Letier, P.; Van Der Linde, R.Q.V.D.; Helm, F. Bowden Cable Actuator for Force-Feedback Exoskeletons. *Comput. Sci.* **2006**. [CrossRef]
43. Grosu, S.; Rodriguez-Guerrero, C.; Grosu, V.; Vanderborght, B. Evaluation and Analysis of Push-Pull Cable Actuation System Used for Powered Orthoses. *Front. Robot. AI* **2018**. [CrossRef]
44. Birouas, F.I.; Tarca, R.C. Development and testing of a mixed feedback control system for robotic hand exoskeleton. In Proceedings of the 2019 15th International Conference on Engineering of Modern Electric Systems (EMES 2019), Oradea, Romania, 13–14 June 2019; Institute of Electrical and Electronics Engineers Inc.: Piscataway, NJ, USA, 2019; pp. 17–20.

45. Liu, Y.F.; Li, J.; Zhang, Z.M.; Hu, X.H.; Zhang, W.J. Experimental comparison of five friction models on the same test-bed of the micro stick-slip motion system. *Mech. Sci.* **2015**, *6*, 15–28. [CrossRef]
46. Li, J.W.; Chen, X.B.; An, Q.; Tu, S.D.; Zhang, W.J. Friction models incorporating thermal effects in highly precision actuators. *Rev. Sci. Instrum.* **2009**, *80*, 045104. [CrossRef] [PubMed]
47. Veneman, J.F.; Kruidhof, R.; Hekman, E.E.G.; Ekkelenkamp, R.; Van Asseldonk, E.H.F.; Van der Kooij, H. Design and evaluation of the LOPES exoskeleton robot for interactive gait rehabilitation. *IEEE Trans. Neural Syst. Rehabil. Eng.* **2003**, *11*, 288–293. [CrossRef]
48. Kong, K.; Bae, J.; Tomizuka, M. Torque Mode Control of a Cable-Driven Actuating System by Sensor Fusion. *J. Dyn. Syst. Meas. Control.* **2012**, *135*. [CrossRef]
49. Ding, Y.; Galiana, I.; Asbeck, A.; Quinlivan, B. Multi-joint actuation platform for lower extremity soft exosuits. In Proceedings of the International. Conference Robots Automation (2014 IEEE), Cluj Napoca, Romania, 22–24 May 2014. [CrossRef]
50. Jeong, U.; In, H.; Lee, H.; Cho, K.-J. Investigation on the control strategy of soft wearable robotic hand with slack enabling tendon actuator. In Proceedings of the International Conference Robots Automation (IEEE), Busan, Korea, 13–16 October 2015. [CrossRef]
51. In, H.; Kang, B.B.; Sin, M.; Cho, K.-J. Exo-Glove: A Wearable Robot for the Hand with a Soft Tendon Routing System. *IEEE Robot. Autom. Mag.* **2015**, *22*. [CrossRef]
52. Jeong, U.; Cho, K.-J. Feedforward Friction Compensation of Bowden-Cable Transmission Via Loop Routing. In Proceedings of the 2015 IEEE/RSJ International Conference on Intelligent Robots and Systems (IROS), Hamburg, Germany, 28 September–2 October 2015. [CrossRef]
53. Birouas, F.I.I.; Avram, F.; Tarca, R.C.C. Anthropometric measurements for hand rehabilitation robotic devices using video processing. *IOP Conf. Ser. Mater. Sci. Eng.* **2018**, *444*, 052028. [CrossRef]
54. Tedrake, R. *Underactuated Robotics: Learning, Planning, and Control. for Efficient and Agile Machines Course Notes for MIT*; Massachusetts Institute of Technology: Cambridge, MA, USA, 2009.
55. Zhang, F.; Lin, L.; Yang, L.; Fu, Y. Design of an Active and Passive Control System of Hand Exoskeleton for Rehabilitation. *Appl. Sci.* **2019**, *9*, 2291. [CrossRef]
56. Zhang, W.J.; Van Luttervelt, C.A. Toward a resilient manufacturing system. *CIRP Ann. Manuf. Technol.* **2011**, *60*, 469–472. [CrossRef]

© 2020 by the authors. Licensee MDPI, Basel, Switzerland. This article is an open access article distributed under the terms and conditions of the Creative Commons Attribution (CC BY) license (http://creativecommons.org/licenses/by/4.0/).

Article

Location Selection of a Manufacturing Facility from the Perspective of Supply Chain Sustainability

Sun-Weng Huang [1,2], James J.H. Liou [1,*], William Tang [3] and Gwo-Hshiung Tzeng [2]

1. Department of Industrial Engineering and Management, National Taipei University of Technology, Taipei 10608, Taiwan; t107379004@ntut.org.tw
2. Graduate Institute of Urban Planning, College of Public Affairs, National Taipei University, New Taipei City 23741, Taiwan; ghtzeng@gm.ntpu.edu.tw
3. College of Management, National Taipei University of Technology, Taipei 10608, Taiwan; t107749008@ntut.edu.tw
* Correspondence: jhliou@ntut.edu.tw; Tel.: +886-27712171 (ext. 2332)

Received: 23 June 2020; Accepted: 19 August 2020; Published: 26 August 2020

Abstract: When threatened with catastrophic political or economic fluctuations, a firm might be forced to consider relocating their supply chain to reduce the risk. Such a relocation necessitates a series of changes, so making the right decision is crucial for sustainable development of the company. In the past, various models have been developed to help managers to select the optimal location. However, most of these considered the factors independently but in the real world, these factors have a mutually influential relationship. This study purposes a hybrid multiple criteria decision making (MCDM) model to provide decision makers with a comprehensive framework to evaluate the best strategies to solve relocation problems, which also considers the interdependency between criteria. The model incorporates the DANP (Decision Making Trial and Evaluation Laboratory-based Analytic Network Process) model (subjective weight) and entropy method (objective weight) to determine the weights of the criteria. Then, the modified VIKOR (VIšekriterijumsko Kompromisno Rangiranje) method is applied to select the optimal alternative for relocation. The usefulness of the model is demonstrated by taking an electronics manufacturing company with a global supply chain as an example. The results indicate that the proposed hybrid model can assist companies in choosing the best locations for their supply chains for sustained development.

Keywords: supply chain; location selection; DANP-mV model; MCDM; performance analysis

---

1. Introduction

With the development of globalization, the establishment of a stable supply chain has become one of the important strategies for the sustained development of an enterprise. However, sometimes, due to the catastrophic economic or political fluctuations, some county or region will lose its original advantages, forcing companies to transfer their supply chain to other countries to reduce the possible risk. Faced with these types of disruptive challenges, companies need to respond rapidly and in a timely manner to retain their competitive advantages. How to transfer the original supply chain and select the best alternatives are critical decisions for managers. In the past, it has been suggested that production processes and supply chains can be adjusted to respond with decentralized production [1–4]. Some researchers believe that relocating the supply chain can strengthen an enterprise's competitive advantage [5,6]. Many studies have confirmed that the choice of production line is one of the most important strategic decisions for corporate development, directly affecting the costs and benefits of corporate operations [7–9]. The choice of supply chain also plays a very important role in building a company's competitive advantage and ensuring its sustainable development. The relocation of production lines plays a key in sustainable supply chain management in today's competitive markets.

In prior research on manufacturing, considerations for location selection include economies and markets, government and governance, business efficiency, infrastructure, human capital and education in the evaluation framework [7,9–11]. However, few studies have incorporated the concepts of sustainability and innovation as criteria in the evaluation system or systematically discussed the entire evaluation framework. Wang et al. [12] pointed out that environmental regulations will certainly have an impact on some locations and will have different effects on different types of industries. Mudambi et al. [13] found that site selection decisions are related to creative activities and the resources required to carry these out, which can create new assets and lay the ground work for a competitive advantage. Therefore, it is necessary to include the dimensions of sustainability and innovation in the study of location selection.

Many studies have used statistical models to explore the issues of location selection. For example, Ye et al. [14] surveyed 3558 new foreign manufacturing enterprises in China's Pearl River Delta and found that the heterogeneity of the enterprise interacts with location selection. Zheng and Shi [15] found that industrial land supply and allocation policies interact with corporate site selection. Industrial land allocation policies have positive effects on corporate site selection. On the other hand, multiple criteria decision making (MCDM) models have already been used to explore the issue of location selection. For example, Liu [6] used a fuzzy Delphi method combined with a Decision Making Trial and Evaluation Laboratory (DEMATEL) method to evaluate the choice of investment location and output an impact diagram. Marinković et al. [11] used the two round Delphi method to confirm decision indicators combined with an Analytic Hierarchy Process (AHP) method to facilitate location selection for new sectors in the Information and Communication Technology (ICT) industry. Although qualitative or quantitative methods have been used in many studies to confirm the relationship between the factors or criteria, the applied models often overlook the interdependency between criteria [12,14–17]. The DANP-mV (DEMATEL-based ANP- modified VIKOR) model is very appropriate for handling the problem of interdependency and easy to operate compared with the original DANP model [18]. However, decisions on location selection, due to the complexity and interaction of the evaluation criteria, often involve lead to a dilemma between rationality and sensitivity. Chang and Lin [19] pointed out that location selection is usually based solely on the subjective preferences of senior managers, so decisions are normally biased. To avoid the subjective weight problem of the DANP-mV model, this study incorporates the entropy method to obtain objective weights for inclusion in the model. Then, the modified VIKOR (VIšekriterijumsko Kompromisno Rangiranje) method is applied to select the optimal alternatives for the relocation of a production line [20–23]. Finally, an empirical analysis by implementing the proposed DANP-mV model is conducted onto an electronic product manufacturer that is suffering from the impact of international economics and trade. The company's supply chain has a global layout and has 175 service spots. The company has a goal of being sustainability. For this vision, this study focuses on the relocation of manufacturing plants for the sustainable development.

The contribution of this study is that the method should help managers to evaluate possible locations, solving the problem through a comprehensive and scientific process, so the results can be closer to reality. The following improvements are made:

1. A complete innovative evaluation framework is proposed, which differs from those used in the past because it integrates the dimensions of sustainability and innovation into the evaluation.
2. The proposed model considers the evaluation framework as an integrated system and transforms the causality of a complex evaluation system into a visualization analysis. In also integrates both subjective and objective weights obtained by the DANP and entropy method, which remedies the reliance in prior models on the experts' subjective opinions.

The rest of the paper is organized as follows—a systematic review of the research on location selection problems is given in Section 2. The revised DANP-mV model is introduced in Section 3. An empirical example is illustrated in Section 4 and the results and management implications are presented in Section 5. Finally, Section 6 provides the findings and future research directions.

2. Literature Review on Location Selection

The sustainable development of supply chains has been a hot topic in recent years. In the past, a lot of research has focused on the discussion of supply chain management framework and evaluation methods [24–27]. Kusi-Sarpong et al. [25] raised the viewpoints of sustainable innovation to discuss supply chain management and believed that the sustainability of supply chain management will depend on innovation. Other scholars held different opinions, discussing the location and sustainability of production plants and finally determined that environmental, social and economic perspectives are important factors influencing location decisions [28–30]. The choice of location is an important company level decision-making problem. It can be divided into two parts—"how" (ownership and governance strategies) and "where" (location strategy) [31]. This study will focus on the analysis of the "where" part, specifically by design in a framework for the "selection of the best geographical location" for manufacturing plants. Past methods used for analyzing location selection can roughly be divided into two categories—qualitative and quantitative models. Most of the quantitative models are based on statistical or economic models. For example, Reference [32] used an economic model to analyze the factors affecting location selection. They found that per capita gross domestic product (GDP), GDP growth rate, agglomeration and government spending have a significant influence on location selection. Some studies argue that institutional quality and natural resources are also important factors influencing location selection [33]. Shuyan and Fabuš [34] used the spatial economic model to analyze the problem of location selection and found that market size and investment freedom were the most important factors for Chinese companies investing in the EU. In addition, the market size, technical level and investment freedom of the host country all have significant influences on location selection for China's foreign direct investment in the EU. He and Romanos [35] used regional taxation as the basis of analysis via regression models of the companies' location preferences and explored influence relationships in vertical and horizontal industrial linkages. The results indicate that both types of links have significant positive impacts. They also found that high taxation will hinder companies from choosing locations in these areas. Wyrwa [36] constructed a theoretical model based on structural equation modeling to explore influence of market size, labor costs, workforce quality and workforce availability on site selection. In contrast, the number of studies using qualitative methods have been relatively few. Wang et al. [37] used triangulation data collection combined with a qualitative research method to explore the determinants of location selection for enterprises in the biotechnology industry from the perspective of market expansion. Rahman and Kabir [38] used the Geographic Information System (GIS) to analyze the location pattern, then applied qualitative analysis to discuss the causes of forming clusters or localization for the manufacturing industry.

The above quantitative models which rely upon data collection, economic or statistical model analysis and hypothesis testing need long term and massive data collection, which might not be practical or reflective of rapid changes in the markets. In the past few decades, the MCDM method has been applied in the location selection problems. The advantages of MCDM are that it is—(1) simple to operate and suitable for complex practical problems; (2) can provide decision makers with clear information for reference; (3) more comprehensive in relation to the level of consideration and criteria, which is helpful to recognize the problem status; (4) supports the evaluation of multiple alternatives with qualitative or quantitative data [39–42].

The most popular MCDM method is Satty's AHP. Marinković et al. [11] used a two stage Delphi and AHP methodology to analyze and formulate the determinants for location selection for the ICT industry and confirmed the relative significance of these factors. They found human resource availability to be the primary factor, followed by the political and economic environment. Some have used the Delphi, AHP, Preference ranking organization method for enrichment evaluation (PROMETHEE) methods to select the location of manufacturing factories, with consideration of factors such as skilled workers, expansion possibilities, availability of required materials, investment costs and on-site risk assessment [7]. Wang et al. [43] given the consideration of human semantic ambiguity, used fuzzy Analytic Network Process (ANP) to explore the issue of location selection and found that small and medium-sized enterprises give priority to costs over regulations and communities, while large enterprises give priority to regulations over costs and community.

AHP and ANP are quite mature in the application of MCDM field. Although these methods can evaluate a complicate system based on the pairwise comparisons between the criteria, it is a time-consuming process and not easy to obtain the consistent results. Therefore, in recent years, there have been many advantages by using Best-worst method (BWM) [25,44]. This method selects the best and worst criteria first and then compares them with other criteria in pairs, effectively reducing the number of pairwise comparisons and obtaining better consistent results. In addition, some scholars use different methods. For example, Rocha et al. [45] used evolutionary game theory and input–output analysis to evaluate a company's strategic location selection. They considered many exogenous factors—potential markets, local productive interdependence, tax incentives and macroeconomic stability. Studies have found that a location in a tax-free market is not necessarily the best choice and that there is a direct relationship between government incentives and regional attractiveness. Liu [6] applied the DEMATEL technology to analyze the causality and discuss the key factors for location selection. Their results showed production costs to be the most influential and industry characteristics to be the least influential factor.

Although the methods discussed above perform well, most of them ignore the fact that the criteria are actually interactive in the real world [42,46]. The DANP-mV model is suitable for improving this weakness and has been applied in many fields [47–52]. However, the DANP-mV is based on the subjective opinions of decision-makers. To remedy this shortcoming, the entropy method can be combined with the DANP method, thereby effectively reducing the limitation of subjective weighting in the DANP method. In practice, one also can adjust the ratio between subjective and objective weights based on decision needs. Therefore, the new model has the merit of being closer to the real environment.

3. Proposed Model

This section introduces the advantages of the DANP-mV model, its limitations and the calculation steps, for a detailed list of symbols, see Table A1 in Appendix A.

3.1. Advantages of the Hybrid Weights

The DANP-mV model is derived from the integration of DEMATEL, DANP and modified VIKOR, three models. It has a strong comprehensive effect due to the synergy of these three methods. Recently, the effectiveness of the DANP-mV model has been proven in many studies in different fields [47–52]. The model has several advantages such as consideration of the interdependencies between the criteria, needing fewer pairwise comparisons and ease of calculation. The DANP-mV model can be applied to solve decision problems in the real world, treating the process of decision-making as a whole evaluation system and focusing on the fundamental cause of the problem. Although the DANP-mV model has some advantages, it still relies on the subjective opinions of experts. Zavadskas and Podvezko [53] pointed out that the criterion weight is critical in MCDM problems. If the criterion weights are only dependent on expert judgements, there will be potential uncertainty which affects the results [20,54]. Therefore, some have proposed the use of objective weights in the decision models [21–23,55].

Among the methods for determining objective weights, the entropy method has a solid theoretical foundation and has proven to be suitable for decision-making problems in different fields. The criterion weight is mainly determined based on the relationship between the original data and does not need decision-maker opinions [20,21,23,54].

During the process of decision-making, if only relies on subjective preferences of make decisions, the final decision-making results are easily influenced by subjective preferences and lose objectivity [19]. The empirical case of this study is to choose the manufacturing location of the factory. In the past, the company only relied on the subjective preferences of senior management to make decisions.

Thus, in this study, the entropy method is combined with the DANP method, to effectively reduce the limitation of subjective weighting in the DANP method. In practice, we can also adjust the ratio between subjective and objective weights based on decision needs.

The DANP-mV model proposed in this study retains the characteristics and advantages of the original DANP-mV model and at the same time considers the objective weights into the system. Therefore, the proposed model will be applicable to real-world decision-making. However, this study assumes that the integrated strategy coefficient of the combined weight is 0.5, which means that subjective and objective preferences are considered equally important.

3.2. Proposed DANP-mV Model

The proposed DANP-mV model is a hybrid research tool that contains the followed methods—DANP, entropy and modified VIKOR. DANP is used to evaluate the network relationship between the criteria and the influential weights of the criteria. The entropy method is mainly used for confirmation of the objective weights and the modified VIKOR method is applied for alternative selection. The complete operating process illustrated in Figure 1 can be divided into four phases:

1. Pairwise comparisons between criteria through experts' judgements for constructing the network relationship by the DEMATEL method to draw the influential network relationship map (INRM).
2. Application of the DANP model to derive subjective weights and calculation of the objective weights based on the entropy method.
3. Decide upon the coefficient, then combine the subjective and objective weights.
4. Use the modified VIKOR method to select the best alternative.

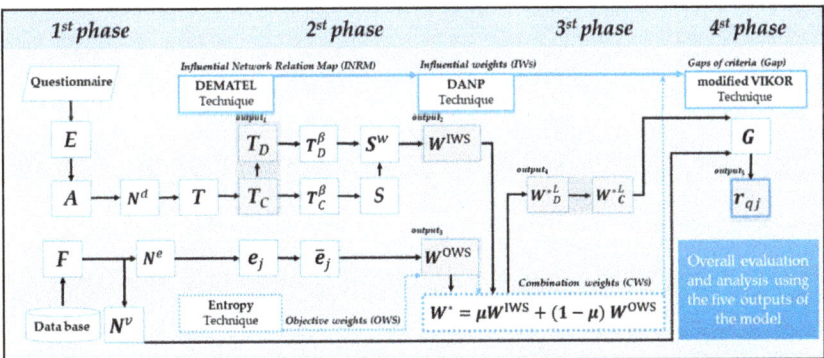

Figure 1. Analytical processes.

3.2.1. Phase 1: Construct the Network Relationship

Step 1: Establish the initial direct influence relationship matrix E

This step encodes the data obtained from the questionnaire responses of the K experts to get an initial direct influence relationship matrix E (Equation (1)) for each expert. Data collection is conducted through interviews with experts. The questionnaire scale is evaluated using scores from 0 to 4—(0) no influence, 1 (low influence), 2 (medium influence), 3 (high influence), 4 (extremely high influence). Experts are asked to specify the degree of influence between all criteria through pairwise comparisons.

The initial direct influence matrix is expressed as $E^K = \left[e_{ij}^k\right]_{n \times n}$ for $k = 1, 2, \cdots, k$:

$$E = \begin{bmatrix} e_{11} & \cdots & e_{1j} & \cdots & e_{1n} \\ \vdots & & \vdots & & \vdots \\ e_{i1} & \cdots & e_{ij} & \cdots & e_{in} \\ \vdots & & \vdots & & \vdots \\ e_{n1} & \cdots & e_{nj} & \cdots & e_{nn} \end{bmatrix}. \tag{1}$$

Step 2: Calculate the average direct influence relationship matrix A

The direct influence relationship matrixes for the K experts are aggregated and divided by K to obtain the average direct influence relationship matrix A as shown in Equation (2).

$$A = E^{AVG} = a_{ij} = \frac{1}{k}\sum_{k=1}^{k} e_{ij}^k = \begin{bmatrix} a_{11} & \cdots & a_{1j} & \cdots & a_{1n} \\ \vdots & & \vdots & & \vdots \\ a_{i1} & \cdots & a_{ij} & \cdots & a_{in} \\ \vdots & & \vdots & & \vdots \\ a_{n1} & \cdots & a_{nj} & \cdots & a_{nn} \end{bmatrix}. \tag{2}$$

Step 3: Calculate the normalized directly influence relationship matrix N^d

The average direct influence relationship matrix is normalized to obtain the normalized direct influence relationship matrix N^d as shown in Equation (3).

$$N^d = A/x \tag{3}$$

$$x = \max\left[\max_{1 \le i \le n}\sum_{j=1}^{n} a_{ij}, \max_{1 \le j \le n}\sum_{i=1}^{n} a_{ij}\right]. \tag{4}$$

Step 4: Derive total influence relationship matrix T

Use the normalized direct influence relationship matrix to obtain the total influence relationship matrix T (Equation (5)). The total influence relation matrix is an n by n matrix, $T = T_C = \left[t_{ij}\right]_{n \times n}$ for $i, j = 1, 2, \cdots, n$.

$$T = A + A^2 + \cdots + A^Z = A(I - A)^{-1} \text{ for } \lim_{z \to \infty} A^Z = [0]_{n \times n}. \tag{5}$$

Step 5: Build (criteria/dimension) total influence relationship matrix T_C and T_D

From the total influence relationship matrix T, the total influence relationship matrix of the criterion T_C and the total influence relationship matrix of the dimensions T_D can be obtained. The calculation of the total influence relationship matrix for criterion T_C is expressed as in Equation (6), where D_m is the m-th dimension (cluster); c_{mm} is the m-th criterion in the m-th dimension; t_c^{ij} is the sub-matrix of the criterion influence relationship obtained by comparing the i-th dimension with the j-th dimension.

$$T_C = \begin{array}{c} D_1 \\ \vdots \\ D_i \\ \vdots \\ D_m \end{array} \begin{array}{c} c_{11} \\ c_{12} \\ \vdots \\ c_{1m_1} \\ \vdots \\ c_{i1} \\ c_{i2} \\ \vdots \\ c_{im_i} \\ \vdots \\ c_{m1} \\ c_{m2} \\ \vdots \\ c_{mm_m} \end{array} \begin{array}{ccccc} D_1 & & D_j & & D_m \\ c_{11}...c_{1m_1} & \cdots & c_{j1}...c_{jm_j} & \cdots & c_{m1}...c_{mm_m} \end{array} \begin{bmatrix} t_C^{11} & \cdots & t_C^{1j} & \cdots & t_C^{1m} \\ \vdots & & \vdots & & \vdots \\ t_C^{i1} & \cdots & t_C^{ij} & \cdots & t_C^{im} \\ \vdots & & \vdots & & \vdots \\ t_C^{m1} & \cdots & t_C^{mj} & \cdots & t_C^{mm} \end{bmatrix} \quad m_j \times m_j | m < n, \sum_{j=1}^{m} m_j = n \quad (6)$$

The total influence relationship matrix of the dimension T_D is shown in Equation (7).

$$T_D = \begin{bmatrix} t_{11} & \cdots & t_{1j} & \cdots & t_{1m} \\ \vdots & & \vdots & & \vdots \\ t_{i1} & \cdots & t_{ij} & \cdots & t_{im} \\ \vdots & & \vdots & & \vdots \\ t_{m1} & \cdots & t_{mj} & \cdots & t_{mm} \end{bmatrix}_{m \times m} \quad (7)$$

Step 6: Degree of influence and the degree it is influenced between systems

The total influence relationship matrix is summed up to obtain the degree of influence and the degree it is influenced between systems. As shown in Equations (8) and (9), r_i represents the sum of the rows on the i-th row of matrix T, which means the sum of the direct and indirect effects of criterion i on the other criteria; c_j represents the sum of the columns in the j-th column of matrix T which means the sum of the direct and indirect influence on criterion j of the other criteria.

$$r = (r_1, \cdots, r_i, \cdots, r_n)' = (r_i)_{n \times 1} = \left[\sum_{j=1}^{n} r_{ij} \right]_{n \times 1} \quad for\ i, j = 1, 2, \cdots, n. \quad (8)$$

$$c = (c_1, \cdots, c_j, \cdots, c_n)' = (c_j)_{n \times 1} = (c_j)'_{1 \times n} = \left[\sum_{i=1}^{n} c_{ij} \right]'_{n \times 1} \quad for\ i, j = 1, 2, \cdots, n. \quad (9)$$

Finally, the degree of influence to and from the dimensions are calculated for the total influence relation matrix (T_D).

Step 7: Draw the influence relationship map INRM

The degree of influence to and from are marked in coordinates to obtain the influence relationship map. Here, $(r_i + c_i)$ represents the sum of the influence of the criterion and the influence, which is also called the total influence degree which represents the importance of criterion i in the entire system. The $(r_i - c_i)$ represents the difference between the degree of influence of the criteria minus the degree it is influenced or the degree of net influence. This index represents the causal relationship between the criteria. Taking $(r_i + c_i)$ as the x axis and $(r_i - c_i)$ as the y axis, we can draw the INRM.

3.2.2. Phase 2: Derive the Subjective and Objective Weights

Step 1: Define the unweighted super matrix S

The total influence relationship matrix of the criterion is normalized and transposed to generate an unweighted super matrix S. The normalization is expressed as in Equation (10) and the unweighted super matrix S is shown in Equation (11).

$$T_C^\beta = \begin{array}{c} \\ D_1 \\ \\ \vdots \\ \\ D_i \\ \\ \vdots \\ \\ D_m \\ \end{array} \begin{array}{c} c_{11} \\ c_{12} \\ \vdots \\ c_{1m_1} \\ \vdots \\ c_{i1} \\ c_{i2} \\ \vdots \\ c_{im_i} \\ \vdots \\ c_{m1} \\ c_{m2} \\ \vdots \\ c_{mm_m} \end{array} \begin{array}{c} \overbrace{c_{11}\ldots c_{1m_1}}^{D_1} \quad \cdots \quad \overbrace{c_{j1}\ldots c_{jm_j}}^{D_j} \quad \cdots \quad \overbrace{c_{n1}\ldots c_{mm_m}}^{D_m} \\ \left[\begin{array}{ccccc} T_C^{\beta 11} & \cdots & T_C^{\beta 1j} & \cdots & T_C^{\beta 1m} \\ \vdots & & \vdots & & \vdots \\ T_C^{\beta i1} & \cdots & T_C^{\beta ij} & \cdots & T_C^{\beta im} \\ \vdots & & \vdots & & \vdots \\ T_C^{\beta m1} & \cdots & T_C^{\beta mj} & \cdots & T_C^{\beta mm} \end{array} \right] \end{array}_{m_j \times m_j | m < n,\ \sum_{j=1}^{m} m_j = n}. \quad (10)$$

$$S = (T_C^\beta)' = \begin{array}{c} \\ D_1 \\ \\ \vdots \\ \\ D_j \\ \\ \vdots \\ \\ D_m \\ \end{array} \begin{array}{c} c_{11} \\ c_{12} \\ \vdots \\ c_{1m_1} \\ \vdots \\ c_{j1} \\ c_{j2} \\ \vdots \\ c_{jm_j} \\ \vdots \\ c_{m1} \\ c_{m2} \\ \vdots \\ c_{mm_m} \end{array} \begin{array}{c} \overbrace{c_{11}\ldots c_{1m_1}}^{D_1} \quad \cdots \quad \overbrace{c_{i1}\ldots c_{im_i}}^{D_i} \quad \cdots \quad \overbrace{c_{m1}\ldots c_{mm_m}}^{D_m} \\ \left[\begin{array}{ccccc} s^{11} & \cdots & s^{i1} & \cdots & s^{m1} \\ \vdots & & \vdots & & \vdots \\ s^{1j} & \cdots & s^{ij} & \cdots & s^{mj} \\ \vdots & & \vdots & & \vdots \\ s^{1m,} & \cdots & s^{im} & \cdots & s^{mm} \end{array} \right] \end{array}_{n \times n | m < n,\ \sum_{j=1}^{m} m_j = n}. \quad (11)$$

Step 2: Construct a weighted super matrix S^w

First, normalize the total influence relationship matrix of the dimensions. Normalization is done by dividing each element by d_i, as shown in Equation (12).

$$T_D^\beta = \begin{bmatrix} t_{11}^{\beta D} & \cdots & t_{1j}^{\beta D} & \cdots & t_{1m}^{\beta D} \\ \vdots & & \vdots & & \vdots \\ t_{i1}^{\beta D} & \cdots & t_{ij}^{\beta D} & \cdots & t_{im}^{\beta D} \\ \vdots & & \vdots & & \vdots \\ t_{m1}^{\beta D} & \cdots & t_{mj}^{\beta D} & \cdots & t_{mm}^{\beta D} \end{bmatrix}_{m \times m} = \begin{bmatrix} t_D^{11}/d_1 & \cdots & t_D^{1j}/d_1 & \cdots & t_D^{1m}/d_1 \\ \vdots & & \vdots & & \vdots \\ t_D^{i1}/d_i & \cdots & t_D^{ij}/d_i & \cdots & t_D^{im}/d_i \\ \vdots & & \vdots & & \vdots \\ t_D^{m1}/d_m & \cdots & t_D^{mj}/d_m & \cdots & t_D^{mm}/d_m \end{bmatrix}_{m \times m}. \quad (12)$$

Next, calculate the weighted super matrix s^w (Equation (13)).

$$S^w = T_D^\beta S = \begin{matrix} & & & & D_1 & & D_i & & D_m \\ & & & & c_{11} \ldots c_{1m_1} & \cdots & c_{i1} \ldots c_{im_i} & \cdots & c_{m1} \ldots c_{mm_m} \end{matrix} \begin{matrix} D_1 \begin{Bmatrix} c_{11} \\ c_{12} \\ \vdots \\ c_{1m_1} \end{Bmatrix} \\ \vdots \\ D_j \begin{Bmatrix} c_{j1} \\ c_{j2} \\ \vdots \\ c_{jm_j} \end{Bmatrix} \\ \vdots \\ D_m \begin{Bmatrix} c_{m1} \\ c_{m2} \\ \vdots \\ c_{mm_m} \end{Bmatrix} \end{matrix} \begin{bmatrix} t_{11}^{\beta D} \times s^{11} & \cdots & t_{i1}^{\beta D} \times s^{i1} & \cdots & t_{m1}^{\beta D} \times s^{m1} \\ \vdots & & \vdots & & \vdots \\ t_{1j}^{\beta D} \times s^{1j} & \cdots & t_{ij}^{\beta D} \times s^{ij} & \cdots & t_{mj}^{\beta D} \times s^{mj} \\ \vdots & & \vdots & & \vdots \\ t_{1m}^{\beta D} \times s^{1m} & \cdots & t_{im}^{\beta D} \times s^{im} & \cdots & t_{mm}^{\beta D} \times s^{mm} \end{bmatrix}. \quad (13)$$

Step 3: Derive the influence weight of the entire system W^{IWS}

Limit the derivation of the weighted super matrix S^w to obtain the overall influence weight W^{IWS} as shown in Equation (14). The matrix will eventually become stable and a set of overall priority vectors $w_1^{iw}, \cdots, w_2^{iw}, \cdots, w_3^{iw}$ obtained, which is called the influential weight W^{IWS}.

$$W^{IWS} = \lim_{q \to \infty} (s^w)^q. \quad (14)$$

Step 4: Establish the performance evaluation matrix F

Extract performance data from the database to obtain a performance evaluation matrix F as shown in Equation (15).

$$F = \begin{matrix} \\ a_1 \\ \vdots \\ a_i \\ \vdots \\ a_q \end{matrix} \begin{matrix} C_1 & \cdots & C_j & \cdots & C_n \end{matrix} \begin{bmatrix} f_{11} & \cdots & f_{1j} & \cdots & f_{1n} \\ \vdots & & \vdots & & \vdots \\ f_{1i} & \cdots & f_{ij} & \cdots & f_{in} \\ \vdots & & \vdots & & \vdots \\ f_{m1} & \cdots & f_{mj} & \cdots & f_{mn} \end{bmatrix}. \quad (15)$$

Step 5: Calculate the normalized performance evaluation matrix N^e

Normalize the performance evaluation matrix to obtain the normalized performance evaluation matrix N^e as shown in Equation (16).

$$N^e = n^e_{ij} = \frac{f_{ij}}{\sum_{i=1}^{m} f_{ij}}. \tag{16}$$

Step 6: Derive the variation degree of the criterion e_j

The normalized performance evaluation matrix is deduced from the variation degree to obtain the entropy value e_j for the degree of variation for each criterion (Equation (17)). The p is a constant. Let $p = (ln(q))^{-1}$ be used to ensure that $e_j (j = 1, 2, \cdots, n)$ belongs from 0 to 1.

$$e_j = -p \sum_{j=1}^{n} n^e_{ij} \ln n^e_{ij}. \tag{17}$$

Step 7: Calculate the degree of the divergence coefficient $\bar{e}_j$

The entropy vector is used to calculate the degree of deviation and each degree of the divergence coefficient $\bar{e}_j$ is obtained, as shown in Equation (18). The $\bar{e}_j (j = 1, 2, \cdots, n)$ represents the inherent intensity of contrast between j criteria. The higher the value of $\bar{e}_j$ in the criteria, the greater the relative importance of the role it plays in the whole system.

$$\bar{e}_j = 1 - e_j. \tag{18}$$

Step 8: Derive the objective weight of the entire system W^{OWS}

The divergence coefficient $\bar{e}_j$ is deduced by simple additive normalization to obtain the objective weight W^{OWS} of the entire system as shown in Equation (19).

$$W^{OWS} = e_j / \sum_{k=1}^{n} e_j. \tag{19}$$

3.2.3. Phase 3: Integrate the Subjective and Objective Weight w^*

The influential weight and the objective weight are combined to obtain the integrated weight w^* of the entire system. As shown in Equation (20), the μ is a strategic coefficient which can be adjusted according to different cases. The preset value is 0.5, which indicates equal importance between the subjective and objective weights.

$$w^* = \mu W^{IWS} + (1 - \mu) W^{OWS}. \tag{20}$$

3.2.4. Phase 4: Use the Modified VIKOR to Perform the Evaluation

The concept of VIKOR originated from the problem of multi-objective planning [56]. Opricovic [57] applied it to the research of civil engineering. Opricovic and Tzeng [58] made a comparison between VIKOR and TOPSIS and their results showed that performance evaluation using VIKOR would be more reasonable and effective. For the detailed operation processes of original VIKOR, please refer to References [58–60]. In this study, modified VIKOR will be used as the following steps:

Step 1: Define the aspiration level and the worst value

Decision-makers define the aspiration level and the worst value based on their expectations. In past performance evaluation methods using the positive and negative ideal solutions as the basis for evaluation, one may be caught in the dilemma of finding a good apple in a barrel of rotten apples.

Therefore, it is better to replace those "ideal" solutions with the aspiration level and the worst value. In this study, the scales range from 0 to 100, where $f^{asp} = 100$ indicates the aspiration level and the $f^{wst} = 0$ is set as the worst value.

Step 2: Calculate the normalized performance evaluation matrix N^v

Normalize the performance evaluation matrix to obtain the normalized performance evaluation matrix N^v as shown in Equation (21). Normalize the performance of j criteria in q alternatives and calculate the distance between each performance and the aspiration level at the same time.

$$N^v = \left(\left|f^{asp} - f_{qj}\right|\right) / \left(\left|f^{asp} - f^{wst}\right|\right). \tag{21}$$

Step 3: Evaluate the overall performance of each alternative

The normalized performance evaluation matrix is weighted to obtain the overall benefit evaluation matrix G and the average group utility vector r_{qj} as shown in Equations (22) and (23). Hence, the normalized performance evaluation matrix means the difference between each criterion and the aspiration level for each alternative. The w_j^* is the integrated weight and the overall performance evaluation will be generated through the interaction of the two matrices.

$$G = N^v w^* \tag{22}$$

$$r_{qj} = \sum_{j=1}^{n} N^v. \tag{23}$$

The original VIKOR considers two types of differences, the average group utility and the maximum regret. Since the purpose of the DANP-mV model is to focus on the decision-making process it can incorporate more references. The model uses the mean group utility r_{qj} only. Here, r_{qj} means the comprehensive difference between the various alternatives and the aspiration level, this difference will be based on the average group utility.

4. Empirical Example

The data collected and the analytical process are introduced below. Furthermore, based on the INRM and performance evaluation results, we provide some strategic suggestions for supply chain layout.

4.1. Description of the Problem

The case company is one of the world's leading manufacturers of electronics. Its products include energy-saving equipment, hardware for automation facilities and ICT infrastructure. The company has long been concerned with environmental protection, so continues to develop innovative energy-saving products and solutions and constantly strives to improve the energy conversion efficiency of its products. Headquartered in Taiwan, it is committed to innovation and research and development. It has locations all over the world including China, Japan, Singapore, Thailand, the United States and Europe. It has 175 operating locations, 37 production locations and 69 research and development centers.

In March 2018, US President Trump signed the "Section 301 Investigation" officially launching the China-US trade war, which has caused a lot of turbulence and had a major impact on manufacturing in Asia and around the world [61]. Shocked companies have had to consider countermeasures in advance, to strategically adjust the layout of their global supply chain, speed up automation, accelerate mergers and acquisitions and supply chain transfers and strengthen cross-border management capabilities in order to reduce the negative impact of trade friction [62]. The major production lines of the case company have been heavily influenced by the impact of international economics and trade. To respond to the rapidly changing international trade situation and keep its core competitive advantage, the company set up a relevant project working group to conduct an evaluation and selection of possible transfer locations. The company has some experience and certain standards for the evaluation of such locations. First, global competitiveness indexes were used to evaluate the possible alternatives. After several rounds of discussion and field surveys, five potential locations for final decision were made, which included Croatia (HRV), India (IND), Taiwan (TWN), Uganda (UGA) and Vietnam (VNM). The company is now faced with how to make the choice of a new location that will affect the business performance of the enterprise and ultimately whether development can be sustained. It should be noted that the selected five possible locations were based on the needs of the case company. The other company might have other alternatives due to their specified requirements and operational environments.

4.2. Identification Criteria for Location Selection

The criteria for location selection have been discussed in many studies. They mainly depend on the characteristics of the enterprise and the operational environment. Therefore, the working group of the case company considered its needs and situation and identified 16 evaluation criteria. The evaluation criteria are summarized and divided into 5 dimensions, which include Economy and Market, Government and Governance, Business Dynamism, Infrastructure, Sustainability and Innovation (Table 1).

Table 1. Dimensions and criteria for the evaluation system.

Dimensions/Criteria	Explanation	References
Economy and Market (D_1)		
Macroeconomic stability (C_1)	Refers to the overall evaluation of local inflation and debt dynamics.	[6,11,37,43,63,64]
Financial system (C_2)	Refers to the overall evaluation of local systems and the depth and stability of the financial system.	[6,10,11,43]
Product market (C_3)	Refers to the overall evaluation of local and domestic market competition, trade openness, market size.	[6,10,11,37,63,64]
Government and Governance (D_2)		
Security (C_4)	Refers to the overall evaluation of local organized crime, homicide rate, terrorist incidents and reliability of police services.	[6,9,43,65]
Institutions (C_5)	Refers to the overall evaluation of local budget transparency, judicial independence, legal fairness and press freedom.	[6,7,11,63,64]
Property (C_6)	Refers to the overall evaluation of local inflation and debt dynamics, protection and management of ownership.	[6,43]
Corporate governance (C_7)	Refers to the overall evaluation of local corporate governance.	[6,64]
Business dynamism (D_3)		
Administrative requirements (C_8)	Refers to the overall evaluation of local entrepreneurial costs, entrepreneurial time, bankruptcy recovery rate and bankruptcy supervision framework.	[6,10,37,43,63,64]
Entrepreneurial culture (C_9)	Refers to the overall evaluation of local attitudes towards entrepreneurial risk, willingness to delegate authority.	[6,7,9,10,63,64]
Infrastructure (D_4)		
Transportation system (C_{10})	Refers to the overall evaluation of local road, railroad, air and sea transport.	[6,9,43,65]
Utility infrastructure system (C_{11})	Refers to the overall evaluation of local electricity and water supply.	[6,9,43,65]
ICT adoption (C_{12})	Refers to the overall evaluation of local mobile-cellular telephone subscriptions, mobile-broadband subscriptions, fixed-broadband internet subscriptions, fiber internet subscriptions, internet usage.	[6,11,43]
Skill (C_{13})	Refers to the overall evaluation of the current and future local workforce.	[6,7,10,63,64]
Labor market (C_{14})	Refers to the overall evaluation of local labor market flexibility, meritocracy and incentivization.	[6,7,63,64]
Sustainability and Innovation (D_5)		
Sustainable planning (C_{15})	Refers to the overall evaluation of local government's long-term vision, energy efficiency regulation, renewable energy regulation, environment-related treaties in force.	[6,9,10,64]
Innovation foundation (C_{16})	Refers to the overall evaluation of local labor market flexibility, meritocracy and incentivization, diversity and collaboration, research and development, commercialization, growth of innovative companies, companies embracing disruptive ideas, etc.	[6–8,63]

The "economic and market" dimension refers to the local economy, prices, exchange rates, financial system, market share and market openness. We will evaluate the macroeconomic stability, financial system and product market of the country or region. The "government and governance" dimension refers to the evaluation of the political stability and local security of the country or region. The assessment of the "business dynamism" dimension refers to the assessment of the administrative costs of the country, local administrative efficiency, operational risks, regulatory systems and corporate culture. "Infrastructure" refers to the assessment of the completeness of infrastructure construction, which includes local transportation infrastructure, water and electricity supply systems, ICT communications and labor adequacy. "Sustainability and innovation" refers to the attitude of the country or region dedicated to sustainable development and leading innovation development. Local sustainability policies/regulations and the cultivation of innovative resources have a significant impact on the sustainable development of enterprises.

4.3. Data Collection, Analysis and Results

The data were collected in two parts from expert opinions and public databases. Since the importance of the evaluating criteria reflects the company's needs, the opinions of the working group must be included in the survey to obtain the influential weights. In the survey, experts were asked to make pairwise comparisons of the degree of influence from criterion i to j. After the survey, a 16 by 16 matrix was obtained based on each expert's opinions, called the direct relationship matrix E. All the experts' results were calculated using Equation (2) to obtain the average direct impact relationship matrix E^{AVG}. Table 2 shows the average direct-influence relationship matrix. It can be found that C_4 and C_5 have a maximum impact (4 points) on C_1, which shows that Security and Institutions have a high degree of impact on Macroeconomic stability.

Table 2. Average direct-influence relation matrix of each criteria.

E^{AVG}	C_1	C_2	C_3	C_4	C_5	C_6	C_7	C_8	C_9	C_{10}	C_{11}	C_{12}	C_{13}	C_{14}	C_{15}	C_{16}
C_1	0	0.333	0.667	3.000	2.000	0.333	1.333	1.000	1.333	0.667	0.667	1.000	0.333	1.000	0.667	1.000
C_2	0.333	0	2.000	0.333	0.333	1.333	0.667	1.667	0.667	0.000	0.000	0.333	1.000	0.333	0.667	0.333
C_3	0.667	2.667	0	0.667	0.667	0.667	0.333	1.333	0.333	0.667	1.000	0.667	0.000	0.000	0.333	0.667
C_4	4.000	0.333	0.667	0	2.000	0.333	1.333	1.000	1.333	0.667	0.667	1.000	0.333	1.000	0.667	1.000
C_5	4.000	0.333	0.667	3.000	0	0.333	1.333	1.000	1.333	0.667	0.667	1.000	0.333	1.000	0.667	1.000
C_6	0.333	4.000	2.000	0.333	0.333	0	0.667	1.667	0.667	0.000	0.000	0.333	1.000	0.333	0.667	0.333
C_7	1.333	0.667	0.333	1.333	1.333	0.667	0	1.333	1.667	1.000	1.000	2.667	1.333	2.333	1.000	0.667
C_8	1.000	3.000	2.000	1.000	1.000	1.000	1.000	0	0.667	0.000	0.000	1.000	0.333	1.333	0.667	0.333
C_9	1.333	0.667	0.333	1.333	1.333	0.667	3.333	1.333	0	1.000	1.000	2.667	1.333	2.333	1.000	0.667
C_{10}	0.667	0.000	1.333	0.667	0.667	0.000	1.000	0.000	1.000	0	3.667	1.333	2.000	0.667	1.000	0.667
C_{11}	0.667	0.000	1.333	0.667	0.667	0.000	1.000	0.000	1.000	2.000	0	1.333	2.000	0.667	1.000	0.667
C_{12}	2.000	0.333	0.667	1.667	1.333	0.333	3.333	1.000	2.000	1.333	1.333	0	1.000	1.667	0.667	1.000
C_{13}	0.333	1.333	0.000	0.333	0.333	0.667	1.333	0.333	1.333	1.333	2.667	1.000	0	1.000	1.333	0.333
C_{14}	1.000	0.333	0.000	1.000	1.000	0.333	1.667	1.000	1.333	1.333	2.667	1.667	2.333	0	1.333	0.333
C_{15}	0.667	1.667	0.333	0.667	0.667	1.000	3.000	0.667	1.667	1.000	1.000	2.000	2.000	1.333	0	0.667
C_{16}	3.000	0.333	1.667	2.333	1.667	0.333	0.667	0.333	0.667	1.000	1.333	1.000	0.333	0.333	0.667	0

The scales 0, 1, 2, 3 and 4 represent the range from "no influence (0)" to "extremely high influence (4)", respondents by experts.

In the second part of the data collection process, data for the five potential locations were collected from the public database of the World Economic Forum (see Table 3). The data shows that Taiwan has the highest score on Macroeconomic. Prior studies have also found that Macroeconomic stability has significant impact on foreign investment [66]. Therefore, Macroeconomic stability is one of Taiwan's important advantages in attracting foreign investment.

Tables 3 and 4 show the input data of analysis used by the proposed DANP-mV model. Following the steps outlined in Section 3, five outputs are obtained—(1) the INRM; (2) influential weights (IWs); (3) objective weights (OWs); (4) combination weights (CWs); (5) comparison and ranking of alternatives. DEMATEL can be used to derive the INRM (Figure 2) which provides a visual basis to help decision makers formulate sustainable development strategies for improvement. An examination of Figure 2 shows that Sustainability and Innovation (D_5) and Business dynamism (D_3) are causal factors in the whole system, whereas Government and Governance (D_2), Infrastructure (D_4) and Economy and Market (D_1) are affected factors. In addition, this study finds that Government and Governance (D_2) has the greatest influence on the entire evaluation system, which is similar to the results of Janssen and Van Der Voort [67]. This also shows that the quality of local governance plays an important role. A stable, more credible and effective and less corrupt system will affect the choice of this location for foreign investors.

Table 3. Performance of five potential alternatives.

F	Criteria	HRV	IND	TWN	UGA	VNM
C_1	Macroeconomic stability	90.000	90.000	100.000	74.159	75.000
C_2	Financial system	61.918	69.478	88.438	50.297	63.865
C_3	Product market	53.164	50.389	66.339	49.064	53.994
C_4	Security	78.710	56.377	85.836	63.544	77.217
C_5	Institutions	35.772	66.376	62.609	50.165	50.661
C_6	Property	60.429	44.729	82.566	39.159	46.014
C_7	Corporate governance	60.699	74.160	77.203	51.846	51.064
C_8	Administrative requirements	71.762	64.592	85.902	59.846	62.567
C_9	Entrepreneurial culture	37.530	55.479	60.219	52.854	50.433
C_{10}	Transportation system	62.054	66.429	79.359	48.488	52.208
C_{11}	Utility infrastructure system	94.393	69.757	94.021	47.273	79.641
C_{12}	ICT adoption	60.686	32.106	82.294	29.351	69.034
C_{13}	Skill	63.470	50.455	76.220	42.258	56.957
C_{14}	Labor market	55.958	53.907	72.738	59.959	58.243
C_{15}	Sustainable planning	60.392	69.332	72.045	50.941	64.262
C_{16}	Innovation foundation	34.913	55.200	61.620	40.648	45.429

The scale will be between 0 and 100, with higher values indicating better performance. [2] Data base at www.weforum.org/gcr/rankings [68].

Table 4. Combination weights based on influence weights and objective weights.

Code	Dimensions/Criteria	Influential Weights	Objective Weights	Combination Weights (CWs) Global Weight	Local Weight
D_1	Economy and Market	0.063	0.097		0.142
C_1	Macroeconomic stability	0.028	0.022	0.054	0.376
C_2	Financial system	0.017	0.055	0.055	0.383
C_3	Product market	0.018	0.020	0.034	0.241
D_2	Government and Governance	0.267	0.280		0.253
C_4	Security	0.094	0.037	0.051	0.201
C_5	Institutions	0.072	0.069	0.062	0.247
C_6	Property	0.024	0.125	0.077	0.306
C_7	Corporate governance	0.077	0.049	0.062	0.246
D_3	Business dynamism	0.268	0.066		0.140
C_8	Administrative requirements	0.116	0.029	0.062	0.443
C_9	Entrepreneurial culture	0.152	0.038	0.078	0.557
D_4	Infrastructure	0.221	0.467		0.344
C_{10}	Transportation system	0.037	0.050	0.043	0.124
C_{11}	Utility infrastructure system	0.045	0.090	0.067	0.196
C_{12}	ICT adoption	0.055	0.244	0.149	0.433
C_{13}	Skill	0.036	0.064	0.053	0.154
C_{14}	Labor market	0.049	0.019	0.032	0.093
D_5	Sustainability and Innovation	0.179	0.090		0.121
C_{15}	Sustainable planning	0.089	0.023	0.053	0.440
C_{16}	Innovation foundation	0.090	0.067	0.068	0.560

Combination weights will be obtained using Equation (20) and the strategy coefficient $\mu = 0.5$.

From the Sustainability and Innovation (D_5) and Business dynamism (D_3) dimensions, Sustainable planning (C_{15}), Innovation foundation (C_{16}) and Entrepreneurial culture (C_9) are the causal criteria, whereas Administrative requirements (C_8) is the affected criteria. Given that factors have an interactive relationship, managers should first focus attention on the causal dimensions such as Sustainability and Innovation and Business dynamism. Improving these causal factors will eventually remedy problems with the affected factors. Similarly, at the criterion level, manager should focus on Planning (C_{15}), Innovation foundation (C_{16}) and Entrepreneurial culture (C_9) for improvement.

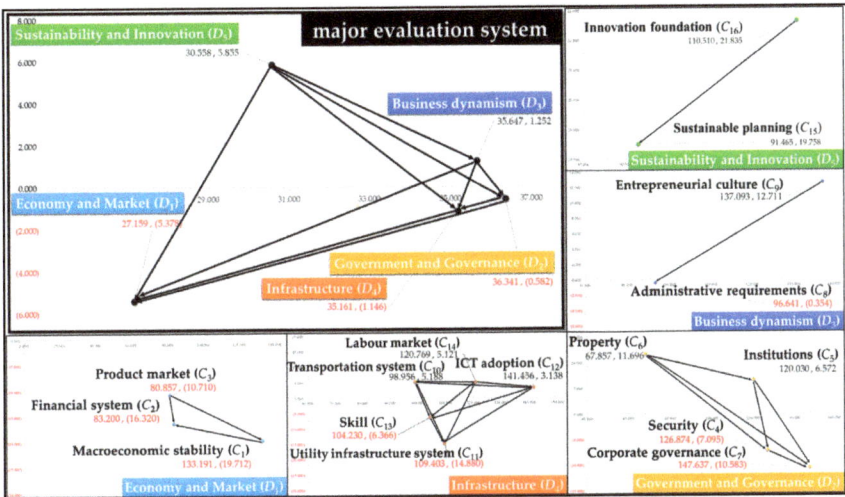

Figure 2. Overall INRM (Influential Network Relation Map).

The proposed DANP model integrates the objective weights to avoid reliance upon the subjective preferences of decision-makers. The entropy method is used to calculate the objective weights. The calculation is based on the performance of alternatives. The objective weights of the criteria can be calculated based on the deviation of performance among alternatives using Equations (15)–(19). The combined weights are then found using Equation (20) as indicated in Table 4. It is worth noting that the ratio between the subjective and objective weights can be adjusted according to the needs of the company. After discussion with the working group of the case company, this study proposes setting the strategy coefficient μ to 0.5, indicating equal importance between the subjective and objective weights.

To visualize the results, the dimension and criterion weights are shown in Figure 3. The order of the dimensions found is Infrastructure (D_4) (0.344), Government and Governance (D_2) (0.253), Economy and Market (D_1) (0.142), Business dynamism (D_3) (0.140), Sustainability and Innovation (D_5) (0.121). In other words, if the company wants to effectively grasp the geographical advantages, it must give priority to the local Infrastructure followed by Government and Governance (D_2), Economy and Market (D_1), Business dynamism (D_3), Sustainability and Innovation (D_5). At the criterion level, the top three criteria are ICT adoption (C_{12}) (0.149), Entrepreneurial culture (C_9) (0.078) and Property (C_6) (0.077). This result is consistent with the results of expert interviews. The ICT adoption and Entrepreneurial culture are essential factors for selection the manufacturing location because these are necessary infrastructures for sustainable development.

Table 5 lists the gaps for each alternative as determined by Equations (21)–(23). The results show that TWN's has a total gap 0.217, followed by HRV at 0.391, VNM at 0.398, IND at 0.421 and UGA at 0.519. In other words, the optimal location is Taiwan, followed by Croatia, Viet Nam, India and finally Uganda. It is worth noting that TWN performs best in the Economy and Market (D_1) dimension at 0.006, followed by Infrastructure (D_4) at 0.012, Government and Governance (D_2) at 0.015, Business dynamism (D_3) at 0.020 and Sustainability and Innovation (D_5) at 0.021. Taiwan has better macroeconomic stability and financial system and relatively good transportation system, utility infrastructure system and labor market. Although Taiwan is the best choice, more attention should be paid to the performance of Entrepreneurial culture, ICT adoption and Innovation foundation, which have larger aspiration gaps. The foundation of Taiwan's economics is dominated by small and medium-sized enterprises. The decentralization of power by individual businesses and family-owned businesses is often insufficient. In recent years, the international community has been continuously committed to the promotion of 5G communication technology but Taiwan's population and market size restrictions will not be conducive to the development of ICT adoption. Therefore, Taiwan still has limited disruptive ideas, so Innovation foundation still has much room for improvement.

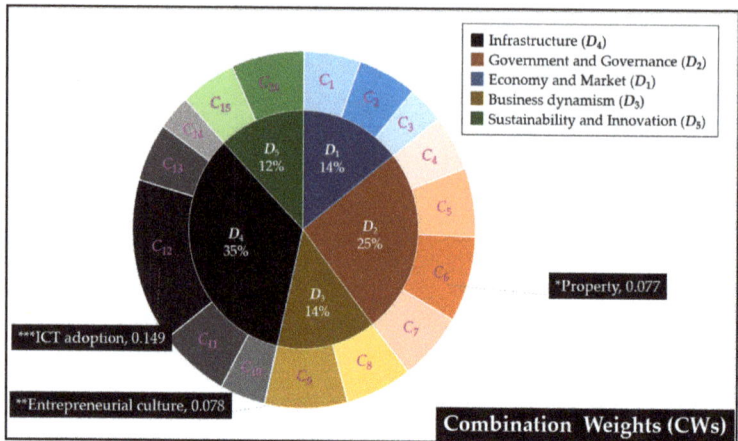

Figure 3. Local Weights for Dimensions and Global Weights for Criteria.

Table 5. Gap analysis for the possible alternatives.

Code	Dimensions/Criteria	CWs	HRV Gap	HRV Rank	IND Gap	IND Rank	TWN Gap	TWN Rank	UGA Gap	UGA Rank	VNM Gap	VNM Rank
D_1	Economy and Market	0.142	0.014	1	0.013	1	0.006	1	0.019	1	0.016	1
C_1	Macroeconomic stability	0.054	0.005	2	0.005	1	0.000	1	0.014	2	0.013	3
C_2	Financial system	0.055	0.021	9	0.017	6	0.006	3	0.027	8	0.020	7
C_3	Product market	0.034	0.016	5	0.017	7	0.012	8	0.017	3	0.016	5
D_2	Government and Governance	0.253	0.026	3	0.025	3	0.015	3	0.032	3	0.029	4
C_4	Security	0.051	0.011	3	0.022	11	0.007	4	0.019	4	0.012	1
C_5	Institutions	0.062	0.040	13	0.021	9	0.023	13	0.031	11	0.031	12
C_6	Property	0.077	0.031	12	0.043	15	0.013	10	0.047	15	0.042	15
C_7	Corporate governance	0.062	0.024	11	0.016	4	0.014	11	0.030	9	0.030	11
D_3	Business dynamism	0.140	0.033	5	0.028	4	0.020	4	0.031	2	0.031	5
C_8	Administrative requirements	0.062	0.017	7	0.022	10	0.009	6	0.025	6	0.023	10
C_9	Entrepreneurial culture	0.078	0.049	15	0.035	14	0.031	16	0.037	13	0.039	14
D_4	Infrastructure	0.344	0.022	2	0.035	5	0.012	2	0.041	5	0.023	2
C_{10}	Transportation system	0.043	0.016	6	0.014	2	0.009	7	0.022	5	0.020	8
C_{11}	Utility infrastructure system	0.067	0.004	1	0.020	8	0.004	2	0.036	12	0.014	4
C_{12}	ICT adoption	0.149	0.059	16	0.101	16	0.026	15	0.105	16	0.046	16
C_{13}	Skill	0.053	0.019	8	0.026	12	0.013	9	0.030	10	0.023	9
C_{14}	Labor market	0.032	0.014	4	0.015	3	0.009	5	0.013	1	0.013	2
D_5	Sustainability and Innovation	0.121	0.033	4	0.023	2	0.021	5	0.033	4	0.028	3
C_{15}	Sustainable planning	0.053	0.021	10	0.016	5	0.015	12	0.026	7	0.019	6
C_{16}	Innovation foundation	0.068	0.044	14	0.030	13	0.026	14	0.040	14	0.037	13
	Total		0.391		0.421		0.217		0.519		0.398	
	Rank			2		4		1		5		3

Croatia is another feasible choice if improvements can be made to the local Entrepreneurial culture and ICT adoption. For Viet Nam, the local Entrepreneurial culture and ICT adoption are the two critical items which need to be improved. India has good performance in the Economy and Market dimension but needs to pay attention to local ICT adoption and Entrepreneurial culture. Uganda should improve its innovation foundation.

5. Discussion

The proposed DANP mV model adds a combination weight assessment to the traditional model foundation. The combination weights (CWs) are set according to different strategic requirements and will eventually produce different assessment results. The influential weights (IWs), objective weights

(OWs) and combination weights (CWs) for each dimension are shown on the left side of Table 6, while the results of the evaluation based on the different weights are shown on the right-hand side. The order of the influential weights, from highest to lowest, is Government and Governance (D_2), Infrastructure (D_4), Business dynamism (D_3), Economy and Market (D_1) and finally Sustainability and Innovation (D_5). The order of the objective weights (OWs) from highest to lowest is Infrastructure (D_4), Government and Governance (D_2), Economy and Market (D_1), Sustainability and Innovation (D_5) and Business dynamism (D_3). The order of the combination weights (CWs) from highest to lowest is Infrastructure (D_4), Government and Governance (D_2), Economy and Market (D_1), Business dynamism (D_3) and Sustainability and Innovation (D_5).

Table 6. Comparison of weights and ranking.

Dimensions	Weight			Alternative	IWs		OWs		CWs	
	DANP	Entropy	Combination		r_{kj}	RANK	r_{kj}	RANK	r_{kj}	RANK
D_1	0.188 4	0.097 3	0.142 3	TWN	0.227	1	0.208	1	0.217	1
D_2	0.226 1	0.28 2	0.253 2	HRV	0.393	3	0.39	2	0.391	2
D_3	0.213 3	0.066 5	0.140 4	VNM	0.399	4	0.396	3	0.398	3
D_4	0.220 2	0.467 1	0.344 1	IND	0.378	2	0.464	4	0.421	4
D_5	0.153 5	0.09 4	0.121 5	UGA	0.477	5	0.561	5	0.519	5

As indicated in Table 6, the final selection order is TWN, HRV, VNM, IND, UGA based on the combined weights. However, if only the DANP weight is considered, the final selection order will become TWN, IND, HRV, VNM and UGA. The results reveal that adding the objective weights to the model has a significant effect on the results. This is consistent with the study of Chang and Lin [19]. If the final evaluation decision is only dependent on subjective weights, the results will be easily influenced by the subjective preferences of senior managers.

Figure 4 shows the weight distribution among the dimensions and criteria and the gaps from the aspiration level for each alternative. From the DANP weight distribution, we can see that the most important dimension is Government and Governance (D_2) and Infrastructure (D_4), which is consistent with the opinions of the experts as given during the interview process. The greatest incentives for the case company to invest in China would be the various policy subsidies in the Hercynian Special Economic Zone and the large amount of cheap labor and the stable water and electricity supply. However, the greatest risk would be the uncertainty of the government's authoritarian regime and regulations.

It is worth noting that Infrastructure (D_4) dominates the importance of the dimensions, regardless of whether for DANP or entropy analysis, where ICT adoption is the most important criterion in the Infrastructure dimension. The development of ICT infrastructure is essential for the governments of various countries who have been actively promoting Industry 4.0 and smart manufacturing in recent years. This results also show that the levels of ICT adoption have a critical effect on firms considering relocation of their production lines. Although the results indicate that TWN should be given the first priority, various gaps to the aspiration level remain in each dimension or criterion.

This study compares the original and modified VIKOR and the results are shown in Figure 5. The left side of the panel is the total gap of five countries. Orange is the modified calculation result and black is the original calculation result. It can be found that if using the original VIKOR, Taiwan's total Gap is only 0.008, which means almost perfect performance. From the right side of the panel, the results of original VIKOR have zero gap in each criterion except in C_5 Institutions with 0.008. This result might not reflect the real situation. Our proposed model can fix this problem. There are different gaps in each criterion to reach the aspiration level.

The case company should formulate and choose the supply chain layout in a more systematic way, to move towards the goal of sustainable operations. Based on the analysis, the assessed sites can be divided into a primary group (TWN, HRV) and a secondary group (VNM, IND, UGA). Although the countries in the primary group have the higher priority, there is still much room for improvement in their entrepreneurial culture, foundations of innovation and ICT adoption (Table 5). Based on the INRM (Figure 2), one can see that ICT adoption belongs in the Infrastructure dimension, which will be influenced by the Government and Governance, Business dynamism, Sustainability and Innovation dimensions. In addition, entrepreneurial culture belongs to the dimension of Business Dynamism, which is also influenced by the Sustainability and Innovation dimensions. Therefore, the Sustainability and Innovation dimensions are causal, being the driving force in the whole system. It is worth noting that the Sustainability and Innovation dimensions include innovation foundation and sustainable planning. Also, from the INRM, it can be seen that innovation foundation is causal and is the key item that the case company needs to develop and prepare for in advance. It is suggested that the case company set up an in-house innovation department and keep an eye on international economic trends and industry dynamics, to get first-hand information, to enable it to respond to rapid market changes. In summary, this study not only provides the optimal location for relocation of the production line but also offers suggested directions for improvement directions for the case company.

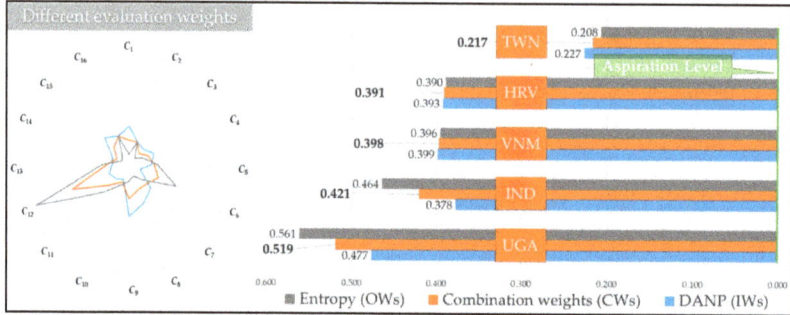

Figure 4. Overall ranking and performance of each alternative.

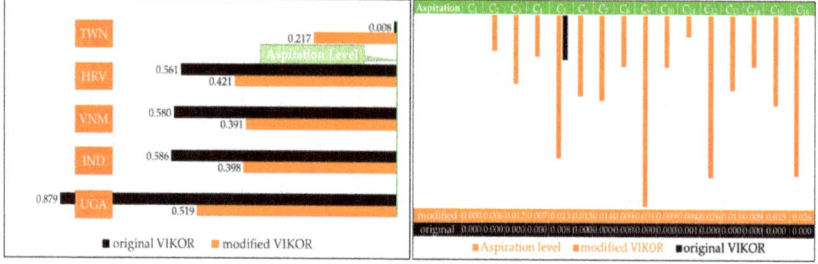

Figure 5. VIKOR (VIšekriterijumsko Kompromisno Rangiranje) method Comparative that from to original and modification.

6. Conclusions

This paper explores a method based on the DANP-mV model for the location selection of production lines which have to be moved due to economic fluctuations and trade wars, which is for sustainable development. We propose a hybrid model that considers both subjective and objective weights thereby avoiding the shortcomings of the original DANP model. The model can help companies determine the optimal location for relocation and provide directions for improvement based on the INRM and gap analysis. We conducted an empirical study to demonstrate the usefulness of the proposed model. The following findings are derived:

1. The proposed DANP-mV model has been verified by real cases, which can fix the shortcomings of original VIKOR method.

2. The entrepreneurial culture, innovation foundation and ICT adoption are the three items that most possible alternatives need to strengthen to attract foreign investment.
3. Sustainability and Innovation is the driving dimension in the system for the company's sustainable development.
4. Setting up an in-house innovation department could be an effective way in cope with deficiencies of the innovation foundation in the potential countries.

Although this study makes some contributions to the location selection problem, there are some suggestions for future study. First, the survey method is a time-consuming process. How to reduce the number of questions and still obtain reliable results could be the subject of further study. Second, different subjective and objective assessment methods can be compared with those used in the current study. Third, the current study used an average to represent the various experts' opinions. Other techniques such as rough number or fuzzy theory could be considered to integrate the different opinions. Fourth, an electronics manufacturing company was used for the case study. The model can be applied in different industries for comparison. Finally, this study finds that sustainable development and innovation is an important factor driving the sustainable development of enterprises. It is suggested that follow-up research can be directed towards discussing how to effectively improve national policies based on the viewpoint of sustainable development and innovation.

Author Contributions: S.-W.H. literature review, article writing, analyzed the data and formatting. W.T. collected the data and article writing. J.J.H.L. writing—Review and editing. Finally, G.-H.T. writing—Review. All authors have read and agreed to the published version of the manuscript.

Funding: This research was funded by the Ministry of Science and Technology, Taiwan, grant number MOST 107-2410-H-305 -038 -MY3, MOST 108-2221-E-305 -002 -MY3 and MOST 109-2410-H-305-056.

Acknowledgments: The authors are extremely grateful for the symmetry editorial team's valuable comments on improving the quality of this article.

Conflicts of Interest: The authors declare no conflict of interest.

Appendix A

Table A1. List of symbols for this study.

Term	Definition
E	Initial direct influence relationship matrix
K	Number of experts
A	Average direct influence relationship matrix
N^d	Normalized directly influence relationship matrix
N^e	Normalized performance evaluation matrix of entropy
N^v	Normalized performance evaluation matrix of modified VIKOR
T	Total influence relationship matrix
T_D	Total influence relationship matrix of the dimensions
T_C	Total influence relationship matrix of the criterion
r	Degree of influence
c	Degree of to be influenced
$(r+c)$	Total influence degree
$(r-c)$	The degree of net influence
S	Unweighted super matrix
S^w	Weighted super matrix
w^{iws}	Influence weight of the entire system
F	Performance evaluation matrix
e_j	Variation degree of the criterion
p	Constant
$\bar{e}_j$	Degree of the divergence coefficient
w^{ows}	Objective weight of the entire system
w^*	Combination weights
f^{asp}	Aspiration level
f^{wst}	Worst value
G	Overall benefit evaluation matrix
r_{qj}	Average group utility

Table A2. List of abbreviations for this study.

Term	Definition
MCDM	Multiple criteria decision making
DEMATEL	Decision Making Trial and Evaluation Laboratory
AHP	Analytic hierarchy process
ANP	Analytic network process
BWM	Best-worst multi-criteria decision-making method
DANP	DEMATEL-based ANP
modified VIKOR	Modified višekriterijumsko Kompromisno Rangiranje
DANP-mV	DEMATEL-based ANP- modified VIKOR
ICT	Information and Communication Technology
GDP	Gross domestic product
GIS	Geographic information system
INRM	Influential network relationship map
IWs	Influential weights
OWs	Objective weights
CWs	Combination weights

References

1. Lin, F. Fragmented production in east Asia: What are their implications for the Sino-U.S. trade. In Proceedings of the 13th Global Congress on Manufacturing and Management (GCMM 2016), Zhengzhou, China, 28–30 November 2016.
2. Olhager, J.; Pashaei, S.; Sternberg, H. Design of global production and distribution networks: A literature review and research agenda. *Int. J. Phys. Distrib. Logist. Manag.* **2015**, *45*, 138–158. [CrossRef]
3. Akkermans, H.; Van Wassenhove, L.N. Supply chain tsunamis: Research on low-probability, high-impact disruptions. *J. Supply Chain Manag.* **2018**, *54*, 64–76. [CrossRef]
4. Maswood, S.J. *Revisiting Globalization and the Rise of Global Production Networks*, 1st ed.; Palgrave Macmillan: London, UK, 2018; pp. 81–112.
5. Partovi, F.Y. An analytic model for locating facilities strategically. *Omega* **2006**, *34*, 41–55. [CrossRef]
6. Liu, W.K. Using FDM and DEMATEL approaches to evaluate the location selection of investment. *Int. J. Inf. Educ. Technol.* **2015**, *5*, 732–739. [CrossRef]
7. Mousavi, S.M.; Tavakkoli-Moghaddam, R.; Heydar, M.; Ebrahimnejad, S. Multi-criteria decision making for plant location selection: An integrated Delphi–AHP–PROMETHEE methodology. *Arab. J. Sci. Eng.* **2013**, *38*, 1255–1268. [CrossRef]
8. Tavakkoli, M.R.; Mousavi, S.M.; Heydar, M. An integrated AHP-VIKOR methodology for plant location selection. *Int. J. Eng.* **2011**, *24*, 127–137.
9. Liou, J.J.; Chuang, Y.C.; Tzeng, G.H. A fuzzy integral-based model for supplier evaluation and improvement. *Inf. Sci.* **2014**, *266*, 199–217. [CrossRef]
10. Jain, N.K.; Kothari, T.; Kumar, V. Location choice research: Proposing new agenda. *Manag. Int. Rev.* **2016**, *56*, 303–324. [CrossRef]
11. Marinković, S.; Nikolić, I.; Rakićević, J. Selecting location for a new business unit in ICT industry. *Čas. Ekon. Teor. Praksu* **2018**, *36*, 801–825.
12. Wang, X.; Zhang, C.; Zhang, Z. Pollution haven or porter? The impact of environmental regulation on location choices of pollution-intensive firms in China. *J. Environ. Manag.* **2019**, *248*, 109248. [CrossRef]
13. Mudambi, R.; Narula, R.; Santangelo, G.D. Location, collocation and innovation by multinational enterprises: A research agenda. *Ind. Innov.* **2018**, *25*, 229–241. [CrossRef]
14. Ye, Y.; Wu, K.; Xie, Y.; Huang, G.; Wang, C.; Chen, J. How firm heterogeneity affects foreign direct investment location choice: Micro-evidence from new foreign manufacturing firms in the Pearl River Delta. *Appl. Geogr.* **2019**, *106*, 11–21. [CrossRef]
15. Zheng, D.; Shi, M. Industrial land policy, firm heterogeneity and firm location choice: Evidence from China. *Land Use Policy* **2018**, *76*, 58–67. [CrossRef]
16. Chou, C.C. Application of a fuzzy MCDM model to the evaluation of plant location. *Int. J. Innov. Comput. Inf. Control* **2010**, *6*, 2581–2594.

17. Chen, C.T. A fuzzy MCDM method based on interval analysis for solving plant location selection problem. *J. Chin. Inst. Ind. Eng.* **2000**, *17*, 111–120. [CrossRef]
18. Qu, G.B.; Zhao, T.Y.; Zhu, B.W.; Tzeng, G.H.; Huang, S.L. Use of a modified DANP-mV model to improve quality of life in rural residents: The empirical case of Xingshisi village, China. *Int. J. Environ. Res. Public Health* **2019**, *16*, 153. [CrossRef]
19. Chang, P.Y.; Lin, H.Y. Manufacturing plant location selection in logistics network using Analytic Hierarchy Process. *J. Ind. Eng. Manag.* **2015**, *8*, 1547–1575. [CrossRef]
20. Yang, K.; Zhu, N.; Chang, C.; Wang, D.; Yang, S.; Ma, S. A methodological concept for phase change material selection based on multi-criteria decision making (MCDM): A case study. *Energy* **2018**, *165*, 1085–1096. [CrossRef]
21. Qin, Q.; Liang, F.; Li, L.; Wei, Y.M. Selection of energy performance contracting business models: A behavioral decision-making approach. *Renew. Sustain. Energy Rev.* **2017**, *72*, 422–433. [CrossRef]
22. Lotfi, F.H.; Fallahnejad, R. Imprecise Shannon's entropy and multi attribute decision making. *Entropy* **2010**, *12*, 53–62. [CrossRef]
23. Lee, H.C.; Chang, C.T. Comparative analysis of MCDM methods for ranking renewable energy sources in Taiwan. *Renew. Sustain. Energy Rev.* **2018**, *92*, 883–896. [CrossRef]
24. Mathivathanan, D.; Kannan, D.; Haq, A.N. Sustainable supply chain management practices in Indian automotive industry: A multi-stakeholder view. *Resour. Conserv. Recycl.* **2018**, *128*, 284–305. [CrossRef]
25. Kusi-Sarpong, S.; Gupta, H.; Sarkis, J. A supply chain sustainability innovation framework and evaluation methodology. *Int. J. Prod. Res.* **2019**, *57*, 1990–2008. [CrossRef]
26. Li, Y.; Mathiyazhagan, K. Application of DEMATEL approach to identify the influential indicators towards sustainable supply chain adoption in the auto components manufacturing sector. *J. Clean. Prod.* **2018**, *172*, 2931–2941. [CrossRef]
27. Sauer, P.C.; Seuring, S. Sustainable supply chain management for minerals. *J. Clean. Prod.* **2017**, *151*, 235–249. [CrossRef]
28. Chen, L.; Olhager, J.; Tang, O. Manufacturing facility location and sustainability: A literature review and research agenda. *Int. J. Prod. Econ.* **2014**, *149*, 154–163. [CrossRef]
29. Anvari, S.; Turkay, M. The facility location problem from the perspective of triple bottom line accounting of sustainability. *Int. J. Prod. Res.* **2017**, *55*, 6266–6287. [CrossRef]
30. Zandiatashbar, A.; Hamidi, S.; Foster, N. High-tech business location, transportation accessibility, and implications for sustainability: Evaluating the differences between high-tech specializations using empirical evidence from US booming regions. *Sustain. Cities Soc.* **2019**, *50*, 101648. [CrossRef]
31. Kim, J.U.; Aguilera, R.V. Foreign location choice: Review and extensions. *Int. J. Manag. Rev.* **2016**, *18*, 133–159. [CrossRef]
32. Kurtović, S.; Maxhuni, N.; Halili, B.; Talović, S. The determinants of FDI location choice in the Western Balkan countries. *Post Communist Econ.* **2020**, 1–22. [CrossRef]
33. Kamal, M.A.; Hasanat Shah, S.; Jing, W.; Hasnat, H. Does the quality of institutions in host countries affect the location choice of Chinese OFDI: Evidence from Asia and Africa. *Emerg. Mark. Financ. Trade* **2020**, *56*, 208–227. [CrossRef]
34. Shuyan, L.; Fabuš, M. Study on the spatial distribution of China's Outward Foreign Direct Investment in EU and its influencing factors. *Entrep. Sustain. Issues* **2019**, *6*, 1080–1096. [CrossRef]
35. He, Z.; Romanos, M. Spatial agglomeration and location determinants: Evidence from the US communications equipment manufacturing industry. *Urban Stud.* **2016**, *53*, 2154–2174. [CrossRef]
36. Wyrwa, J. Analysis of determinants of the inflow of foreign direct investment to Poland. Part I—Theoretical considerations. *Management* **2019**, *23*, 238–262. [CrossRef]
37. Wang, K.J.; Lestari, Y.D.; Yang, T.T. Location determinants of market expansion in China's second-tier cities: A case study of the biotechnology industry. *J. Bus. Ind. Mark.* **2015**, *3*, 139–152. [CrossRef]
38. Rahman, S.T.; Kabir, A. Factors influencing location choice and cluster pattern of manufacturing small and medium enterprises in cities: Evidence from Khulna city of Bangladesh. *J. Glob. Entrep. Res.* **2019**, *9*, 61. [CrossRef]
39. Breedveld, S.; Craft, D.; Van Haveren, R.; Heijmen, B. Multi-criteria optimization and decision-making in radiotherapy. *Eur. J. Oper. Res.* **2019**, *277*, 1–19. [CrossRef]

40. Cinelli, M.; Kadziński, M.; Gonzalez, M.; Słowiński, R. How to support the application of multiple criteria decision analysis? let Us Start with a comprehensive taxonomy. *Omega* **2020**, *96*, 102261. [CrossRef]
41. Katsikopoulos, K.V.; Durbach, I.N.; Stewart, T.J. When should we use simple decision models? A synthesis of various research strands. *Omega* **2018**, *81*, 17–25. [CrossRef]
42. Tzeng, G.H.; Shen, K.Y. *New Concepts and Trends of Hybrid Multiple Criteria Decision Making*, 1st ed.; CRC Press: London, UK, 2017.
43. Wang, K.J.; Lestari, Y.D.; Tran, V.N.B. Location selection of high-tech manufacturing firms by a fuzzy analytic network process: A case study of Taiwan high-tech industry. *Int. J. Fuzzy Syst.* **2017**, *19*, 1560–1584. [CrossRef]
44. Khokhar, M.; Hou, Y.; Rafique, M.A.; Iqbal, W. Evaluating the Social Sustainability Criteria of Supply Chain Management in Manufacturing Industries: A Role of BWM in MCDM. *Probl. Ekorozw. Probl. Sustain. Dev.* **2020**, *15*, 185–194.
45. Rocha, A.; Silveira, D.; Perobelli, F.; Vasconcelos, S. Modelling the location choice: Evidence from an evolutionary game based on regional input-output analysis. *Reg. Stud.* **2019**, *53*, 1734–1746. [CrossRef]
46. Liou, J.J. New concepts and trends of MCDM for tomorrow–in honor of Professor Gwo-Hshiung Tzeng on the occasion of his 70th birthday. *Technol. Econ. Dev. Econ.* **2013**, *19*, 367–375. [CrossRef]
47. Liou, J.J.; Lu, M.T.; Hu, S.K.; Cheng, C.H.; Chuang, Y.C. A hybrid MCDM model for improving the electronic health record to better serve client needs. *Sustainability* **2017**, *9*, 1819. [CrossRef]
48. Lin, S.H.; Wang, D.; Huang, X.; Zhao, X.; Hsieh, J.C.; Tzeng, G.H.; Chen, J.T. A multi-attribute decision-making model for improving inefficient industrial parks. *Environ. Dev. Sustain.* **2020**, 1–35. [CrossRef]
49. Tsuei, H.J.; Tsai, W.H.; Pan, F.T.; Tzeng, G.H. Improving search engine optimization (SEO) by using hybrid modified MCDM models. *Artif. Intell. Rev.* **2020**, *53*, 1–16. [CrossRef]
50. Lin, P.J.; Shiue, Y.C.; Tzeng, G.H.; Huang, S.L. Developing a sustainable long-term ageing health care system using the DANP-mV model: Empirical case of Taiwan. *Int. J. Environ. Res. Public Health* **2019**, *16*, 1349. [CrossRef]
51. Peng, K.H.; Tzeng, G.H. Exploring heritage tourism performance improvement for making sustainable development strategies using the hybrid-modified MADM model. *Curr. Issues Tour.* **2019**, *22*, 921–947. [CrossRef]
52. Huang, J.Y.; Shen, K.Y.; Shieh, J.C.; Tzeng, G.H. Strengthen financial holding companies' business sustainability by using a hybrid corporate governance evaluation model. *Sustainability* **2019**, *11*, 582. [CrossRef]
53. Zavadskas, E.K.; Podvezko, V. Integrated determination of objective criteria weights in MCDM. *Int. J. Inf. Technol. Decis. Mak.* **2016**, *15*, 267–283. [CrossRef]
54. Zhao, J.; Ji, G.; Tian, Y.; Chen, Y.; Wang, Z. Environmental vulnerability assessment for mainland China based on entropy method. *Ecol. Indic.* **2018**, *91*, 410–422. [CrossRef]
55. Vujičić, M.D.; Papić, M.Z.; Blagojević, M.D. Comparative analysis of objective techniques for criteria weighing in two MCDM methods on example of an air conditioner selection. *Tehnika* **2017**, *72*, 422–429. [CrossRef]
56. Duckstein, L.; Opricovic, S. Multiobjective optimization in river basin development. *Water Resour. Res.* **1980**, *16*, 14–20. [CrossRef]
57. Opricovic, S. Multicriteria Optimization of Civil Engineering Systems. Ph.D. Thesis, Faculty of Civil Engineering, University of Belgrade, Belgrade, Serbia, 1998.
58. Opricovic, S.; Tzeng, G.H. Compromise solution by MCDM methods: A comparative analysis of VIKOR and TOPSIS. *Eur. J. Oper. Res.* **2004**, *156*, 445–455. [CrossRef]
59. Tzeng, G.H.; Huang, J.J. *Multiple Attribute Decision Making: Methods and Applications*, 1st ed.; CRC Press: London, UK, 2011.
60. Liou, J.J.; Chuang, Y.T. Developing a hybrid multi-criteria model for selection of outsourcing providers. *Expert Syst. Appl.* **2010**, *37*, 3755–3761. [CrossRef]
61. Kao, R.S. Sino-US trade war and its possible impact on Taiwan's industries. *J. Strateg. Secur. Anal.* **2018**, *150*, 59–68.
62. Chen, J.L. Discussion on the impact of Sino-US trade war on Taiwanese manufacturing. *Int. J. Bus. Manag.* **2019**, *14*, 70–76. [CrossRef]
63. Ray, A.; De, A.; Dan, P.K. Facility location selection using complete and partial ranking MCDM methods. *Int. J. Ind. Syst. Eng.* **2015**, *19*, 262–276. [CrossRef]

64. Gupta, P.; Mehlawat, M.K.; Grover, N. Intuitionistic fuzzy multi-attribute group decision-making with an application to plant location selection based on a new extended VIKOR method. *Inf. Sci.* **2016**, *370*, 184–203. [CrossRef]
65. Tabari, M.; Kaboli, A.; Aryanezhad, M.B.; Shahanaghi, K.; Siadat, A. A new method for location selection: A hybrid analysis. *Appl. Math. Comput.* **2008**, *206*, 598–606. [CrossRef]
66. Shah, M.H. The effect of macroeconomic stability on inward FDI in African developing countries. International. *J. Bus. Stud. Rev.* **2016**, *1*, 1–11.
67. Janssen, M.; Van Der Voort, H. Adaptive governance: Towards a stable, accountable and responsive government. *Gov. Inf. Quart.* **2016**, *33*, 1–5. [CrossRef]
68. Global Competitiveness Index 4.0. Available online: www.weforum.org/gcr/rankings (accessed on 15 November 2019).

© 2020 by the authors. Licensee MDPI, Basel, Switzerland. This article is an open access article distributed under the terms and conditions of the Creative Commons Attribution (CC BY) license (http://creativecommons.org/licenses/by/4.0/).

Article

A Novel Extension of the TOPSIS Method Adapted for the Use of Single-Valued Neutrosophic Sets and Hamming Distance for E-Commerce Development Strategies Selection

Darjan Karabašević [1,*], Dragiša Stanujkić [2], Edmundas Kazimieras Zavadskas [3], Predrag Stanimirović [4], Gabrijela Popović [1], Bratislav Predić [5] and Alptekin Ulutaş [6]

1. Faculty of Applied Management, Economics and Finance, University Business Academy in Novi Sad, Belgrade, Serbia, Jevrejska 24, 11000 Belgrade, Serbia; gabrijela.popovic@mef.edu.rs
2. Technical Faculty in Bor, University of Belgrade, Vojske Jugoslavije 12, 19210 Bor, Serbia; dstanujkic@tfbor.bg.ac.rs
3. Institute of Sustainable Construction, Vilnius Gediminas Technical University, LT 10223 Vilnius, Lithuania; edmundas.zavadskas@vgtu.lt
4. Faculty of Sciences and Mathematics, University of Niš, Višegradska 33, 18000 Niš, Serbia; pecko@pmf.ni.ac.rs
5. Faculty of Electronic Engineering, University of Niš, Aleksandra Medvedeva 14, 18000 Niš, Serbia; bratislav.predic@elfak.ni.ac.rs
6. Department of International Trade and Logistics, Faculty of Economics and Administrative Sciences, Sivas Cumhuriyet University, Sivas 58140, Turkey; aulutas@cumhuriyet.edu.tr
* Correspondence: darjan.karabasevic@mef.edu.rs or darjan.karabasevic@gmail.com

Received: 23 June 2020; Accepted: 3 July 2020; Published: 30 July 2020

Abstract: Neutrosophic sets have been recognized as an effective approach in solving complex decision-making (DM) problems, mainly when such problems are related to uncertainties, as published in numerous articles thus far. The use of the three membership functions that can be used to express accuracy, inaccuracy, and indeterminacy during the evaluation of alternatives in multiple-criteria DM can be said to be a significant advantage of these sets. By utilizing these membership functions, neutrosophic sets provide an efficient and flexible approach to the evaluation of alternatives, even if DM problems are related to uncertainty and predictions. On the other hand, the TOPSIS method is a prominent multiple-criteria decision-making method used so far to solve numerous decision-making problems, and many extensions of the TOPSIS method are proposed to enable the use of different types of fuzzy as well as neutrosophic sets. Therefore, a novel extension of the TOPSIS method adapted for the use of single-valued neutrosophic sets was considered in this paper.

Keywords: multiple-criteria decision-making; neutrosophic; single-valued neutrosophic sets; TOPSIS; Hamming distance; Euclidean distance; e-commerce development strategies

1. Introduction

As one of the essential elements of the modern world economy and the increasing use of advanced information and communication technology (ICT), technological changes have driven fundamental changes in the economic and social environments, thereby transforming society from the industrial into the information age [1]. The increasing use of ICT has significantly changed the way we live, learn, and work, transforming the direction of the interaction of people, business systems, and public institutions. The development of information technologies, and in particular, the advancement of Internet technologies, enables existing businesses to progress and the opening of new businesses, leading to the growth of e-business and the digital economy [2,3].

The Internet has contributed to the extremely dynamic development of e-commerce within e-business. In its simplest sense, e-commerce implies the purchase and sale of goods or services online as well as advertising revenue. Without the Internet, e-commerce would be virtually non-existent. Therefore, e-commerce includes all activities of buying and selling products and services that are performed via the Internet or other electronic communication channels [4]. First of all, e-commerce consists of distributing, buying, selling, marketing, and servicing products and services through the Internet. It also incorporates electronic money transfer, supply chain management, e-marketing, electronic data exchange, and automated data collection systems [5]. Over time, e-commerce has transformed from a mechanism for online retail sales into something much broader [6]. This is why it is of great importance which e-commerce strategy the company will choose to implement [7]. The selection of an optimal strategy is vital because the strategy defines the future direction and actions of the organization or part of the organization [8]. Developing an e-commerce strategy requires combining existing approaches to business and developing an information systems strategy. In order to achieve a competitive advantage, it is crucial to join innovative techniques in traditional strategic approaches [9]. The implementation of an adequate strategy may help the company to achieve and maintain its competitive advantage in the long run [10].

Many of the real problems are often characterized by a number of mostly antagonistic criteria. Multiple-criteria decision-making (MCDM) is a notable part of operational research. It considers the issues in which we are faced with a greater number of, most often conflicting, criteria when making a decision [11–13]. The extraordinarily rapid and dynamic development of MCDM worldwide has contributed to a number of MCDM methods and techniques proposed by scholars to solve a wide variety of problems [14,15]. Some of the prominent methods that are most applied are the AHP method (Analytic hierarchy process) [16], the ELECTRE method (Elimination et choix traduisant la realité) [17], the PROMETHEE method (Preference ranking organization method for enrichment evaluations) [18], the TOPSIS method (Technique for order preference by similarity to ideal solution) [19], the COPRAS method (Complex proportional assessment of alternatives) [20], the VIKOR method (Visekriterijumska optimizacija i kompromisno resenje) [21], the MOORA method (Multi-objective optimization on basis of ratio analysis) [22], the MULTIMOORA method (Multi-objective optimization by ratio analysis plus the full multiplicative form) [23], and so on.

Hwang and Yoon [19] develop the TOPSIS method (Technique for Order Preference by Similarity to Ideal Solution). To solve a broader range of problems when problems are related to uncertainties, ambiguities, and vagueness, the TOPSIS method has a proper extension based on the application of fuzzy, intuitionistic, grey, and neutrosophic numbers to be able to cope with these problems. To date, the TOPSIS method has been applied to solving many cases, often in combination with other techniques, some of which are as follows: the application of TOPSIS when deciding on a discipline, course, and university [24]; the application of entropy TOPSIS-F for the performance assessment of green suppliers [25]; the evaluation of solar power technologies based on the application of the intuitionistic fuzzy TOPSIS [26]; hotel evaluation and selection based on the modified TOPSIS decision support algorithm [27]; the evaluation of the sustainable energy planning strategies based on the SWOT-AHP method and Fuzzy TOPSIS method [28]; supplier evaluation and selection based on the green innovation ability based on the BWM and fuzzy TOPSIS [29]; website assessment by employing the interval type-2 fuzzy number TOPSIS approach [30]; assessment in civil engineering [31–33]; evaluation and selection of personnel [34–37]; and so on.

Neutrosophic sets were established by Smarandache [38] to deal with complex DM problems related to uncertainties, which are followed by inconsistent and indeterminate information. The use of the three membership functions in order to express accuracy, indeterminacy, and inaccuracy during the evaluation of alternatives in MCDM can be said to be a very important and significant advantage of neutrosophic sets. So far, neutrosophic sets have been utilized in different fields such as medical analysis [39–42], transport [43,44], information and communication technology [45–47], MCDM [48–52], and so forth.

Therefore, a novel extension of the TOPSIS method adapted for the application of single-valued neutrosophic sets is the subject matter of consideration in this manuscript. The applicability and usability of the developed single-valued neutrosophic TOPSIS extension are demonstrated on a numerical illustration of the evaluation and selection of e-commerce development strategies. For all of the preceding reasons, the remainder of the manuscript is based on the following global organization of sections. The preliminaries are presented in Section 2; in Section 3, the TOPSIS method customized to the use of single-valued neutrosophic numbers (SVNNs) and group decision-making is presented; Section 4 contains a presentation of the numerical clarification, whereas Section 5 presents a discussion and a comparison analysis. Finally, concluding remarks are specified at the end of the manuscript.

2. Preliminaries

In this part of the manuscript, some fundamental definitions and notations of neutrosophic sets (NS), single-valued neutrosophic set (SVNS), and single-valued neutrosophic numbers (SVNN) are given.

Definition 1. *[53] Let X denote the universe of discourse. The NS A in X has the following form*

$$A = \{\langle x, \mu_A(x), \pi_A(x), v_A(x) \rangle | x \in X\}, \tag{1}$$

where $\mu_A(x)$ denotes the truth–membership function; $\mu_A \in\ ]^-0, 1^+[$; $\pi_A(x)$ denotes the falsity-membership function; $\pi_A \in\ ]^-0, 1^+[$; and $v_A(x)$ denotes the falsity–membership function, $v_A \in\ ]^-0, 1^+[$. These membership functions must satisfy the following constraint $^-0 \leq \mu_A(x) + \pi_A(x) + v_A(x) \leq 3^+$.

Definition 2. *[54] Let X be a nonempty set. The SVNS A in X has the following form*

$$A = \{\langle x, \mu_A(x), \pi_A(x), v_A(x) \rangle | x \in X\} \tag{2}$$

wheremembership functions T_A, I_A, and $F_A \in [^-0, 1^+]$ and satisfy the following constraint $0 \leq \mu_A(x) + \pi_A(x) + v_A(x) \leq 3$.

Definition 3. *[54] A SVNN $a = \langle t_a, i_a, f_a \rangle$ is a special case of a SVNS on the set of real numbers $\mathcal{R}$, where $t_a, i_a, f_a \in [0, 1]$ and $0 \leq t_a + i_a + f_a \leq 3$.*

Definition 4. *[53] Let $x_1 = \langle t_1, i_1, f_1 \rangle$ be a SVNN and $\lambda > 0$. The multiplication SVNNs and λ are as follows:*

$$\lambda x_1 = \langle 1 - (1 - t_1)^\lambda, i_1^\lambda, f_1^\lambda \rangle \tag{3}$$

Definition 5. *Let $X = (x_1, x_2, ..., x_n)$ and $Y = (y_1, y_2, ..., y_n)$ be two n-dimensional vectors, $x_i = \langle t_{xi}, i_{xi}, f_{xi} \rangle$ and $y_i = \langle t_{yi}, i_{yi}, f_{yi} \rangle$. The Hamming distance between X and Y is defined as*

$$h_{(X,Y)} = \frac{1}{3n} \sum_{i=1}^{n} \left(|t_{xi} - t_{yi}| + |i_{xi} - i_{yi}| + |f_{xi} - f_{yi}| \right). \tag{4}$$

Definition 6. *Let $X = (x_1, x_2, ..., x_n)$ and $Y = (y_1, y_2, ..., y_n)$ be two n-dimensional vectors, $x_i = \langle t_{xi}, i_{xi}, f_{xi} \rangle$ and $y_i = \langle t_{yi}, i_{yi}, f_{yi} \rangle$. The Euclidean distance between X and Y is defined as*

$$e_{(X,Y)} = \frac{1}{3n} \sqrt{\sum_{i=1}^{n} \left((t_{xi} - t_{yi})^2 + (i_{xi} - i_{yi})^2 + (f_{xi} - f_{yi})^2 \right)}. \tag{5}$$

Definition 7. [55] Let $x = <t, i, f>$ be a SVNN. The score function s of x is defined as

$$s = (1 + t - 2i - f)/2, \qquad (6)$$

where $s \in [-1, 1]$.

Definition 8. [56] Let $x = <t, i, f>$ be a SVNN. The cosine similarity measure of x is the expression

$$c = \frac{t}{\sqrt{t^2 + i^2 + f^2}} \qquad (7)$$

Definition 9. [55] Let $a_j = <t_j, i_j, f_j>$ be a collection of SVNSs and $W = (w_1, w_2, \ldots, w_n)^T$ be an associated weighting vector. The Single-Valued Neutrosophic Weighted Average (SVNWA) operator of a_j is

$$SVNWA(a_1, a_2, \ldots, a_n) = \sum_{j=1}^{n} w_j a_j = \left(1 - \prod_{j=1}^{n}(1-t_j)^{w_j}, \prod_{j=1}^{n}(i_j)^{w_j}, \prod_{j=1}^{n}(f_j)^{w_j}\right), \qquad (8)$$

where w_j is the element j of the weighting vector, $w_j \in [0, 1]$ and $\sum_{j=1}^{n} w_j = 1$.

3. The TOPSIS Method Customized to the Use of SVNNs and Group Decision-Making

3.1. The TOPSIS Method

The TOPSIS method, originated by Hwang and Yoon [19], is a very prominent and frequently used MCDM method. Compared to other MCDM methods, this method has a characteristic approach to determine the most acceptable alternative and is based upon the concept that an alternative is defined on the basis of the shortest distance to the ideal solution and the longest distance to the anti-ideal solution. The relative distance C_i of the ith alternative to the ideal and anti-ideal solutions is calculated as

$$C_i = \frac{d_i^-}{d_i^+ + d_i^-}, \qquad (9)$$

where d_i^+ and d_i^- denote the distance of the alternative i from the ideal and anti-ideal solutions, respectively, and $C_i \in [0, 1]$.

The distance of each alternative from the ideal and anti-ideal solutions are computed as follows:

$$d_i^+ = \left\{ \sum_{j=1}^{n} + (w_j(r_{ij} - r_j^+))^2 \right\}^{0.5} \qquad (10)$$

and

$$d_i^- = \left\{ \sum_{j=1}^{n} (w_j(r_{ij} - r_j^-))^2 \right\}^{0.5}. \qquad (11)$$

In Equations (10) and (11), w_j denotes the weight of the criterion j; r_j^+ and r_j^- denote the coordinate j of the ideal and anti-ideal solutions, respectively; and r_{ij} is the normalized rating of the alternative i to the criterion j.

The ordinary TOPSIS method utilizes the Euclidean distance to determine the separation measures. However, some authors such as Chang et al. [57], Shanian and Savadogo [58], and Hwang and Yoon [19], have also considered the application of the Hamming distance for that purpose:

$$d_i^+ = \sum_{j=1}^n w_j |r_{ij} - r_i^+|, \text{ and} \tag{12}$$

$$d_i^- = \sum_{j=1}^n w_j |r_{ij} - r_i^-|. \tag{13}$$

In the numerous extensions of the TOPSIS method that were later proposed, the application of the Hamming distance has become more common such as in the research of Gautam and Singh [59], Izadikhah [60], and Chen and Tsao [61].

The ordinary TOPSIS method uses the vector normalization procedure for the calculation of normalized ratings, as

$$r_{ij} = \frac{x_{ij}}{\left(\sum_{i=1}^n x_{ij}^2\right)^{1/2}} \tag{14}$$

where r_{ij} is the normalized rating of the alternative i to the criterion j, and x_{ij} is the rating of the alternative i to the criterion j.

In some extensions of the TOPSIS method, however, this normalization procedure is followed with a simpler normalization procedure [31,62], as follows:

$$r_{ij} = \frac{x_{ij}}{x_j^+}. \tag{15}$$

In Equation (15), it is assumed that x_j^+ denotes the largest rating of the criterion j.

The ideal A^* and the anti-ideal A^- solutions are defined by

$$A^+ = \left\{r_1^+, r_2^+, \ldots, r_n^+\right\} = \left\{\max_i r_{ij} | j \in \Theta_{\max}), (\min_i r_{ij} | j \in \Theta_{\min})\right\}, \tag{16}$$

$$A^- = \left\{r_1^-, r_2^-, \ldots, r_n^-\right\} = \left\{\min_i r_{ij} | j \in \Theta_{\max}), (\max_i r_{ij} | j \in \Theta_{\min})\right\}, \tag{17}$$

where r_j^+ denotes the coordinate j of the ideal solution; r_j^- denotes the coordinate j of the anti-ideal solution; and $\Theta_{\max}$ and $\Theta_{\min}$ denote the sets of beneficial and non-beneficial criteria, respectively.

3.2. An Extension of the TOPSIS Method Adapted for the Use of SVNNs

The typical MCDM problem that includes m alternatives and n criteria can concisely be presented in the following matrix form:

$$D = [x_{ij}]_{m \times n}, \tag{18}$$

$$W = [w_j]_n. \tag{19}$$

The entry x_{ij} in the evaluation matrix D means the rating of the alternative i with respect to the criterion j and entries w_j in W of the weight vector denote the weights of the criterion j, for each $i = 1, \ldots m$ and $j = 1, \ldots, n$.

However, many practical DM problems require the participation of more decision-makers or experts in the evaluation process. Therefore, in multiple-criteria group decision-making (MCGDM), there is more than one decision-making matrix

$$D^k = [x_{ij}^k]_{m \times n}, k = 1, \ldots, K, \quad (20)$$

where D^k denotes an evaluation matrix formed by the decision-maker and/or expert k; x_{ij}^k is the rating of the alternative i with respect to the criterion j obtained from the decision-maker and/or expert k; and K denotes the number of decision-makers and/or experts.

In the MCGDM process, decision-makers and/or experts often have different experiences and/or specific knowledge of the problem that has to be solved, which is why another weighting vector can be used to express the impact of the decision-makers and/or experts on the final evaluation, namely as follows:

$$[\omega_k]_K. \quad (21)$$

The value ω_k is the significance or impact of the decision-maker and/or expert k on the overall evaluation.

Using the weighting vector that expresses the impact of decision-makers on the overall evaluation, the individual evaluation matrix obtained from the decision-makers and/or experts, and a sort of aggregation operator, an overall group decision-making matrix can be constructed.

Taking into consideration the foregoing facts pertaining to the MCGDM, the specifics of SVNNs and operations over them as well as the previously proposed extension of the TOPSIS method [54,63,64], a thorough step-by-step procedure of the adapted TOPSIS method, as shown in Figure 1, can be accurately presented through the following basic steps:

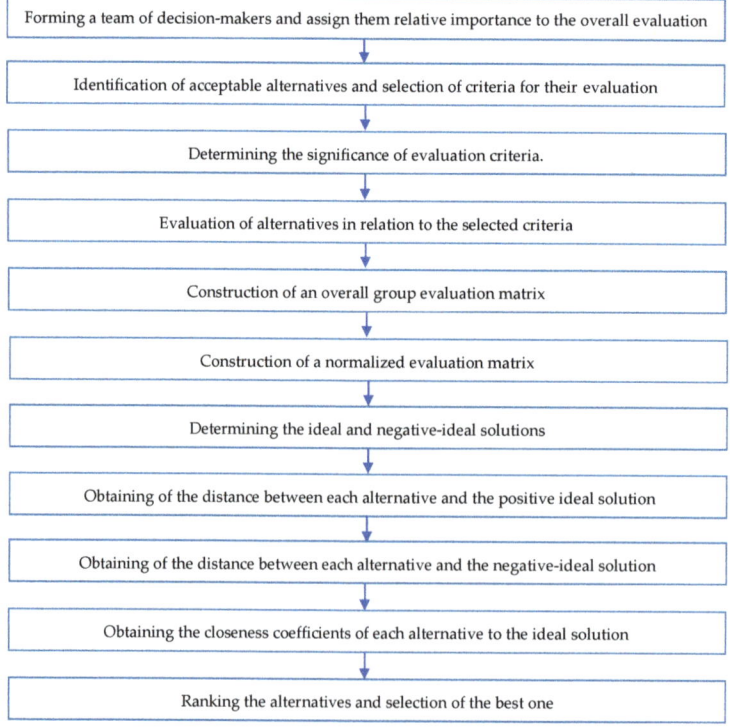

Figure 1. Computational procedure of the adapted TOPSIS method.

Step 1. Forming a team of decision-makers and assigning them relative importance to the overall evaluation. In the first step, a team of decision-makers and/or experts is formed and relative importance is assigned to each of them, if necessary. In many cases, all decision-makers and/or experts have equal importance to the final evaluation.

Step 2. Identification of acceptable alternatives and selection of criteria for their evaluation. In the second step, the team of decision-makers identified the feasible alternatives and determined a set of evaluation criteria.

Step 3. Determining the significance of evaluation criteria. In this step, the team of decision-makers and/or experts determined the weights of the evaluation criteria. A number of methods that can be used to determine criteria weights have been considered in many papers published in scientific and professional journals [16,65–68].

Step 4. Evaluation of alternatives in relation to the selected criteria. In the fourth step, each decision-maker performs an evaluation and forms their own evaluation matrix, in which the ratings are expressed by using SVNNs. As a result of performing this step, a K evaluation matrix is formed as follows:

$$D^k = [x_{ij}^k]_{m \times n} = [< t_{ij}^k, i_{ij}^k, f_{ij}^k >]_{m \times n}, \quad (22)$$

where $< t_{ij}^k, i_{ij}^k, f_{ij}^k >$ denotes the rating of the alternative i with respect to the criterion j, obtained from the decision-maker expert k.

Step 5. Construction of an overall group evaluation matrix. In this step, the individual attitudes of the decision-makers involved in the evaluation are transformed into one overall group evaluation matrix by using a SVNWA operator (i.e., by applying Equation (8)). As a result of performing this step, a matrix of the following form is formed:

$$D = [x_{ij}]_{m \times n} = [< t_{ij}, i_{ij}, f_{ij} >]_{m \times n}, \quad (23)$$

where $< t_{ij}, i_{ij}, f_{ij} >$ denotes the rating of the alternative i in relation to the criterion j.

Step 6. Construction of a normalized evaluation matrix. The normalization of the overall group evaluation matrix can be performed by applying Equation (3) and the following λ:

$$\lambda = \frac{1}{\max(\max_i t_{ij}, \max_i i_{ij}, \max_i f_{ij})}. \quad (24)$$

This step is not necessary if all ratings belong to the interval [0, 1].

Step 7. Determining the ideal and negative-ideal solutions. In the case when all evaluation criteria are beneficial, the ideal and negative ideal solutions are calculated as follows:

$$A^+ = \left\{ r_1^+, r_2^+, \ldots, r_n^+ \right\} = \left\{ < \max_i t_{ij}, \min_i i_{ij}, \min_i f_{ij} > \right\}, \quad (25)$$

$$A^- = \left\{ r_1^-, r_2^-, \ldots, r_n^- \right\} = \left\{ < \min_i t_{ij}, \max_i i_{ij}, \max_i f_{ij} > \right\}. \quad (26)$$

Step 8. Obtaining the distance between each alternative and the positive ideal solution. The distances between the alternatives and the positive ideal solution can be determined by applying Equations (4) or (5).

Step 9. Obtaining the distance between each alternative and the negative-ideal solution. The distances between the alternatives and the negative ideal solution can be determined in a similar manner as the distances to the ideal solution.

Step 10. Obtaining the closeness coefficients of each alternative to the ideal solution. Applying Equations (4) and (5), SVNNs are transformed into the resulting crisp values, thus allowing the application of Equation (9) to determine the closeness coefficients to the ideal solution, as in the ordinary TOPSIS method.

Step 11. Ranking the alternatives and selection of the best one. The final ranking of the considered alternatives remains the same as in the ordinary TOPSIS method, which means that an alternative with a higher value of the closeness coefficient is more preferable.

4. A Numerical Illustration

To demonstrate the efficiency and the applicability of the proposed extension, an example of the evaluation of e-commerce strategies adopted from Stanujkić et al. [69] is the subject matter of consideration in this section of the paper. Suppose a team of three decision-makers should evaluate three e-commerce development strategies based on five criteria. The e-commerce development strategies (ECDS) and the evaluation criteria are shown in Tables 1 and 2.

Table 1. E-commerce development strategies.

Alternatives	Designation
A_1—E-customization and personalization—Ansari & Mela [70]	ECDS1
A_2—Social E-commerce adoption model—Hajli [71]	ECDS2
A_3—Strong search engine optimization (SEO)—Sen [72]	ECDS3

Table 2. E-commerce development strategy evaluation criteria.

Criteria	Designation
C_1—Feasibility of the strategy	FS
C_2—Implementation speed	IS
C_3—Compliance with the corporate strategy	CS
C_4—Compliance of the strategy with the mission and vision of the company	MV
C_5—General acceptance	GA

The ratings obtained from the three decision-makers for the proposed strategies are shown in Tables 3–5.

Table 3. The ratings received from the first decision-maker.

	FS	IS	CS	MV	GA
ECDS1	<0.6, 0.1, 0.1>	<0.6, 0.1, 0.1>	<0.6, 0.1, 0.1>	<0.4, 0.1, 0.1>	<0.4, 0.1, 0.1>
ECDS2	<1.0, 0.0, 0.0>	<0.8, 0.0, 0.0>	<1.0, 0.1, 0.1>	<1.0, 0.1, 0.3>	<1.0, 0.0, 0.1>
ECDS3	<0.6, 0.0, 0.2>	<0.6, 0.2, 0.1>	<0.8, 0.2, 0.1>	<1.0, 0.2, 0.3>	<1.0, 0.0, 0.2>

Table 4. The ratings received from the second decision-maker.

	FS	IS	CS	MV	GA
ECDS1	<0.5, 0.0, 0.1>	<0.7, 0.1, 0.1>	<0.5, 0.0, 0.1>	<0.4, 0.1, 0.1>	<0.4, 0.0, 0.1>
ECDS2	<0.9, 0.0, 0.0>	<0.7, 0.1, 0.0>	<0.9, 0.0, 0.0>	<1.0, 0.0, 0.1>	<0.7, 0.0, 0.2>
ECDS3	<0.7, 0.0, 0.0>	<0.6, 0.1, 0.1>	<0.8, 0.1, 0.2>	<0.9, 0.1, 0.3>	<0.8, 0.0, 0.2>

Table 5. The ratings received from the third decision-maker.

	FS	IS	CS	MV	GA
ECDS1	<0.5, 0.0, 0.0>	<0.8, 0.1, 0.1>	<0.6, 0.0, 0.1>	<0.5, 0.0, 0.0>	<0.5, 0.1, 0.1>
ECDS2	<0.8, 0.0, 0.1>	<0.7, 0.0, 0.0>	<1.0, 0.0, 0.0>	<0.9, 0.0, 0.1>	<0.6, 0.0, 0.1>
ECDS3	<0.8, 0.1, 0.1>	<0.7, 0.0, 0.0>	<0.8, 0.0, 0.1>	<0.9, 0.1, 0.2>	<0.8, 0.0, 0.0>

After that, a group evaluation matrix was determined by using Equation (6), whereby all the decision-makers had the same importance $\omega_1 = \omega_2 = \omega_3 = 0.33$. The group evaluation matrix is presented in Table 6.

Table 6. The group evaluation matrix.

	FS	IS	CS	MV	GA
ECDS1	<0.5, 0.0, 0.0>	<0.7, 0.1, 0.1>	<0.6, 0.0, 0.1>	<0.4, 0.0, 0.0>	<0.4, 0.0, 0.1>
ECDS2	<1.0, 0.0, 0.0>	<0.7, 0.0, 0.0>	<1.0, 0.0, 0.0>	<1.0, 0.0, 0.1>	<1.0, 0.0, 0.1>
ECDS3	<0.7, 0.0, 0.0>	<0.6, 0.0, 0.0>	<0.8, 0.0, 0.1>	<1.0, 0.1, 0.3>	<1.0, 0.0, 0.0>

In the following step, the ideal and negative ideal solutions shown in Table 7 are determined by applying Equations (23) and (24).

Table 7. The ideal and negative ideal solutions.

	FS	IS	CS	MV	GA
$ECDS^+$	<1.0, 0.0, 0.0>	<0.7, 0.0, 0.0>	<1.0, 0.0, 0.0>	<1.0, 0.0, 0.0>	<1.0, 0.0, 0.0>
$ECDS^-$	<0.5, 0.0, 0.0>	<0.6, 0.1, 0.1>	<0.6, 0.0, 0.1>	<0.4, 0.1, 0.3>	<0.4, 0.0, 0.1>

The calculation details obtained by applying the TOPSIS method and the two distance measures are presented in Tables 8 and 9.

Table 8. The computational details obtained by using the Hamming distance.

	d_i^+	d_i^-	C_i	Rank
ECDS1	0.87	0.69	0.44	3
ECDS2	0.38	1.08	0.74	1
ECDS3	0.63	0.66	0.51	2

Table 9. The computational details obtained by using the Euclidean distance.

	d_i^+	d_i^-	C_i	Rank
ECDS1	3.38	3.24	0.490	3
ECDS2	1.70	4.25	0.714	1
ECDS3	2.60	2.54	0.495	2

The calculation details obtained by utilizing the TOPSIS method and the Hamming distance are presented in Table 8. In this case, all the criteria had the same importance of $w_j = 0.20$.

As can be observed from Table 8, the most acceptable alternative (i.e., e-commerce development strategy) is designated as ECDS2, which means that the most appropriate e-commerce development strategy is the "social e-commerce adoption" alternative.

5. Discussion and Comparison Analysis

In order to confirm the obtained results, similar calculations were performed by applying the TOPSIS method with the Euclidean distance, and the two commonly used approaches in the case of applying neutrosophic sets (i.e., the score function and the cosine similarity measure).

The calculation details obtained by using the TOPSIS method and the Euclidean distance are presented in Table 9. As can be observed from Table 9, the application of the TOPSIS method with the Euclidean distance produced the same ranking results.

To check the stability of the obtained ranking order of the alternatives, the calculation was repeated five times with the weighting vectors shown in Table 10.

Table 10. The weighting vectors used for the recalculation.

	w_1	w_2	w_3	w_4	w_5	Σw_j
W_1	0.40	0.15	0.15	0.15	0.15	1.00
W_2	0.15	0.40	0.15	0.15	0.15	1.00
W_3	0.15	0.15	0.40	0.15	0.15	1.00
W_4	0.15	0.15	0.15	0.40	0.15	1.00
W_5	0.15	0.15	0.15	0.15	0.40	1.00

The ranking results obtained by using the five different weighting vectors and the two distances are given in Tables 11 and 12.

Table 11. The ranking results obtained by using the Hamming distance and different W_i.

	W_1		W_2		W_3		W_4		W_5	
	C_i	Rank	C_i	Rank	C_i	Rank	C_i	Rank	C_i	Rank
ECDS1	0.45	3	0.51	2	0.44	3	0.39	3	0.43	3
ECDS2	0.74	1	0.70	1	0.72	1	0.75	1	0.78	1
ECDS3	0.50	2	0.43	3	0.54	2	0.59	2	0.49	2

Table 12. The ranking results obtained by using the Euclidean distance and different W_i.

	W_1		W_2		W_3		W_4		W_5	
	C_i	Rank	C_i	Rank	C_i	Rank	C_i	Rank	C_i	Rank
ECDS1	0.49	3	0.56	2	0.48	3	0.44	3	0.48	2
ECDS2	0.72	1	0.67	1	0.70	1	0.73	1	0.76	1
ECDS3	0.50	2	0.41	3	0.54	2	0.57	2	0.46	3

The use of different weighting vectors caused changes in the ranking order in two cases, namely: W_2 and W_5. In the first case (W_2), both distances gave the same ranking order, whereas in the second case (W_5), there was a difference in the second- and third-ranked alternatives.

Based on the foregoing, it can be concluded that the developed extension of the TOPSIS method can be employed with any of the two previously considered distances (i.e., with the one easier to calculate such as the Hamming distance, or the one slightly more complex to calculate in the case of using SVNNs like Euclidean distance).

To finally verify the ranking results obtained by the developed adaptation of the TOPSIS method, an additional ranking of the strategies was performed by using two commonly used approaches (i.e., the score function and the cosine similarity measure). The values of the score function and the cosine similarity measure for the considered alternatives were determined by applying Equations (6) and (7), respectively, to the overall ratings calculated by applying Equation (8). In this calculation, all the criteria again had the same importance of $w_j = 0.20$. The achieved ranking results are shown in Table 13.

Table 13. The ranking by using the score function and the cosine similarity measure.

	Overall Ratings	Score	Rank	Cosine	Rank
ECDS1	<0.55, 0.00, 0.00>	0.78	3	0.55	3
ECDS2	<1.00, 0.00, 0.00>	1.00	1	1.00	1
ECDS3	<1.00, 0.00, 0.00>	1.00	1	1.00	1

Table 13 allows us to note that the obtained results were partly different from the results shown in Tables 8 and 9. The difference occurs with the alternative ECDS3, which now shared first place with the alternative ECDS2, whereas the alternative ECDS1 ranked second when using the TOPSIS method.

Generally speaking, the alternative ECDS2 was the best-ranked when using all the approaches (as seen in Figure 2), although some deviations in the ranking orders obtained by using different approaches were expected. Possible deviations in the ranking orders obtained by using different approaches are caused by the differences and specificities of the calculation procedures applied in different approaches, whereas deviations usually reflect in the case of worse-ranked alternatives.

Figure 2. Ranking results achieved by utilizing different procedures.

6. Conclusions

As a generalization of fuzzy sets and their various extensions, neutrosophic sets introduce three membership functions, thus enabling an easier and more efficient evaluation of alternatives in the cases of solving problems associated with ambiguities and uncertainties. Therefore, several approaches have been proposed for ranking neutrosophic numbers, and numerous MCDM methods have been adapted for the purpose of their use.

The TOPSIS method is a prominent MCDM method that has been used so far to solve numerous decision-making problems, and many extensions of the TOPSIS method have been proposed to enable using different types of fuzzy as well as neutrosophic numbers. Based on a previously proposed extension, a new adaptation to use single-valued neutrosophic numbers is being considered. The additional goal of this study was to confirm the applicability of the Hamming distance alternatively to the Euclidean distance. The results of the considered numerical illustration and the conducted comparative analysis indicate the justified application of the Hamming distance with a less complex calculation procedure instead of the Euclidean distance with a much more complex calculation procedure, especially in the case of neutrosophic set application. Furthermore, the proposed approach has enabled the use of the Hamming distance and/or Euclidean distance.

Based on the conducted numerical illustration, the most acceptable alternative is ECDS2, the Social E-commerce adoption model. Furthermore, the reliability of the TOPSIS extension based on SVNNs was additionally verified by utilizing the score function and cosine similarity measure. It is noticeable that alternatives ECDS2 and ECDS3 had the same ranking result. Additionally, alternative ECDS2, the Social E-commerce adoption model, was the best-ranked when using different ranking approaches (ranking based on Hamming distance and Euclidean distance, and ranking based on score function and cosine similarity measure).

The proposed TOPSIS extension based on SVNNs proved to be efficient and easy to use when solving decision-making problems that are complex, multifaceted, and often associated with ambiguities and uncertainties. In addition, TOPSIS SVNNs is a good choice when it comes to the evaluation and selection of e-commerce development strategies.

Author Contributions: Conceptualization, D.K., P.S., and G.P.; Methodology, D.K., D.S., and E.K.Z.; Validation, B.P. and A.U.; Investigation, B.P.; Data curation, G.P.; Writing—original draft preparation, D.S. and E.K.Z.;

Writing—review and editing, P.S. and A.U.; Supervision, D.K. All authors have read and agreed to the published version of the manuscript.

Funding: This research received no external funding.

Conflicts of Interest: The authors declare no conflicts of interest.

References

1. Magnusson, D.; Hermelin, B. ICT development from the perspective of connectivity and inclusion—The operation of a local digital agenda in Sweden. *Nor. Geogr. Tidsskr. Nor. J. Geogr.* **2019**, 81–95. [CrossRef]
2. Sandberg, K.W.; Håkansson, F. Strategical Use of ICT in Microenterprises: A Case Study. *Int. J. E Entrep. Innov.* **2020**, *10*, 1–13. [CrossRef]
3. Nica, E. ICT innovation, internet sustainability, and economic development. *J. Self Gov. Manag. Econ.* **2015**, *3*, 242–249.
4. Chaffey, D.; Hemphill, T.; Edmundson-Bird, D. *Digital Business and E-Commerce Management*; Pearson: London, UK, 2019.
5. Goyal, S.; Sergi, B.S.; Esposito, M. Literature review of emerging trends and future directions of e-commerce in global business landscape. *World Rev. Entrep. Manag. Sustain. Dev.* **2019**, *15*, 226–255. [CrossRef]
6. Laudon, K.C.; Traver, C.G. *E-Commerce: Business, Technology, Society*; Pearson: Essex, UK, 2016.
7. Hua, N.; Hight, S.; Wei, W.; Ozturk, A.B.; Zhao, X.R.; Nusair, K.; DeFranco, A. The power of e-commerce. *Int. J. Contemp. Hosp. Manag.* **2019**, *31*, 1906–1923. [CrossRef]
8. Johnson, G.; Whittington, R.; Scholes, K.; Angwin, D.N.; Regnér, P. *Exploring Strategy*, 11th ed.; Pearson: London, UK, 2017.
9. Thompson, F.M.; Tuzovic, S.; Braun, C. Trustmarks: Strategies for exploiting their full potential in e-commerce. *Bus. Horiz.* **2019**, *62*, 237–247. [CrossRef]
10. Ćurčić, N.; Piljan, I.; Simonović, Z. Marketing concept in insurance companies. *Ekonomika* **2019**, *65*, 21–23. [CrossRef]
11. Jauković Jocić, K.; Jocić, G.; Karabašević, D.; Popović, G.; Stanujkić, D.; Zavadskas, E.K.; Thanh Nguyen, P. A Novel Integrated PIPRECIA—Interval-Valued Triangular Fuzzy ARAS Model: E-Learning Course Selection. *Symmetry* **2020**, *12*, 928. [CrossRef]
12. Hassanpour, M.; Pamucar, D. Evaluation of Iranian household appliance industries using MCDM models. *Oper. Res. Eng. Sci. Theory Appl.* **2019**, *2*, 12–15. [CrossRef]
13. Karabašević, D.; Maksimović, M.; Stanujkić, D.; Brzaković, P.; Brzaković, M. The evaluation of websites in the textile industry by applying ISO/IEC 91264-standard and the EDAS method. *Ind. Text.* **2018**, *69*, 4894.
14. Fazlollahtabar, H.; Smailbašić, A.; Stević, Ž. FUCOM method in group decision-making: Selection of forklift in a warehouse. *Decis. Mak. Appl. Manag. Eng.* **2019**, *2*, 49–65. [CrossRef]
15. Karabasević, D.; Stanujkić, D.; Maksimović, M.; Popović, G.; Momčilović, O. An Approach to Evaluating the Quality of Websites Based on the Weighted Sum Preferred Levels of Performances Method. *Acta Polytech. Hung.* **2019**, *16*, 195–215.
16. Saaty, T.L. *The Analytic Hierarchy Process: Planning, Priority Setting, Resource Allocation*; McGraw-Hill: New York, NY, USA, 1980.
17. Roy, B. The outranking approach and the foundation of ELECTRE methods. *Theory Decis.* **1991**, *31*, 49–73. [CrossRef]
18. Brans, J.P.; Vincke, P. Note—A Preference Ranking Organisation Method: (The PROMETHEE Method for Multiple Criteria Decision-Making). *Manag. Sci.* **1985**, *31*, 647–656. [CrossRef]
19. Hwang, C.L.; Yoon, K. *Multiple Attribute Decision Making: Methods and Applications*; Springer: New York, NY, USA, 1981.
20. Zavadskas, E.K.; Kaklauskas, A.; Sarka, V. The new method of multicriteria complex proportional assessment of projects. *Technol. Econ. Dev. Econ.* **1994**, *1*, 131–139.
21. Opricović, S. *Multicriteria Optimization of Civil Engineering Systems*; Faculty of Civil Engineering: Belgrade, Serbia, 1998.
22. Brauers, W.K.M.; Zavadskas, E.K. The MOORA method and its application to privatization in a transition economy. *Control Cybern.* **2006**, *35*, 445–469.

23. Brauers, W.K.M.; Zavadskas, E.K. Project management by MULTIMOORA as an instrument for transition economies. *Technol. Econ. Dev. Econ.* **2010**, *16*, 52–54. [CrossRef]
24. Nanayakkara, C.; Yeoh, W.; Lee, A.; Moayedikia, A. Deciding discipline, course and university through TOPSIS. *Stud. High. Educ.* **2019**, 1–16. [CrossRef]
25. Dos Santos, B.M.; Godoy, L.P.; Campos, L.M. Performance evaluation of green suppliers using entropy-TOPSIS-F. *J. Clean. Prod.* **2019**, *207*, 498–509. [CrossRef]
26. Cavallaro, F.; Zavadskas, E.K.; Streimikiene, D.; Mardani, A. Assessment of concentrated solar power (CSP) technologies based on a modified intuitionistic fuzzy topsis and trigonometric entropy weights. *Technol. Forecast. Soc. Chang.* **2019**, *140*, 258–270. [CrossRef]
27. Kwok, P.K.; Lau, H.Y. Hotel selection using a modified TOPSIS-based decision support algorithm. *Decis. Support Syst.* **2019**, *120*, 95–105. [CrossRef]
28. Solangi, Y.A.; Tan, Q.; Mirjat, N.H.; Ali, S. Evaluating the strategies for sustainable energy planning in Pakistan: An integrated SWOT-AHP and Fuzzy-TOPSIS approach. *J. Clean. Prod.* **2019**, *236*, 117655. [CrossRef]
29. Gupta, H.; Barua, M.K. Supplier selection among SMEs on the basis of their green innovation ability using BWM and fuzzy TOPSIS. *J. Clean. Prod.* **2017**, *152*, 242–258. [CrossRef]
30. Efe, B. Website Evaluation Using Interval Type-2 Fuzzy-Number-Based TOPSIS Approach. In *Multi-Criteria Decision-Making Models for Website Evaluation*; IGI Global: Hershey, PA, USA, 2019; pp. 166–185.
31. Wang, Y.M.; Elhag, T.M. Fuzzy TOPSIS method based on alpha level sets with an application to bridge risk assessment. *Expert Syst. Appl.* **2006**, *31*, 309–319. [CrossRef]
32. Abdulsalam, K.; Ighravwe, D.; Babatunde, M. A fuzzy-TOPSIS approach for techno-economic viability of lighting energy efficiency measure in public building projects. *J. Proj. Manag.* **2018**, *3*, 197–206. [CrossRef]
33. Ranjbar, H.R.; Nekooie, M.A. An improved hierarchical fuzzy TOPSIS approach to identify endangered earthquake-induced buildings. *Eng. Appl. Artif. Intell.* **2018**, *76*, 21–39. [CrossRef]
34. Kelemenis, A.; Askounis, D. A new TOPSIS-based multi-criteria approach to personnel selection. *Expert Syst. Appl.* **2010**, *37*, 4999–5008. [CrossRef]
35. Sang, X.; Liu, X.; Qin, J. An analytical solution to fuzzy TOPSIS and its application in personnel selection for knowledge-intensive enterprise. *Appl. Soft Comput.* **2015**, *30*, 190–204. [CrossRef]
36. Samanlioglu, F.; Taskaya, Y.E.; Gulen, U.C.; Cokcan, O. A fuzzy AHP–TOPSIS-based group decision-making approach to IT personnel selection. *Int. J. Fuzzy Syst.* **2018**, *20*, 1576–1591. [CrossRef]
37. Kelemenis, A.; Ergazakis, K.; Askounis, D. Support managers' selection using an extension of fuzzy TOPSIS. *Expert Syst. Appl.* **2011**, *38*, 2774–2782. [CrossRef]
38. Smarandache, F. *Neutrosophy, Neutrosophic Probability, Set and Logic*; American Res. Press: Rehoboth, DE, USA, 1998.
39. Abdel-Basset, M.; Mohamed, M. A novel and powerful framework based on neutrosophic sets to aid patients with cancer. *Future Gener. Comput. Syst.* **2019**, *98*, 144–153. [CrossRef]
40. Abdel-Basset, M.; Gamal, A.; Manogaran, G.; Long, H.V. A novel group decision making model based on neutrosophic sets for heart disease diagnosis. *Multimed. Tools Appl.* **2019**, 1–26. [CrossRef]
41. Abdel-Basset, M.; Mohamed, M.; Elhoseny, M.; Chiclana, F.; Zaied AE, N.H. Cosine similarity measures of bipolar neutrosophic set for diagnosis of bipolar disorder diseases. *Artif. Intell. Med.* **2019**, *101*, 101735. [CrossRef] [PubMed]
42. Ulucay, V.; Kılıç, A.; Şahin, M.; Deniz, H. A new hybrid distance-based similarity measure for refined neutrosophic sets and its application in medical diagnosis. *Matematika* **2019**, *35*, 83–94. [CrossRef]
43. Pratihar, J.; Kumar, R.; Dey, A.; Broumi, S. Transportation problem in neutrosophic environment. In *Neutrosophic Graph Theory and Algorithms*; IGI Global: Hershey, PA, USA, 2020; pp. 180–212.
44. Smith, P. Exploring public transport sustainability with neutrosophic logic. *Transp. Plan. Technol.* **2019**, *42*, 257–273. [CrossRef]
45. Elhassouny, A.; Idbrahim, S.; Smarandache, F. Machine learning in Neutrosophic Environment: A Survey. *Neutrosophic Sets Syst.* **2019**, *28*, 58–68.
46. Jayaparthasarathy, G.; Little Flower, V.F.; Dasan, M.A. Neutrosophic Supra Topological Applications in Data Mining Process. *Neutrosophic Sets Syst.* **2019**, *27*, 80–97.

47. Sengur, A.; Budak, U.; Akbulut, Y.; Karabatak, M.; Tanyildizi, E. A survey on neutrosophic medical image segmentation. In *Neutrosophic Set in Medical Image Analysis*; Academic Press: Cambridge, MA, USA, 2019; pp. 145–165.
48. Tuan, T.M.; Chuan, P.M.; Ali, M.; Ngan, T.T.; Mittal, M. Fuzzy and neutrosophic modeling for link prediction in social networks. *Evol. Syst.* **2019**, *10*, 629–634. [CrossRef]
49. Kahraman, C.; Otay, İ. *Fuzzy Multi-Criteria Decision-Making Using Neutrosophic Sets*; Springer: Berlin, Germany, 2019.
50. Luo, M.; Wu, L.; Zhou, K.; Zhang, H. Multi-criteria decision making method based on the single valued neutrosophic sets. *J. Intell. Fuzzy Syst.* **2019**, *37*, 2403–2417. [CrossRef]
51. Zhang, H.Y.; Ji, P.; Wang, J.Q.; Chen, X.H. An improved weighted correlation coefficient based on integrated weight for interval neutrosophic sets and its application in multi-criteria decision-making problems. *Int. J. Comput. Intell. Syst.* **2015**, *8*, 1027–1043. [CrossRef]
52. Peng, J.J.; Wang, J.Q.; Zhang, H.Y.; Chen, X.H. An outranking approach for multi-criteria decision-making problems with simplified neutrosophic sets. *Appl. Soft Comput.* **2014**, *25*, 336–346. [CrossRef]
53. Smarandache, F. *A Unifying Field in Logics. Neutrosophy: Neutrosophic Probability, Set and Logic*; American Research Press: Rehoboth, DE, USA, 1999.
54. Wang, H.; Smarandache, F.; Zhang, Y.; Sunderraman, R. Single valued neutrosophic sets. *Rev. Air Force Acad.* **2010**, *1*, 10–14.
55. Sahin, R. Multi-criteria neutrosophic decision making method based on score and accuracy functions under neutrosophic environment. *arXiv*, 2014; arXiv:1412.5202.
56. Ye, J. Multicriteria decision-making method using the correlation coefficient under single-valued neutrosophic environment. *Int. J. Gen. Syst.* **2013**, *42*, 386–394. [CrossRef]
57. Chang, C.H.; Lin, J.J.; Linc, J.H.; Chiang, M.C. Domestic open-end equity mutual fund performance evaluation using extended TOPSIS method with different distance approaches. *Expert Syst. Appl.* **2010**, *37*, 4642–4649. [CrossRef]
58. Shanian, A.; Savadogo, O. TOPSIS multiple-criteria decision support analysis for material selection of metallic bipolar plates for polymer electrolyte fuel cell. *J. Power Sources* **2006**, *159*, 1095–1104. [CrossRef]
59. Gautam, S.S.; Singh, S.R. An improved-based TOPSIS method in interval-valued intuitionistic fuzzy environment. *Life Cycle Reliab. Saf. Eng.* **2018**, *7*, 81–88. [CrossRef]
60. Izadikhah, M. Using the Hamming distance to extend TOPSIS in a fuzzy environment. *J. Comput. Appl. Math.* **2009**, *231*, 200–207. [CrossRef]
61. Chen, T.Y.; Tsao, C.Y. The interval-valued fuzzy TOPSIS method and experimental analysis. *Fuzzy Sets Syst.* **2008**, *159*, 1410–1428. [CrossRef]
62. Yang, T.; Hung, C.C. Multiple-attribute decision making methods for plant layout design problem. *Robot. Comput. Integr. Manuf.* **2007**, *23*, 126–137. [CrossRef]
63. Broumi, S.; Ye, J.; Smarandache, F. An extended TOPSIS method for multiple attribute decision making based on interval neutrosophic uncertain linguistic variables. *Neutrosophic Sets Syst.* **2015**, *8*, 22–31.
64. Elhassouny, A.; Smarandache, F. Neutrosophic-simplified-TOPSIS multi-criteria decision-making using combined simplified-TOPSIS method and neutrosophics. In Proceedings of the 2016 IEEE International Conference on Fuzzy Systems (FUZZ-IEEE), Vancouver, BC, Canada, 24–29 July 2016; pp. 2468–2474.
65. Srinivasan, V.; Shocker, A.D. Linear programming techniques for multidimensional analysis of preferences. *Psychometrika* **1973**, *38*, 337–369. [CrossRef]
66. Kersuliene, V.; Turskis, Z. Integrated fuzzy multiple criteria decision making model for architect selection. *Technol. Econ. Dev. Econ.* **2011**, *17*, 645–666. [CrossRef]
67. Pamucar, D.; Stevic, Z.; Sremac, S. A new model for determining weight coefficients of criteria in MCDM models: Full consistency method (FUCOM). *Symmetry* **2018**, *10*, 393. [CrossRef]
68. Stanujkić, D.; Zavadskas, E.K.; Karabašević, D.; Smarandache, F.; Turskis, Z. The use of Pivot Pair-wise Relative Criteria Importance Assessment method for determining weights of criteria. *Rom. J. Econ. Forecast.* **2017**, *20*, 116–133.
69. Stanujkić, D.; Karabašević, D.; Maksimović, M.; Popović, G.; Brzaković, M. Evaluation of the e-commerce development strategies. *Quaestus* **2019**, *1*, 144–152.

70. Ansari, A.; Mela, C.F. E-customization. *J. Mark. Res.* **2003**, *40*, 131–145. [CrossRef]
71. Hajli, M. A research framework for social commerce adoption. *Inf. Manag. Comput. Secur.* **2013**, *21*, 144–154. [CrossRef]
72. Sen, R. Optimal search engine marketing strategy. *Int. J. Electron. Commer.* **2005**, *10*, 9–25. [CrossRef]

© 2020 by the authors. Licensee MDPI, Basel, Switzerland. This article is an open access article distributed under the terms and conditions of the Creative Commons Attribution (CC BY) license (http://creativecommons.org/licenses/by/4.0/).

Article

Similarity Measures of Quadripartitioned Single Valued Bipolar Neutrosophic Sets and Its Application in Multi-Criteria Decision Making Problems

Subhadip Roy [1], Jeong-Gon Lee [2,*], Anita Pal [1] and Syamal Kumar Samanta [3]

1. Department of Mathematics, National Institute of Technology Durgapur, Durgapur 713209, India; subhadip_123@yahoo.com (S.R.); anita.pal@maths.nitdgp.ac.in (A.P.)
2. Division of Applied Mathematics, Wonkwang University, 460, Iksan-daero, Iksan-Si, Jeonbuk 54538, Korea
3. Department of Mathematics, Visva Bharati, Santiniketan 731235, India; syamal_123@yahoo.co.in
* Correspondence: jukolee@wku.ac.kr

Received: 9 May 2020; Accepted: 11 June 2020; Published: 16 June 2020

Abstract: In this paper, a definition of quadripartitioned single valued bipolar neutrosophic set (QSVBNS) is introduced as a generalization of both quadripartitioned single valued neutrosophic sets (QSVNS) and bipolar neutrosophic sets (BNS). There is an inherent symmetry in the definition of QSVBNS. Some operations on them are defined and a set theoretic study is accomplished. Various similarity measures and distance measures are defined on QSVBNS. An algorithm relating to multi-criteria decision making problem is presented based on quadripartitioned bipolar weighted similarity measure. Finally, an example is shown to verify the flexibility of the given method and the advantage of considering QSVBNS in place of fuzzy sets and bipolar fuzzy sets.

Keywords: neutrosophic sets; quadripartitioned bipolar neutrosophic sets; similarity measure; decision making

1. Introduction

Multiple-criteria decision making (MCDM) is a branch of decision making theory where the aim of an individual is to select the most acceptable alternatives among the feasible ones under some criteria. This criteria dependence in decision can be found in real life on a regular basis. While handling some real life decision making problems, a decision maker often faces trouble due to the presence of several kinds of uncertainties in the data, which is very natural. An attempt was made for the first time by Zadeh [1] by introducing a novel concept of fuzzy set theory. Immediately after that, several improvisations of fuzzy sets were made and implemented in the decision making process. For instance, rough sets by Pawlak [2], intuitionistic fuzzy sets [3], interval valued intuitionistic fuzzy sets [4] by Atanassov, soft sets by Molodtsov [5], etc. Unlike the classical logic, a fuzzy set associates a degree of membership value to every element of the universe of discourse, which can range from 0 to 1, whereas an intuitionistic fuzzy set associate a degree of membership $\mu \in [0,1]$ and a degree of non-membership $\nu \in [0,1]$, where $0 \leq \mu + \nu \leq 1$. The margin of indeterminacy or hesitation π is defined as $\pi = 1 - \mu - \nu$. Smarandache in [6,7] proposed neutrosophic sets. In neutrosophic sets, the indeterminacy membership function walks along independently of the truth membership or of the falsity membership. Neutrosophic theory has been widely explored by researchers (see [8–13]) for application purpose in handling real life situations involving uncertainty. Although the hesitation margin of neutrosophic theory is independent of the truth or falsity membership, looks more general than intuitionistic fuzzy sets yet. Recently, in [14] Atanassov et al. studied the relations between inconsistent intuitionistic fuzzy sets [15], picture fuzzy sets [16], neutrosophic sets [7] and intuitionistic fuzzy sets [3]; however, it remains in doubt that whether the indeterminacy associated to a particular element occurs due to the belongingness of the element or the non-belongingness. This has been pointed out by Chattejee et al. [17] while introducing a more general structure of neutrosophic set viz. quadripartitioned single valued neutrosophic set (QSVNS). The idea of QSVNS is actually stretched from Smarandache's four numerical-valued neutrosophic logic [18] and Belnap's four valued logic [19], where the indeterminacy is divided into two parts, namely, "unknown" i.e., neither true nor false and "contradiction" i.e., both true and false. In the context of neutrosophic study however, the QSVNS looks quite logical. Also in their study, Chatterjee et al. [17] analyzed a real life example for a better understanding of a QSVNS environment and showed that such situations occur very naturally. They have also solved a decision making problem pertaining to pattern recognition showing the application capability of QSVNS.

Bipolarity often reflects the tendency of the human mind in reasoning to make a decision on the basis of +ve and -ve information. Lee [20,21] introduced bipolar fuzzy set as an extension of fuzzy set. Bipolar fuzzy model with some hybrid structures were studied in [22–25] shows the flexibility of bipolar fuzzy sets for solving decision making problems. Bipolar fuzzy set and neutrosophic set have been put together for a more general framework viz. bipolar neutrosophic sets (BNS) by Deli et al. [26]. Sahin et al. [27,28] introduced the Jaccard vector similarity measure, hybrid vector similarity measure, and dice similarity measure with applications to decision making problems. Jamil et al. [29] applied bipolar neutrosophic Hamacher averaging operator in group decision making problems. Bipolar neutrosophic sets help in handling uncertain information in a reliable way. It is an extension of the bipolar fuzzy set and neutrosophic set, which can deal with real life problems involving positive and negative information. Looking at the work of Chatteree et al. [17], unlike neutrosophic set, it is in doubt whether the negative indeterminacy associated to some elements of the universe of discourse is due to the occurrence of the counter-property or the non-occurrence of the counter-property.

To overcome the aforesaid situation we merged the bipolar neutrosophic set and QSVNS to introduce a more general structure, namely, quadripartitioned single valued bipolar neutrosophic sets (QSVBNS). The word "quadripartitioned" refers to four values i.e., in case of QSVBNS the negative indeterminacy of the BNS is divided into two parts alongside truth and falsity membership alike QSVNS.

First, we develop some set theoretic results on QSVBNS and then formulas for similarity measures were framed, and finally a real life problem was dealt with using the MCDM method in this setting. A comparison was made in application of a real life problem, where it is seen that the use of QSVBN system gives a better result compared to fuzzy sets and bipolar fuzzy sets. The paper is organized as follows: Section 2 recalls some preliminaries results. In Section 3, QSVBNS is introduced and some basic operations on QSVBNS are dealt with; an example of QSVBNS is also presented. Several similarity measures between QSVBNS are defined and their properties are studied in Section 4. In Section 5 we give an algorithm based on quadripartitioned bipolar weighted similarity measure to deal with the multi-criteria decision making problem in a QSVBN environment. Based on the given algorithm, a real life problem in decision making is solved in Section 6. A detailed discussion about the obtained result is analyzed in Section 7. Finally, Section 8 concludes the paper.

2. Preliminaries

Definition 1 ([7]). *Let X be a universal set. A single valued neutrosophic set A over X is defined as, $A = \{\langle x, \langle T_A(x), I_A(x), F_A(x) \rangle \rangle : x \in X\}$, where, $T_A(x), I_A(x), F_A(x)$ are respectively called truth-membership function, indeterminacy-membership function and falsity-membership function. These are defined by $T_A : X \to [0,1]$, $I_A : X \to [0,1]$, $F_A : X \to [0,1]$ respectively with the property that $0 \leq T_A(x) + I_A(x) + F_A(x) \leq 3$.*

Definition 2 ([17]). *Let X be a universal set. A quadripartitioned neutrosophic set (QSVNS) A, over X is defined as, $A = \{\langle x, \langle T_A(x), C_A(x), U_A(x), F_A(x) \rangle \rangle : x \in X\}$, where $T_A(x), C_A(x), U_A(x), F_A(x)$ are respectively called truth-membership function, contradiction-membership function, ignorance-membership function, and falsity-membership function. These are defined by $T_A : X \to [0,1]$, $C_A : X \to [0,1]$, $U_A : X \to$*

$[0,1]$, $F_A : X \to [0,1]$ respectively with the property that $0 \leq T_A(x) + C_A(x) + U_A(x) + F_A(x) \leq 4$. When X is discrete, A is represented as, $A = \sum_{k=i}^{n} \langle T_A(x_i), C_A(x_i), U_A(x_i), F_A(x_i), \rangle / x_i$, $x_i \in X$. When X is continuous, A is represented as, $\int_X \langle T_A(x), C_A(x), U_A(x), F_A(x) \rangle / x$, $x \in X$.

Definition 3 ([26]). *A bipolar neutrosophic set (BNS) A in X is defined to be an object of the form $A = \{\langle x, T^+(x), I^+(x), F^+(x), T^-(x), I^-(x), F^-(x)\rangle : x \in X\}$, where, T^+, I^+, F^+ are functions from X to $[0,1]$ and T^-, I^-, F^- are functions from X to $[-1,0]$. The +ve membership degrees $T^+(x), I^+(x), F^+(x)$ denote respectively the truth-membership, indeterminate-membership, and falsity-membership of $x \in X$ corresponding to a bipolar neutrosophic set A and the -ve membership degrees $T^-(x), I^-(x), F^-(x)$ denote respectively the truth-membership, indeterminate-membership, and falsity-membership $x \in X$ to some implicit counter-property corresponding to a bipolar neutrosophic set A.*

Definition 4 ([17]). *Let A and B be two QSVNS. Then*

(1) $A \subseteq B$ if $T_A(x) \leq T_B(x), C_A(x) \leq C_B(x), U_A(x) \geq U_B(x), F_A(x) \geq F_B(x)$ for all $x \in X$.

(2) *The complement of A is denoted by A^c and is defined as $A^c = \sum_{i=1}^{n} \langle F_A(x_i), U_A(x_i), C_A(x_i), T_A(x_i), \rangle / x_i$, $x_i \in X$, where $T_{A^c}(x_i) = F_A(x_i), C_{A^c}(x_i) = U_A(x_i)$ and $U_{A^c}(x_i) = C_A(x_i), F_{A^c}(x_i) = T_A(x_i)$.*

(3) $A \cup B$ *is defined as* $A \cup B = \sum_{i=1}^{n} \langle T_A(x_i) \vee T_B(x_i), C_A(x_i) \vee C_B(x_i), U_A(x_i) \wedge U_B(x_i), F_A(x_i) \wedge F_B(x_i) \rangle / X$.

(4) $A \cap B$ *is defined as* $A \cap B = \sum_{i=1}^{n} \langle T_A(x_i) \wedge T_B(x_i), C_A(x_i) \wedge C_B(x_i), U_A(x_i) \vee U_B(x_i), F_A(x_i) \vee F_B(x_i) \rangle / X$.

Definition 5 ([26]). *Let $A_1 = \langle x, T_1^+(x), I_1^+(x), F_1^+(x), T_1^-(x), I_1^-(x), F_1^-(x) \rangle$, $A_2 = \langle x, T_2^+(x), I_2^+(x), F_2^+(x), T_2^-(x), I_2^-(x), F_2^-(x) \rangle$ be two bipolar neutrosophic sets (BNS) over the universe of discourse X. Then,*

(1) $A_1 \subseteq A_2$ if $T_1^+(x) \leq T_2^+(x), I_1^+(x) \leq I_2^+(x), F_1^+(x) \geq F_2^+(x)$ and $T_1^-(x) \geq T_2^-(x), I_1^-(x) \geq I_2^-(x), F_1^-(x) \leq F_2^-(x)$.

(2) $A^c = \langle x, 1 - T_A^+(x), 1 - I_A^+(x), 1 - F_A^+(x), -1 - T_A^-(x), -1 - I_A^-(x), -1 - F_A^-(x) \rangle$.

(3) $A_1 \cup A_2 = \langle x, max(T_1^+(x), T_2^+(x)), \frac{I_1^+(x) + I_2^+(x)}{2}, min(F_1^+(x), F_2^+(x)), min(T_1^-(x), T_2^-(x)), \frac{I_1^-(x) + I_2^-(x)}{2}, max(F_1^-(x), F_2^-(x)) \rangle$ for all $x \in X$.

(4) $A_1 \cap A_2 = \langle x, min(T_1^+(x), T_2^+(x)), \frac{I_1^+(x) + I_2^+(x)}{2}, max(F_1^+(x), F_2^+(x)), max(T_1^-(x), T_2^-(x)), \frac{I_1^-(x) + I_2^-(x)}{2}, min(F_1^-(x), F_2^-(x)) \rangle$ for all $x \in X$.

3. Quadripartitioned Single Valued Bipolar Neutrosophic Sets

In this section, we introduce the concept of quadripartitioned single valued bipolar neutrosophic sets (QSVBNS).

Definition 6. *A quadripartitioned single valued bipolar neutrosophic set (QSVBNS) A in X defined as an object of the form $A = \langle x, T_A^P(x), C_A^P(x), U_A^P(x), F_A^P(x), T_A^N(x), C_A^N(x), U_A^N(x), F_A^N(x) \rangle : x \in X$, where, $T_A^P, C_A^P, U_A^P, F_A^P : X \to [0,1]$ and $T_A^N, C_A^N, U_A^N, F_A^N : X \to [-1,0]$. The positive membership degrees $T_A^P(x), C_A^P(x), U_A^P(x), F_A^P(x)$ denote respectively the truth-membership, a contradiction-membership, an ignorance membership, and falsity membership of $x \in X$ corresponding to a QSVBNS A. The negative membership degrees $T_A^N(x), C_A^N(x), U_A^N(x), F_A^N(x)$ denote respectively the truth-membership, a contradiction-membership, an ignorance membership, and falsity membership of $x \in X$ to some explicit counter-property corresponding to a QSVBNS A.*

With respect to $(T_A^P(x), F_A^P(x))$ and $(C_A^P(x), U_A^P(x))$ and +ve and -ve membership grade, there is a sense of symmetry in the structure of QSVBNS.

Example 1. Suppose an environment organization desires to know peoples opinion on the following statement: "The fashion industry has helped economic growth but it also has a bad impact on the environment due to a large amount of carbon emissions".

To help the cause, a group of four experts, say $X = \{x_1, x_2, x_3, x_4\}$, has been asked to give their opinion. The statement can be divided into two parts as:

(a) The fashion industry has helped economic growth and to a counter property of that:
(b) The fashion industry has a bad impact on the environment due to a large amount of carbon emissions.

It may so happen that the opinion has the following outcomes: "a degree of agreement with statement (a) and disagreement with statement (b)", "a degree of agreement and disagreement with both the statements (a) and (b)", "a degree of neither agreement nor disagreement regarding both the statements", and "a degree of disagreement with statement (a) and agreement with statement (b)". According to the views of the four experts, the outcome represented in terms of QSVBNS as follows:

$$\langle 0.9, 0.4, 0.3, 0.1, -0.1, -0.4, -0.3, -0.9 \rangle / x_1 + \langle 0.3, 0.8, 0.2, 0.3, -0.4, -0.4, -0.9, -0.5 \rangle / x_2 +$$
$$\langle 0.2, 0.5, 0.8, 0.4, -0.2, -0.1, -0.8, -0.3 \rangle / x_3 + \langle 0.2, 0.5, 0.5, 0.9, -0.8, -0.1, -0.4, -0.2 \rangle / x_4$$

the above QSVBNS reflects that the expert x_1 agrees to the fact that the fashion industry has helped economic growth, whereas the expert x_2 believes that fashion industry might have helped economic growth but it also has affected the environment a bit. On the other side the expert x_3 is ignorant regarding the truth of both the statements and the expert x_4 opines that fashion industry does not have much impact on the world economy but he believes that it causes damage to the environment.

Remark 1. The relationship between QSVBNS and other extensions of fuzzy sets are diagrammatically depicted in the following figure (Figure 1).

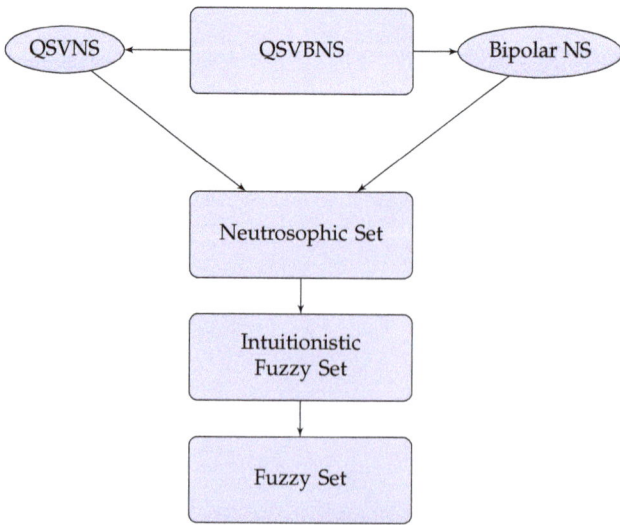

Figure 1. Relationship of quadripartitioned single valued bipolar neutrosophic sets (QSVBNS) with other extensions of fuzzy sets.

Definition 7. A QSVBNS, A over a universe X is said to be an absolute QSVBNS, denoted by **X**, if for each $x \in X$, $T_A^P(x) = 1$, $C_A^P(x) = 1$, $U_A^P(x) = 0$, $F_A^P(x) = 0$, $T_A^N(x) = -1$, $C_A^N(x) = -1$, $U_A^N(x) = 0$, $F_A^N(x) = 0$.

Definition 8. A QSVBNS, A over a universe X is said to be a null QSVBNS, denoted by Θ, if for each $x \in X$ the membership values are respectively $T_A^P(x) = 0$, $C_A^P(x) = 0$, $U_A^P(x) = 1$, $F_A^P(x) = 1$, $T_A^N(x) = 0$, $C_A^N(x) = 0$, $U_A^N(x) = -1$, $F_A^N(x) = -1$.

Alongside this, we expound some set theoretic operations on quadripartitioned single valued bipolar neutrosophic sets over a universe X and analyze some of their properties.

Definition 9. Let A and B be two QSVBNS over X. Then A is said to be included in B, denoted by $A \subseteq B$, if for each $x \in X$, $T_A^P(x) \leq T_B^P(x)$, $C_A^P(x) \leq C_B^P(x)$, $U_A^P(x) \geq U_B^P(x)$, $F_A^P(x) \geq F_B^P(x)$ and $T_A^N(x) \geq T_B^N(x)$, $C_A^N(x) \geq C_B^N(x)$, $U_A^N(x) \leq U_B^N(x)$, $F_A^N(x) \leq F_B^N(x)$.

Definition 10. Two QSVBNSs A and B are said to be equal if for each $x \in X$, $T_A^P(x) = T_B^P(x)$, $C_A^P(x) = C_B^P(x)$, $U_A^P(x) = U_B^P(x)$, $F_A^P(x) = F_B^P(x)$ and $T_A^N(x) = T_B^N(x)$, $C_A^N(x) = C_B^N(x)$, $U_A^N(x) = U_B^N(x)$, $F_A^N(x) = F_B^N(x)$.

Definition 11. The complement of a QSVBNS A, denoted by A^c, is defined as, $A^c = \langle x, F_A^P(x), U_A^P(x), C_A^P(x), T_A^P(x), F_A^N(x), U_A^N(x), C_A^N(x), T_A^N(x)\rangle : x \in X$, where, $T_{A^c}^P(x) = F_A^P(x)$, $C_{A^c}^P(x) = U_A^P(x)$, $U_{A^c}^P(x) = C_A^P(x)$, $F_{A^c}^P(x) = T_A^P(x)$ and $T_{A^c}^N(x) = F_A^N(x)$, $C_{A^c}^N(x) = U_A^N(x)$, $U_{A^c}^N(x) = C_A^N(x)$, $F_{A^c}^N(x) = T_A^N(x)$, $x \in X$.

Definition 12. The union of two QSVBNS A and B, denoted by $A \cup B$ is defined as, $A \cup B = \langle x, T_A^P(x) \vee T_B^P(x), C_A^P(x) \vee C_B^P(x), U_A^P(x) \wedge U_B^P(x), F_A^P(x) \wedge F_B^P(x), T_A^N(x) \wedge T_B^N(x), C_A^N(x) \wedge C_B^N(x), U_A^N(x) \vee U_B^N(x), F_A^N(x) \vee F_B^N(x)\rangle : x \in X$.

Definition 13. The intersection of two QSVBNS, A and B, denoted by $A \cap B$ is defined as, $A \cap B = \langle x, T_A^P(x) \wedge T_B^P(x), C_A^P(x) \wedge C_B^P(x), U_A^P(x) \vee U_B^P(x), F_A^P(x) \vee F_B^P(x), T_A^N(x) \vee T_B^N(x), C_A^N(x) \vee C_B^N(x), U_A^N(x) \wedge U_B^N(x), F_A^N(x) \wedge F_B^N(x)\rangle : x \in X$.

Example 2. For two QSVBNS A and B over X given by $A = \langle 0.8, 0.6, 0.4, 0.1, -0.2, -0.3, -0.5, -0.7\rangle/x_1 + \langle 0.6, 0.5, 0.2, 0.3, -0.5, -0.4, -0.7, -0.8\rangle/x_2 + \langle 0.2, 0.5, 0.6, 0.7, -0.6, -0.1, -0.5, -0.7\rangle/x_3$ and $B = \langle 0.6, 0.5, 0.4, 0.3, -0.4, -0.7, -0.5, -0.6\rangle/x_1 + \langle 0.4, 0.5, 0.7, 0.5, -0.6, -0.4, -0.3, -0.4\rangle/x_2 + \langle 0.3, 0.7, 0.4, 0.2, -0.2, -0.1, -0.4, -0.8\rangle/x_3$

(1) $A^c = \langle 0.1, 0.4, 0.6, 0.8, -0.7, -0.5, -0.3, -0.2\rangle/x_1 + \langle 0.3, 0.2, 0.5, 0.6, -0.8, -0.7, -0.4, -0.5\rangle/x_2 + \langle 0.7, 0.6, 0.5, 0.2, -0.7, -0.5, -0.1, -0.6\rangle/x_3$.
(2) $A \cup B = \langle 0.8, 0.6, 0.4, 0.1, -0.4, -0.7, -0.5, -0.6\rangle/x_1 + \langle 0.6, 0.5, 0.2, 0.3, -0.6, -0.4, -0.3, -0.4\rangle/x_2 + \langle 0.3, 0.7, 0.4, 0.2, -0.6, -0.1, -0.4, -0.7\rangle/x_3$.
(3) $A \cap B = \langle 0.6, 0.5, 0.4, 0.3, -0.2, -0.3, -0.5, -0.6\rangle/x_1 + \langle 0.4, 0.5, 0.7, 0.5, -0.5, -0.4, -0.7, -0.8\rangle/x_2 + \langle 0.2, 0.5, 0.6, 0.7, -0.6, -0.2, -0.5, -0.8\rangle/x_3$.

Theorem 1. Under the aforesaid set-theoretic operation, the quadripartitioned single valued bipolar neutrosophic sets satisfy the following properties:

(1) Identity law:

- $A \cup \Theta = A$ and $A \cap \mathbf{X} = A$.

(2) Commutative law:

- $A \cup B = B \cup A$ and $A \cap B = B \cap A$.

(3) Associative law:

- $(A \cup B) \cup C = A \cup (B \cup C)$ and $(A \cap B) \cap C = A \cap (B \cap C)$.

(4) Distributive law:

- $A \cup (B \cap C) = (A \cup B) \cap (A \cup C)$ and $A \cap (B \cup C) = (A \cap B) \cup (A \cap C)$.

(5) De-Morgan's law:

- $(A \cup B)^c = A^c \cap B^c$ and $(A \cap B)^c = A^c \cup B^c$.

Proof. Proofs are plain-dealing. □

4. Similarity Measure of Quadripartitioned Bipolar Neutrosophic Sets

Here we provide the definition of similarity measure between two QSVBNS A, B over a universe X.

Definition 14. *Let QSVBNS(X) indicate the set of all QSVBNS over the universe X. Let* $S : QSVBNS(X) \times QSVBNS(X) \rightarrow [0,1]$ *be a function satisfying the following properties for all* $A, B \in QSVBNS(X)$:

(S1) $0 \leq S(A,B) < 1$ and $S(A,B) = 1$ iff $A = B$,
(S2) $S(A,B) = S(B,A)$,
(S3) for any $A, B, C \in QSVBNS(X)$ with $A \subseteq B \subseteq C$, $S(A,C) \leq S(A,B) \wedge S(B,C)$.

then S is said to be a similarity measure.

Based on the membership functions of two QSVBNS, we prescribe some functions which measures the differences between the membership values of two QSVBNS. Let $A, B \in QSVBNS$. For each $x_k \in X$, $k = 1, 2, ..., n$ and for each $i = 1, 2, 3, 4$ and $j = 1, 2$ define the functions $\delta_i^{A,B}$, $\lambda_j^{A,B}$: $QSVBNS(X) \times QSVBNS(X) \rightarrow [0,1]$ respectively,

- $\delta_1^{A,B}(x_k) = \frac{1}{2}(|T_A^P(x_k) - T_B^P(x_k)| + |T_A^N(x_k) - T_B^N(x_k)|)$,

- $\delta_2^{A,B}(x_k) = \frac{1}{2}(|F_A^P(x_k) - F_B^P(x_k)| + |F_A^N(x_k) - F_B^N(x_k)|)$,

- $\delta_3^{A,B}(x_k) = \frac{1}{4}(\delta_1^{A,B}(x_k) + \delta_2^{A,B}(x_k) + |C_A^P(x_k) - C_B^P(x_k)| + |C_A^N(x_k) - C_B^N(x_k)|)$,

- $\delta_4^{A,B}(x_k) = \frac{1}{2}(|U_A^P(x_k) - U_B^P(x_k)| + |U_A^N(x_k) - U_B^N(x_k)|)$,

- $\lambda_1^{A,B}(x_k) = \frac{1}{4}(|T_A^P(x_k)C_A^P(x_k) - T_B^P(x_k)C_B^P(x_k)| + |T_A^N(x_k)C_A^N(x_k) - T_B^N(x_k)C_B^N(x_k)| + |C_A^P(x_k) - C_B^P(x_k)| + |C_A^N(x_k) - C_B^N(x_k)|)$,

- $\lambda_2^{A,B}(x_k) = \frac{1}{4}(\delta_1^{A,B}(x_k) + \delta_2^{A,B}(x_k) + |U_A^P(x_k) - U_B^P(x_k)| + |U_A^N(x_k) - U_B^N(x_k)|)$.

Remark 2. *The function* $\mathcal{T}_1(A, B)$ *defined by* $\mathcal{T}_1(A,B) = 1 - \frac{1}{4n}\sum_{k=1}^{n}\sum_{i=1}^{4}\delta_i^{A,B}(x_k)$, $A, B \in QSVBNS(X)$ *is shown to be a similarity measure in the following theorem.*

Theorem 2. $\mathcal{T}_1(A, B)$ *is a similarity measure between two quadripartitioned bipolar neutrosophic sets A and B over X.*

Proof. Since $T_A^P(x_k), C_A^P(x_k), U_A^P(x_k), F_A^P(x_k) \in [0,1]$ and $T_A^N(x_k), C_A^N(x_k), U_A^N(x_k), F_A^N(x_k) \in [-1,0]$ for all $x_k \in X$ it follows that $\delta_1^{A,B}(x_k)$ attains its maximum value 1 whenever one of the positive truth membership values corresponding to A and B is 1 and the other is 0 and one of the negative truth membership values corresponding to A and B is -1 and the other is 0. Similarly for each $x_k \in X$, $\delta_1^{A,B}(x_k)$ attains its minimum value 0 whenever $T_A^P(x_k) = T_B^P(x_k)$ and $T_A^N(x_k) = T_B^N(x_k)$. Thus for all $x_k \in X$, $0 \leq \delta_1^{A,B}(x_k) \leq 1$, $\forall x_k \in X$. Likewise it can be shown that $0 \leq \delta_2^{A,B}(x_k), \delta_3^{A,B}(x_k), \delta_4^{A,B}(x_k) \leq 1$. Therefore for all $x_k \in X$ we have,

$$0 \leq \delta_1^{A,B}(x_k) + \delta_2^{A,B}(x_k) + \delta_3^{A,B}(x_k) + \delta_4^{A,B}(x_k) \leq 4$$
$$\implies 0 \leq \tfrac{1}{4}[\delta_1^{A,B}(x_k) + \delta_2^{A,B}(x_k) + \delta_3^{A,B}(x_k) + \delta_4^{A,B}(x_k)] \leq 1$$
$$\implies 0 \leq \tfrac{1}{4n} \sum_{k=1}^n \sum_{i=1}^4 \delta_i^{A,B}(x_k) \leq 1$$
$$\implies -1 \leq -\tfrac{1}{4n} \sum_{k=1}^n \sum_{i=1}^4 \delta_i^{A,B}(x_k) \leq 0$$
$$\implies 0 \leq 1 - \tfrac{1}{4n} \sum_{k=1}^n \sum_{i=1}^4 \delta_i^{A,B}(x_k) \leq 1$$
$$\implies 0 \leq \mathcal{T}_1(A,B) \leq 1$$

Again, $\mathcal{T}_1(A,B) = 1 \iff \sum_{k=1}^n \sum_{i=1}^4 \delta_i^{A,B}(x_k) = 0 \iff \delta_1^{A,B}(x_k) = \delta_2^{A,B}(x_k) = \delta_3^{A,B}(x_k) = \delta_4^{A,B}(x_k) = 0 \iff T_A^P(x_k) = T_B^P(x_k), C_A^P(x_k) = C_B^P(x_k), U_A^P(x_k) = U_B^P(x_k), F_A^P(x_k) = F_B^P(x_k)$ and $T_A^N(x_k) = T_B^N(x_k), C_A^N(x_k) = C_B^N(x_k), U_A^N(x_k) = U_B^N(x_k), F_A^N(x_k) = F_B^N(x_k) \iff A = B$.

It is easy to prove that $\mathcal{T}_1(A,B) = \mathcal{T}_1(B,A)$.

Finally let $A \subset B \subset C$. Then for all $x_k \in X$, we have
$T_A^P(x_k) \leq T_B^P(x_k) \leq T_C^P(x_k)$, $T_A^N(x_k) \geq T_B^N(x_k) \geq T_C^N(x_k)$, $C_A^P(x_k) \leq C_B^P(x_k) \leq C_C^P(x_k)$, $C_A^N(x_k) \geq C_B^N(x_k) \geq C_C^N(x_k)$, $U_A^P(x_k) \geq U_B^P(x_k) \geq U_C^P(x_k)$, $U_A^N(x_k) \leq U_B^N(x_k) \leq U_C^N(x_k)$, $F_A^P(x_k) \geq F_B^P(x_k) \geq F_C^P(x_k)$, $F_A^N(x_k) \leq F_B^N(x_k) \leq F_C^N(x_k)$.

Then, $|T_A^P(x_k) - T_B^P(x_k)| \leq |T_A^P(x_k) - T_C^P(x_k)|, |T_A^N(x_k) - T_B^N(x_k)| \leq |T_A^N(x_k) - T_C^N(x_k)|$.

Therefore, $\tfrac{1}{2}(|T_A^P(x_k) - T_B^P(x_k)| + |T_A^N(x_k) - T_B^N(x_k)|) \leq \tfrac{1}{2}(|T_A^P(x_k) - T_C^P(x_k)| + |T_A^N(x_k) - T_C^N(x_k)|) \implies \delta_1^{A,B}(x_k) \leq \delta_1^{A,C}(x_k), \forall x_k \in X$ ....(*)

Considering a similar process, it can be shown that $\delta_2^{A,B}(x_k) \leq \delta_2^{A,C}(x_k), \delta_3^{A,B}(x_k) \leq \delta_3^{A,C}(x_k)$ and $\delta_4^{A,B}(x_k) \leq \delta_4^{A,C}(x_k)$.

Therefore,

$$\sum_{i=1}^4 \delta_i^{A,C}(x_k) \geq \sum_{i=1}^4 \delta_i^{A,B}(x_k)$$

$$\Rightarrow \sum_{k=1}^n \sum_{i=1}^4 \delta_i^{A,C}(x_k) \geq \sum_{k=1}^n \sum_{i=1}^4 \delta_i^{A,B}(x_k)$$

$$\Rightarrow 1 - \frac{1}{4n}\sum_{k=1}^n \sum_{i=1}^4 \delta_i^{A,B}(x_k) \geq 1 - \frac{1}{4n}\sum_{k=1}^n \sum_{i=1}^4 \delta_i^{A,C}(x_k)$$

$$\Rightarrow \mathcal{T}_1(A,B) \geq \mathcal{T}_1(A,C).$$

Similarly $\mathcal{T}_1(B,C) \geq \mathcal{T}_1(A,C)$. Therefore, $\mathcal{T}_1(A,C) \leq \mathcal{T}_1(A,B) \wedge \mathcal{T}_1(B,C)$. Hence the proof. □

Remark 3. *Define* $\mathcal{T}_2(A,B) = 1 - \left[\tfrac{1}{n}\sum_{k=1}^n \left(\tfrac{1}{4}(\delta_1^{A,B}(x_k) + \delta_2^{A,B}(x_k) + \lambda_1^{A,B}(x_k) + \lambda_2^{A,B}(x_k))\right)^p\right]^{\frac{1}{p}}$, *where* p, *a positive integer, is defined to be the order of the similarity.*

Theorem 3. $\mathcal{T}_2(A,B)$ *is a similarity measure between two quadripartitioned bipolar neutrosophic sets* A *and* B *over* X.

Proof. $T_2(A, B) = T_2(B, A)$ is quite obvious.
Under any of the the following condition $\lambda_1^{A,B}(x_k)$ attains its maximum value 1,

(1) $T_A^P(x_k) = C_A^P(x_k) = 1$ and at least one of $T_B^P(x_k)$ or $C_B^P(x_k)$ is 0 or $T_B^P(x_k) = C_B^P(x_k) = 1$ and at least one of $T_A^P(x_k)$ or $C_A^P(x_k)$ is 0,
(2) $T_A^N(x_k) = C_A^N(x_k) = -1$ and at least one of $T_B^N(x_k)$ or $C_B^N(x_k)$ is 0 or $T_B^N(x_k) = C_B^N(x_k) = -1$ and at least one of $T_A^N(x_k)$ or $C_A^N(x_k)$ is 0,
(3) $C_A^P(x_k) = 1$ and $C_B^P(x_k) = 0$ or $C_A^P(x_k) = 0$ and $C_B^P(x_k) = 1$,
(4) $C_A^N(x_k) = -1$ and $C_B^N(x_k) = 0$ or $C_A^N(x_k) = 0$ and $C_B^N(x_k) = -1$.

Also the minimum value of $\lambda_1^{A,B}(x_k)$ is 0. Thus $0 \leq \lambda_1^{A,B}(x_k) \leq 1$ for all $x_k \in X$. Also $0 \leq \lambda_2^{A,B}(x_k) \leq 1$ follows from similar arguments. Therefore,

$$0 \leq \delta_1^{A,B}(x_k) + \delta_2^{A,B}(x_k) + \lambda_1^{A,B}(x_k) + \lambda_2^{A,B}(x_k) \leq 4$$
$$\Longrightarrow 0 \leq (\tfrac{1}{4}(\delta_1^{A,B}(x_k) + \delta_2^{A,B}(x_k) + \lambda_1^{A,B}(x_k) + \lambda_2^{A,B}(x_k)))^p \leq 1, \forall p \geq 1$$
$$\Longrightarrow 0 \leq \sum_{k=1}^{n} (\tfrac{1}{4}(\delta_1^{A,B}(x_k) + \delta_2^{A,B}(x_k) + \lambda_1^{A,B}(x_k) + \lambda_2^{A,B}(x_k)))^p \leq n$$
$$\Longrightarrow 0 \leq \tfrac{1}{n}\sum_{k=1}^{n} (\tfrac{1}{4}(\delta_1^{A,B}(x_k) + \delta_2^{A,B}(x_k) + \lambda_1^{A,B}(x_k) + \lambda_2^{A,B}(x_k)))^p \leq 1$$
$$\Longrightarrow 0 \leq \Big[\tfrac{1}{n}\sum_{k=1}^{n} (\tfrac{1}{4}(\delta_1^{A,B}(x_k) + \delta_2^{A,B}(x_k) + \lambda_1^{A,B}(x_k) + \lambda_2^{A,B}(x_k)))^p\Big]^{\tfrac{1}{p}} \leq 1$$
$$\Longrightarrow 0 \leq 1 - \Big[\tfrac{1}{n}\sum_{k=1}^{n} (\tfrac{1}{4}(\delta_1^{A,B}(x_k) + \delta_2^{A,B}(x_k) + \lambda_1^{A,B}(x_k) + \lambda_2^{A,B}(x_k)))^p\Big]^{\tfrac{1}{p}} \leq 1$$
$$\Longrightarrow 0 \leq T_2(A, B) \leq 1$$

To show the triangular inequality suppose $P \subset Q \subset R$. Then for all $x_k \in X$, we have, $T_P^P(x_k) \leq T_Q^P(x_k) \leq T_R^P(x_k)$, $T_P^N(x_k) \geq T_Q^N(x_k) \geq T_R^N(x_k)$, $C_P^P(x_k) \leq C_Q^P(x_k) \leq C_R^P(x_k)$, $C_P^N(x_k) \geq C_Q^N(x_k) \geq C_R^N(x_k)$, $U_P^P(x_k) \geq U_Q^P(x_k) \geq U_R^P(x_k)$, $U_P^N(x_k) \leq U_Q^N(x_k) \leq U_R^N(x_k)$, $F_P^P(x_k) \geq F_Q^P(x_k) \geq F_R^P(x_k)$, $F_P^N(x_k) \leq F_Q^N(x_k) \leq F_R^N(x_k)$.

Then $\delta_1^{P,R}(x_k) \geq \delta_1^{P,Q}(x_k)$ and $\delta_2^{P,R}(x_k) \geq \delta_2^{P,Q}(x_k)$ follows from (*) of Theorem 2. Next consider $\lambda_1^{P,Q}(x_k)$ and $\lambda_1^{P,R}(x_k)$. From above inequalities we have, $T_P^P(x_k)C_P^P(x_k) \leq T_Q^P(x_k)C_Q^P(x_k) \leq T_R^P(x_k)C_R^P(x_k) \Rightarrow |T_P^P(x_k)C_P^P(x_k) - T_Q^P(x_k)C_Q^P(x_k)| \leq |T_P^P(x_k)C_P^P(x_k) - T_R^P(x_k)C_R^P(x_k)|$.

Similarly, $|T_P^N(x_k)C_P^N(x_k) - T_Q^N(x_k)C_Q^N(x_k)| \leq |T_P^N(x_k)C_P^N(x_k) - T_R^N(x_k)C_R^N(x_k)|$ and $|C_P^P(x_k) - C_Q^P(x_k)| \leq |C_P^P(x_k) - C_R^P(x_k)|$, $|C_P^N(x_k) - C_Q^N(x_k)| \leq |C_P^N(x_k) - C_R^N(x_k)|$.

Then, $\tfrac{1}{4}(|T_P^P(x_k)C_P^P(x_k) - T_R^P(x_k)C_R^P(x_k)| + |T_P^N(x_k)C_P^N(x_k) - T_R^N(x_k)C_R^N(x_k)| + |C_P^P(x_k) - C_R^P(x_k)| + |C_P^N(x_k) - C_R^N(x_k)|) \geq \tfrac{1}{4}(|T_P^P(x_k)C_P^P(x_k) - T_Q^P(x_k)C_Q^P(x_k)| + |T_P^N(x_k)C_P^N(x_k) - T_Q^N(x_k)C_Q^N(x_k)| + |C_P^P(x_k) - C_Q^P(x_k)| + |C_P^N(x_k) - C_Q^N(x_k)|)$
$\Rightarrow \lambda_1^{P,R}(x_k) \geq \lambda_1^{P,Q}(x_k)$

Similarly it can shown that $\lambda_2^{P,R}(x_k) \geq \lambda_2^{P,Q}(x_k)$.

$\tfrac{1}{4}(\delta_1^{P,R}(x_k) + \delta_2^{P,R}(x_k) + \lambda_1^{P,R}(x_k) + \lambda_2^{P,R}(x_k)) \geq \tfrac{1}{4}(\delta_1^{P,Q}(x_k) + \delta_2^{P,Q}(x_k) + \lambda_1^{P,Q}(x_k) + \lambda_2^{P,Q}(x_k))$

$\Rightarrow \sum_{k=1}^{n}(\tfrac{1}{4}(\delta_1^{P,R}(x_k) + \delta_2^{P,R}(x_k) + \lambda_1^{P,R}(x_k) + \lambda_2^{P,R}(x_k)))^p \geq \sum_{k=1}^{n}(\tfrac{1}{4}(\delta_1^{P,Q}(x_k) + \delta_2^{P,Q}(x_k) + \lambda_1^{P,Q}(x_k) + \lambda_2^{P,Q}(x_k)))^p$
$\Rightarrow 1 - \Big[\tfrac{1}{n}\sum_{k=1}^{n}(\tfrac{1}{4}(\delta_1^{P,R}(x_k) + \delta_2^{P,R}(x_k) + \lambda_1^{P,R}(x_k) + \lambda_2^{P,R}(x_k)))^p\Big]^{\tfrac{1}{p}} \leq 1 - \Big[\tfrac{1}{n}\sum_{k=1}^{n}(\tfrac{1}{4}(\delta_1^{P,Q}(x_k) + \delta_2^{P,Q}(x_k) + \lambda_1^{P,Q}(x_k) + \lambda_2^{P,Q}(x_k)))^p\Big]^{\tfrac{1}{p}}$
$\Rightarrow T_2(P, R) \leq T_2(P, Q)$

It is identical to show $\mathcal{T}_2(P,R) \leq \mathcal{T}_2(Q,R)$. Therefore, $\mathcal{T}_2(P,R) \leq \mathcal{T}_2(P,Q) \wedge \mathcal{T}_2(Q,R)$. This completes the proof. □

We define below the weighted similarity measure between two QSVBNS A, B over a universe X.

Definition 15. *The weighted similarity measure of two QSVBNS A, B is defined as,* $\mathcal{T}_2^w(A,B) = 1 - \left[\frac{1}{n}\sum_{k=1}^{n} w_k \left(\frac{1}{4}(\delta_1^{A,B}(x_k) + \delta_2^{A,B}(x_k) + \lambda_1^{A,B}(x_k) + \lambda_2^{A,B}(x_k))\right)^p\right]^{\frac{1}{p}}$, *where,* $(w_1, w_2, \ldots w_n)^T$ *is the weight vector assigned to the element* $x_1, x_2, \ldots x_n$ *of the universe X, such that* $0 \leq w_k \leq 1$, $k = 1, 2, \ldots, n$ *and* $\sum_{k=1}^{n} w_k = 1$. *It is effortless to find out that* $\mathcal{T}_2^w(A,B)$ *satisfies the conditions of similarity measure.*

Remark 4. *We define the following functions based on one particular membership function for two QSVBNSs A and B over the universe of discourse X, provided the denominators never vanish*

$$\mathcal{T}_T^P(A,B) = \frac{\sum_{k=1}^{n} \min\left(T_A^P(x_k), T_B^P(x_k)\right)}{\sum_{k=1}^{n} \max\left(T_A^P(x_k), T_B^P(x_k)\right)}, \quad \mathcal{T}_C^P(A,B) = \frac{\sum_{k=1}^{n} \min\left(C_A^P(x_k), C_B^P(x_k)\right)}{\sum_{k=1}^{n} \max\left(C_A^P(x_k), C_B^P(x_k)\right)},$$

$$\mathcal{T}_U^P(A,B) = \frac{\sum_{k=1}^{n} \min\left(U_A^P(x_k), U_B^P(x_k)\right)}{\sum_{k=1}^{n} \max\left(U_A^P(x_k), U_B^P(x_k)\right)}, \quad \mathcal{T}_F^P(A,B) = \frac{\sum_{k=1}^{n} \min\left(F_A^P(x_k), F_B^P(x_k)\right)}{\sum_{k=1}^{n} \max\left(F_A^P(x_k), F_B^P(x_k)\right)},$$

$$\mathcal{T}_T^N(A,B) = \frac{\sum_{k=1}^{n} \max\left(T_A^N(x_k), T_B^N(x_k)\right)}{\sum_{k=1}^{n} \min\left(T_A^N(x_k), T_B^N(x_k)\right)}, \quad \mathcal{T}_C^N(A,B) = \frac{\sum_{k=1}^{n} \max\left(C_A^N(x_k), C_B^N(x_k)\right)}{\sum_{k=1}^{n} \min\left(C_A^N(x_k), C_B^N(x_k)\right)},$$

$$\mathcal{T}_U^N(A,B) = \frac{\sum_{k=1}^{n} \max\left(U_A^N(x_k), U_B^N(x_k)\right)}{\sum_{k=1}^{n} \min\left(U_A^N(x_k), U_B^N(x_k)\right)}, \quad \mathcal{T}_F^N(A,B) = \frac{\sum_{k=1}^{n} \max\left(F_A^N(x_k), F_B^N(x_k)\right)}{\sum_{k=1}^{n} \min\left(F_A^N(x_k), F_B^N(x_k)\right)}.$$

The following is a definition of generalized similarity measure between two QSVBNS A, B whose value set is the set of all 2×4 matrices over $\mathbb{R}$.

Definition 16. *Let $X = \{x_1, x_2, \ldots, x_n\}$ be a finite universe of discourse. For two QSVBNSs A, B define a mapping* $\mathcal{L}: QSVBNS(X) \times QSVBNS(X) \to \mathbb{M}_{2 \times 4}(\mathbb{R})$ *by*

$$\mathcal{L}(A,B) = \begin{pmatrix} \mathcal{T}_T^P(A,B) & \mathcal{T}_C^P(A,B) & \mathcal{T}_U^P(A,B) & \mathcal{T}_F^P(A,B) \\ \mathcal{T}_T^N(A,B) & \mathcal{T}_C^N(A,B) & \mathcal{T}_U^N(A,B) & \mathcal{T}_F^N(A,B) \end{pmatrix},$$

and a partial order relation "$\preceq$" on $\mathbb{M}_{2 \times 4}(\mathbb{R})$ *as:*

$$\begin{pmatrix} a_1 & a_2 & a_3 & a_4 \\ a_5 & a_6 & a_7 & a_8 \end{pmatrix} \preceq \begin{pmatrix} b_1 & b_2 & b_3 & b_4 \\ b_5 & b_6 & b_7 & b_8 \end{pmatrix}, \quad \text{if } a_i \leq b_i \; \forall i.$$

Also define

$$\tilde{0} = \begin{pmatrix} 0 & 0 & 0 & 0 \\ 0 & 0 & 0 & 0 \end{pmatrix} \text{ and } \tilde{1} = \begin{pmatrix} 1 & 1 & 1 & 1 \\ 1 & 1 & 1 & 1 \end{pmatrix}.$$

Remark 5. *Then for $A, B \in QSVBNS(X)$*

(1) $\tilde{0} \preceq \mathcal{L}(A, B) \preceq \tilde{1}$,
(2) $\mathcal{L}(A, B) = \mathcal{L}(B, A)$,
(3) *for $A \subset B \subset C$, $\mathcal{L}(A, C) \preceq \mathcal{L}(A, B) \wedge \mathcal{L}(B, C)$.*

We give an outline of the proof as:
Let $A \subset B \subset C$. Then for all $x_k \in X$, $T_A^N(x_k) \geq T_B^N(x_k) \geq T_C^N(x_k)$. Consequently, $\min\left(T_A^N(x_k), T_B^N(x_k)\right) = T_B^N(x_k)$, $\max\left(T_A^N(x_k), T_B^N(x_k)\right) = T_A^N(x_k)$, $\min\left(T_A^N(x_k), T_C^N(x_k)\right) = T_C^N(x_k)$, $\max\left(T_A^N(x_k), T_C^N(x_k)\right) = T_A^N(x_k)$.

Then we have, $\sum_{k=1}^{n} T_B^N(x_k) \geq \sum_{k=1}^{n} T_C^N(x_k) \Rightarrow \dfrac{1}{\sum_{k=1}^{n} T_B^N(x_k)} \leq \dfrac{1}{\sum_{k=1}^{n} T_C^N(x_k)} \Rightarrow \dfrac{\sum_{k=1}^{n} T_A^N(x_k)}{\sum_{k=1}^{n} T_B^N(x_k)} \geq \dfrac{\sum_{k=1}^{n} T_A^N(x_k)}{\sum_{k=1}^{n} T_C^N(x_k)}$

$\Rightarrow \mathcal{T}_T^N(A, B) \geq \mathcal{T}_T^N(A, C)$.
A similar process follows for $\mathcal{T}_T^N(B, C) \geq \mathcal{T}_T^N(A, C)$. Hence $\mathcal{T}_T^N(A, C) \leq \mathcal{T}_T^N(A, B) \wedge \mathcal{T}_T^N(B, C)$.
Hence $\mathcal{L}$ is a generalized similarity measure.

Definition 17. *Let $d : QSVBNS(X) \times QSVBNS(X) \to \mathbb{R}^+ \cup \{0\}$ be a mapping satisfying the following conditions:*

(d1) $d(A, B) \geq 0$ and $d(A, B) = 0$ iff $A = B$,
(d2) $d(A, B) = d(B, A)$,
(d3) $d(A, C) \leq d(A, B) + d(B, C)$.

Then d is said to be a distance based measure between two QSVBNS A and B.

We now define the Hamming distance, normalized Hamming distance, Euclidean distance, and normalized Euclidean distance between two QSVBNSs $A, B \in QSVBNS(X)$,

(1) The Hamming distance:
- $d_H(A, B) = \sum_{k=1}^{n} \Big(|T_A^P(x_k) - T_B^P(x_k)| + |C_A^P(x_k) - C_B^P(x_k)| + |U_A^P(x_k) - U_B^P(x_k)| + |F_A^P(x_k) - F_B^P(x_k)| + |T_A^N(x_k) - T_B^N(x_k)| + |C_A^N(x_k) - C_B^N(x_k)| + |U_A^N(x_k) - U_B^N(x_k)| + |F_A^N(x_k) - F_B^N(x_k)| \Big)$,

(2) Normalized Hamming distance:
- $d_{NH}(A, B) = \frac{1}{8n} d_H(A, B)$,

(3) The Euclidean distance:
- $d_E(A, B) = \Big(\sum_{k=1}^{n} \big(|T_A^P(x_k) - T_B^P(x_k)|^2 + |C_A^P(x_k) - C_B^P(x_k)|^2 + |U_A^P(x_k) - U_B^P(x_k)|^2 + |F_A^P(x_k) - F_B^P(x_k)|^2 + |T_A^N(x_k) - T_B^N(x_k)|^2 + |C_A^N(x_k) - C_B^N(x_k)|^2 + |U_A^N(x_k) - U_B^N(x_k)|^2 + |F_A^N(x_k) - F_B^N(x_k)|^2 \big) \Big)^{\frac{1}{2}}$,

(4) Normalized Euclidean distance:
- $d_{NE}(A, B) = \frac{d_E(A, B)}{2n\sqrt{2}}$.

5. QBN-Multi-Criteria Decision Making Method

Definition 18. Let $U = (u_1, u_2, ..., u_m)$ be a set of alternatives, $A = (a_1, a_2, ..., a_n)$ be the set of attributes, $w = (w_1, w_2, ..., w_n)^T$ be the weight vector assigned to a_j $(j = 1, 2, ...n)$ such that $w_k \geq 0$ and $\sum_{k=1}^{n} w_k = 1$.

Let $[b_{ij}]_{m \times n} = \langle T_{ij}^P, C_{ij}^P, U_{ij}^P, F_{ij}^P, T_{ij}^N, C_{ij}^N, U_{ij}^N, F_{ij}^N \rangle$ represents the rating values of the alternatives in term of QSVBNS.

Then,
$$\begin{pmatrix} & a_1 & a_2 & \cdots & a_n \\ u_1 & b_{1,1} & b_{1,2} & \cdots & b_{1,n} \\ u_2 & b_{2,1} & b_{2,2} & \cdots & b_{2,n} \\ \vdots & \vdots & \vdots & \ddots & \vdots \\ u_m & b_{m,1} & b_{m,2} & \cdots & b_{m,n} \end{pmatrix}$$
is called the QBN-multi-attribute decision making matrix.

The positive ideal QBN solution of the decision matrix $[b_{ij}]_{m \times n}$ is defined as: $\bar{b}_j^* = \langle \max_i \{T_{ij}^P\}, \max_i \{C_{ij}^P\}, \min_i \{U_{ij}^P\}, \min_i \{F_{ij}^P\}, \min_i \{T_{ij}^N\}, \min_i \{C_{ij}^N\}, \max_i \{U_{ij}^N\}, \max_i \{F_{ij}^N\}, \rangle$. The negative ideal QBN solution of the decision matrix $[b_{ij}]_{m \times n}$ is defined as:

$$\underline{b}_j^* = \langle \min_i \{T_{ij}^P\}, \min_i \{C_{ij}^P\}, \max_i \{U_{ij}^P\}, \max_i \{F_{ij}^P\}, \max_i \{T_{ij}^N\}, \max_i \{C_{ij}^N\}, \min_i \{U_{ij}^N\}, \min_i \{F_{ij}^N\}, \rangle.$$

We now propose an algorithm based on the quadripartitioned weighted similarity measure to select the best alternative for multi-attribute decision making problem in quadripartitioned bipolar neutrosophic enviornment which is given in Algorithm 1:

Algorithm 1: Algorithm based on The quadripartitioned weighted similarty measure

---

Step 1. Give the QBN-multi-attribute decision making matrix $[b_{ij}]_{m \times n}$ to the decision maker.
Step 2. Compute the positive ideal QBN solution $\bar{b}_j^*$ and negative ideal QBN solution $\underline{b}_j^*$ for the decision matrix $[b_{ij}]_{m \times n}$.
Step 3. Determine $\mathcal{T}_2^w(\bar{b}_j^*, b_i)$ for $j = 1, 2, ..., m$, the weighted quadripartitioned similarity measure between positive ideal solution $\bar{b}_j^*$ and $b_i = [b_{ij}]_{1 \times n}$ for $i = 1, 2, ..., m$ and $j = 1, 2, ..., n$ and $\mathcal{T}_2^w(\underline{b}_j^*, b_i)$ for $j = 1, 2, ..., m$, the weighted quadripartitioned similarity measure between negative ideal solution $\underline{b}_j^*$ and $b_i = [b_{ij}]_{1 \times n}$ for $i = 1, 2, ..., m$ and $j = 1, 2, ..., n$ as:

- $\mathcal{T}_2^w(\bar{b}_j^*, b_i) = 1 - \left[\frac{1}{n} \sum_{k=1}^{n} w_k \left(\frac{1}{4} (\delta_1^{\bar{b}_j^*, b_i}(x_k) + \delta_2^{\bar{b}_j^*, b_i}(x_k) + \lambda_1^{\bar{b}_j^*, b_i}(x_k) + \lambda_2^{\bar{b}_j^*, b_i}(x_k)) \right)^p \right]^{\frac{1}{p}}$,

- $\mathcal{T}_2^w(\underline{b}_j^*, b_i) = 1 - \left[\frac{1}{n} \sum_{k=1}^{n} w_k \left(\frac{1}{4} (\delta_1^{\underline{b}_j^*, b_i}(x_k) + \delta_2^{\underline{b}_j^*, b_i}(x_k) + \lambda_1^{\underline{b}_j^*, b_i}(x_k) + \lambda_2^{\underline{b}_j^*, b_i}(x_k)) \right)^p \right]^{\frac{1}{p}}$,

Step 4. Figure out the non-increasing order of the average ideal solution, $\frac{\mathcal{T}_2^w(\bar{b}_j^*, b_i) + \mathcal{T}_2^w(\underline{b}_j^*, b_i)}{2}$ for $j = 1, 2, ..., m$ and select the best alternatives.

---

6. Illustrative Example

The following group decision making problem, which has been studied by Wu et al. [30], is taken into consideration in a quadripartitioned bipolar neutrosophic environment. Climate change in a global environment is a worrying sign. Industries have shifted their focus toward green production. A car company is eager to choose the most suitable green supplier for one of the key elements in its manufacturing process. After the pre-evaluation, four suppliers $\mathcal{A}_i$, $(i = 1, 2, 3, 4)$, have been short-listed for evaluation on the basis of the concerned criteria: a_1: is the product quality, a_2: is technological capability, and a_3: is pollution control. The weight vector of the concerned criteria are $\{w_1, w_2, w_3\}^T = \{0.3, 0.3, 0.4\}^T$. To determine the decision information an expert is appointed to gather the criteria values for the four possible alternatives in a QBN environment which is given in Algorithm 2.

Algorithm 2: Decision making algorithm for the four possible alternatives in a QBN environment

Step 1. The decision matrix $[b_{ij}]_{4\times 3}$ given by the expert shown in Table 1.
Step 2. The positive ideal quadripartitioned bipolar neutrosophic solution and negative ideal quadripartitioned bipolar neutrosophic solutions are calculated as: $\tilde{A}^* = [\langle 0.8, 0.6, 0.2, 0.2, -0.6, -0.6, -0.4, -0.4\rangle, \langle 0.9, 0.4, 0.2, 0.2, -0.5, -0.3, -0.2, -0.4\rangle,$
$\langle 0.9, 0.6, 0.4, 0.3, -0.5, -0.4, -0.1, -0.3\rangle]$ and $\underline{A}^* = [\langle 0.4, 0.2, 0.5, 0.5, -0.2, -0.3, -0.7, -0.8\rangle, \langle 0.6, 0.1, 0.6, 0.5, -0.1, -0.2, -0.5, -0.6\rangle,$
$\langle 0.6, 0.1, 0.5, 0.7, -0.1, -0.2, -0.6, -0.8\rangle]$
Step 3. The weighted quadripartitioned similarity measure $T_2^w(\tilde{A}^*, A_i)$, $i = 1, 2, 3, 4$, and $T_2^w(\underline{A}^*, A_i)$, $i = 1, 2, 3, 4$ (shown in Table 2) are computed.

Table 1. Decision making matrix.

	a_1	a_2	a_3
$\mathcal{A}_1$	$\langle 0.4, 0.5, 0.3, 0.2, -0.6,$ $-0.4, -0.5, -0.7\rangle$	$\langle 0.6, 0.1, 0.2, 0.3, -0.4,$ $-0.3, -0.2, -0.5\rangle$	$\langle 0.8, 0.6, 0.5, 0.7, -0.3,$ $-0.2, -0.1, -0.4\rangle$
$\mathcal{A}_2$	$\langle 0.6, 0.4, 0.2, 0.5, -0.4,$ $-0.5, -0.7, -0.8\rangle$	$\langle 0.6, 0.2, 0.3, 0.4, -0.5,$ $-0.2, -0.3, -0.4\rangle$	$\langle 0.7, 0.4, 0.5, 0.6,$ $-0.1, -0.3, -0.4, -0.5\rangle$
$\mathcal{A}_3$	$\langle 0.7, 0.2, 0.4, 0.3,$ $-0.2, -0.6, -0.4, -0.5\rangle$	$\langle 0.9, 0.3, 0.6, 0.5,$ $-0.2, -0.2, -0.5, -0.4\rangle$	$\langle 0.6, 0.1, 0.5, 0.4,$ $-0.2, -0.4, -0.6, -0.3\rangle$
$\mathcal{A}_4$	$\langle 0.8, 0.6, 0.5, 0.3,$ $-0.5, -0.3, -0.6, -0.4\rangle$	$\langle 0.6, 0.4, 0.3, 0.2,$ $-0.1, -0.3, -0.4, -0.6\rangle$	$\langle 0.9, 0.6, 0.4, 0.3,$ $-0.5, -0.3, -0.6, -0.8\rangle$

7. Discussion

In this section, a detailed analysis about the above introduced algorithm and the obtained result based on the algorithm is carried through. The weighted quadripartitioned similarity measure between the alternatives ($\mathcal{A}_j$, $j = 1, 2, 3, 4$) and the positive ideal quadripartitioned bipolar neutrosophic solution is shown in Table 2 and the same with the negative ideal quadripartitioned bipolar neutrosophic solution is given in Table 2. The main objective of the proposed algorithm i.e., the average ideal solution is obtained. The ranking results based on these similarity measures is highlighted in the final Table (Table 3).

Deli et al. [28] and Sahin et al. [27], in their study on bipolar neutrosophic sets, obtained the ranking result without considering the negative ideal solution. From their algorithm, it can be seen that if the decision maker is asked to choose an alternative emphasizing more on the satisfaction degree of the given criteria than the satisfaction degree of the counter-property of the criteria, the similarity measure with the positive ideal solution can be used to get the most suitable alternatives. In the reverse case, the similarity measure with negative ideal solution will be more fruitful.

In the case of QSVBNS, our algorithm follows the same footstep as Deli et al. [28]; however, the major difference is that we have used the average of the measure values of positive ideal solution and negative ideal solution. From the proposed algorithm, it seems that the ranking results to choose the best alternatives using a positive ideal solution and a negative ideal solution will give exactly the opposite ranking, but this is not the case, as can be seen in Table 2. The similarity index p in the weighted quadripartitioned similarity measure also has a big role to play. From the study, we have found that as the similarity index starts to take more higher values, the formula predicts more accurately, as the difference between the first two choices of the alternatives starts increasing for higher values of p. From Figure 2, it is observed that for $p = 1, 2$, the alternative values are quite close and $\mathcal{A}_3$ comes out as the best alternative with a very small margin from $\mathcal{A}_1$. For $p = 3$, $\mathcal{A}_1$ overtakes $\mathcal{A}_3$ as the best alternative and as p stars increasing, $\mathcal{A}_1$ remains the best among the four alternatives and the margin of the second best choice $\mathcal{A}_3$ starts increasing. The differences between the alternative values is shown in Figure 2 for $p = 1, 2, 3$. In Figure 3, it can be observed that for $p = 4, 5, 6$, $\mathcal{A}_1$ enlarge by a bit more margin than $\mathcal{A}_3$. In Figure 4, the comparison between the best two alternatives $\mathcal{A}_1$ and $\mathcal{A}_3$ is shown. It can be seen that for a very large value of p, $\mathcal{A}_1 - \mathcal{A}_3 \approx 0.1$.

Table 2. Similarity measures for different values of p.

Similarity Index	Positive Ideal Solution	Negative Ideal Solution	Average Ideal Solution
$p = 1$	$\mathcal{T}_2^w(\bar{\mathcal{A}}^*, \mathcal{A}_1) = 0.952416$	$\mathcal{T}_2^w(\underline{\mathcal{A}}^*, \mathcal{A}_1) = 0.94$	$\mathcal{T}_2^w(\mathcal{A}^*, \mathcal{A}_1) = 0.946208$
	$\mathcal{T}_2^w(\bar{\mathcal{A}}^*, \mathcal{A}_2) = 0.929125$	$\mathcal{T}_2^w(\underline{\mathcal{A}}^*, \mathcal{A}_2) = 0.954604$	$\mathcal{T}_2^w(\mathcal{A}^*, \mathcal{A}_2) = 0.941864$
	$\mathcal{T}_2^w(\bar{\mathcal{A}}^*, \mathcal{A}_3) = 0.936681$	$\mathcal{T}_2^w(\underline{\mathcal{A}}^*, \mathcal{A}_3) = 0.960833$	$\mathcal{T}_2^w(\mathcal{A}^*, \mathcal{A}_3) = 0.948757$
	$\mathcal{T}_2^w(\bar{\mathcal{A}}^*, \mathcal{A}_4) = 0.957291$	$\mathcal{T}_2^w(\underline{\mathcal{A}}^*, \mathcal{A}_4) = 0.928791$	$\mathcal{T}_2^w(\mathcal{A}^*, \mathcal{A}_4) = 0.943041$
$p = 2$	$\mathcal{T}_2^w(\bar{\mathcal{A}}^*, \mathcal{A}_1) = 0.917337$	$\mathcal{T}_2^w(\underline{\mathcal{A}}^*, \mathcal{A}_1) = 0.895453$	$\mathcal{T}_2^w(\mathcal{A}^*, \mathcal{A}_1) = 0.906395$
	$\mathcal{T}_2^w(\bar{\mathcal{A}}^*, \mathcal{A}_2) = 0.874914$	$\mathcal{T}_2^w(\underline{\mathcal{A}}^*, \mathcal{A}_2) = 0.921020$	$\mathcal{T}_2^w(\mathcal{A}^*, \mathcal{A}_2) = 0.897967$
	$\mathcal{T}_2^w(\bar{\mathcal{A}}^*, \mathcal{A}_3) = 0.889566$	$\mathcal{T}_2^w(\underline{\mathcal{A}}^*, \mathcal{A}_3) = 0.927222$	$\mathcal{T}_2^w(\mathcal{A}^*, \mathcal{A}_3) = 0.908394$
	$\mathcal{T}_2^w(\bar{\mathcal{A}}^*, \mathcal{A}_4) = 0.923766$	$\mathcal{T}_2^w(\underline{\mathcal{A}}^*, \mathcal{A}_4) = 0.870422$	$\mathcal{T}_2^w(\mathcal{A}^*, \mathcal{A}_4) = 0.897094$
$p = 3$	$\mathcal{T}_2^w(\bar{\mathcal{A}}^*, \mathcal{A}_1) = 0.900428$	$\mathcal{T}_2^w(\underline{\mathcal{A}}^*, \mathcal{A}_1) = 0.873755$	$\mathcal{T}_2^w(\mathcal{A}^*, \mathcal{A}_1) = 0.887092$
	$\mathcal{T}_2^w(\bar{\mathcal{A}}^*, \mathcal{A}_2) = 0.847426$	$\mathcal{T}_2^w(\underline{\mathcal{A}}^*, \mathcal{A}_2) = 0.904713$	$\mathcal{T}_2^w(\mathcal{A}^*, \mathcal{A}_2) = 0.876069$
	$\mathcal{T}_2^w(\bar{\mathcal{A}}^*, \mathcal{A}_3) = 0.866476$	$\mathcal{T}_2^w(\underline{\mathcal{A}}^*, \mathcal{A}_3) = 0.907610$	$\mathcal{T}_2^w(\mathcal{A}^*, \mathcal{A}_3) = 0.887043$
	$\mathcal{T}_2^w(\bar{\mathcal{A}}^*, \mathcal{A}_4) = 0.905738$	$\mathcal{T}_2^w(\underline{\mathcal{A}}^*, \mathcal{A}_4) = 0.839067$	$\mathcal{T}_2^w(\mathcal{A}^*, \mathcal{A}_4) = 0.872402$
$p = 4$	$\mathcal{T}_2^w(\bar{\mathcal{A}}^*, \mathcal{A}_1) = 0.890553$	$\mathcal{T}_2^w(\underline{\mathcal{A}}^*, \mathcal{A}_1) = 0.860959$	$\mathcal{T}_2^w(\mathcal{A}^*, \mathcal{A}_1) = 0.875756$
	$\mathcal{T}_2^w(\bar{\mathcal{A}}^*, \mathcal{A}_2) = 0.830665$	$\mathcal{T}_2^w(\underline{\mathcal{A}}^*, \mathcal{A}_2) = 0.895086$	$\mathcal{T}_2^w(\mathcal{A}^*, \mathcal{A}_2) = 0.862875$
	$\mathcal{T}_2^w(\bar{\mathcal{A}}^*, \mathcal{A}_3) = 0.852716$	$\mathcal{T}_2^w(\underline{\mathcal{A}}^*, \mathcal{A}_3) = 0.894353$	$\mathcal{T}_2^w(\mathcal{A}^*, \mathcal{A}_3) = 0.873535$
	$\mathcal{T}_2^w(\bar{\mathcal{A}}^*, \mathcal{A}_4) = 0.893862$	$\mathcal{T}_2^w(\underline{\mathcal{A}}^*, \mathcal{A}_4) = 0.819565$	$\mathcal{T}_2^w(\mathcal{A}^*, \mathcal{A}_4) = 0.856714$
$p = 5$	$\mathcal{T}_2^w(\bar{\mathcal{A}}^*, \mathcal{A}_1) = 0.884025$	$\mathcal{T}_2^w(\underline{\mathcal{A}}^*, \mathcal{A}_1) = 0.852444$	$\mathcal{T}_2^w(\mathcal{A}^*, \mathcal{A}_1) = 0.868235$
	$\mathcal{T}_2^w(\bar{\mathcal{A}}^*, \mathcal{A}_2) = 0.819257$	$\mathcal{T}_2^w(\underline{\mathcal{A}}^*, \mathcal{A}_2) = 0.888633$	$\mathcal{T}_2^w(\mathcal{A}^*, \mathcal{A}_2) = 0.853945$
	$\mathcal{T}_2^w(\bar{\mathcal{A}}^*, \mathcal{A}_3) = 0.843424$	$\mathcal{T}_2^w(\underline{\mathcal{A}}^*, \mathcal{A}_3) = 0.884681$	$\mathcal{T}_2^w(\mathcal{A}^*, \mathcal{A}_3) = 0.864052$
	$\mathcal{T}_2^w(\bar{\mathcal{A}}^*, \mathcal{A}_4) = 0.885108$	$\mathcal{T}_2^w(\underline{\mathcal{A}}^*, \mathcal{A}_4) = 0.806328$	$\mathcal{T}_2^w(\mathcal{A}^*, \mathcal{A}_4) = 0.845718$
$p = 6$	$\mathcal{T}_2^w(\bar{\mathcal{A}}^*, \mathcal{A}_1) = 0.879341$	$\mathcal{T}_2^w(\underline{\mathcal{A}}^*, \mathcal{A}_1) = 0.846318$	$\mathcal{T}_2^w(\mathcal{A}^*, \mathcal{A}_1) = 0.862830$
	$\mathcal{T}_2^w(\bar{\mathcal{A}}^*, \mathcal{A}_2) = 0.810950$	$\mathcal{T}_2^w(\underline{\mathcal{A}}^*, \mathcal{A}_2) = 0.883926$	$\mathcal{T}_2^w(\mathcal{A}^*, \mathcal{A}_2) = 0.847438$
	$\mathcal{T}_2^w(\bar{\mathcal{A}}^*, \mathcal{A}_3) = 0.836617$	$\mathcal{T}_2^w(\underline{\mathcal{A}}^*, \mathcal{A}_3) = 0.877287$	$\mathcal{T}_2^w(\mathcal{A}^*, \mathcal{A}_3) = 0.856952$
	$\mathcal{T}_2^w(\bar{\mathcal{A}}^*, \mathcal{A}_4) = 0.878257$	$\mathcal{T}_2^w(\underline{\mathcal{A}}^*, \mathcal{A}_4) = 0.796801$	$\mathcal{T}_2^w(\mathcal{A}^*, \mathcal{A}_4) = 0.837529$

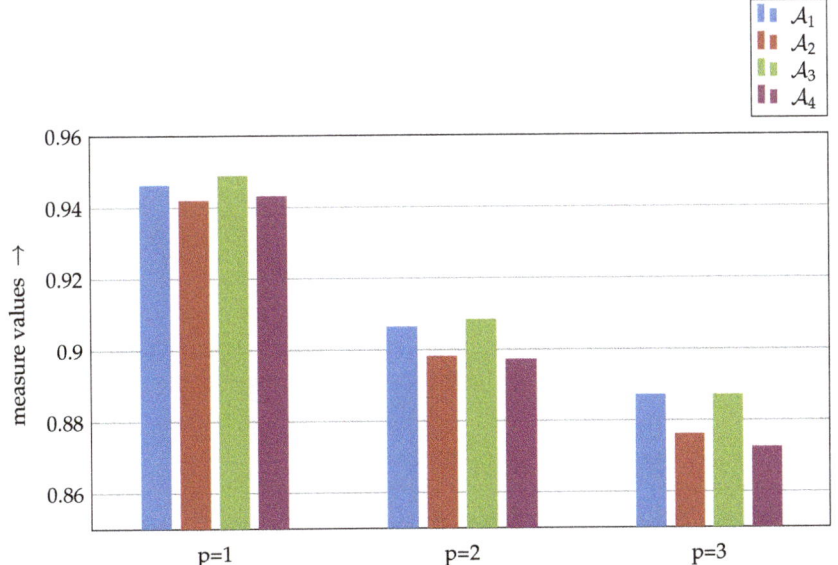

Figure 2. Comparison between the alternatives for different similarity indexes.

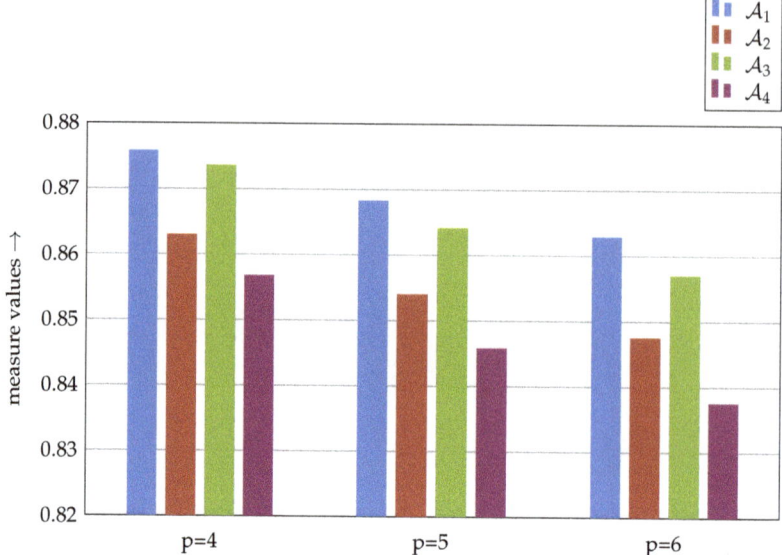

Figure 3. Comparison between the alternatives for different similarity indexes.

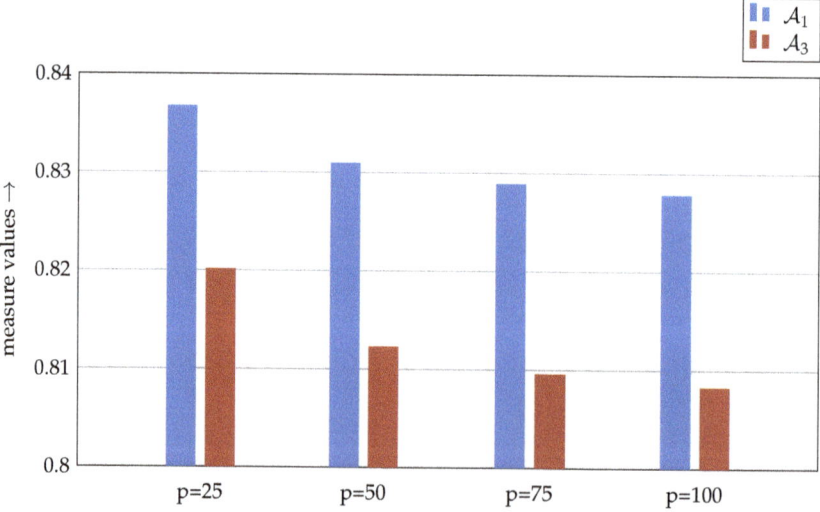

Figure 4. Comparison between the best two alternatives $\mathcal{A}_1$ and $\mathcal{A}_3$ for some higher similarity index.

From the above analysis it is clear that $\mathcal{A}_1$ is the most suitable alternative to the decision maker. The proposed method can get the better of the decision making problem with quadripartitioned bipolar neutrosophic information. Also, the higher similarity index produces a more accurate method by indicating clear differences between the alternatives. A comparison of the above discussed MCDM problem is made in a fuzzy system and a bipolar fuzzy system, where it is observed that in a fuzzy system, the same conclusion is reached at $p = 5$ and in bipolar fuzzy system the result fluctuate between $\mathcal{A}_1$ and $\mathcal{A}_3$. So, we think that the proposed method can serve immensely in decision making purpose.

Table 3. Ranking results.

Similarity Index	Based on Positive Ideal Solution	Based on Negative Ideal Solution	Based on Average Value
$p=1$	$A_4 \succ A_1 \succ A_3 \succ A_2$	$A_3 \succ A_2 \succ A_1 \succ A_4$	$A_3 \succ A_1 \succ A_4 \succ A_2$
$p=2$	$A_4 \succ A_1 \succ A_3 \succ A_2$	$A_3 \succ A_2 \succ A_1 \succ A_4$	$A_3 \succ A_1 \succ A_2 \succ A_4$
$p=3$	$A_4 \succ A_1 \succ A_3 \succ A_2$	$A_3 \succ A_2 \succ A_1 \succ A_4$	$A_1 \succ A_3 \succ A_2 \succ A_4$
$p=4$	$A_4 \succ A_1 \succ A_3 \succ A_2$	$A_2 \succ A_3 \succ A_1 \succ A_4$	$A_1 \succ A_3 \succ A_2 \succ A_4$
$p=5$	$A_4 \succ A_1 \succ A_3 \succ A_2$	$A_2 \succ A_3 \succ A_1 \succ A_4$	$A_1 \succ A_3 \succ A_2 \succ A_4$
$p=6$	$A_1 \succ A_4 \succ A_3 \succ A_2$	$A_2 \succ A_3 \succ A_1 \succ A_4$	$A_1 \succ A_3 \succ A_2 \succ A_4$

8. Conclusions

This paper introduces a novel concept of QSVBNS. Some set theoretic operations and several similarity measures have been stated. Also, a real life example of QSVBNS is presented for brief understanding. Decision making problem has been considered in a QSVBN environment and dealt with successfully.

BNS has been a successful tool for decision maker as bipolarity often occurs as a common phenomenon in human thinking. QSVBNS comes handy in situations where a person is unsure about the truth, false, both true and false or neither of them while handling a bipolar information system. The introduction of QSVBNS will help the cause of decision making problems and open new branch of neutrosophy. Future work may involve study of aggregation operators involving QSVBNS while dealing with decision making problems.

Author Contributions: Created and conceptualized ideas, S.R. and J.-G.L.; writing—original draft preparation, S.R.; writing—review and editing, A.P. and S.K.S.; funding acquisition, J.-G.L. All authors have read and agreed to the published version of the manuscript.

Funding: This research was partially supported by a Basic Science Research Program through the National Research Foundation of Korea (NRF) funded by the Ministry of Education (2018R1D1A1B07049321).

Conflicts of Interest: The authors declare no conflict of interest.

References

1. Zadeh, L.A. Fuzzy sets. *Inform. Control* **1965**, *8*, 338–353. [CrossRef]
2. Pawlak, Z. Rough sets. *Int. J. Comput. Inf. Sci.* **1982**, *11*, 341–356. [CrossRef]
3. Atanassov, K.T. Intuitionistic fuzzy sets. *Fuzzy Sets Syst.* **1986**, *20*, 87–96. [CrossRef]
4. Atanassov, K.T. Interval valued intuitionistic fuzzy sets. *Fuzzy Sets Syst.* **1989**, *31*, 343–349. [CrossRef]
5. Molodtsov, D. Soft set theory-first results. *Comput. Math. Appl.* **1999**, *37*, 19–31. [CrossRef]
6. Smarandache, F. Neutrosophic set, a generalization of the intuitionistic fuzzy sets. *Int. J. Pure. Appl. Math.* **2005**, *24*, 287–297.
7. Wang, H.; Smarandache, F.; Zhang, Q.; Sunderraman, R. Single valued neutrosophic sets. *Multispace Multistruct.* **2010**, *4*, 410–413.
8. Broumi, S.; Smarandache, F. Cosine similarity measures of interval valued neutrosophic sets. *Neutrosophic Sets Syst.* **2013**, *5*, 115–20.
9. Broumi, S.; Smarandache, F. Several similarity measures of neutrosophic sets. *Neutrosophic Sets Syst.* **2013**, *1*, 54–62.
10. Chahhtterjee, R.; Majumdar, P.; Samanta, S.K. Similarity Measures in Neutrosophic Sets-I, Fuzzy Multi-criteria Decision-Making Using Neutrosophic Sets. *Stud. Fuzziness Soft Comput.* **2019**, *369*, 249–294.
11. Jiang, W.; Shou, Y. A novel single-valued neutrosophic set similarity measure and its application in multi-criteria decision making. *Symmetry* **2017**, *9*, 127. [CrossRef]
12. Jun, Y. Similarity measures between interval neutrosophic sets and their application in multicriteria decision-making. *J. Int. Fuzzy Syst.* **2014**, *26*, 165–172.
13. Majumdar, P.; Samanta, S.K. On similarity and entropy of neutrosophic sets. *J. Int. Fuzzy Syst.* **2014**, *26*, 1245-1252. [CrossRef]

14. Atanassov, K.T.; Vassilev, P. Intuitionistic fuzzy sets and other fuzzy sets extensions representable by them. *J. Int. Fuzzy Syst.* **2020**, *38*, 525–530. [CrossRef]
15. Hinde, C.; Patching, R. Inconsistent intuitionistic fuzzy sets. Development in Fuzzy sets, Intuitionistic Fuzzy sets. *Gen. Nets Relat. Top.* **2008**, *1*, 133–153.
16. Cuong, B.C.; Kreinovich, V. Picture fuzzy sets—A new concept for computational intelligence problems. In Proceedings of the Third World Congress on Information and Communication Technologies WICT'2013, Hanoi, Vietnam, 15–18 December 2013; pp. 1–6.
17. Chahhtterjee, R.; Majumdar, P.; Samanta, S.K. On some similarity measures and entropy on quadripartithioned single valued neutrosophic sets. *J. Int. Fuzzy Syst.* **2016**, *30*, 2475–2485.
18. Smarandache, F. n-valued Refined Neutrosophic Logic and its Applications to Physics. *arXiv* **2014**, arXiv:1407.1041.
19. Belnap, N.D., Jr. A Useful Four Valued Logic, Modern Uses of Multiple Valued Logic. In *Modern Uses of Multiple-Valued Logic*; Dunn, J.M., Epstein, G., Eds.; D. Reidel: Dordrecht, The Netherlands, 1977; Volume 2, pp. 9–27.
20. Lee, K.M. Bipolar-valued fuzzy sets and their operations. In Proceedings of the International Conference on Intelligent Technologies, Bangkok, Thailand, 13–15 December 2000; pp. 307–312.
21. Lee, K.J. Bipolar fuzzy subalgebras and bipolar fuzzy ideals of BCK/BCI-algebras. *Bull. Malayas. Math. Sci. Soc.* **2009**, *32*, 361–373.
22. Alghamdi, M.A.; Alshehri, N.O.; Akram, M. Multi-criteria Decision Making Methods in Bipolar Fuzzy Environment. *Int. J. Fuzzy Syst.* **2018**, *20*, 2057–2064. [CrossRef]
23. Al-Qudah, Y.; Hassan, N. Bipolar fuzzy soft expert set and its application in decision making. *Int. J. Appl. Decis. Sci.* **2017**, *10*, 175–191. [CrossRef]
24. Bosc, P.; Pivert, O. On a fuzzy bipolar relation algebra. *Inform. Sci.* **2013**, *219*, 1–13. [CrossRef]
25. Malik, N.; Shabir, M. Rough fuzzy bipolar soft sets and application to decision-making problems. *Soft Comput.* **2019**, *23*, 1603–1614. [CrossRef]
26. Deli, I.; Ali, M.; Smarandache, F. Bipolar neutrosophic sets and their application based on multi-criteria decision making problems. In Proceedings of the International Conference on Advanced Mechatronic Systems (ICAMechS), Beijing, China, 22–24 August 2015; pp. 249–254.
27. Sahin, M.; Deli, I.; Ulcay, V. Jaccard vector similarity measure of bipolar neutrosophic sets based on multi-criteria decision making. In Proceedings of the International conference on natural science and engineering (ICNASE'16), Kilis, Turkey, 19–20 March 2016.
28. Ulucay, V.; Deli, I.; Sahin, M. Similarity measures of bipolar neutrosophic sets and their application to multi criteria decision making. *Neural Comput. Appl.* **2018**, *29*, 739–748. [CrossRef]
29. Jamil, M.; Abdullah, S.; Khan, M.Y.; Smarandache, F.; Ghani, F. Application of the bipolar neutrosophic hamacher averaging aggregation operators to group decision making: An illustrative example. *Symmetry* **2019**, *11*, 698. [CrossRef]
30. Wu, J.; Cao, Q.W. Same families of geometric aggregation operators with intuitionistic trapezoidal fuzzy numbers. *Appl. Math. Model.* **2013**, *37*, 318–327. [CrossRef]

© 2020 by the authors. Licensee MDPI, Basel, Switzerland. This article is an open access article distributed under the terms and conditions of the Creative Commons Attribution (CC BY) license (http://creativecommons.org/licenses/by/4.0/).

Article

A Novel Integrated PIPRECIA–Interval-Valued Triangular Fuzzy ARAS Model: E-Learning Course Selection

Kristina Jaukovic Jocic [1], Goran Jocic [1], Darjan Karabasevic [1,*], Gabrijela Popovic [1], Dragisa Stanujkic [2], Edmundas Kazimieras Zavadskas [3] and Phong Thanh Nguyen [4]

1. Faculty of Applied Management, Economics and Finance, University Business Academy in Novi Sad, Jevrejska 24, 11000 Belgrade, Serbia; kristina.jaukovic@mef.edu.rs (K.J.J.); goran.jocic@mef.edu.rs (G.J.); gabrijela.popovic@mef.edu.rs (G.P.)
2. Technical Faculty in Bor, University of Belgrade, Vojske Jugoslavije 12, 19210 Bor, Serbia; dstanujkic@tfbor.bg.ac.rs
3. Institute of Sustainable Construction, Vilnius Gediminas Technical University, LT 10223 Vilnius, Lithuania; edmundas.zavadskas@vgtu.lt
4. Department of Project Management, Ho Chi Minh City Open University, Ho Chi Minh City 7000000, Vietnam; phong.nt@ou.edu.vn
* Correspondence: darjan.karabasevic@mef.edu.rs or darjan.karabasevic@gmail.com

Received: 14 May 2020; Accepted: 1 June 2020; Published: 2 June 2020

Abstract: The development of information and communication technologies has revolutionized and changed the way we do business in various areas. The field of education did not remain immune to the mentioned changes; there was a gradual integration of the educational process and the mentioned technologies. As a result, platforms for distance learning, as well as the organization of e-learning courses of various types, have been developed. The rapid development of e-learning courses has led to the problem of e-learning course selection and evaluation. The problem of the e-learning course selection can be successfully solved by using multiple-criteria decision-making (MCDM) methods. Therefore, the aim of the paper is to propose an integrated approach based on the MCDM methods and symmetry principles for e-learning course selection. The pivot pairwise relative criteria importance assessment (PIPRECIA) method is used for determining the weights of criteria, and the interval-valued triangular fuzzy additive ratio assessment (ARAS) method is used for the ranking of alternatives i.e., e-learning courses. The suitability of the proposed integrated model is demonstrated through a numerical case study.

Keywords: ARAS; interval-valued triangular fuzzy numbers; e-learning courses; MCDM

1. Introduction

The role of information and communication technologies (ICT) has become very important in all aspects of life and business. These technologies have a very significant role in information elaboration and its transformation into knowledge, which is the main condition for someone to become an efficient part of the information society [1]. The information has become accessible and transferable from anywhere in the world. Also, education and its availability have an important role in the modern world and therefore, ICT has become an integral part of people's lives in all aspects [2]. The rapid and dynamic development of information and communication technologies has led to significant changes in people's personal, social, and work lives. Currently, people live in an information society that relies on the use of information and communication technologies, which is also a society of knowledge, intangible capital and learning, in which progress is based on knowledge and creativity [3].

The education did not remain immune to the spreading of the mentioned technologies and therefore, these technologies had integrated into the learning process, as well.

Education is the constitutive element of the knowledge society and global economy of knowledge if it is structured in line with information and communication technologies. Furthermore, the integration of these technologies could make education more available, but also could change the cultural context of education, as well as the language of learning [4]. These impacts change the way of learning because the students do not receive the knowledge passively as they have previously but they are actively involved in the learning process. Wang and Woo [5] state that the integration of information and communication technologies is often seen as a process of deploying any ICT (including resources on the Internet, multimedia programs, learning objects, and other tools) with the aim of improving student learning. Although the primary function of ICT use is not only in the field of education, it can be said that information and communication technologies are a tool for achieving learning goals [6].

In this competitive world, the future of the education sector is based on knowledge of ICT. The integration of ICT into education through e-learning courses enables active learning, discussion, sharing of ideas, immediate feedback, and easy access to digital content [7]. When it comes to technology integration into education, three main components should be taken into account: content, pedagogy, and technology [8]. The integration of ICT in educational processes is often defined as the process of applying any ICT (including Internet resources, multimedia programs, learning subjects, and other tools) with the aim to improve student learning and achieve desired outcomes [5,9].

Effective integration of ICT and learning processes through e-learning courses has great potential to involve and engage students on a larger scale. For example, the use of multimedia for presenting authentic and poorly structured problems in problem-based learning can motivate and engage students and thus help them to develop problem-solving skills [10]. An and Reigeluth [11] emphasize that groups can have "different learning needs based on their interests and problem-solving plans, even though if they were working on the same problem". E-learning courses can support different types of interaction: student–content, student–student, student–lecturer, and student–interface [12]. These types of interactions make the learning process more interactive, and students more active and engaged.

Studies have shown that online education can be just as effective as the traditional way of education, and in some cases, it has even been shown to be better [13,14]. According to Stavredes and Herder [15], creating an effective e-learning course begins with understanding the needs of future students. Therefore, it is necessary to identify the needs and requirements of future users in order to create such a course that will successfully meet the stated needs. Also, it is important to point out that the e-learning courses have enabled the acquisition of quality education to those participants for whom education would not be available in other circumstances.

As stated, integration of the learning process and information and communication technologies has led to the development of the e-learning courses. In that way, the educational resources are available to the individuals who, in different conditions, are able to attend the lectures. The very important question is the design of the course so that it is understandable and easy to use for different kinds of students. The creators of the e-learning courses should pay attention to the features that enable the smooth operation of the course, which is very important. The appearance of the e-learning courses initiated the need to find suitable methods for their evaluation and selection.

Multiple-criteria decision-making (MCDM) is often associated with the selection of an alternative from a set of alternatives, but it can also be used for ranking alternatives [16,17]. Until now, a number of MCDM methods have been proposed, such as: SAW [18], AHP [19], TOPSIS [20], PROMETHEE [21], ELECTRE [22], VIKOR [23], and so forth.

Notable progress in solving real-world complex decision-making problems appeared after Zadeh [24] and his introduction to the fuzzy sets theory. As a part of the fuzzy set theory, fuzzy numbers that are usually based on triangular or trapezoidal shapes, which are much more adequate for modeling and solving a number of complex decision-making problems were introduced.

Based on the previously mentioned fuzzy sets theory, somewhat later Bellman and Zadeh [25] introduced the fuzzy MCDM-based methodology, which was later widely accepted in the scientific community as well as being used to solve many decision-making problems. With the aim to solve a variety of complex MCDM problems, some extensions to the fuzzy set theory have been proposed, such as intuitionistic fuzzy sets [26], interval-valued fuzzy sets [27], bipolar fuzzy sets [28], and so on.

The interval-valued fuzzy numbers (IVFNs), as a particular form of fuzzy numbers, provide much more possibilities for solving the real-world MCDM problems. Hence, some of the prominent multiple-criteria decision-making methods have proper extensions based on IVFNs. It is worth mentioning some of them: ELECTRE [29], VIKOR [30,31], MULTIMOORA [32], TOPSIS [33–35], and so forth.

The additive ratio assessment (ARAS) method was developed by Zavadskas and Turskis [36]. The ARAS method has been applied to solve various decision-making problems. So, for example, Zavadskas and Turskis [36] have applied the ARAS method to evaluate the microclimate in office rooms, Zavadskas et al. [37] have applied the ARAS method to select the most appropriate foundation installment alternative, Karabašević et al. [38] have applied the ARAS method for personnel selection. Besides that, the ARAS method has also been applied for the ranking of companies according to the CSR indicators [39], selection of the software testing method [40], mineral prospectivity mapping [41], reduction of greenhouse gas emission [42], and so on.

In order to extend the applicability of the ARAS method and to enable the use of grey and fuzzy numbers, Turskis and Zavadskas [43] proposed a proper fuzzy extension (ARAS-F) and a grey extension (ARAS-G) [44]. It is also important to note that on the basis of the ARAS method, some other approaches are proposed. In this context, it is worth mentioning the ARCAS approach proposed by Stanujkic et al. [45] that is based on ordinary SWARA and ARAS methods and is adapted for negotiations.

Based on all the above, the main aim of this paper is to propose an integrated approach based on the MCDM methods for the selection of the e-learning course. The proposed approach is based on the use of the interval-valued triangular fuzzy (IVTFN) ARAS method for the ranking of alternatives and the PIPRECIA method for the determining weights of the criteria.

Therefore, the rest of this paper is organized as follows. Section 2 demonstrates the proposed methodology, based on the PIPRECIA and extended ARAS method. In order to highlight the proposed MCDM methodology, in Section 3 a case study of e-courses evaluation is considered. The discussions and conclusions are given at the end of the manuscript.

2. Methods

The proposed methodology for the evaluation of the e-courses is based on the PIPRECIA method and interval-valued triangular fuzzy ARAS method. The PIPRECIA method is used for defining weights of the criteria whereas the interval-valued triangular fuzzy ARAS method is used for the ranking of alternatives.

2.1. PIPRECIA Method

The pivot pairwise relative criteria importance assessment (PIPRECIA) method for determining the weights of criteria was proposed by Stanujkic et al. [46], as one of the extensions of the step-wise weight assessment ratio analysis (SWARA) method. Although it is a relatively new method, so far, the PIPRECIA method is applied for solving problems of personnel selection [47], assessment of ICT [48,49], supplier selection [50], mining method selection [51], and so forth.

The computational procedure of the PIPRECIA method can be demonstrated through the following steps [46]:

Step 1. Determination of the set of the evaluation criteria.

Step 2. Starting from the second criterion, it is necessary to determine the relative importance s_j of the criterion j in relation to the previous $(j-1)$ criterion:

$$s_j = \begin{cases} >1 & \text{when significance of } C_j > C_{j-1} \\ 1 & \text{when significanse of } C_j = C_{j-1} \\ <1 & \text{when significance of } C_j < C_{j-1} \end{cases}. \quad (1)$$

Step 3. Calculation of the coefficient k_j as follows:

$$k_j = \begin{cases} 1 & j=1 \\ 2-s_j & j>1 \end{cases} \quad (2)$$

Step 4. Calculation of the recalculated weight q_j as follows:

$$q_j = \begin{cases} 1 & j=1 \\ \frac{q_{j-1}}{k_j} & j>1 \end{cases}. \quad (3)$$

Step 5. Calculation of the relative weights of the evaluation criteria as follows:

$$w_j = \frac{q_j}{\sum_{k=1}^{n} q_k} \quad (4)$$

where w_j represents the relative weight of the criterion j.

2.2. An Extension of the ARAS Method Based on the Use of Interval-Valued Fuzzy Numbers

Based on Stanujkic et al. [52], the computational procedure for selecting the most acceptable alternative by applying the IVTFN-ARAS method that includes only beneficial criteria could be demonstrated through the following steps:

Step 1. Determination of the optimal performance rating for each criterion.

$$\tilde{x}_{0j} = [(l_{0j}, l'_{0j}), m_{0j}, (u'_{0j}, u_{0j})], \quad (5)$$

with

$$l_{0j} = \max_i l_{ij}, \quad (6)$$

$$l'_{0j} = \max_i l'_{ij}, \quad (7)$$

$$m_{0j} = \max_i m_{ij}, \quad (8)$$

$$u'_{0j} = \max_i u'_{ij} \quad (9)$$

$$u_{0j} = \max_i u_{ij} \quad (10)$$

where $\tilde{x}_{0j}$ represents the interval-valued fuzzy optimal performance rating of criterion j.

Step 2. Calculation of the normalized decision matrix.

$$\tilde{r}_{ij} = \left[\left(\frac{a_{ij}}{c_j^+}, \frac{a'_{ij}}{c_j^+} \right), \frac{b_{ij}}{c_j^+}, \left(\frac{c'_{ij}}{c_j^+}, \frac{c_{ij}}{c_j^+} \right) \right], \quad (11)$$

where $\tilde{r}_{ij}$ represents the normalized interval-valued fuzzy performance rating of alternative i in relation to the criterion j, $c_j^+ = \sum_{i=0}^{m} c_{ij}$.

Step 3. Calculation of the weighted interval-valued normalized fuzzy decision matrix.

$$\widetilde{v}_{ij} = w_j \cdot \widetilde{r}_{ij} \tag{12}$$

where $\widetilde{v}_{ij}$ represents the weighted normalized interval-valued fuzzy performance rating of alternative i in relation to the criterion j.

Step 4. Calculation of the overall interval-valued fuzzy performance ratings.

$$\widetilde{S}_i = \sum_{j=1}^{n} w_j \widetilde{r}_{ij}, \tag{13}$$

where $\widetilde{S}_i$ represent overall interval-valued fuzzy performance rating of alternative i.

Step 5. Calculation of the degree of utility, for each alternative. As a result of performing the previous steps, the obtained overall performance ratings are IVFNs. Therefore, overall performance ratings have to be defuzzified before the calculation of the overall degree of utility. In this way, the same equation as in the ordinary ARAS method is used to determine the overall degree of utility.

Step 6. Ranking of alternative selections by the most efficient. This step is the same as in the original ARAS method.

3. A Numerical Case Study

This section describes the process of the selection of an e-learning course based on the opinions of twenty-four respondents by using the PIPRECIA method and the IVTFN-ARAS method. Four e-learning courses in the field of programming are evaluated, designated as: A_1—Cubes (www.cubes.edu.rs); A_2—ITAcademy (www.it-akademija.com); A_3—Link-eLearning (www.link-elearning.com), and A_4—Ok School (www.ok-school.com). The criteria used for the evaluation of the e-learning courses are obtained based on the analysis of the relevant literature [53–55], and their weights are determined by using the PIPRECIA method. Evaluation criteria and their corresponding weights that represent the attitudes of the group are shown in Table 1.

Table 1. The group evaluation criteria and their weights.

Criteria		w_j
C_1	Level of content	0.14
C_2	Presentation method	0.14
C_3	Teaching method	0.13
C_4	e-learning environment	0.14
C_5	Learning materials	0.15
C_6	Quality of multimedia content	0.14
C_7	Group work and interactivity	0.15

At the beginning of the evaluation, all twenty-four respondents evaluated alternatives using the five-point Likert scale. The Likert scale was chosen because it is easy to use and its usage is understandable for respondents. Ratings obtained from three randomly selected respondents are shown in Tables 2–4 and Figures 1–3.

Table 2. The ratings obtained from the fist of twenty-four respondents.

Criteria	C_1	C_2	C_3	C_4	C_5	C_6	C_7
A_1	4	3	3	4	2	4	5
A_2	3	5	2	4	4	4	4
A_3	5	5	4	5	3	3	2
A_4	4	5	5	4	4	4	4

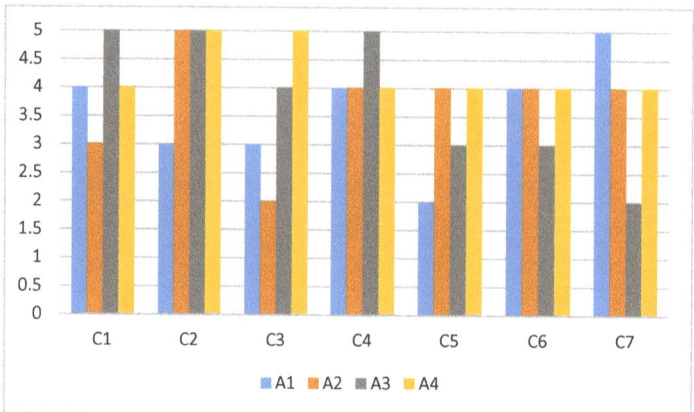

Figure 1. The ratings obtained from the fist of twenty-four respondents.

Table 3. The ratings obtained from the second of twenty-four respondents.

Criteria	C_1	C_2	C_3	C_4	C_5	C_6	C_7
A_1	2	3	5	5	2	3	2
A_2	4	5	4	5	4	4	5
A_3	5	4	4	5	5	5	3
A_4	3	5	3	4	4	5	4

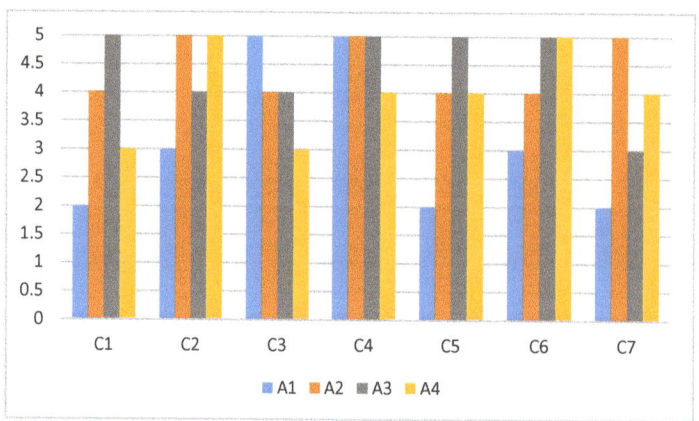

Figure 2. The ratings obtained from the second of twenty-four respondents.

Table 4. The ratings obtained from the third of twenty-four respondents.

Criteria	C_1	C_2	C_3	C_4	C_5	C_6	C_7
A_1	3	3	3	4	5	4	4
A_2	2	4	4	3	2	5	5
A_3	5	4	4	3	4	5	3
A_4	5	5	5	3	3	4	4

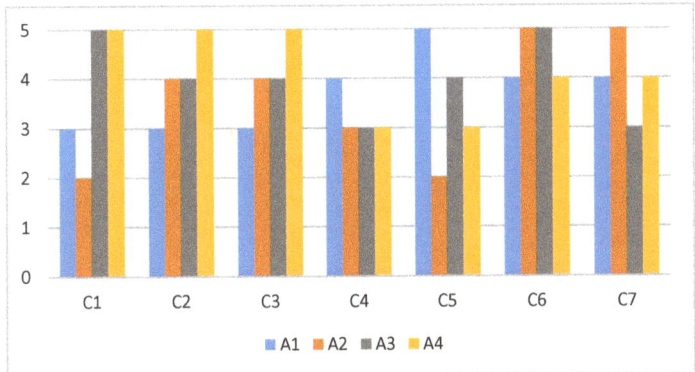

Figure 3. The ratings obtained from the third of twenty-four respondents.

Subsequently, in the next step, a group decision matrix was formed. The elements of this matrix, shown in Table 5, are IVTFNs formed by the transformation of crisp ratings into IVTFNs, as is explained in Stanujkic [52].

Based on the data from Table 5, the optimal performance ratings are determined by using Equation (5). The obtained optimal performance ratings are shown in Table 6.

In the next two steps, normalized and weighted normalized decision-making matrices are calculated using Equations (11) and (12). The normalized and weighted normalized decision-making matrices are shown in Tables 7 and 8.

Table 5. IVTF group decision-making matrix.

	C_1	C_2	C_3	C_4	C_4	C_6	C_7
A_1	[(1, 2.5), 3.25, (4.3, 5)]	[(2, 2.67), 3.5, (4.33, 5)]	[(2, 2.75), 3.63, (4.5, 5)]	[(1, 2.11), 3.46, (4.27, 5)]	[(1, 2.4), 3.13, (4.33, 5)]	[(1, 2), 3.04, (4.27, 5)]	[(1, 2.33), 3.13, (4.44, 5)]
A_2	[(2, 2.69), 3.29, (4.5, 5)]	[(2, 2.92), 3.71, (4.64, 5)]	[(2, 2.4), 3.5, (4.29, 5)]	[(2, 2.44), 3.54, (4.2, 5)]	[(1, 2.44), 3.46, (4.07, 5)]	[(2, 2.17), 3.71, (4.22, 5)]	[(1, 2.44), 3.58, (4.27, 5)]
A_3	[(1, 2.8), 3.92, (4.71, 5)]	[(1, 2.64), 3.71, (4.62, 5)]	[(1, 2.31), 3.17, (4.18, 5)]	[(1, 2.3), 3.79, (4.86, 5)]	[(1, 2.83), 3.54, (4.25, 5)]	[(1, 2.4), 3.63, (4.5, 5)]	[(2, 2.53), 3.13, (4.57, 5)]
A_4	[(2, 2.58), 3.46, (4.33, 5)]	[(1, 3), 4, (4.67, 5)]	[(2, 2.58), 3.63, (4.67, 5)]	[(1, 2.3), 3.38, (4.14, 5)]	[(1, 2.5), 3.79, (4.44, 5)]	[(1, 2.15), 3.13, (4.27, 5)]	[(2, 2.5), 3.38, (4.25, 5)]

Table 6. The optimal IVTF performance ratings.

	C_1	C_2	C_3	C_4	C_4	C_6	C_7
A_0	[(2, 2.8), 3.92, (4.71, 5)]	[(2, 3), 4, (4.67, 5)]	[(2, 2.75), 3.63, (4.67, 5)]	[(2, 2.44), 3.79, (4.86, 5)]	[(1, 2.83), 3.79, (4.44, 5)]	[(2, 2.4), 3.71, (4.5, 5)]	[(2, 2.53), 3.58, (4.57, 5)]

Table 7. The normalized IVTF performance rating.

	C_1	C_2	C_3	C_4	C_4	C_6	C_7
A_0	[(0.4, 0.56), 0.78, (0.94, 1)]	[(0.4, 0.6), 0.8, (0.93, 1)]	[(0.4, 0.55), 0.73, (0.93, 1)]	[(0.4, 0.49), 0.76, (0.97, 1)]	[(0.2, 0.57), 0.76, (0.89, 1)]	[(0.4, 0.48), 0.74, (0.9, 1)]	[(0.4, 0.51), 0.72, (0.91, 1)]
A_1	[(0.2, 0.5), 0.65, (0.86, 1)]	[(0.4, 0.53), 0.7, (0.87, 1)]	[(0.4, 0.55), 0.73, (0.9, 1)]	[(0.2, 0.42), 0.69, (0.85, 1)]	[(0.2, 0.48), 0.63, (0.87, 1)]	[(0.2, 0.4), 0.61, (0.85, 1)]	[(0.2, 0.47), 0.63, (0.89, 1)]
A_2	[(0.4, 0.54), 0.66, (0.9, 1)]	[(0.4, 0.58), 0.74, (0.93, 1)]	[(0.4, 0.48), 0.7, (0.86, 1)]	[(0.4, 0.49), 0.71, (0.84, 1)]	[(0.2, 0.49), 0.69, (0.81, 1)]	[(0.4, 0.43), 0.74, (0.84, 1)]	[(0.2, 0.49), 0.72, (0.85, 1)]
A_3	[(0.2, 0.56), 0.78, (0.94, 1)]	[(0.2, 0.53), 0.74, (0.92, 1)]	[(0.2, 0.46), 0.63, (0.84, 1)]	[(0.2, 0.46), 0.76, (0.97, 1)]	[(0.2, 0.57), 0.71, (0.85, 1)]	[(0.2, 0.48), 0.73, (0.9, 1)]	[(0.4, 0.51), 0.63, (0.91, 1)]
A_4	[(0.4, 0.52), 0.69, (0.87, 1)]	[(0.2, 0.6), 0.8, (0.93, 1)]	[(0.4, 0.52), 0.73, (0.93, 1)]	[(0.2, 0.46), 0.68, (0.83, 1)]	[(0.2, 0.5), 0.76, (0.89, 1)]	[(0.2, 0.43), 0.63, (0.85, 1)]	[(0.4, 0.5), 0.68, (0.85, 1)]

Table 8. The weighted IVTF performance ratings.

	C_1	C_2	C_3	C_4	C_4	C_6	C_7
w	0.14	0.14	0.13	0.14	0.15	0.14	0.15
A_0	[(0.06, 0.08), 0.11, (0.14, 0.14)]	[(0.06, 0.08), 0.11, (0.13, 0.14)]	[(0.05, 0.07), 0.1, (0.13, 0.13)]	[(0.06, 0.07), 0.11, (0.14, 0.14)]	[(0.03, 0.09), 0.11, (0.13, 0.15)]	[(0.06, 0.07), 0.11, (0.13, 0.14)]	[(0.06, 0.08), 0.11, (0.14, 0.15)]
A_1	[(0.03, 0.07), 0.09, (0.12, 0.14)]	[(0.06, 0.07), 0.1, (0.12, 0.14)]	[(0.05, 0.07), 0.1, (0.12, 0.13)]	[(0.03, 0.06), 0.1, (0.12, 0.14)]	[(0.03, 0.07), 0.09, (0.13, 0.15)]	[(0.03, 0.06), 0.09, (0.12, 0.14)]	[(0.03, 0.07), 0.09, (0.13, 0.15)]
A_2	[(0.06, 0.08), 0.1, (0.13, 0.14)]	[(0.06, 0.08), 0.1, (0.13, 0.14)]	[(0.05, 0.06), 0.09, (0.12, 0.13)]	[(0.06, 0.07), 0.1, (0.12, 0.14)]	[(0.03, 0.07), 0.1, (0.12, 0.15)]	[(0.06, 0.06), 0.11, (0.12, 0.14)]	[(0.03, 0.07), 0.11, (0.13, 0.15)]
A_3	[(0.03, 0.08), 0.11, (0.14, 0.14)]	[(0.03, 0.07), 0.1, (0.13, 0.14)]	[(0.03, 0.06), 0.09, (0.11, 0.13)]	[(0.03, 0.07), 0.11, (0.14, 0.14)]	[(0.03, 0.09), 0.11, (0.13, 0.15)]	[(0.03, 0.07), 0.1, (0.13, 0.14)]	[(0.06, 0.08), 0.09, (0.14, 0.15)]
A_4	[(0.06, 0.07), 0.1, (0.13, 0.14)]	[(0.03, 0.08), 0.11, (0.13, 0.14)]	[(0.05, 0.07), 0.1, (0.13, 0.13)]	[(0.03, 0.07), 0.1, (0.12, 0.14)]	[(0.03, 0.08), 0.11, (0.13, 0.15)]	[(0.03, 0.06), 0.09, (0.12, 0.14)]	[(0.06, 0.07), 0.1, (0.13, 0.15)]

Finally, the overall interval-valued triangular fuzzy performance ratings, obtained by using Equation (13), are shown in Table 9.

Table 9. The overall IVTF performance ratings.

A_0	[(0.07, 0.11), 0.15, (0.19, 0.2)]
A_1	[(0.05, 0.1), 0.13, (0.17, 0.2)]
A_2	[(0.07, 0.1), 0.14, (0.17, 0.2)]
A_3	[(0.05, 0.1), 0.14, (0.18, 0.2)]
A_4	[(0.06, 0.1), 0.14, (0.18, 0.2)]

In order to determine the quality of the e-courses, these values must be defuzzified using some of the well-known procedures [52].

Results obtained using the simplest of all of the considered defuzzification procedures are shown in Table 10. The relative quality, i.e., the degree of utility, of analyzed e-courses as well as their ranking orders, are also shown in Table 10.

Table 10. The degree of utility and ranking order of analyzed e-courses.

Alternatives	BNP	Q_i	Rank
A_0	0.143		
A_1	0.130	0.910	4
A_2	0.136	0.951	1
A_3	0.134	0.936	3
A_4	0.135	0.941	2

As can be seen from Table 10, the best alternative, i.e., e-course, is the alternative designated as A_2.

By varying the coefficient λ, greater importance can be given to l and u in relation to l' and u', and vice versa. The results obtained using Equation (16) for some characteristic values of the coefficient λ are shown in Table 11.

Table 11. The degree of utility and ranking order of analyzed e-course for some characteristic values of λ.

	$\lambda = 0$			$\lambda = 0.5$			$\lambda = 1$		
Alternatives	S_i	Q_i	Rank	S_i	Q_i	Rank	S_i	Q_i	Rank
A_0	0.42			0.43			0.44		
A_1	0.39	2.72	4	0.39	2.73	4	0.39	2.73	4
A_2	0.41	2.87	1	0.41	2.87	1	0.41	2.87	1
A_3	0.40	2.81	3	0.40	2.81	3	0.40	2.81	3
A_4	0.41	2.83	2	0.41	2.83	2	0.41	2.83	2

In this case, the alternative denoted as A_2 remains the best alternative i.e., an e-learning course in all cases. This indicates the stability of the chosen e-learning course.

However, in many cases variation of the coefficient lambda may have an impact on the ranking order of the considered alternatives, and this approach may be useful to analyze different scenarios such as pessimistic, realistic, and optimistic.

4. Discussion and Conclusions

The main aim of the paper is to introduce a methodology suitable for e-learning course evaluation and selection. The emergence of e-courses as the modern way of learning has provoked the need for finding the methods ideal for their assessment. In this paper, the methodology based on the PIPRECIA and the interval-valued triangular fuzzy ARAS methods is proposed. The applicability of the proposed methodology is presented through a numerical case study. When defining criteria, special attention was dedicated to the issues of organization and teaching. So, in this case, the attention was not directed on the technical and informational performance of an e-learning course, but towards the quality of the offered content and how the teaching process was implemented.

Based on the data obtained from the respondents, the PIPRECIA method was applied, and the weights of the criteria for each of the twenty-four respondents were obtained, as is shown in Table 1. The obtained results show that the weights of the criteria are approximate, which impose the fact that the given features are nearly equally important to all respondents. This is entirely understandable because the e-learning course should satisfy all the requirements and, in that way, offer the quality of "service" to the users.

The reason for applying the PIPRECIA method for the determination of the weights lies in its simplicity and suitability for use in cases where a large number of decision-makers are involved in the evaluation process. The advantage of the PIPRECIA method over the well-known and widely used AHP method is reflected in a more straightforward computational procedure that does not diminish the reliability and relevance of the results obtained. Also, when interviewing respondents who are not familiar with the MCDM methods, the process of evaluating weights by using the PIPRECIA method is far more understandable to respondents, than is the case with the AHP method. If the PIPRECIA method is compared with the SWARA method (on which the PIPRECIA method was developed), it can be concluded that the PIPRECIA method has certain advantages over it. Namely, the SWARA method requires that the evaluation criteria should be sorted according to their intended significance, which complicates its application in group decision cases. Many complex decision-making problems require the participation of a group of respondents. In such cases, the individual attitudes of the respondents have to be transformed into group attitudes, with an as small as possible loss of information. In order to take into account the uncertainty and imprecision of the data on which decision-making is very often based, the application of the interval-valued triangular fuzzy ARAS method is proposed. The approach in which individual ratings are transformed into interval-valued triangular fuzzy numbers can be very useful in this regard. The interval-valued triangular fuzzy ARAS method may use such information to rank alternatives and/or analyze different scenarios. Thus, by applying this method, decision-makers have been given the opportunity to express their optimistic, pessimistic, and realistic attitudes.

In this paper, the numerical case study of the e-learning course selection was examined. The reason for that relies on the increasing importance of this kind of learning. In order to create the high quality e-learning course, it is necessary to determine the pros and cons of the considered course and its position relative to the competition. In that way, the creators will know what aspects of the course should be improved and what are of satisfactory quality. The application of the proposed integrated approach has proven to be quite justified and appropriate in this case. The reason is that if the e-learning courses were evaluated based solely on the use of crisp numbers, the obtained results would not include uncertainty. This would result in a decision that would not be completely realistic and, ultimately, unreliable. The obtained results confirmed this point of view. To get the most reliable results and to make the best possible decisions, it is necessary to respect the risk and uncertainty to the maximum extent possible. So, based on the conducted numerical case study, the e-learning course designated as A_2 is the best in terms of evaluated criteria.

As the examination of the literature has shown, the authors used different approaches for e-course evaluations. Chao and Chen [56] examined which factors are crucial for the quality of the e-learning courses. They applied the consistent fuzzy preference relations (CFPR) with AHP methodology. They evaluated four groups of factors that are elaborated in a particular number of criteria. The final results showed that the most influential criteria are: the e-learning material, friendly user interface, using the web discussion zone, and distant learning without time and space. The main point of this paper is the quality of the content of the e-learning courses. The assessment of the evaluation criteria showed that e-learning material has the greatest influence together with the group work and interactivity, which is in line with the results obtained from the mentioned authors.

Garg and Jain [57] applied the combination of the methods for defining the best e-learning website. They divide the evaluation criteria into two groups called quality factors and e-learning specific factors. The second group of factors is pointed to the quality of e-learning content and their results showed that the most important criterion is the ease of learning community, which could be considered as a counterpart to the group work and interactivity presented here.

Besides the mentioned works, others present the utilization of different MCDM techniques for e-learning course evaluation and selection. For the resolving of the problem of evaluation of e-course quality, the authors have proposed the application of the proximity indexed value (PIV) model [58], fuzzy ANP [59], DANP and VIKOR [60], and so on. The conducted numerical case study presented in this paper, as well as the comparison with the results of the given authors, confirmed that the proposed approach is also very beneficial for e-learning course evaluation and selection because the obtained results clearly outlined the crucial characteristics and the position of the specific e-learning course comparing to the others.

Therefore, the proposed integrated PIPRECIA-IVTFN-ARAS model has proven to be useful and feasible, especially in circumstances where it is essential to make the most relevant and realistic decision possible. The proposed integrated model can be extended to other areas of the business as well.

As a direction for future research, a significantly larger sample could be used in order to obtain results from a macro point of view. Besides that, the learning outcomes of the learners that would study the ranked courses can be further investigated as well.

Author Contributions: Conceptualization, K.J.J., D.K., and G.P.; methodology, D.K., D.S., and E.K.Z.; validation, G.J.; investigation, G.J.; data curation, G.P.; writing—original draft preparation, D.S. and E.K.Z.; writing—review and editing, K.J.J. and P.T.N.; supervision, D.K.; funding acquisition, P.T.N. All authors have read and agreed to the published version of the manuscript.

Funding: The APC was funded by: Department of Project Management, Ho Chi Minh City Open University, Ho Chi Minh City, Vietnam; and Faculty of Applied Management, Economics and Finance, University Business Academy in Novi Sad, Belgrade, Serbia.

Conflicts of Interest: The authors declare no conflict of interest.

References

1. Grimus, M. ICT and Creative Computing, Austrian Perspective in Teacher Education. In *Educational Technology: Opportunities and Challenges*; University of Oulu: Oulu, Finland, 2007; pp. 86–104.
2. Trehan, A.; Trehan, R. ICT in Education Sector and its Impacts. *Int. J. Manag. IT Eng.* **2019**, *7*, 281–288.
3. Plomp, T.; Anderson, R.E.; Law, N.; Quale, A. (Eds.) *CrossNational Information and Communication Technology Policies and Practices in Education*, 2nd ed.; IAP: Charlotte, NC, USA, 2009.
4. Pulkkinen, J. *Cultural Globalization and Integration of ICT in Education. Educational Technology: Opportunities and Challenges*; University of Oulu: Oulu, Finland, 2007; pp. 13–23.
5. Wang, Q.; Woo, H.L. Systematic planning for ICT integration in topic learning. *J. Educ. Technol. Soc.* **2007**, *10*, 148–156.
6. Altun, S.A.; Kalayci, E.; Avci, U. Integrating ICT at the Faculty Level: A Case Study. *Turkish Online J. Educ. Technol. -TOJET* **2011**, *10*, 230–240.
7. García-Alcaraz, P.; Martínez-Loya, V.; García-Alcaraz, J.L.; Sánchez-Ramírez, C. The role of ICT in educational innovation. In *Managing Innovation in Highly Restrictive Environments*; Springer: Berlin/Heidelberg, Germany, 2019; pp. 143–165.
8. An, Y.-J.; Reigeluth, C. Creating Technology-Enhanced, Learner-Centered Classrooms. *J. Digit. Learn. Teach. Educ.* **2011**, *28*, 54–62. [CrossRef]
9. Al-Samarraie, H.; Teng, B.K.; Alzahrani, A.I.; Alalwan, N. E-learning continuance satisfaction in higher education: A unified perspective from instructors and students. *Stud. High. Educ.* **2017**, *43*, 2003–2019. [CrossRef]
10. Sung, Y.-T.; Chang, K.-E.; Liu, T.-C. The effects of integrating mobile devices with teaching and learning on students' learning performance: A meta-analysis and research synthesis. *Comput. Educ.* **2016**, *94*, 252–275. [CrossRef]

11. An, Y.J.; Reigeluth, C.M. Problem-Based Learning in Online Environments. *Q. Rev. Distance Educ.* **2008**, *9*, 1–16.
12. Chou, C. Interactivity and interactive functions in web-based learning systems: A technical framework for designers. *Br. J. Educ. Technol.* **2003**, *34*, 265–279. [CrossRef]
13. Sachar, M.; Neumann, Y. Twenty years of research on the academic performance differences between traditional and distance learning: Summative meta-analysis and trend examination. *MERLOT J. Online Learn. Teach.* **2010**, *6*, 318–334.
14. Chao, I.T.; Saj, T.; Hamilton, D. Using collaborative course development to achieve online course quality standards. *Int. Rev. Res. Open Distrib. Learn.* **2010**, *11*, 106. [CrossRef]
15. Stavredes, T.; Herder, T. *A Guide to Online Course Design: Strategies for Student Success*; John Wiley & Sons: Hoboken, NJ, USA, 2014.
16. Karabašević, D.; Popović, G.; Stanujkić, D.; Maksimović, M.; Sava, C. An approach for hotel type selection based on the Single-Valued Intuitionistic Fuzzy Numbers. *Int. Rev.* **2019**, *1–2*, 7–14. [CrossRef]
17. Subotić, M.; Stević, B.; Ristić, B.; Simić, S. The selection of a location for potential roundabout construction–a case study of Doboj. *Oper. Res. Eng. Sci. Theory Appl.* **2020**, *3*, 41–56. [CrossRef]
18. MacCrimmon, K.R. *Decision Marking Among Multiple-Attribute Alternatives: A Survey and Consolidated Approach. RAND Memorandum, RM-4823-ARPA*; Rand Corporation: Santa Monica, CA, USA, 1968.
19. Saaty, T.L. *The Analytic Hierarchy Process for Decision in a Complex World*; RWS Publications: Pittsburgh, PA, USA, 1980.
20. Hwang, C.L.; Yoon, K. *Multiple Attribute Decision Making: Methods and Applications*; Springer: Berlin/Heidelberg, Germany, 1981.
21. Brans, J.P.; Vincke, P. A preference ranking organization method: The PROMETHEE method for MCDM. *Manag. Sci.* **1985**, *31*, 647–656. [CrossRef]
22. Roy, B. The outranking approach and the foundations of electre methods. *Theory Decis.* **1991**, *31*, 49–73. [CrossRef]
23. Opricovic, S. *Multicriteria Optimization of Civil Engineering Systems*; Faculty of Civil Engineering: Belgrade, Serbia, 1998. (In Serbian)
24. Zadeh, L. Fuzzy sets. *Inf. Control.* **1965**, *8*, 338–353. [CrossRef]
25. Bellman, R.E.; Zadeh, L.A. Decision-Making in a Fuzzy Environment. *Manag. Sci.* **1970**, *17*, 141–164. [CrossRef]
26. Atanassov, K.T. Intuitionistic fuzzy sets. *Fuzzy Sets Syst.* **1986**, *20*, 87–96. [CrossRef]
27. Wang, G.; Li, X. Correlation and information energy of interval-valued fuzzy numbers. *Fuzzy Sets Syst.* **1999**, *103*, 169–175. [CrossRef]
28. Lee, K.M. Bipolar-valued fuzzy sets and their basic operations. In Proceedings of the International Conference on Intelligent Technologies, Bangkok, Thailand, 12–14 December 2000; pp. 307–317.
29. Vahdani, B.; Hadipour, H. Extension of the ELECTRE method based on interval-valued fuzzy sets. *Soft Comput.* **2010**, *15*, 569–579. [CrossRef]
30. Samantra, C.; Sahu, N.K.; Datta, S.; Mahapatra, S.S. Decision-making in selecting reverse logistics alternative using interval-valued fuzzy sets combined with VIKOR approach. *Int. J. Serv. Oper. Manag.* **2013**, *14*, 175. [CrossRef]
31. Vahdani, B.; Hadipour, H.; Sadaghiani, J.S.; Amiri, M. Extension of VIKOR method based on interval-valued fuzzy sets. *Int. J. Adv. Manuf. Technol.* **2009**, *47*, 1231–1239. [CrossRef]
32. Baležentis, T.; Zeng, S. Group multi-criteria decision making based upon interval-valued fuzzy numbers: An extension of the MULTIMOORA method. *Expert Syst. Appl.* **2013**, *40*, 543–550. [CrossRef]
33. Vahdani, B.; Tavakkoli-Moghaddam, R.; Mousavi, S.M.; Ghodratnama, A. Soft computing based on new interval-valued fuzzy modified multi-criteria decision-making method. *Appl. Soft Comput.* **2013**, *13*, 165–172. [CrossRef]
34. Ye, F. An extended TOPSIS method with interval-valued intuitionistic fuzzy numbers for virtual enterprise partner selection. *Expert Syst. Appl.* **2010**, *37*, 7050–7055. [CrossRef]
35. Park, J.H.; Park, I.Y.; Kwun, Y.C.; Tan, X. Extension of the TOPSIS method for decision making problems under interval-valued intuitionistic fuzzy environment. *Appl. Math. Model.* **2011**, *35*, 2544–2556. [CrossRef]
36. Zavadskas, E.K.; Turskis, Z. A new additive ratio assessment (ARAS) method in multicriteria decision-making. *Technol. Econ. Dev. Econ.* **2010**, *16*, 159–172. [CrossRef]

37. Zavadskas, E.; Turskis, Z.; Vilutiene, T. Multiple criteria analysis of foundation instalment alternatives by applying Additive Ratio Assessment (ARAS) method. *Arch. Civ. Mech. Eng.* **2010**, *10*, 123–141. [CrossRef]
38. Karabašević, D.; Stanujkic, D.; Urošević, S. The MCDM Model for Personnel Selection Based on SWARA and ARAS Methods. *Manag. Sustain. Bus. Manag. Solutions Emerg. Econ.* **2015**, *20*, 43–52.
39. Karabašević, D.; Paunkovic, J.; Stanujkić, D.; Darjan, K.; Jane, P.; Dragisa, S. Ranking of companies according to the indicators of corporate social responsibility based on SWARA and ARAS methods. *Serbian J. Manag.* **2016**, *11*, 43–53. [CrossRef]
40. Karabašević, D.; Maksimović, M.; Stanujkic, D.; Jocić, G.B.; Rajčević, D.P. Selection of software testing method by using ARAS method. *Tehnika* **2018**, *73*, 724–729. [CrossRef]
41. Bahrami, Y.; Hassani, H.; Maghsoudi, A. BWM-ARAS: A new hybrid MCDM method for Cu prospectivity mapping in the Abhar area, NW Iran. *Spat. Stat.* **2019**, *33*, 100382. [CrossRef]
42. Balki, M.K.; Erdoğan, S.; Aydın, S.; Sayin, C. The optimization of engine operating parameters via SWARA and ARAS hybrid method in a small SI engine using alternative fuels. *J. Clean. Prod.* **2020**, *258*, 120685. [CrossRef]
43. Turskis, Z.; Zavadskas, E.K. A new fuzzy additive ratio assessment method (ARAS-F). Case study: The analysis of fuzzy multiple criteria in order to select the logistic centers location. *Transport* **2010**, *25*, 423–432. [CrossRef]
44. Turskis, Z.; Zavadskas, E.K. A Novel Method for Multiple Criteria Analysis: Grey Additive Ratio Assessment (ARAS-G) Method. *Information* **2010**, *21*, 597–610.
45. Stanujkic, D.; Zavadskas, E.K.; Karabasevic, D.; Turskis, Z.; Keršulienė, V. New group decision-making ARCAS approach based on the integration of the SWARA and the ARAS methods adapted for negotiations. *J. Bus. Econ. Manag.* **2017**, *18*, 599–618. [CrossRef]
46. Stanujkic, D.; Zavadskas, E.K.; Karabašević, D.; Smarandache, F.; Turskis, Z. The use of Pivot Pair-wise Relative Criteria Importance Assessment method for determining weights of criteria. *Rom. J. Econ. Forecast.* **2017**, *20*, 116–133.
47. Popović, G. A framework for the quality control manager selection based on the PIPRECIA and WS PLP methods. In *EMAN 2019–Economics & Management: How to Cope with Disrupted Times*, Ljubljana; UdEkoM Balkan: Ljubljana, Slovenia, 2019; pp. 33–43.
48. Tomašević, M.; Lapuh, L.; Stević, Ž.; Stanujkić, D.; Karabašević, D. Evaluation of Criteria for the Implementation of High-Performance Computing (HPC) in Danube Region Countries Using Fuzzy PIPRECIA Method. *Sustainability* **2020**, *12*, 3017. [CrossRef]
49. Stević, Ž.; Stjepanović, Ž.; Božičković, Z.; Das, D.; Stanujkić, D. Assessment of Conditions for Implementing Information Technology in a Warehouse System: A Novel Fuzzy PIPRECIA Method. *Symmetry* **2018**, *10*, 586. [CrossRef]
50. Đalić, I.; Stević, Ž.; Karamasa, C.; Puška, A. A Novel Integrated Fuzzy PIPRECIA–Interval Rough Saw Model: Green Supplier Selection. *Decis. Making Appl. Manag. Eng.* **2020**, *3*, 80–95.
51. Popović, G.; Đorđević, B.; Milanović, D. Multiple criteria approach in the mining method selection. *Industrija* **2019**, *47*, 47–62.
52. Stanujkic, D. Extension of the ARAS Method for Decision-Making Problems with Interval-Valued Triangular Fuzzy Numbers. *Informatica* **2015**, *26*, 335–355. [CrossRef]
53. Al-Alwani, A. Evaluation Criterion for Quality Assessment of E-Learning Content. *E-Learning Digit. Media* **2014**, *11*, 532–542. [CrossRef]
54. Castellanos–Nieves, D.; Fernandez-Breis, J.T.; Peñalvo, F.J.G.; Martínez-Béjar, R.; Iniesta-Moreno, M. Semantic Web Technologies for supporting learning assessment. *Inf. Sci.* **2011**, *181*, 1517–1537. [CrossRef]
55. Tzeng, G.-H.; Chiang, C.-H.; Li, C.-W. Evaluating intertwined effects in e-learning programs: A novel hybrid MCDM model based on factor analysis and DEMATEL. *Expert Syst. Appl.* **2007**, *32*, 1028–1044. [CrossRef]
56. Chao, R.-J.; Chen, Y.-H. Evaluation of the criteria and effectiveness of distance e-learning with consistent fuzzy preference relations. *Expert Syst. Appl.* **2009**, *36*, 10657–10662. [CrossRef]
57. Garg, R.; Jain, D. Fuzzy multi-attribute decision making evaluation of e-learning websites using FAHP, COPRAS, VIKOR, WDBA. *Decis. Sci. Lett.* **2017**, *6*, 351–364. [CrossRef]
58. Khan, N.Z.; Ansari, T.S.A.; Siddiquee, A.N.; Khan, Z.A. Selection of E-learning websites using a novel Proximity Indexed Value (PIV) MCDM method. *J. Comput. Educ.* **2019**, *6*, 241–256. [CrossRef]

59. Ghannadpour, S.F. Fuzzy analytical network process logic for performance measurement system of e-learning centers of Universities. *J. Ind. Syst. Eng.* **2018**, *11*, 261–280.
60. Su, C.-H.; Yang, M.-H.; Wang, W.-C. The Use of a DANP with VIKOR Approach for Establishing the Model of E-Learning Service Quality. *Eurasia J. Math. Sci. Technol. Educ.* **2017**, *13*, 5927–5937. [CrossRef]

© 2020 by the authors. Licensee MDPI, Basel, Switzerland. This article is an open access article distributed under the terms and conditions of the Creative Commons Attribution (CC BY) license (http://creativecommons.org/licenses/by/4.0/).

Article

Application of a Gray-Based Decision Support Framework for Location Selection of a Temporary Hospital during COVID-19 Pandemic

Sarfaraz Hashemkhani Zolfani [1,*], Morteza Yazdani [2], Ali Ebadi Torkayesh [3] and Arman Derakhti [1]

1. School of Engineering, Catholic University of the North, Larrondo 1281, Coquimbo 1780000, Chile; arman.derakhti@alumnos.ucn.cl
2. Department of Management, Universidad Loyola Andalucia, 41704 Seville, Spain; myazdani@uloyola.es
3. Faculty of Engineering and Natural Sciences, Sabanci University, 34956 Tuzla, Turkey; ebaditorkayesh@sabanciuniv.edu
* Correspondence: sarfaraz.hashemkhani@ucn.cl

Received: 3 May 2020; Accepted: 14 May 2020; Published: 30 May 2020

Abstract: The hospital location selection problem is one of the most important decisions in the healthcare sector in big cities due to population growth and the possibility of a high number of daily referred patients. A poor location selection process can lead to many issues for the health workforce and patients, and it can result in many unnecessary costs for the healthcare systems. The COVID-19 outbreak had a noticeable effect on people's lives and the service quality of hospitals during recent months. The hospital location selection problem for infected patients with COVID-19 turned out to be one of the most significant and complicated decisions with many uncertain involved parameters for healthcare sectors in countries with high cases. In this study, a gray-based decision support framework using criteria importance through inter-criteria correlation (CRITIC) and combined compromise solution (CoCoSo) methods is proposed for location selection of a temporary hospital for COVID-19 patients. A case study is performed for Istanbul using the proposed decision-making framework.

Keywords: COVID-19; criteria importance through inter-criteria correlation (CRITIC); combined compromise solution (CoCoSo); gray values; temporary hospital; location selection

1. Introduction

Human beings have always been faced with a diversity of disasters for thousands of years. Some examples of natural disasters include earthquakes, floods, volcanic eruptions, tornados, and the outbreak of diseases [1]. There are different definitions of outbreak disease, and the highest level is a pandemic which involves the worldwide spread of a new disease. Recently, the world faced a big threat highlighting a direct relationship with the mortality rate of human beings. The coronavirus disease (COVID-19) is caused by the SARS-CoV-2 virus [2]. Throughout history, humans experienced different pandemics such as Spanish flu, HIV, SARS, and now COVID-19. With the growth of medical science, technology, and science, the number of deaths was decreased considerably in comparison with the Spanish flu disaster. This could be a consequence of proper decision-making and rapid reaction. The coronavirus originated from Wuhan, Hubei province, China [3] and was reported to the World Health Organization at the last day of 2019 [4]. The spread of COVID-19 was incredibly fast, such that the outbreak was declared a pandemic late January 2020. Almost all countries are affected by the virus with effects on every aspect of people's lifestyle, in terms of social, economic, and other factors.

Due to fast spread of COVID-19, countries faced many limitations in their resources and capacities in order to treat the infected patients. Hospitals became one of the most dangerous locations for patients that are diagnosed with other diseases, since infected patients with COVID-19 increase the risk of virus outbreak even inside the hospitals. The information on high-ranked countries in terms of dead bodies shows that healthcare facilities play the most important role in saving peoples' life. For example, Germany managed the circumstance better than other countries with almost the same number of infected people with the help of a high number of hospitals and hospitality facilities in comparison with Spain or Italy. With a high level of quantitative human resources and facilities, taking care of the patient's situation will be better and it will increase the probability of saving patients. Therefore, healthcare policy-makers are proposing some recommendations toward building new temporary hospitals for COVID-19-infected patients. The establishment of hospitals includes many costs for governments and other stakeholders; thus, important decisions should be taken before each step. Although COVID-19 is a very dangerous and fast-spreading virus, decision-makers cannot only focus on medical capacities when they are planning to establish an exclusive hospital. Ignoring other involved factors may lead to other costs that may have an effect on patients and their process of getting cured. Therefore, location selection for a new a hospital is not only affected by only one factor or only medical-related factors. In other words, multiple location factors are also involved in the process of selecting a suitable location for hospitals. These factors integrate most technical, economic, environmental, and social aspects into the decision-making process in order to select the most appropriate location. COVID-19 increased the importance of the social, economic, and environmental aspects of the location selection process for a hospital during the current critical time. Therefore, decision-makers require reliable and robust decision-making tools which enable them to make decisions during the uncertain period that we are all in.

Multi-criteria decision-making (MCDM) methods are some of the frequently utilized decision-making tools that are well designed for complicated problems that involve multiple criteria with a need to prioritize the alternatives. MCDM methods enable decision-makers to evaluate number of alternatives with various data that are available such as crisp, fuzzy, interval, rough, etc. The criteria importance through inter-criteria correlation (CRITIC) approach is one of the well-known MCDM methods, which is designed to determine the importance of criteria for an MCDM problem [5]. Unlike other MCDM methods that are focused on a weight determination process, the CRITIC method does not require separate pairwise comparisons for the criteria, since it uses the initial decision matrix that is constructed for the comparison of the alternatives. As one of the recently introduced powerful MCDM methods, the combined compromise solution (CoCoSo) method [6] is an MCDM method that enables decision-makers to prioritize the alternatives under multiple criteria. In this paper, we present a decision support framework to address the temporary hospital location selection problem under a gray uncertainty environment. A case study is performed for Istanbul which is one of the top cities in terms of the number of infected COVID-19 cases.

The remainder of the paper is organized as follows: in Section 2, a literature review of the applications of MCDM methods for the location selection problem is presented. In Section 3, the steps of the integrated decision-making framework are given. In Section 4, we perform a real-life case study in order to show the feasibility and applicability of the proposed methodology for the temporary hospital location selection problem in Istanbul, Turkey. Finally, we present conclusions in Section 5.

2. Literature Review

Location selection is always an important issue in decision-making science. Business owners, managers, and decision-makers are always faced with this issue in different circumstances, with an effect on tangible profits or losses. As choosing an appropriate location is a part of decision-making science, multi-criteria decision-making (MCDM) was discussed in many previous studies. These studies can be classified using different themes as follows: construction, energy, and production, with some subsets. As there are many articles which discussed site selection with MCDM methodologies, this study presents the most significant studies in each theme.

Firstly, we present the prior studies that used MCDM techniques in order to select the best choice in a construction theme. Hashemkhani Zolfani et al. [7] implemented a hybrid multi-attribute decision-making (MADM) methodology called SWARA–WASPAS, in order to find a suitable location for a shopping mall with foresight perspective. This hybrid model was presented for the first time in this article. The SWARA technique was used to prioritize criteria and the weighted aggregated sum product assessment (WASPAS) method was applied to assess the alternatives. Moreover, Ijadi Maghsoodi et al. [8] propounded BWM–CODAS for site selection in terms of a mega-structure project involving a shopping mall in Iran.

Finding the best place for constructing a forest road was considered in [9]. The article presented the site selection of a forest road among three places in an expanded forested region in Iran. AHP was implemented to calculate the importance of criteria; then, COPRAS-G methodology was applied to evaluate places in order to find the best location. Rezaeiniya et al. and Haghnazar Kouchaksaraei et al. [10,11] presented hybrid models to find the best location for a greenhouse. Rezaeiniya et al. [10] studied the importance of finding an appropriate site for a greenhouse by using the ANP method to weight the criteria and applying COPRAS-G to rate the selected places. In addition, presented the SWARA–COPRAS hybrid model to find a suitable location for a glasshouse. With this description, choosing an optimum place for a glasshouse is a significant decision because it needs an incredibly large area and must have financial feasibility. SWARA was applied to weight and COPRAS was applied to rate the important places. Two new methodologies were applied to find a proper location for waste disposal systems in previous studies [12,13]. Kahraman et al. [12] proposed an intuitionistic fuzzy EDAS method to evaluate solid waste disposal site alternatives. Moreover, Krylovas et al. [13] applied the KEMIRA-M method find the best place for constructing a non-hazardous waste incineration plant in Lithuania. The KEMIRA-M methodology is based on searching solutions of an optimization problem.

The site selection of professional workplaces was also discussed in prior studies [14,15]. While considering environmental risk, Suder & Kahraman [15] proposed the fuzzy TOPSIS method to find the most suitable location for a faculty university in Turkey. Rock or soil structure, remoteness to health facilities, transportation availability, and transportation costs were prioritized as having high to low importance, respectively. Computer workstation selection was achieved with hesitant fuzzy linguistic term sets (HFLTS) by using AHP and TOPSIS in [14], where a new fuzzy quality function was deployed in order to solve a real industrial application.

This study focuses on Istanbul in Turkey as a case study in order to determine the optimum location for a temporary hospital for infected people. Some previous studies discussed the same topic such as [16], who proposed a mixed integer linear programming method to select the location of temporary shelter sites in terms of unpredictable earthquakes in Istanbul, Turkey. A cause-and-effect model for the location of temporary shelters in disaster operations management was proposed by [17]. Furthermore, an MCDM method called DEMATEL was presented in a fuzzy environment with 14 different criteria. Iqbal et al. [18] studied the effectiveness of natural disaster management using stochastic model and Mont Carlo simulation. Then, in order to check the sampled numbers from a random space, they proposed a statistical model to check for relief supply location and distribution related to the healthcare system in natural disaster management.

Another subject that was discussed in the MCDM framework was finding the best residential place, which was proposed [19,20]. Neighborhood selection was presented for a newcomer in Chile by (Hashemkhani Zolfani et al. 2020). BWM and revised MAIRCA were applied to investigate which neighborhoods were appropriate, and the approach was compared with three other MADM methods: MABAC, VIKOR, and CODAS. Karasan et al. [20] proposed the hesitant fuzzy CODAS method to find the optimum location for a construction site and implemented a sensitivity analysis to stabilize the ranking result. Hotel site selection was proposed by [21], where BWM–WASPAS methodologies were presented with a sustainable perspective.

The last part of the construction theme is related to healthcare system site selection. Lin & Tsai [22] developed an integrated model consisting of ANP and TOPSIS to determine the best ranking for hospital selection. A case study was performed in China for foreign investment. Furthermore, Senvar et al. [23] considered hesitant fuzzy sets and TOPSIS to locate the best site for constructing a hospital in Istanbul. Establishing a well-organized and distributed network of a hospital in order to deliver healthcare services to patients was considered and discussed in the study. In addition, Kutlu Gündoğdu et al. [24] presented a new hesitant fuzzy EDAS with TOPSIS method to find the best place for an organ transplantation hospital. This novel model is an extension of classical EDAS which considers the hesitancies of decision-makers. The last study in the construction theme and healthcare subset applied the flexible and interactive tradeoff (FITradeoff) method in order to evaluate healthcare facility stakeholders in order to select an optimum site for a hospital in Milan, Italy.

Secondly, we introduce publications which discussed site selection using MCDM methodologies in the energy theme. Currently, renewable energies have a high priority in the energy industry; thus, site selection of new energy resources were investigated by different researchers from different countries all around the world. The number of energy site selection publications is too extensive to cover in this literature review; thus, we refer only to some of them. Vafaeipour et al. [25] prioritized regions for solar power plants in Iran by applying a hybrid model SWARA–WASPAS. Many criteria such as environmental, economic, technical, social, and risk factors were considered in 25 cities by using a GIS map of the country. Moreover, Marques-Perez et al. [26] studied photovoltaic power plant site selection by applying PROMETHEE and AHP methods with a GIS-based approach in Spain. Furthermore, Ekmekçioglu et al. [27] proposed a SWOT analysis model and then developed this model by applying fuzzy TOPSIS and fuzzy AHP methods to find an optimum location for nuclear power plants in Istanbul. Another renewable energy which is a hot issue in energy science is wind energy. Moradi et al. [28] implemented the AHP methodology to determine an appropriate location for a wind farm. Structural, topological, and ecological criteria were discussed based upon an ArcGIS map.

Finally, the last theme in our classification, i.e., production, introduces previous studies that discussed site selection by applying MCDM methods in the manufacturing industry. Athawale et al. [29] proposed the PROMETHEE II method to achieve facility location selection in the manufacturing industry. This application is faced with complex problems, and the best decision can result in better economic benefits by increasing productivity and qualified network distribution. Logistic center site selection was brought up as a complex decision problem in [30], which was solved with a multi hybrid model. As a first step, communities were compared using DEA to find beneficial alternatives. In the next step, a model was constructed to assess the performance of efficient communities with the R-FUCOM method and they were prioritized with R-COCOSO. The discussed literature is presented in Table 1, containing study subjects and methodologies.

Table 1. Application of multi-criteria decision-making (MCDM) in location selection.

Study Subject	Methodologies	References
Hospital site selection	ANP, TOPSIS	[22]
Forest road location	AHP, COPRAS-G	[9]
Nuclear power plant selection	Fuzzy AHP, Fuzzy TOPSIS	[27]
Greenhouse location	ANP, COPRAS-G	[10]
Shopping mall location	SWARA, WASPAS	[7]
Assessment of region priority for implementation of solar projects in Iran	SWARA, WASPAS	[25]
Glasshouse location	SWARA, COPRAS	[11]
Computer workstation selection	Hesitant fuzzy sets, TOPSIS, AHP	[14]
Hospital site selection	Hesitant fuzzy TOPSIS	[23]
Solid waste disposal site selection	Fuzzy EDAS	[12]
Hospital selection in terms of organ transplantation	Fuzzy EDAS, Hesitant fuzzy TOPSIS	[24]
Hotel location	BWM, WASPAS	[21]
Residential construction site selection	Hesitant fuzzy CODAS	[20]
Waste disposal location selection	VIKOR, ELECTREE III	[31]
Offshore wind–PV–seawater pumped storage power plant	Fuzzy TODIM	[32]
Neighborhood selection	BWM, Revised-MAIRCA	[19]
Location selection of logistic centers	DEA, R-FUCOM, R-CoCoSo	[30]
Wind farm site selection	AHP	[28]

After reviewing different studies on site selection with MCDM techniques, it was concluded that the MCDM framework can enable better decision-making, especially in disaster situations. However, there were not many studies which worked on hospital locations in a pandemic or disaster circumstance with multi-criteria decision-making. This issue motivated us to implement hybrid MADAM techniques to find an optimum location in Turkey during the coronavirus pandemic in 2020. This fact shows the novelty of this study which can be used as a guide for future studies.

3. Methodology

The procedure of the proposed integrated decision support framework is presented in this section. Gray-based CRITIC and CoCoSo methods are applied to determine the importance of criteria and to prioritize the location alternatives, respectively.

3.1. Criteria Importance through Inter-Criteria Correlation (CRITIC)

In MCDM problems, the identification of criteria and the determination of their weights are very important processes, since weights of criteria can significantly affect the final output of the decision-making framework. The CRITIC method [5] is one of the frequently used MCDM methods to obtain the importance of criteria. In this method, the objective importance of the criteria is obtained by applying the contrast intensity of each criterion, which is considered as the standard deviation, while conflicts between criteria are considered as the correlation coefficient between criteria. Steps of the CRITIC method for an MCDM problem with m alternatives and n criteria are presented below.

Step 1. The decision-maker constructs the initial decision matrix.

$$x_{ij} = \begin{bmatrix} x_{11} & \cdots & x_{1n} \\ \vdots & \ddots & \vdots \\ x_{m1} & \cdots & x_{mn} \end{bmatrix} (i = 1, 2 \ldots, m \text{ and } j = 1, 2, \ldots, n). \tag{1}$$

The elements (x_{ij}) of the decision matrix (X) represent the performance value of the i-th alternative on the j-th criterion.

Step 2. Equations (2) and (3) normalize the initial decision matrix considering the benefit and cost criteria.

$$r_{ij} = \frac{x_{ij} - \min_{i} x_{ij}}{\max_{i} x_{ij} - \min_{i} x_{ij}} \text{ for benefit criterion.} \tag{2}$$

$$r_{ij} = \frac{\max_{i} x_{ij} - x_{ij}}{\max_{i} x_{ij} - \min_{i} x_{ij}} \text{ for cost criterion.} \tag{3}$$

Step 3. A symmetric linear correlation matrix (m_{ij}) is calculated by the decision-maker.

Step 4. In order to obtain the objective importance of a criterion, the standard deviation and the correlation of each criterion with other criteria are calculated. With this information, the importance of each criterion can be determined via Equation (4).

$$W_j = \frac{C_j}{\sum_{j=1}^{n} C_j}, \tag{4}$$

where C_j is the amount of information contained in the criterion j and is calculated using Equation (5).

$$C_j = \sigma \sum_{j=1}^{n} 1 - m_{ij}. \tag{5}$$

In Equation (5), σ is the standard deviation of the j-th criterion. In fact, the CRITIC method assigns higher weights to criteria with higher values of σ and lower correlation with the other criteria. A higher value of C_j denotes a higher amount of information included in a specific criterion; therefore, it is assigned a higher weight value.

3.2. Gray Numbers

In this section, we provide the fundamental principles and functions of gray numbers and their integration with the recently developed CoCoSo method [6].

The exact value of a gray number is uncertain; however, we know that it is within a range or a closed interval. Gray numbers can be continuous gray numbers within an interval. On the other hand, values from a finite number or a set of numbers are labeled as discrete gray numbers. A combined approach for both continuous and discrete gray numbers provided a new definition for gray numbers [33,34].

Definition 1. *Suppose that S is a gray value. If $\forall s \in S$ and $\widetilde{s} = [a, b]$, then $\widetilde{s}$ is known as an interval gray number, where a and b are the upper and lower bounds of $\widetilde{s}$ and $a, b \in R$.*

Definition 2. *Assume that $\widetilde{s}_1 = [a, b]$ and $\widetilde{s}_2 = [c, d]$ are two interval gray numbers, and $\lambda > 0$, $\lambda \in R$. The arithmetic operations are defined as follows [34,35]:*

$$1. \widetilde{s}_1 + \widetilde{s}_2 = [a + c, b + d]; \tag{6}$$

$$2. -s_1 = [-b, -a]; \tag{7}$$

$$3. \widetilde{s}_1 - \widetilde{s}_2 = [a - d, b - c]; \tag{8}$$

$$4. \lambda \widetilde{s}_1 = [\lambda a, \lambda b]. \tag{9}$$

Definition 3. *For a gray number S, if $S = \bigcup_{i=1}^{n} [a_i, b_i]$, then S is called an extended gray number (EGN). We consider S as a union of a set of closed or open intervals, while n is an integer and $0 < n < \infty$, $a_i, b_i \in R$, and $b_{i-1} < a_i \leq b_i < a_{i+1}$ [33].*

Theorem 1. *If S is an EGN, then the following properties hold:*

(1) $S = [a_1, b_n]$ iss a continues EGN if and only if $a_i \leq b_{i-1}$ ($\forall i > 1$) or $n = 1$.
(2) $S = \{a_1, a_2, \ldots, a_n\}$ is a discrete EGN if and only if $a_i = b_i$.
(3) S is a mixed EGN if only some of its intervals integrate to crisp numbers and the others remain intervals.

Definition 4. *For two EGNs $S_1 = \bigcup_{i=1}^{n} [a_i, b_i]$ and $S_2 = \bigcup_{j=1}^{m} [c_j, d_j]$, let $a_i \leq b_i (i = 1, 2, \ldots, n)$, $c_i \leq d_i (j = 1, 2, \ldots, m)$, $\lambda \geq 0$, and $\lambda \in R$. Then, the arithmetic operations can be defined as follows [34]:*

$$1. S_1 + S_2 = \bigcup_{i=1}^{n} \bigcup_{j=1}^{m} [a_i + c_j, b_i + d_j], \tag{10}$$

$$2. -S = \bigcup_{i=1}^{n} [-b_i, -a_i], \tag{11}$$

$$3. S_1 - S_2 = \bigcup_{i=1}^{n} \bigcup_{j=1}^{m} [a_i - d_j, b_i - c_j], \tag{12}$$

$$4. \frac{S_1}{S_1} = \bigcup_{i=1}^{n}\bigcup_{j=1}^{m} [\min\left\{\frac{a_i}{c_j}, \frac{a_i}{d_j}, \frac{b_i}{c_j}, \frac{b_i}{d_j}\right\}, \max\left\{\frac{a_i}{c_j}, \frac{a_i}{d_j}, \frac{b_i}{c_j}, \frac{b_i}{d_j}\right\}], \quad (13)$$

where $c_j \neq 0, d_j \neq 0,$ and $(j=1,2,\ldots,m)$.

$$5. S_1 * S_2 = \bigcup_{i=1}^{n}\bigcup_{j=1}^{m}[\min\{a_i c_j, a_i d_j, b_i c_j, b_i d_j\}, \max\{a_i c_j, a_i d_j, b_i c_j, b_i d_j\}], \quad (14)$$

$$6. \lambda S_1 = \bigcup_{i=1}^{n}[\lambda a_i, \lambda b_i], \quad (15)$$

$$7. S_1{}^\lambda = \bigcup_{i=1}^{n}[\min(a_i{}^\lambda, b_i{}^\lambda), \max(a_i{}^\lambda, b_i{}^\lambda)]. \quad (16)$$

Definition 5. *The length of a gray value $S = [a, b]$ is measured as*

$$L(S) = [b-a]/b. \quad (17)$$

3.3. Gray-Based Combined Compromise Solution (CoCoSo)

For the first time in the literature related to MCDM methods, [6] proposed the CoCoSo method as an alternative ranking tool for multi-criteria problems. Since its introduction, the CoCoSo method was used for multiple problems in its initial form or in an extended form. In this paper, we use the gray-based CoCoSo method. The steps of the gray-based CoCoSo are described below.

Step 1. The decision-maker identifies decision factors and alternatives.

Step 2. In this step, the decision-maker constructs the initial gray-based decision matrix.

$$X = \begin{bmatrix} \cup [a_{11}, b_{11}] & \cup [a_{12}, b_{12}] & \cdots & \cup [a_{1m}, b_{1m}] \\ \cup [a_{21}, b_{21}] & \cup [a_{22}, b_{22}] & \cdots & \cup [a_{2m}, b_{2m}] \\ \vdots & \vdots & \cdots & \vdots \\ \cup [a_{n1}, b_{n1}] & \cup [a_{n2}, b_{n2}] & \cdots & \cup [a_{nm}, b_{nm}] \end{bmatrix}, \quad (18)$$

where a_{ij} represents the lower bound, while b_{ij} represents the upper bound, for $i = 1, 2, \ldots, m$, $j = 1, 2, \ldots, n$.

Step 3. The constructed initial decision matrix is normalized using Equations (18) and (19) considering benefit and cost criteria.

$$r = \bigcup[c_{ij}, d_{ij}] = \frac{\cup[a_{ij}, b_{ij}] - \min_i \cup [a_{ij}, b_{ij}]}{\max_i \cup [a_{ij}, b_{ij}] - \min_i \cup [a_{ij}, b_{ij}]}; \text{ for the benefit criterion.} \quad (19)$$

$$r = \bigcup[c_{ij}, d_{ij}] = \frac{\max_i \cup [a_{ij}, b_{ij}] - \cup [a_{ij}, b_{ij}]}{\max_i \cup [a_{ij}, b_{ij}] - \min_i \cup [a_{ij}, b_{ij}]}; \text{ for the cost criterion.} \quad (20)$$

Step 4. The weighted normalized matrix and the sum of power weights of comparability sequences for each alternative are calculated using Equations (20) and (21).

$$S_i = \sum_{j=1}^{n}(w_j \bigcup[c_{ij}, d_{ij}]). \quad (21)$$

$$P_i = \sum_{j=1}^{n}(\bigcup[c_{ij}, d_{ij}]^{w_j}). \tag{22}$$

Step 5. The relative weights of alternatives using three aggregation strategies are calculated in various ways. We use three appraisal score strategies to calculate the relative weights of other options using Equations (22)–(24).

$$H_{ia} = [h_{1ij}, h_{2ij}] = \frac{P_i + S_i}{\sum_{i=1}^{m}(P_i + S_i)}. \tag{23}$$

$$L_{ia} = [l_{1ij}, l_{2ij}] = \frac{S_i}{\min_i S_i} + \frac{P_i}{\min_i P_i}. \tag{24}$$

$$M_{ia} = [m_{1ij}, m_{2ij}] = \frac{\lambda S_i + (1-\lambda)(P_i)}{\lambda \max_i S_i + (1-\lambda)\left(\max_i P_i\right)}, \text{ for } 0 \leq \lambda \leq 1. \tag{25}$$

The final preference order of the alternatives according to the CoCoSo-G method is calculated using Equation (25).

$$K_i = (H_{ia} * L_{ia} * M_{ia})^{\frac{1}{3}} + \frac{1}{3}(H_{ia} + L_{ia} + M_{ia}), \tag{26}$$

where λ (normally $\lambda = 0.5$) is chosen by the decision-makers. Different values of λ can have a significant effect on the flexibility and stability of the proposed CoCoSo.

Step 6. To rank the alternatives, we obtain the length of the gray values shown by the above equation (based on Definition 5).

4. Case Study

In big cities with high population, healthcare centers are very important facilities which are designed to deal with health issues. Location selection for healthcare centers, specifically hospitals, is a very important and very complicated decision for authorities and decision-makers, since multiple decision factors are involved in the decision-making process for this problem. The significance of location selection process for a hospital is implied by many direct or indirect relationships with economic, environmental, and social factors. Moreover, the location selection problem for a hospital is more important in critical time periods such as a disease outbreak. Starting in December 2019, COVID-19 became one of the biggest disease outbreaks of the last century. Soon after its emergence in China, COVID-19 became the most important issue to deal with for most countries in the world. In most countries, daily reports showed a sharp increasing trend in the number of infected patients. The high number of infected patients brought forward many problems in terms of the capacity of hospitals, such as hardware resources or specialized human resources to treat these patients. On the other hand, the presence of COVID-19-infected patients in hospitals increases the risk of its outbreak inside those hospitals, which would have a great effect on patients in other wards. In this matter, governments decided to construct well-resourced temporary hospitals to exclusively treat COVID-19-infected patients. As the first country affected, China constructed a hospital, with 100 beds, for patients that were suspected to be infected by COVID-19. After construction of this special hospital by China, the necessity of constructing such hospitals was understood by other governments.

Istanbul is an international city with a population of more than 15 million people living on both Asian and European sides of the city. Istanbul is one of the biggest transportation and business hubs in the world, where more than hundreds of flights move people worldwide through Istanbul each day. The medical system in Turkey is divided into public and private sectors. Due to the population increase in Istanbul, many public and private hospitals were constructed in recent decades. Turkey remained one of the safest countries during the first days of the COVID-19 outbreak. However, a few months later, the COVID-19 outbreak happened very quickly with an increasing trend in most cities in Turkey, especially Istanbul, which has the highest number of infected patients. Istanbul can play a key role in treating and preventing infections in a pandemic circumstance. The first case in Turkey was officially confirmed on 11 March 2020, and, as of 29 April, based upon a Johns Hopkins university report [36], 4,673,809 people were infected and 312,646 people died due to this disease around the world. Furthermore, according to the health ministry of Turkey [37], the total number of tests administered was 991,613, of which 117,589 returned positive, with 3081 passing away, whereas the total number of intensive care patients is 1574 and 44,040 patients are recovered. In order to treat COVID-19-infected patients, as well as prevent its outbreak in other hospitals, there is a necessity to construct a temporary hospital which serves only clients that are suspected to be infected by COVID-19. With respect to the geographical features of Istanbul, selecting a suitable location for the establishment of a new hospital is a very complicated process.

To show the feasibility and applicability of the proposed decision-making framework, we applied the decision support framework to Istanbul in order to select a suitable location for a temporary hospital for COVID-19 patients. Istanbul is a very big city which is divided into Asian and European sides, where the population ratio is not the same on both sides. There are 25 districts on the European side and 14 districts on the Asian side, giving a total of 39 districts. The population of the European side is almost two times that of the Asian side, which is approximately 5.5 million. With this information in mind, five districts were selected as potential location alternatives for the hospital location selection problem. Due to the spread of the population and geographical features in Istanbul, three of these districts were located on the European side and the two other districts were located on the Asian side. As shown in Figure 1, the five districts of Beykoz (A1), Bakırköy (A2), Büyükçekmece (A3), Eyüp (A4), and Pendik (A5) were selected as potential locations for this case study.

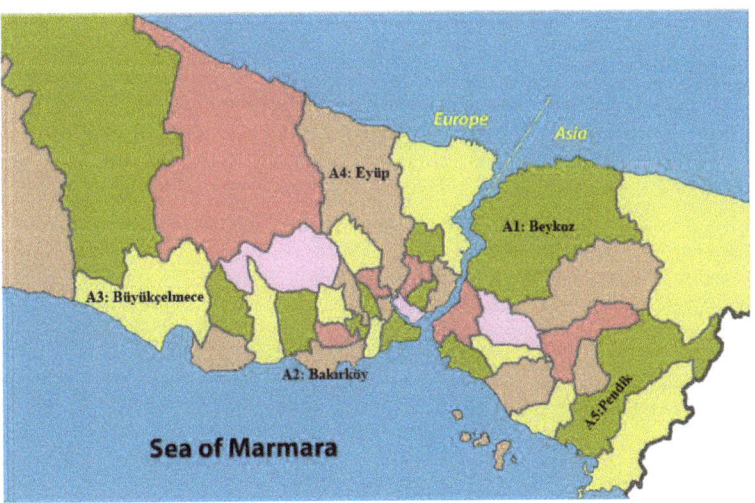

Figure 1. Location alternatives in Istanbul.

Based on the characteristics of stakeholders, several criteria were identified and defined using the location selection studies in the literature. The identified criteria were categorized into three main groups of technological, economic, and social criteria. Firstly, we defined the technological criteria involved in the decision-making process. Traffic congestion (C1) was defined as a qualitative criterion to measure the level of traffic congestion in each district. Ease of transportation is very important when promptly delivering patients to a hospital. Accessibility via roads (C2) denotes how many different roadways are available in the district in order to deliver patients. Accessibility via airports (C3) measures the distance of the hospital to its closest international or local airport, which can be used to deliver patients in a critical situation. Health centers in the district (C4) measure how many hospitals are in the district that the hospital would be built in. The distance from populated residential areas (C5) measures how far the hospital is from areas with a high population density. Land price, transportation cost, and future expansion potential are considered as economic criteria. Land price (C6) measures the range of land cost for an infrastructure like a hospital. Transportation cost (C7) measures transportation cost in terms of transportation means available to deliver patients in different districts. Future expansion potential (8) denotes the possibility of expanding the temporary hospital to a permanent one with respect to financial indexes. We considered two criteria for environmental and social aspects. The distance from industrial areas (C9) measures how far the hospital is from industrial areas with respect to the fact that the emissions of factories in an industrial area can have a negative effect on the air quality level. Local regulation (10) represents a series of official and unofficial regulations related to each district with respect to its demography characteristics.

Table 2 shows a comparison among alternatives with respect to the defined criteria for Istanbul. In the first step, an initial decision matrix was constructed using gray values (Table 3). For each criterion, a gray value was indicated for each alternative with respect to expert experience, knowledge, etc. In Table 4, the initial decision matrix values were normalized using Equations (2) and (3) based on the benefit and cost criteria in step 2 of the CRITIC method. In the next step, the matrix of correlation was generated, as presented in Table 5, where the correlations of each pair of criteria are shown. Finally, we calculated the weights of criteria using Equations (4) and (5), as shown in the last row of Table 6. The distance from industrial areas (C9), future expansion potential (8), and land price (C6) were determined as the most important criteria.

After determining the weights of the criteria, we normalized the initial gray-based decision matrix using Equations (18) and (19), as presented in Table 7. In the next step of the gray-based CoCoSo method, we constructed the weighted decision matrix by multiplying the normalized decision matrix and weight vector using Equation (20), as presented in Table 7. Gray S_i values were calculated for each alternative in Table 8. In Table 9, we calculated the power-weighted normalized decision matrix using Equation (21). Gray P_i values were calculated for each alternative in Table 9. In order to prioritize the alternatives, three appraisal score strategies were used with respect to Equations (22)–(24). As shown in Table 10, we calculated the gray-based relative weights of alternatives, and the results were finally combined using Equation (25) as K_i values. Using K_i values, the ranking of alternatives was determined using gray lengths. As represented in Table 10, the Beykoz (A1) and Bakırköy (A2) districts were ranked as the first and second priorities to build a temporary hospital. Pendik (A5) and Eyüp (A4) were ranked as the third and fourth preferred locations. Büyükçekmece (A3) was the least preferred location to build a temporary hospital.

Table 2. Profile of experts.

# of Expert	Gender	Degree	Field
1	Male	PhD	Business Management
2	Male	PhD	Industrial Engineering
3	Male	PhD	Civil Engineering
4	Male	PhD	Construction Technology and Management
5	Male	PhD	Transport Engineering
6	Female	MD	Medical doctor
7	Male	M.Sc.	Urban Planning
8	Male	M.Sc.	Industrial Engineering
9	Male	M.Sc.	Data Science
10	Female	M.Sc.	Architecture

Table 3. Performance value matrix.

Alternatives	C_1		C_2		C_3		C_4		C_5		C_6		C_7		C_8		C_9		C_{10}	
A1	20.0	30.0	5.0	10.0	30.0	37.0	5.0	15.0	30.0	65.0	45.0	70.0	65.0	70.0	15.0	30.0	5.0	15.0	10.0	20.0
A2	80.0	90.0	90.0	100.0	5.0	40.0	50.0	70.0	40.0	55.0	85.0	90.0	10.0	25.0	70.0	85.0	5.0	15.0	65.0	75.0
A3	70.0	80.0	20.0	30.0	30.0	45.0	25.0	40.0	65.0	70.0	50.0	70.0	60.0	65.0	60.0	70.0	5.0	15.0	25.0	45.0
A4	45.0	60.0	15.0	25.0	15.0	20.0	75.0	90.0	70.0	80.0	50.0	75.0	70.0	75.0	10.0	20.0	5.0	15.0	20.0	35.0
A5	40.0	55.0	35.0	55.0	5.0	10.0	65.0	80.0	65.0	70.0	45.0	70.0	60.0	65.0	55.0	70.0	5.0	15.0	45.0	50.0

Table 4. Transformations of performance values.

C_1		C_2		C_3		C_4		C_5		C_6		C_7		C_8		C_9		C_{10}	
0.00	0.14	1.00	0.95	0.63	0.80	1.00	0.88	0.75	0.38	0.00	0.56	0.85	0.92	0.93	0.73	0.00	1.00	1.00	0.85
0.86	1.00	0.11	0.00	0.00	0.88	0.47	0.24	1.00	0.63	0.89	1.00	0.00	0.23	0.20	0.00	0.00	1.00	0.15	0.00
0.71	0.86	0.84	0.74	0.63	1.00	0.76	0.59	0.38	0.25	0.11	0.56	0.77	0.85	0.33	0.20	0.00	1.00	0.77	0.46
0.36	0.57	0.89	0.79	0.25	0.38	0.18	0.00	0.25	0.00	0.11	0.67	0.92	1.00	1.00	0.87	0.00	1.00	0.85	0.62
0.29	0.50	0.68	0.47	0.00	0.13	0.29	0.12	0.38	0.25	0.00	0.56	0.77	0.85	0.40	0.20	0.00	1.00	0.46	0.38

Table 5. Correlation coefficient.

1	−0.732	0.171	−0.363	0.107	0.681	−0.611	−0.757	0.272	−0.782
−0.732	1	0.172	0.414	−0.488	−0.755	0.88	0.771	−0.176	0.955
0.171	0.172	1	0.477	−0.097	0.176	0.15	−0.081	0.48	0.136
−0.363	0.414	0.477	1	0.436	−0.328	0.048	0.143	−0.27	0.502
0.107	−0.488	−0.097	0.436	1	0.189	−0.799	−0.284	−0.455	−0.295
0.681	−0.755	0.176	−0.328	0.189	1	−0.591	−0.526	0.639	−0.748
−0.611	0.88	0.15	0.048	−0.799	−0.591	1	0.632	0.173	0.761
−0.757	0.771	−0.081	0.143	−0.284	−0.526	0.632	1	−0.252	0.837
0.272	−0.176	0.48	−0.27	−0.455	0.639	0.173	−0.252	1	−0.302
−0.782	0.955	0.136	0.502	−0.295	−0.748	0.761	0.837	−0.302	1

Symmetry **2020**, *12*, 886

Table 6. The weights of decision-making criteria.

	1	2	3	4	5	6	7	8	9	10
Sum	4.8172	4.6337	3.2765	3.0359	4.0419	5.0372	5.3323	5.2074	5.1487	4.4837
Cj	1.517	1.527	1.144	0.991	1.112	1.752	1.662	1.791	2.574	1.369
wj	0.098	0.099	0.074	0.064	0.072	0.113	0.108	0.116	0.167	0.089

Table 7. Normalized matrix for CoCoSo-G.

	1	2	3	4	5	6	7	8	9	10
1	0.143	0	0.053	0.63	0.800	0	0.118	0.25	0.625	0
2	1.000	0.89	0	0	0.875	0.53	0.765	0	0.375	0.89
3	0.857	0.16	0.263	0.63	1.000	0.24	0.412	0.63	0.750	0.11
4	0.571	0.11	0.211	0.25	0.375	0.82	1.000	0.75	1.000	0.11
5	0.500	0.32	0.526	0	0.125	0.71	0.882	0.63	0.750	0

Table 8. The weighted normalized matrix.

	1	2	3	4	5	6	7	8	9	10
1	0.014	0.000	0.005	0.046	0.059	0.000	0.008	0.018	0.045	0.000
2	0.098	0.088	0.000	0.000	0.065	0.059	0.083	0.000	0.027	0.079
3	0.084	0.016	0.026	0.046	0.074	0.015	0.045	0.072	0.054	0.010
4	0.056	0.011	0.021	0.019	0.028	0.053	0.108	0.087	0.167	0.010
5	0.049	0.031	0.052	0.000	0.009	0.045	0.095	0.073	0.125	0.000

Table 9. Power weighted normalized matrix.

	1	2	3	4	5	6	7	8	9	10	Si	Pi
1	0.826	0.000	0.802	0.972	0.984	0.000	0.783	0.853	0.922	0.000	3.58	9.03
2	1.000	0.989	0.000	0.000	0.991	0.932	0.972	0.000	0.847	0.990	5.88	9.76
3	0.985	0.833	0.902	0.971	1.000	0.847	0.911	0.947	0.952	0.819	8.23	9.62
4	0.946	0.800	0.896	0.914	0.932	0.978	1.000	0.966	1.000	0.819	7.19	9.40
5	0.934	0.892	0.954	0.000	0.857	0.963	0.987	0.947	0.952	0.000	6.58	9.55

344

Table 10. The CoCoSo-G ranking for alternatives.

	P + S		H(ia)		L(ia)		M(ia)		Ki		Gray Length	Rank
A1	3.7465	9.5319	0.0738	0.2877	2.0000	5.6137	0.3532	0.8987	1.1826	3.3988	0.6520654	1
A2	6.3559	10.6068	0.1252	0.3201	4.5555	7.9210	0.5992	1	2.4591	4.444	0.4466384	2
A3	8.6134	10.3503	0.1697	0.3124	4.6589	7.1376	0.8121	0.9758	2.7428	4.1044	0.3317302	5
A4	7.4879	10.0395	0.1475	0.3030	3.8245	6.5497	0.7060	0.9465	2.295	3.8336	0.4013361	4
A5	6.9320	10.2406	0.1365	0.3090	3.9810	6.8912	0.6535	0.9655	2.2986	3.9935	0.424416	3

5. Managerial Insights and Conclusions

The hospital location selection problem is an important issue for big cities with respect to the fact that the location selection problem is influenced by various decision factors and dimensions in the context of technical, environmental, economic, and social aspects. Therefore, a logical analysis of location alternatives considering all criteria will enable policy-makers to better address the location selection problem. The importance of the hospital location selection problem relies on the fact that any consequences from the medical services directly affect the mortality rate in societies. On the other hand, the COVID-19 outbreak, as one of the biggest threats of the last century, spread to most countries in the world. The high number of infected patients and the limited medical resources to treat the patients resulted in healthcare sectors facing many issues. Thus, policy-makers in the healthcare sector suggested establishing temporary hospitals for only patients diagnosed with COVID-19. In this situation, the location selection problem becomes more important than ever due to the critical situation that the health sectors are in.

To show the efficiency of the proposed decision support framework, we performed a case study using Istanbul, which is one of the world's biggest cities with more than 15 million people. Results indicated that the Beykoz and Bakırköy districts are the most suitable locations for the establishment of a temporary hospital for COVID-19 patients. The populations of Beykoz and Bakırköy districts are very close together. However, the population density in Bakırköy is 7734 per km^2, whereas the same parameter for Beykoz is only 800 per km^2. The distance from industrial and production areas is greater for Beykoz than Bakırköy. In addition, the traffic congestion in Beykoz is way lower than in Bakırköy. On the other hand, Bakırköy is one of the closest districts to local and international airports, which can be used to deliver patients that are being transported using air medical services. The establishment of a temporary hospital in Beykoz would also benefit this district in the future. With a high future expansion potential, a big hospital in this area would play a great role in its gentrification. In other words, transportation factors and the applicability of the area will improve, which would certainly bring more profit and satisfaction for all stakeholders in the healthcare sector.

In this paper, we addressed the location selection problem for a temporary hospital in the era of the COVID-19 outbreak. A gray-based decision support framework was presented for the decision-making process, considering the uncertain nature of the information related to location alternatives. The CRITIC and CoCoSo methods were implemented under gray values to determine the weights of criteria and to prioritize the location alternatives, respectively. For a case study in Istanbul, we selected five possible districts for the establishment of a temporary hospital in Istanbul.

Some future research directions can be identified. One may use the proposed decision support framework for the location selection problem in other industries such as waste management, hotels, power plants, airports, and so on. In another direction, one may implement the proposed decision-making approach with other uncertainty models such as fuzzy set theory, rough numbers, neutrosophic sets, etc.

Author Contributions: Main idea, conceptualization, supervision, editing, and writing-original by S.H.Z.; Methodology, supervision, editing, and writing-original by M.Y., main idea, case study, methodology, and writing-original by A.E.T., Literature review, general background review, and writing-original by A.D. All authors have read and agreed to the published version of the manuscript.

Funding: This research received no external funding.

Conflicts of Interest: The authors declare no conflict of interest.

References

1. Simonovic, S.P. Approach to management of disasters—A missed opportunity? *J. Integr. Disaster Risk Manag.* **2015**, *5*, 70–83. [CrossRef]
2. Pambuccian, S.E. The COVID-19 pandemic: Implications for the cytology laboratory. *J. Am. Soc. Cytopathol.* **2020**, *9*, 202–211. [CrossRef] [PubMed]

3. Huang, C.; Wang, Y.; Li, X.; Ren, L.; Zhao, J.; Hu, Y.; Zhang, J.; Fan, G.; Xu, J.; Gu, X.; et al. Clinical features of patients infected with 2019 novel coronavirus in Whuan, China. *Lancet* **2020**, *395*, 497–506. [CrossRef]
4. WHO (World Health Organization). WHO Timeline—Covid-19. 2020. Available online: https://www.who.int/news-room/detail/27-04-2020-who-timeline---covid-19 (accessed on 25 April 2020).
5. Diakoulaki, D.; Mavrotas, G.; Papayannakis, L. Determining objective weights in multiple criteria problems: The CRITIC method. *Comput. Ops. Res.* **1995**, *22*, 763–770. [CrossRef]
6. Yazdani, M.; Zarate, P.; Kazimieras Zavadskas, E.; Turskis, Z. A combined compromise solution (CoCoSo) method for multi-criteria decision-making problems. *Manag. Decis.* **2019**, *57*, 2501–2519. [CrossRef]
7. Hashemkhani Zolfani, S.; Aghdaie, M.H.; Derakhti, A.; Zavadskas, E.K.; Morshed Varzandeh, M.H. Decision making on business issues with foresight perspective; An application of new hybrid MCDM model in shopping mall locating. *Expert Syst. Appl.* **2013**, *40*, 7111–7121. [CrossRef]
8. Ijadi Maghsoodi, A.; Rasoulipanah, H.; Martínez López, L.; Liao, H.; Zavadskas, E.K. Integrating interval-valued multi-granular 2-tuple linguistic BWM-CODAS approach with target-based attributes: Site selection for a construction project. *Comput. Ind. Eng.* **2020**, *139*, 106147.
9. Hashemkhani Zolfani, S.H.; Rezaeiniya, N.; Zavadskas, E.K.; Turskis, Z. Forest roads locating based on AHP and COPRAS-G methods: An empirical study based on Iran. *E M Ekon. Manag.* **2011**, *14*, 6–21.
10. Rezaeiniya, N.; Zolfani, S.H.; Zavadskas, E.K. Greenhouse locating based on ANP-COPRAS-G methods—An empirical study based on Iran. *Int. J. Strateg. Prop. Manag.* **2012**, *16*, 188–200. [CrossRef]
11. Haghnazar Kouchaksaraei, R.; Hashemkhani Zolfani, S.; Golabchi, M. Glasshouse locating based on SWARA-COPRAS approach. *Int. J. Strateg. Prop. Manag.* **2015**, *19*, 111–122. [CrossRef]
12. Kahraman, C.; Keshavarz Ghorabaee, M.; Zavadskas, E.K.; Cevik Onar, S.; Yazdani, M.; Oztaysi, B. Intuitionistic fuzzy EDAS method: An application to solid waste disposal site selection. *J. Environ. Eng. Landsc. Manag.* **2017**, *25*, 1–12. [CrossRef]
13. Krylovas, A.; Zavadskas, E.K.; Kosareva, N. Multiple criteria decision-making KEMIRA-M method for solution of location alternatives. *Econ. Res. Ekon. Istraz.* **2016**, *29*, 50–65. [CrossRef]
14. Çevik Onar, S.; Büyüközkan, G.; Öztayşi, B.; Kahraman, C. A new hesitant fuzzy QFD approach: An application to computer workstation selection. *Appl. Soft Comput. J.* **2016**, *46*, 1–16. [CrossRef]
15. Suder, A.; Kahraman, C. Minimizing Environmental Risks Using Fuzzy TOPSIS: Location Selection for the ITU Faculty of Management. *Hum. Ecol. Risk Assess.* **2015**, *21*, 1326–1340. [CrossRef]
16. Kilci, F.; Kara, B.Y.; Bozkaya, B. Locating temporary shelter areas after an earthquake: A case for Turkey. *Eur. J. Oper. Res.* **2015**, *243*, 323–332. [CrossRef]
17. Celik, E. A cause and effect relationship model for location of temporary shelters in disaster operations management. *Int. J. Disaster Risk Reduct.* **2017**, *22*, 257–268. [CrossRef]
18. Iqbal, S.; Sardar, M.U.; Lodhi, F.K.; Hasan, O. Statistical model checking of relief supply location and distribution in natural disaster management. *Int. J. Disaster Risk Reduct.* **2018**, *31*, 1043–1053. [CrossRef]
19. Hashemkhani Zolfani, S.; Ecer, F.; Pamucar, D.; Raslanas, S. Neighborhood selection for a newcomer via a novel BWM-based Reised MAIRCA integrated model: A case from the Coquimbo-La Serena conurbation, Chile. *Int. J. Strateg. Prop. Manag.* **2020**, *24*, 102–118. [CrossRef]
20. Karasan, A.; Zavadskas, E.K.; Kahraman, C.; Keshavarz-Ghorabaee, M. Residential construction site selection through interval-valued hesitant fuzzy CODAS method. *Informatica (Netherlands)* **2019**, *30*, 689–710. [CrossRef]
21. Hashemkhani Zolfani, S.; Mosharafiandehkordi, S.; Kutut, V. A pre-planning for hotel locating according to the sustainability perspective based on BWM-WASPAS approach. *Int. J. Strateg. Prop. Manag.* **2019**, *23*, 405–419. [CrossRef]
22. Lin, C.T.; Tsai, M.C. Location choice for direct foreign investment in new hospitals in China by using ANP and TOPSIS. *Qual. Quant.* **2010**, *44*, 375–390. [CrossRef]
23. Senvar, O.; Otay, I.; Bolturk, E. Hospital site selection via hesitant fuzzy TOPSIS. *IFAC Pap.* **2016**, *49*, 1140–1145. [CrossRef]
24. Kutlu Gündoğdu, F.; Kahraman, C.; Civan, H.N. A novel hesitant fuzzy EDAS method and its application to hospital selection. *J. Intell. Fuzzy Syst.* **2018**, *35*, 6353–6365. [CrossRef]
25. Vafaeipour, M.; Hashemkhani Zolfani, S.; Morshed Varzandeh, M.H.; Derakhti, A.; Keshavarz Eshkalag, M. Assessment of regions priority for implementation of solar projects in Iran: New application of a hybrid multi-criteria decision making approach. *Energy Convers. Manag.* **2014**, *86*, 653–663. [CrossRef]

26. Marques-Perez, I.; Guaita-Pradas, I.; Gallego, A.; Segura, B. Territorial planning for photovoltaic power plants using an outranking approach and GIS. *J. Clean. Prod.* **2020**, *257*, 120602. [CrossRef]
27. Ekmekçioglu, M.; Can Kutlu, A.; Kahraman, C. A fuzzy multi-criteria swot analysis: An application to nuclear power plant site selection. *Int. J. Comput. Intell. Syst.* **2011**, *4*, 583–595. [CrossRef]
28. Moradi, S.; Yousefi, H.; Noorollahi, Y.; Rosso, D. Multi-criteria decision support system for wind farm site selection and sensitivity analysis: Case study of Alborz Province, Iran. *Energy Strategy Rev.* **2020**, *29*, 100478. [CrossRef]
29. Athawale, V.M.; Chatterjee, P.; Chakraborty, S. Decision making for facility location selection using PROMETHEE II method. *Intern. J. Ind. Syst. Eng.* **2012**, *11*, 16–30. [CrossRef]
30. Yazdani, M.; Chatterjee, P.; Pamucar, D.; Chakraborty, S. Development of an integrated decision making model for location selection of logistics centers in the Spanish autonomous communities. *Expert Syst. Appl.* **2020**, *148*, 113208. [CrossRef]
31. Ebadi Torkayesh, A.; Fathipoir, F.; Saidi-Mehrabd, M. Entropy-based multi-criteria analysis of thermochemical conversions for energy recovery from municipal solid waste using fuzzy VIKOR and ELECTRE III: Case of Azerbaijan Region. Iran. *J. Energy Manag. Technol.* **2019**, *3*, 17–29.
32. Wu, Y.; Zhang, T.; Xu, C.; Zhang, B.; Li, L.; Ke, Y.; Yan, Y.; Xu, R. Optimal location selection for offshore wind-PV-seawater pumped storage power plant using a hybrid MCDM approach: A two-stage framework. *Energy Convers. Manag.* **2019**, *199*, 112066. [CrossRef]
33. Yang, Y.J. Extended grey numbers and their operations. In Proceedings of the 2007 IEEE International Conference on Fuzzy Systems and Intelligent Services, Man and Cybernetics, Montreal, QC, Canada, 7–10 October 2017; pp. 2181–2186.
34. Liu, S.F.; Dang, Y.G.; Fang, Z.G.; Xie, N.M. *Grey Systems Theory and Its Applications*; Science Press: Beijing, China, 2010.
35. Zhou, H.; Wang, J.; Zhang, H. Grey Stochastic Multi-criteria Decision-making Approach Based on Prospect Theory and Distance Measures. *J Grey Syst.* **2017**, *29*, 15–33.
36. Johns Hopkins University & Medicine. Corona Virus Resource Center. 2020. Available online: https://coronavirus.jhu.edu/map.html (accessed on 1 April 2020).
37. The Ministry of Health. Türkiye'deki Güncel Durum. 2020. Available online: https://covid19.saglik.gov.tr/ (accessed on 1 April 2020).

© 2020 by the authors. Licensee MDPI, Basel, Switzerland. This article is an open access article distributed under the terms and conditions of the Creative Commons Attribution (CC BY) license (http://creativecommons.org/licenses/by/4.0/).

MDPI
St. Alban-Anlage 66
4052 Basel
Switzerland
Tel. +41 61 683 77 34
Fax +41 61 302 89 18
www.mdpi.com

Symmetry Editorial Office
E-mail: symmetry@mdpi.com
www.mdpi.com/journal/symmetry